Handbooks of Sociology and Social Research

Series editor
John DeLamater
University of Wisconsin, Madison, WI, USA

Each of these Handbooks survey the field in a critical manner, evaluating theoretical models in light of the best available empirical evidence. Distinctively sociological approaches are highlighted by means of explicit comparison to perspectives characterizing related disciplines such as psychology, psychiatry, and anthropology. These seminal works seek to record where the field has been, to identify its current location and to plot its course for the future.

If you are interested in submitting a proposal for this series, please contact senior editor, Esther Otten: esther.otten@springer.com.

More information about this series at http://www.springer.com/series/6055

Pinar Batur · Joe R. Feagin

Editors

Handbook of the Sociology of Racial and Ethnic Relations

Second Edition

 Springer

Editors
Pinar Batur
Department of Sociology
Vassar College
Poughkeepsie, NY
USA

Joe R. Feagin
Department of Sociology
Texas A&M University
College Station, TX
USA

ISSN 1389-6903   ISSN 2542-839X   (electronic)
Handbooks of Sociology and Social Research
ISBN 978-3-319-76755-0   ISBN 978-3-319-76757-4   (eBook)
https://doi.org/10.1007/978-3-319-76757-4

Library of Congress Control Number: 2018939308

Printed on acid-free paper

This Springer imprint is published by the registered company Springer International Publishing AG part of Springer Nature
The registered company address is: Gewerbestrasse 11, 6330 Cham, Switzerland

To the memory of Hernán Vera,
Roderick D. Bush, Felix M. Berardo,
and the tomorrow of all of our students

Contents

Editors and Contributors

About the Editors

Pinar Batur is a Professor of Sociology at Vassar College, where she has chaired multidisciplinary programs in Urban Studies (1999–2006), International Studies (2007–2010) and Environmental Studies (2012–2016). She also served the college as the Director of Research (2002–2005) and the elected chair of the research committee (2013–2016). She has authored books and articles on global racism and anti-racism, including The Global Color Line (1999), and White Racism (2000). She is the author of several articles examining racism, anti-racism, and political discourse, including "Heart of Violence: Global Racism, War and Genocide," and "Centering on Global Racism and Anti-Racism: From Everyday Life to Global Complexity." Her new interest area is environmental thought and she works on Turkish authors and intellectuals, such as Yaman Koray and Halikarnas Balıkçısı, and on green discourse and eco-consciousness. She has received grants from SSRC, IREX, The Kennan Institute at the Woodrow Wilson Center, the Hoover Institution, HR Guggenheim Foundation, SENCER, InTeGrate and the Dreyfus Foundation, among others.

Joe R. Feagin Ella C. McFadden Professor and University Distinguished Professor at Texas A&M University, does research on racism, sexism, and classism issues. He has published many scholarly books and hundreds of scholarly articles in these research areas. Among his books are Systemic Racism (Routledge 2006); Two-Faced Racism (Routledge 2007, with L. Picca); The White Racial Frame (2nd ed; Routledge 2013); Racist America (3rd ed; Routledge 2014); White Party, White Government (Routledge 2012); Latinos Facing Racism (Paradigm 2014, with J. Cobas); The Myth of the Model Minority (2nd ed., Paradigm, 2015, with R. Chou); Liberation Sociology (3rd ed., Paradigm, 2015, with H. Vera, K. Ducey); and How Blacks Built America (Routledge, 2016). He has served as Scholar-in-Residence at the U.S. Commission on Civil Rights and is the recipient of the American Association for Affirmative Action's Fletcher Lifetime Achievement Award and the American Sociological Association's W. E. B. Du Bois Career of Distinguished Scholarship Award. He was the 1999–2000 president of the American Sociological Association.

Contributors

Carlos Alamo-Pastrana Department of Sociology, Vassar College, Poughkeepsie, NY, USA

Pinar Batur Department of Sociology and the Program in Environmental Studies, Vassar College, Poughkeepsie, NY, USA

Felix M. Berardo Emeritus Professor of Sociology, University of Florida, Gainesville, FL, USA

Melanie E. L. Bush Department of Sociology, Adelphi University, Garden City, NY, USA

Jorge A. Bustamante Department of Sociology, University of Notre Dame, Notre Dame, IN, USA

Rodney D. Coates University of Miami, Miami, OH, USA

Danielle Dirks Independent Researcher, Detroit, MI, USA

Karen Manges Douglas Department of Sociology, Sam Houston State University, Huntsville Texas, TX, USA

Kimberley Ducey Department of Sociology, The University of Winnipeg, Winnipeg, MB, Canada

David G. Embrick Department of Sociology and African Studies, University of Connecticut, Storrs, CT, USA

Danielle Falzon Department of Sociology, Brown University, Providence, RI, USA

Joe R. Feagin Department of Sociology, Texas A&M University, College Station, TX, USA

James V. Fenelon Department of Sociology and Center of Indigenous Peoples Studies, California State University, San Bernardino, CA, USA

M. Elizabeth Fore Department of Community and Public Health, Idaho State University, Pocatello, ID, USA

Charles A. Gallagher Department of Sociology, La Salle University, Philadelphia, PA, USA

Chong-Suk Han Department of Sociology and Anthropology, Middlebury College, Middlebury, VT, USA

Yanick St. Jean Department of Sociology, Northwest Arkansas Community College, Bentonville, AR, USA

Debra Walker King Department of English, University of Florida, Gainesville, FL, USA

Peter Kivisto Department of Sociology, Augustana College, Rock Island, IL, USA

Isaac Sohn Leslie Department of Sociology, University of Wisconsin-Madison, Madison, WI, USA

Amir Marvasti Department of Sociology, Penn State Altoona, Altoona, PA, USA

Karyn McKinney Department of Sociology and Women's, Gender and Sexuality Studies, Penn State University, Altoona, PA, USA

Maria Cristina Morales Department of Sociology and Anthropology, University of Texas at El Paso, El Paso, TX, USA

Amanda Moras Department of Sociology, Sacred Heart University, Fairfield, CT, USA

Jennifer C. Mueller Department of Sociology, Skidmore College, Saratoga Springs, NY, USA

Eileen O'Brien Saint Leo University, St. Leo, FL, USA

Deborah Parra-Medina Department of Mexican American and Latina/o Studies, University of Texas at Austin, Austin, TX, USA

Brad Pinter Department of Psychology, Penn State University, Altoona, PA, USA

Victor Ray Department of Sociology, University of Tennessee, Knoxville, TN, USA

Andrey Rezaev St. Petersburg State University, Petersburg, Russia

Rogelio Sáenz Dean of the College of Public Policy, University of Texas at San Antonio, San Antonio, TX, USA

Constance Shehan Department of Sociology and Criminology & Law, University of Florida, Gainesville, FL, USA

Gideon Sjoberg Department of Sociology, University of Texas at Austin, Austin, TX, USA

Jesus G. Smith Ethnic Studies, Lawrence University, Appleton, WI, USA

Roberta Spalter-Roth Center for Social Science Research, George Mason University, Fairfax, VA, USA

Ruth Thompson-Miller Department of Sociology, University of Dayton, Dayton, OH, USA

Hernán Vera Emeritus Professor of Sociology, University of Florida, Gainesville, FL, USA

Lynn Weber Department of Psychology and Women's and Gender Studies Program, University of South Carolina, Columbia, SC, USA

Monica M. White Nelson Institute for Environmental Studies and the Department of Community and Environmental Sociology, University of Wisconsin-Madison, Madison, WI, USA

Apryl Williams Department of Sociology, Susquehanna University, Selinsgrove, PA, USA

Ruth Enid Zambrana Department of Women's Studies, University of Maryland, College Park, MD, USA

Introduction

Pinar Batur, Joe R. Feagin and Hernán Vera

Racial and Ethnic Relations Today

In this *Handbook of Racial and Ethnic Relations*, we foster and put forth cutting-edge analyses of racial and ethnic topics from a critical perspective. To develop this volume, we began with a list of important scholars in these racial and ethnic fields and asked them to tell us what topics they thought should be included in a major reference work of this kind and which topics they felt capable of taking on. Their well-informed responses yielded, after considerable work and interactive discussion, the highly informative contents of this handbook. These authors are authoritative researchers on the important range of racial and ethnic topics they deal with.

For several decades now, critical social scientists have made a clear distinction between prejudice, bias, and discrimination as individual phenomena and institutional and systemic racism as societal practice. At least since the early 1900s, some North American social scientists have demonstrated that white-imposed racism involves at its heart an institutionalized social practice. White-imposed racism constitutes a way of acting, framing, and feeling that society's dominant white group sanctions and makes legitimate through a pervasive white racial framing of society. Today, calling white racism—the deliberate exclusion of racialized others from the resources and opportunities society offers to whites of European origin—by terms like hatred, intolerance, prejudice, and animus tends to euphemistic obfuscation and hides the deliberate and systemic character of still extensive racial exclusion and discrimination. What people call "race" is a set of real or imagined physical traits—such as skin color, facial form, hair type—thought to be indicative of intellectual ability, as well as moral and spiritual caliber.

As we put this volume together, we are missing Hernán Vera. Over two decades of teaching, Hernán, our late friend and the coeditor of the first edition of this *Handbook,* generated classroom data on the socially constructed racist stereotypes in U.S. society's racial framing. He asked numerous classes, "What do we know about 'spics'?" as he underlined that abusive epithet on the blackboard. Before students had recovered their breath, he would say, "Everyone knows we are great lovers!" and when the relieved laughter subsided, he would write "oversexed" under the underlined term of abuse. Little by little, students would venture into well-known abusive characterizations: "They stick to their families," "they are lazy," "they are dumb," "they have rhythm," "they talk funny," "they deal drugs," "they cannot control their emotions," and so forth. When the list was exhausted, Vera would say "let's do 'nigas'" now as he wrote and underlined that abusive epithet on the blackboard and took time to explain what these terms of abuse are and how they are racist stereotypes. He used the abusive terms to make the important sociological point that they made no reference to real people, but to broad social constructions in the dominant white racial frame. Then he would ask the class to answer question on societal views: "Are 'nigas' oversexed?" "Are they lazy?" and down the typically racist list, making checkmarks by each of the racially framed traits that they listed.

With minor variations, the two groups, African Americans and Latinos, turned out to be similar in the typical white racial framing. When the list was finished, Vera would do the same with other conventional epithets and other racial-ethnic groups: "wops," "micks," "polacks," and then "kikes" and "chinks." In all cases, with the exception of the last two, the targeted groups ended up having student-listed negative traits similar to those initially attributed to "spics." In decades of teaching he found a strong consensus: Many "racial" groups are viewed in similar terms in the old conventional white racial framing of society. In the class exercise, students were asked to think through this list and search for critical explanations. The classes were lively, but over the years many students mentioned how "tired" and "depressed" they were after the exercise that they would never forget. Often numerous students would insist that there had to be a kernel of truth in the abusive characterizations or they would not exist.

In this introduction, we cannot reproduce the richness of the conceptual and emotional discoveries that students made with this exercise. In the essays in which they wrote their reflections on the exercise, the consensual and socially constructed nature of the traits and images that emerged was surprising to most students. "I cannot believe, that up to this day, I had never questioned the truth of these stereotypes," wrote a student that captured the central comment that his peers had also made in these essays. "That blackboard will haunt me," wrote another student, "because that thinking has shaped all of my life to this point." Here we will only note that the similarity in undesirable traits among groups so different in heritages and cultures stems from the fact that they are ongoing expressions of fears of the same hegemonic white mindset and its long-term white racial framing of society. This is so because all people in this society are constantly bombarded, from cradle to grave, with this white racial framing—from parents, peers, teachers, clergy, and the mainstream media.

The blackboard, with its consistent and provocative data, accents the centuries-old consensual nature of "race" framing in U.S. society, and how it is a socially constructed, taken-for-granted, and normative way of thinking. For more than four centuries, European Americans have developed a racialized framing of society that has created, and still constantly legitimizes, numerous white privileges and powers exerted over peoples who contemporary European Americans and their ancestors have systematically conquered and subordinated. How else can anyone compel servitude from, and impose long-term suffering over, other peoples if not by establishing an unbridgeable social difference between themselves and those being oppressed? Note too that in human history only whites have developed such an extensive framing that accents "racial" differences to justify centuries of extensive exploitation and oppression.

The authors in this book often analyze from a critical perspective exploring these long-established, well-institutionalized, and systemic racial realities. In our view, one of the concepts that is most promising to the sociology of racism is that of *systemic racism*. Systemic racism is a social concept that should guide much social science and other research on matters of societal racial oppression. In his conceptual and empirical work, one of the editors, Joe Feagin, has stepped back and offered an analysis of U.S. oppression from a critical perspective that contextualizes and accents the complex whole and foundational character of systemic racism for the U.S. case (Feagin 2000, 2006, 2013). Working with diverse students and colleagues, he has extensively examined how this racist social system was initially constructed, how it has functioned as a political-economic and symbolic-ideological societal foundation for centuries, and who constantly profits and loses from it. Drawing here on Feagin's work, we use the term *systemic* as an approximate synonym for "ubiquitous," "total," "well-institutionalized," and "foundational." Systemic racism is that which penetrates every significant "nook and cranny" of the society we live in. "*Racist relations*—are not *in*, but rather *of* this society" (Feagin 2000:17).

Concepts such as systemic racism have come, not out of preestablished theorizing, but out of extensive field research—from examining many of the lives, experiences, and interpretations of those "organic intellectuals" who have had to endure and survive racial oppression in this society for decades. This concept of systemic racism is designed to open, not close, the analytical assessments of the social fields to which they are applied. When we use the concept of systemic racism, we do not seek to establish one truth about things societal, but rather encourage people to look at this and other societies in a much more critical, contextualized, and systematic fashion, from a deeper perspective that questions official truths and "established knowledge." We recognize the need for flexibility as we dig deeper into the foundational realities of U.S. racism. Feagin (1973:4) put this matter of flexibility thus in introducing his early social science anthology, *The Urban Scene*: "The selections will provide divergent and provocative interpretations which one may or may not be able to synthesize into a whole. The intention thus is to provoke the reader to formulate and integrate his or her own hypotheses and conclusions about the whys and wherefores of urban life."

In the U.S. case, white racism is centuries-old and extraordinarily well-institutionalized, one reason for the failure of most mainstream analysts to see its deeply imbedded, foundational, and systemic reality. Beginning in the early seventeenth century, the European American elite, working with its acolytes, established lasting colonies by killing off and stealing land from already existing indigenous peoples, and concurrently, systematically establishing an extensive slavery system that involved enslaving millions of African Americans for nearly two and a half centuries. That all-embracing slavery society was soon followed by comprehensive legal (Jim Crow) segregation targeting African Americans and other Americans of color for yet another 90 years. Altogether, slavery and Jim Crow oppression made up most (*83%*) of U.S. history. That long era of extreme racial domination laid a solid political-economic and legal foundation on which the many institutionalized forms, wide-ranging impacts, and constant oscillations of U.S. racial oppression have developed ever since.

The marginal status of African Americans within U.S. society is also the source of a form of "dual consciousness" regarding personal, communal, and national identity that assists in placing the sociopolitical strategies of African Americans in the bridge between securing the globalizing "American Dream" and international social justice efforts. The first edition of this volume included an article "Acting for a Good Society: Racism and Black Liberation in the *Longue Durée*," by Rod Bush (CITE), our dear departed friend, a radical Black scholar, and an inspirational scholar on social movements, in particular of African-descended peoples and the world systems. In his contribution to the previous volume, Rod Bush focused on what has become to be known as "the long twentieth century." Key in his examination are the critical events of historical capitalism and the pan-European project of world domination starting in the late 1800s. He argued that, before and during this era, the oppressive efforts to integrate people of African descent into the United States have been symptomatic of the troubled relationship between the white European world and the world of those defined by whites as the "dark others." The latter are often people of African descent, who have a distinctive position historically in the globalizing capitalistic political-economic system. Since pan-European world hegemony has frequently relied on pan-European racist thinking, the social psychology of emancipation for oppressed populations of color has tended to take the form of counter-hegemonic strategies emphasizing the rise of the "darker world" against oppressive whiteness. Indeed, the marginal status of African Americans within U.S. society is also the source of a form of "dual consciousness" regarding personal, communal, and national identity that assists in placing the sociopolitical strategies of African Americans in the bridge between securing the globalizing "American Dream" and international social justice efforts.

Our ideas here about the systemic character of white racism are influenced by W. E. B. du Bois's and Emile Durkheim's idea that sociology should be the *science* of institutions and advanced by a social constructionist perspective; this approach to racial matters has been reinvigorated in social science since the 1960s. Awareness of the systemic nature of U.S. racism does not deny the fact that similar types of racial oppression have been institutionalized around the world, with some of the latter significantly shaped by already existing U.S. racism. For instance, Nazi Germany's leaders were influenced in their systemic oppression of European Jews by their study of the operation of the legal segregation and other oppression of black and Native Americans in the United States. Adolf Hitler even celebrated this oppression in a speech, in which he noted that U.S. whites had systematically reduced "millions of Redskins to a few hundred thousand, and now keep the modest remnant under observation in a cage" (Whitman 2017: 9).

The U.S. elite and the colonialist and imperialist European elites shared a pervasive "white racial frame" and have long utilized it to maintain a global system of racial oppression. On a global level, this white racial frame enables systemic racist practices by providing a well-defined and socially maintained "organized set of racialized ideas, stereotypes, emotions, and inclinations to discriminate" (Feagin 2006: 25). The white racial frame is a key element of systemic racism, attached to other terms of racial oppression to forge systemic coherency and provide mutable rationalization, changing to fit a variety of situations, institutions, and processes. The white racial frame was globalized through racist colonial oppression. In this context, white racial framing defined the terms of racist systems of oppression and enabled the global spread of a racial geography of exploitation and violence. In this volume, we point out that the key to understanding the expansion of the dominant white racial frame is comprehension of the synergistic relationship between racist systems of oppression and the capitalist system of exploitation. In the age of industrial capitalism, this synergy manifested imperialism and colonialism. In the age of advanced capitalism, it is articulating also as intensified violence, war, and genocide (Batur 2007). As numerous authors in this volume demonstrate, white elites have for centuries engaged in overseas colonialism and imperialism, thereby imposing systemic forms of white racism on peoples of color across the globe.

The future of racial oppression and resistance to that oppression, in the United States and across the world, will depend to a large extent on the way ordinary people choose to look at and react to that oppressive reality. The concept of systemic racism invites us all to look at both the objective reality and subjective experience of everyday racism, avoiding the scientific error of adopting the official definitions of others, as radically different realities. In our view, much depends on how social scientists enable and empower people to analyze accurately and struggle successfully against one of the most significant human evils in the history of the world. If the multiple racial genocides of the nineteenth through the twenty-first centuries, legitimized in perpetrators' minds by notions of "race," are no longer going to be allowed, then we need to live up to the challenge of acknowledging and subverting the totality of the systemic racism that engulfs almost all of us.

Our collective works here begin with the core arguments of the field regarding the racial categorization of as white and "superior" and others as "inferior," and is about the dynamics of power to maintain the "color line." Charles A. Gallagher, a leading U.S. expert in this area, notes that whiteness remains a relatively invisible way to classify human beings. Other people are classified as minorities; some have a "race"; others have ethnicity; and others are just different. Whiteness often remains implicit and unstated, but still held in the mind. Yet viewing "white" as a racial identity helps to support the societal fiction that inferior and superior "race" characteristics—rather than racial exploitation, imposed poverty, or institutionalized exclusion—are responsible for the inequality between and among people of different skin colors in the United States and overseas. Contrary to much popular belief, human populations cannot be placed without ambiguity and error into discrete, mutually exclusive categories based on anatomical and visual features. The idea that "races" are stable features of humanity has long been contradicted by the constant change that these categories undergo in current popular debates and older scholarly debates. The U.S. census itself provides an example of how definitions of white and other racial categories defined by contrast to it have changed substantially over several decades.

The chapter by James Fenelon, a leading scholar on indigenous issues, traces the origins of indigenous peoples in the Americas, their struggles to survive and resist during European and Eurocentric-American conquests and domination over centuries and continents, and the nature of contemporary indigenous conflicts and revitalization strategies. Several important themes are accented, including the origins of indigenous peoples, the definitions used as political identities, and historical and current sociopolitical usage. Fenelon explores the intergroup identities of those termed "American Indians" in terms of nationhood and struggles over sovereignty. He examines the larger indigenous struggles with a focus on the modern states of the Americas, as well as on the burgeoning anti-globalization and cultural contestation conflicts over indigeneity, autonomy, and the nature of community. His section concludes with an analysis of the centrality and predictive location of indigenous peoples in the Americas—which partly explains the great diversity of indigenous cultures, experiences, histories, and names.

For decades, the n-word has been accepted as a bonding tool in various social groups, and often a sign of cultural coolness. Noting in her chapter that the use of the word is a question of conscience and consciousness, Debra King, a leading humanities scholar, suggests there is much more to this issue than is usually recognized. Approaching the word via Pierre Bourdieu's provocative theory of symbolic violence—which is defined as "the gentle, invisible form of violence, which is never recognized as such, and is not so much undergone as chosen"—she challenges certain assumptions about black cultural acceptance of a ritualistic grammar that wounds. She shows that the word *nigger* has a tremendous ability to control and silence those using it or allowing themselves to be defined through it. Because it is greatly empowered as a marker or code of acceptance, it has the ability to shift hierarchical relationships and condemn, denounce, divide, or unify individuals, almost simultaneously. The n-word is a signifier of guilt and innocence; and, as such, it has gained the power to challenge and compromise this country's official advocacy of free speech. Through a discussion of these important issues, including the tension that arose when the President of the United States, Barack Obama, was addressed as "my nigga" at a White House Correspondents' Dinner, King concludes that no matter how much people claim an unproblematic transition from hurtful to healthy nominative possession when using this word, the *pain* of derogatory name-calling endures and runs deep in personalities and in society.

A leading sociological scholar and poet, Rodney D. Coates, provides an important chapter examining certain issues of racial hegemony and counter-hegemony in the formation and destruction of the racial state. For this important purpose, he uses and improves the concept of the "racial state" and explores how the racial state was strengthened by national racial fault lines, especially evident after the last presidential election. He also contemplates how we can get together to forge a transformative political movement to destroy this racial state. He argues that transformative political movements depend on peoples' evaluating, transforming, and eliminating the hegemony of the racial state–and thus by building intersectional political coalitions.

The section on the institutions that shaped and reshaped power struggle and racial conflict is led by Jennifer Mueller, Apryl Williams, and Danielle Dirk's work on the relationship between popular culture and systemic white racism. Talented younger scholars working on cutting-edge cultural issues, they illuminate the many ways in which white-racist representations of blackness of the past have endured to distort, shape, and misrepresent African Americans and other groups of color today, both in the United States and across the globe. They provide a brief history of U.S. popular culture's racist past to illustrate that the manufactured images, ideas, and material goods of the present are generally recycled remnants of the dominant racialized ideologies and actions of the past. Especially looking at how racialization is currently reflected in digital media, they point out that while "we perform and live race offline, we now also "do race online." While U.S. popular culture appears to be in a state of constantly new invention, this is often not the case when it comes to centuries-old racist imagery and racism. In their view, however, it is possible to mold the medium to the needs of anti-racist movements, thereby reinforcing anti-racist voice, image, community, and the unity of struggle and resistance.

African Americans have been at the heart of white racial oppression since the 1600s, but much of the social science literature on African American families has adopted a perspective that mostly stresses the negative impact of slavery on evolving black family structures and relationships over time. This mainstream literature often speaks of the alleged "demise," "disorganization," and "pathologies" of black families that are thought to be grounded in the realities of hierarchical slavery. These controversial social science analyses have too often reflected the biases and prejudices preponderant in larger society at particular periods of time. In their probing chapter on African American families, Amanda Moras, Constance Shehan, and the late Felix Berardo, influential family sociologists, examine questions and critiques that generally focus on the many strengths of much-maligned black families. They assess the complexities of racialized slavery in the shaping and adaptation of family life for African Americans and the continuing structural-racial oppressions that shape their family experiences and reactions. They point out that while the socioeconomic conditions of African American families are getting somewhat better, they still face segregation, institutional racism and violence even as Black Lives Matter and other resistance movements struggle to confront the racialized system.

Roberta Spalter-Roth, an important sociologist researching U.S. employment issues, seeks in her chapter to understand the workings of the U.S. labor market, employer practices, and worker efforts to understand why workers of color often end up at the bottom of the employment ladder. She draws attention to the metaphoric "job queue" as a useful instrument for evaluating structural inequalities and their impact on workers. She explores what will happen to the job queue in the future, and points out that the existing and growing racial polarization, encouraged by the white right wing and presidents like Donald Trump, means that constructive cooperation between increasingly diverse U.S. workers is extremely unlikely.

Lynn Weber, Ruth Zambrana, and Elizabeth Fore address several critical aspects of the relationship between health institutions and intersecting systems of racial, ethnic, and other inequalities. They argue that racial and ethnic differences define health conditions and health care in the United States. They also provide an overview of contemporary data on racial-ethnic differences in health and health care. Nowhere is the severity and impact of white racism on the United States and its people clearer and more profound than in the arena of health care—where racism is often literally a matter of life and death. Since the middle of the twentieth century, extensive population studies have repeatedly documented the lower life quality, lesser life expectancy, and restricted life chances that people of color endure in the United States and, for the most part, worldwide. Whether obesity or cancer, or mental health, systemic racism reduces the possibilities for healthy life. The authors persuasively point out that the transformation of U.S. health care requires significant confrontations with all systems of social oppression.

Victor Ray, a keen sociological observer and scholar of racial relations, explores the relationship between the U.S. "racial project" and the U.S. military, arguing that this centuries-old and highly developed militarization is a key component of the domestic construction of racial relations. He points out how much social violence radiates from the military experience to everyday life, dehumanizing all in a continuing cycle of decline under systems of institutional racial domination and racial repression both at home and abroad.

To examine further the rationalization of the U.S. racial and racist hierarchy, Peter Kivisto and Andrey Rezaev argue that, if applied to the United States, the idea of a racial democracy can be a valuable analytic tool to understand the implications of "race" for structurally determined and persistent patterns of inequality. In this meaning "racial democracy" can be defined as a racially diverse nation that is *not* characterized by significant racial inequality. This ideal of "racial democracy" as a political tool took root in Brazil and was over time applied to that country and several others in Latin America. There is a creative irony here insofar as, in its earliest articulations, the idea of a racial democracy was intended to distinguish the racial dynamics in Brazil from that of the United States. Moreover, in recent decades the term has been challenged by anti-racist groups and movements as very inaccurate for a highly racist Brazil and for other Latin American countries. In these cases, it actually operates as a pernicious myth serving as an ideological rationale for existing racial oppression and inequalities. Cognizant of these latter realities, Kivisto and Rezaev make a case for the utility of the ideal of a "racial democracy" as an analytical tool for the United States.

Amir Marvasti, Karyn McKinney, and Brad Pinter are important scholars working on issues of racial inequality. Here, they substantially interrogate the concept of "diversity" and ask what diversity goals truly are. They argue for more demanding and more critical tools to measure the effectiveness of existing and projected diversity programs. They argue that this society needs to set up important long-term and short-term goals that will actually enable meaningful and corrective reassessment and monitoring, as well as reinforcing realistic diversity goals with more creative societal resources and strategies.

In their provocative chapter, Ruth Thompson-Miller, leading scholar on forms of symbolic racism, and Joe R. Feagin provide an overview analysis of the long legal segregation (Jim Crow) era in the United States. They examine how during the near-slavery realities of this legal segregation epoch, African Americans were under quite *extreme* social, economic, and political control, which was often backed up with white racial violence such as lynchings. They also demonstrate how individual African Americans and their families had to cope on a daily basis with one of the most oppressive systems of racial oppression ever developed, one often paralleling the patterns of the South African system of violent apartheid. Drawing on in-depth interviews from many older African Americans in two southern areas they detail the views, understandings, and experiences of older African Americans who lived for decades under legal segregation. These interviews reveal, among other important things, how these men and women are still, even today, greatly affected by the severely negative experiences of legal segregation.

In her chapter, Melanie Bush, an innovative scholar who has done much interviewing of younger Americans on racial matters, examines constructions and imaging in the United States and calls for a moratorium on the dominant equation of "being American" with being white. She examines commonplace assumptions and attitudes about national identity in the United States and various social constructions of which groups are considered to be "real" citizens, and under what circumstances. Exploring the mechanisms that reinforce global and national racialized structures, she examines new configurations of identity that have emerged as the contradictions of white world supremacy have become increasingly apparent in the modern world. Today, in innumerable public and private constructions, U.S. nationalism and white racism have become largely indistinguishable.

In examining colonial legacies and the postcolonial realities, in his chapter on international migrants, Jorge A. Bustamante, a leading immigration scholar, examines the critical policies that governments adopt concerning immigration, policies that mark indelibly the racial and ethnic thinking of a country's leader. He navigates the historical, empirical, and theoretical aspects of Mexican immigration to the United States. The mobilization of people in multiple directions makes such cross-border migrations impossible to disassociate from ongoing globalization and the question of the human rights of immigrants. Bustamante's dialectical analysis notes the apparent contradiction between the universality of human rights and the notion of international immigrants as under the sovereign control of a particular country's government, which can thus distinguish between its own "nationals" and "foreigners." He examines how most government constitutions define relations between these supposed nationals and foreigners. This governmental process is explained through a diagram of the dialectics of vulnerability, and a historical perspective is used in order to analyze the salient aspects of a *de facto* international labor market in which a particular type of immigration takes place.

Not all Americans of African descent have come into the complex society that is the United States through the involuntary immigrations of the slavery era, as Yanick St. Jean makes clear in her chapter. St. Jean, a talented sociologist who works on both racism and religion issues, takes a different approach by examining writings on Haitian Americans. She reviews the literature on this neglected group of relatively new Americans to examine their situation over recent decades. Haitian immigrants, who have come to the United States over roughly the same period as many Cuban immigrants, have had quite different entry and development experiences from the Cubans. This is, in large part, because of their differential, often racialized, treatment by those whites in control of the U.S. immigration process over the last few decades. Cuban immigrants got a great deal of U.S. government aid and support, while Haitian immigrants received little such support. St. Jean identifies some trends from this slowly growing literature and draws attention to some benefits for understanding racial matters in the United States that comes from research examining Caribbean Americans separately from other Americans of color, specifically African Americans.

Kimberley Ducey, a leading Canadian scholar on contemporary racial relations, explores the white racial frame and systemic racism to understand the history of white privilege in Canada. She focuses on how white racial framing shaped the thoughts and actions of elite white women who governed a low-income housing project, which is based on an ethnography Ducey conducted. She successfully shows how black residents routinely respond to white racial framing with counter-framing, effectively challenging the white racial frame. Regardless of the commonplace Canadian claim of growing racial and ethnic equality, it is impossible to understand complex Canadian relations without understanding racism's systemic impact on institutions in the society. Her analysis provides critical tools for understanding the racial realities of Canadian society.

Racial oppression is not unique to the United States, as we have already noted, but indeed has become a global reality—usually with the assistance of major U.S. government actors. Over the last two centuries, racial oppression has encompassed the establishment of racial hierarchies and the institution-alization of racial segregation, the confinement and exclusion of certain racialized peoples, and the elimination of those considered racially inferior through group genocide. In the context of global racism, racialized genocide and war are frequently seen as natural and inevitable—indeed sometimes they are not even seen or noticed by many people. Pinar Batur, who works on global racism, explores the changing terms and realities of racist oppression and anti-racist struggles, using case studies ranging from Iraq, to New Orleans in the United States, to the Sudan. She explores the new terms of exclusion and the paths to persisting war and genocide, as well as the integrality of war and genocide to the framework of global anti-racist confrontation and organization.

Carlos Alamo-Pastrana, a critical scholar of racial and ethic relations in the Puerto Rican and Latin American communities, analyzes the utilization and limitations of a comparative methodology as a tool to study race, gender, ability, and sexuality. By concentrating on political cartoons in the United States and in Puerto Rico, he argues that the study of these cartoons cannot develop well without full consideration of the larger racial regimes and institutions within which they arise. He suggests innovative methodological interventions that are not haunted by their past or obscured by dominant racist contexts.

Whereas the relationship of food production and racial matters is typically discussed through the lens of economic production and consumption related to food systems, Isaac Leslie and Monica White, major scholars on these food system issues, explain instead how farmers of color have used agriculture as a site of racial resistance and collective agency throughout U.S. history. Focusing on U.S.-born black and immigrant Latino\a farmers, they dissect how twentieth and twenty-first century U.S. agricultural policies have systematically disadvantaged farmers of color. They highlight these farmers' collective strategies of resistance. As contemporary alternative food movements redesign food systems to focus on personal and environmental health, they also reproduce racialized racial and other social inequalities; this is challenged by the Food Justice movement. Leslie and White argue that contemporary food movements can contribute to racial justice by building on the historical resistance strategies of U.S. farmers of color. Leslie and White thus take an asset-based approach by demonstrating how farmers of color continue to use agriculture to disrupt racial oppression and to construct important alternatives that prioritize healthy communities and racial justice.

In this highly provocative work, an excellent team of observers and analysts of racial relations and racism, Karen Douglas, Gideon Sjoberg, Rogelio Sáenz and David Embrick, reveal the importance of the prison industrial complex to the American economy, and explore some mechanisms to reverse course. They expose how institutions and knowledge have long been structured to serve best the interests of those in power. They advance several arguments. First, the prison industrial complex as it is presently constituted is a product of the economic, social, and political transformation associated with market-oriented policies over the past forty-plus years. Second, race and racism are defining features in present-day mass incarceration. Third, few social scientists recognize the importance of knowledge in the development and advancement of the modern world. Its importance becomes more apparent when we see what is happening in its neglect. Lastly, they elaborate on a counter-system that will serve to buttress the population as we transition away from the prison economy and reverse course from the undemocratic path we have been traveling.

Jesus G. Smith, Cristina Morales, and Chong-Suk Han, shouldering a fresh new analysis, innovatively examine the concept of racism in regard to analyzing sexual desire issues in GLBTQ studies. In their chapter, they explore how sexual racism impacts erotic capital among black and black mixed-race men. In their view, this type of racism greatly influences their erotic capital and thereby shapes the social status order. Sexual racism is prevalent in all areas, resulting in black men acquiring less erotic capital even though they possess all the qualities of sexual desirability. This is primarily because they are operating in a society where the superiority of whiteness is hegemonic.

Danielle Falzon, a young scholar of environmental racism and environmental justice policy, and Pinar Batur, in their study of global environmental racism argue that in the face of global climate change, Pacific Islanders face a societal future that is far more uncertain than the rest of the world. They point out that this future is forged by environmentally racist and unjust practices and policies on a global level. Global institutions such as the United Nations often ignore the racist character of such unjust practices, and the voices and concerns of climate vulnerable nations become marginalized to the economic wants of those countries with more resources and power.

In her probing chapter, Eileen O'Brien, a leading expert on whites who have joined anti-racist organizations, argues that "anti-racism" can be understood, in its broadest sense, as any theory or practice, whether personal or organizational, that seeks to challenge, reduce, or eliminate manifestations of white racism in a society. In her analysis, she demonstrates that the issue of what particular ideas and practices qualify as "anti-racist" is difficult to answer, given that scholars in the field of racial relations operate from different definitions of racism. In her view, anti-racism cannot be merely understood as the inverse of racism because many practices that some label "anti-racist" may be taken to perpetuate contemporary racism by yet another definition. She suggests that, in contrast to feminist research that has better defined and theorized what feminism is, anti-racism research has not yet developed an agreed-upon typology and interpretations in regard to what is racist and anti-racist.

The volume's concluding chapter, by Joe Feagin and Hernán Vera, accents the idea of racism as a *total* social phenomenon, a theoretical perspective that opens to research several aspects of racial and ethnic relations thus so far unexplored. One emphasis in this regard is on the empirical reality of a global elite-white-male dominance system that encompasses not only systemic racism but also systemic sexism (heterosexism) and systemic classism (capitalism). Much of the chapter then examines the use of counter-system framing and analysis by important organizations—such as the United Nations–and many black and other social justice movements. The latter seek to dismantle the systemic racism central to this elite-white-male dominance system and thus to expand real human rights and democracy.

The scholar Etienne Balibar famously argues that we all have a tendency to give great importance to the events of our youth. But not just our youth, for the entirety of our lives is reflected in our work, scholarship, and agency. As our inspirations change, as the challenges we face alter, and as the scars of the period in which we live get integrated into our work, ideology, and actions, as sociologists we strive to ask the next revolutionary question and explore its possibilities. As a result, we exist in a forever expanding universe of possibilities. Next year (2018) and thereafter, most entering college students will have known only this new twenty-first century, yet they still will be confronting the centuries-old global color line. Their possibilities are endless, but their futures are already marred by social confrontation and struggle—while they try to make a living in this new century of white-imposed racism, with its still extensive racist framing and racial discrimination. As their social universe expands with education and experience, they will doubtless feel these many challenges deeply in their hearts!

As we finish this volume, we are witnessing troubling societal realities across the globe and an even more troubling global future. Agency is about teaching and learning participation, understanding equality is a form of praxis, and counter-hegemony is about not standing for passive inclusion in politics or cultural practice. Our challenge as educators is to face the increasing responsibility to realistically represent what we know, experience, and struggle about systemic racial oppression. Our commitment and responsibility is to integrate anti-racist praxis in order to enable more community, justice, and equality. This volume shows that many social scientists have shouldered new educational possibilities and responsibilities to make sure that we break down oppressive racial and ethnic barriers and to open up classroom walls to include difficult problems of everyday life and the challenges of being a progressive and activist citizen, forever defending equality and anti-racist commitments. As our students, like ourselves, learn to question, participate, and coordinate, and thereby feel powerful, our struggle continues!

References

Batur, P. (2007). Heart of violence: Global racism, war and genocide. In H. Vera & J. Feagin (Eds.), *Handbook of the sociology of racial and ethnic relations,* pp. (441–54). Springer.

Batur, P. (2012). Colonialism and post-colonialism: The global expansion of racism (updated and revised). In J. Feagin & C. B. Feagin (Eds.), *Racial and ethnic relations* (10th ed.) Prentice-Hall.

Feagin, J. R. (2006). *Systemic racism: A theory of oppression.* New York and London: Routledge.

Feagin, J. R. (1973). *The urban scene: Myths and realities.* New York: Random House.

Feagin, J. R. (2000). *Racist america: Roots, current realities, and future reparations.* New York and London: Routledge.

Feagin, J. R. (2013). *The white racial frame* (2nd ed.). New York: Routledge.

Whitman, J. Q. (2017). *Hitler's american model: The united states and the making of nazi race law.* Princeton, NJ: Princeton University Press.

Part I
Classical Debates: Upholding the Color Line

White

Charles A. Gallagher

Contents

In everyday vernacular the racial category white is understood as a group of people who share a common set of phenotypes (skin color, hair texture, facial features) and trace their genealogical roots to Europe. This account where Caucasian, European ancestry and "fair" skin color are synonymous with whiteness is problematic for a number of reasons, most notably the ahistorical and homogenizing treatment of whiteness and the omission of how white as a social identity is inextricably linked to power, privilege and dominance.

Popular accounts that reduce whiteness to simply a matter of geography and skin pigment reveal the hegemonic nature of this identity. Whiteness remains a relatively unmarked and invisible category yet white supremacy, since its ascendancy in the 17th century, continues to define, construct and control a global order organized around race.

The inherent power of whiteness is the confluence of multiple social and political fictions that have transformed this category into the dominant, universal racial norm other racialized groups are forced to mirror. The maintenance of whiteness as both a hegemonic and normative racial identity is achieved through the international reach of the western media, geo-politics and the marketing white patterns of consumption and lifestyles around the globe. Given that whiteness is often viewed as status symbol it is not surprising that a marketing study in 2006 found that 40% of women in Hong Kong, Malaysia, the Philippines South Korea and Taiwan routinely use skin whitening creams (Fuller 2006). In these countries "whiter" skin functions as mark of beauty for women, a tangible asset that privileges those with lighter skin above those who are darker or less white. "Whiter" Asian women are perceived to be more attractive to men and hence more likely to have the opportunity to "marry up" socio-economically. Far from a benign act of status enhancement these whitening creams can disfigure, burn, scar and lead to various forms of skin cancers. This example of whitening points to the complicated ways whiteness is bound up in patriarchy, class location, cultural imperialism and how white desires reflect

C. A. Gallagher (✉)
Department of Sociology, La Salle University, Philadelphia, PA, USA
e-mail: gallagher@lasalle.edu

© Springer International Publishing AG, part of Springer Nature 2018
P. Batur and J. R. Feagin (eds.), *Handbook of the Sociology of Racial and Ethnic Relations*,
Handbooks of Sociology and Social Research, https://doi.org/10.1007/978-3-319-76757-4_1

a racist form of rational choice modeling (Knowles 2003; Gabriel 1998; Dyer 1997).

Given that the dictionary definition of whiteness is how most individuals (at least in the West) understand this word it is instructive to quickly outline what this definition excludes. Mainstream explanations of what constitutes membership in the category white ignores the socio-historic process that created a hierarchical social system based on white supremacy (Allen 1994; Smedley 1993; Fanon 1968). Nor do everyday accounts of whiteness acknowledge the relational, socially situated and inherently political foundation that constructs all racial categories (Omi and Winant 1994; Roediger 1991; Lipsitz 1998). Popular understandings of whiteness are typically unconscious of how a classification scheme based on pseudo-science and religious dogma became globally hegemonic (Smedley 1993; Baum 2006). Missing from the common sense understanding of white is how an amalgamation of diverse and warring populations from what is now Europe came to see themselves and their own self interests as whites, place themselves at the top of this hierarchy, and impose a system of racial stratification on the rest of the world (Jacobson 1998; Baum 2006). Contemporary understandings of white does not begin to map the emergence of a new racialized system of global stratification that quickly shifts whiteness from mere phenotypic description to one that signifies white privilege and domination (Baum 2006; Omi and Winant 1986). There is no acknowledgment in the current definition of this racial category concerning the plasticity, instability and changing parameters of whiteness. Present-day accounts of whiteness do not detail the genealogy of this category; what is or was considered white in one social, historic or geographical context is outside the bounds of whiteness in another (Hartigan 1999; Perry 2004; Jacobson 1998; Rodriguez and Cordero Guzman 1992; Twine 1998). Missing from this definition where white is reduced to simply being the relative absence of melanin is the assumption that whiteness is a naturally occurring, unproblematic, unchanging and uniform social identity rather than one was and continues to be forged

out of political contestation, coercion and violence (Omi and Winant 1994; Lopez 1996; Gallagher 2004; Bonilla-Silva 2001). The unacknowledged privileges that accrue to whites because of their skin color, the role racist ideology plays in normalizing white supremacy and a history of racism that is peripheral to most whites is why whiteness is often invisible to those who occupy this racial category. The incomplete and truncated definition of "white" one finds in a dictionary mirrors how the general population, particularly whites, have come to understand this racial category; one that is situationally or only partially marked as a racial identity but one that continues to confer unearned privileges to its members (Gallagher 1997; Harris 1993; Lipsitz 1998).

The belief that human populations can be placed neatly into discreet, non-overlapping, mutually exclusive categories based on anatomical features is not only false, it is, relatively speaking, a rather recent development (Smedley 1993; Allen 1994). The discredited view that race is a valid scientific category that correlates perfectly with phenotypes comes into being around 1500 as Europeans exploring new regions for natural resources and potential colonial conquest interact with populations in Africa, Asia and the Americas. Prior to these contacts there is simply no record of race being used as it is *now* currently, generally, and incorrectly understood (Smedley 1993; Baum 2006).

Creating a system of social and economic stratification where the category white could become hegemonic required the creation of mutually reinforcing binaries where white cultural practices and belief systems could be put in place by Europe's colonial projects. Eminent 18th century scientists like Carolus Linnaeus and Johann Blumenbach fused cultural bias, religious dogma and ethnocentrism with the assumed inferior behavioral and psychological traits of non-Northern European human populations to create a hierarchical taxonomy organized around skin color. Not surprisingly the "civilized" white race was situated on the upper reaches of this hierarchy while lesser "races" occupied lower rungs of this pecking order. The term

"Caucasian" itself reflects the extent to which these groupings mirror cultural bias and ethnocentrism. Blumenbach choose the word Caucasian to represent the "white" race "because he felt that the women of the Caucasus region in Russia were the most beautiful in all of Europe" (Smedley p. 167). The construction and reification of racial categories through a now discredited branch of science not only justified European cultural and economic domination throughout the globe but the rise of white supremacy becomes the rationalization for equally nefarious activities, namely slavery, colonialism, genocide and the eugenics movement.

Writing in the 18th century scientists like Count de Buffon, Carolus Linnaeus and Johann Blumenbach debated if human population were divided into three, four, five or six distinct races. By the end of the 19th century these categories were collapsed into the three Great Races: Caucasoid, Mongoloid and Negroid. Once this racial ideology was in place, race and whiteness became synonymous with power and privilege as European military and technological superiority allowed these nations to colonize much of the "new" world. The new system of conquest, slavery, and colonial control destroyed indigenous social, religious and economic systems, extracted wealth in the form of slavery and natural resources and imposed a framework throughout Asia, Latin America, Africa and Australia where the colonizers could lord over those who were colonized (Fanon 1963; Allen 1994; Omi and Winant 1994).

The classification of the earth's population into racial categories ostensibly based on sound scientific principles was nothing more then the religious dogma of the day given a veneer of respectability by the scientific community. Almost every scientific theory that justified and normalized white over non-white had some rationalization, empirical starting point or assumption based in Holy Scripture. The supposed essential races of mankind (Negroid, Mongoloid and Caucasoid) and which groups were destined to dominate becomes a scientific retelling of the curse of Ham, manifest destiny and God's will that heathens (anyone not white

and Christian) must be converted, controlled or eliminated. Science confirmed what Christian theologians knew all along: the white race was God's chosen people and as such had the right to claim all natural resources and to subjugate any population deemed culturally inferior, heathen, pagan or uncivilized.

This self-serving Biblical mandate to enlighten created the "white man's burden" to civilize (through slavery if need be) the non-white masses. The narrative that emerges from white colonizers is one that depicts those colonized as quasi-human, atavistic throwbacks occupying a branch far down the tree of human evolutionary history. In relatively short order a hierarchical social system that sorts people by physical characteristics is unilaterally imposed on Europe's far-flung colonies in the Americas Africa and Asia, placing the architects of this system, the European colonizers themselves atop this racist social order.

Although the struggle over the meaning of racial categories has been in play for over 500 years there remains the tendency to see race as a static entity. The category white, like all racial categories, is in a constant state of flux and contestation. The parameters of what constitutes racial binaries are constantly being recalibrated and redrawn through various political, cultural and economic pressures. There has never been, nor is there now, one definition of white. The construction of the category white, however loose, variable or inconsistent this classification was or continues to be, signifies the supremacy of one socially defined population over others based on physical characteristics deemed meaningful and important through the political and social process of racialization. The racial formation perspective holds that "social, economic, and political forces determine the content and importance of racial categories, and by which they are in turn shaped by racial meanings" (Omi and Winant 1994, p. 55). Once this racial formation process is set in motion a "racialized social order" (Bonilla-Silva 2001) is cemented in place where all levels of society (politics, economics, ideology) organized, reproduce and allocate resources along racial lines.

The US Census's definition of which groups were considered white provides a clear example of both the instability of whiteness as a social category and the role institutions play in structuring the racial order. Starting with the first decennial census in 1790 the US Census has changed, redefined or recategorized who was "officially" white numerous times (Baum 2006; Lopez 1996; Prewitt 2005). The official government definition of who was inside or outside the bounds of whiteness decided who would be a slave, who could own land, who one could marry, who could vote, where individuals could live, who would be targeted for lynching and who could fill menial versus primary sector jobs. Jurisprudence and the courts have also played an important role in shaping the contours of whiteness. One such example is the 1923 Supreme Court case revolving around Bhagat Singh Thind, a college educated man born in India who had petitioned for citizenship after living in the United States for ten years. The Supreme Court argued that although some anthropologist might categorize Mr. Thind as "Caucasian" he did not have the right to naturalized citizenship because the "common man" would not consider this individual white (Lopez 1996). The Supreme Court rejected Thind's contention that his Aryan (and not Mongolian) roots, high caste status and his animosity towards racial minorities established his whiteness. The court took the position that the social definition of white was what the man on the street understood it to be, not the musings of the "scientific" community. Drawing on the cultural biases of the day these judges decided by fiat what constituted membership in the white race and hence the rights of citizenship of Mr. Thind, and by extension all "Asians" in the United States.

Social definitions of what constitutes the category white are even more slippery and expansive than those divined by the census or the courts, in part because what constitutes membership in the category white is always mutating. The inclination is however, to view racial categories as unchanging entities that reflect a "natural" order in a fixed racial hierarchy. What is quickly forgotten by each subsequent generation is that these racial designations are social definitions forged out of conflict and contest. From 1619 through the early 1800s enslaved West Africans representing a myriad of cultures, ethnic identities and languages collectively became "Negroes" upon arrival into the United States. Diverse ethnic groups like Russian Jews, Greeks, Southern Italians and the Irish, each at one time outside of what the "common man" would consider was part of the white dominant racial group in the United States became, through an act of social alchemy and racism, white (Ignatiev 1995). James Baldwin succinctly puts the process of White On Arrival (WOA) for European immigrants in this way "No one was white before he/she came to America. It took generations, and a vast amount of coercion, before this became a white country" (Baldwin 1984, p. 178). From a material resource perspective there was much to be gained by European immigrants embracing a white identity. Beyond the "psychological wage of whiteness" which meted out status and social honor based on membership in the white race, new immigrants who could reposition themselves as being marked as white could (eventually) enter the first rung on an industrial occupational ladder that was by and large upward. In discussing how whiteness served as a wage David Roediger explains that "the Problem is not that the white working class is at critical junctures manipulated into racism, but that it comes to think of itself and its interests as white" (Roediger 1991, p. 12). Just as class cleavages shaped the process of white racialization for European immigrants so to did newly emerging nation states, through the action of elites and institutions they controlled, consciously forge a national identity across antagonistic and often warring white ethnic populations. In the United States and South Africa, and to a lesser extent in Brazil, a national identity was achieved by embracing white supremacy. The unification of intra-ethnic white populations was accomplished primarily by sacrificing the rights and lives of non-whites to achieve peace and stability in countries that were experiencing civil wars and insurrections which threatened their existence as emerging or new nations (Marx 1998).

The US Census includes in its definition of who is white people having origins in "the Middle East and North Africa" but this official definition of who is part of the dominant group and who can claim the privileges such membership provides has changed significantly since the 9/11 terrorist attacks on US targets (Akram and Johnson 2002). Before the smoke had cleared from the terrorist attacks Arab and Arab-Americans went from being white Americans (albeit marginally) to the racial "other". The profiling, detainment, harassment and discrimination directed towards Arab-Americans since 9/11 is an example of how whiteness, and the civil rights normally granted to this population can be revoked or suspended.

If the category white has meant different things at different times in various locals in the United States such incoherence and confusion pale in comparison to the multiplicity of white identities throughout the world. Someone considered something other than or not quite white in the context of the United States' racial hierarchy could easily glide into the category white in Brazil (Twine 1998), Puerto Rico (Rodriguez 1992) or South Africa (Steyn 2001). In the United States half of all Latinos (recognized as an ethnic group by the US government) define themselves as white in the decennial census. A segment of the Asian-American and Latino population is, according to recent research on identity construction in this community, "whitening" in ways that parallel how the Irish, Italians and Jews came to see themselves and be defined as white (Gans 1999; Bonilla-Silva 2001; Gallagher 2003a, b).

All racial categories are by definition social relations of power. Within this system of racial stratification being white typically affords a disproportionate share of status and greater relative access to the material resources that shape life chances. It is for these reasons that white is defined as a form of property (Harris 1993) that yields both tangible assets (land, jobs) and privileges (citizenship, social honor) to whites that are or have been denied to non-whites. The "possessive investment in whiteness" as George

Lipsitz puts it, is the bundle of perks, benefits and privileges that accrue to whites simply because of their skin color and can, like most assets, be passed down from one generation to the next (Lipsitz 1998). These societal perks of whiteness are by no means uniformly distributed to all whites. White privilege is not, as Ruth Frankenberg points "absolute but rather crosscut by a range of other axes of relative advantage or subordination; these do not erase or render irrelevant race privilege, but rather inflect and modify it" (Frankenberg 2001, p. 76).

It is within this context where whiteness, privilege and the institutional arrangements that reproduce racial hierarchies that the category white itself should be understood as a racial project. Omi and Winant (1994) define a racial project as being "simultaneously an interpretation, representation or explanation of racial dynamics, and an effort to reorganize and redistribute resources along particular racial lines (p. 56)... [it is] racist if it creates or reproduces structures of domination based on essentialist categories of race" (p. 71). Institutions and social practices redistribute resources along racial lines in ways that are often made invisible or justified through racist ideology. For hundreds of years religion and science justified white supremacy on epistemological and moral grounds. These institutions were, and in many ways continue to be, racial projects because they maintain, reproduce and normalize white privilege. Just as a geocentric view of earth's relationship to the sun was replaced with a heliocentric one, so to have geneticists, biologists and social scientists come to accept the idea that race is a social construction. The fact race (and hence whiteness) is now defined by the scientific community as a social construction does not, however, change the perception among most individuals that race is responsible for traits like intelligence, criminality, motivation, behavior or athletic prowess. The power that white as an identity continues to hold is the fiction that race itself, rather that social inequality, poverty or institutional racism, is responsible for social inequality between races.

References

Allen, T. W. (1994). *The invention of the white race: Racial oppression and social control*. New York: Verso.

Baldwin, J. (1984). On being "white" ... and other lies. In D. Roediger (Ed.), *Black on white: Black writers on what it means to be white*. New York: Schocken Books.

Baum, B. (2006). *The rise and fall of the Caucasian Race: A political history of racial identity*. New York: New University Press.

Bonilla-Silva, E. (2001). *White supremacy and racism in the post-civil rights era*. Boulder: Lynne Rienner Publishers.

Doane, A. W., & Bonilla-Silva, E. (2003). *White out: The continuing significance of Racism*. New York: Routledge.

Dyer, R. (1997). *White*. New York, NY: Routledge.

Fanon, F. (1968). *The wretched of the earth*. New York: Grove Press Inc.

Frankenberg, R. (2001). The mirage of an unmarked whiteness. In B. B. Rasmussen, E. Klinenberg, I. Nexica, & M. Wray (Eds.), *The making and unmaking of whiteness*. Durham, NC: Duke University Press.

Fuller, T. (2006). *International Herald Tribune*, 31 May.

Gabriel, J. (1998). *Whitewash: Racialized politics and the media*. London: Routledge.

Gallagher, C. A. (1997). White racial formation in the twenty-first century. In R. Delgado & J. Stefancic (Eds.), *Critical white studies: Looking behind the mirror*. Philadelphia, PA: Temple University Press.

Gallagher, C. A. (2003a). Color-blind privilege: The social and political functions of erasing the color-line in post-race America. *Race, Gender Class, 10*(4), 22–37.

Gallagher, C. A. (2003b). Racial redistricting: Expanding the boundaries of whiteness. In H. Dalmage (Ed.), *The politics of multiracialism: Challenging racial thinking*. Albany, NY: SUNY Press.

Gans, H. (1999). The possibility of a new racial hierarchy in the twenty-first century United States. In C. A. Gallagher (Ed.) *Rethinking the color line: Readings in race and ethnicity*. New York: McGraw-Hill Publishers, Third Edition, 2007.

Harris, C. (1993). Whiteness as property. *Harvard Law Review, 106*, 1710–1795.

Hartigan, J., Jr. (1999). *Racial situations: Class predicaments of whiteness in Detroit*. Princeton: Princeton University Press.

Hartigan, J., Jr. (2005). *Odd tribes: Towards a cultural analysis of white people*. Durham: Duke University Press.

Jacobson, M. F. (1998). *Whiteness of a different: European Immigrants and the alchemy of race*. Cambridge, MA: Harvard University Press.

Knowles, C. (2003). *Race and social analysis*. London: Sage Press.

Lipsitz, G. (1998). *The possessive investment in whiteness: How white people profit from identity politics*. Philadelphia: Temple University Press.

Lopez, I. F. (1996). *White by law: The legal construction of race*. New York: New York University Press.

Marx, A. (1998). *Making race and nation: A comparison of South Africa, The United States and Brazil*. New York: Cambridge University Press.

Omi, M., & Winant, H. (1994). *Racial formation in the United States: From the 1960s to the 1990s*. New York: Routledge.

Perry, P. (2004). *Shades of white: White kids and racial identities in high school*. Durham: Duke University Press.

Rodriguez, C., & Cordero Guzman, H. (1992). Placing Race in Context. *Ethnic and Racial Studies, 14*, 1.

Roediger, D. R. (1991). *The wages of whiteness: Race and the making of the American working class*. New York: Verso.

Roediger, D. R. (2005). *Working towards whiteness: How America's Immigrants became white: The strange journey from Ellis Island to the suburbs*. New York: Basic Books.

Steyn, M. (2001). *"Whiteness just isn't what it used to be": White identity in a changing South Africa*. Albany: State University of New York Press.

Twine, F. W. (1998). *Racism in a racial democracy: The maintenance of white supremacy in Brazil*. New Brunswick: Rutgers University Press.

The Struggle of Indigenous Americans: A Socio-Historical View

James V. Fenelon

Contents

Abstract

This chapter traces out the origins of Indigenous Peoples in the Americas, their struggles to survive and resist during European and American conquest and domination over the continent, and the nature of contemporary conflicts and revitalization strategies. We will cover four thematic/historical periods, including the origins of indigenous peoples, along with definitions used as political identifies, historically and current socio-political usage; conflicts of "American Indians" in terms of nations and struggles over sovereignty; larger Indigenous struggles in Latin America with a focus on the three modern states of North America; and anti-globalization and cultural contestation conflicts over Indigeneity, autonomy and the nature of community. The work concludes analyzing indigenous peoples in the Americas, partly explaining a great diversity of cultures, experiences, histories and even names, through the contemporary conflicts at Standing Rock and over natural resources around the globe.

2.1 Origins and Definitions

Indigenous Peoples and modern science differ in key ways as to their original locations, resembling philosophical differences in approach toward "creation" and "tribalism" which debatedly resonate in contemporary disagreements found in mainstream society. Perhaps the most fundamental of these is the nature of creation and sacred origin stories. American Indians generally believed they were created from the spirits and

J. V. Fenelon (✉)
Department of Sociology and Center of Indigenous Peoples Studies, California State University, San Bernardino, CA, USA
e-mail: JFenelon@csusb.edu

© Springer International Publishing AG, part of Springer Nature 2018   9
P. Batur and J. R. Feagin (eds.), *Handbook of the Sociology of Racial and Ethnic Relations*,
Handbooks of Sociology and Social Research, https://doi.org/10.1007/978-3-319-76757-4_2

the land, thereby connecting their philosophies with particular places, and with all forms of life. (Important to note in this respect is the great similarity with the Biblical creation story written in Genesis, while most American Indian peoples followed their oral traditions) Western societies used their ocean-going technologies to explore the Caribbean area, supported by their vast militaries and war-like approaches, following news from the Columbus expedition. These religion-driven societies called their invasion "discovery" and exploited their technological superior warfare and notions of race and "savagery" with utter disregard for the societies that they encountered, "conquered" and then set to work on the lands taken from them. So a socio-historical view of indigenous Americans must include these histories of conquest, racial stratification and at times genocide, and perhaps most important, the effects on the culture and societies of Native Nations.

2.1.1 Racial Construction of Indians and Blacks for Conquest and Enslavement (1490–1620)

Indigenous Peoples as Native Nations were incredibly complex with great diversity of social systems, ranging from the Aztecan city of Tenochtitlan as one of the largest cities in the world, to transhumance peoples in central plains of North and South America—from great multi-national political confederacies such as the Haudenosaunee, or sea-borne alliances of Island Arawakan in the Caribbean or the Northwestern peoples, to great highland empires such as the Inka—from the numerous Mayan temple cities to vast agricultural nations such as the Coosa in southeastern North America or the Guarani of South America (Mann 2005).

Initial formation of "race" for Indigenous Americans, became salient shortly after 1492.[1]

The first practical usage is over indigenous peoples by the Catholic Church and various Southern European nation-states interested in colonial expansion in the "New World." Taino-Arawak peoples living on the large islands later called Hispaniola are perfectly representative of this initial stage of European conquest.[2] A few were taken back by Columbus to Spain on his first voyage, were shown to the monarchs to prove their existence as "*los Indios*" and then sold in the slave markets of Seville. These indigenous Natives represented racially identified peoples,

---

The inquisition in Spain and southern Europe was instigating these terms against the Moors and especially against Jews (Frederickson 2002), along religious lines, which transported well to the Spanish colonies using Catholic church ideologies. One apparent place to observe this is a continuing tradition in Europe to use more expansive terms of race to include religious minorities, that is less explicitly about the skin-tone identification arising in the Americas.

[2]The Taino Arawak people living on Hispaniola, in the area now called the country of Haiti, was the first place that the first Columbus expedition stopped and spent a significant amount of time, and actually left the better part of the crew of one of his ships that had foundered just off the city called Cape Haitian. When Columbus returned on his second voyage, they had been wiped out after heaping much abuse on women and the local leaders, called "*caciques*" and so Columbus started killing off large scores of them, forcing even more to work in the mines in his feverish search for gold to pay for the expeditions and *conquista*, quickly reducing the overall numbers from an estimated three million indigenous peoples to somewhere around twenty to thirty thousand within thirty years. Having eliminated his workforce, and having new constructs of categorizing people by race rather than ethnicity or national origin, Spain began to import Blacks from Africa to be the first race-based slaves in the Americas, so by 1540 the complete genocide of the Taino-Arawak and the construction of the world's first race-based slave population was constructed. Later the French wrested this incredibly rich and forested colony away from the Spanish, and built what is now known as Haiti, destroying the country's environment and entrenching a brutal system of slavery, ending only with the Haitian Slave Revolution successfully fending off all the colonial armies of the day, leading to the impoverished and often occupied black nation of Haiti in the French West Indies. Thus, egalitarian and community based indigenous societies, often lead by women, living in one of the most beautiful places on earth, were turned into a ravaged environment of the descendants of black slaves, what is now the poorest country in the western hemisphere.

---

[1]"Race" was not used as a term during this first formation period, rather "savages" were connoted to be non-Christian and uncivilized, terms that were conflated.

rather than their own cultures or ethno-national constructs. On the western half of Hispaniola, a nearly complete genocide of Arawakan peoples by 1542 caused a lack of indigenous labor force, which had been replaced by the importation of "blacks" from Africa to be slaves in the colonies, ending in the country Haiti becoming a "black" nation in the western hemisphere. Las Casas and other priest-philosophers of the time later regretted having supported the enslavement of black Africans to replace the indigenous Arawaks.[3] Similarly, within a few decades, Cortez and his military force conquered the Aztecs, reducing them and all indigenous peoples in Mexico to the lowered status of "Indian" although they ruled over one of the world's great empires. Skin-tone visibility, compounded by vast cultural differences, allowed the dominating groups to have instant and permanent recognition of status by "race" stratification (Berkhofer 1978; Fenelon 2002). In this way, notions of the "savage" were connoted to have "racial" distinctions that were inescapable and lifelong. The conquistadors, and their descendants for generations, were thereby in a permanent elite status over the "native" populations. Various racial hierarchies would continue to be utilized for three centuries by the Spanish, until they became essentially unmanageable, partly because of all the racial miscegenation that began to blur any coherent system.[4] However, the effect on native

peoples in the "new world" was always the same, either outright genocidal destruction or racial subordination with an attending loss of culture, (Dippie 1982) and more powerfully the loss of sovereignty and freedom.

Thus millions of peoples and hundreds of societies were racially reduced, ranging from the relatively beautiful and egalitarian Taino-Arawak peoples of Hispaniola to the great cities and empires of the Aztecan peoples ruling over the diverse Native peoples living in what is now called Mexico. This same pattern was enacted throughout Central and South America, including the great Incan peoples of the Andes, the Calusas of the Floridian peninsula, and in one of the huge genocidal romps of history, a destruction of the Mobile peoples and other large Native Nations by deSoto in what would later be the southeastern United States. The de Soto expedition, like Pizarro and others before them including Cortez, introduced another incredibly destructive element into the Americas, diseases such as smallpox that spread like wildfire among the peoples that had no resistance, literally killing hundreds of thousands of American Indians, sometimes as much as 70–80% of a particular community or nation (Thornton 1987). But even if it was only 20 or 30%, Native Nations across the eastern North American continent were devastated and destabilized to the extent that they could no longer pose effective resistance to the "guns, germs and steel" of the Europeans (Diamond 1999).

Movement of racial distinctions into clear demarcation within social institutions was therefore considerably more ambiguous in Caribbean colonies dominated by Spain and France, than systems the English developed over the Irish, and later transported to their American

---

[3]This requires explanation and a disclaimer related to contemporary race theory. "Indios" were a lower order race of people, partially enslaved and killed off in large numbers. As Las Casas, and in Mexico Bernal Diaz and others, decried the brutalization, in a set of debates with Supelveda and European theorists from the Church, colonists began replacing the slave labor force with blacks, initiating race-based slavery into forms as we now know them. However, the Spanish systems always had fractionation of heritage related to manumission and civil status. Two or more trajectories of race began during this time period, one of conquest by race over the Indian, and the other as enslavement by race over the Black. It would take the English to harden and institutionalize these systems into the forms and typologies we know today.

[4]It is important to note that the *repartimiento* (apportionment) and *encomienda* (landed labor or slavery) systems were developed by Columbus and fully enforced by 1502, institutionalized as a base of operations for Spanish

conquest expansion before Cortez invaded Mexico and toppled Tenochtitlan. By 1550 the plantations of the rich colony relied upon Black slaves imported from Africa. When the French retained the *conquista* rights over western Hispaniola, which they renamed *San Domingue*, they inherited fully developed, race-based slavery plantations over 100 years old, which they built into the richest colonial holdings in the world, intensifying the oppression until the Haitian slave revolution overthrew colonial domination.

colonies. "Savage" tribes and chieftains of Ireland were systematically excluded from social institutions within the English system, and subsequently barred by religion and "national" (cultural) origin (Smedley 1999). However, when the English moved this system into their colonies in the Americas, they married this conceptually with notions of the "race" of Indians and subsequently of Blacks, and sub-human status of savagery and lack of civilization. Origins of Indigenous peoples and "Indians" in the Americas, in terms of Race, ethno-nationalism and racism, from the Caribbean through colonial conquest and domination, and later the English colonies and the development of the United States, lifted "race" above all categories of ethnicity, national origin or culture. These are the racial categories nearly all scholars use today, although they were considerably more fluid from 1600 to 1800.[5]

The first major colonies of England in the Americas represents these relationships very well, with the Jamestown settlement in Virginia starting about 1607 and the Plymouth settlements in early Massachusetts, starting about 1620. Both of these colonies were preceded by English ships on fishing, trading and sometimes slaving expeditions along the coastal areas, and usually caused violent conflicts. Both of these settlements tried to befriend some of the local indigenous communities to get food and supplies, but also betrayed any agreements with armed conflicts, usually over land and leadership. After numerous colonists migrated into the region, settlements expanded and entered into many wars with the local Native Nations, often interrupted by agreements and treaties. Both

colonies broke their treaties, with Powhatan and Wampanoag confederacies respectively, under the justification that Indians were not civilized or Christian, and thus could not enter into such agreements with civilized peoples. In both cases, and numerous others, Native peoples were eliminated upwards of 90% of their population, and those who survived were either hiding in small isolated villages, or were sold into slavery (Jennings 1975). The political philosophy behind this genocidal expansion over Native nations as indigenous peoples was racist grouping of diverse peoples collectively called "Indians."

When English colonists in Virginia first bought and kept black "African" slaves, before 1619, they simply adapted existing systems of race-based slavery to their own knowledge of how to maintain dominance over subordinated peoples through laws in their existing social institutions. "Race" thereafter became immutable and permanently stratifying[6] (Hannaford 1996) precisely because of the typification of different races for different purposes—conquest and thereby elimination for Native Nations or indigenous peoples; enslavement and subordination for the people called Negro or Black of African descent; and supremacy and cultural domination for those people first considered Christian, Anglo, and then gradually as "white" of European descent (Frederickson 2002).

The United States of America inherited this system, at least for its agricultural economies in the southern and central colonies that became states. It replicated central institutional features, social engines for setting up and maintaining systems of domination and perpetual stratification, that were so highly developed in Ireland. These were laws governing the control over property, land-holdings and inheritance, education, political participation, exclusion from systems of law, control over the military and police forces, taxation, trade, language, religion, and manipulation over family systems.

---

[5]Again, the racial categories and labels were in formation throughout this period, so the Spanish enforced racial enslavement/ genocide against the Arawak Indians in Hispaniola, replacing them with black slaves, even as they brutalized and partially enslaved Indian peoples in Mexico, but leading to *mestizaje* (mixing) rather than clear racial boundaries. It took the English, over the following hundred years, to institutionalize and harden the racial categories of Indian (to be eliminated) and Black (to be enslaved), and another two hundred years to clarify Whites (with the U.S.) and therefore the typologies we know today.

---

[6]It is important to note that this was "race" in formation, taking a hundred years or more to take shape into the immutable and hardened categories that the U.S. inherited and further developed.

Clearly, "blacks" under race-based slavery had every one of these component spheres of their life either highly regulated or completely denied to them. "Indians" presented a much more complex group to control in this manner, since many Native Nations were still very strong around the new country with their own social systems, under constant attack and erosion. Also, there were many treaties that required legal interpretation, and existing land tenure and socio-economic relations. These systems were controlled through the simple expedient of denying all indigenous peoples' citizenship in the new country that was built on the very lands they once controlled (Wilkins 1997).

The central sociological features of racial domination in the first years of the United States were built around three foundations—the most obvious and powerful feature that overlapped all others was the construction of laws, social policies, and legal practices that maximized and enforced the deep-set stratification and race-based inequality that fueled the entire system[7] (Montague 1997). The controlling systems

of racism were built over, around and for social institutions that separated Christian "white" immigrant Americans from "black" slaves and "Indian" peoples. At first, the English borrowed from the pre-existing enslavement of Native Nations throughout the southeastern area of North America by the Spanish and sometimes the French. However, in utilizing the systems identified above, reaching from the 1620s until 1690 and on to 1700 and even beyond, English colonies hardened their racial codification systems, coding all the "Indian" peoples for elimination, often paying bounties for "redskins" and making alignments with treaties that were repealed as soon as external threats were gone. For indigenous peoples coming into contact and conflict with expanding systems of colonization, this meant a construction of Anglo or "white" with early purity rules that excluded them, hardening of racial rules for Blacks, and underpinnings of

---

[7]These three systemic foundations would now be identified as—laws and social policies, social institutions structured around inequality in all sectors, and the ideological underpinnings. While the ideologies may shift and be transformed over time and changing societal conditions, they are set in place in the 16th century, beginning around 1493 and continuing until the late 1500's, when an advanced slave system over Indian peoples in the Americas, was inherited by the English. The English quickly transported existing systems of domination over the Irish to the Americas, taking its present form around 1619, when "black" slaves were bought and sold in the Virginia colony. Here is where the English slavery system began to diverge from the Spanish and French systems. Non-English systems, while race-based and slipping between genocide of indigenous peoples, slavery over all non-Europeans, and vast land control and labor stratification, such as *encomienda*, were complex and allowed for some mobility. The English, borrowing from their Irish colonies, created immutable racial barriers of English or white, and uncivilized inferior non-white "races." Other Europeans were thus still "civilized" even as it became necessary to wage war with them over lands and new colonies. However, the uncivilized "non-whites" began to be broken into two major groupings—those destined for slavery, and those destined for elimination. For the next one hundred fifty years this system gradually became dichotomous with two racial

domination systems—non-English (mostly Blacks and Indians) versus "English" and later European descent peoples, (typically represented as the black–white dichotomy today) as the overarching racial hierarchy;—and differential treatment toward Blacks and Indians as differing races. Thus social institutions become constructed around these systems of racial hierarchy and treatment. More importantly, laws and social policies favoring English and Europeans in the American colonies, are constructed around enhancing and refining slavery systems over Blacks, and another set are then constructed for continuing elimination of Native peoples and development of legally justified dehumanization, destruction and removal of "foreign" savages with no claim to any citizenship. These essential constructions, of European "whites" over racially inferior "people of color," along with a race-based slavery for Blacks and a race-based social destruction for Indians, are precisely the systems inherited by the fledgling United States of America in the late 18th century, and codified into law (Feagin 2002). Therefore, the United States of America developed its constitution with clearly stated laws about racial slavery only for Blacks and racial domination only for Indians, that were constructed into the well-known racialized social institutions of the 19th century, extended in various permutations toward Mexicans and Asians, and continued to be the ideological underpinnings of 20th century racial inequalities and racism. In this way, the ideologies of racism have survived and transformed themselves many times over the 500 years of racial domination in the Americas, even as policies, laws and social institutions are violently constructed and then violently deconstructed with the changing socio-political orientations toward race, racism and racial hegemony in the Americas.

Indian "blood" descent, not acknowledging national origin, and refusing them full citizenship.[8] Nearly a hundred Native Nations were destroyed and subsumed along the North American east coast (Josephy 2002 [1994]).

2.2 Conflicts of American Indians

The struggles of indigenous Americans and Native Nations in a North American context, over a four hundred year period, would focus especially on sovereignty and their survival in the face of genocide and culturicide (Fenelon 1998), by the colonies and the countries that grew out of their expansion, the United States and Canada. The indigenous nations resisted these invasions and their policies of domination, a main subject of this chapter. We also need to discuss the construction of laws, by race and racism as well as by nation, that discriminated against American Indians, and the ideological apparatus put into place to justify their oppression, that coincides with the rise of scientific racism.

The first actions respecting colonial claims of "sovereignty" over Native Nations occur with the 1493 Inter-Caetera Papal Bull,[9] (Newcomb

2008) declared after Columbus's return. In this time of developing European nation-states, there was no separation of church and state, hence Spanish and other western sea-faring powers intent on taking new lands, were given justification to wage war on native peoples, under "Christianizing" ideologies for conquering peoples with less developed "souls" (Lyons 1992; Berman 1992). The "race" of "*los indios*" was initially constructed with religious differentiation that also marked the racially perceived level of civilization.

The two primary legal principles employed in this grand scheme were the Prince's "Rights to Conquest" (for Europeans only), and the developing "Doctrine of Discovery" (over indigenous peoples in "New World" America) (Wright 1992; Deloria and Lytle 1984). Sundry forms of conquest directed solely for the western hemisphere were put in place. Mechanisms for using these tactics were formalized in "laws" such as the Requerimiento, composed about 1512 by Palacios Rubios (Berkhofer 1978)[10] appearing to give natives "choice" in the manner of a coming domination and destruction, but amounting to little more than legal cover for war. This was deeply embedded in English colonial reasoning as a "Cant of Conquest" (Jennings 1975)[11] in

---

[8]These three forms continue formation in the English and later American systems, from the 17th until mid-19th century political and legal constructions. Purity for "Whites" is mostly Anglo and Christian at first, although there are periodic references to "free white" in colonial and American documents. Hardening of racial hypodescent rules for Blacks occurs during the later 1600's and early 1700's, but is formally fixed by U.S. laws and court decisions throughout the 19th and into the 20th century, often noted as "one drop rule" by later scholars and critical race theorists. Indians as firm racial category are under attack from 1492 on, yet all Treaties and agreements are made with specific Native Nations, leading to further fractionation in the mid-19th century with distinction of "full bloods" and "mixed bloods" ultimately forming into diverse ":blood quantum" rules by the 20th century. The formations for all three racial categories are only complete as the United States move into the early 20th century. However, the scientific underpinnings were classified during the years of the American Revolution by Blumenbach, defended by Kant, and utilized by Thomas Jefferson with clear racial hierarchies placing the Caucasian on top (see Feagin 2002: 33, 81on).

[9]This theological position statement placed the Native peoples in quite inferior positions, requiring European civilization dominance. Expeditions to a "new world" therefore had "just" cause to conquer and civilize in the name of "God and Righteousness." (Lyons 1992; Berman 1992; Wilkins 1997).

[10]To legalize this view of forceful conquest and prove its righteousness, Spanish policy required that a document, probably composed around 1512 by Palacios Rubios, an authority on just-war doctrine, be read to native populations about to be colonized. Although ship captains had the Requerimiento, read from their ship deck as they approached an island, or brave commanders had it delivered in safe but empty places far from the Indian enemies to be attacked, the natives were to understand that they possessed a choice of peace or war as a result of the history of God's creation of the world, and the patronage of the Catholic Church ... (Berkhofer 1978: 123).

[11]These historical roots were central to establishing European-based sovereignty, with future interpretations for institutional legitimation. This meant leaving residual, and very real claims to sovereignty. At this point a "Cant

American colonies, leading to formal application of the "Great White Father" (Prucha 1984) first to colonial administrators and later the United States President when dealing with the Native Nations that stood in the way of their expansion (Berkey 1992).

These claims of legitimate conquest and extinguishing of aboriginal title to lands, usually but not always enacted under various "treaties" between nations, lead to complex forms of "multiple sovereignty" (Todorov 1984; Cornell 1988)[12] and (Wunder 1994), contested in terms of establishing a "Manifest Destiny" ideology that allowed the US Congress and other federal bodies, sufficient interpretation to avoid following treaties, even those made by the U.S. itself (Berkey 1992).

2.2.1 U.S. Claims to Sovereignty as Racism and Genocide

The Declaration of Independence referred to Native peoples as "merciless savages" even as the United States brought Indian Nations into sovereignty discourse under an infamous "Indians not Taxed" clause (representation without taxation), leading to the Non-Intercourse Act of 1790 that formally established nation-to-nation relationships, albeit with an intent of conquest. Already controlling the entire east coast, especially with Washington's destruction of the Haudenosaunee in the north, the Louisiana "Purchase" (1803, Lewis and Clark 1804–1806) was another formal relationship. Essentially, "rights to conquest" using the "doctrine of discovery" were "purchased" by the U.S. (hence, the "voyage of discovery" expedition title).

President Jefferson ordered Lewis and Clark to make declarations of "sovereignty" and "great white father" to Indian nationss, especially the *Tetonwon*-Sioux (Lakota) throughout the journey, similar to the "*Requerimiento*" both in content and delivery (Ronda 1984; Prucha 1984). Jefferson had complicated, often opposing views of Americans Indians, sometimes being paternalistic and seeing them as more assimilable than blacks, as in his *Notes on the State of Virginia.*, and at other times calling for their outright elimination. In this way he was the supreme racist hypocrite, celebrating the Noble Savage while he called for the "rights of all men," conversely holding black slaves and warring upon Native Nations and peoples.

As the United States continued its expansion westward, and its attempts at extinguishing Indian land claims through the treaty-making and war-waging process were successful, the already internalized Indian Nations posed problems to "sovereign" relationships. None stand out more in this respect, than the so-called "Five Civilized Tribes" including the Cherokee Nation. Not only did these people refuse to be removed to the "Frontier" or "Indian Country" as other Native nations were so forced, but they began sophisticated attempts at bi-cultural assimilation, including with U.S. laws. Local states, especially the Carolinas and Georgia, took umbrage at this resistance, and attempted taking Cherokee land by force with a unilateral declaration of sovereign dominance. This led to the next round of official relationships between the United States and Indian Nations (Deloria and Lytle 1984; Champagne 1992).

The Cherokee, with limited support by some missionaries, took legal action to resist continued state encroachment over their lands, leading to a set of U.S. Supreme Court decisions, first being *Johnson v. Mc'Intosh, (1823)*, where the court acknowledged a limited "sovereignty" but sided with individual states.[13] Following that was the

---

of Conquest" (Jennings 1975) meant "claims to sovereignty" were not completely extinguished, provided a potential threat to hegemonic domination.

[12]Todorov (1984) has expressed these claims as issues of "multiple sovereignty," in situations of collective action and revolution. Although untempered by a "complex unfoldings of multiple conflicts" that take into consideration conditions of how a "situation emerged in the first place" (Deloria and Wilkins 1999), the presence of multiple claims, (real or potential), on legitimate sovereignty, greatly informs processes and outcomes of U.S. struggles with Native Nations.

---

[13]The Court did not, however, acknowledge Native Nation "ownership" of the land, ironically forcing legal discussion of group/tribal "trust" rights, therefore sovereignty (Wilkins 1997).

moot *Cherokee Nation v. Georgia, 30 U.S. (5 Pet.) 1 (1831)* that called the Cherokee "domestic dependent nations," thereby setting the precedent as sovereigns. Finally, the court ruled against Georgia in *Worcester v. Georgia (1832),* and in a limited way for Indian Nations, although introducing concepts leading to "plenary power" of the federal government.

Sovereignty, decided by Supreme court majority decision under Chief Justice Marshall, therefore was accorded the Cherokee Nation (and by legal precedent all Indian Nations), although still under federal sovereignty, with ambiguous relationship to the individual states. Nonetheless, U.S. President Jackson broke the constitutional interpretation and began removing Indian peoples from the Southeast states, cajoling Congress into passing the Indian Removal Act of the 1830s (from 1834 to 1868), and thus causing the genocidal "Trail of Tears," extinguishing Indian land claims for a lack of sovereignty (Wallace 1993), based, primarily on essentialist notions of the "race" of American "Indians."

Many indigenous peoples or Native Nations attempted to adapt their culture and socio-political relations to the invasive society. The "five civilized tribes" (Cherokee, Choctaw, Creek, Seminole and Chickasaw) stand out in this respect, but ultimately it was only their status as "Indians" that mattered. The death rates of Indian Removal by military force along the routes to "Indian Country" ran from 20 to 40%, without counting the dead after arrival in what would later be Oklahoma and Kansas. Many traditionalists went into hiding in the mountains and forests, and tried to hold on to their culture ways of life. So-called "Indian Wars" on an expanding "Frontier" caused Native Nations in Ohio, Indiana, Michigan and New York, and all the territories to experience similar suppression (Mohawk 2000). Many had barely survived the domino effects of slave-raiding and the fur trade, developing and maximizing inter-tribal warfare, during the colonialism era, when they came into violent conflict with the United States. While militaristic coalitions arose in opposition to the advancing U.S. imperialism, as under Tecumseh, others attempted peaceful revitalization

movements. All were met with massive military destruction, whether the peoples had entered into non-aggression pacts or not. Near perfect genocide was conducted by states such as California from 1848 to 1868 (Fenelon and Trafzer 2014; Lindsay 2014) extending an oppressive Spanish Mission system toward complete extermination.

This ruthless rejection of even its own laws concerning sovereignty was continued by U.S. administrations along with Congressional oversight all the way until the Treaties Statute of 1871 ended treaty-making and future nation-to-nation status in agreements with "Indians." This was firmly connected to the U.S. —"Sioux Nation of Indians" (Lakota) Fort Laramie Treaty of 1868, (Lazarus 1991) determining land claims that should have been inextinguishable (Fenelon 1998). For twenty years, during battles over the Black Hills, and in the southwest with the Apache, U.S. lawmakers and military leaders lied to and coerced Indian Nations about legal issues concerning sovereignty. The killings at Wounded Knee and death of the Ghost Dance in 1890, ended the conflicts, as the General Allotment (or Dawes) Act of 1887 was now utilized across the United States to allot Indian land to "non-Indians" on "treaty" reservations and "trust" lands. Civilian and military authorities in the U.S. predicted that early in the twentieth century Indian (nations) "tribes" would disappear forever (Cadwalader and Deloria 1984).

However, first reports of a demise of Indian nations were both premature and untrue. Long-term protracted struggle over the cultural existence of Indian people, ensued throughout the first decades of this last century, leading to many struggles, whether understood as "tribal," or originating from "Indian Nations" in treaties. This is where sharp differences between American Indians as Race and Native Nations began to emerge, with the former becoming a racialized "minority" without citizenship or civil rights in the dominant society (Feagin 2000), but the latter with sovereignty claims and an existing sense of social membership as "citizens" in traditional societies. This became the underpinning of all law as well as treatment of indigenous

Americans. This is when racial categories for Blacks and Indians go in sharply different directions.[14]

The United States centralized Federal Sovereignty as the overall authority, especially international. However, individual State sovereignty as an outgrowth of the colonial concerns and differences, maintained effective control over social institutions within purview of the states, especially their taxation, judicial system, public education, transportation, and many economic enterprises. This meant that any conflict (or cooperation) between federally recognized Indian Nations and/or "tribes" operating within these and other regulated activity within states, was and is dealing with two sovereigns. While Federal sovereignty was supposed to be over-arching and the only required relationship, states often exercised their real economic and political power to force Indian "tribes" to the table, especially when there are financial resources at stake (Pommersheim 1995; Deloria and Wilkins 1999). The most contested relationships in the 20th century were between the "Tribal" (Indian Nation) sovereignty and individual State (each U.S. "state") sovereignty, even as the public continued racially identifying indigenous peoples as "Indians." Confusion over racial, political and ethno-national identities persisted to the present day.

2.2.2 Historical and Current Struggles Over Tribal Sovereignty

Cyclical struggles over sovereignty led to a long series of policies meant to eliminate, suppress, or subordinate the cultures and resistance of indigenous peoples—as tribes or nations—that have often produced just the opposite effects from the desired results—namely the cultural continuance of Indian peoples and therefore their ability to resist total assimilation into the dominant society. In the twentieth century two distinct forms of this struggle over sovereignty began to emerge—socio-political sovereignty, usually related to Supreme Court decisions and jurisdictional relationships with individual states, and "cultural" sovereignty—the ability of a people to speak their own languages, practice their spirituality, and raise their families with "traditional" values, similar to cultural self-determination.[15] Also, arising during and after the civil rights movement and urbanization of many Indian families in the U.S., social movements converged on many related issues, such as the American Indian Movement (AIM). However, first we need to identify governmental policies that show development of these conflicts (Deloria 1992).

First are the "Indian Offences" (1882) and "Tribal" Courts involving tribal jurisdiction. These policies specifically outlawed many cultural practices, even traditional religious and educational practices, with ostensible purposes of assimilation into a mainstream, dominant "white" American society, albeit without citizenship or other polity rights. Traditionalists from Native societies, such as the Lakota, were put into conflict with U.S. government backed "progressive" groups who rejected the primitive "savage." Perhaps the most clear attacks on cultural sovereignty were prohibitions against the Sun-Dance, a community religious practice. Coercive assimilation against group property and kinship holdings, such as with the *tiyospaye*, broken up by allotment in the 1887 Dawes Act, were other forms of Culturicide (Fenelon 1998).

Second are the Indian Reorganization Act (1934) policies and resulting Tribal Councils —"Tribal" Governments put into place and

---

[14]Blacks become the most-despised of all racial minority groups, and their subordinate marker overcomes all others, contributing to reification of the so-called "one drop rule." American Indians are increasingly fractionated by "blood quantum" rules for ethno-national identification and are subsumed into other racial groups whenever mixing occurs, except of course for Anglo whites. Some analysts believe demographic pressures were no longer a "threat" to racial hegemony, with Natives less than 1% of the population.

[15]Wallace Coffey and Rebecca Tsosie observe "Cultural Sovereignty" as critical to survival for Indian Nations, in their article "Rethinking the Tribal Sovereignty Doctrine: Cultural Sovereignty and the Collective Future of Indian Nations (Stanford Law & Policy Review, Volume 12:2, Spring 2001).

supported by the various agencies of the United States. This continued the practices of re-formulating Indian "governments" that answered to and were funded by federal authorities, that to a large extent were opposed by "traditionalists" and "treaty" groups, who wanted to retain cultural practices such as their own language and value systems (White Hat 1999; Biolsi 1992).

Third were the Termination policies (1954) and the Relocation programs (50s and 60s)—accompanied by resistance and Tribal recognition that focused on reservations, Indian agencies, and some reconfigured "tribes" around such historical legacies as missions, or removal locations (Fixico 1986). Sovereignty became highly contested, often revolving around "internal colonial" social structures, and external political groups, that themselves were designed to suppress "sovereignty" claims arising from cultural knowledge (Coffey and Tsosie 2001; Fenelon 2002).

A fourth grouping involves various economic development strategies that are connected to federally recognized "tribes" and political structures, chief among them an Indian Gaming Regulatory Act (1988) and its regulatory controls that act like tribal economic "confederacies." Herein lies the dilemma of competing notions of sovereignty locked into historical struggles. Sovereignty, often based on a treaty, an agency or reservation, or a reconfigured "tribal" group, remains separate from individual state governments, yet is still under the federal government. Traditionalists may oppose any or all three of the politically sovereign groups (Young Bear and Theisz 1994). Tribal governments must negotiate with state governments concerning compacts and elaborate tax plans in order to implement development like Indian Gaming (Fenelon 2002, 1998). Many states interpret these negotiations as subordination to state sovereignty. Iconic imagery of "Indians" as "noble savage" or as "hostiles" played an important part of these relations, including with sports mascots and team names. Thus the resistance activism growing around the nation protested the ongoing use of these racist symbols.

During the 1960s and into the early 70s, mostly in the cities of the northern region, there arose urban movements to struggle against the extreme discrimination that many American Indians experienced. Starting in the Twin Cities of Minnesota, and quickly spreading throughout the United States, AIM and other forms of resistance linked up with ongoing struggles on Indian reservations, especially the embattled Lakota in the Dakotas. These movements garnered considerable press, as did the occupation of Alcatraz Island, under a claim to federal land arising from the 1868 Fort Laramie Treaty. This helped to lead the Train of Broken Treaties caravan to Washington, DC, where the protest groups ended up occupying the buildings for the Department of the Interior. The Federal Bureau of Investigation had already launched counter movement activities, COINTELPRO, leading to conflicts across the nation, and finally a spectacular re-occupation of the hamlet of Wounded Knee, where the last genocidal act of the United States military had taken place against surrendered Lakota families in the winter of 1890. The summer of 1973 struggles were put down after a three month siege by the U.S. army, and the federal government began aggressive actions upon anyone associated with AIM, or the reservations with civil war like conditions, such as on Pine Ridge in South Dakota. By 1975 there had been many arrests, some false imprisonment, selective assassinations, and a virtual prison industry against American Indian activists across the nation, finally coming to a head, again on Pine Ridge, when two FBI agents were killed as they tried to enforce a chase unto the Jumping Bull complex[16] where traditionalists had accepted help from AIM members. Within the next

---

[16]The FBI agents were allegedly chasing after a Lakota teenager who *it was said* had stolen a pair of cowboy boots in Rapid City. They came in shooting, and were wounded and then killed, leading to one of the greatest manhunts in FBI history, and months later arrests of some AIM members who were present, and who were ultimately acquitted by a jury in federal court. The FBI extracted the one other alleged AIM member from Canada, Leonard Peltier, cooked up the case against him and got a conviction on falsified evidence and tainted testimony, putting Peltier into prison for life in the most

few years, the movement was deeply suppressed even as the great sovereignty movements of the 1980s came into their own strength. Activism stayed alive, especially in the cities and as linked up with other movements, especially in the universities, but most traditionalists were more concerned with cultural retention, that allowed for tribal groups or Indian Nations to survive in the first place, (Ortiz 1984) while some tribal governments entered into Indian Gaming, increasing their financial base but bringing them squarely into legal systems of the federal government.

As we shall see shortly, all these conflicts came to a head in the 21st century at Standing Rock in North Dakota, including the use of heavily armed, militarized forces.

2.2.3 Case Study—The Lakota

The Lakota (and Dakota) people make an excellent example of how these various forces have worked out over time and in political frameworks. The traditional "Lakota Oyate" and the U.S. defined "Sioux Nation" were socio-political identities. There are three major phases of Lakota "constructions" that can be identified: the ancient and traditional "Oceti Sakowin;" two separate "Nations;" followed by six separate Lakota—"Sioux" Indian Reservations, (Fenelon 1997). There arose two separated "Nations" of "Santee" Dakota and "Teton" Lakota. Ironically, in 1851 the United States conducted treaties with these two "Sioux Indian Nations"—the Dakota peoples in the "Traverse-de-Sioux"—Dakota nation treaty, and a first "Fort Laramie" treaty—Lakota multi-national (multi-tribal) compact (treaty). This was followed by the 1868 Treaty with the "Sioux Nation of Indians"—the Lakota ("Teton Sioux") in the other more well-known Fort Laramie Treaty that established the United States and the Lakota ("Teton-Sioux") geo-political boundaries. This was a direct result of two

years of warfare. However, the United States broke the agreement to get the gold mines and natural resources of the Black Hills, after many Lakota adjusted to or were dependent on reservation life and rations. Many Lakota and Cheyenne resisted these illegal incursions, and defeated the U.S. army at the Battle of the Little Big Horn in 1876, but had to flee when the U.S. responded with a relentless quasi-genocidal pursuit.

As the century ended, the United States divided the 1868 treaty lands into six separated Lakota—"Sioux" reservations, thus formally and unilaterally breaking up the "Lakota Oyate." By 1890 the "Sioux" Agencies had become reservations divided by "band" into six separated BIA agencies, bounded in 1889, with the two Dakota states accompanied by land-takings. Agencies made the Lakota into dependent people, with great corruption, even denying them meager rations owed by treaty law, while creating the aforesaid laws to suppress them and destroy their cultural systems. When the 1889–1890 Ghost Dance came into the region as a religious revitalization movement, the United States government and its military responded by arresting and killing intransigent leaders, including Sitting Bull, and purposefully slaughtering over three hundred people they surrounded at Wounded Knee Creek.

By 1934 the Indian Reorganization Act had created the "Standing Rock Sioux Tribe" (one "agency" from six reservations acting politically separate as "tribes") into a separate council and (BIA) tribal identity. This evolved into six individual claims of a "tribal sovereignty" so that in 1990 Standing Rock "Nation" (Standing Rock "Sioux" Indian Reservation) operated both as a reservation and as an Indian Nation (tribal government) within the United States, one of six Lakota divisions with Dakota people relocated too.[17] Although the treaty was made with the "Sioux Nation of Indians" meaning the Lakota

---

hardcore conditions possible, where he still is (see Peter Matthiesson's *In the Spirit of Crazy Horse.*).

[17]Typically the Indian Office would locate different peoples together on one reservation, which would deny some their traditional lands and become a constant source of friction for enrollment and local politics.

people as a whole, the sovereignty which continued was allocated only to reservations that had survived from the original agencies, producing new and smaller socio-political constructs that further eroded traditional life.[18]

Lakota often use the phrase *ikce wicasa* ("common" or just a man) when they undertake many leadership roles which can be glossed to mean, "I am no better or worse then the people." Herein we observe how resistance to western and colonial forms of cultural domination, especially personal aggrandizement, is also often linked to revitalization of traditional lifestyles further connected to ongoing oppression and injustice, such as treaty rights and lawful or ethical behavior. This is also demonstrated when Frank Fools Crow and "headsman" Frank Kills enemy were selected to represent the traditional Lakota in terms of monetary "settlement" for treaty-breaking that led to the loss of land. Again, land is perceived spiritually and collectively, just as relations with "the people" are understood to change the behavior and orientation of a person selected to be "leader" which is better called a "spokesperson" for the councils of elders to represent the people.

We shall never sell our sacred black hills
Joint statement of Chief Frank Fools Crow and Frank Kills Enemy
on Behalf of the **Traditional Lakota Treaty Council** (Fools Crow 1976)
Kola (friends)... I am Frank Fools Crow, Lakota Chief, and I am here today with Frank Kills Enemy, respected headsman and expert on Indian treaty rights...
We have come here from Pine Ridge today to discuss this house bill which permits the tribal councils to get interest on the award given by the Indian Claims Commission... Our people have been holding meetings on the Black Hills for many years and we have just held such a meeting at Porcupine... the people authorized us to come to this hearing today and speak for them. *The people unanimously reaffirmed our long-standing position that the Black Hills are not for sale under any circumstances.* We are therefore standing behind the resolution we passed at Fort Yates, reading:

Resolution on 1868 Treaty
Whereas a meeting of all Sioux Tribes concerned with the 1868 Treaty was called by the Standing

Rock Sioux and all elected and traditional leaders were invited... Be It Resolved, the delegates of the eight Sioux Reservations have unanimously agreed that all land involved in the 1868 Treaty is not for sale, and all monies appropriated for such sale will not be accepted by members of the Traditional people of each reservation.

I want to repeat that there can never be an acceptance this bill or the total Black Hills Claim under any circumstances. This is the wish of the people. We have a treaty and it requires ¾ of all adult male members to sign before our land can be sold. I believe that this provision was stuck in the treaty by the whiteman because Lakota do not sell their land. The whiteman claims that he is not bound by the ¾ provision of the treaty... The treaty was broken by the whiteman before it was even signed by him. But we Lakota are more honorable men. We have signed the treaty and we will try to live by it, and respect it. Even though this treaty may not be binding on the whiteman, it is binding on us until we vote it out. It says that ¾ of Lakota adult male members must sign before land can be sold and the Lakota people can never accept any payment until this provision is fully complied with. The Black Hills are sacred to the Lakota people. Both the sacred pipe and the Black Hills go hand and hand in our region. The Black Hills is our church, the place where we worship. The Black Hills is our burial grounds. The bones of our grandfathers lie buried in those hills. How can you expect us to sell our church and our cemeteries for a few token whiteman dollars. We will never sell.

There are two important points to make in this chapter from the above passage—first, traditional people can be sophisticated in their understanding of treaty relations, and law-making; and second, value-systems of indigenous peoples are inter-connected with orientations to land, community and spirituality. This is doubly important in a society that is undergoing forms of globalization, subordinating all people and communities and societal values to economic determination. It is not just that many indigenous peoples are most often at the bottom of this stratification system, but that their very values and beliefs are under attack, and that they have rather sophisticated responses to these attacks, including the electoral legal systems of the dominant society.

We have observed these long-term processes of incorporation and suppression within Lakota traditional societies as essential features of

---

[18]See Fenelon (1997) (Summer, 1997).

resistance for societal survival, and how traditional groups have continued their historical, treaty-based interpretations of these issues. Now we ask, considering all indigenous Nations, whether these issues of the Lakota "traditionalists" resonate on a "pan-ethnic" level? We observe in the 1993 "Statement of Vision Toward the Next 500 Years"[19] similar declarations were made by delegates from many tribes and nations, (*italics* mine) representative of American Indians socio-historical perspectives.

> Statement of Vision Toward the Next 500 Years from the Gathering of United Indigenous People at the Parliament of World Religions, Chicago, 1993[20]
>
> We as Indigenous peoples and Native Nations, honoring our ancestors and for our future generations do hereby declare our present and continuing survival with our sacred homelands.
>
> Since time immemorial, we have lived in a spiritual way in keeping with sacred laws, principles and values given to us by the Creator. That way of life is predicated on a sense of honor and respect for the Earth, a sacred regard for all our relations, and a continuation of our languages, cultures and traditions. In the presence of this world gathering we call for recognition of the past, acknowledgement of the present, and a commitment to support our just demands for dignity, justice and human rights. These rights include: the right to practice our *spiritual traditions* without interference or restrictions, the right to raise our children in *our own cultures*, and the right to *sovereignty and self-determination*.
>
> One hundred years ago, at the 1893 Parliament of the World's Religions, we, Original Nations of the Western Hemisphere were not invited. A century later, even as this Parliament convenes, the following issues have yet to be addressed: * The destruction of Native spiritual traditions; * Historical and continuing genocide and holocaust against our peoples; * Repatriation and reburial of *sacred artifacts* and funerary remains; * Protection or return of *sacred sites and traditional lands*; * Legitimization of native medicinal, and health practices; * The *cultural education* of *our children*,

including spirituality; * Misrepresentation and theft of *spiritual traditions*, and ethnic fraud; * Teaching and learning of *traditional language and culture*; * Environmental abrogation of *sacred sovereign rights*; * Respect and awareness of prophecies and *traditional teachings*; * Church silence and complicity in dominating native spirituality; * Ongoing federal policies designed to destroy our way of life.

2.3 Indigenous Struggles in Latin America(s)

Indigenous struggles in the Americas, especially in Latin American contexts, includes the contemporary conflicts above, Zapatistas in Mexico, uprisings in many other countries, including the Miskito against the Sandinistas, "Quechuan" peoples linked up in Ecuador, Venezuela, the Aymara in Bolivia, Mapuche in Chile, and other Central and South American countries where resistance and rebellion is underway.

> Popol Vuh
> They tore off our fruits, they broke off our branches, they burnt our trunks, but they could not kill our roots. (Popol vuh)[21]

Indigenous peoples are involved in struggles over local autonomy, land tenure, community relations, and socio-economic "development" that are often viewed as anti-globalization efforts. In many parts of the world, these struggles take on definitive forms of de-colonization strategies, none more poignantly than Mexico and other Latin American countries. In this section, I consider situations and perspectives of indigenous peoples in Mexico and Latin America, and then make comparative analysis with other cases and struggles by indigenous peoples in other locations in the Americas.

> Mexico Profundo
> The recent history of Mexico, that of the last five hundred years, is the story of permanent confrontation between those attempting to direct the country toward the path of Western civilization and those, rooted in Mesoamerican ways of life, who resist. (Bonfil Batalla 1996: xv)

---

[19]The document "Statement of Vision Toward the Next 500 Years from the Gathering of United Indigenous People at the Parliament of World Religions, Chicago, 1993" was created by "multi-tribal" Indian Nation delegates as reported in Fenelon (1998).

[20]Fenelon (1998: 310) I was the rapporteur for the traditional spiritual leaders who congregated there, taking down these notes that were delivered to the United Nations representative and news agencies.

[21]quote from *America Profunda*, 2003 meetings held in Mexico City, by and for Indigenous scholars.

We immediately observe from Bonfil's quote that the struggles of indigenous peoples extends back over time and space from before conquest and invasion occurs, identified as five centuries within the Americas. Bonfil furthers states that it is only after European invasion and the installation of the colonial regime that the country becomes "unknown territory" whose contours and secrets need to be "discovered" (1996: 8–9). Thus essential features of indigeneity also become a partial foundation, however denied, for the nation-state and new cultural forms built over those who preceded it. Bonfil identifies this as "De-Indianization" as a "historical process through which populations that originally possessed a particular and distinctive identity, based on their own culture, are forced to renounce that identity, with all the consequent changes in their social organization and culture" (1996: 17). What I believe Bonfil identified, however, was a targeted cultural destruction of individual "Indian" or indigenous communities, nations, cultures and collectivities for the purposes of domination, and the subsequent building of racialized concepts of "the Indian" that no longer has these diverse relationships, but only represents the primitive and undeveloped. Thus stark contrasts on the nature of the land, autonomous socio-political relationships, and community as a collectivity, emerge in relationship to "modernity" and capitalist expansion over increasingly large territories. "The clear and undeniable evidence of our Indian ancestry is a mirror in which we do not wish to see our own reflection." (Bonfil Batalla 1996: 18)

Activist scholars in Mexico call American indigenous communities "*Pueblos Indios*" for convenience as to identify important differences from other groups resisting domination and potential erasure. I refer to the United Nations definition:

> Indigenous communities, peoples and nations are those who have a continuous historical connection with pre-colonial societies that preceded the invasion... that have the determination to preserve, develop and transmit to future generations their ancestral lands and their ethnic identity... (Cobo 1987)

As noted earlier (Bonfil Batalla 1996: 88), one of the basic relationships of indigenous peoples is having a relationship to the land. This relationship is often sacred, rarely has direct economic value, and is usually held collectively, rather than individual ownership. This orientation to the land is indirect opposition to how modern, capitalistic society, approaches land, with direct economic values and individual title.

> The larger problem for the Indians was the struggle against breaking up the communal lands. The Liberals made private property sacred ... the communal ownership of land in Indian communities became an obstacle to be removed. (Bonfil Batalla 1996: 100)

Bonfil, as do a host of scholars working on indigenous peoples of the Americas, identifies other areas of social organization that differ markedly from dominant groups, and mainstream "modern" society, including medicine (pg. 34) community service, *cargo* systems in Mexico that are "simultaneously civil, religious, and moral." (36) Thus we observe that it is the collective nature of indigenous life which is at conflict with modern social systems, invading and incorporating the indigenous. This collectivity includes the land, distributive economics, shared decision-making and the community. Invasive systems want to take over the land, stratify the economy to build a power elite, centralize political systems into hierarchies they control, and relate all social issues to ever-larger urban areas that dominate in all arenas the surrounding communities. Since indigenous peoples utilize alternative systems of social organization, and do not dissolve relationships, they are seen as obstacles, and if they resist, they are seen as "enemy."

> In seeing the "Indian as Enemy" Bonfil observes (1996: 103–104):
> The radical denial of the imaginary Mexico. The struggle over land, involved one side, which wanted free trade and individual property, while the other side protested the land was communal and inalienable.

With the ensuing conflict over resources, and increasingly played out over culture, indigenous peoples literally become the enemy, of dominants and later civilization itself. Value systems, one placing private property and maximum monetary profits as mainstay, and the other with community relations at heart, come into sharp conflict, with violence employed by the invasive systems, and often by the defending systems.

> "To civilize" is meant to pacify them, domesticate them, end *their* violence. (Bonfil Batalla 1996: 105)

Western colonial powers and later the U.S. created a "minority" group—the "Indian"—while they tried to destroy the culture, history and knowledge of individual Native nations or cultures. Even as this process occurred, place names and land based knowledge systems evolved from the previous indigenous systems. In Mexico, I refer to "Day of the Dead" posters and celebrations, that in Oaxaca represent the "prehispanic origin of the celebration of the dead" that is now understood to be Mexican culture. These layers of domination—500 years and more in Mexico—reveal Bonfil's Mexico Profundo, the indigenous "Indian" foundation even as oppression stratifies every aspect of life —cultural, political, economic and social. Therefore the indigenous represents both the foundation of society itself, and the "enemy" to be overtaken and destroyed. Once we dispel the notion of primitive people without historical memory, we need to address how indigenous peoples understand our histories, often denied and/or distorted by dominant historical perspectives. Murals painted over the walls of a mostly indigenous in Mexico City, the barrio Santo Domingo in their cultural center "*La Escuelita*" itself the site of resistance, demonstrate the detailed knowledge and perspectives of these relationships, even among urbanized peoples. Similar to how urban resistance arose in the United States, indigenous peoples in Mexico build new sites of revitalization, resistance and survival, inevitably revolving around indigenous ideas of social justice.

The Zapatistas indigenous resistance and revitalization movement, at times revolutionary and always about transformational change positive for autonomous communities, represents recent attempts to fuse traditional indigenous social justice with responsive and reflexive "governance" that are representative of those communities choosing to participate. I discuss these and other examples in this section of the chapter.

Indigenous peoples in the extremely poor but resource rich state of Chiapas alongside Guatemala have experienced deep discrimination, and saw opportunities to challenge the destructive forces of globalization with the NAFTA agreements, opening up their regions to further "development." From 1984 until 1994, these people met with revolutionaries in the Lacandon jungle, and planned out uprisings that would restore justice and fairness in their lives. On the same day that Mexico woke up to celebrate business with the United States, New year's 1994, the EZLN armed uprising took the capitol San Cristobol and most of the countryside. Withheld from military pacification because of the possibility of indigenous uprisings throughout the country, especially in Oaxaca and Guerrero, and because of international human rights groups observing the *Encuentros* and mediating talks, Mexico entered into protracted agreements with the Zapatistas, and thus changed the entire orientation toward "*Pueblos Indigenas*" and their movements. Although para-militaries arose as arms of the national army, and engaged in suppression such as a massacre at Acteal, indigenous resistance proved successful in the state of Chiapas.

Zapatista-led communities organized in ways that attempted to respect traditional culture, but sowed new patterns as well, including equality and involvement for women, direct challenges to local and state authorities, and community self-defense. Conflicts took various forms, forcing struggles with para-militaries, government officials, military forts, restive localities, peasant organizations, and a depressed economy. One set of social changes by the Zapatistas was to form offices called "*Junta del Buen Gobierno*" that heard local issues and resolved them for the betterment of harmonious relations within the community (Ramirez 2003), similar to the restorative justice systems of North American Indian Nations such as the Lakota wrote them in the 19th century (Fenelon 1998). These exemplify mediating social structures that place community relations as the highest value.

Zapatistas use *"normas y costumbres"* (Bonfil Batalla 1996) in their conflict mediation in the Junta del Buen Gobierno, where they defer to indigenous cultural norms and values defined by the communities themselves. People may take any set of issues, whether a property problem, or labor-related, or even familial including the nature of divorce, child-care, and domestic abuse, to have a fair and open hearing. The government systems of "justice" have been corrupted with politics and bribery, so the Zapatistas banned monetary restitution for the Juntas or any others, and keep a focus on conflict resolution to restore harmony for those community members affected.

Community organizations in Los Altos and other contested regions, where conflicts between indigenous and government supported forces were common, transformed basic socio-political relations so they were both modern and responsive to contemporary issues, and yet traditional and sensitive to local concerns. A municipal sign at *San Pedro Polho* represents this well, identifying itself as an autonomous rebel community banning drugs, stolen property such as cars, and alcohol abuse as threats to local lifestyle, exemplified with the phrase *"Aqui el pueblo manda y el gobierno obedece"* (here the people speak and the government obeys...)

Latin America's Indian struggles as compared to First Nations in the United States and Canada, mostly revolve around formal recognition issues arising from their treaty relationships, development of racialized "minority" groups, and their historical change. Our work discusses these relationships as long term social change (Hall and Fenelon 2004), with focus on three major socio-political relations—sovereignty, autonomy and minority status. Indigenous peoples with historical treaties have established various forms of legal sovereignty, in the United States and Canada. Indigenous peoples established both recognized and unrecognized autonomous zones and communities in various locales in the

Americas and globally, with Nicaraguan Miskito and Mexican Mayan-descent Zapatistas standing out. Indigenous peoples still considered or seen solely as "minority" groups within their nations are the most vulnerable, and often form resistance groups and/or movements, such as *Communidades Indigenas* in Oaxaca (Maldonado Alvarado 2002).

The key comparative issues here are fourfold (contrasting across the Americas):

Sovereignty is recognized in First Nations, though they are historically genocidal states.

Minority or conflicted autonomy in Latin America, although historically *mestizo* states, confers neither sovereignty claims nor clear legal protections for its indigenous peoples. Therefore, indigenous peoples experience different relationships depending on their spatial (place) and temporal (over time) conditions. Within Mexico and throughout most of Latin America, the indigenous peoples are suppressed and held down to the lowest rungs of the economic order, although they did not experience as powerfully a genocidal regime in earlier centuries, as the colonies that preceded the United States and Canada did practice upon the indigenous (American Indian) nations falling under their conquest. This is directly correlated with race and racism for the last two or three hundred years, coinciding with racist systems developed in North America that sometimes used genocide or war to suppress indigenous nations, and always kept American Indians in subordinate roles through racist laws, coercive assimilation, and lack of access to full citizenship. Now, making up no more than one percent of the total population, Canada and the United States broker sovereignty struggles to maintain an appearance of democracy and freedom, allowing limited recognition of sovereignty as First Nations or American Indian Tribes. Mestizo states in Mexico and most of Latin America, while periodically resorting to war, brutal suppression and segregated status, rarely rose to the level of genocide after colonial powers were installed. The creation of a *mestizaje* population, although highly stratified, kept indigenous peoples as significant, low-level presence of their respective countries, constantly struggling for autonomy and recognition. In some parts of Mexico as noted, and in some countries, especially Peru, Ecuador and notably Bolivia, indigenous peoples make up a large percentage of the total population, yet have little socio-political status, although with Evo Morales as president of Bolivia there is more recognition. This is one of the many anomalies of indigenous peoples in the Americas.

Perhaps the most important element of indigenous struggles for observing resistance to globalization, is a connectedness that many movement groups see with other indigenous peoples. For Zapatistas this is lead to actual invitations, referred to as international *Encuentros* and Inter-Continentals, represented in the Four directions of hands united mural image on a headquarters building in Oventik, Chiapas, with the words *Democracia* (democracy), *Libertad* (liberty), *Justicia* (justice), and *Paz* (peace) over the meeting hands with fists, put in a medicine wheel design with the surrounding words *Unidad y Victoria*. The colors used are Lakota traditions which vary from those used by Mayan, (Tzotzil) and so two very different indigenous traditions and social movements are connected in their vision and struggle. It is this set of relationships to which we now turn.

Comparative analysis is important, as the basis of indigenous resistance and consciousness and as absolutely integral to all of Latin@ America; from revitalization resistance of Zapotecs in southern Mexico to recognition fights of the Wampanoag in the United States; and from movement resistance of Zapatistas, compared with Lakota resistance forces, to overall indigeneity and its many intersections with resistance to globalization and "neo-liberalism" of a Washington consensus. We now turn to this indigenismo as a collective orientation to social organization.

2.3.1 Basis of Indigenous Resistance/Consciousness Integral to Latin America

Indigenous peoples represent significant percentages of the population of many Latin American countries, and in some cases, when grouped together, they constitute the majority. This is certainly the case in Bolivia, where we reference an indigenous leader, Felipe Quispe Huanca (*Aymara*) Head of the Indian Movement *Pachacuti*, that initiated protests in Bolivia that contributed to the downfall of the sitting president. (Washington Times, March 3, 2004)

> We believe in the reconstruction of the Kollasuyu, our own ancestral laws. our own philosophy... We have... our political heritage (that) can be successful in removing and destroying neoliberalism, capitalism and imperialism.
> It is community-based socialism... That is what the brothers of our communities hold as model... In the Aymara and Quechua areas, primarily in La Paz, we have been working since 1984 on fostering awareness of community-based ideologies.

Felipe Quispes speaks of social movements arising throughout "Indian" Latin America, shared struggles, that are based on a diversity of indigenous peoples and nation-states. While each is reconstructing traditions unique to their culture, and often relative to the specific lands they inhabit, they are also finding commonalities across many fronts, notably in opposition to cultural domination and capitalist expansion over their lands. Even as the essence of a community, economic cooperatives, shared decision-making, and land tenure relations vary, indigenous peoples seem to rely on these foundations both to resist in their individual situations, and increasingly in global networks.

Ecuador is an outstanding example, with recent protests and insurrection rising to levels of revolutionary activity, some of it in concert with mainstream military forces, leading to the Quito accords, and ultimately a broken alliance. Indigenous peoples are often in the middle of social unrest and rebellion, especially when there are high numbers and they are well organized. Unfortunately, all too often they are left out of resolutions and agreements arising out of the conflict. This marginalization has been a distinctive feature of indigenous social movements, and when accompanied with cultural suppression and oppression has caused revitalization movements to arise. Usually the dominant society reacts with military pacification reminiscent of the *conquista* hundreds of years ago. We can observe current resistance and attempted revitalization in social conflicts in Canada, with the Mohawk, in the U.S. over federal recognition fights and sacred lands dispute, with the Wampanoag, or Lakota over Bear Butte, in Mexico with Zapatistas in Chiapas and Zapotecan resistance in Oaxaca, in Ecuador with the Quechuan land tenure fights, Guarani in Brazil and Argentina, and notably with Aymara coca-leaf growers aligning with leftist unions in Bolivia.

Mayan-descent peoples in Guatemala, and in the states of Chiapas and Oaxaca, Mexico, moved away from Liberation Theology to indigenous "Liberation Philosophy" which are partly based on traditional understandings of culture, the land and community. These epistemological movements that reject not only the hierarchy of European social orders, but the very nature of their social organization.

The Nicaragua Miskito communities realized their "autonomous" zones of *Zelaya Norte*, first in armed conflict with the Sandinistas who were in low intensity war with Contras funded by the United States, (part of resistance to capitalist globalization as socialism, but more importantly as community responsibility and resisting privatization), and later with coalition governments. This has led to a series of legal challenges by Nicaraguan indigenous groups, all of which further the causes of resistance and cultural revitalization.

Mapuche peoples in Chile have also organized their resistance along cultural lines, again relating their struggle to community and land. While many of these inter-ethnic conflicts find flash points around some major economic activity, as mining or land appropriation for large scale agricultural development in some cases, their underlying issues remain focused on maintaining traditional lifestyles in order to retain community cohesion. (Fenelon and Hall 2005)

As Quispes describes above, as Evo Morales speaks as the elected head of Bolivia, and as traditionalists throughout the history and the current reality of the United States and Canada's indigenous nations have struggled with, it is the essence of community, economic cooperatives, traditional decision-making, and land tenure relations that sometimes lead to violent uprising or a more localized economic re-organization. Yet indigenous peoples rely on these foundations to resist in their individual situations, and within global networks (Ramirez 2003; Sklair 2002). Increasingly communities in Amazonian regions where oil extraction is ongoing, have risen up and even brought lawsuits against oil companies. These new movements have collective orientation toward communities that are transparently anti-globalization, and specifically target neo-liberalism as modern "evil" for the poor, indigenous, marginalized peasants making up their constituency. Examples such as coca leaf growing in Bolivia, disconnected from United States cocaine markets, as indigenous horticultural practices, challenge regional dominance and hegemony operated by corporate economic practices. Similar issues are addressed in the Declaration on the Rights of Indigenous Peoples passed by the United Nations, supported by the Mohawk of Canada, the U.S. Lakota, *Pueblos Indigenas* of Mexico, and Indigenous movements throughout the Americas.

Herein we see how the historically developed concepts of the "hostile" against the U.S. conquest or domination, are realized in 21st century Latin and North American conflicts. We also observe how important such racist icons and symbology are in American society, why they are fought over in many universities and social institutions by dominant groups, and how they connect with hegemonic histories and struggles over racialized imagery. Autonomy movements such as the Zapatistas in southern Mexico,

Aymara in Bolivia, have become typified as "socialist" or even as "terrorist" in nature, even though they actually represent over 500 years of indigenous struggle in the Americas.

2.4 Global Conflicts Over Indigeneity and Conclusion

Some of the most important issues for contemporary Indigenous Peoples are their socio-political struggles with dominant modern "state" structures, as seen in Canada, the United States and Mexico. These three large nation-states represent the entire North American continental areas, and reflect the differing trajectories that arise from the socio-historical circumstances. In terms of identity relationships, Champagne (2005: 4) differentiates indigenous claims toward "government, land ownership … resource management and community organization and identity" and calls for a "multinational" state structure that respects Indigenous People's rights and societies. In other work Champagne finds that "most Native nations are striving to gain greater responsibility over their communities through strategies of economic development, renegotiating relations between tribal and federal governments, and reintroducing Native history and culture into reservation institutions, education, and government." (Champagne and Goldberg 2005)

International borders often run across and divide traditional lands of indigenous people. Shrum (2005) analyzes U.S. "border crossings" of the *Kumeyaay* and *Tohono O'odham* (now resisting the Trump wall) with Mexico and the Iroquois and Blackfoot Confederacy with Canada, finding linkage and policy shifts over two centuries, that is still fractionating communities and tribal identities, somehow managing to survive. But that survival has come at some cost, even when limited sovereignty is recognized, within the United States and Canada. Dempsey discusses definitions of a "status Indian" in Canada, how this was historically based on gender discrimination, and how many new governmental policies divides aboriginal

communities in terms of changing membership, often polarizing First Nations (2005). In each of these cases, we see how socio-historical struggles have shaped contemporary realities, and cause us to re-evaluate embedded concepts of race and racism rather than ethno-national struggles, leading us closer to Champagne's call for using a multi-national model, inclusive of indigenous peoples.

In Central and South America, we identify the indigenous perspective on social problems arising from hundreds of years of conquest, colonization and ongoing cultural domination of North America. Marcos tells us how *Zapatismo* incorporates traditional family approaches to critically assess colonization gender constructs that have stratified Mexican society and indigenous women, and how *Commandanta* Esther's speech to Parliament in Mexico, represents the EZLN and Zapatistas, showing how indigenous struggle informs non-indigenous society as well (2005). The Zapatistas, reformulated from initial revolutionary uprising, had negotiations over limited autonomy during the San Andreas Accords, now support community development strategies in the areas under their control. Their uprising has caused Mexico to begin indigenous relations in earnest, with limited progress happening across the nation.

Nash identifies the "Mayan Quest" for indigenous forms of autonomy in southern Mexico and Guatemala, noting the genocidal repression in Guatemala against indigenous peoples who resisted the "threat of dislocation brought about by neoliberal trade and economic policies." (2005: 122). By identifying the "practice of autonomy" as "deeply embedded" she sees a primary struggle as collective interests against state supported corporate interests, or as Mayas say "ants and bees" (working together in cell-like organizations of flexibility), with inherent tendencies to "listen" and "obey." The *Juntas de Buen Gobierno* run by the Zapatistas are emblematic of this resistance, borne out of violent uprising but with metamorphosis into a blending of traditionalism and modernity, also engaging in resistance and revitalization. As noted earlier, these movements see a certain solidarity and common purpose in maintaining their traditional culture in a modern world that continues to discriminate against them collectively, therefore racially. As stated by Fools Crow, often against treaties and agreements, with the Black Hills for the Lakota, the San Andreas accords for Zapatistas, indigenous peoples see their struggle in a global context.

Indigenous struggles of resistance and survival, linked to social movements, internally over sovereignty and autonomy, and externally as anti-Globalization movements, contest dominant versions of social organization and dialectics of history, especially in contemporary "development" discourse, and the nature of democracy. The Hodenosaunee or Iroquois Confederation, composed of more than five Native Nations, better represented their people in civil discourse than the fledgling and deeply racist, sexist and class-ist American systems before, during and after the Revolutionary War. Women, especially maternal Grandmothers, could hold important positions in society, while their Anglo counterparts could only plead a legal case to an all male jury through their husbands or fathers. Yet American history has depicted this early League of Nations as "primitives" and "savages" with its primary military leader and first President George Washington waging genocidal war against them to the extent that the Onondagas still refer to him as "Town Destroyer." The Zapatistas, representing more than five indigenous peoples in their uprising in the highlands and rainforests of Chiapas, have provided better local justice systems than the Mexican government ever has, or probably ever will. They have highlighted their traditional family systems, evidenced in the *Tzotzil* communities, placing special offices for women to find support and dignity in male dominated areas. Yet Mexican government officials have typified them as "insurgents" and "terrorists," with para-military pacification strategies that have a long history of western domination. Bolivian indigenous leaders Felipe Quispes and Evo Morales have clearly stated their support for the poorest indigenous communities in their attempts at social change in the poorest South American country with the largest

percentage of indigenous peoples. Yet, the United States and powerful corporate forces have consistently charged them with being socialist pawns, or simple-minded rural activists, rather than community leaders arising to resist oppression and to reinforce the revitalization of indigenous cultures.

Conversely, the United States Justice Department refused to believe its own analysis, finding that of all racially or ethnically defined groups in the U.S., Native Americans were the most likely to be victims of violent crime, exceeding even African Americans, and that they were the only people primarily attacked by members of other racial groups, mostly "whites" in and around border-town regions. So at a time that a few Indian "tribes" or nations have managed to lift off the floor of poverty and discrimination within the United States through Indian Gaming or other economic development actions, historical systems continue to oppress and stratify these indigenous peoples in America. Much of the historical oppression is now realized through the United States and a few other core nation-states with advanced capitalist systems, exporting labor exploitation and expropriating property and profits from other poorer countries, with especially strong deleterious effects on the indigenous peoples in those societies, who continue to occupy the lowest strata in their countries, and who continue to be the target of discriminatory systems that target whatever natural resources, land-holdings or labor they may have. Liberation movements, each specific to their own situation just as the American Indian Movement joined up with the traditionalists in the United States, are thereby viewed or perceived as a "threat" to the well-being of the same nation-states that oppressed them. Struggles for local autonomy and cultural sovereignty rage across the Americas, being the legacy of invasion, conquest and domination over indigenous peoples.

In describing the modern constructs of empire, George Steinmetz describes the early steps in the process as "Colonialism entails the seizure of sovereignty from locals and the formation of a separate colonial state apparatus" (2005: 344). But countering that, recently elected

Bolivian President Evo Morales (*Aymara* 'Indian') has stated "With the unity of the people, we're going to end the colonial state and the neoliberal model." Morales went on to speak for indigenous peoples throughout the Americas, in stating: "The time has come to change this terrible history of looting our natural resources, of discrimination, of humiliation, of hate,' Morales said." (Associated Press 2006).[22] Struggles of Indigenous Peoples in the Americas has come full circle in sociological terms, with Native Americans resisting ongoing racism against the "race" of "Indians" and for sovereignty within their nation-states, and with indigenous peoples throughout the hemisphere engaged in struggles for recognition and autonomy against the nation-state, and when possible, as agents for change that could indeed prove better for all peoples.

All of these issues were found in the "standoff at Standing Rock" where an oil pipeline rerouted from white communities and was relocated next to the reservation and an historical treaty land (1851, 1868). Starting as a peaceful prayer camp by youth and Dakota women (Sacred Stone) as state police made arrests to suppress the NoDAPL movement, other Indian Nations joined in solidarity, rising to 10,000 people in a main camp named after traditional alliances, the Oceti Sakowin. Indigenous Peoples from around the world joined the struggle, each ceremoniously asking to join the Standing Rock Sioux on their land. North Dakota state, heavily reliant on fracking oil profits, (Bakken) blocked the main road and increased militarized police after pipeline security forces put dogs on the "water protectors," leading to uneven conflicts with Indian forces and their allies, with assault vehicles and less (non) lethal firing on the resistance. With the election of Trump (invested in oil pipelines) and heavy losses of their reservation community, finally the tribal council voted to remove the

camps but not give up the fight, resulting in a March 10, 2017 march on Washington.

2.5 Conclusions

The expansion of Europeans into the Americas produced conflicts with devastating results for indigenous peoples, and the racialization of "Indians" in North America. European colonizers of American Indians continued to use the "Doctrine of Discovery" and "Rights to Conquest" to justify the racialized destruction of Native Nations.

The U.S. further developed these racist ideologies, at times resorting to genocide policies, found in the Trail of Tears (1823–1838), elimination of California Indians (1850–1880), and acts of mass killing such as at Wounded Knee (1890). After nadir of the American Indian population, around 1900 north of Mexico, historical and contemporary struggles in the U.S. and Canada were over sovereignty, tribal and ethno-national, even as the "Indian" was still racially defined.

As a case study for the U.S., the Lakota make an excellent example, extending from the "purchase" by President Jefferson, through invasion and conquest, and then cultural domination and internal colonialism of the twentieth century. The Lakota also exemplify resistance over sovereignty by maintaining their claim to the Black Hills through the 1868 Fort Laramie Treaty, in AIM/traditionalist conflicts at Pine Ridge, and now at Standing Rock.

Indigenous struggles in Latin America, were less racialized over time, but just as intense in terms of stratification and oppression at the bottom of their respective societies. Just as important is the underlying basis of indigenous resistance/consciousness being integral to Latin America identity, as found in Mexico Profundo and lately in Bolivian resistance. Racist iconography of the 'hostile" from North America, still existing in social discourse, have been transported to fights over indigenous movements.

Conflicts over indigeneity have become more universal over time. Similar to what scholars now

---

[22]Reported by the Associated Press, also in: Forero, Juan and Larry Rohter, "Bolivia's Leader Solidifies Region's Leftward Tilt" January 22, 2006 The New York Times (electronic, nytimes.com).

refer to as "global racism" the frames and labels used during the conquest of American Indians are now generically applied to indigenous peoples around the world. The struggles of Black Americans at the bottom of a U.S. racial and economic hierarchy, closely resembles the stratified positions of Indians elsewhere in the Americas, and many indigenous peoples globally. Historically developed racist systems in the United States have been transformed into the international social struggles of Indigenous Americans.

References

Associated Press (2006) Bolivian President-elect Evo Morales Seeks Blessing in Indian Temple. Fiona Smith, Associated Press, 22 Jan 2006.

Berkey, C. G. (1992). United States-Indian relations: The constitutional basis. In O. Lyons & J. Mohawk (Eds.), *Exiled in the land of the free: Democracy, Indian Nations, and the U.S.* Santa Fe, NM: Clear Light Publishers.

Berkhofer, R. (1978). *The white man's Indian*. New York: Random House.

Berman, H. R. (1992). Perspectives on American Indian Sovereignty and international law, 1600 to 1776. In O. Lyons & J. Mohawk (Eds.), *Exiled in the Land of the Free: democracy, Indian Nations, and the U.S.* Santa Fe: Clear Light Publishers.

Biolsi, T. (1992). *Organizing the Lakota: The political economy of the new deal on the Pine Ridge and Rosebud reservations*. Tucson: University of Arizona Press.

Bonfil Batalla, G. (1996) Mexico Profundo—reclaiming a civilization (P. A. Dennis, Trans.). University of Texas PressAustin.

Cadwalader, S. D., & Deloria, V. (Eds.). (1984). *The aggressions of civilization: Federal Indian policy since the 1880's*. Philadelphia: Temple University Press.

Champagne, D. (1992). Organizational change and conflict: A case study of the Bureau of Indian Affairs. In F. J. Lyden & L. M. Legters (Eds.), *Native Americans and public policy*. Pittsburgh: University of Pittsburgh Press.

Champagne, D. (2005). Rethinking native relations with contemporary nation-states. In D. Champagne, K. J. Torjesen, & S. Steiner (Eds.), *Indigenous peoples and the modern state* (pp. 3–23). Walnut Creek, CA: AltaMira Press.

Champagne, D., & Goldberg, C. (2005). Changing the subject: Individual versus collective interests in Indian Country Research. *Wicazo Sa Review, 20*(1), 49–69.

Cobo, J. R. M. (1987). *Estudio del problema de la discriminacion contra las poblaciones indigenas* (vol. V, Conclusiones, propuestas y recomendaciones). Nueva york: Nationes Unidas.

Coffey, W., & Tsosie, R. (2001). Rethinking the tribal sovereignty doctrine: Cultural sovereignty and the collective future of Indian Nations. *Stanford Law & Policy Review, 12*, 2.

Cornell, S. (1988). *The return of the native: American Indian political resurgence*. New York: Oxford University Press.

Deloria, V., Jr. (1992). The application of the constitution to the American Indian. In O. Lyons & J. Mohawk (Eds.), *Exiled in the land of the free: Democracy, Indian Nations, and the U.S.* Santa Fe, NM: Clear Light Publishers.

Deloria, V., Jr., & Lytle, C. (1984). *The nations within, the past and future of American Indian sovereignty*. New York: Pantheon Books.

Deloria, V., Jr., & Wilkins, D. E. (1999). *Tribes, treaties, and constitutional tribulations*. Austin: University of Texas Press.

Dempsey, L. J. (2005). Status Indian: Who defines you? In D. Champagne, K. J. Torjesen, & S. Steiner (Eds.), *Indigenous peoples and the modern state*. Walnut Creek, CA: AltaMira Press.

Diamond, J. (1999 [1997]). *Guns, germs, and steel: The fates of human societies* (new edition), New York: Norton Publishers.

Dippie, B. W. (1982). *The Vanishing American, white attitudes and U.S. Indian policy*. Middletown, CT: Wesleyan University Press.

Feagin, J. R. (2000). *Racist America: Roots, current realities, and future reparations*. New York: Routledge.

Fenelon, J. V. (1997). From peripheral domination to internal Colonialism: Socio-political change of the Lakota on standing rock. *Journal of World-Systems Research, 3*(2), 259–320. http://jwsr.ucr.edu/index.php.

Fenelon, J. V. (1998). *Culturicide, resistance, and survival of the Lakota (Sioux Nation)*. New York: Garland Publishing.

Fenelon, J. V. (2002). dual sovereignty of native nations, the United States, & traditionalists. *Humboldt Journal of Social Relations, 27*(1), 106–145.

Fenelon, J. V., & Hall, T. D. (2005). Indigenous struggles over autonomy, land and community: Anti-globalization and resistance in world systems analysis. In R. Grosfoguel, N. Maldonado-Torres, & J. D. Saldivar (Eds.), *Latin@s in the world-system: Towards THE DECOLONIZATION of the US empire in the 21st century* (pp. 107–122). Boulder: Paradigm Press.

Fenelon, J. V., & LeBeau, D. (2006). Four directions for Indian Education: Curriculum models for Lakota/Dakota teaching & learning. In D. Champagne & I. Abu-Saad (Eds.), *indigenous and minority education*. Beer Sheva, Israel: Negev Center for Regional Development.

Fenelon, J. V., & Trafzer, C. E. (2014). From colonialism to denial of California genocide to misrepresentations. *American Behavioral Scientist, 58*(1), 3–29.

Fixico, D. (1986). *Termination and relocation, federal Indian policy 1945–1960*. Albuquerque: University of New Mexico Press.

Fools Crow, F. (1976). To My People from Eagle Bear, Better Known as Chief Frank Fools Crow. In recording *Fools Crow*, Tatanka Records: Denver, Colorado.

Frederickson, G. M. (2002). *Racism: A short history* (p. 2002). Princeton, NJ: Princeton University Press.

Hall, T. D., & Fenelon, V. J. (2004). The futures of Indigenous peoples: 9/11 and the trajectory of indigenous survival and resistance. *Journal of World Systems Research, IX*(3), 153–197.

Hannaford, I. (1996). *Race: The history of an idea in the west*. Baltimore, Maryland: Johns Hopkins University Press.

Jennings, F. (1975). *The Invasion of America—Indians, colonialism and the cant of conquest*. New York: W. W. Norton & Company.

Josephy, A. (2002 [1994]). *500 Nations*. New York: Knopf, Gramercy [Random House].

Lazarus, E. (1991). *Black Hills, white justice. The Sioux Nation versus the United States, 1775 to the present*. New York: Harper Collins.

Lindsay, B. C. (2014). *Murder state: California's Native American genocide, 1846–1873*. Lincoln: University of Nebraska Press.

Lyons, O. R. (1992). The American Indian in the past. In O. Lyons & J. Mohawk (Eds.), *Exiled in the land of the free: Democracy, Indian Nations, and the U.S.* Santa Fe, NM: Clear Light Publishers.

Maldonado Alvarado, B. (2002). *Autonomia y Communalidad India, enfoques y propuestas desde Oaxaca* (p. 2002). Secretaria de Asuntos Indigenas, CEDI, Oaxaca, Mexico: INAH.

Mann, C. C. (2005). *1491: New revelations of the Americas before Columbus*. New York: Alfred A. Knopf.

Marcos, S. (2005). We come to ask for justice, not crumbs. In D. Champagne, K. J. Torjesen, & S. SteinerIndigenous (Eds.), *Peoples and the Modern State* (pp. 97–107). Walnut Creek, CA: AltaMira Press.

Mohawk, J. C. (2000). *Utopian legacies: A history of conquest and oppression in the western world*. Santa Fe, NM: Clear Light Publishers.

Montague, A. (1997[1942]). *Man's most dangerous myth: The fallacy of Race*. Walnut Creek, CA: AltaMira Press.

Nash, J. (2005). The mayan quest for pluricultural autonomy in Mexico and Guatemala. In D. Champagne, K. J. Torjesen, & S. Steiner (Eds.), *Indigenous peoples and the modern state* (pp. 121–142). Walnut Creek, CA: AltaMira Press.

Newcomb, S. (2008). *Pagans in the promised land: Decoding the doctrine of Christian discovery*. Golden, Colorado: Fulcrum Publishing.

Ortiz, R. D. (1984). *Indians of the Americas, human rights and self-determination*. New York: Praeger.

Pommersheim, F. (1995). *Braid of feathers: American Indian Law and contemporary tribal life*. Berkeley: University of California Press.

Prucha, F. (1984). *The great father, the United States government and the American Indians*. Lincoln: Univ. of Nebraska Press.

Ramirez, G. M. (2003). *EZLN: 20 y 10, el fuego y la palabra*. Mexico City: Revista Rebeldia.

Ronda, J. P. (1984). *Lewis and Clark among the Indians*. Lincoln: University of Nebraska.

Shrum, S. J. (2005). Border crossings/crossing borders: Native Americans and the issue of border crossing. In D. Champagne, K. J. Torjesen, & S. Steiner (Eds.), *Indigenous peoples and the modern state* (pp. 24–32). Walnut Creek, CA: AltaMira Press.

Sklair, L. (2002). *Globalization: Capitalism and its alternatives* (3rd ed.). Oxford: Oxford University Press.

Smedley, A. (1999). *Race in North America, origins and evolution of a worldview* (2nd ed.). Boulder, CO: Westview Press.

Steinmetz, G. (2005). Return to empire: The new U.S. imperialism in comparative historical perspective. *Sociological Theory, 23*(4), 339–367.

Thornton, R. (1987). *American Indian holocaust and survival*. Norman: University of Oklahoma Press.

Todorov, T. (1984). *The conquest of America. The question of the other*. New York: Harper & Row.

Wallace, A. (1993). *The long and bitter trail: Andrew Jackson and the Indians*. Philadelphia: Hill and Wang.

White Hat, A., et al. (1999). *Reading and writing the Lakota language: lakota Lyapi UN Wowapi Nehan Yawapi*. Utah: University of Utah Press.

Wilkins, D. E. (1997). *American Indian Sovereignty and the U.S. Supreme Court: The masking of justice*. Austin: University of Texas Press.

Wright, R. (1992). *Stolen continents, the "New World" through Indian eyes*. Boston: Houghton Mifflin Company.

Wunder, J. R. (1994). *"Retained by the people": A history of American Indians and the Bill of Rights*. New York: Oxford University Press.

Young Bear, S., & Theisz, R. D. (1994). *Standing in the light, a Lakota way of seeing*. Lincoln: University of Nebraska Press.

The Not-So-Harmless Social Function of a Word that Wounds

3

Debra Walker King

Contents

Nigger hurts. Always. Whether ending with an "a" or an "er;" whether spoken or written, the word has the power to assault racial dignity, silence voices, compromise social parity and threaten freedom of speech. Because of its relationship to a history of overt racism, it has been labeled "the filthiest, dirtiest, nastiest word in the English language." It is a dangerous word, a violent word, which "hits in the gut, catches the eye, knots the stomach, jerks the knee, [and] grabs the arm." No matter how diligently individuals or groups of individuals try to challenge it, co-opt it or revise it, this word remains "the nuclear bomb of racial epithets," a word that trumps other racial epithets in it fearsomeness, danger and noxious historical associations. Although most Black scholars, activists and public intellectuals understand the reasons behind these assessments of the word, not everyone agrees. Law Professor Randal Kennedy, for instance, contends such claims are flawed, primarily because they necessitate comparisons of oppressions that prioritize victimiza-

tion, something he finds even more repulsive than the word.[1]

Instead of arguing degrees of violation, Kennedy suggests discussions about the word should investigate the depth and variety of its potential to "mean." *Nigger*, he advises, must be taken in context for its meaning to be clear and germane to any discussion. According to him, context can transform this hurtful word into a more benign one.[2] Kennedy explains that *nigger* "can mean many different things, depending upon, among other variables, intonation, the location of the interaction, and the relationship between the speaker and those to whom he [or she] is speaking."[3] Having heard this theory frequently, I felt it was worth testing. Below, I offer four context-specific and, seemingly, innocent examples of the word's use in hopes of doing just that.

1997

Aboriginal Australian Stephen Hagan attends a rugby game at an Australian sports stadium–the Toowoomba Sports Ground. There he finds his

D. W. King (✉)
Department of English, University of Florida, Gainesville, FL, USA
e-mail: dwking@ufl.edu

---

[1]Chris Darden, prosecutor in the infamous OJ Simpson trial, quoted in Margaret (1997). Williams (2002). Farai (1999, p. 9). Kennedy (2002, p. 28).
[2]Kennedy. *Nigger.* pp. 174–76.
[3]Kennedy. *Nigger.* p. 54.

seat and prepares his family for an afternoon of pleasure, watching a game he's loved his entire life. That is, until he discovers the name of the section in which his family sits. Above his head, written in large letters are the words "E.S. 'Nigger' Brown Stand." Although the word, *nigger*, is meant to recall the childhood nickname of a blond, blue-eyed rugby hero and Too-woomba politician, Hagan finds the word offensive and begins a legal campaign to remove it from the stadium. Even in the light of the word's "harmless" revival among a few Australian white and Aborigine teenagers, which Hagan claims is due to American hip-hop popularity in Australia, most Black Australians find the word "extremely offensive" and humiliating. For Hagan and others like him, its presence and continued use, no matter how void of disparaging intent, is a painful reminder of the "increasing incidence of racist violence against [B]lack Australians."[4]

January 2004

Philadelphia fitness expert, David Sylvester, joins thirty-nine other professional and amateur bikers for Tour d'Afrique, a one hundred day cycling event beginning in Cairo, Egypt and ending in Cape Town, South Africa. Sylvester rides to raise money for a scholarship honoring his dear friend and fellow African American Kevin Bowser who died in the 9/11 tragedy. Near the end of the trip he arrives in Lilongwe, Malawi where he discovers a hip-hop clothing store called "Niggers." Thinking at first, "this is a very bad joke," Sylvester investigates further. After talking with the two attending salesmen, Sylvester concludes, "This is no joke … The bottom line is this: I rode over 12,000 miles on two continents through 15 states and 13 countries and broke two bikes in the process, to get to a store in Africa called *Niggers*." He feels guilty for his role in the vulgar ritual grammar that has grown to *infect* the continent he calls *the moth-erland*. "I am willing to step [up] and admit my part in the havoc that we have wrought on our mindset," he writes in an email posted on his

website in 2005, "but I think that we all are to blame."[5]

September 13, 2005

During a live NBC broadcast of a Hurricane Katrina disaster relief concert, three-time Grammy winner, rapper Kanye West comments that the federal government's response to the hurricane was slower than desired because "Bush doesn't care about Black People." Eleven days later his image and the phrase "Nigga, please!" become the focus of a major controversy at the University of Florida. That day *The Independent Florida Alligator*, a student-run newspaper, publishes Andy Marlette's political cartoon rejecting the value of West's statement. In a full color cartoon, he depicts West standing silently, as if in shock, with beads of sweat springing from his forehead, holding a joker face card identified as "the race card." US Secretary of State, Condoleezza Rice, stands across from him with her arms folded. A bubble above her head reads, "Nigga Please!"[6]

---

[4]Monaghan (2005).

[5]Sylvester (2005).
[6]Marlette (2005a). The cartoon spurred protest rallies and forums at the university and beyond. UF administrators, including then-President Bernard Machen and Vice President of Student Affairs Patricia Telles-Irvin, denounced its inflammatory and disrespectful content. Tremendous national responses of anti-cartoon support followed and the editor of the newspaper received death threats. Debate about the word's use increased dramati-cally as news that Kanye West, who uses the word frequently in his music, was scheduled to perform in the University's O'Connell Center in exactly one month. References to his visit once again raised questions of who can and cannot use the "N" word outside a culturally "acceptable" community of discourse production. One month later, after Kanye West performed at the University of Florida, *The Independent Alligator* featured a cartoon depicting the rapper alongside University of Florida President Bernard Machen. This time West is speaking (rapping actually), the lyrics of his Billboard hit "Gold Digger": "NOW I AIN'T SAYIN' SHE A GOLD DIGGA BUT SHE AIN'T MESSIN' WIT NO BROKE …." President Machen, microphone in hand, eyes crossed and feet dancing, responds, "AFRICAN AMERICAN." In this instance, even the absence of the word does not soften its impact of verbal assault. Marlette (2005b).

4:45 pm, October 21, 2005

An email circulates in Gainesville, Florida (and perhaps beyond) titled "Why is it Always Black Folks." It reads:

> There were a total of 15 passengers boarding a small plane on their way to Florida. One Black mother and her child were on their way to visit relatives while the other passengers consisted of the KKK on their way to a convention. The plane took off and after flying for approximately 12 min an announcement came over the intercom from the pilot saying: "We have overloaded this flight. We are going to have to start throwing luggage out the window so the plane won't go down." Two minutes later you could see luggage being thrown out the window. Five minutes after that, the pilot made a second announcement. "We are still experiencing problems. We're sorry, but the plane is still overloaded and we're going to have to get rid of some of the weight so the plane won't go down. We're going to have to ask some passengers to jump out of the window when we call you by your name. To make it fair, we'll go alphabetically. We'll start with A. Will all the African Americans please jump now?" The [B]lack woman and her child continued to sit. The pilot came over the intercom system. "Next is B. Will all the Black people please jump now"? The Black woman and child continued to sit. The pilot came over the intercom system again. "Next is C. Will all the colored people please jump now? All the KKK were now staring at the mother and child. The [B]lack woman and child continued to sit. The child then looked up at her Mom and said: "Mom aren't we all of those?" The mother then replied to her daughter, "Baby, we niggers tonight and the K's come before the N's." -Unknown

April 16, 2016

The President of the United States is addressed publically as "my nigga." The words send shockwaves throughout the nation. Questions of appropriateness, insult, and disgrace ripple like water around the person addressing the first Black president in such a manner—not only because of the familiarity the phrase calls forth but also because the name-calling occurs during a formal, public and nationally broadcast Whitehouse event: the president's last Correspondents' Dinner. Ending a comedy skit that is insulting on many levels, comedian and Saturday Night Live host, Larry Wilmore concludes the night by reminding the president of their brotherhood, "You did it, my nigga." In the audience tensions rise, shoulders tighten, eyes fall, hearts skip a beat and no one laughs. In a moment reminiscent of when Malcolm X quieted the harassment of a Black associate professor during a public speech by reminding him racists still identify Black professors as 'niggers," Wilmore waved a double edged sword of camaraderie and assault. The sword strikes America deeply with shame.

Did presenting the word "in context" soften the impact of seeing it on the page or reading about reactions to it? Did it seem harmless? Perhaps not. In fact, each story begs the question of whether *nigger* can ever be harmless. The last two examples are especially poignant in this regard. They demand reconsideration of how (and whether) self-naming practices undermine or transform the meaning potential of the word, particularly when the cultural, national and social contexts, or environments, surrounding those it names remain racially hostile, fragile or potentially injurious. Much like the comedy routines of Richard Pryor, Chris Rock and others who use *nigger* as a comedic hook and intercultural bonding tool, the word's inclusion in the emailed joke and the Wilmore comedic blast brings an element of shock and defiant pleasure to the laughter (or lack thereof) that follows it. But, when we look closer, we discover the joke suggests something more ominous than we might have first thought.

The Black woman and child at the emailed joke's center are situated within a space of potential violation and harm; yet, they sit confident of their survival. Why? Because they choose to be *niggers*. The joke suggests that when Black people are faced with situations of racist hostility and danger, the decision to identify oneself as a "nigger" can save not only one's own life but also the life of one's children. The word used during President Obama's last Whitehouse Correspondents' Dinner functions to remind both the president and all of America that regardless of how high a Black man (or woman, for that matter) may ascend in this country black skin is always "nigga" skin. In both instances a verbal assault, a death threat or a leveling of honor are present subliminally even though they are meant to be funny. We might even laugh, especially if a member of what we consider a permissible in-group forwards the joke to us or speaks it in public. Regardless of race, most readers and hearers of the jokes admit experiencing an uneasiness that compromises their blind appreciation of the intended comedy.[7]

Neither the jokes nor the laughter they may promote diminish the impact of verbal abuse and vulgarity the word *nigger* brings into the stories I've reviewed here. The history and the crimes of murder, disfranchisement, disempowerment and human injury remain part of the word's historical content even when the context of its use is comical. Considering these observations, the following pages contend that whether *nigger* is the name of a section in an Australian rugby stadium, a store in Africa or the punch line in a cartoon or joke, it remains, as always, a racist insult–a word that wounds.

History distinguishes *nigger* as a racial insult from other words of "mere insult" and ultimately renders it a word that wounds. According to Richard Delgado, who first framed the word's effects this way, "[r]acial insults are different qualitatively because they conjure up the entire history of racial discrimination in this country."[8] Like other racial insults, nigger has a social history, which it can never escape. The derogatory influence and power of this word arrived with its seventeenth century invention by people who were just beginning to identify themselves as "white." The connotation of inhuman and barbarian inferiority built into that invention provided white racism with an onomastic tool primed to injure those it names as well as to justify slavery and the inhumane treatment of

African Americans.[9] In this way, the word is *always already* a racial and dehumanizing insult. Its conjurational force and social violence as a racially specific or racially associated affront calls forth and makes present a history of hatred, murder and fear each time it is mentioned regardless of context. In other words, *Nigger*, not only names an entity and calls forth a presence, it embodies the presence called forth.

During the 1960s Black scholars referred to this conjurational power as a "nommo force," the spiritual-physical energy of words that enables them to call forth being. According to Paul Carter Harrison and others, nommo, the seed of word, water and life, brings to the body its vital human force–its nyama or essential self.[10] Through nyama we become (in spirit if not always in action) what we claim through our names, nicknames, and our participation in ritualistic or ceremonial events. Under these terms, one might ask: what does *nigger* call forth? What do Black people become when we claim it or align ourselves with it in ritualistic, verbal play? What violence do we claim and thereby validate?

In John Singleton's *Rosewood*, the character Sara declares: "Nigga, just another word for guilty." And, indeed, for the residents of Black owned towns and districts from Rosewood, Florida to Greenwood (also known as Black Wall Street) in Tulsa Oklahoma, during the twentieth-century "nigga" did indeed conjure guilt. In each of these cases, guilt associated with a charge of rape gave entire communities of

---

[7]Readers asked about their response to the email reported noticing a slight discomfort with their own reaction to the joke, but admitted they quickly overcame the feeling by ignoring it.

[8]Delgado and Stefancic (2004, p. 13).

[9]In a personal communication with the editors of the present text, Joe Feagin and Hernan Vera pointed out that "the N word is a U.S. invention that it is very hard to translate. We have seen it translated as 'negro apestoso' but this term is not included in the Dictionary of Latin American Racial and Ethnic Terminology (UF Press 1989), which suggests that it is a translator's invention. In Portuguese, the expressions 'negro ruim' and 'negro sujo' are nowhere near the N word in negative valence. Mexicans use the term 'chango,' that designates a monkey, but this is a regional usage; in other regions it is a term of endearment. 'Changó' and 'chango prieto' have negative connotations in some regions of Latin America, but it is also used to refer to whites and to Indians, both as a racial insult and as term of endearment" (email communication, December 25, 2005).

[10]Harrison (1972).

racists the "right" to condemn and destroy neighbors whose skin color marked them as *nigger*. Rosewood was burned and Black Wall Street was bombed from the air. Today, we have not moved far beyond defining *nigger* as another word for guilty. In fact, we have not moved beyond it at all. We have just added a new twist to the destructive potential of the word by redirecting its ability to condemn. Our society's desperate need for blinding itself to the possibility that racism continues to structure our sense of justice shifts the possessor of guilt from the subject of name-calling to the name-caller—especially if that name caller is not Black.

The most notorious example of this inversion and its consequences occurred in 1995 during the OJ Simpson Trial when Mark Fuhrman's use of the word marked him as not only a racist but also a liar. In the midst of a trial many Americans thought would end in the conviction of Simpson for murder, the cry of "Nigger!" condemned a white man of deception while playing a major role in the legal exoneration of a Black man. Perhaps, for the first time in history, *nigger* was "just another word for white men's guilt."

The events occurring in Judge Ito's courtroom involving this word produced the politically correct use of a ridiculous acronym, a description of a horror and a defeat. Suddenly, few beyond the boundaries of the Black race dare speak the word without concern for repercussions. Instead, everyone speaks freely about "the N-word." This name fragmentation does little to erase the bloody history of racism the original word conjures. In fact, it illustrates that history by drawing a tortured picture of the word itself. Through abbreviations, dashes and, sometimes, quotation marks the word *nigger* is castrated but not rendered impotent. Because of this linguistic castration, however, even the most racist player on the field can be washed clean, while, his or her use of the euphemism slashes the souls of Black folk just as violently, just as successfully, as the word it signifies.

Appropriation and structural revisions, such as "*the N-word*," cannot erase *nigger's* historical content; neither can it situate the word beyond the onomastic desires (or history of intentions) fueling its pejorative meanings. Instead historical content is always there keeping hurtful meanings and memories alive, empowering signification and building conjurational force beyond the site of current or "harmless" semantic intent. Joe Feagin and Karyn McKinney make note of this in *The Many Costs of Racism*. They asked respondents:

> "Why [is this word] and other common racist epithets often an irritating and painful experience for African Americans? …one experienced African American psychologist … explained to Joe Feagin that, when he hears the epithet "nigger," in the back of his mind he often sees a black man hanging from a tree. This is not surprising, because he grew up in the segregation era when lynchings of [B]lack men were more common than it is today. In this way, past experience informs and contextualizes present events. Indeed, the impact of racist epithets is often underestimated by outside, especially white, observers. Some whites have the audacity to counsel African Americans as to how they can or should ignore such comments. The psychologist indicated in his further comment that his liberal white friends will sometimes tell him to "let go" of such racist comments from white bigots and quickly "move on." Thus, it appears that many whites believe that as long as one has a strong sense of self, or as long as one does not exemplify whatever racist remarks seem to signify, such insults are "only words" and thus should not hurt or cause psychological damage. Such a white perspective suggests that its advocates have not been the recipients of regular put-downs and routine questioning of one's worth. Most whites also do not realize that it is not just the attacks on one's own person that a [B]lack person must face and process, but also the harmful attacks by whites that are held in the collective memories of one's family and community."[11]

What Feagin and McKinney identify here as collective memory is the historical content of the word—a nommo force that does not transform nor diminish in impact in spite of attempts to re-appropriate or reinscribe the word. Regardless of how it is spelled or spoken, n-i-g-g-a-h, n-i-g, n-i-g-g-a, n-i-g-g-u-h, or n-i-g-g-a-z, historical recall and social injury is always threatening to erupt beyond the boundaries of suppressed connotative value. This occurs because, in each case,

---

[11]Feagin and McKinney (2003, p. 48).

meaning can only occur if the word's relationship with a history of subordination and murder is disguised, maintained and monitored—kept just beneath the surface, but kept just the same. The violence inherent to the word's revision is evident when its function as an acceptable marker of Black identity crosses racial boundaries as it does in the following example.

> [I]n San Jose, California, a judge allowed a white high school student to escape punishment after the student, angry at an African-American teacher who had suspended his best friend, scrawled "Thanks, Nigga" on a school wall. The judge was swayed by an argument that "nigga" is not the same as "nigger" but rather an inoffensive rap music term of endearment common among soul brothers.[12]

Although the judge buys this argument, not many blacks would consider general public use of the word acceptable in this or any other context. The assaultive nature of the word is highlighted, but ignored, in this example—particularly because it brings to light a judge's choice to align his legal decision with the word's assumed popular use without regard for its history of offense. Had he considered the full story of the term's function as a, so-called, term of endearment he might have recognized its violent history and become aware of its cultural censorship.

Musicians, comedians, writers and other artists have for decades tried to transform *nigger* into a sign of cultural "cool," a bonding tool used by members of racially exclusive in-groups. The attempt, however, has yielded little more that the global marketing of self-naming practices grounded in acts of ritualistic vulgarity. The use of the word in popular culture, as indicated in the example above, has led many to believe the word is harmless and, therefore, acceptable for general cross-racial and cross-cultural use. But, as Eric Dyson claims, this word has "never been cool when spit from white lips."[13] In fact, it is so "not-cool" the very popular and outspoken white rapper Eminem doesn't use the word. "That word," he claims, "is not even in [his]

vocabulary."[14] James Weldon Johnson summarizes the rules of cultural censorship Eminem honors in *The Autobiography of an Ex-Colored Man* (1912). His protagonist, observes, while visiting a poor Black community, that "among this class of colored man the word 'nigger' was freely used in about the same sense as the word 'fellow,' and sometimes as a term of endearment: but I soon learned that its use was positively and absolutely prohibited to white men."[15]

African Americans use the term to remain mindful of social realities or (in other words) "to keep it real." Some use it to "rope off turf" for profit in the music industry and in comedy. Others recognize it as a means of gaining empowerment and defying racial subordination while distinguishing themselves from (the culturally self-ostracized) assimilated "Negro."[16] In a small way, black intercultural uses of the word, *nigger*, clear a space for linguistic empowerment and communal privilege in a world where socio-economic power and black racial privilege do not exist. But in order to do this, the pain, insult and defensive outrage that result from the word's ability to wound must be acknowledged internally. In other words, the word must be allowed to hurt, if only briefly. It must be allowed leverage to recoup its historical meanings; otherwise, why would white American's be barred from using it?

Class, race (and, sometimes, educational) distinctions make all the difference in terms of permissibility and linguistic "turf." But even when shared between streetwise associates within restricted racial boundaries *nigger* has the power to wound, scar, denigrate and silence those it names. The word is so potent as an instrument of harm it has only to be written, to appear in print, to contribute in a big way to the physical injury and "little murders" Black people experience daily.[17]

One of its most powerful influences of *nigger* as a word that wounds is its ability to suppress

---

[12]Williams, Patricia J. "Sensation." p. 9.
[13]Dyson (1999). Quoted in Kennedy (2002, p. 51).

[14]Ibid. Kennedy. p. 51.
[15]Johnson (1912: p. 67).
[16]Kennedy. *Nigger*, pp. 47–49.
[17]Feagin and Sikes (1994, p. 54).

meaningful discourse whenever and wherever it is used. Legal scholar Charles Lawrence claims words like it (including *bitch*, *whore*, *spic*, and *kike*, among others) can "temporarily disable the victim, and the perpetrators often use these words with the intention of producing this effect."[18] Clearly the phrase "Nigga Please!" in *The Independent Alligator* is used to silence arguments that President Bush devalued the lives of those effected by Hurricane Katrina's devastation, most prominently Black people. As mentioned earlier, West is depicted in the cartoon as dumbfounded by Condoleezza Rice's use of the word.

Using this phrase as leverage for silencing an opponent or adversary is an old trick. Throughout the twentieth century, the phrase was used to question the integrity, sincerity and worth of words spoken and ideas shared amongst Black friends or associates. It was used to silence but in a friendly, so-called, "endearing" way. "Nigga, Please," someone would say, dismissively. Laughter, a chuckle maybe, but never more than this, usually followed. It was suitable for both parties to offer a laugh just bold enough to signal a successful moment of bonding and brief enough to choke the subtle pain of a signifin' game played against a backdrop of horror and shame, a haunting milieu of collective memory. Even amidst in-group laughter, the poison of the phrase's dismissive discourse, hidden yet coolly brandished amongst peers, had the power to silence the addressee while giving power and control to the name-caller. And, although no one wanted to admit it, the words pinched like poorly fitting shoes.

The pain of subjecting oneself to such violence is rarely acknowledged among Black peers who understand its function within a code of honorability. Within the code, *nigger* delivers cultural capital to those who are named by it. Within that social space, it not only controls and silences but also offers prestige to members of the in-group. If acknowledgement of the word's violence does occur, it is quickly and explicitly dismissed. Better to keep the wounds, such name-calling carves in the soul, private and out of view. It wouldn't be honorable or prestigious

for someone accepted into social comradeship as a fellow "nigga" to cry or resist such social branding. To remain safe from group alienation and suspicion of betrayal, the person so-named must accept the capital of honorability offered to them. Pain must be swallowed whole in order for social allegiance to be framed and confirmed.

This in-group silencing operates without regard to who is being named. If, for instance, a member of the Black in-group calls a white teenager *nigger*, the teenager raises in status among members of that in-group. As an outsider-within, he must be careful of using the term himself, however. And, most importantly, he must not reject the labeling or the brotherhood (or culture) of pain into which he is called by name. If he does, he shows disrespect and will be rejected—perhaps with overt violence and physical force. In this way, the destructive operations of silence and submission merge with a ritual grammar of domination and control to form a very precarious social bond.

The ritual grammar in which *nigger* offers those it names cultural capital and prestige is useful as a mechanism for adversarial or combative silencing—even when Black-to-Black interlocutory exchanges exist outside the sphere of communal play and "street talk." As mentioned earlier, Malcolm X solved a potentially explosive situation during a public encounter with an African American who insisted on being an intellectual heckler. In a moment of certain frustration, if not also anger, Malcolm X called upon the word's inherent duplicity to provide him with the ability to silence his opponent while also claiming a pain-laden fraternity with him. He tells the story in his autobiography as follows:

> [A] 'token-integrated' black Ph. D associate professor ... was ranting about what a "divisive demagogue" and what a "reverse racist" I was. I was racking my head, to spear that fool; finally I held up my hand, he stopped. "Do you know what white racists call black Ph.D's?" He said something like, "I believe that I happen not to be aware of that"—you know, one of these ultra-proper-talking Negroes. And I laid the word down on him, loud: "NIGGER!" (Haley 284).[19]

---

[18]Lawrence (1993).

[19]Haley (1964, p.284).

The epithet used in Malcolm X's staged interrogation stands at a crossroad of meaning. There the professor may choose to yield to a coded message of bonding and "common history" or experience the word's ability to deflate, wound and quiet all who resist as an outsider. The question and its answer suggest that in the eyes of a racist all Blacks are inferior, no matter how educated or distinguished by class, rank, training or pretense. Literary scholar and critic, Kimberly Benston comments that through the word's use Malcolm X "remind[s] the professor of a shared origin, returning him to the debasing ground of middle passage and slavery." In other words, beneath the intellectual fray and animosity of Malcolm X's name-calling, an entire history of "a nation dispossessed" speaks and claims the professor as one of its own, the denigrated and denied of a racist society.[20]

Nigger, in this case, disrupts, but does not deny, the horror at its core. With racism hovering boldly over the audience, occupying its attention, a more subtle ritual grammar, a grammar of vulgarity and harm, speaks from the worldview of the dispossessed, the angry, the humiliated, the sullen and the banished. This subtle discourse conjures the familiarity assumed by a bonded fate that at once shames while it silences and unifies. Although Malcolm X resorts to a ritual grammar of humor and sarcasm to communicate what his earnest elocution does not, his use of a name that wounds is a serious affair the "brother" who hears it understands.[21]

This leads one to ask: "did President Obama hear and understand a similar or different ritual grammar present in the words "my nigga" when he was addressed in this manner? Obama's response when asked was one of understanding. He advised his aids that he "appreciated the spirit" in which the name was used. Wilmore was talking about the growth of a nation that can move from racists hate to a black man as president in the Whitehouse when he used the phrase. Although the president offered his appreciation of the spirit in which Wilmore uttered the epithet,

it is only because of the name's horrific historical content that this "spirit" is called forth. As such it served to not only acknowledge the nation's growth but to harangue its still present racism.

The ritual grammar Malcolm and Wilmore employ oscillates between a horrible history of racist social, legal and political corruption and Black pain as a source of empowered Black identity and voice. As a ritual, this linguistic practice gains meaning and influence through repetition. And, as a grammar, it follows certain rules of permissibility, syntax and usage, outlined above. Considering the word's meaning potential within Black interlocutory exchanges, it is easy to consider the situation facing Malcolm X an ideal example of when one might effectively employ the word and Wilmore's as questionable. In fact, the Los Angeles times reports that Reverend Al Sharpton denounced the use of the word for all occasions adding, however, "to say that to the President of the United States in front of the top people in media was at best in poor taste."[22] Malcolm's impressive use of the word (as a tool for silencing a "brother" who appears to have forgotten his past and his connection to a people's struggle) doesn't make the name any less painful or any less poor in taste, however. This is why the online and forum discussions about the appearance of "Nigga, Please" in *The Independent Alligator* were necessary and why the UF Black students' demand for an apology should be applauded.

Unfortunately, the discussion caused an immediate disruption of energies and meaningful discourse focused on the welfare of the powerless, poor and Black victims of Hurricane Katrina. Those whose survival depended upon a federal response to a natural disaster (that, for many, never came) where suddenly second place to a fight against a white cartoonist's use of a word. In this way "action" became reaction and dialogue about the crisis at hand was consumed by the word's function as a silencing agent—if only for a few days. The point of West's original comment, whether truthful or a racially provoked misperception, was deflected as long as the

---

[20]Benson (1984, pp. 151–152).
[21]King (1998, pp. 114–115).

[22]Korte (2016).

central focus of discourse and outrage was the violence and violating presence of a word that wounds.

Patricia Hill Collins delves into questions concerning the utility of struggling with words like *nigger* in her 1998 book *Fighting Words*. She admits this word is considered one of several "insults of such dimension that they either urge people to violence or inflict harm" but cautions her readers that fighting about words does not solve problems.[23] However, if *nigger* is not silenced, it will continue to do injury to social parity and justice. *Nigger* is a fighting word in the both the street and legal sense. It is an instrument of "assaultive speech" degrading to those it labels—especially when presented in clearly racist contexts. What appears to be less accepted is that it functions outside a racist context in similar degrading and hurtful ways. Context does not matter when the subject of discussion is the word *nigger*. The violence and the threat of violence, at its core can never be diminished or successfully minimized—regardless of cultural, social or national context.

Theories suggesting the repetition of the word in racially neutral contexts can somehow cleanse it are flawed mainly because the word itself is not neutral. I was utterly perplexed when I discovered the central objective of an "interactive" session I attended at the 2004 National Conference on Race and Ethnicity was to move people, Black and white, beyond their discomfort with this word by saying it repeatedly.[24] The room was filled to capacity and no one objected to what was certainly a raising dis-ease with the format. Instead, the facilitator controlled the group, clearly identified as his temporary "in-group," by making their fear of this word and their sense of guilt-by-association with it the cornerstone of what he called a "Message of Madness." Perhaps the point was to encourage the audience's experience of the word's awful violence and thereby assist recognition that its continual in-group social use is madness.

No matter how much those who use the word *nigger* in social games of verbal play claim an unproblematic transition from hurtful to healthy (and often ritualistic) nominative possession, the pain of derogatory naming-calling endures. By denying this pain, Black people, who self-identify using the word, become complicit with it. Pierre Bourdieu calls this type of self-inflicted social and communal harm and domination *symbolic violence*: "the gentle, invisible form of violence, which is never recognized as such, and is not so much undergone as chosen."[25] It is "violence which is exercised upon a social agent with his or her complicity."[26] It is not the same as the brutal exploitation and overt violence of lynching or murder; yet, it yields similar regulatory and disciplinary effects.

While overt violence is often bloody and unquestionably offensive, symbolic violence manifests itself as domination through individual or communal acceptance of naturalized racial markings, social hierarchies and codes of honorability. Acceptance of symbolic violence, through which relations of dominance are concealed, works to legitimize strategies of exclusion and build the political, economic, cultural and social capital of the status quo. Within this lexicon, for instance, *nigga* is a "misrecognizable, socially recognized domination" through which black bodies become, once again, property under surveillance and containment.[27] This function of the word is most clear in the endearing phrase "my nigga," which cloaks while communicating its hidden relationship to a history of ownership and racially prescribed containment.

Symbolic violence acts as a mechanism to encourage containment of anything or anyone, group or individual, that the established social order deems unsavory, unwanted or unnecessary. This type of violence exists as long as the social injury and wounding history the words contain are euphemized or censored. When we accept appropriation as an act that changes, instead of one that

---

[23]Collins (1998, p. 84).
[24]Eddie (2004).

[25]Bourdieu (1972, p. 192).
[26]Bourdieu and Wacquant (1992, p. 167).
[27]Bourdieu. Outline, 192.

fails to chance, the impact and meaning content of a violent word, we censor social injury and history but we do not eliminate them. The boundary crossing poison of the word is always present and claims supreme influence in all situations.

Maintaining misinterpretation (or what Bourdieu calls misrecognition) requires anyone who uses the word to qualify intent either through an assumed racial alliance or through argument and justifications that posture innocence. Unfortunately, such justifications must always contend with race and in so doing expose the work of racist injury and historical violence existing within the word. In the Australian context sample opening this chapter, Stephen Hagan discovered the injurious word labeling the "E.S. 'Nigger' Brown Stand" was intended as a "term of endearment" honoring a white man "who was so blond and blue-eyed that when he was just a few years old, his brothers gave him the nickname as a joke."[28] According to the stadium owners, the name had nothing to do with dark skinned Australian Aborigines. Still, only the word's symbolic violence was evident to Hagan upon first seeing it:

> I'm 45 years of age now, and all my life I've only heard [*nigger*] used in the derogatory sense. ... In primary school, in secondary school, people called Aboriginal people niggers if they wanted to make fun of them or belittle them, or try to put them off their game, be it on the football field or in life. Later, socially, as young teenagers, at discos, if they wanted to pick a fight with you they'd call you a boong or a coon or an abo or a nigger. Those were just demeaning terms that were used throughout my life. I certainly haven't heard *nigger* used as a term of endearment."[29]

Present with the word is the memory of a violent past in which dark-skinned Aboriginal people were lynched and physically abused. This presence, called forth through the word *nigger*, is what builds the irony of the white man's nickname. It is so strong in its appearance that it outweighs the signifying intent of those who named the stand in 1960. That intent does not resound as loudly as the hidden truths of the word's inherent violence. Hagan rejects that violence and his potential complicity with it by rejecting the word and, in 2008, succeeding in his quest to have the stand demonished.

The idea implicit in the contextual defense used by the stadium owners, that the word identifies a white man, implies that one does not have to be Black to be called a nigger. Sociologist John Hartigan cites a similar claim made by a participant in his study of white identity politics in Detroit. The respondent he quotes felt the need to justify his white on white use of the word *nigger* by claiming "[y]ou don't have to be black to be a nigger. Niggers come in all colors ... We are all colored."[30] For Randal Kennedy, who also cites Hartigan's study, this justification is enough to remedy any racially specific "misinterpretation" that might ensue from this white man's use of the term. Although these defining elements influence meaning, we cannot dismiss the historical content that gives the word its linguistic power and social determination.

The argument that "[w]e are all colored" does not minimize the figure of blackness or its influence in terms of how meaning is accrued—the analogy merely qualifies and refines meaning. Without Black history and its relationship to racist name-calling, murder and hate, the word is meaningless. Whether the context and intent of the speaker is innocent, inflammatory or "friendly," when blackness, as a racial signifier, and the history of shame surrounding it inform meaning in any way —which it does in every case I can imagine—, *nigger* can do little more than act as a censored social compress.

This leads me back to my original question: Who do Black people become when we claim as a sign of identity a word linked to a history of pain and racist animosity? What do our children become when they hear their idols in song, poetry, prose, and on the streets call themselves (and those who wish to be like them) names that wound? What do we conjure when we fill our verbal play with a ritualistic grammar calling out to Black pain and the sting of historical rejection and dehumanization—mocking it while also

---

[28]Monahan. "Taking a Stand," p. A16.

[29]Monaghan. "Taking a Stand," p. A16.

[30]Hartigan (1999, p. 116).

depending upon it to solidify moments of racialized, experiential bonding? Some would say we become "bad," but only in the "non-insulting" way. And they would be right.

Aside from Kennedy's support of the word's not-so-hostile use by whites when distinguishing "good" from "bad" niggers is another history, one more layered and culturally distinct. It is a history of symbolic violence cloaked in myth and folklore. For two centuries, Black folk heroes like Stackolee and John Henry stood on opposite ends of a spectrum characterizing the "bad nigger"–the former acting with profound rage and amorality in disregard to African American communal values and the latter moving through moments of anger and hopelessness in order to survive racism within acceptable moral limits. Contemporary images of the "bad nigger" follow suit. Through it Black people become justified brutes living outside morality and community, unconventional men surviving the world's hostility through unconventional means, counter-culture intellectuals fighting battles for the Black underclass, self-proclaimed whores intent on "getting paid" or, according to Maya Angelou's softer take on Black women's struggle, "phenomenal" women living phenomenally. All are *baddd* niggers.

Both the nice (or good) and the ugly find their reflections in the oral culture of today's black youth. We hear Queen Pen, for instance, rap (with pride) using words like: "I got mad bitches just wantin' me./And I got mad niggaz just checkin' for me."[31] Today "bad niggaz" are "mad niggaz" and Stackolee's moral wisdom (or the lack thereof) and rebellious flavor combs the airwaves like thunder. Young boys (and, in some cases, girls too) who claim the name "nigga" pride themselves on being pseudo-gangsters, pimps and thugs—"mad niggaz" in pants they can barely keep on their hips and with a glide perfectly harmonized to the tune of a ghetto fabulous, cool only they can hear. While their clothes glorify prison life (and the prisoner's lack of belts) their walk and reputation harks back to past characterizations of the "bad nigger."

James Earl Hardy, author of the hip-hop love story *B-Boy Blues* (1994), describes the male figure in this coupling this way:

> Here are 'men' who throw their masculinity around for the entire world to not only see but swallow … of course, it is a rather grotesquely exaggerated take on manhood. But, when you are on your way to growing into a man (at least in years) and nobody has told you how to be one and almost all the "men" you see around you walk, talk, dress, and act like this, how else do you prove that you are a man but by joining them? Yes, you too have to be one bad mothafucka, the one they'll fear the most…only the roughest survive.[32]

Yes, the "bad nigga" survives, but will the child who claims this persona find prosperity, education, political power and upward mobility beyond the field of containment prescribed for his self-proclaimed "badness" by the status quo: the world of drugs, violence and jail? Without breaking with an identity under constant surveillance by a non-Black, non-accepting majority, can the "nigga" cross the bar of class and race to survive whole? Can black children move beyond the culture of grotesque masculinity promoted by "mad niggaz" without code switching in dress, manner and, most importantly, in self-naming practices? History's record suggests not. Furthermore, Black activists and political leaders have insisted historically that only a full and eternal break with this word will suffice. In 1920, for instance, Blacks attending a convention in New York rejected the painful reality and insulting power of the word *nigger* by saying so in the "Declaration of the Rights of Negro People of the World." Marcus Garvey in cooperation with other convention participants wrote:

> [t]hat the Negro people of the world, through their chosen representatives in convention assembled in Liberty Hall, in the City of New York and United States of America, from August 1 to August 31, in the year of our Lord, one thousand nine hundred and twenty protest against the wrongs and injustices they are suffering at the hands of their white brethren, and state what they deem their fair and just rights, as well as the treatment they propose to demand of all men in the future.[33]

---

[31]Queen (1997).

[32]Hardy (1994, p. 27).
[33]UNIA-ACL (1920).

"The Declaration of Rights" is intended to encourage Black people globally to higher standards and higher social expectations than the word *nigger* can provide. Of special note here are the following two entries on the list of rights:

> 11. We believe all men entitled to common human respect, and that our race should in no way tolerate any insults that may be interpreted to mean disrespect to our color.
> 12. We deprecate the use of the term 'nigger' as applied to Negroes."[34]

This word's use in an Australian rugby stadium, as the name of a hip-hop clothing store in Africa and in twenty-first century cartoons and jokes defies both the spirit and the law of this declaration. These occurrences and others like them insult and assault Black history, Black people and Black pride globally. But what hurts most about the contemporary use of this word is that some African Americans choose to act with complicity by using it in self-naming practices. When Black people allow this word to enter ritual grammars that define moments of social bonding, a nommo force of evil and hate follows; reminding us all that there is no way to escape the past cleanly—no way to banish horror from the core of words that wound.

So, how do we empty a word like this of its assaultive effects when its relationship to a history of pain, struggle and victories won at great cost, great sacrifice are what give it life and meaning? We do not. Every time we laugh at this word's lighthearted use, we drive a hole into everything decades of Black pain and black struggles to gain respect and equity have purchased. Sanctioning the right of African Americans to call each other *niggers* does not soften the blow of hearing the word spoken or weaken the silencing shock of its appearance, unexpectedly, in print. Nothing makes the word less painful or insulting and nothing ever will. Beneath the rhetoric of in-group appropriation, bonding and comic liberation is a sword pressed against the neck of social and political progress. Each time Black people use this word, each time we forget or ignore its relationship to suffering,

discrimination and disenfranchisement, we dig the edge of that sword into our own flesh until we can no longer deny: *NIGGER* hurts!

References

Benson, K. W. (1984). I Yam What I Am: Topos of (Un)naming in Afro-American literature. In H. L. Gates Jr. (Ed.), *Black literature and literary theory* (pp. 151–72). New York: Methuen.

Bourdieu, P. (1972). *Outline of a theory of practice* (Trans. 1977). Cambridge: Cambridge University Press.

Bourdieu, P., & Wacquant, L. J. D. (1992). *An invitation to reflexive sociology*. Chicago: University of Chicago Press

Collins, P. H. (1998). On fighting words with 'fighting words'. In *Fighting words: Black women and the search for justice* (pp. 79–94). Minneapolis: University of Minnesota Press.

Delgado, R., & Stefancic, J. (2004). *Understanding words that wound*. Bolder, Colorado: Westview Press.

Dyson, M. E. (1999). Nigga gotta stop. *The Source*.

Eddie, M., Jr. (2004). The Nigger word: A message of madness. In *Presented at the National Conference on Race and Ethnicity. Miami Beach, Florida*, June 1–5.

Farai, C. (1999). *The color of our future: Race for the 21st century*. New York: William Morrow and Company.

Feagin, J. R., & McKinney, K. D. (2003). *The many costs of racism*. Lanham, Maryland: Rowman & Littlefield Publishers Inc.

Feagin, J. R., & Sikes, M. P. (1994). *Living with racism: The black middle class experience*. Boston: Beacon Press.

Haley, A. (1964). *The autobiography of Malcolm X*. New York: Random House, Ballantine Books.

Hardy, J. E. (1994). *B-Boy Blues*. Boston: Alyson.

Harrison, P. C. (1972). *The drama of Nommo*. New York: Grove Press.

Hartigan, J. (1999). *Racial situations: Class predicaments of whiteness in Detroit*. Princeton: Princeton University Press.

Johnson, J. W. (1912). *The autobiography of an Ex-Colored Man* (p. 1990). New York: Penguin Books.

Kennedy, R. (2002). *Nigger: The strange career of a troublesome word*. New York: Pantheon Books.

King, D. W. (1998). *Deep talk: Reading African-American literary names*. Charlottesville: University of Virginia Press.

Korte, G. (2016, May 2). Obama has no problem with Larry Wilmore's use of racial slur, Aide Says. *USA Today*. Accessed June 24, 2016. http://www.usatoday.com/story/news/politics/theoval/2016/05/02/obama-wilmore-white-house-correspondents-dinner-comedy/83831334/.

Lawrence, C. R. III. (1993). If he hollers let him go: regulating racist speech on campus. In M. J. Matsuda, C. R. Lawrence III, R. Delgado, & K. Crenshaw (Eds.), *Words that wound: Critical race theory,*

---

[34]Ibid.

assaultive speech, and the first amendment (pp. 53–88). Bolder: Westview.

Margaret, M. R. (1997). Representing race: Beyond 'sellouts' and 'race cards': Black attorneys and the straightjacket of legal practice. *Michigan Law Review,* 95, 765.

Marlette, A. (2005). Cartoon. *Independent alligator* (p. 6). 99.14.

Marlette, A. (2005). Cartoon. *The independent alligator* (p. 6). 99.36, October 13.

Monaghan, P. (2005). Taking a stand: An aboriginal Austrian researcher battles to strip a stadium of a derogatory word. *The Chronicle of Higher Education* (p. A16–A18), July 29.

Queen, P. (1997). Girl friend. In *My melody.* Interscope Records.

Sylvester, D. (2005). The Nigger email [pdf]. Kevin Bowser Scholarship. Accessed October 16, 2005. http://www.contribute2.org/.

UNIA-ACL. (1920). Declaration of rights of the Negro people of the world. Oct 21, 2005. http://www.unia-acl.org/archive/declare.htm.

Williams, P. J. (2002). Diary of a mad law professor: 'Sensation.' *The Nation,* 274.17, May 6, 2002 (p. 9).

The Racial State

4

Rodney D. Coates

Contents

The racial state is one that is intricately associated with the origins, development and apparent permanence of particularly, modern, western nation states. These states, associated with European expansion, imperialism, and exploitation, created race as a means of organizing and legitimizing its existence (Omi and Winant 2015). Cazenave (2011), analyzing what he terms as the urban racial state, adds that the racial state provides numerous links and other organizational and institutional structures (such as courts, schools, private foundations, research centers, state and local governments) which foster and sustain white racial supremacy (25–26). The racial state uses state coercion or repression, to not only normalize racial governance but also to nullify or delegitimize resistance. (Cazenave, ibid.: 25–26, 30) Specifically, the racial state creates political institutions to regulate and insinuate race throughout most, if not all, institutions within the society. The racial state stipulates a specific racial hierarchy and hegemony which further determines how racial conflict and accommodation will be accomplished between specific racial groups, ideas, and institutions within the society. The president, as the chief executive officer, is often the official face and voice of the racial state. This chapter will investigate how the President of the United States has served in this capacity.

As the forty-fifth president of the United States, Donald Trump lost the popular vote in the 2016 but won the majority of the Electoral College vote to take the highest office of the land. Trump's upset threw into sharp relief the already

R. D. Coates (✉)
University of Miami, Miami, OH, USA
e-mail: coatesrd@miamioh.edu

© Springer International Publishing AG, part of Springer Nature 2018
P. Batur and J. R. Feagin (eds.), *Handbook of the Sociology of Racial and Ethnic Relations*,
Handbooks of Sociology and Social Research, https://doi.org/10.1007/978-3-319-76757-4_4

existing intersectional divide between race, gender and education. Geographically speaking, Trump dominated rural and suburban areas, while Clinton was strongest in urban areas (Morin 2016). Most of Trump's vote came from White, non-Hispanic voters, while Blacks and Hispanics preferred Clinton (Tyson and Maniam 2016). As we shall see, this election demonstrated an extremely fragmented and polarized electorate. The election also served to reinforce the reality of the racial state.

In general, the 2016 election revealed the significant gap between those with and without college degrees. Clinton did quite well among voters with college degrees (garnering 52% of the vote), while Trump scored similar support among those without college degrees (52%). While Trump's electoral support among whites without college degrees was in accord with projections, (he obtained 67% of non-college white's votes). He, contrary to projections, also did quite well among white, college graduates (49%). Trump clearly dominated among White non-Hispanic voters (58%). In addition, Clinton scored major victories among Blacks (80%). In the largest gender gap since 1972, women were slightly more likely to support Clinton (54%), while more men supported Trump (53%). Young voters (ages 18–29) preferred Clinton to Trump by a wide margin (53–45%) (Tyson and Maniam 2016).

The election of Mr. Trump did not create the racial state, nor did it cause these gaps it merely highlighted them. The racial state, highlighted by racial faultiness, aggravated by class, gender, and geography, has increasingly become evident within our nation. Across our nation, the evidence of such is not only the apparent increased levels of racial violence, harassment, and discrimination, but also increased levels of stress and anxiety (Williams and Medlock 2017).

4.1 The Development of the Racial State

Typically on multiple levels, through ceremonial events and occasions, we preserve the myth that our nation is a democracy in which every citizen,

regardless of identifying characteristics, has a vote and a voice in the political process. Further, while recognizing that inequalities exists, the myth ignores that inequalities associated with race (as well as class, gender, ethnicity, and sexual orientation) are more than aberrant but part of our core values as a state. Thus the myth preserves the "dream" that we are a nation of immigrants, equally embraced and embracing freedom, justice and the pursuit of happiness. That is the dream. Unfortunately, for all too many, the reality for much of the history of the racial state is more akin to a night-mare.

Revealing the contours of the racial state demonstrates the historical moments that coincide with its development. Feagin (2014) argues that the racial state, though it political processes, not only create and maintain the racial status quo, but it also serves to extend its reach throughout the social structure. He identifies what he calls as racial frames which allows us to see the contours of these processes. Consequently, with our knowledge of history we can identity at least four major racial frames associated with the development and perpetuation of our nation as a racial state. These are associated with: (1) *nation building,* (2) *exclusionism,* (3) *identity politics and political machines* and (4) *coalitional politics and social movements.* For each of these racial frames we shall identify specific sets of events that served to construct, maintain, and transform the racial state. As we'll see next, each of these periods also roughly corresponds to a specific phase of political development in the Unites States. Lastly, as a process often these racial frames overlapped as different geographies of politics unfold.

4.1.1 Nation Building

In the process of becoming a nation, many events led to the development of the first elements of the racial state. In this state residents were explicitly racialized, gendered and classed. For example, colonial women's rights and privileges were directly related to their marital status, race, class and religion. Unmarried English women could not own property, enter contracts, sue or be sued. Once married, their rights and properties were under the control of the husband. Married English couples were considered as "one person at law" where the wife and all children were considered the husband's property. Dowries provided the only degree of financial liberty. A widow could receive as much as one-third of her husband's property as her dowager's rights and could manage her husband's business. Black and Native American women had even fewer rights. White indentured female servants, after their period of service, could claim the same rights as other white Colonial women.

Black slave women had no rights. White indentured servants could claim the same rights as other white Colonial women after their servitude ended. Colonial Quaker women shared almost all the same rights as Quaker men. The shortage of men in English Colonial America provided some liberties not enjoyed by their English peers. Thus, filling roles left vacant by men, women such as Anne Dudley Bradstreet (Poet) and Anne Marbury Hutchinson (theologian) were able to step out of the narrow roles reserved for women.

> If natural law did not suffice, then the law also in the earlier stages of social confederacies, we find this connection between master and servant established.
> If this had been contrary to the law of nature, it could never have been tolerated under the Jewish theocracy. Yet that it was so tolerated, Holy writ affords us ample testimony. (Robin et al. vs. Hardaway et al. 1772)

To a significant extent, racial hierarchies also came into being as a means of controlling who could sleep with whom. Religious ideologies often were expressed in early court cases and other legal pronouncements throughout the early 1700s that further solidified the racial hierarchy. Thus, we find in the Act of 1705 explicit racial and gendering of the other:

> If any woman servant shall have a bastard child, by a Negro or mulatto, or if a free Christian white woman shall have such bastard child by a Negro or mulatto; in both the said cases the churchwardens shall bind the said child to be a servant until it shall

be of thirty-one years of age. (Act of 1705, c. 49. s. 18, see Howell vs. Netherland 1770)

Of interest is that this act also removes a slight glitch in previous laws relative to religious freedom. Prior to this act, some confusion existed regarding what was to be done with Baptized slaves. By this act, we further note,

> Baptism of slaves doth not exempt them from bondage; and all children shall be bond or free according to the condition of their mothers and the particular directions of this act. (Howell vs. Netherland 1770)

The purpose of slavery was to dehumanize, delegitimize, and restrict agency among those trapped in its clutches. Nevertheless, while slavery victimized several generations of blacks, whites, and Native Americans—it did not destroy their ability to act on their own or collaboratively. Such action demonstrates the human will to survive, and the ability to fight regardless of how horrible the situation. Let us see how these voices of resistance challenged the English colonial authority.

One of the chief forms of resistance is associated with rebellions on the part of not only slaves, but White indentured servants. The first significant rebellion during our nation building, known as Bacon's Rebellion, did much to advance racial identity during this period. Bacon's Rebellion, similarly, linked European indentured servants and African slaves, and would lead to even more racialized set of laws and fears. Students of history point out that Bacon's Rebellion pitted wealthy white planters against "an amalgam of indentured servants and slaves, of poor whites and blacks, of landless freemen and debtors" (Breen 1973). This varied group of labor constituted a serious threat to the Virginian class structure. The elite response to Bacon's Rebellion in 1676 served not only to consolidate white male dominance and public culture, but also contrived to create a culture of racism, sexism, and patriarchy. In order to understand this threat, we must understand the labor situation in 16th century Virginia.

Labor demands for tobacco production in the middle of the 17th century was immense.

Planters, in search of a large inexpensive labor force, opted for the importation of white indentured servants. Between one-half to two-thirds of all white immigrants to the British colonies from 1630 to the Revolutionary period were indentured servants (Galenson 1984). Thousands of indentured servants flooded into Virginia beginning in the 1650s. With the promises of transportation, food, clothing and shelter—many willingly signed their papers of indenturement. Governors in both Virginia and Maryland operated what came to be known as the "Headright System" where planters were provided with incentives to import such labor (e.g., 50 acres of land per laborer). Upon completion of their contract, typically from 5 to 7 years, the servant was to receive "freedom dues"—typically land, money, a gun, clothes or food. As few as 40% of the indentured servants actually received such dues—leading to resentment. Other European servants were tricked or forced into indentured contracts by "spirits," unscrupulous merchants who "preyed upon the poor, young and unsuspecting. Some…enticed to the New World with stories of quick riches; others were coerced" (Breen ibid. 4).

Planters became increasingly hostile toward and disappointed with their "servants" frequently accusing merchants of delivering "the very scum and off-scouring" of England (Pestana 2004). These complaints were used by planters to extend the terms of the contracts or declare them invalid. The "Headright System" provided the basis for a small group of planters to monopolize the markets and labor and maximize their profits at the expense of both labor and other planters—creating a monopoly—and effectively pushing smaller producers out of the market. The resulting fluctuations in the price of tobacco, as cycles of overproduction became endemic of the system, also undermined the salaries of "free" labor.

> Freemen found themselves tied to an economic system over which they had little control. Fluctuations in the price of tobacco could reduce wage earners and small planters to abject poverty. It was not a question of work habits. According to an account in 1667, a man, on the average, could produce 1200 pounds of tobacco each year, which after taxes left him with approximately 50

> shillings. It left so little, in fact, that the colony's secretary marvelled, "I can attribute it to nothing but the great mercy of God … that keeps them [the small planters] from mutiny and confusion. (Breen ibid.: 6)

By the early 1670s a new source of cheap labor was available—Africans. These Africans—indentured, free, and enslaved—initially provided greater labor flexibility and reliability for the planter class. Therefore, what started out as a trickle was a torrent as from three to four thousand Africans streamed into Virginia. What made these Africans different than others is that they were probably imported from English speaking Barbados ultimately allowing black and white servants to communicate, identify their common grievances, and plan their insurrection. Fears arose and led to a series of laws designed to decrease political and social collaborations. These laws not only prohibited and sanctioned fraternization but also sexual liaisons and relationships between Africans and Europeans, either free or bound. The latter laws, known as anti-miscegenation laws, continued in Virginia well into the 20th century (Thompson 2009).

Tensions reached a head in 1663 as black and white servants banded together in what has become known as the Gloucester County Revolt. In the wake of this revolt, a Gloucester court in 1663 accused nine "laborers" of conspiring to violently overthrow the government of Virginia. Bacon's Rebellion, of 1676, was the most significant challenge to the class structure. In this revolt consisting of black, Irish, Scotts, and English bond servants pitted against small and nervous planter elite. What makes this particular revolt of interest is that many historians point to this specific event, at this specific time, as the moment that "white" as a racial category came into being (Roediger 2007). More to the point, this revolt was not about race but about class. And the consequence of this revolt was the invention of race, racial hierarchies, and all the baggage that goes with it. Let's investigate how this came into being.

Oddly enough, the revolt did not start with the bonded class but with a disgruntled member of the colonial elite—Nathaniel Bacon. Bacon, a member of the colonial council was a fierce opponent of Virginia's land policy. As reported in a Royal commission:

> He was said to be about four or five and thirty years of age, indifferent tall but slender, black-hair'd and of an ominous, pensive, melancholly Aspect, of a pestilent and prevalent Logical discourse tending to atheisme.... He seduced the Vulgar and most ignorant people to believe (two thirds of each county being of that Sort) Soe that their whole hearts and hopes were set now upon Bacon. Next he charges the Governour as negligent and wicked, treacherous and incapable, the Lawes and Taxes as unjust and oppressive and cryes up absolute necessity of redress. Thus Bacon encouraged the Tumult and as the unquiet crowd follow and adhere to him, he listeth them as they come in upon a large paper, writing their name circular wise, that their Ringleaders might not be found out. Having connur'd them into this circle, given them Brandy to wind up the charme, and enjoyned them by an oath to stick fast together and to him and the oath being administered, he went and infected New Kent County ripe for Rebellion.[1]

What lies at the heart of Bacon's complaint? Bacon, a member of displaced white labor, found himself and his group literally between a rock and a hard place. The real issues were three-fold—the increasing use of Africans as bonded labor forced an increasingly large group of white labor out of their positions. The irony of this is that while the planter class was gaining land grants with each new allotment of workers no such provisions were being made for those displaced by increasing cheaper forms of labor.

> Negro slavery displaced white servitude [in the South] because of certain economic advantages to the planters. There was, first, the fact that it was more difficult for the Negro than for the white servant to escape and lose himself among the colonists. Then there was the economic advantage of employing the black women as field hands since white women were as a rule exempted from such work. (Frazier 1949: 30)

To deal with this displaced labor, the Virginia Colonial authority began a policy encouraging them to settle land that had previously been allocated to the Native Americans. The problem was that while the lands of the elite were being

protected by the Crown and local militia, those in the possession of displaced whites were not. The results were frequent and predictable. The frontiersmen were trapped between the landed aristocracy in and the Native Americans.

Crop failures in 1676 provided the fuel for the violence that followed. The revolt quickly became a mass rebellion of bond-laborers who aimed to level the government, class structure and ultimately provide for what today we might call "true democracy." In this rare event we should note that there was no racial antagonism separating the various labor groups. More precisely the various groups were divided by class and not by race. Thousands of bond-labors linked by a common situation joined hands. Over six thousand European Americans and two thousand African Americans took up arms and fought against a tiny-Anglo-American slave-owning planter class. They marched to take over the garrisons and military arsenal at West Point. They forced the military governor to flee and shut down all tobacco production for the next 14 months.

The rebellion threatened the very heart of the British colonial authority by challenging the existence and dominance of the Anglo-American slave owning and planter elite. The rebellion of labor represented one of the worst fears of the ruling elite. They responded by solidifying slavery into a racial caste system. This racial caste system by definition created racial categories, racial privileges, racial sanctions, and racial hierarchies. As noted by Allen—"The solution was to establish a new birthright not only for Anglos but for every European-American, the 'white' identity that 'set them at a distance, 'to use Sir Francis (Bacon's) phrase from the laboring-class African Americans, and enlisted them as active, or at least passive, supporters of lifetime bondage of African American" (Allen 2012: 248). This is clearly seen in the various codes and almost obsession with race from this point onward from the various *Virginia Codes* through the *Black Codes* (post-emancipation) and the *Jim Crow codes*. The ultimate purpose of the Virginia code of 1705 was:

---

[1]Cited at http://www.historyisaweapon.com/defcon1/zinnvil3.html.

The exclusion of free African Americans from the intermediate stratum was a corollary of the establishment of the 'white' identity as a mark of social status. If the mere presumption of liberty was to serve as a mark of social status for masses of European-Americans without real prospects of upward social mobility, and yet induce them to abandon their opposition to the plantocracy and enlist them actively, or at least passively, in keeping down the Negro bond-laborers with whom they had made common cause in the course of Bacon's Rebellion, the presumption of liberty had to be denied to free African Americans. (Allen 2012: 24)

Consequently, by the time we began contemplating the political structure of the U.S. the intersectional lines established the first racial frame and became enshrined within our very core. This intersectionality is clearly evidence in the very first enactments. One of the most significant aspects of power within any political system is to whom citizenship is granted. Citizenship reflects the legal process countries use to regulate national identity, membership, and rights. Citizenship also establishes the political boundaries that defines who is and who is not included in the democratic franchise.[2] The 1790 Naturalization Act granted citizenship to "free white aliens" with two years' residence but withheld it from slaves and women. The link between Whiteness and citizenship was further elaborated in the Militia Act of 1792, which described White male citizens as vital to the national defense. While all Whites after establishing residency, only property-owning men could exercise the right to vote or hold political office (Tehranian 2000).

> [E]ach and every **free able-bodied white male citizen** of the respective States, residents therein, who is and shall be of age of eighteen years, and under the age of forty-five (except as herein after excepted) shall severally and respectively be enrolled in the militia ... (Second Congress, 1 Stat. 272 cited in Tehranian ibid.)

---

[2]Citizenship clearly a part of the nation building process was and is a major device by which exclusionism operates. We shall explore this in greater detail in the next section. This category also demonstrates the grey areas between the categories and the blinding of historical periods.

Once established, this racial frames continued to dominate political behavior, identities, and issues until tensions within the nation forced change. These tensions associated that culminating with Civil War, various wars with Native Americans, and Asian immigration. The racial frames that developed served to legitimize the racial contract that established segregation, reservations, and exclusionary immigration policies.

4.2   Exclusionism

The previous sections outlined how during nation building the 1st racial frame came into being. This racial frame established white masculinity as a privileged intersectional identity. We also witnessed how blacks were systematically marginalized and ultimately excluded from the political sphere. Similar exclusionary processes were also operant involving Native Americans, Asian Americans and women.

Shortly after the American Revolution, the United States instituted a set of laws and policies that called for the systematic exclusion and removal of Native American tribes from the southwest. These tribes, originally recognized as autonomous nations, consisted of the Chickasaw, Choctaw, Muscogee-Creek, Seminole and the Cherokee. The Seminoles were among the first to establish long standing relationships with runaway slaves by allowing them safe havens in areas that they control. To a great extent, Andrew Jackson was instrumental in creating the "Indian Problem" as he burned Indian villages, pursued runaway slaves and precipitated the first Seminole wars that took place between 1814 and 1818 (Wright 1968). And as Andrew Jackson the Indian Fighter became Andrew Jackson the president he pushed through congress the Indian Removal Act. In 1830 President Andrew Jackson signed into law the Indian Removal Act. The removal of these tribes allowed southern Whites to forcibly take these lands. Jackson justified his actions by stating that it represented progress and that:

> Humanity has often wept over the fate of the aborigines of this country and philanthropy has long been busily employed in devising means to

avert it, but its progress has never for a moment been arrested, and one by one have many powerful tribes disappeared from the earth. ... But true philanthropy reconciles the mind to these vicissitudes as it does to the extinction of one generation to make room for another. ... Philanthropy could not wish to see this continent restored to the condition in which it was found by our forefathers. What good man would prefer a country covered with forests and ranged by a few thousand savages to our extensive Republic, studded with cities, towns, and prosperous farms, embellished with all the improvements which art can devise or industry execute, occupied by more than 12,000,000 happy people, and filled with all the blessings of liberty, civilization, and religion? (Brands 2006: 490)

Although this forced exclusion led to what has come to be termed as the "Trail of Tears", many forms of resistance were advanced by various Native American groups. Intersectional analysis of Seminole resistance in Florida reveals many insights. The Seminole Nation, under its warriors and chiefs decided war was preferable to expulsion from their lands. Seminole leaders, even while facing apparent defeat, continued to resist. On multiple occasions, while apparently conceding defeat, they would call a halt to the fighting and agree to emigrate. But this turned out to be strategy used to gain time to reorganize, gather supplies, ammunitions and disappear back into the everglades. This the second Seminole war, claimed the lives of thousands on both sides, costs the United States government an estimated fifteen million dollars, and resulted in armistice in 1842. While an estimated 3000 Seminoles were removed to Indian Territory, resistance again surfaced a decade later. This, the Third Seminal War, lasting from 1855 to 1858, continued to surface as small groups of insurgents fought over land. Even after the cessation, and the removal of hundreds of other Seminoles, many remained in hiding. Today, almost 3500 of their descendants still call Florida their home.[3]

While we the U.S. government was prosecuting its war of exclusion against the Native Americans, it was also pursuing a course that would ultimately lead to the Civil War. And

while much is known about this war, few highlight the role of intersectionality played in the abolitionist movement.

Many prominent names in the U.S. early feminist movement were equally part of the abolitionist social movement. These women, representing both black (for e.g., Maria Stewart and Sojourner Truth) and white (for e.g., Lydia Maria Child, Angelina and Sara Grimke, and Elizabeth Cady Stanton) marshalled the collective forces of women across the country to create an elaborate anti-slavery network. This anti-slavery network not only included formal organizations involved with public actions and protests, pamphlet writing, and lobbying but also informal ones to include the "Underground Railroad." Collectively, these social movements served to highlight the necessity for change but also pushed ultimately for the resolution of the slave issue. Unfortunately, the resolution would only come after one of the most costly and bloodiest wars this nation has ever faced While most black soldiers fought for the north, a few actually fought for the south. Hispanics soldiers also were represented on both sides. While, indigenous scouts and guides, hoping to regain both land and their freedom, served both north and south. The battle to end slavery, unfortunately did not end injustice. In fact, in many ways the aftermath of the civil war served to redefine a whole assortment of injustices that impacted all racial, gendered, and class groups. But it was not until after the infamous Dred Scott decision of 1857, in which the Supreme Court said blacks could not be citizens, and the Civil War, which lasted from 1861 to 1865, that Congress extended citizenship to "aliens of African nativity and to persons of African descent" (Tehranian 2000). The 14th Amendment to the U.S. Constitution, ratified in 1868, attempted to address the issue of naturalization. It reads: "All persons born or naturalized in the United States and subject to the jurisdiction thereof are citizens of the United States and of the State wherein they reside."

Quickly, the southern states, however, led by Florida and Mississippi, instituted laws that not only challenged but also limited the hard-won

---

[3]Excerpted from "Indian Resistance and Removal" by the Seminole Tribe of Florida. Accessed on line at URL: http://www.semtribe.com/History/IndianRemoval.aspx.

rights of Blacks. In Florida, the poll tax, in effect between 1889 and 1910, effectively disenfranchised most Blacks and many poor Whites and others, because paying the tax was a prerequisite for voting in federal elections. In Mississippi, state-sanctioned literacy tests were utilized to deny suffrage to African Americans. Although Whites were exempted from these requirements, other groups such as Asians, Hispanics, some Europeans, and other recent immigrants were equally denied the right to vote for several generations. The battle over voters' rights continues to be fought. In June 2013, the Supreme Court "effectively struck down the heart of the Voting Rights Act of 1965 by a 5-to-4 vote, freeing nine states, mostly in the South, to change their election laws without advance federal approval" (Liptak 2013).

4.2.1 Asian Americans

Asian-Americans also found their identities, political and civil rights circumscribed and marginalized as they encountered the American political project. A series of specific treaties, laws, and decrees served to deprive them of humanity, citizenship, and property. In this case, Wong Kim Ark, born in San Francisco to Chinese parents around 1871, was denied re-entry into the United States after a trip overseas. His case specifically challenged laws which restricted Chinese immigration and those prohibiting immigrants from China ability to claim so called "native born" rights of citizenship. Asian-Americans, through the Chinese Exclusionary laws, were blatantly and bureaucratically subjected to demeaning discrimination, oppression, and began a long history toward self-actualization and political enfranchisement. Asians were effectively disenfranchised in 1878 when a federal court upheld the bar against naturalizing Chinese immigrants. *American exclusionists*, concerned with halting what they perceived as the flood of Chinese being born in the United States began to challenge "birthright citizenship" in the late 1880s (Slayer 1995: 99). Those who argued against this right held that

Chinese were so culturally different that they could always be subjects of the Chinese empire. In *United States v Wong Kim Ark (1898)* the United States Supreme Court decided that all persons born in the United States were U.S. citizens. This case not only challenged the meaning of citizenship, but it also established the rights of citizens even born on American soil. This decision established and clarified the Citizenship Clause of the 14th Amendment to the U.S. Constitution. It was not until 1943 that Chinese Americans were first permitted to vote. A U.S. Supreme Court Ruling in 1944 *(Smith v. Allwright/Texas)* effectively outlaws all *White primaries*. Japanese-Americans were systematically reduced to victims, as their lands were confiscated and their freedoms were stripped as thousands were forced to live in internment camps during the World War II. While Asian Indians were allowed to vote in 1946, it was not until 1952 that Japanese Americans and other Asian Americans could vote (Jacobson 2006).

4.3 Women's Rights and Political Activism

Woman constituted one of the largest single groups that were excluded from political participation, by both law and practice. Many women, who had given up their push for the right to vote (suffrage) for what they perceived as the greater injustice of slavery, felt betrayed when the 15th Amendment expressly gave rights to vote to "black men". Thus in 1869, while some, such as Lucy Stone, thought that any improvement was good, others such as Elizabeth Cady Stanton and Susan B. Anthony thought the bill granting black men the right to vote and excluding women was dangerous. Susan B. Anthony, and other suffragettes, challenged this in the 1872 presidential election. They argued that if they had the right of citizenship, then they should have the right to vote. The Supreme Court, in its 1875 decision in *Minor V. Happersett* ruled that women could only receive the vote as a result of explicit legislation or constitutional amendment (Lind 1994: 169–174).

At the turn of the century, alliances forged during abolition began to resurface. Their efforts were largely successful as they linked hundred women's organizations, to include working-class and immigrant women. Their first major victory came in 1913 when Illinois legislature gave all women in the state suffrage for both local and national elections. The victory was, however, limited, in that their right to vote was still linked to the status of their husbands. It was not until the 1920 national amendment that all women were granted the right to vote and the National American Women Suffrage Association was formally disbanded and was replaced by the League of Women Voters (Flanagan 2005). Thus, by forging intersectional alliances, women learned to effectively challenge exclusionary political practices.

4.3.1 Identity Politics and Political Machines

The election of Roosevelt, the New Deal, is associated with the birth of identity politics. Marginalized racial and ethnic groups coalesced into organized political organizations as a means of promoting economic and social progress. These political organizations known as **political machines** operated under a single boss who rewarded followers. These bridged the racial and ethnic divide and challenged the prevailing racial frames.

With political machines and identity politics in place, patronage jobs and important decision-making positions were now being allocated to the newly enfranchised. As a consequence, in those Northern and Midwestern cities dominated by machine politics, the Irish came to dominate the police and fire departments and Blacks were more likely to obtain jobs in street maintenance and sanitation. Thus despite the illusion of racial egalitarianism, in the 1930s even patronage jobs served to reinforce the racial and ethnic hierarchy. While neither egalitarian

nor without strife, however, a new racial frame came into being. This frame, associated with the New Deal, was led by formerly disenfranchised White ethnics, including unionized working-class Jews, Irish, and Italians as they fought to become truly white and incorporated into the new racial frame. This frame was the key to the electoral victory of Franklin D. Roosevelt and dominated U.S. politics through the middle of the twentieth century (Ross 2008; King and Smith 2008).

The number, diversity, and persistence of racial and ethnic identity groups in the United States is not a surprise when we consider that it is a country founded and populated—both by choice and by force—by immigrants with political ties to their homeland and ethnic ties throughout the world (Ambrosio 2002). Several different factors helped accelerate the development of ethnic identity or consciousness. During World War I, for example, many European ethnics forged alliances with each other in efforts to lobby Washington for favorable treatment of overseas kin (DeConde 1992).

During the Cold War, the influence of ethnic identity politics was somewhat muted as the United States focused on perceived threats associated with communism. The U.S. social and political landscapes were shifted again by the Civil Rights Movements, in which domestic racial and ethnic identity groups significantly changed the language of politics. Now pluralism and multiculturalism became the language of the day, just as sit-ins, marches, rallies, litigation, and protests became the new political instruments of change.

4.3.2 Coalitional Politics and Social Movements

The political dominance of such racial frames was severely disrupted by the success of the Civil Rights Movement of the 1950s and 1960s. Perhaps no single movement captured the new

coalition form of politics better than the Black Civil Rights Movement. In this movement, Southern Blacks—in partnership with their northern allies both White and Black- not only challenged but effectively nullified the intimidation and segregation of the Old South.

Although much of the public memory regarding the Montgomery Bus Boycott (1955–56) features the role of King and the N.A.A.C.P, the role of black women tends to be dismissed. Even the mention of Rosa Parks as the "mother of the" movement rails to recognize that she was picked according to King: "Mrs. Parks was ideal for the role assigned to her by history" because "her character was impeccable and her dedication deep-rooted" (King 1958: 44). But it was the thousands of "nameless cooks and maids who walked endless miles for a year to bring about the breach in the walls of segregation" (Burks 1990: 82). King in his memories recalls one grandmother who said that she had "joined the boycott not for her own benefit but for the good of her children and grandchildren (King 1958: 78).

When Democratic President Lyndon B. Johnson signed the Civil Rights Act of 1964, pledging the immense power of the federal government in dismantling Jim Crow America, many Southern Democrats rebelled. As Johnson remarked, with the signing of this bill the Democrats had "just lost the South for a generation" (Quoted in Pohlmann and Whisenhunt 2002:215). But just how effective was the Civil Rights Act of 1964? Clearly, the Act was highly effective as demonstrated by analysis provided by Arnwine and Johnson-Blanco (2013):

- In 1962, only 1.4 million of the more than 5 million Blacks of voting age in the South's 11 states were registered to vote.
- In five southern states, Alabama, Georgia, Mississippi, North Carolina, and South Carolina, fewer than 25% of voting-age African Americans were registered to vote. In

Mississippi, fewer than 6% of voting-age African Americans were registered, compared with almost 95% of Whites.
- In Selma, Alabama, in 1965, fewer than 2% of eligible Blacks were registered to vote.

All too often the complicated sets of intersectional coalitions associated with the Civil Rights Act get blurred. One such coalition resulted in Section VII of that Act. Intersectionality, linking women of color activism against both sex and race based discrimination, was at the core of this section. As pointed out by Mayeri (2015) it served to effectively expand the definition of sexual discrimination (by including sexual harassment, pregnancy discrimination, and discrimination against unmarried parents) and in developing constitutional protections against sex equality (ibid.: 715). The identity intersections associated with this coalition demonstrates that politics often produces strange alliances. In this coalition, Mayeri notes not only White and Black feminist, but also white female liberal and segregationist conservative congresspersons. White feminist and segregationist backed the bill to ensure that white women would not be the "last at the hiring gate". (ibid. 718). Many progressive White Democrats came close to sinking the legislation until they were convinced that the section would protect white women "since employers, fearing prosecution for race discrimination under the act, will tend to give preference to Negro women (and Negro men) over white women (ibid. 719). Black civil rights attorney Pauli Murray argued that "Jane Crow" was just as devastating as Jim Crow. Murray recast the debate, by arguing that it was not a contest pitting Negro Women against White Women, or Negros against whites, but reflected the intersectional reality that the success of the Civil Rights Movement and Act were linked directly to the success and status of Negro Women. He argued:

...both Negro and white women will share a common fate of discrimination, since it is exceedingly difficult for a Negro woman to determine whether or not she is being discriminated against because of race or sex. These two types of discrimination are so closely intertwined [sic] and so similar that Negro women are uniquely qualified to affirm their interrelatedness. (Murray cited in Mayeri: 719)

Many viewing the Civil Rights Movement only look toward the gains of Blacks. However, in reality there were other significant movements taking place among other identity groups. One such example resulted in a new form of political protest. Another form of political coalitions were forged. In September 8, 1965, a group of mostly male, Filipino American grape workers, members of the Agricultural Workers Organizing Committee, walked off the fields and began a strike against the Delano-Area Table and Wine Grape Growers Association. The workers were protesting decades of poor pay, living conditions and lack of benefits. Cesar Chavez, leader of the mostly Latino National Farm Workers Association was asked to join their strike. Cesar, a veteran union activist, understood how growers historically pitted different racial groups against each other. Therefore when Cesar's union voted to join the Filipino workers by walking out on Mexican Independence day, September 16, 1965 they orchestrated the development of a coalition that bridged two different, and often-adversarial racialized labor groups. Soon the strike became a national boycott. As Latino and Filipino strikers banded together they were able to connect poor farm workers and their families with middle-class families in the big cities. Millions of every families just stopped buying and eating grapes. And by 1970 the table grape growers admitted defeat and agreed to sign the first union contacts granting workers increased benefits and salaries.[4]

4.4 Retreat from Civility

The 60s with so much promise was soon dwarfed as the racial state reemerged with a vengeance. The retreat from civility associated with extreme right wing politics pushed the nation sharply to the right. Ultra conservative candidates such as Barry Goldwater articulated the need to return to the racial state and helped articulate a modern version of the white identity politics. Driving both processes was what has since been termed Angry White Male Syndrome (AWMS) (Kimmel 2014).

It's been around for some time, you know, Angry White Men. But some may think it a new phenomenon. Angry White Male Syndrome (AWMS) has been part and parcel to the United States almost as long as there has been a United States. It has manifested itself most force-ably in many episodes of violence and mayhem targeting "others". These episodic situations typically are preceded by significant challenges to white, male identity, privilege, status and power. In the past these episodes have been cleverly masked within several foils such as Nation Building, White Man's Burden, and Family Values. In the process we almost annihilated the Indigenous people of this continent, fostered slavery and colonialism resulting in the devastation, genocide and exploitation, and the justification for sexual violence, homophobia, and gendered discrimination. AWMS has also given rise to various movements, euphemistically called wars such as the war on poverty, war on drugs and more recently the war on terror. Strangely, these so called wars have actually targeted women, minorities, and Muslims, respectively, and have done little to actually decrease poverty, the availability of illegal drugs, and the rising tide of terrorism. What they have accomplished is the preservation of a system that protects fragile white, male egos, status, power, privileges and status.

Politically, AWMS has given rise to a number of quite effective campaigns where candidates have been able to manipulate and capitalize upon these pint up frustrations. George Wallace, during the early 60s articulated their views when he declared "In the name of the greatest people that

---

[4]Excerpted from The Official Web Page of the United Farm Workers of America. http://www.ufw.org/_board.php?mode=view&b_code=cc_his_research&b_no=10482.

have ever trod this earth, I draw the line in the dust and toss the gauntlet before the feet of tyranny, and I say segregation now, segregation tomorrow, segregation forever". This was what Ronald Reagan described as a "silent majority" which was neither silent nor a majority. This 'silent majority' represented the disenfranchised, core of Americans who rejected civil rights and women rights, and were staunchly pro-American defenders of militarism, capitalism, and imperialism. In 1992, Ross Perot and Patrick Buchanan tried to ride this wave of white male paranoia into the House. Newt Gingrich and then George Bush would also tap into this fear, or what Jude Davies calls a "crises of representation" where at the core one finds discontent by perceptions of being displaced by "others". The current manifestation of AWMS is being played out in the GOP campaigns with the most obvious example being Donald Trump. Unfortunately, the milder versions of Rubio and Cruz are no less adamant in their appeal.

So what is the threat? The answer is really quite obvious. A fear that white dominance will be supplanted by women, blacks, Hispanics, Muslims, gays, etc. Why now, transposing a phrase from an earlier period—"its demographic stupid". The demographic reality is that white male hegemony is on a decline. This decline is not only with reference to population majorities that will soon be represented by blacks and Hispanics, but also global markets that point to an extremely unstable U.S. and European production and consumer base. Lastly, the global dominance of the Western military has been in decline at least since Vietnam, but continues to decline in the face of not only China, but also violent non-state actors to include ISIS, Taliban, and dozens of warlords, insurgents, and organizations. Gone are the good old days when in the name of "the White Man's Burden" the U.S. can go into any country of its choosing -rape, pillage, plunder and colonize with impunity. Now, such things are not only frowned upon, but utterly impossible given the reality of a newly emerging global political-economy. This reality, unfortunately does not assuage white, male fears no, instead it actually aggravates Angry White Male Syndrome. And no, we cannot just tell the patient to take two aspirin and call me in the morning. Rather, a strong dose of humility and personal responsibility and a willingness to work with all these "others" as collaborators and not subjects is what is needed.

4.5 Our Current Realities and Moving Forward

Black, Hispanic, women, and highly educated youth formed a coalition that rocked American politics by electing the first ever Black as president in 2008. As we deconstruct this vote we see the clear patterns of this ethnic, gendered, classed coalition.

Voter Turnout Rates in Presidential Elections, 1988-2012

(% of eligible voters)

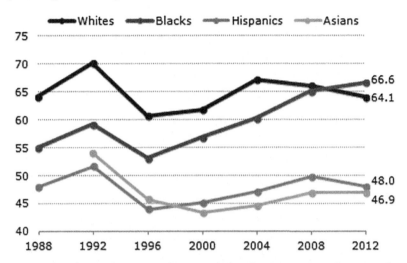

Note: White, black and Asian populations include only non-Hispanics who reported a single race. Native Americans and mixed-race groups not shown. The estimated number of votes cast is based on individual voting self-reports.

Source: Pew Research Center tabulations from the Current Population Survey, November Supplements

PEW RESEARCH CENTER

Source http://www.pewresearch.org/fact-tank/2013/06/11/eligible-latino-voters-who-didnt-go-to-polls-in-2012-out-numbered-those-who-did/

In the 2012 Presidential election, about 129 million voters participated. While this was slightly down from the 2008 election, it still reflected about 60% political participation among all voters. Among all groups, the participation rate among Blacks was the most dramatic. From less than 50% participation rates, during the 1996 election, we note significant jumps for the next three presidential elections. And by the 2012 election, Black voter turnout rates led the nation. Although White turnout increased from 1995 through 2004, we note significant declines for the two elections thereafter.

For recent presidential elections, voters with higher levels of education and greater income were more likely to vote. This is especially true when we consider race and ethnicity. Consequently, among college educated voters, whites (64%), blacks (57%), Hispanics (56%), and Asian Americans (40%) led the path to the voter's booth. This takes on even greater meaning when we consider the marginally smaller number of eligible voters who had college education among whites (31%), blacks (18%), Hispanics (15%) and Asian Americans (47%). The typical voter is also more likely to be younger (70%).

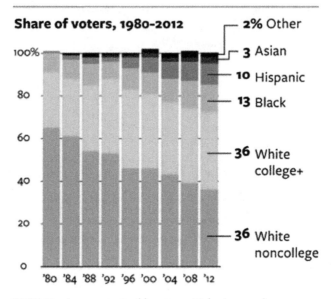

The Shrinking White Electorate

Since 1980, whites without a college degree, now the most Republican-leaning group, have plummeted as a share of the electorate. The more-competitive college whites have grown slightly, and Democratic-leaning minorities have more than doubled.

Share of voters, 1980-2012

2% Other
3 Asian
10 Hispanic
13 Black
36 White college+
36 White noncollege

'80 '84 '88 '92 '96 '00 '04 '08 '12

NOTE: Numbers may not add up to 100% due to rounding.

Source http://www.theatlantic.com/politics/archive/2013/09/republicans-cant-win-with-white-voters-alone/279436/

The voting electorate has become more diverse over the past 3 decades and more liberal. As shown in the figure above, whites without college has historically represented the republican base. That Republican base is shrinking. Every Democratic presidential nominee since 1980 has received considerably more votes from white women than white men. While white men and women voted equally in 1984, in 2012 the percentage of women (38%) outpaced that of men (34%). If we look at voting by race, gender and education the patterns become even more apparent. Exit polls taken after the 2012 presidential election found that college-educated whites cast 36% of the total vote. This was the first time that they equaled working class whites. And leading this increase were white, college educated women who outvoted their male counterparts regardless of educational levels. A total of 10.6 million new registered voters (143.1% increase) were reported during the period 1996–2012. Latinos or Asians and Pacific Islanders accounted for 9.8 million. Native Born whites accounted for the smallest percentage of growth (Ewing and Cantor 2014).

4.6 Data Literacy Exercise

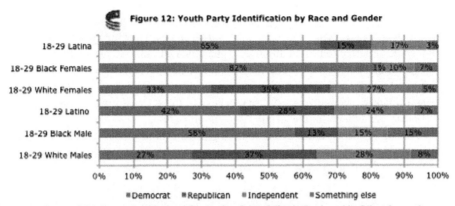

Figure 12: Youth Party Identification by Race and Gender

Source: CIRCLE Analysis of National Election Day Exit Poll (2012) Conducted by Edison Research

Source http://www.civicyouth.org/quick-facts/235-2/

Clear patterns of youth involvement by race, ethnicity, and gender are obvious among American voters. One of these patterns is the overwhelming Democratic Party identification among both Black and Hispanic youths, another is the significantly larger representation of females, across all groups, that identify as Democrats. While whites tend to be republicans, they also have the highest percentage of independent party affiliations.

have risen. Nationwide, over 100 groups targeting Muslims have come into being since 2015 alone. Hate violence have spiked, where nearly 1100 bias attacks have been recorded by the SPLS. Among these, 37% make direct reference to either campaign slogans, statements or President-elect Trumps infamous sexual assault remarks (Chen 2017). Clearly, something more than talk must be done. We must have a strategic plan where we can began to reframe the discourse. .

4.6.1 The Election of Donald Trump: The Retreat from Civility

Donald Trump was pushed into office as many white, particularly white males, believed that their America was quickly disappearing. For many, Trump's pledge to make America great again' is likened to the world of Archie Bunker where we return not only to a more conservative but also a vastly whitened America (Reiner 2017). For those who remember, the 1990s our nation seemed consumed with paramilitary-style "Patriots". Further, Trump's rhetoric, policies, and late night 'tweets' have fueled a drastic rise in hate groups, radical right activities, and attacks. For two straight years, radical right groups, encouraged by the candidacy of Trump,

4.6.2 So What Is to Be Done— Diversity Must Become a Reality

At the core of truth and justice is empathy equity, and community. People, groups, communities, even nations responding to fear, pain, and insecurity often set aside their high morals and revert to defensive of offensive postures that targets and attacks others. Thus principal is replaced with practicality and these become normative destructive cycles.

All too often, when we talk about diversity, we tend to do in in compartmentalized spaces. That is, we tend to discuss race, then gender, then sexuality, then disability, and maybe class. In all of these spaces, we fail to recognize that they are interrelated, intersectional, and irreducible to its various parts. In addition, the trend is to paint these conversations in terms of victims and victimizers. We name and shame, we raise up some standard as the Holy Grail, and condemn all those who fall short of perfection. In addition, as often is the case, white straight males tend to be isolated, castigated, and cast as the ultimate (implicitly or explicitly) victimizers. Alternatively, we relegate all others to the status as victims, rarely seeing how they too may be both agents and enablers. Such conversations rarely produce anything more than a mild sense of accomplishment, while all parties retreat to their respective safe zones—until another incident happens when we have to have yet another discussion regarding diversity.

Living, working, and interacting within various institutional settings, where memberships are constantly fluctuating, means that such we are constantly being challenged to incorporate increasingly diverse sets of identities. This by definition means that we will constantly have various types of episodes that are a natural part of change. Rather than seeing these as natural, we typically respond as if they are adherent aberrations that must be condemned, sanctioned, controlled and immediately remedied. I would argue that these are logical and tied to the dynamic nature of our institutions. Therefore, our response is to view these as teachable moments. As teachable moments, they become not something to stigmatize, but to embrace and recognize that it is part of who we all are. How should we proceed?

Our responses across this country, in our communities, in our universities has been to have more discussions, more lectures, more evidence—in the hope that as more people become aware of the problems, equipped with even more sophisticated knowledge we will develop the will to fix the problems, fix the system, or fix the individuals. Such hope has been in vain. Moreover, if, as Einstein suggested, continuing to do the same thing and expecting a different result is the definition of insanity, how might our efforts for these last decades be characterized. If we want to

transform the structures that produce racial hierarchies, we must engage these structures in processes that are more deliberate. These structures, such as education, legal, economic, and housing, are not isolated components but systemic arenas in which and by which racial hierarchies are created, manipulated, and sustained. If indeed, we are to transform the racial hierarchies our processes must equally be systemic. We propose that the keys to these transformative processes lie within our educational institutions. Specifically, we recognize that educational institutions link or has the potential to link all other major societal/community institutions. At the core, we recognize that to think globally/nationally we must act locally means that our efforts must be geared to local community interactions and processes. Specifically, we believe that our Universities are uniquely embedded in communities which are able to impact upon their regional sphere of influence and can be the catalyst for bringing about these transformative processes.

Many of us learn of difference and others second hand through our schools, television, social media, friends, and others. Much of this knowledge, filtered through various layers, becomes sterile and easily dispensed. Many of us spend most of our time in rather segregated, isolated islands. (Research documents that our schools, neighborhoods are as segregated today as they were before Brown v. Topeka. And Sunday, between the hours of 9–12 we are most segregated.) Consequently, is it no wonder that we continue to have racial incidents, hostilities, animosities and anxieties. We don't know each other or our various stories.

Our realities are a composite of the multiplicity of stories, layered, nuanced, and rehearsed. These stories, reflecting the many lived stories of place and space, time and distance, perceived and experienced are constantly produced and reproduced. Novelist Chimamanda Adichie (2009) warns of what happens when all we here is a single story, about a single people, country or group. When this is the case, we make critical mistakes as we stereotype, marginalize, and delegitimize others. When on the one hand we have thousands upon thousands of stories that rehearse the wonders of white culture; while that of the Asian, African, Middle Easterner only comes to life during contestations with Europeans (often where they are being subjugated)—we are essentially reifying whiteness at the expense of others. The problem comes in not knowing these other stories. Our task in this volume has been in trying to tell these other stories. Stories are at once about power, whose stories get told, who gets to tell it, and from which vantage point. The number, variety, and richness of stories are also about power, as dominance is associated with not only quantity but also quality. Whose story is considered the norm, and which is deviant speaks of power. Achebe quips:

> There is that great proverb — that until the lions have their own historians, the history of the hunt will always glorify the hunter. That did not come to me until much later. Once I realized that, I had to be a writer. I had to be that historian. It's not one man's job. It's not one person's job. But it is something we have to do, so that the story of the hunt will also reflect the agony, the travail — the bravery, even, of the lions. (Achebe cited by Brooks 2016)

Palestinian poet Mourid Barghouti writes, if you want to dispossess a people, start by simply starting their story with "secondly". Begin by talking about the Native American savages, the African slaves, not with the arrival of the Spanish, French and English. Ignore their rich histories before they encountered the Europeans, and stress only their problems since. Talk about the increasing black on black crime, the racial gap in education, the failure of Post-colonial Africa. For if you start with the Native Americans before Columbus, the Africans civilizations that preceded and perhaps seeded the European contentment then you have a very different story (Adichie ibid.).

The differences we perceive that divide us are not real, they are socially constructed lens that shapes our perceived realities. None of us sees clearly, no matter how hard we try. We must diversify our discourse, reimagine our narratives, and rearticulate our differences. The fundamental value that underscores democracy is the right to make choices, not constrained by our individual or collective differences. In fact, the very presence of differences is both antecedent to and the resultant of such choices. Our differences should not be the basis of our status, nor in the roles that we choose, but the power to choose those roles should be the basis of our realities. In essence, we must all embrace the nobility of differences.

Unless we choose to be vulnerable, we cannot have true dialogue. Hiding behind our various titles, academic identities or status groups, we cannot see each other. We all have our quirks, we all have our phobias, we all have our biases, and we all have our identities. The only way that we can breach the walls that divide us is to use our own stories to bridge the divide.

This process will demonstrate that differences we perceive that divide us are not real, they are socially constructed lens that shapes our perceived realities. None of us sees clearly, no matter how hard we try. Students will learn how to diversify their discourse, reimagine our narratives, and rearticulate our differences. These discourses will underscore the fundamental value of democracy is diversity and the right to make choices, not constrained by our individual or collective differences. In essence, the students will learn to embrace the nobility of differences by first understanding how they themselves (whether black or white, Hispanic or Jewish) are a vital part of this thing we call diversity. Students will learn that we are all vulnerable, we all have experience some form of discrimination, and bias. This is a good starting point. Because, unless we choose to be vulnerable, we cannot have true dialogue. Hiding behind our various titles, academic identities or status groups, we cannot see each other. We all have our quirks, we all have our phobias, we all have our biases, and we all have our identities. The only way that we can breach the walls that divide us is to use our own stories to bridge the divide.

And once we do bridge this divide, maybe then we can began to discuss how to actually come together to forge a transformative political movement which can destroy the racial state. The political will that joined radically different political identities to elect the first Black president demonstrates that we can accomplish just that. This transformative political moment occurred as we learned to talk, organize, and politicize across our various identities to produce an intersectional political coalition. Our progressive future lies in our ability to turn this moment into a movement. And that future looks bright.

References

Adichie, C. (2009). The danger of a single story. *Ted Talk*. https://www.ted.com/talks/chimamanda_adichie_the_danger_of_a_single_story. Accessed June 30, 2017.

Allen, T. W. (2012). *The invention of the white race, Volume 2: The origin of racial oppression in Anglo-America*. Brooklyn, NY: Verso Books.

Ambrosio, T. (2002). *Ethnic identity groups and U.S. foreign policy*. Westport, CT: Praeger Publishers.

Arnwine, B. & Johnson-Blanco, M. (2013). Voting rights at the crossroads: The supreme court decision in shelby is the latest challenge in the "Unfinished March" to full black access to the ballot. *Economic Policy Institute*. http://www.epi.org/publication/voting-rights-crossroads-supreme-court-decision/. Accessed October 10, 2013.

Brands, H. W. (2006). *Andrew Jackson: His life and times* (p. 488). New York: Anchor. ISBN 978-1-4000-3072-9.

Breen, T. H. (1973). A changing labor force and race relations in Virginia 1660–1710. *Journal of Social History, 7*, 3–25.

Brooks, D. (2016). The danger of a single story. *The New York Times*. https://www.nytimes.com/2016/04/19/opinion/the-danger-of-a-single-story.html. Accessed June 30, 2017.

Burks, M. F. (1990). Trailblazers: Women in the Montgomery Bus Boycott. In Crawford et al. (Eds.), *Women in the Civil Rights Movement*.

Cazenave, N. A. (2011). *The urban racial state: Managing race relations in American cities*. Lanham, MD: Rowman & Littlefield.

Chen, M. (2017). Donald Trump's Rise Has Coincided With an Explosion of Hate Groups. *The Nation*. https://www.thenation.com/article/donald-trumps-rise-has-coincided-with-an-explosion-of-hate-groups/. Accessed April 18, 2018.

DeConde, A. (1992). *Ethnicity, race and American foreign policy*. Lebanon, NH: Northwestern University Press.

Ewing, W. A. & Guillermo, C. (2014). New Americans in the voting booth: The growing electoral power of immigrant communities. *American Immigration Council*. http://www.immigrationpolicy.org/special-reports/new-americans-voting-booth-growing-electoral-power-immigrant-communities. Accessed January 28, 2015.

Feagin, J. R. (2014). *Racist America: Roots, current realities, and future reparations*. New York: Routledge.

Flanagan, M. A. (2005). Suffrage. In *Encyclopedia of Chicago history*. http://www.encyclopedia.chicagohistory.org/pages/1217.html. Accessed June 30, 2017.

Frazier, E. F. (1949). *The Negro in the United States*. New York: The MacMillan Co.

Galenson, D. (1984). The rise and fall of indentured servitude in the americas: An economic analysis. *The Journal of Economic History, 44*(1), 1–26.

Howell vs. Netherland. (1770). http://www2.vcdh.virginia.edu/saxon/servlet/SaxonServlet?source=/xml_docs/slavery/documents/jeffcase70.xml&style=/xml_docs/slavery/documents/display_doc.xsl/. Accessed June 30, 2017.

Jacobson, R. (2006). Characterizing consent: Race, citizenship, and the new restrictionists. *Political Research Quarterly, 59*(4, December), 645–654.

King, Jr, M. L. (1958). *Stride toward freedom*. Boston: Beacon Press.

Kimmel, M. (2014). *Angry white men: American masculinity at the end of an era*. New York: Nation Books.

King, D. S., & Smith, R. M. (2008). Strange bedfellows? Polarized Politics? The quest of racial equity in contemporary America. *Political Research Quarterly, 61*(4, December), 687–703.

Lind, J. (1994). Dominance and Democracy: The legacy of woman suffrage for the voting right. *UCLA Women's Law Journal, 5*, 104–216. http://escholarship.org/uc/item/4r4018j9#page-113. Accessed June 30, 2017.

Liptak, A. (2013). Supreme court invalidates key part of voting rights act. *The New York Times*. http://www.nytimes.com/2013/06/26/us/supreme-court-ruling.html. Accessed June 30, 2017.

Mayeri, S. (2015). Intersectionality and title VII: A brief (pre-) history. *Boston University Law Review, 95*, 713–731.

Morin, R. (2016). *Behind Trump's win in rural, white America: Women joined men in backing him*. Fact Tank, Pew Research Center, November 17. http://www.pewresearch.org/fact-tank/2016/11/17/behind-trumps-win-in-rural-white-america-women-joined-men-in-backing-him. Accessed January 15, 2017.

Omi, M., & Winant, H. (2015). *Racial Formation in the United States* (3rd ed.). New York: Routledge.

Pestana, C. G. (2004). *The English Atlantic in an age of revolution, 1640–1661*. Cambridge, MA: Harvard University Press.

Pohlmann, M., & Whisenhunt, L. V. (2002). *Student's guide to landmark congressional laws on civil rights*. Westport, CT: Greenwood Press.

Reiner, R. (2017). Is Donald Trump the new Archie Bunker? *NBC News*. http://www.nbcnews.com/meet-the-press/video/is-donald-trump-the-new-archie-bunker-734259267724. Accessed June 30, 2017.

Robin et al. vs. Hardaway et al. (1772). https://lva.omeka. net/items/show/19. Accessed June 30, 2017.

Roediger, D. R. (2007). *The wages of whiteness*. New York: Verso.

Ross, S. J. (2008). A new democratic coalition. *The Washington Independent*, August 22. Accessed online at URL: http://washingtonindependent.com/6/a-new-democratic-coalition.

Salyer, L. E. (1995). *Laws harsh as tigers: Chinese immigrants and the shaping of modern immigration laws*. Chapel Hill: The University of North Carolina Press.

Tehranian, J. (2000). Performing whiteness: Naturalization litigation and the construction of racial identity in America. *Yale Law Journal, 109*(4), 817–848.

Thompson, D. (2009). Racial ideas and gendered intimacies: The regulation of interracial relationships in North America. *Social and Legal Studies, 18*(3), 353–371.

Tyson, A., & Shiva, M. (2016). *Behind Trump's victory: Divisions by race, gender, education*. Fact Tank, Pew Research Center, November 9. http://www. pewresearch.org/fact-tank/2016/11/09/behind-trumps-victory-divisions-by-race-gender-education. Accessed June 17, 2017.

Williams, D. R., & Morgfan M. M. (2017). Health Effects of Dramatic Societal Events-Ramifications of the Recent Presidential Eleciton. *The New England Journal of Medicine, 376*, 2295–2299. http://www. nejm.org/doi/full/10.1056/NEJMms1702111. Accessed April 18, 2018.

Wright, J. L. (1968). A note on the First Seminole War as seen by the Indians, Negros, and their British advisers. *The Journal of Southern History, 34*(4), 565–575.

Part II
Institutions that Bind: History Matters!

Racism and Popular Culture: Representation, Resistance, and White Racial Fantasies

5

Jennifer C. Mueller, Apryl Williams and Danielle Dirks

Contents

5.1 Introduction

At times people play with racism, quite literally. Consider *Ghettopoly*. Originally released in 2003, the *Monopoly* parody sold in Urban Outfitters chains around the nation. Wielding game pieces made to look like crack rock, 40-ounce malt liquor bottles, and marijuana leaves, *Ghettopoly's* "playas" are promised the fun of "buying stolen properties, building crack houses and projects," and "pimpin' hoes" (Ghettopoly 2016). Railroads and utilities of the original are now liquor stores and chop shops; instead of taxes, players risk landing on spaces threatening police shakedowns and car-jackings. Gamers "steal money" every time they pass "Let$ Roll" and draw "Hustle" cards to reap rewards—"You got your whole neighborhood addicted to crack. Collect $50" (Bergstrom 2003).

Ghettopoly's endless stereotypes about black cultural deviance proved more than just popular—they were profitable. Following a lawsuit with Hasbro over copyright infringement, David Chang, the game's creator, testified he had sold upwards of 50,000 copies of the game by 2006,

J. C. Mueller (✉)
Department of Sociology, Skidmore College,
Saratoga Springs, NY, USA
e-mail: jmueller@skidmore.edu

A. Williams
Department of Sociology, Susquehanna University,
Selinsgrove, PA, USA
e-mail: williamsaa@susqu.edu

D. Dirks
Independent Researcher, Detroit, MI, USA
http://danielledirks.com

© Springer International Publishing AG, part of Springer Nature 2018
P. Batur and J. R. Feagin (eds.), *Handbook of the Sociology of Racial and Ethnic Relations*,
Handbooks of Sociology and Social Research, https://doi.org/10.1007/978-3-319-76757-4_5

garnering profits between $400,000 and $500,000; the Court estimated a net closer to $900,000 (Hasbro, Inc. v. Chang 2006). Though pulled from shelves following civil rights protest, over a decade later *Ghettopoly* still generates an active Twitter, YouTube, and Facebook following and remains available for purchase online.

As product, controversy, and sustained curiosity, *Ghettopoly* highlights many elements at the nexus of racism and popular culture. So often the terrain of popular culture appears dynamic, even progressively evolving. New mediums emerge and become embedded in markets, institutions, and everyday life. Social media grabs our collective consciousness with ever-newer modes for self-presentation and communication. Technological innovations shrink cultural divides once imposed by geographical distance further and further. Even traditional mediums—like TV and film—undergo routine facelifts, appearing to 'liberalize' in content and form. Yet, in the face of these apparent transformations many continuities remain clear. Perhaps nowhere is this more obvious than with respect to race.

5.2 Exploring Racism Through Popular Culture

In its rawest form, race is a fiction of the imagination. Neither naturally discrete nor biologically fixed, 'races' are continuously made and remade (Carbado 2011; Omi and Winant 2014). Despite the fluidity implied, however, these processes of 'making race' are never divorced from white supremacy. Indeed, 'race'—specifically 'whiteness' contrasted against racial 'otherness'—is first and foremost a Euro-American invention; an ideological technology developed to facilitate colonialism and slavery by making human divisions appear natural and inviolable, and thus conquest and racial domination morally reasonable (Allen 2012; Coleman 2009). In this sense, race remains forever inseparable from white supremacy, a system of racial hierarchy around which the global world has been organized; one which structures everyday and institutional practices and ideologies (Mills 1997).

Given connections to dominant social institutions and the ubiquity of everyday life, popular culture offers a powerful lens for considering how racial ideologies and everyday logics work to reinforce white supremacy as a global system. Popular culture draws influence not simply from its expansive reach, but also its quotidian nature (Pérez 2016). From cherished pastimes and amusing artifacts, to written, spoken, and visual representations that make us laugh one moment and bring us to tears the next, popular culture is woven deeply and often very intimately into the fabric of everyday life. While it may be tempting to imagine such amusements and attachments as apolitical, popular culture both reflects and plays a significant role in contouring how we think, feel, and act in the world, for better and often for worse (Hall 2006; hooks 2009).

In this chapter, we explore how popular culture helps bolster white supremacy, both historically and today. We work to elevate how dominant racial groups have deployed and engaged popular culture to naturalize and defend white power and racial domination (hooks 2009; Jewell 1993; Pieterse 1992); and further, how these abstractions—even many that appear racially progressive on their face—mask the structural elements of white supremacy and whites' own involvement reproducing systemic racism across eras (Bonilla-Silva 2015; Mueller and Issa 2016). Our analysis highlights numerous examples demonstrating both how popular culture has been used to construct and circulate whites' racist fantasies about white virtue and 'racial deviance,' but also the important and strategic ways people of color have worked to resist, defend against, challenge and think beyond these "controlling images" (Collins 2009: 76).

5.3 White Supremacy Logics and Early U.S. Popular Culture

In her innovative essay, "Heteropatriarchy and the Three Pillars of White Supremacy" (2012), Andrea Smith argues that white supremacy has been organized by three distinct logics used to secure power, privilege, and wealth—logics that appear persistent over history. The *logic of slavery* serves as the ideological anchor of capitalism, rendering black people "inherently slaveable," like an object of "property" (p. 286). Beyond legitimizing the historical institution of trans-Atlantic slavery, slavery logics also support other institutions and practices by which the bodies and labor of people of color are commodified for the unjust enrichment of white people (e.g., through migrant labor, the prison industrial complex). The *logic of genocide* reinforces the belief that indigenous people and cultures must disappear (and indeed, are *always* 'disappearing'). Using genocidal logics whites defend the plunder of land and other physical, cultural, and spiritual resources held by people of color, even as these practices rest on violence, coerced assimilation, and cultural theft. Finally, the *logic of Orientalism* grants civility to non-Western peoples and nations, but marks them inevitably inferior and thus permanent foreign threats to U.S. empire. Orientalism logics have been deployed throughout U.S. history to bolster and defend resurgent anti-immigrant policy and practices (e.g., internment, racial profiling) and continual war-making, both domestically and abroad (e.g., the "War on Drugs," "War on Terror").

White supremacy logics are united in naturalizing 'whiteness' and white interests as normal and superior, tacitly if not explicitly; while marking the bodies and practices of 'racial others' as deviant, inferior, even sub-human, by comparison (Feagin 2013; Bracey et al. 2017). Below we draw on Smith's framework to unpack the logical 'substance' of controlling images deployed in popular culture over U.S. history. Indeed, tracing some of the earliest examples of U.S. popular culture illuminates how heavily the logics of slavery, genocide, and Orientalism figured in the popular culture of a burgeoning U.S. nation-state.

5.3.1 "Our Only Original American Institution"

In many regards, minstrelsy appears the earliest form of American popular culture. Many 19th-century Americans boasted minstrelsy was the first distinct form of American entertainment; the "only true American drama," as some proudly claimed (Pilgrim 2012; Toll 1977: v). Despite such romantic conventions, however, most whites referred to blackface performances more simply—as "nigger minstrelsy" or "coon shows."

Emerging around the 1820s, minstrel shows peaked in popularity by the 1840s, capturing audiences—"from the White House to the California gold fields, from New Orleans to New England, from riverboats and saloons to 2500-seat theaters"—for over half a century (Lott 2013; Toll 1977: 31). While popularity among white working class audiences is well-documented, blackface minstrelsy enjoyed significant favor among elites, as well. Minstrel troupes performed at President John Tyler's inauguration and before Queen Victoria; even "The Great Emancipator," Abraham Lincoln, was known to be a spectacular fan, using blackface shows as an amusing distraction from the pressures of war (Bennett 1997; Roediger 2007).

It is perhaps unsurprising, though no less appalling to see how heavily explicit anti-blackness featured in early American popular culture, given how central slavery was in supporting the U.S. nation-state (Baptist 2014; Feagin 2014). Early minstrelsy featured troupes of white men in burnt cork 'blackface' make-up, performing song, dance, and comedy claimed to be authentically 'Negro.' White minstrels executed outlandish caricatures of blackness, drawing on heavy mocking dialect, bulging eyes, and gaping lips to popularize racist fantasies that Blacks were inherently lazy, dimwitted, and subhuman—certainly incapable of self-determination (Pilgrim 2012; Toll 1977). Black Americans began replacing white minstrels toward the latter half of the nineteenth century, blackening their own faces and engaging in similarly exaggerated performances to make a living. This tragic twist reinforced the credibility of minstrel images further, as white audiences imagined Black minstrels to be "genuine Negroes" displaying "natural impulses" (Toll 1977: 202).

As the above examples begin to capture, minstrelsy worked not only to rationalize the exercise of white domination, but also to assuage whites' various social, moral, and political anxieties in an evolving nation. Toll (1977) documents that minstrelsy adopted more unequivocal pro-slavery stances as the abolitionist movement began to expand. Enslaved blacks were portrayed as happy-go-lucky, while depictions of Northern society featured free but frivolous "dandies" and homesick ex-slaves. Such characterizations of blacks as indolent, improvident, and ignorant were "the very antithesis of what white men liked to believe about themselves," and served as "ego-boasting scapegoats" to confirm blacks could not, nor even desired to play a constructive role in free society (Toll 1977: 71; see also Pérez 2014, 2016; Roediger 2007). Lott (2013) argues the relentless, literal dehumanization "of black people into things" in minstrelsy—a "sheer overkill of songs in which black men are roasted, fished for, smoked like tobacco, peeled like potatoes, planted in the soil, or dried up and hung as advertisements"—exposes working class whites' sense of racial panic as opposed to racial power. The extreme aggression of such portrayals provided reassurance about the racial order of economic relations many ordinary whites feared insecure (p. 155).

Minstrelsy also capitalized on genocidal and Orientalist logics. For example, early portrayals of Native Americans emphasized hyper-generalized notions about indigenous nobility, fierce independence, and connection to the "natural world"—characteristics white, European settlers wished to appropriate in crafting a unique identity as 'Americans' (Deloria 1998). Nonetheless, as "occupants of the land 'destined' for white Americans," settlers could imagine "literally no 'place'" for actual Native peoples in the U.S. social order (Toll 1977: 168). As such, "Injin" minstrelsy expanded from the occasional 'sympathetic' tale of pitiable indigenous victims to more consistent portrayals marking Indians as barbaric savages to be defended against or otherwise controlled. Such stories increased particularly following the Civil War, as white settlers escalated war-making to secure indigenous land ever further Westward. Controlling images increasingly characterized Native Americans as not just threatening, but literal and figurative obstacles to America's manifest (white) destiny.

Whites also used minstrelsy to cope with anxiety-provoking demographic shifts connected to 19th century immigration. European ethnic groups, including Germans and Irish Catholics, were sometimes depicted unfavorably. While negative portrayals of European groups gave way as they were incorporated into whiteness, those legitimizing the exclusion of sustained 'racial outsiders' held firm root. For example, anti-Chinese minstrelsy commonly featured immigrants' engaged in alien cultural practices—showcasing preference for "disgusting" foods, mocking Asian language with nonsense song lyrics, and implying Asians engaged in deviant drug use. Performances also regularly featured unsuspecting white citizens ensnared by Asians' wicked habits due to their alluring exoticism. These portrayals capture the paradox of Orientalist logic—emphasizing Asians as backward and degenerate (and thus *inferior* and *non-threatening*), but also dangerous (and thus *threatening*), reinforcing the need to exclude and segregate "Oriental heathens," and, if necessary, use violence to protect the white polity (Lee 2012; Toll 1977).

5.3.2 "Contemptible Collectibles"

White supremacist logics also have a long history in U.S. material culture—that is, in the physical objects of popular culture. White consumption of blackness—through minstrel performances and popular images and material goods—marked an easy, if figurative, transition from the trade in actual black bodies in the postbellum South. As legalized segregation emerged alongside an expanding post-slavery economy, merchants of U.S. popular culture imported common racist stereotypes to a burgeoning market of mass-produced goods.

While products sometimes featured anti-Asian, anti-Indian, and anti-Mexican imagery, anti-black representations appeared ubiquitous and especially vicious (Behnken and Smithers 2015; Carrillo 2003). From lawn ornaments to kitchen items, coffee, ashtrays, hair products, and detergents, postcards, even children's toys, white manufacturers plastered insidious anti-black iconography on virtually every type of product imaginable (Pilgrim 2012; Turner 2002). The image of the "coon" was particularly common, depicted as unreliable, lazy, stupid, and child-like, and known for his quaking, superstitious nature—an ideal target for abuse. Other controlling images included the wide-eyed "picaninny," the subservient "Tom," and of course, "mammy," a rotund, smiling, benevolent, black female caretaker (Bogle 2016; Collins 2009: 46; Jewell 1993).

Indeed, despite updates to the well-known icon, mammy continues to hold happy watch over pancakes and waffles today under the brand name "Aunt Jemima." Inspired by a late nineteenth century minstrel show character, white flour mill entrepreneurs capitalized on the hope Aunt Jemima would help sell a pancake mix "so easy to make that it was almost as if your black servant had done it for you" (Behnken and Smithers 2015: 23; Pilgrim 2012). For all her popularity, no other image has been so well debunked as a fiction of white imagination than mammy. Social historians document how rare if not implausible 'real' mammies would have been in the antebellum South; even her imagined corpulent physique appears absurd given the context of slavery and slavers' severe rationing of food (Clinton 1982; Turner 2002). The image of this obsequious and docile black woman has nonetheless survived and remains immortalized in the mass production (and reproduction) of thousands of household and kitchen items.

Postcards depicting blacks in various states of childishness, deprivation, and danger provide some of the most remarkable and disturbing snapshots of white thinking and imagination at the time. As if some bizarre aesthetic rule, black adults and children appear coupled near universally with watermelons in these print media artifacts (Pilgrim 2012). Even more unsettling is the vast array of alligator-themed postcards and 'artwork' depicting the snarling reptiles chasing

and on the brink of devouring small black children and infants. Consumption, in the all too literal Freudian sense, cannot be understated among this sub-genre of 'memorabilia;' like alligators, white Americans appeared to share an insatiable appetite for black destruction, even among the most vulnerable.

Far from limited to adult enjoyment, children's noisemakers, story books, dolls, games, and other toys reveal some of the most pernicious socialization to white racist thinking at the time. Costumes—like a "Negro make-up outfit" described in a 1912 Sears, Roebuck & Co. catalog as "the funniest and most laughable outfit ever sold"—encouraged white children to "play at being a 'Negro'" by dressing-up in wigs, masks, and blackface makeup (Wilkinson 1974: 105). Popular toys have helped habituate children to genocidal and Orientalist logics, as well. Consider, for example, persistent interest in "Cowboys and Indians" and other war-making games. Though numerous mass-marketed toys reinforce the U.S. commitment to war-making, perhaps none are as ubiquitous as the "five and dime store" figurines made famous in the early twentieth century. Production of miniature figures connected to the "wild west" and various domestic and international wars exploded with the advent of plastics in the mid-century U.S. (Sheil and Sheil 2002; Tawzer 2009). *Time* named "Army Men" one of the "all-time greatest" and most influential toys in U.S. history (Townsend 2011). Ultimately, however, these toys rest on white fantasies about the glory of genocide, settler colonialism, and empire-building.

5.4 The Strange, Contemporary Career of Racist Throwbacks: "Something Old, Something New, Something Borrowed, Something…"

In *Ethnic Notions*, his award-winning documentary exploring the history of minstrelsy and anti-black collectibles, film-maker Marlon Riggs contends, "the history of our national conscience" is "[c]ontained in these cultural images; … a conscience striving to reconcile the paradox of racism in a nation founded on human equality—a conscience coping with this *profound contradiction* through caricature" (Riggs 1987). And yet, as our analysis begins to account, this "national conscience" captures not some uniform cognitive dissonance shared by all Americans, but rather the specific moral complications of whiteness (Bracey et al. 2017). In that sense, racist controlling images must be understood not just as "fictions" *of* the white imagination, but fictions created *for* "the white self" (Vera and Gordon 2003: ix; Doane 2017; Mueller 2017).

In light of this perspective, it is powerful to see how resonant historical racist iconography remains during an era regarded by many as *less* racist and racially *progressing*, if not 'post-racial.' Consider, for example, pervasive contemporary interest in anti-black memorabilia. Racist artifacts like those described above are easily purchased in antique stores across the nation today; some originals fetch several thousands of dollars apiece. While these "contemptible collectibles" are often sold under the more euphemistic "Black Americana" label—as if these images were generated by the creative endeavors of black Americans themselves (Turner 2002: 12)—the description is as misleading as it is insulting. Nonetheless, the market for such goods has exploded in the wake of the Internet. An eBay search in the early months of 2017 turned up literally tens of thousands of items —both original *and* reproduction: "jolly nigger banks;" mammy salt and pepper shakers; sambo toothpick holders and door stops; product tins, boxes, and labels; postcards with watermelons and 'pickaninnies' in every style imaginable—all readily available with a few keyboard strokes.[1] David Pilgrim, curator for the Jim Crow Museum

of Racist Memorabilia, notes that "[t]here is so much money in these things that people are even creating fake vintage items, to fool those who collect them" (Carrillo 2003).

How are we to make sense of popular interest in anti-black 'throwback' items during an era where black Americans are supposedly no longer enslaved nor non-citizens? We approach this question by tracing the tangled fate linking Spike Lee's film *Bamboozled* (2000) and the tumultuous, real life events leading to the demise of black comedian Dave Chappelle's wildly successful, *Chappelle's Show* (2003–2006). Even with the space of time, their striking connections remain a revealing testament to the durability and sustained utility of white supremacy logics.

5.4.1   Satire Appropriated: *Bamboozled* and *Chappelle's Show*

Released in 2000, Spike Lee's *Bamboozled* replants minstrelsy in contemporary historical soil to raise questions about faith in U.S. racial progress.[2] The film is narrated posthumously by the main character, Pierre Delacroix (Damon Wayans), an African American executive 'buppie.' Already disenchanted by his work at a major television network, Delacroix is pushed to the edge when network administrators approach him about developing a new show to launch slumping ratings, one that is "dope, sexy, and funny." Tired of the constant microaggressions, Delacroix plans to get himself fired. Aiming recklessly toward his goal, he pitches a pilot he assumes will do the trick—*Mantan: The New Millennium Minstrel Show*. However, rather than reject Delacroix' idea as outrageously offensive and racist, his white boss, Thomas Dunwitty (Michael Rappaport), appears elated. Boasting that his black wife and biracial children make him "blacker" than the reserved and tightly hemmed Delacroix, Dunwitty jumps on

---

[1]EBay prohibits items that "promote or glorify hatred, violence, racial, sexual, or religious intolerance," or "portray graphic violence or victims of violence, unless they have substantial social, artistic, or political value." Despite their implicit, racially offensive nature, Black Americana listings—whether original *or reproduction*— are excepted by virtue of their presumed "historical significance." Ebay's full "offensive material policy" is available from: http://pages.ebay.com/help/policies/offensive.html.

[2]For two longer reviews of *Bamboozled*, see Barlowe (2003) and Epp (2003).

production and begins marketing the new show, featuring "two real coons" who are "keepin' it real."

Mantan premieres with a live-audience and house band ('The Alabama Porch Monkeys'), on a set arranged to look like a watermelon (i.e., "nigger apple") patch. Following classic minstrel predecessors, the show chronicles the dull-witted and unlucky antics of tap-dancing 'Mantan' and his sidekick, 'Sleep 'n Eat.' The sitcom earns rapid, national praise, and by the end of the film audience members of all races appear in black-face, excitedly proclaiming themselves "real niggers." Though others praise Delacroix as a "creative genius," he finds his intended satire has been lost in translation; worse, people assume "the show can't be racist because he's black." Free of the social restrictions that might otherwise inhibit their racist pleasures, viewers become obsessed with *Mantan*, delighting in restaging a nostalgic era where "a man could be a man, a woman could be a woman, and a nigger knew his place."

Interestingly, even before *Bamboozled*'s release, *The New York Times* blocked an advertisement featuring a watermelon-eating pickaninny, perhaps concerned Lee's satirical focus would be lost on *Times* readers, too. Blending real life with fiction, the film weaves images of *Ethnic Notions* (Riggs 1987) throughout. Juxtaposing historical reality with a fictional socio-political future, *Bamboozled* reminds viewers that racist icons from the not-so-distant past can—and have been—resurrected and commercialized with relative ease, revealing a sustained cultural appetite for buffonish portrayals of blackness.

In a remarkable twist of fate, *Bamboozled's* art-imitates-life lessons came to ironic fruition with the rise of African American comedian Dave Chappelle's Comedy Central Network program, *Chappelle's Show*. With sketches like "The Racial Draft," "The Niggar Family," and "The Life of Clayton Bigsby"—a blind white supremacist unaware he is black—*Chappelle's Show* turned American racial politics on their head with humorous satire, enjoying two wildly successful seasons. Fans were thus shocked in early 2005 when Comedy Central announced the third season would be delayed indefinitely. After having signed a $50 million dollar contract, Chappelle fled the country, and speculations about drug addiction and mental breakdown quickly followed (Farley 2005).

Chappelle's Show rightly earned a broad, multiracial fan-base; nonetheless audiences' divergent responses to the show's material and dramatic end are telling. Chappelle's sharp satire, which mocked the absurdities of white racism and particularly white stereotypes of blackness, appeared to resonate with black audiences.[3] For example, one well-known skit featured a fictional news report announcing congressional disbursement of a trillion dollars for black reparations. Reporters chronicle black citizens wasting "reparations checks" on frivolous things, like clothes and bootleg cigarettes, and paying delinquent phone bills. For a critically decoding audience, the skit laid bare the racial politics of white resistance to the very defensible idea of reparations—specifically a failure to imagine meaningful ways to redress centuries of black immiseration, and worse, total inability to envision black Americans as worthy of atonement.

Nonetheless, it is clear, and became upsettingly apparent to Chappelle that not all audiences were discerning antiracist meaning from the comic's satire. In a revealing interview recorded shortly after his departure, Chappelle was eager to dispel rumors about his instability. Recounting an incident from what would be his last taping, Chappelle discussed a skit where he played the role of a magical blackfaced pixie who tries to convince other black people to act in stereotypical ways. Chappelle recalled one spectator, a white man, laughed particularly loud and long: "When he laughed, it made me uncomfortable. As a matter of fact, that was the

---

[3]In a recent piece exploring his own gratitude, black writer and cultural critic, Brown (2013) described *Chappelle's Show* as "revolutionary" and "the most important show" of his life. In more light-hearted fashion, Browne opined Chappelle should earn "an American Sociological Association Lifetime Achievement Award" for one of his most well-known sketches, "The Niggar Family."

last thing I shot... Because my head almost exploded" (Farley 2005).

In haunting parallel with *Bamboozled's* protagonist, Chappelle also testified to his increasing leeriness about praise from people around him: "'You're a genius!'; 'You're great!'; 'That's your voice!' But I'm not sure that they're right." And, indeed, Chappelle revealed longer standing concerns about material created with colleagues, and his breakdown in trust. In illuminating counterpoint, Comedy Central and Chappelle's long-time white writing partner, Neal Brennan, appeared unable or unwilling to hear Chappelle's concerns, particularly surrounding the racial politics of their humor. Brennan said, "We'd write [a sketch]. He'd love it, say, 'I can't wait to do it.' We'd shoot it, and then at some point he'd start saying, 'This sketch is racist, and I don't want this on the air.' And I was like, 'You like this sketch. What do you mean?' There was this confusing contradictory thing: he was calling his own writing racist" (Farley 2005). Like Delacroix, Chappelle's white colleagues not only doubted Chappelle's insights, but also his right to consider social responsibility in producing black imagery, and his ability to determine—and right to honor—elements of his own experience that felt personally compromising.

In the end, the fictional Delacroix and real-life Dave Chappelle both earned hard-won clarity on a lesson pinpointed by critical film analyst, Armond White (1995); namely, black artists—and popular artists of color more broadly—"can take nothing for granted" (p. 62). As Chappelle himself noted, those not willing to tow the line in the multinational media outlet become obstacles to manage when dollars and comforting racist fantasies hang in the balance. As if portending his own fate, Chappelle remarked well before his departure, "I was replaceable. I'm still replaceable now. That's what's so crazy about show business" (Chaney 2005). And, indeed, when Chappelle attempted to end his show permanently, Comedy Central quickly rebounded to feed hungry white audiences with or without him. Dropping Chappelle's popular live opening monologue format and eschewing worries about authenticity, the network scraped together pieces from unused filming for a truncated third season—dubbed "The Lost Episodes."

The fate of *Mantan* and *Chappelle's Show* end the same: each show taking on a life of its own, even in the absence of its creators. In *Bamboozled*, when Mantan and Sleep n' Eat finally decide to end their degrading roles, their characters are quickly replaced by another desperate actor waiting in the wings. Comedy Central, too, attempted to further fill the vacuum left by Chappelle, launching a new show, *Mind of Mencia*. The program featured Latino comic, Carlos Mencia, and his "unflinching" brand of racial humor. Perhaps attempting to re-capture what they thought drew Chappelle's viewers, the show's web page promised Mencia would show "no mercy as he skewers current events and culture, unleashing his one-of-a-kind observations in the studio and out on the street."[4]

Unlike the clever satirical formula central to Chappelle's humor, however, *Mind of Mencia* appeared far less nuanced and socially analytical. Indeed, Mencia held few comic punches, relying on unsophisticated stereotypes to "punch down" more frequently than "up," and mocking everyone from Mexican immigrants to the disabled. If white audiences found ways to bypass Chappelle's smart (and antiracist) satire, decoding racist messages instead, that task was made positively easier by Mencia's skewering, "no-mercy" approach. It is perhaps unsurprising to learn these were the precise reasons Chappelle came to question his role generating sharp-witted satire only to have the message destroyed upon delivery. While Chappelle's comedy is not beyond critical reproach, Chappelle proved unwilling to approach the work he loved without mercy for himself or communities important to him. In compelling defense of his unexpected retreat, Chappelle appealed, "I want to make sure I'm dancing and not shuffling.... Your soul is priceless" (Farley 2005).[5]

---

[4]Retrieved March 10, 2017 from http://www.cc.com/shows/mind-of-mencia.

[5]See also Chappelle's recent March 21, 2017 interview with CBS News (http://www.cbsnews.com/news/dave-chappelle-netflix-comedy-fame-leaving-chappelles-show/).

5.4.2 Controlling Images as "Symbolic Reservoir"

As Chapelle's drama reveals, white supremacy logics are not simply historical; they are durable and often reworked for contemporary consumption. King (2013) argues this kind of sustained preoccupation reveals how useful such representations are to filling the "symbolic reservoirs" from which we construct meanings about self and society (p. xiii). Far from limited to anti-black representations, scholars also demonstrate persistent recycling of genocidal and Orientalist logics in popular culture. Examining artifacts spanning the 13th century to the present, Tchen and Yeats (2014) expose steady anti-Asian paranoia in the Western racial imagination, as captured in images marking Asia and Asians a "yellow peril" and constant existential threat to "the West." In similar vein, Shaheen (2014) reveals a century of Hollywood films have worked to represent Arabs as "brutal, heartless, uncivilized religious fanatics and 'money-mad' cultural 'others' bent on terrorizing civilized Westerners" (Shaheen 2014: 8). Meanwhile, Delgado and Stefancic (1992) document how Mexican-American portrayals alternated from a genocidal focus, accenting Mexicans as "shifty, brutal, and treacherous" (as the U.S. was seizing and settling Mexican territory in the Southwest); to a more Orientalist focus, emphasizing Mexicans as base, unassimilable simpletons (as immigration escalated in the early 20th century and poor Mexican workers entered the economy en masse) (see also Pérez 2014).

Beyond looking at artifacts and images themselves, we can learn a great deal by looking at how white people actively *use* these in everyday life—not just to mark racial otherness, but to construct and stabilize imagined white selves. For example, whites have long relied on the practice of 'playing Indian'—using props and spectacled performances assumed to be authentically indigenous—"to make powerful statements about themselves that they might not be able to otherwise enunciate" (Deloria 1998; King 2013: 30). Though examples are plentiful, Native American sports mascots offer one of the most literal and commonplace ways non-Natives play Indian.

American Indian mascots remain largely ubiquitous despite decades of protest from indigenous groups and organizations. While fans commonly claim mascots reflect a deep reverence for Native Americans, their reliance on flattened, often false images of indigeneity (feathered headdresses; buckskin pants; mythical dances, rhythms, and tomahawk chops); mutilation of cultural practices considered sacred; and often militant resistance to retiring mascots expose an uglier reality. Indeed, Green (1988) argues 'playing Indian' rests on a tacit genocidal logic that requires the literal and psychological removal of *actual*, living Indians. After all, "why would non-Native peoples need to play Indian … if they thought Indians were still alive and perfectly capable of being Indian themselves?" (Smith 2012: 287–288).

By isolating Native Americans in a romanticized history of noble savages disappeared long-ago, whites who play Indian render living Native Americans invisible, denying indigenous people a meaningful socio-political identity in contemporary public life (Strong 2005). Moreover, indigenous appropriation expresses a tacit 'imperialist nostalgia' about the theft and violence involved in European conquest, as performances often invoke a sentimental longing, even psuedo-mourning over that which whites destroyed (Deloria 1998; King 2013). Movie portrayals capture this 'sentimentalized destruction,' too. In common form, white characters enter indigenous communities on colonizing missions, but find themselves so captivated by indigenous culture they 'go native.' Examples include Kevin Costner's Army-lieutenant-turned-Lakota-warrior in *Dances with Wolves* (1990), and Tom Cruise's Army-captain-turned-samurai in *The Last Samurai* (2003). Such plots crescendo with white characters 'switching sides' to fight nobly against encroaching but ultimately irrepressible Western forces.

Like playing Indian, white consumers use hip hop and its association with blackness to construct imagined white selves—selves that are cool, masculine, progressive, unique, "realer," even more "human" (Hughey 2012: 158; Hurt 2006; Rodriquez 2006). Historical diversity notwithstanding, the language, styles, and attitudes associated with commercial hip hop tend to be "coded and understood and performed as 'black'" (Perry 2004; Rose 2008: xii). Hip hop legend, Chuck D once remarked that the move to hyper-commodify hip hop in the mid-1990s reflected corporate elites' belief they could "put soul in a bottle" to attract a broad consumer base (Hurt 2006). During a period when other genres experienced declines, hip hop's market share rose rapidly as white consumers flocked from the early 1990s onward. Research confirms that since then white consumers have comprised 70–75% of the hip hop customer base (Rose 2008).

Moreover, as globalization circulates U.S. culture ever further, the symbolic reservoir of 'black soul' has become popular export. For example, analysts have identified striking throwback black imagery in contemporary 'K-pop,' an immensely popular musical genre originating out of South Korea (Britton 2017; Morrissey 2012). In one salient example, female quartet, the Bubble Sisters made headlines when they deployed a "blackface gimmick" to market themselves, performing in black makeup and hairstyles, and dancing in pajamas with grotesquely caricatured rubber lips (Morrissey 2012). Responding to criticism, one of the group's members explained they "loved music by black people…. We happened to have black makeup. With the makeup we felt good, natural, free and energized. In taking the real album cover photos, we finally decided to go for it" (KOCCA 2003). Again, imagined 'blackness' appears captured, like magic, in a makeup bottle. In a strikingly more 'modern' example, Snapchat made the technique of blackface even more simple, commemorating

the 4/20 pot-smoking 'holiday' by enabling users to "blacken" selfies with a rastafarian, dreadlocked "Bob Marley" filter (Smith 2016).

5.5 Representation, Resistance, and Contemporary Racial Fantasies

Given cultural representation is so tightly bound to actual practices of racial domination, popular culture often becomes a site of significant contestation (hooks 2009; Smith and Thakore 2016). Targeted racial groups often resist, protest, and engage in protracted organizing over controlling, racist images. Historical examples are plentiful. When Frito-Lay introduced a marketing campaign in 1967 featuring the 'Frito Bandito'—a greasy, gun-toting Mexican bandit, so driven by his love for Fritos corn chips he'll stop at nothing—reaction was swift. Chicano groups, including the National Mexican-American Anti-Defamation Committee and Mexican-Americans in Gainful Endeavors, joined forces to place unrelenting pressure on the Frito Lay Company to retire the image. Appearing tone-deaf to activists' moral pleas, Frito Lay hoped to quell resistance by sanitizing the image—removing the character's gun and gold tooth and making him appear less grimacing. Only after four years of organizing and the threat of a class action anti-defamation lawsuit on behalf of the 6.1 million Mexican Americans in the U.S. did Frito-Lay finally drop the corporate mascot, following years of racist profiteering (Behnken and Smithers 2015; Noriega 2000).

Social movements against Native American mascots remain some of the most visible examples of indigenous activism and socio-cultural resurgence. As noted above, white interests reflect an unjust sense of entitlement and commitment to 'owning,' using, and indeed, profiting from these mythologized racist fantasies. Despite their sustained ubiquity, nearly 1500 Native mascots have been changed, retired, or reworked since anti-mascot organizing escalated in the 1970s (King 2013). In one particularly creative example of resistance, American Indian students at the University of Northern Colorado (UNC) worked to flip the tables to pressure a local high school team to retire their tenure as the 'Fightin' Reds.' Changing their intramural basketball team name to the 'Fightin' Whites,' the group began selling t-shirts featuring an archetypical 1950s-styled middle-aged white male mascot, and the motto "Every thang's gonna be all white!" Though the high school refused to budge, the group's efforts sparked wide media interest, inspiring similar efforts and driving merchandise sales; enough to donate $100,000 to the UNC Foundation, for a Fightin' Whites Minority Scholarship endowment (Ochoa 2003; Washington Times 2003).

Though inspiring, examples like these highlight the steep challenges people of color face resisting institutionalized, corporate white power. To be sure, battles over the right to be self-determining and control one's own/group image most often occur on battlegrounds shaped by vastly unequal power, status, and resources. Moreover, the normative context of colorblindness today sets the stage for even more complicated negotiations.

5.5.1 Race-Neutrality, Race-Progress, and Post-racialism in the Popular Imagination

In 2003, retail giant, Abercrombie and Fitch, came under fire after launching a line of t-shirts featuring mocking Asian portrayals—with images of slant-eyed, smiling caricatures donning rice hats, and slogans like "Wong Brothers Laundry Service: Two Wongs Make it White." Asian Americans and student groups mobilized quickly, writing letters, organizing online petitions, and staging protests in shopping malls. Revealing they had not "test-marketed" the idea, Abercrombie's spokesperson announced the company would pull the shirts from stores and online, adding:

We personally thought Asians would love this T-shirt. We are truly and deeply sorry we've offended people.... We never single out any one group to poke fun at. We poke fun at everybody, from women to flight attendants to baggage handlers, to football coaches, to Irish Americans to snow skiers. There's really no group we haven't teased. (Strasburg 2002)

Abercrombie's claims of racial innocence appear reaching in light of a subsequent class action discrimination lawsuit brought by applicants and employees of color, which resulted in a $50 million dollar settlement in 2005 (Lieff Cabraser Heimann & Bernstein 2017). Nonetheless, as Doane (2017) explains, these kinds of 'racial morality plays'—where public figures or, in this case, corporate entities verbally atone and seek exoneration following racist transgressions—remain commonplace in contemporary public life. Indeed, Abercrombie's company line appears solidly bent on restoring an image of colorblindness. To do so, they peddle illusions of a post-racial world where the playing field has been leveled, freeing everyone to enjoy 'equal opportunity' teasing across differences now assumed socially insignificant and detached from power. Read this way, Abercrombie's apology sounds more like #sorrynotsorry.

Popular culture plays a central role in normalizing these kinds of colorblind ideological fantasies, so common in contemporary life (Nilsen and Turner 2014). Importantly, colorblind ideology is not about *not* seeing race, but rather about the evolving ways that whites evade and downplay the persistent social significance of race (Bonilla-Silva 2015; Doane 2017; Mueller 2017). Segregation patterns ensure most white people have little meaningful contact with people of color. Meanwhile, popular culture provides a constant barrage of styles, products, and programs that *signify* color, while downplaying race as connected to a system of white domination, one to which we are all bound. Popular culture thus not only facilitates white fantasies of a more widely integrated and racially egalitarian world than actually exists; it makes it possible to consume race in a way that appears to erase the material inequalities and social distance dividing white people from people of color in real life (Gallagher 2003: 22; see also Durham 2015).

Elevating colorblindness in racially-themed films assumed to be progressive proves particularly illuminating. While problems with under-representation and recycled, stereotypically racist tropes remain (see, e.g., Bogle 2016; Jewell 1993; Russell-Brown 2008; Vera and Gordon 2003), films that address racism as a serious social issue are often taken as reassuring evidence of racial progress. Indeed, filmmakers and producers often hope they will contribute to a slow, but presumably inevitable social evolution by developing and circulating films that tackle racism 'head on' (Mueller and Issa 2016).

Consider two new-millennium films that earned numerous honors, including the Academy's highest praise, Oscar gold for Best Picture. The first, Crash (released in 2005), was hailed by critics and audiences for its seemingly forthright treatment of race in America. Popular review aggregating website, Rotten Tomatoes (2017a) describes the film as a "raw and unsettling" examination of the "dangers of bigotry and xenophobia in the lives of interconnected [Los] Angelenos." Many believed Crash was quite courageous in unmasking sustained explicit white bigotry, from the heinous abuses of a racist white cop (played by Matt Dillon) to the purse-clutching-prejudices of a wealthy white woman (Sandra Bullock). Equally striking, however, were Crash's messages surrounding racism as an equal-opportunity-structure of prejudice. Not only did white characters regularly spout racist dialogue; nearly all characters in the film engaged in interpersonal interactions commonly regarded as racist in form—from African Americans, to Asian Americans, to Arab Americans. The net effect is, again, a leveling of the racial playing field with a psychic payout. The film's message reduces racism to an individual-level phenomenon captured in prejudicial thinking. Moreover, white moviegoers brave enough to be "unsettled" by "raw" white prejudice will find comfort in the notion that racism is not a white problem, but rather a shared human condition. Prejudice may become

discrimination in the context of institutional positions, but racism appears detached from structures, resting solutions in the hope of mustering a *collective* willingness to struggle against common, potentially "rational" and unavoidable,[6] but nonetheless immoral prejudicial tendencies.

Like *Crash*, Oscar-winner *12 Years A Slave* (2013) could be filed alongside the spate of contemporary movies "that pretend 'a conversation about race'," as one black critic chided (White 2013). Unlike *Crash*, however, *12 Years A Slave* was not the brainchild of white minds, but developed rather from the efforts of a black writer and director (John Ridley and Steve McQueen, respectively; though in relationship to white institutional production and support). Critics notwithstanding, popular consensus appeared to be that the film, which tackles American slavery, may be "far from comfortable viewing," but is nonetheless "brilliant—and quite possibly essential—cinema" (Rotten Tomatoes 2017b). It is difficult to imagine white-washing racism in a film about slavery, let alone one so "unflinchingly brutal" (Rotten Tomatoes 2017b). Beyond violent, as an institutionalized system, slavery is unambiguously connected to racial exploitation and white dominance. Moreover, the film is based on the autobiography of an actual historical figure, Solomon Northrup (played by Chiwetel Ejiofor), a black man born free in New York, but kidnapped and sold into slavery in the antebellum Louisiana south. Nonetheless, as one analysis reveals, the film represents slavery and black suffering through means that appear to acknowledge race and certain structures of racial hierarchy while paradoxically facilitating racial

---

[6]*Crash* injects a variety of 'moral dilemmas' to bring seemingly provocative racial questions forward. In the end, however, these tend to exculpate white actors by suggesting racism-as-prejudice is almost irresistible (a white character's 'irrational' prejudices appear 'rational' when she is car-jacked by two black characters; the non-racist 'good'" white cop ends up murdering a black character because of involuntary, knee-jerk biases); and that even the worst racists are redeemable under the right circumstances (as when an egregiously racist cop saves a black female character he sexually violated earlier in the film).

ignorance. Specifically, Mueller and Issa (2016) find the film supports a variety "racial illusions" that obscure the material and relational basis of race, mystify the totalizing nature of white supremacy, and elevate anemic ideas about antiracism to rescue whiteness.

5.5.2 About Us, by Them, for Whom?: (Re-)Imagining Interracial Romance on Film

By way of providing one final set of examples that demonstrate the pliability of white racial illusions—and how they might be creatively challenged—we compare several additional films separated by historical distance, but united in contemplating "racial integration of the most intimate kind" (Obasogie 2013: 109). Sex, marriage, and family have long operated as sites of social control under white supremacy (Collins 2009; Smith 2012). While space prevents full accounting, popular renditions of racialized sexuality have often focused on the sexual deviance of people of color. Typically, this deviance is presumed in extremes, alternating between characterizations that imply people of color are hypersexual and thus sexually threatening; or aesexual, sexually impotent, and thus no threat at all (i.e., to idealized white femininity, white male virility) (Collins 2009; Delgado and Stefancic 1992; Fung 2005).

There is, of course, a deep projection involved in these kinds of white fantasies, given how whites engage sexual control and violence as tools of, and privileges accorded by domination (Harris 2017; Russell-Brown 2008; Smith 2015). Historically speaking, controlling images of women of color as promiscuous temptresses have conditioned and legitimated much white sexual violence. Relatedly, controlling images cast men of color as sexually criminal—and the primary threats to white female purity—emboldening whites' violence and, too often, deadly force (Harris 2017). Indeed, this trope is centered in a movie widely exalted as a revolutionary achievement in cinematic history despite being vitriolically racist—*Birth of a Nation* (1915)

(Calney 1993). The film gave broad, cinematic life to images of black men as depraved, lascivious beasts, bent on destroying "Southern Civilization" and "mongrelizing the races," and positioned the Ku Klux Klan as righteous defenders of white women, and the South more generally (Calney 1993). Massive nationwide black protest and legal efforts to ban or at minimum censor the film proved largely futile, and *Birth of a Nation* became the first film ever screened in the White House.

Considering how severe social prohibitions against interracial sexual relations were in principle if not whites' actual practice, the 1967 release of *Guess Who's Coming to Dinner?* appeared a watershed moment in cinematic history. The film took for granted an idea totally foreclosed by generations of controlling racialized sexual images; namely that genuine, romantic love across the boundaries of race was possible. Indeed, *Guess Who's Coming to Dinner?* made its release just six months following the Supreme Court's landmark decision in *Loving v. Virginia*, declaring state laws prohibiting interracial marriage unconstitutional.

Guess Who's Coming to Dinner? centers the moral crisis of a sympathetic white father (played by Spencer Tracey), forced to confront his own internalized racism after his daughter returns home announcing her surprise engagement to a black physician (Sidney Poitier). The movie's emphasis on prejudice and rosy message—that racial divides can be overcome if only whites and blacks embrace a spirit of openness and goodwill—are certainly not beyond critical reproach. Nonetheless, the film did take particular aim at white audiences and their ostensible racial liberalism in the wake of the civil rights movement, forcing viewers "render a verdict" about whether race should matter when it comes to "affairs of the heart" (Obasogie 2013: 111; Vera and Gordon 2005).

It is striking to consider, by contrast, the evolution of form and message in 2005's remake, *Guess Who?* Replacing drama with comedy, *Guess Who?* attempts to flip the racial script, substituting a middle-class black father (Bernie Mac) challenged to accept his daughter's white boyfriend (Ashton Kutcher). Laughter is the vehicle that makes this update and its messages about race innocuous at best, hardly as challenging as its predecessor. Like *Crash*, *Guess Who?* levels the racial playing field; here, blacks' racial prejudice is made to appear immorally equivalent to whites—a message likely to resonate with viewers who believe that 'reverse' discrimination and racism are plausible, if not genuine social issues. The historical context that figured so centrally as backdrop to the original appears entirely erased, replaced by a fantastical white reinterpretation only made intelligible through the lens of contemporary colorblind ideology (Obasogie 2013; Vera and Gordon 2005).

Notably, none of these film treatments deal realistically with the long, structured legacy of systemic white supremacy in the U.S. *Birth of a Nation* deploys interracial intimacy as an existential threat, to rationalize anti-black violence and re-establish the necessity of white rule. By contrast, with their emphasis on racism-as-prejudice, *Guess Who's Coming to Dinner?* and *Guess Who?* elide the material significance of race in a post-Civil Rights world still structured around white dominance. Arguably, these three films are also united in centering white audiences, either directly or implicitly, by virtue of their grounding in palatable, white fantasies.

In these regards, 2017's breakout success, *Get Out* stands in stark contrast. Written and directed by black actor, comedian, and film-maker, Jordan Peele, *Get Out* uses the genre of horror to satirize black terror under the "kinder, gentler" hands of liberal white racism. The film centers around the terrifying trials of a young, black photographer, Chris (played by Daniel Kaluuya), during a visit to meet the family of his white girlfriend, Rose (Allison Williams). Despite their apparent comfort, even approval, Chris slowly uncovers Rose's family —and indeed, the whole surrounding white community—are in the business of harvesting black bodies for the purposes of literally colonizing them. Chris finds himself the latest victim of a patterned routine: Rose manipulates unsuspecting black partners using sex, love, and

white female innocence; her mother uses hypnotism to groom and paralyze them; Rose's brother remains available to play the 'heavy,' should brute violence become necessary; and finally—after a slave-like auction—Rose's father transplants the high-bidder's brain into the lobotomized victim's body, which can now be used to enjoy fetishized black attributes (e.g., physical and sexual prowess, 'cool' aesthetic viewpoint).

Presenting a diversity of characters, *Get Out* opens itself to a highly intersectional reading.[7] Indeed, as Harris (2017) argues, "part of the genius of *Get Out* is the way Peele plays with and subverts over a century's worth of racist on-screen imagery," particularly with respect to white female innocence vis-à-vis the hyper-sexed "black brute." Moreover, using the metaphor of "The Sunken Place"—the terrifying and paralyzing psychological space black victims are sent to during hypnosis and colonization—*Get Out* implies whiteness exacts *continual terror* on the black psyche under white supremacy. Relatedly, by virtue of this unrelenting domination, black resistance appears ever-present, though often disarmed and repressed.[8] Perhaps most distinctive, *Get Out* may appeal to white audiences, but is not oriented around white pleasure, understanding, nor validation. Indeed, Jones and Ware (2017a) suggest the film takes black understanding for granted, and "proceed[s] from that knowing," inevitably leaving many white viewers 'out of the loop' on the film's deeply encoded racial messages. In the end, *Get Out* forecloses trust in white liberalism and interracial intimacy as signs of racial progress, urging viewers *never* underestimate white people's collective commitment and power to preserve white supremacy (Mitchum 2017).

---

[7]In addition to Harris (2017), see Jones and Ware (2017a, b) for more developed analyses of the film.

[8]Jones and Ware (2017b) suggest the film offers an implicit critique of racist cultural indoctrination through popular culture, specifically television.

5.5.3 New Media: (Re-)New(ed) Racism, (Re-)New(ed) Resistance

Racialization that takes place offline in traditional forms is now mirrored, broadened and expanded by digital media and online networking platforms. Scrolling through comments on almost any YouTube video or virtual news post reveals the polarization of race on the Internet. From friendly Facebook threads to NFL players tweeting about the George Zimmerman trial, many can and do participate in the social construction of race online. But beyond conversations *about* race, the Internet itself *is* racialized—or, Andre Brock (2009) argues, race has been built *into* the Internet. Race and racism persist online in ways both new and unique to the Internet, but which also co-exist "alongside vestiges of centuries-old forms that reverberate both offline and on" (Daniels 2013: 696). Early internet studies (pre-social media) theorized the web as a race-neutral space (because users were not privy to the race of others). On the purely text-based web, gender and race were imagined as concealed. With the advent of social media, representations of race were reimagined, regulated, and recodified simultaneously.

Indeed, just as we perform and live race offline, we also "do" race online (Pitcher 2014) in ways that reflect an ongoing process of negotiation. Research on Internet cultures confirms that familiar social mechanisms—race play, race work, racial projects, and racial identity-making—operate in largely the same fashion as they do offline. Consider backlash to several versions of the *Grand Theft Auto* video game franchise. For example, in *Grand Theft Auto: San Andreas* players to take on the role of a young black man, "Carl Johnson" in a form of 'digital race play':

> Carl Johnson, a Black man who, having left his home to escape the violence engulfing his life and community, returns to San Andreas, Carl is accosted by the police, framed for a crime he did not commit, and warned that he had better stay out of trouble. The game's quest-based storyline takes the player on a violent, but heavily satirical, trip to becoming a criminal kingpin... Players are invited to try on the personae of an inner-city gang member, experiencing some of what it means to live in a stylized 1990s rap world. (DeVane 2008: 266)

With the added dimension of connectivity, users play out race collectively, engaging online with other players. Massively multiplayer online games (MMOG) are particularly enmeshed with race play in these virtual meeting spaces, which provide access to new types of symbolic reservoirs (King 2013). Indeed, online gaming communities privilege the narratives of white men (Gray 2014) who, through video games, can take on roles as diverse as a disenfranchised black man (Carl Johnson in *Grand Theft Auto*) or a white U.S. marine gunning down Middle Eastern civilians (*Call of Duty: Modern Warfare*). Indeed, the collective play afforded by games like *Grand Theft Auto* uses this variety to reinforce themes all too familiar—about the inherent deviance and criminality of people of color and pleasureable, justified violence and militarism.

Further, in a space that paradoxically reinforces dissolved social distance alongside stereotypical, racist images, media forms also become more entangled. Recently, televised and digital media have coalesced to reinvigorate consumption of extralegal violence perpetrated against people of color. Online news media portrays race-based violence in much the same manner as video games with one exception—news media harness the power of digital technologies to increase the consumption of *real* black death and white violence against racial-others. Amidst the expanding new millennium Movement for Black Lives (MBL), videos capturing violent police brutality and sanctioned extralegal murder are legion.[9]

Broad media circulation and subsequent sharing across social media platforms reflects, at least in part, belief in an "empathic fallacy"—that is, in the faulty hope that white people can talk,

---

[9]Included among examples, too numerous to name, are dash cam video documenting police shooting 12-year-old Tamir Rice dead; bystander video of police choking 43-year-old Eric Garner to death; and again, eyewitness video capturing police violently hurling young black women to the ground - from a school desk in South Carolina; and at a pool party in Texas.

read, write and *watch* their way "out of bigotry and narrow-mindedness, out of… limitations of experience and perspective" to deepen empathy and "achieve new levels of sensitivity and fellow-feeling" (Delgado and Stefancic 1992: 1261). Nonetheless, widespread attention often fails to achieve such ends. Instead, black death and racial violence become banal, extending people of color's trauma while buttressing white fantasies further. Indeed, normalizing black and brown suffering and death not only reinforces the reasonableness of whites' common racial apathy (Forman and Lewis 2006); it also creates perverse fodder for racist humor and play, like the horrific trend of "Trayvoning," where young whites posted photos across Twitter, Instagram, and Tumblr re-enacting the image of black teen, Trayvon Martin's dead body (Durham 2015). Alternately, white audiences can engage in "consuming" people of color's pain as a self-referential morality exercise, using their willingness to bear witness as a symbolic act of contrition that reinforces one's (and one's groups') "goodness" (Mueller and Issa 2016). Whatever one's politics, these videos and sequential everyday practices serve as a consistent and, for white people, reassuring reminder of who holds power in society (Jones and Ware 2017b).

Just as new media have created novel venues for the proliferation of white supremacist images and ideas, however, new media provide powerful new spaces for creative resistance among networked and highly savvy users. Digital, social media often allow for oppositional discussions across political and social lines, while pushing the politics of respectability concerning public discussion of race. While platforms such as Twitter act as a space for the circulation of news and identity-politics based discourse (Williams and Gonlin 2017), they have also birthed new forms of community organizing and resistance. Indeed, because they have been more broadly democratized than many traditional forms, social media platforms have extended means for people of color to mount and amplify counter-frames to racism in real time (Williams 2017). Nowhere is this more evident than Black Twitter—a virtual community of active, primarily African-American Twitter users. "Proving adept at bringing about a wide range of sociopolitical changes" (Jones 2013), Black Twitter has generated a cultural zeitgeist, promptly responding to white-framed ways of being in popular culture and beyond. This participatory culture, as some scholars have called it (see Jenkins 2006), has ushered in a new era of 'clapback'—swift, targeted public comeuppances. Black Twitter's hashtag campaigns challenge antiblack racism, cultural theft, and black degradation (Brock 2012; Florini 2013). Revelations of celebrity chef Paula Deen's use of the "n-word" were swiftly met with a painfully hilarious Twitter campaign challenging her overt racism under the #PaulasBestDishes hashtag. In its aftermath, Deen's cooking empire crumbled and she reportedly lost over 10 million dollars in endorsements and deals. Black Twitter's #OscarsSoWhite campaign expressed disgust and called for a boycott over the Academy of Motion Picture Arts and Sciences' all-white nominations for lead and supporting actors in 2016 for the second year in a row. Within a week, the Academy unanimously agreed to make changes to expand the racial and gender diversity of Oscar voters by the year 2020.

To be sure, online campaigns and movements are made up of real individuals; as such, these often exist as an extension of offline groups and communities. Movements such as Black Lives Matter (BLM) have been successful precisely because there are real communities that are willing to, and have, put boots on the ground in the offline world. As compared with historical movements, like the Civil Rights Movement, contemporary movements benefit from new media in very concrete ways (Riemer 2016). For example, Civil Rights movement-building relied on communities sending delegates to meet in a central location to plan national direct actions. Today, digital media, such as Twitter allow communities to organize nation-wide collective action without meeting in a single, physical location. In the same vein, though not universal, increased access to the Internet has facilitated more democratic forms of resistance, leaving movements less beholden to classism.

Not only have digital media influenced how communities mobilize; the meaning of collective action itself has also shifted. Routines that we typically think of as mundane, such as watching television or online shopping can take on new meaning in light of digital media and participatory culture. In fact, the digital mundane offers a multitude of opportunities for shaping resistance discourse. Fan communities discuss the latest music videos, performances, television series, and award shows—calling out cultural appropriation, inaccurate cultural representations, and disingenuous behavior in the process. They also use their collective voice to reinforce positive portrayals of identities. For instance, viewers of the television series *Scandal* dialogue regularly about the contested representation of interracial relationships between the main characters. Responding to viewers' claims that the main character, a black woman, appears powerless in her relationship with a white married man, producers developed subsequent episodes that explored the power dynamics of their relationship. Audiences can successfully change the nature and outcome of a series because networks want to maintain their continued viewership. Viewers of color get to influence the narratives that depict their communities, taking back power to tell their own stories.

Such campaigns do not exist solely on Twitter of course, but anywhere visually-driven content can challenge racist representations through participatory culture. When Vogue magazine discovered "big butts," the *New York Times* unveiled "urban fabulous" babyhair, and the *Los Angeles Times* unearthed corn rows for "white ladies," social media users quickly sprung into action across Tumblr, Instagram, Facebook and other platforms to identify the erasure of women of color and revisionist histories presented by these media outlets (Brown 2014). Similar resistance campaigns can be seen across the blogosphere challenging cultural appropriation. White women's use of headdresses at Coachella music festival have been called out. Fashion designers have taken to their own social media accounts to address cultural theft of design. All of these conversations extend an arena of

participatory culture that allows for discussion at the intersections race, politics, culture, and everyday life. New media facilitate a virtual meeting place where ongoing discourse about power and representation build community (Williams 2016). In turn, users of color mobilize their communities to act as powerful, multi-faceted collectives committed to political and cultural change.

5.6 Conclusion

Reflecting on the pervasiveness of anti-blackness in American life, James Baldwin once remarked that the future the U.S. rested in white people's willingness to broach a single, pivotal question:

> What white people have to do is try to find out in their own hearts why it was necessary to have a nigger in the first place. Because I'm not a nigger. I am a man. But if you think I am a nigger, it means you need him…. If I'm not a nigger here and you, the white people invented him, then you've got to find out why.[10]

Baldwin's reproach of whites speaks beyond the boundaries of anti-black constructions. We can ask, too—why was it necessary to have a noble savage? Why was it necessary to have a foreign heathen? Moreover, why *is* it necessary to have an alien? A terrorist? A thug? Why must natives be disappeared into "the past"? Why so many conversations about racism that ignore so many deeply important truths? To be sure, these are not simply historical questions.

Racism in popular culture is paradoxical in some respects—simultaneously ubiquitous and yet so shrouded in white fantasies as to appear natural, unproblematic, even just. Indeed, white moral outrage over racism tends to be trapped in a "time-warp;" whites' willingness to acknowledge racism as "glaringly and appallingly wrong" reserved mostly for "the racism of other times and places," or people removed from

---

[10]From Baldwin's 1963 interview with Dr. Kenneth Clark for the public broadcast, "The Negro and the American Promise." Transcript available at: http://www.pbs.org/wgbh/americanexperience/features/bonus-video/mlk-james-baldwin/.

oneself. Meanwhile, racism "of our own place and time strikes us, if at all, as unexceptionable, trivial, or well within literary license;" so many "acquiesce in today's version with little realization… that a later generation will 'How could they?' about *us*" (Delgado and Stefancic 1992: 1278; Mueller and Issa 2016).

It would be false to claim popular culture "causes" racism—racism is generated, not strictly from ideas but from concrete, material relations between groups (Bonilla-Silva 2015; Feagin 2014). Nonetheless, under white supremacy, ideas—and the institutions and mediums through which ideas are circulated—become weaponized in support of domination. As such, the broad reach and capacity to circulate and nurture logics of white domination mark popular culture as inevitably political. As our analysis demonstrates, popular culture has been used to sustain many psychic and cognitive fantasies conducive to white supremacy (Bracey et al. 2017; Feagin 2013; Mills 1997). Toward that end, the controlling images circulated through popular culture do more than just rationalize commodifying, excluding, and hoarding resources from people of color; these white fantasies are essential to making white domination easier to execute and enjoy psychologically by helping white people hide the ways they collude in domination from themselves (Bonilla-Silva 2015; Mueller 2017).

Of course, if popular culture is not the "cause" of racism, it can neither be the "cure" (Delgado and Stefancic 1992). Nonetheless, we can do more than just resist oppressive representations and popular practices when they emerge. Looking to examples like #BlackLivesMatter, people of color and radical allies can weaponize popular culture and its mediums in even more liberation-driven ways. There is a long history of revolutionary cultures from which to draw—grounded in art, music, film-making, humor, and written narrative (Brown 2010; Deloria 2004; Kelley 2003; Perry 2004; White 1995; Womack 2013). They include artists, like Peele, who provide legitimating and pleasurable insider critiques of white supremacy (Harris 2017; Jones and Ware 2017a). They include voices who move from "behind the veil," to offer ideas and strategies for constructing healthy subjectivities disassociated from an internalized white gaze (Brown 2010; Jones and Ware 2017b). And perhaps most exciting, they include the freedom dreamers, who dare truly wild fantasies—about the selves and worlds that not yet are, but in a different, more just and humane world *could be* (Imarisha and Brown 2015; Kelley 2003).

Acknowledgements The authors extend special thanks to Glenn Bracey, Christopher Chambers, Sarah Gatson, Kishonna Gray, Katisha Greer, and Kristen Lavelle for support and helpful feedback. Dedicated to the late Hernán Vera—beloved scholar/teacher/activist. Direct correspondence to: Jennifer Mueller, Department of Sociology, Skidmore College, 815 North Broadway, Saratoga Springs, NY 12866. E-mail: jmueller@skidmore.edu.

References

Allen, T. W. (2012). *The invention of the white race* (2nd ed.). New York: Verso.

Baptist, E. E. (2014). *The half has never been told: Slavery and the making of American capitalism.* Philadelphia, PA: Perseus Books.

Barlowe, J. (2003). 'You must never be a misrepresented people': Spike Lee's Bamboozled. *Canadian Review of American Studies, 33*(1), 1–16.

Behnken, B. D., & Smithers, G. D. (2015). *Racism in American popular media.* Santa Barbara, CA: Praeger.

Bennett, L. (1997). *Forced into glory: Abraham Lincoln's white dream.* Chicago: Johnson Publishing Co.

Bergstrom, B. (2003, December 12). 'Ghettopoly' game called 'Racist'. *NBC New.* Retrieved October 1, 2016. (http://www.nbcnews.com/id/3158402/#. V88LuldWJg0).

Bogle, D. (2016). *Toms, coons, mulattoes, mammies, and bucks.* New York: Bloomsbury (New expanded 21st century ed).

Bonilla-Silva, E. (2015). More than prejudice: Restatement, reflections, and new directions in critical race theory. *Sociology of Race and Ethnicity, 1*(1), 75–89.

Bracey, G., Chambers, C., Lavelle, K., & Mueller, J. C. (2017). The white racial frame: A roundtable discussion. In R. Thompson-Miller & K. Ducey (Eds.), *Systemic racism: Making liberty, justice, and democracy real* (pp. 41–75). New York: Palgrave.

Britton, L. M. (2017, March 7). K-Pop Girl Group Mamamoo apologise after performing 'Uptown Funk' in blackface. *NME.* Retrieved April 1, 2017. http://www.nme.com/news/music/k-pop-girl-group-mamamoo-apologise-performing-uptown-funk-blackface-2005297.

Brock, A. (2009). Life on the wire: Deconstructing race on the internet. *Information, Communication & Society, 12*(3), 344–363.

Brock, A. (2012). From the blackhand side: Twitter as a cultural conversation. *Journal of Broadcasting & Electronic Media, 56*(4), 529–549.

Brown, K. (2014, September 23). The LA times covers corn rows, the hot new trend for white ladies. *Jezebel.* Retrieved June 20, 2016. http://jezebel.com/the-la-times-covers-cornrows-the-hot-new-trend-for-whi-1638168328.

Brown, K. N. (2010). *Writing the black revolutionary diva.* Bloomington, IN: Indiana University Press.

Brown, R. (2013, January 22). A battle for the best Chappelle's show sketch ever. *Grantland.* Retrieved March 15, 2017. http://grantland.com/features/a-battle-best-chappelle-show-sketch-ever/.

Calney, M. (1993, January 11). D. W. Griffith and 'The Birth of A Monster': How the confederacy revived the KKK and created hollywood. *The American Almanac.* Retrieved April 2, 2017. http://members.tripod.com/~american_almanac/griffith.htm.

Carbado, D. W. (2011). Critical what what? *Connecticut Law Review, 43*, 1593–1643.

Carrillo, K. J. (2003). Highly offensive: Karen Juanita Carrillo examines the ongoing currency of racist curios. Retrieved November 6, 2016. http://www.ferris.edu/news/jimcrow/links/newslist/offensive.htm.

Chaney, J. (2005, May 24). 'Chappelle's show': It's a celebration. *WashingtonPost.com.* Retrieved March 10, 2017. http://www.washingtonpost.com/wp-dyn/content/article/2005/05/23/AR2005052300794.html.

Clinton, C. (1982). *The plantation mistress.* New York: Pantheon.

Coleman, B. (2009). Race as technology. *Camera Obscura, 24*(1), 177–207.

Collins, P. H. (2009). *Black feminist thought.* New York: Routledge.

Daniels, J. (2013). Race and racism in internet studies: A review and critique. *New Media & Society, 15*(5), 695–719.

Delgado, R., & Stefancic, J. (1992). Images of the outsider in American law and culture: Can free expression remedy systemic social ills?" *Cornell Law Review, 77*(6), 1258–1297.

Deloria, P. J. (1998). *Playing Indian.* New Haven, CT: Yale University Press.

Deloria, V. (2004). Indian humor. In: L. Heldke & P. O'Connor (Eds.), *Oppression, privilege, and resistance* (pp. 611–625). New York: McGraw Hill.

DeVane, B. (2008). The meaning of race and violence in *Grand Theft Auto. Games and Culture, 3*(3–4), 264–285.

Doane, A. W. (2017). Beyond color-blindness: (Re)theorizing racial ideology. *Sociological Perspectives, 60*(5), 975–991.

Durham, A. (2015). _____ While black: Millennial race play and the post-hip-hop generation. *Cultural Studies ↔ Critical Methodologies, 15*(4), 253–259.

Epp, M. H. (2003). Raising minstrelsy: Humour, satire and the stereotype in *The Birth of a Nation* and *Bamboozled. Canadian Review of American Studies, 33*(1), 17–35.

Farley, C. J. (2005, May 15). On the beach with Dave Chappelle. *Time.com.* Retrieved March 10, 2017. http://content.time.com/time/arts/article/0,8599,1061415,00.html.

Feagin, J. R. (2013). *The white racial frame* (2nd ed.). New York: Routledge.

Feagin, J. R. (2014). *Racist America* (3rd ed.). New York: Routledge.

Florini, S. (2013). Tweets, tweeps, and signifyin' communication and cultural performance on 'Black Twitter'. *Television & New Media, 15*(3), 223–237.

Forman, T. A., & Lewis, Amanda E. (2006). Racial apathy and Hurricane Katrina: The social anatomy of prejudice in the post-civil rights era. *Du Bois Review, 3*(1), 175–202.

Fung, R. (2005). Looking for my penis: The eroticized Asian in gay video porn. In K. A. Ono (Ed.), *A companion to Asian American studies* (pp. 235–253). Malden, MA: Blackwell.

Gallagher, C. A. (2003). Color-blind privilege: The social and political functions of erasing the color line in post race America. *Race, Gender & Class, 10*(4), 22–37.

Ghettopoly. (2016). *Ghettopoly.* Retrieved August 15, 2016. http://www.ghettopoly.com.

Gray, K. L. (2014). *Race, gender, and deviance in Xbox live: Theoretical perspectives from the virtual margins.* Oxford: Routledge.

Green, R. (1988). The tribe called wannabee: Playing Indian in America and Europe. *Folklore, 99*(1), 30–55.

Hall, S. (2006). Encoding/decoding. In M. G. Durham & D. Kellner (Eds.), *Media and cultural studies* (pp. 163–173). Malden, MA: Blackwell.

Harris, A. (2017, March 7). How *Get Out* positions white womanhood as the most horrifying villain of all. *Slate.* Retrieved April 10, 2017. http://www.slate.com/blogs/browbeat/2017/03/07/how_get_out_positions_white_womanhood_as_the_most_horrifying_villain_of.html.

Hasbro, Inc. v. Chang, CA 03–482 T. (2006). *Report and recommendation.* Retrieved August 29, 2016. http://www.rid.uscourts.gov/menu/judges/opinions/martin/05302006_1-03CV0482T_MJM_HASBRO_V_CHANG_RR.pdf.

hooks, B. (2009). *Reel to real: Race, sex, and class at the movies.* New York: Routledge Classics.

Hughey, M. W. (2012). *White bound: Nationalists, antiracists, and the shared meanings of race.* Stanford, CA: Stanford University Press.

Hurt, B. (2006). *Beyond beats and rhymes.* Northampton, MA: Media Education Foundation.

Imarisha, W., Brown, A. M. (Eds.). (2015). *Octavia's brood: Science fiction stories from social justice movements.* Oakland, CA: AK Press.

Jewell, K. S. (1993). *From mammy to Miss America and beyond.* New York: Routledge.

Jenkins, H. (2006). Quentin Tarantino's Star Wars? Digital cinema, media convergence, and participatory culture. In M. G. Durham & D. M. Kellner (Eds.), *Media and cultural studies: KeyWorks* (pp. 549–576). Malden, MA: Blackwell Publishing.

Jones, F. (2013, July 17). Is Twitter the underground railroad of activism? *Salon*. Retrieved June 20, 2016. http://www.salon.com/2013/07/17/how_twitter_fuels_black_activism/.

Jones, R. Jr., & Ware, W. (2017a). Get the fuck outta here: A dialogue on jordan peele's *Get Out*. *Son of Baldwin*, February 27. Retrieved April 10, 2017. https://medium.com/@SonofBaldwin/get-the-fuck-outta-here-a-dialogue-on-jordan-peeles-get-out-831fef18b2b3.

Jones, R. Jr., & Law, W. (2017b). "Get the fuck outta here, the sequel: Further consideration of Jordan Peele's *Get Out*. *Son of Baldwin*, March 10. Retrieved April 10, 2017 (https://medium.com/@SonofBaldwin/get-the-fuck-outta-here-the-sequel-further-consideration-of-jordan-peeles-get-out-81c19658ebc5).

Kelley, R. D. G. (2003). *Freedom dreams: The black radical imagination*. Boston, MA: Beacon Press.

King, C. R. (2013). *Unsettling America: The uses of Indianness in the 21st century*. Lanham, MD: Rowman & Littlefield.

KOCCA (Korea Culture and Content Agency). (2003, February 25). Trouble bubbles up around pop group's look. http://www.kocca.or.kr/ctnews/eng/SITE/data/html_dir/2003/02/25/200302250128.html. Retrieved November 6, 2005.

Lee, R. (2012). Chinese American stereotypes in nineteenth-century minstrelsy. Pgs. 46–48 in *Major Problems in American Popular Culture*, edited by K. Franz & S. Smulyan. Boston, MA: Wadsworth.

Lieff Cabraser Heimann & Bernstein, LLP. (2017). Summary of the settlement of the Abercrombie & Fitch Class Action Lawsuit. *AF Justice*. Retrieved April 11, 2017. http://www.afjustice.com/.

Lott, E. (2013). *Love and theft: Blackface minstrelsy and the American working class*. New York: Oxford University Press. (20th Anniversary ed.).

Mills, C. W. (1997). *The racial contract*. Ithaca, NY: Cornell University Press.

Mitchum, P. (2017, March 10). *Get out* reminds us only we can save ourselves. *theGrio*. Retrieved April 17, 2017. http://thegrio.com/2017/03/10/get-out-reminds-us-only-we-can-save-ourselves/.

Morrissey, T. E. (2012, March 1). WTF is up with K-Pop and blackface?!" *Jezebel*. Retrieved April 12, 2017. http://jezebel.com/5889705/omg-wtf-is-up-with-k-pop–blackface.

Mueller, J. C. (2017). Producing colorblindness: Everyday mechanisms of white ignorance. *Social Problems, 64*(2), 219–238.

Mueller, J. C., & Issa, R. (2016). Consuming black pain: Reading racial ideology through the lens of cultural appetite for *12 Years A Slave*. In J. Smith & B. Thakore (Eds.), *Race and contention in 21st century U.S. Media* (pp. 131–147). New York: Routledge.

Nilsen, S., & Turner, S. E. (Eds.). (2014). *The colorblind screen*. New York: New York University Press.

Noriega, C. (2000). *Shot in America: Television, the state and the rise of Chicano cinema*. Minneapolis: University of Minnesota Press.

Obasogie, O. (2013). *Blinded by sight*. Stanford, CA: Stanford University Press.

Ochoa, J. (2003, January 29). Fightin' whites will donate scholarship money to UNC. *The Tribune*. Retrieved March 20, 2017. http://www.greeleytribune.com/news/local/fightin-whites-will-donate-scholarship-money-to-unc/.

Omi, M., & Winant, Howard. (2014). *Racial formation in the United States* (3rd ed.). New York: Routledge.

Pérez, R. (2016). Racist humor: Then and now. *Sociology Compass, 10*, 928–938.

Pérez, R. (2014). Brownface minstrelsy: 'José Jiménez', the civil rights movement, and the legacy of racist comedy. *Ethnicities, 16*(1), 40–67.

Perry, I. (2004). *Prophets of the hood*. Durham, NC: Duke University Press.

Pieterse, J. N. (1992). *White on black: Images of Africa and blacks in western popular culture*. New Haven, CT: Yale University Press.

Pilgrim, D. (2012). *Jim Crow Museum of racist memorabilia*. Retrieved October 30, 2017. http://www.ferris.edu/jimcrow/ .

Pitcher, B. (2014). *Consuming race*. New York: Routledge.

Riemer, N. J. (2016). New media and new possibilities: The online engagement of young black activists. In J. Smith & B. Thakore (Eds.), *Race and contention in 21st century U. S. Media* (pp. 41–56). New York: Routledge.

Riggs, M. T. (1987). *Ethnic notions*. Berkeley, CA: California Newsreel.

Rodriquez, J. (2006). Color-blind ideology and the cultural appropriation of hip-hop. *Journal of Contemporary Ethnography, 35*(6), 645–668.

Roediger, D. (2007). *The wages of whiteness*. New York: Verso. (new edition).

Rose, T. (2008). *The hip hop wars*. New York: Basic Books.

Rotten Tomatoes. (2017a). *Crash*. Retrieved March 31, 2017. https://www.rottentomatoes.com/m/1144992_crash.

Rotten Tomatoes. (2017b). *12 years a slave*. Retrieved March 31, 2017. https://www.rottentomatoes.com/m/12_years_a_slave.

Russell-Brown, K. (2008). *The color of crime* (2nd ed.). New York: New York University Press.

Shaheen, J. (2014). *Reel bad Arabs* (3rd ed.). Northampton, MA: Olive Branch Press.

Sheil, T, & Sheil, A. (2002). *The army men homepage*. Retrieved September 18, 2016. http://www.thortrains.net/armymen/armymen1.htm.

Smith, A. (2012). Heteropatriarchy and the three pillars of white supremacy. In E. Martínez, M. Meyer, & M. Carter (Eds.), *We have not been moved* (pp. 285–294). Oakland, CA: PM Press.

Smith, A. (2015). *Conquest: Sexual violence and American Indian genocide*. Durham, NC: Duke University Press.

Smith, J. (2016, May 2). The 'technique' of blackface. *Cyborgology*. Retrieved August 16, 2016. https://thesocietypages.org/cyborgology/2016/05/02/the-technique-of-blackface/.

Smith, J., & Thakore, Bhoomi (Eds.). (2016). *Race and contention in 21st century U.S. media*. New York: Routledge.

Strasburg, J. (2002, April 19). Abercrombie recalls t-shirts many found offensive. *San Francisco Chronicle*. Retrieved March 8, 2017. http://www.sfgate.com/cgi-bin/article.cgi?file=/c/a/2002/04/19/MN102999.DTL.

Strong, P. T. (2005). The mascot slot: Cultural citizenship, political correctness, and pseudo-Indian sports symbols. *Journal of Sport & Social Issues, 28,* 79–87.

Tawzer, A. (2009). Five and dime cowboys and Indians. *Plastic Soldier Review*. Retrieved September 18, 2016 (http://www.plasticsoldierreview.com/ShowFeature.aspx?id=50).

Tchen, J. K. W., & Yeats, D. (2014). *Yellow peril! An archive of anti-Asian fear*. New York: Verso.

Toll, R. C. (1977). *Blacking up: The minstrel show in nineteenth-century America. New* (edition ed.). New York: Oxford University Press.

Townsend, A. (2011, February 16). All-Time 100 greatest toys. *Time.com*, February 16. Retrieved September 18, 2016. http://content.time.com/time/specials/packages/article/0,28804,2049243_2048649_2049009,00.html.

Turner, P. A. (2002). *Ceramic uncles and celluloid mammies*. Charlottesville, VA: The University of Virginia Press.

The Washington Times. (2003, January 6). *Fighting whites inspire imitators*. Retrieved April 11, 2017. http://www.washingtontimes.com/news/2003/jan/6/20030106-010101-5452r/.

Vera, H., & Gordon, A. M. (2003). *Screen Saviors*. Lanham, MD: Rowman & Littlefield.

Vera, H., & Gordon, A. M. (2005). On How to Dissolve Racial Taboos. *Contexts, 3*(4), 68–69.

White, A. (1995). *The resistance: Ten years of pop culture that shook the world*. New York: Overlook Books.

White, A. (2013, October 16). Can't trust it. *City Arts*. Retrieved September 28, 2014. http://cityarts.info/2013/10/16/cant-trust-it/.

Wilkinson, D. Y. (1974). Racial socialization through children's toys: A sociohistorical examination. *Journal of Black Studies, 5*(1), 96–109.

Williams, A. (2016). On Thursdays we watch *Scandal*: Communal viewing and Black Twitter. In J. Daniels, K. Gregory, & T. McMillan Cotton (Eds.), *Digital sociologies* (pp. 273–293). Chicago, IL: University of Chicago Press.

Williams, A. (2017). Fat people of color: Emergent intersectional discourse online. *Social Sciences, 6*(1), 15–31.

Williams, A., & Gonlin, V. (2017). I got all my sisters with me (on black twitter): Second screening of *How to Get Away with Murder* as a discourse on black womanhood. *Information, Communication & Society, 20*(7), 984–1004.

Womack, Y. L. (2013). *Afrofuturism: The world of black sci-fi and fantasy culture*. Chicago: Lawrence Hill Books.

African American Families: History and Contemporary Forces Shaping Family Life and Studies

Amanda Moras, Constance Shehan and Felix M. Berardo

Contents

A. Moras (✉)
Department of Sociology, Sacred Heart University,
Fairfield, CT, USA
e-mail: morasa@sacredheart.edu

C. Shehan
Department of Sociology and Criminology & Law,
University of Florida, Gainesville, FL, USA
e-mail: cshehan@ufl.edu

F. M. Berardo
Emeritus Professor of Sociology, University of
Florida, Gainesville, FL, USA

6.1   Introduction

Any attempt to examine sociological and historical information regarding African American families is fraught with broad and controversial literatures. Much of this reflects a perspective that generally stressed the negative impacts of slavery on evolving Black family structures and relationships, often speaking of the alleged "demise" and "pathologies" of Black families. This perspective is largely reflective of culturally

© Springer International Publishing AG, part of Springer Nature 2018
P. Batur and J. R. Feagin (eds.), *Handbook of the Sociology of Racial and Ethnic Relations*,
Handbooks of Sociology and Social Research, https://doi.org/10.1007/978-3-319-76757-4_6

ociological analyses, and racism endemic ademic study and larger society. The literature emphasized here in turn questions and critiques these analyses, generally stressing the strengths of Black families, the complexities of slavery in the shaping and adaptation of family life, and the continued structural oppressions that shape these experiences. This work is not intended to be a definitive statement regarding the experiences of largely diverse groups of families, but instead a critical look at the structural forces that affect the lives of Black families and the systematic racism that informs public discourse about Black families and scholarship.

In crucial respects the experience and the development of African American families in the United States represent a sharp contrast to that of other racial and ethnic groups. The distinct historical circumstances that have impacted Black families have been unusually complicated and in some ways without parallel in comparison to other segments of our multiethnic, multiracial society. The unique experience of forced migration from Africa into a system of extended slavery, and continued systematic exclusion from major U.S. social institutions, coupled with a large history of institutionalized racism characterized by severe violence and oppression, are just a few of the factors that have significantly influenced the structure and well-being of Black families. Furthermore, the diversity of families has created heterogeneous communities in which histories and experiences vary with time, space, and conditions (Billingsley and Billingsley 1968). The contemporary experiences of Black families are intimately connected with the historical, economic, and social conditions encountered by generations past.

6.2 African American Families Under Slavery

In order to understand the continuing impact of historical factors on contemporary African American families, it is necessary to incorporate not only the impact of slavery but also the lasting effects of African family structure. African families represented largely diverse and complex backgrounds, characterized by "large multigenerational groupings of relatives built around a core group known as lineage" (Sudarkasa 1997). While the conditions of slavery largely restricted families from reestablishing and maintaining this heritage, evidence of large extended kin networks have been documented, reflecting the continued importance of extended households and lasting traditions of African culture in Black families (Sudarkasa 1997; Gutman 1976).

Until the 1970s, much of the existing scholarship assumed that slavery had destroyed African American culture and families. Perhaps more so than other immigrant groups, African Americans faced severe restrictions in efforts to reestablish and maintain the traditions of their heritage by conditions associated with the slave system. This disruptive process had its beginnings in Africa, where enslaved people were often separated from their families subsequent to being transported to North America. E. Franklin Frazier asserted that in this new environment slaves were discouraged, if not explicitly forbidden, from practicing traditional customs and forced to adopt the ways of slave owners. He claimed that over generations African heritage had become but a dim memory (Frazier 1966: 15). Since the time of Frazier's writing, however, scholars have challenged this assumption, highlighting how new forms of families were often developed as a social adaptation to difficult social conditions (Baca-Zinn and Eitzen 2001). Frazier largely underestimated and ignored the adaptability and complexity of Black family life under slavery. Gutman (1976) points out in his landmark work, *Black Family in Slavery and Freedom*, that to assume that "slave behavior was primarily a function of slave treatment" denies the historically derived values, customs, and cultures in enslaved Black communities.

The continued existence of families under slavery "was a most precarious existence," one that was constantly dependent on the economic interests of Whites and often supported only by the perseverance of the families themselves (Billingsley and Billingsley 1968: 65). Many circumstances of slavery made it extremely difficult to develop stable family systems. However, in spite of this, most slave communities were characterized by strong family ties and extensive kinship networks (Gutman 1976). Many social scientists have ignored firsthand accounts such as slave narratives that point to the primacy of family and kin in everyday life. Evidences of this centrality are reoccurring themes in works such as Harriet Jacobs, *Incidents in the Life of a Slave Girl*, and William Wells Brown, *My Life in the South*. In the autobiography *Incidents in the Life of a Slave Girl*, Harriet Jacobs repeatedly references her grandmother and other female kin as instrumental forces in her life and remembers her family's repeated attempts to buy her freedom.

Through extensive analysis of plantation and freedman bureau records and letters between families and kin, Gutman's (1976) work illustrated the prevalence of connected families during slavery. Although these families lacked legal protection, many slave families were two-parent households and intimate relationships were often long-lasting unions. "Developing Afro-American culture had at its core common adaptive slave domestic arrangements and kin networks and that enlarged slave communities emerged over time out of these adaptive kin arrangements" (36). While marriage among enslaved people was viewed by many plantation owners as uneconomical and, consequently, was often prohibited, there is evidence to suggest thousands of marriages were performed unofficially by friends, family, and kin, one example of such ceremony being "jumping over the broomstick" (Gutman 1976).

Even when such ties were established husbands and fathers were frequently sold or traded, leaving their wives and children behind. Slave-owners attempted to justify these separations, arguing that "family ties among slaves were either extremely loose or non-existent and that slaves were, therefore, indifferent to separation" (Hope Franklin 2000: 133). As Gutman has illustrated, this argument was false, evidenced by the great lengths many underwent to find and be reunited with family members, as well as the adaptations of family institutions that sustained families in hostile conditions (Gutman 1976; Hope Franklin 2000). Furthermore, enslaved African American men who were separated from their families were in some cases permitted to visit them frequently, thus enabling them to maintain family ties (Baca-Zinn and Eitzen 2001).

Of the approximately 60,000 African Americans who were not enslaved in 1798, 45% of them lived in families, almost 85% of which were headed by men and women (Billingsley 1992). Several factors contributed to this "overwhelming existence of stable patterns of family life." Among these are strong commitment to family among African American peoples and a "social, economic and political environment" (i.e., religious beliefs and economic opportunities) that encouraged the development of families (Billingsley 1992: 98).

6.3 Female-Headed Households: A Historical Perspective

Various scholars have attempted to trace the rapid increase of female-headed households among African Americans to the long-lasting system of slavery. Women did, and continue to, occupy foundational roles in families; however, they did so under extremely harsh conditions. They were frequently subjected to sexual violence and had to endure an enormous amount of backbreaking labor that fell upon all enslaved African people (Hooks 1981). Slavery was a highly gendered institution and the processes of oppression took significantly different forms for Black men and women. Images of Black women as sexually promiscuous were created out of and solidified by the institutionalized rape of Black women at the hands of White men. Furthermore, women's work was largely confined to the boundaries of the plantation keeping them within close proximity of oppressive "masters." Childbearing and rearing were central responsibilities (Gray White 1999) and often this fertility and sexuality was not under women's control (Hill-Collins 2004).

While the number of female-headed households during slavery was substantial, single parent families were not the dominant family type

(Gutman 1976). Women were much more likely to be married or in long-term relationships than their male counterparts, largely due to the vast sex ratio differences of men and women on plantations (Gray White 1999). Researchers who attributed supposed matriarchal structures in Black families to conditions under slavery failed to account for systematic historical data that pointed to the contrary (Burgess 1995). Moynihan's controversial work, The Negro Family: The Case for National Action, for instance, cited the legacy of slavery as the primary force in the disruption of Black families, creating a system of female-headed households that emasculated men and bred a "tangle of pathology." Scholars have since pointed out Moynihan's inaccurate use of historical data and racist assumptions (Gutman 1976; Billingsley 1973), noting that two-parent families were in the majority during slavery and following emancipation.

6.4　Emancipation and Black Families

Following emancipation, large numbers of people who had been previously enslaved sought to solidify their families. Many searched for relations that had been separated either by slavery or the war (Billingsley and Billingsley 1992: 118) and families sought to make their "marriages legal and children legitimate." In 1866, almost 20,000 African Americans in North Carolina who were formerly enslaved registered their marriages in legal records (Hope Franklin 1997: 7). During this period many communities also established formal educational systems for their children.

This period was characterized by various challenges for Black families (including the stabilizing of their families, the establishment of independent economic existences and of permanent social institutions that would represent their interests, as well as securing political liberty). Many found their lives under daily threat by the lack of the basic essentials for survival. Indeed: "For tens of thousands of Blacks, emancipation meant the freedom to die of starvation and

illness" (Billingsley and Billingsley 1968: 69). Due to conditions that prevailed following emancipation, the mother-child relationship became central in many newly "freed" families (Bernard 1966: 19–23).

The years immediately following emancipation seemed promising. During Reconstruction there were huge strides in political participation and economic security. The Thirteenth, Fourteenth, and Fifteenth Amendments abolished slavery, asserted Black civil rights, and guaranteed Black men the right to vote, respectively. Reconstruction, however, lasted only a short time as "a new reign of terror descended over the south which toppled the newly interracial governments, ended reconstruction, and fastened a system of servitude and subservience on the Africans that would last for nearly a century" (Billingsley 1992: 126). Southern White elites, often with the help of White Northerners and politicians, terrorized local reconstruction governments and African Americans. Many of the rights previously guaranteed were rescinded by state legislatures and congressional and judicial actions, not to be regained until the 1950s (Feagin 2000).

The period to follow was far from the racial equality many had dreamed emancipation would bring. The long-standing racial Apartheid of the United States has meant much more than separate and unequal facilities for Whites and Blacks. The Civil Rights Act of 1875 was declared unconstitutional by the Supreme Court in 1883, and the later established Plessey v. Ferguson statute of "separate but equal" was a decision that would shape the United States, and the well-being of Black families, for years to come. Black Codes, Jim Crow legislation, and legal segregation ensured racial inequality that continues to shape the discourse on and lived experiences of Black families. Poll taxes and grandfather clauses were used to deny Black men their right to vote. Polling stations would often be moved to new locations that were hidden from Black voters in an effort to disenfranchise the possible political power of Black communities (Hope Franklin 2000). Furthermore, following slavery, many Black families were promised land by the federal government, the famous "forty acres and a mule," however, few Black families were given this land, and those that were had it confiscated later. The plantation system was replaced by sharecropping systems, which did little to change the economic situations of many Black families (Feagin 2000).

Racism mandated the separation of Blacks and Whites in various spheres of social interaction. Southern states often accomplished this segregation and systematic exclusion through laws, while northern states enforced it largely through customs and traditions. Segregation placed Black families under extreme economic and social strain. Black schools and job opportunities were far from equal. Extremely dangerous working environments and poor pay exacerbated the racially hostile environment. The economic conditions following slavery locked many Black families into poverty, setting up past and present systematic exclusions from wealth and opportunity (Hill-Collins 2004), demonstrating how the historical and contemporary manifestations of institutionalized racism continue to affect the lives of Black families.

White violence took the place of legal slavery: over 3000 lynchings were recorded between 1882 and 1964 (U.S. Census Bureau 1975). Many rigorous historians place this number much higher, pointing out the number of undocumented cases and overall tendency to ignore and/or condone White violence toward Blacks (Wells-Barnett 1969). Over 200 anti-lynching bills have been shot down by Congress over the past 100 years, reflecting the complicity of the U.S. government in this violence. Rape was also used as a tool of racial violence and control. Whereas under slavery, the rape of African American women was a "property" dispute (if the rapist was not her "master"), "free" Black women did not even have this so-called protection. As Hill-Collins points out, "No longer the property of a few White men, African American women became sexually available to all White men … in a climate of violence that meted out severe consequences for either defending themselves or soliciting Black

male protection, Black women could be raped" (Hill-Collins 2004: 65).

6.5 Impact of Migration and Urbanization on Black Families

At the close of the Civil War, well over 90% of all African Americans were still located in the rural South. Beginning with emancipation, however, a pattern of geographic mobility was set into motion that ultimately was to have profound ramifications for family life as well as society. Up to the turn of the 20th century, the migration of ex-slaves was primarily to the towns and cities of the South. Thereafter this population shifted increasingly toward the North and to a lesser extent to the Midwest. In 1900, about 9 of every 10 African Americans still resided in the southern region. One hundred years after the end of the Civil War, only about 54% of African Americans were located there. Periodic failures in the southern economy, labor shortages and job opportunities in the North, the cataclysmic social changes produced by two world wars, racial prejudice and discrimination, and a host of other social forces provided the impetus for this massive redistribution of the Black population. However, since 1970, there has been a return of large numbers of African Americans to the South. It appears that this latest trend accelerated throughout the 1990s and into the 21st century (Stoll 2004; Frey 2004; U.S. Census 2011).

Two explanations have been given for the return of African Americans to the South. One emphasizes the role of deteriorating social and economic conditions in the North caused by deindustrialization and persistent discrimination. This was coupled with improvements in the social and economic climate of the South, including increased integration of schools, improved race relations, and increased capital investment and economic opportunities (Johnson and Brunn 1980). The other explanation for return migration emphasizes historically significant ties African Americans have had to the

South. Cromartie and Stack (1989) argue that Black Northerners, even those who were not born in the South, maintained strong ties to home communities in the region, sharing their connections with younger generations of their families. These kinship ties have been strong predictors of migration decisions.

It is important to note that the initial migration from the South was essentially a movement of millions of individuals and families from rural to primarily urban environments. Moreover, the steady stream of migration was overwhelmingly directed toward the large industrial and metropolitan centers of the country, particularly in the North. The movement of Black Americans to urban areas has been phenomenal, and they now constitute a majority of the population in several large metropolitan communities in the US (Stoll 2004; U.S. Census 2011).

Nearly all of the early migrants had little choice but to settle in the dilapidated housing of the deteriorated slums of the cities. The rapidly increasing numbers eventually overflowed into surrounding neighborhoods, met by both dismay and open antagonism among the White middle-class residents. Racial discrimination and exploitation in housing and employment subsequently produced a pattern of residential segregation that would increasingly Jock some Black families into urban ghettos for decades. However, since the 1970s, the residential patterns of blacks within urban areas have changed. The 2000 Census showed that in metropolitan areas with at least half a million residents, the proportion of African Americans who lived in the central cities declined from 66 to 61%. This has been accompanied by an increasing suburbanization prompted by a desire for home-ownership and pursuit of economic opportunities (Stoll 2004). More recent numbers suggest that while Black people continue to be more likely to live in a "largest principal city" (as defined by the US Census 20 largest US metropolitan areas) compared to other races, they have also experienced the largest decline of the proportion living in largest principal cities (U.S. Census 2011). Likewise, while micro- segregation within metropolitan areas is decreasing (micro-segregation), segregation between suburbs and these cities are increasing (macro-segregation) (Lichter et al. 2015).

6.6 Contemporary African American Families

From the initial adaptation of the African family system under the conditions of slavery to the rapid urbanization of a majority of the Black population, family life has undergone a constant process of change. While a long history of deprivation, segregation, and discrimination has taken its toll, commitment to family has remained strong. African American families have adjusted and shifted with fluctuations in societal conditions and social class (Billingsley 1992). While there have been outstanding professional, educational, and economic gains since the 1960s, institutionalized racism and structural inequality continue to leave many families in severely disadvantaged positions. 36.4% of all Black households have incomes of $50,000 or more; however, 26.2% of African Americans live under the poverty line (this proportion is 38.2% for Black children) compared to 10% of Whites (17% of White children) (U.S. Census 2011, 2015). 24% of Black men and 35% of Black women hold managerial or professional specialty positions, but the unemployment rate for Black people people is about twice that of Whites (BLS 2011). African American families suffer discrimination on both personal and institutional levels. Access to quality education, healthcare, and housing is repeatedly denied regardless of class. Racial profiling happens not only on our streets, but in our schools, re-creating a system of poverty that tracks Black children into the lowest classes and alienates their parents.

A large portion of the existing family research has reflected pervasive cultural biases. Black families are held to a cultural measuring stick in which White, hegemonic, middle-class, nuclear families are posed as the ideal (Hill 2005). Deviations from this norm are construed as maladjustments, and prescriptive research attempts to determine why some Black families have not assimilated into a two-parent nuclear family form. Over the past three decades, many critical scholars have called for the abandonment of a cultural deficiency model (Billingsley 1992; Stack 1974; Hill 2003). Baca-Zinn and Eitzen (2001) urge us to hold the diversity of families as the norm, and understand families within their larger social and economic contexts. When one family type is identified as normative, those who do not meet that standard, specifically families of color, are labeled as "backwards" and products of their "ethnically flawed lifestyles" (Baca-Zinn and Eitzen 2001). African American families are extremely diverse and do not represent a homogeneous experience. Ignorance of structural, economic, regional, and value differences within families has created inaccurate and overly simplistic images. In addition, the diversity of Black families across the Diaspora is often overlooked, assuming that all Black families share the experience of African Americans, or that all African Americans share the same history (Allen and James 1998).

Over the past 200 years the study of Black families has been "held hostage" by White researchers, consistently reinforcing the notion of inherently problematic families (Nobles 1997; Billingsley 1973). A complete analysis of the diverse and complex lives of African American families must acknowledge the reality of White racism and institutionalized oppression and its historical and contemporary effects on families and communities (Nobles 1997: 84). An analysis of oppression (one that constructs race, class, gender, and nation as intersectional forces) is integral to the understanding of Black families. Treating social class as "a fixed static system of social locations" or as "a passive backdrop for active family processes" neglects the active role social class plays in the formation of families' experiences. In addition, the gendered nature of families and state policies regarding families reflects intersectional realities not adequately understood by race or gender alone (Hill-Collins 1998). Therefore, the study of Black families requires a holistic perspective encompassing historical and ecological societal factors that guides us toward incorporating the influence of institutionalized racism.

6.7 Kinship Ties

The presence of extended families and kinship ties has historically been and continues to be a major foundation of African American families. Formal and informal kinship care has been an adaptive response to familial endangerment, poverty, racism and discrimination, potentially offsetting some of those effects through material and emotional support (Scannapieco and Jackson 1996; Garcia Coll et al. 1996; Jarrett et al. 2010; Stack 1974; Hill 2003). For instance, Jarrett et al. (2010) demonstrate the ways in which "network members share resources across households and assist one another with childcare and other domestic tasks to promote positive family functioning and well-being, despite individual and neighborhood impoverishment" (299). Three decades earlier, Stack (1974) similarly documented the importance of kinship ties in African American communities, describing the relationships between blood relatives, married kin, and close non-family ties. Familial networks provide invaluable resources to parents in poor communities. Transportation, housing, food, job contacts, emotional support, and childcare are among the types of support offered (Stack 1974). In an analysis of Meadowview, a small Black suburb in the Midwest, Hicks-Bartlett (2000) observed "loose, family-based networks that minimize risk and center on meeting immediate needs" (29). Billingsley (1992) also documented the presence of these networks as a strong basis for family unity. The diverse structures of African American families are not accidental; they are purposive adaptations to societal challenges. Extended kin networks have been documented for working-class families (McAdoo 1978), families living in poverty (Stack 1974), and middle-class families, contesting popular assertions that "with adequate income and security, racial and cultural characteristics no longer are salient" (McAdoo 1978: 775).

The primary characteristics of Black extended kin systems include geographical closeness of kin, a strong sense of familial obligation, fluid household boundaries exhibited by the willingness to absorb relatives, high familial interactions, and strong systems of mutual aid (Hatchett and Jackson 1999: 173). The varying types of kinship exchange reflect the diversity of African American families. This assistance from extended family members has various positive effects for families including increases in mother's optimism, decreases in maternal depressive symptoms, decreases in adolescent internalization of external problems, increases in maternal emotional support, decreases in "problem behavior," and increases in positive parenting practices (Taylor et al. 2008, 2014; Taylor 2015).

Kin networks continue to operate as support systems for Black families; however, recent studies suggest the prevalence of these networks is declining (Roschelle 1997; Jayakody et al. 1993). In her 1974 study, Stack reported high levels of exchange, in the forms of financial help, food, child care, and clothes. Jayakody et al. (1993) found that only one quarter of never-married mothers received financial assistance from kin, and less than one-fifth received child care. However, four out of five mothers received emotional support from their kin networks. Roschelle (1997) also found that support among Black and Latino families may be less prevalent than past social science literature has suggested. While she cites many possible causes for this, among the most persuasive is the continued poverty affecting disadvantaged families, which strains kin networks at times beyond repair. Seemingly contradicting studies have found that 9 out of 10 respondents report their families being very close or fairly close, and more than two thirds contacted their families every week and reported receiving help from their families (Hatchett and Jackson 1999). Likewise, Jarrett et al. (2010) find that all of the women in their research report some kind of resource sharing among kin networks. These resources often include tangible items such as food, clothing, housing, childcare, and transportation. Across this work, kin networks are neither static nor simplistic. As structural and institutional forces shift, the shape and frequency

and types of kin interaction may change based on resources and needs (Sarkisan and Gerstel 2004).

The inordinate degree of poverty that afflicts African American families threatens these systems. Public welfare and housing policies in the United States that discourage multigenerational households have directly influenced the rising numbers of isolated households (Sudarkasa 1999). Public assistance programs have been based on the assumption of the nuclear family as the ideal functioning unit. Therefore, policies intended to "help" economically disadvantaged Black families have disrupted large extended networks in an effort to force them to conform to White middle-class norms. For many families the only asylum are these networks, often placing stress on relatives who themselves might be poor. As the numbers of families in need increases, it becomes more difficult to meet the needs of everyone. In addition, public housing projects in urban communities have been designed with little regard for the long-term welfare and communal needs of its inhabitants (Barclay-McLaughlin 2000). Living in multigenerational households and maintaining large kinship networks provide protection for poor families. Unlike middle-class families, who can often absorb unexpected economic ebbs and flows, poor households often do not have large savings to pull extra cash from (Stack 1974).

Contemporary forms of kin networks can be traced to structures of African extended families (Sudarkasa 1999). Many distinctive features of those earlier patterns survived the American experience, continually manifesting themselves (Billingsley 1992). Sudarkasa (1999) emphasizes this "earlier structure of African extended families out of which it (kinship networks) evolved" (Sudarkasa 1999: 192). In these communities children were a shared responsibility and there were no illegitimate children (Scannapieco and Jackson 1996). Continuing today, African American children are disproportionately placed into kinship care in the social welfare system and are twice as likely as white children to be placed with relatives (Hill 2004).

6.8   Black Motherhood

Motherhood remains a central institution in African American communities (Hill-Collins 1990; St. Jean and Feagin 1998). Mothers have occupied an integral role in not only caring for families, but also in preserving of cultures and collective memories (St. Jean and Feagin 1998). The glorification of motherhood, however, often requires Black women to repeatedly push their needs behind the needs of all others. "Black motherhood as an institution is both dynamic and dialectical" (Hill-Collins 1990: 176). Women construct motherhood in a myriad of ways, from self-actualization to burdensome worry, often these constructions existing in the same communities or even within the same woman.

In spite of the importance of women in communities, negative imagery of motherhood permeates discussions of Black families. Images of overbearing women and castrated men lead to the false assumption that Black men are being emasculated by powerful Black women, placing the oppression of men onto the shoulders of women, ignoring the White supremacist, capitalist state that actually subordinates Black men and women based on a system of institutionalized racism (Hooks 2004). Therefore, this stereotyping of Black mothers supports patriarchal thinking; the achievement of family harmony could only be achieved by the triumph of men over women in the home. Hill-Collins (1990) also cites "the mammy, the matriarch, and the welfare queen" as oppressive images, tools that control perceptions about Black women's sexuality and fertility. These images subordinate women's roles, falsifying their experiences. These controlling images not only influence mainstream perceptions of Black motherhood and governmental polices; but also how Black mothers themselves navigate identity construction. For instance, in Dow's recent research with middle class Black mothers, she documents the strategies they use to reject and negotiate the assumptions of those around them (particularly white mothers), in regards to prevailing images of Black motherhood such as the "welfare queen" and the "strong Black woman" (Dow 2015).

There is little evidence to support Black women's dominance over Black men. While commonly referred to as matriarchal (the female dominance over males), Black families may be more accurately depicted as matrifocal, in which kin are held together through an extended line of women, grandmothers, mothers, and daughters (Dickerson 1995). "Other-mothers" (women who are not necessarily blood kin yet take on mothering roles), grandmothers, and community mothers are indispensable in the rearing of African American children. Women-centered networks based on kin and community have been central to the institution of Black motherhood.

6.9   Changing Patterns of Marriage, Fertility, and Household Living Arrangements Among African Americans

Since marriage rates, household living arrangements, and childbearing patterns have been at the center of many analyses of African American families, it is important to examine these in a broader context of family-related changes in the United States. A number of major trends have occurred in marriage and fertility patterns in the United States since the 1950s: an increase in the age at first marriage; an increase in non-marital cohabitation; high levels of divorce; lower levels of remarriage, and increased access to legal marriage for same-sex couples (Shehan 2016). The proportion of women who are married has declined among all racial and ethnic groups over this period. The decline has been most pronounced for Latinas and Black women. In the second decade of the 21st century, the racial-ethnic group with the lowest proportion married is African American (26%), in comparison to 56% among Asian Americans, 51% white women, and 43% Latinas (Cruz 2013).

The divorce rate in the US doubled between 1965 and 1980 but has remained stable at a slightly lower level since then. Trends in divorce vary by race and ethnicity. African Americans consistently have the highest rates of divorce, approximately 30 per 1000 married men and women (Payne 2014). The level of childbearing in the United States has declined since the middle of the 20th century, from an average of 3.6 children per woman to approximately two children per woman in 2012. This varies by race and ethnicity, however. Latinos aged 40–50 (considered the end of the child bearing period) had an average of 2.4 children, African American women had an average of 2.0 children over their life time, and white women, 1.8. Latinas were also the most likely to have three or more children (25.2%), whereas only 21.3% of African American had three or more children (Monte and Ellis 2014). The share of births to unmarried mothers increased substantially since 1980. The non-marital birth rate among white women in 1980 was 18.1 per every 1000 unmarried women, while among Black women it was 81.1 per 1000 unmarried women. In 2014, the rate was 29.3 per 1000 for unmarried white women and 71.4 per 1000 for unmarried Black women. However, the 2014 figures represent a six-year decline from the peak in 2007–2008. When the rate was 48.4 per 1000 unmarried white women and 71.4 per 1000 unmarried Black women (Hamilton et al. 2015). It's important to note that over the past 25 years, the majority of births outside of marriage among Latinas and white women have occurred within the context of a cohabiting relationship, whereas the majority of non-marital births to Black mothers have been to women who are not living with a partner (Manning et al. 2015).

In 2015, there were nearly 16.5 million African American households. Twenty-seven percent of those consisted of married couples. Another 6.3% consisted of cohabiting heterosexual couples. Twenty percent involved mothers with no partner present. When only those with children under 18 are Changes in marriage, divorce, and out-of-marriage births have also changed the living arrangements of children. In 1960, for instance, 91% of white children and 67% of African American children lived in two-parent homes. By 2015, this had decreased to 74 and 41%, respectively.

For many the rise of single-parent households has been a cause for alarm. Conservatives cite the dwindling numbers of nuclear families as evidence of deficient family values. High rates of divorce, unwed motherhood, and female-headed households have been identified as the social forces responsible for the supposed decline of the family (Hill-Collins 2008). As Stoll (2004) notes, these trends in family formation, especially the decline in marriage rates, suggest that there are macro-level forces that are influencing all racial groups. However, the question regarding causes of racial differences in American family formation patterns remains. A number of well-documented explanations for these differences have been advanced. One pertains to the long-lasting impact of slavery on African American families. A number of scholars have argued that slavery forced African Americans to adopt a variety of family forms, including extending the roles of more distant family members (Stevenson 1995; Morgan et al. 1993; McDaniel 1994). This reasoning has been extended to contemporary families by Stack (1974) and others (Blum and Deussen 1996), who argue that some poor and working-class African American women share a notion of community-based independence that emphasizes kin-based support networks and long-term partnerships with men, but not necessarily marriage.

Another explanation for the racial difference in marriage rates focuses on Black male marriageability. This argument holds that Black people are less likely than Whites to marry because of the increasing economic marginality of Black men. The decline in the manufacturing sector of the economy has resulted in job loss among African American men compounded by the effects of discriminatory hiring processes and hostile working environments. The fact that the marriage rate among Black families stabilized in the 1990s, a period of relative economic gain, provides some support for this hypothesis. Demographic factors have also been proposed as a contributor to the racial gap in marriage. Sampson (1995) and others (Guttentag and

Secord 1983) argue that an imbalanced sex ratio results in a shortage of Black men available for marriage. Higher mortality and incarceration rates among young Black men produce the sex ratio imbalance. Furthermore, both Black men and women in the United States also continue to suffer the effects of extreme and violent racism and stereotypes and White fear of Black men have created images of them as criminal and dangerous (Feagin 2000). Black men are repeatedly victims of police brutality and White violence. Disproportionate traffic stops, racial profiling, increased police presence in poor and/or Black areas, and the severe over-representation of Black men in the prison industrial complex are only a few of the manifestations of a racist criminal justice system. This extreme marginalization of Black men often forces Black women to assume central roles in Black communities and families. This violence however is not exclusive to Black men as Black women are also disproportionately victims of state violence and police brutality/harassment. As the highly publicized deaths of Sandra Bland, Rekia Boyd, and Korryn Gaines among others and the concurrent #sayhername movement emphasizes, Black women are also repeatedly victimized by the criminal justice system.

It is important to note how social institutions such as racism, economic deprivation, and social stratification shape families and their adaptive patterns. "Examining structural constraints requires that we have an understanding of how the larger social structure-a racist, patriarchal, capitalist system-affects those individuals and the choices available to them" (Elise 1995: 54). Family structure alone does not dictate the well-being of families although popular opinion describes single-mother homes-particularly those in African American communities: as detrimental.

As mentioned earlier, Moynihan's 1965 report is perhaps the most famous assertion of this negative image. In it he referred to Black families as "a tangle of pathology," citing Black mothers as the transmitters of this "culture of poverty."

"Black mothers were accused of failing to discipline their children, of emasculating their sons, of defeminizing their daughters, and of retarding their children's academic achievement" (Hill-Collins 1990). Although Moynihan's data and results have been largely contested, this thinking continues to permeate our public discourse (Dickerson 1995: ix).

This often discredits single mothers, characterizing them as social problems. Scholars and policymakers typically strategize about ways to "deal" with single mothers rather than how to empower them, which could have life-changing generative effects (Billingsley 1992). Those on all sides of the political spectrum, however, are concerned with the situations of children and parents in single-family households. Research has shown that children who grow up in single-parent households are more likely to drop out of school, have lower academic performance, have higher absentee rates, and are more likely to use drugs and alcohol or engage in other delinquent behaviors (Baca-Zinn and Eitzen 2001). While these negative outcomes have been consistently documented, the strategies geared toward bettering the life chances of parents and children differ. Some scholars and political pundits focus on the absence of men (i.e., 80% of all single-parent households are headed by women), others focus on structural stresses and differences in economic resources (Baca-Zinn and Eitzen 2001).

Although single-mother households may be father-absent, often there are other suitable male kin to serve nurturing roles for children. Extensive kin networks are often present in single-mother homes, absorbing part of the responsibilities of these families. African American families have adapted to the presence of single-mother homes, using extended family structures to provide economic and social support (Billingsley 1992). Rates of marriage or non-marriage exaggerate Black-White differences in union formation. When one considers both informal and formal unions, the race differences in the percentages of young women who have entered a union are reduced by about one-half (Seltzer 2000: 1250). Moreover, much of the rise in childbearing outside marriage can be attributed to childbearing in cohabiting unions. Likewise, there are large variations in female-headed households, which may include never-married, divorced, and/or widowed women (Sudarkasa 1999).

Cain and Combs-Orme (2005) found in their research of female-headed households that being a single mother did not predict poor parenting or parenting stress for Black women. Marital status and family structure were not found to be significant predictors of stress. Instead, poverty and the quality of parenting received by the mothers emerged as important variables: "the multigenerational or two-parent family is not necessarily an improvement over single motherhood ... A true commitment to strong families and healthy children begins with a focus on the debilitating effects of poverty in the African American Community" (Cain and Combs-Orme 2005: 34). 30.6% of female headed households are living under the poverty line (U.S. Census Bureau 2015). The urgency of single-mother families, therefore, is not that they are female-headed households; it is the poverty that accompanies being a single mother (Burgess 1995).

Likewise, living in a two-parent family does not safeguard children against poverty. True commitment to families requires critical analysis of the structural forces at work, and gendered racism. Heterosexist, racist, and sexist agendas of "getting" Black women married or molding Black families to fit a two-parent ideal that rarely exists is not a solution for empowering families. Ignorance of economic forces, access to opportunity, and institutionalized racism provide incomplete and inaccurate understandings of the difficulties facing families. For instance, given the median income of Black men in the United States, each two-child household would need to add three Black men to meet the median income of U.S. families, and four to be middle class (Elise 1995: 63). This statistic illustrates the true urgency of poor families.

6.10 The Rising Middle Class

In 1910, only 6% of African Americans were employed in census definitions of trade, professional, clerical work, or governmental service. By 1940, this percentage had only risen to 9% who were employed in either White collar or skilled blue collar labor. Following the civil rights laws of the 1960s, this percentage rose to 32%, demonstrating large growth among a once very small Black middle class (Feagin and Sikes 1994: 27). There is considerable diversity within this population, both in economic situations, and family structure and well-being. Billingsley and Billingsley (1968), for example, identified three strata within the middle classes: the upper middle class, the solid middle middle class, and the precarious lower middle class.

The majority of the Black middle classes are represented in lower middle-class occupations. In addition, because the appearance of a sizeable middle class is relatively new, they lack accumulated wealth. Patillo-McCoy (2000) documented the experiences and lives of several Black families in the middle-class neighborhood of Groveland. She identifies the many circumstances that make Black middle-class experience a racial and class specific reality, which may not be comparable to their White counterparts. They continue to live in largely segregated communities and retain cross-class kin and social ties. Many Black middle-class communities are in close proximity to poor neighborhoods, contrary to White middle-class neighborhoods that are often far removed from such disadvantaged lifestyles. For Middle class Black families who prefer to live in integrated neighborhoods, they on average, "actually live in neighborhoods that are about 60 and 30% white. On the other hand, middle class whites who prefer integrated neighborhoods (or who are more "comfortable" with them) live in neighborhoods that, on average, are only 10% black and 80% white (Adelman 2005: 225–226).

The areas where Black middle-class youth reside typically have higher poverty and crime rates and worse schools than White middle-class youth: "Socioeconomic status is complicated by the crosscutting reality of race, and the ways in which racial discrimination shapes neighborhood contexts" (Patillo-McCoy 2000: 99). Black middle-class families are perceived to have achieved the American dream, evidencing the disappearance of racism and possibility of class mobility, creating the false illusion that the United States has achieved racial equality (Feagin and Sikes 1994). This, however, ignores Black middle-class families' continued confrontations with racism on a daily basis regardless of class status. While their resources could secure quality education and housing, they continue to encounter severe racism when attempting to enter predominately White schools and neighborhoods. Navigating middle-class spaces challenges African American families with daily negotiations of race and racist encounters. Class mobility is usually accompanied by increased contact with large White populations; as a result, White racism is a daily experience for middle-class African Americans (Feagin and Sikes 1994; Allen 2012). In the 1960s, the federal government passed legislation outlawing housing discrimination; however, neighborhoods continue to be very segregated. The racial segregation of neighborhoods is not accidental or voluntary for African Americans. Feagin and Sikes (1994) found in their interviews with 209 middle-class African Americans that many had experienced blatant housing discrimination, ranging from the refusal of real estate agents to return their phone calls, to White homeowners slamming the door in their faces when they showed up to look at a property. Black children in White schools face their own burdens: "life for Black students in mostly White schools often means daily struggle and recurring crises … when Black students say "whiteness" is an omnipresent problem they are not just talking about color or racial identification. They are reporting being at sea in a hostile environment" (Feagin and Sikes 1994: 133). Black middle class students repeatedly encounter "racial micro-aggressions" including "pejorative views of intelligence, assumptions of deviance, and

differential treatment in school discipline" (Allen 2012: 186). African Americans in White middle-class workplaces are repeatedly reminded of "society's negative evaluation of their blackness" (1994: 185). White co-workers claim "reverse discrimination" when Blacks gain valuable positions; when in actuality Black workers continue to be paid less than their White counterparts.

Black middle-class families are also significantly less likely than white middle class families to reproduce middle-class status across generations (Issacs 2007) and may be more negatively affected by economic hardships such as parental job loss. For instance, while parental job loss is correlated with a decreased likelihood of obtaining post-secondary education, the association for Black children is three times as strong when compared to white children (Kalil and Wightman 2011). Residing in middle-class neighborhoods also restricts the growth of kin networks for many Black families. "US middle class family life is based on privatization-buying a big house so that one not need to cooperate with one's neighbors, or even see them" (Hill-Collins 1990: 182). As Hill-Collins points out, the American middle class participates in "the privatization of everything," from health clubs to education. This challenges the traditional value systems of working-class African Americans, making women-centered networks of other mothers and community mothers structurally arduous. In spite of this, many middle-class Black families continue to participate in networks of mutual help, often attributing their own mobility to extensive kin support. Extended family patterns are instrumental for the emotional well-being of African Americans across class lines, demonstrating their viability as cultural capital (McAdoo 1978). Daniel Tatum (1999) documented the importance of extended kin for middle-class families: "The family environment is the primary source of support and rejuvenation in the face of daily stress" (117). This support is especially important for Black families in White communities given the constant degradation of Blackness, and racism encountered in these White spaces.

Understanding these experiences requires intricate analysis of the dynamics of race and class that shape communities, families, and lives. While increased resources differentiate this experience from working-class and economically disadvantaged Black experiences, it is not comparable to that of the White middle classes. With some notable exceptions, Black middle classes have remained largely invisible in the study of families, creating a false monolithic picture of African American communities. Furthermore, mainstream portrayals of middle class African American families, for example, "The Cosby Show," downplay the continued importance of race and experiences of racism in the lives of Black middle-class families.

6.11 Conclusion

Nearly four decades ago, Billingsley (1973) surveyed the major social science scholarship in terms of its treatment of Black families in America, including the myths regarding these families present in the literature. It was clear from this survey that the body of Jay and empirical knowledge available up to that point "viewed the Black family as a pathological entity, emphasizing its weaknesses instead of its strengths." He contends that "no area of American life (is) more glaringly ignored, distorted, or more systematically devalued than black family life" (431). In subsequent decades, sociological research has moved ever so incrementally toward correcting this picture. The new revisionist scholarship now generally presents a more realistic and positive assessment of Black families, in terms of both their historical manifestations as well as their contemporary lives, and stresses the stability of the majority of Black families. The diversities within this family system as well as its strengths are now given much more prominence and help explain the survival of families in a hostile and racist environment.

There is little question that on a variety of indicators the educational and socioeconomic positions of Black families in society are rising. The expanding middle class is illustrative of this progress. However, Black families continue navigate the disparities of pervasive structural and institutional racism, reflected, for instance, in widespread residential segregation. We have noted some of these disparities, such as persistently high unemployment rates and extensive poverty. High infant mortality rates and high death rates continue to be realities for many economically disadvantaged Black families. Recent studies reveal that "African Americans are exposed to more stressful life events and chronic stressors; experience more traumatic events, especially those related to violence; and feel less sense of control and well-being than Whites; they also have a greater sense of alienation and mistrust" (Spalter-Roth et al. 2005: 7). Such conditions clearly pose difficulties for maintaining the health and welfare of today's families. As these authors note: "Reducing poverty, integrating neighborhoods, raising educational levels, and reducing prejudice would improve the likelihood of healthier and longer lives for minority groups" (2005: 11). Black Lives Matter activists and related movements are likewise confronting the myriad of ways that state sponsored violence against people of color continues to manifest through police violence and the larger criminal justice system. BLM is a continuation of a long history of activism among Black communities to challenge oppression and marginalization. Black families and their testimonies have been central to the activism of BLM as partners, fathers, mothers, children and extended kin work to bring often ignored violence against Black people to the center of our national conversation regarding policing and the criminal justice system.

Furthermore, as discussed here, many family researchers remain largely ignorant of the experiences of families of color. In order to develop truly inclusive family studies, we must entirely reformulate how we think about, research, and teach about families. Black families and other families of color remain largely isolated to special topic weeks on race and are rarely studied for their contributions to families in general. Ignorance of the diversity and complexities of families has various manifestations and consequences for academic disciplines as a whole, and reinforces and recreates a system of racial exclusion. The urgency of this project is clear, and it begins with an honest and critical analysis of how racism and White supremacy continue to inform how we conceptualize families.

References

Adelman, R. M. (2005). The roles of race, class, and residential preferences in the neighborhood composition of middle-class Blacks and Whites. *Social Science Quarterly, 86*(1), 209–228.

Allen, Q. (2012). "They think minority means lesser than": Black middle class sons and fathers resisting microaggressions in the school. *Urban Education, 48* (2), 171–197.

Allen, W. R., & James, A. D. (1998). Comparative perspectives on Black family life: Uncommon explorations of a common subject. *Journal of Comparative Family Studies, 29*, 1–12.

Baca-Zinn, M., & Eitzen, D. S. (2001). *Diversity in families*. Boston, MA: Allyn & Bacon.

Barclay-McLaughlin, G. (2000). Communal isolation: Narrowing pathways to goal attainment and work. In S. Danziger, & A. Chih Lin (Eds.), *Coping with poverty: The social contexts of neighborhood, work, and family life in the African American community*. Ann Arbor, MI: University of Michigan Press.

Bernard, J. (1966). *Marriage and family among Negroes*. Englewood Cliffs, NJ: Prentice Hall.

Billingsley, A. (1973). Black families and White social science. In J. Ladner (Ed.), *The death of White sociology*. New York, NY: Random House.

Billingsley, A. (1992). *Climbing Jacob's ladder: The enduring legacy of African American families*. New York: Simon and Schuster.

Billingsley, A., & Billingsley, A. T. (1968). *Black families in White America*. Englewood Cliffs, NJ: Prentice Hall.

Blum, L. M., & Deussen, T. (1996). Negotiating independent motherhood: Working-class African American women talk about marriage and motherhood. *Gender and Society, 10*, 199–211.

Burgess, N. J. (1995). Female-headed households in a socio-historical perspective. In B. Dickerson (Ed.), *African American single mothers: Understanding their lives and families*. Thousand Oaks, CA: Sage.

Cain, D. S. & Combs-Orme, T. (2005). Family structure effects on parenting stress and practices in the African American family. *Journal of Sociology and Social Welfare, 32*(2), 19–40.

Cromartie, J. & Stack, C. B. (1989). Reinterpretation of Black return and Nonreturn migration to the South 1975–1980. *Geographical Review, 79*(3), 297–310.

Cruz, J. (2013). Marriage: More than a century of change (FP-13-13). National Center for Family & Marriage Research. Retrieved from http://ncfmr.bgsu.edu/pdf/familyprofiles/file131529.pdf.

Daniel Tatum, B. (1999). *Assimilation blues: Black families in White communities, who succeeds and why?*. New York, NY: Basic Books.

Dickerson, B. (1995). *African American single mothers: Understanding their lives and families*. Thousand Oaks, CA: Sage.

Dow, D. M. (2015). Negotiating "The welfare Queen" and "The strong Black Woman": African American middle-class mothers' work and family perspectives. *Sociological Perspectives, 58*(1), 36–55.

Elise, S. (1995). Teenaged mothers: A sense of self. In B. Dickerson (Ed.), *African American single mothers: Understanding their lives and families*. Thousand Oaks, CA: Sage.

Feagin, J. (2000). *Racist America*. New York, NY: Routledge.

Feagin, J., & Sikes, M. P. (1994). *Living with racism: The Black middle-class experience*. Boston, MA: Beacon Press.

Frazier, E. Franklin. (1966). *The Negro family in the United States*. Chicago, IL: University of Chicago Press.

Frey, W. H. (2004). *The new great migration: Black Americans' return to the South, 1965–2000*. Washington, DC: Center on Urban and Metropolitan Policy, The Brookings Institute.

Garcia Coll, C. T., et al. (1996). An integrative model for the study of developmental competencies in minority children. *Child Development, 67*, 1891–1914.

Gray White, D. (1999). *Aren't I a woman? Female slaves in the plantation South*. New York NY: W.W Norton & Co.

Gutman, H. G. (1976). *Black family in slavery and freedom, 1750–1925*. New York, NY: Pantheon Books.

Guttentag, M., & Secord, P. F. (1982). *Too many women? The sex ratio question*. Beverly Hills, CA: Sage Publications. 1983.

Hamilton, B. E., Martin, J. A., Osterman, M. J. K., et al. (2015). Births: Final data for 2014. *National Vital Statistics Reports, 64*(12), 1–64.

Hatchett, S. J., & Jackson, J. S. (1999). African American extended kin systems: An empirical assessment in the national survey of Black Americans. In H. P. McAdoo (Ed.), *Family ethnicity: Strength in diversity*. Thousand Oaks, CA: Sage.

Hicks-Bartlett, S. (2000). Between a rock and a hard place: The Labyrinth of working and parenting in a poor community. In S. Danziger & A. Chih Lin (Eds.), *Coping with poverty: The social contexts of neighborhood, work, and family life in the African American community*. Ann Arbor, MI: University of Michigan Press.

Hill, R. (2003). *The strengths of Black families*. Lanham, MD: University Press of America.

Hill, R. B. (2004). Institutional racism in child welfare. In J. Everett, S. Chipungu, & B. Leashore (Eds.), *Child welfare revisited* (pp. 57–76). New Brunswick, NJ: Rutgers University Press.

Hill, S. A. (2005). *Black intimacies: A gender perspective on families and relationships*. Walnut Creek, CA: Altmira Press.

Hill-Collins, P. (1990). *Black feminist thought: Knowledge, consciousness, and the politics of empowerment*. New York, NY: Routledge.

Hill-Collins, P. (1998). Intersections of race, class, gender and nation: Some implications for Black family studies. *Journal of Comparative Family Studies, 29*, 27–35.

Hill-Collins, P. (2004). *Black sexual politics*. New York, NY: Routledge.

Hooks, B. (1981). *Ain't I a Woman*. Boston, MA: South End Press.

Hooks, B. (2004). *We real cool: Black men and masculinity*. New York, NY: Routledge.

Hope Franklin, J. (1997). African American families: A historical note. In H. P. McAdoo (Ed.), *Black families*. Thousand Oaks, CA: Sage.

Hope Franklin, J. (2000). *From slavery to freedom: A history of African Americans*. New York: Alfred A. Knopf.

Issacs, J. B. (2007). *Economic mobility of Black and White families*. Washington DC: The Brookings Institute.

Jarrett, R. L., Jefferson, S. R., & Kelly, J. N. (2010). Finding community in family: Network effects and African American kin networks. *Journal of Comparative Family Studies, 41*(3), 299–328.

Jayakody, R., Chatters, L. M., & Taylor, R. J. (1993). Family support to single and married African American mothers: The provision of financial, emotional, and child care assistance. *Journal of Marriage and Family, 55*(2), 261–276.

Johnson, J. H., & Brunn, S. D. (1980). Spatial and behavioral aspects of the counterstream migration of blacks to the South. In S. D. Brunn & J. O. Wheeler (Eds.), *The American metropolitan system: Present and future* (pp. 59–75). New York, NY: Wiley.

Kalil, A., & Wightman, P. (2011). Parental job loss and children's educational attainment in Black and White middle class families. *Social Science Quarterly, 92*(1), 57–78.

Lichter, D. T., Parisi, D., & Taquino, M. C. (2015). Toward a new macro-segregation? Decomposing segregation within and between Metropolitan cities and suburbs. *American Sociological Review, 80*(4), 843–873.

Manning, W. D., Brown, S. L., & Stykes, B. (2015). Trends in births to single and cohabiting mothers, 1980–2013 (FP-15-03). National Center for Family & Marriage Research. Retrieved from http://www.bgsu.edu/content/dam/BGSU/college-of-arts-and-sciences/NCFMR/documents/FP/FP-15-03-birthtrends-singlecohabitingmoms.pdf.

McAdoo, H. P. (1978). Factors Related to Stability in Upwardly Mobile Black Families. *Journal of Marriage and Family, 40*, 761–776.

McDaniel, A. (1994). Historical racial differences in living arrangements of children. *Journal of Family History, 19*, 55–77.

Monte, L. M., & Ellis, R. R. (2014). *Fertility of women in the United States: June 2012, Current Population Reports, P20-575*. Washington, DC: U.S. Census Bureau.

Morgan, S. P., Antonio, M., Miller, A. T., & Preston, S. H. (1993). Racial differences in household and family structure at the Turn of the Century. *American Journal of Sociology, 98*(4), 799–828.

Nobles, W. N. (1997). African American family life: An instrument of culture. In H. P. McAdoo (Ed.), *Black families*. Thousand Oaks, CA: Sage.

Patillo-McCoy, M. (2000). Negotiating adolescence in a black middle class neighborhood. In S. Danziger & A. Chih Lin (Eds.), *Coping with poverty: The social contexts of neighborhood, work, and family life in the African American community*. Ann Arbor, MI: University of Michigan Press.

Payne, K. K. (2014). Divorce rate in the U.S., 2013 (FP-14-17). National Center for Family & Marriage Research. Retrieved from http://www.bgsu.edu/content/dam/BGSU/college-of-arts-and-sciences/NCFMR/documents/FP/FP-14-17-divorcerate-2013.pdf.

Roschelle, A. (1997). *No more kin: Exploring race, class, and gender in family networks*. Thousand Oaks, CA: Sage.

Sampson, R. J. (1995). Unemployment and imbalanced sex ratios: Race-specific consequences for family structure and crime. In Tucker, M. Belinda & Mitchell-Kernan, Claudia, (Eds.), *The decline in marriage among African Americans: Causes, consequences and policy implications*. New York, NY: Russell Sage Foundation.

Sarkisan, N., & Gerstel, N. (2004). Kin support among Blacks and Whites: Race and family organization. *American Sociological Review, 69*(6), 812–837.

Scannapieco, M., & Jackson, S. (1996). Kinship care: The African American response to family preservation. *Social Work, 41*(2), 190–196.

Seltzer, J. (2000). Families formed outside marriage. *Journal of Marriage and the Family, 62*, 1247–1268.

Shehan, Constance L. (2016). "United States, Families In," pp. In C. L. Shehan (Ed.), *The Wiley Blackwell Encyclopedia of family studies, Volume IV: Q-Z* (pp. 2006–2012). Malden, MA: Wiley.

Spalter-Roth, R., Lowenthal, T. A., & Rubio, M. (2005). Race, ethnicity and the health of Americans. ASA Series on How Race and Ethnicity Matter.

St. Jean, Y., & Feagin, J. (1998). *Double burden: Black women and everyday racism*. New York, NY: M.E. Sharpe.

Stack, C. (1974). *All our kin*. New York, NY: Harrer & Row.

Stevenson, B. E. (1995). *Black family structure in colonial and Antebellum Virginia: Amending the revision African Americans causes, consequences and policy implications.* New York, NY: Russell Sage Foundation.

Stoll, M. A. (2004). *African Americans and the color line.* New York: Russell Sage Foundation. Washington, DC: Population Reference Bureau.

Sudarkasa, N. (1997). African American families and family values. In H. P. McAdoo (Ed.), *Black families.* Thousand Oaks, CA: Sage.

Sudarkasa, N. (1999). African American Females as Primary Parents. In H. P. McAdoo (Ed.), *Family ethnicity: Strength in diversity.* Thousand Oaks, CA: Sage.

Taylor, R. D. (2015). Kin social undermining, adjustment and family relations among low-income African American mothers and adolescents: Moderating effects of kin social support. *Journal of Child and Family Studies, 24,* 1271–1284.

Taylor, R. D., Seaton, E., & Dominquez, A. (2008). Kinship support, family relations and psychological adjustment among low-income African American mothers and adolescents. *Journal of Research on Adolescence, 18,* 1–22.

Taylor, R. D., et al. (2014). Family financial pressure and maternal and adolescent socioemotional adjustment: Moderating effects of kin social support in low income African American families. *Journal of Child and Family Studies, 23,* 242–254.

U.S. Census. (2011). *Child poverty in the United States 2009 and 2010: Selected Race Groups and Hispanic Origin. American Community Survey Briefs.* Washington, DC: U.S. Government Printing Office.

U.S. Census. (2015). *Income and poverty in the United States: 2014, current population reports.* Washington, DC: U.S. Government Printing Office.

U.S. Census Bureau. (1975). *Historical statistics of the United States, Colonial Times to 1970, Bicentennial Edition, Part 2.* Washington, DC: U.S. Government Printing Office.

U.S. Census Bureau. (2011). *The Black population: 2010.* Washington, DC: U.S. Government Printing Office.

U.S. Census Bureau (2015). Current Population Survey, March and Annual Social and Economic Supplements, 2015 and earlier. Source of 1960 data: U.S. Bureau of the Census, 1960 Census of Population, PC(2)-4B, "Persons by Family Characteristics," tables 1 and 19.

Wells-Barnett, I. B. (1969). On lynching: Southern horrors, a red record, Mob Rule in New Orleans. New York.

Race and Ethnicity in the Labor Market; Changes, Restructuring, and Resistance 2000–2014

7

Roberta Spalter-Roth

Contents

7.1   Introduction

The labor market consists of a set of arrangements with employers ranking workers in terms of preferences and characteristics and workers trying to obtain the best jobs they can. The results of the ranking and sorting process have been described in metaphorical terms as a "job queue"—a line in which jobs are ranked by workers from best to worst, and workers are ranked from best to worst by employers (Reskin and Roos 1990; Stainback and Tomaskovic-Devey 2012). In a perfectly competitive labor market, according to neo-classical economic theory, those who buy labor and those who offer their labor for sale would have perfect information, employers would find the employee they want at the wages they want to pay, and workers would find jobs at the wages they are willing the accept. Unemployment would be inconsequential. In theory, this ideal market is "race blind" because it is costly for employers to discriminate, at least in the long run (Becker 1971).

With the assistance of Justin Lowery, State University of Plattsburg; Hank Leland, Independent Researcher.

R. Spalter-Roth (✉)
Center for Social Science Research, George Mason University, Fairfax, VA, USA
e-mail: rspalter@gmu.edu

© Springer International Publishing AG, part of Springer Nature 2018
P. Batur and J. R. Feagin (eds.), *Handbook of the Sociology of Racial and Ethnic Relations*,
Handbooks of Sociology and Social Research, https://doi.org/10.1007/978-3-319-76757-4_7

In this chapter, we argue that this process is *not* race, ethnicity, or gender blind. The neo-classical model does not explain the racial dynamics of the complex ranking and sorting process. Employers (and secondarily, employees) bring a set of assumptions, stereotypes, preferences, and discriminatory practices to the process (Bobo and Suh 2000; Feagin and Sikes 1994; Hamilton et al. 2011; Tomaskovic-Devey 2016). Nor is this process the result of an unseen hand that determines which workers get jobs and whether they move ahead with their careers. Instead, the labor market consists of a set of employer practices including hiring, firing, integrating or segregating jobs and workers, outsourcing functions or keeping them in house, and union busting (Appelbaum et al. 2006; Weil 2014). In their turn, workers bring a multiplicity of different kinds of attributes, skills, credentials, preferences, networks, and information to the process. Employers prefer some of these attributes, skills, and credentials to others, because they are considered to be proxies for productivity, profits, or ability to fit in. Key indicators and studies show that race and ethnicity play significant roles in determining rates of unemployment, job placement, career opportunities, and wages (Darity et al. 1997; Hamilton et al. 2011; Spalter-Roth and Lowenthal 2005; Stainback and Tomaskovic-Devey 2012). Employers also discriminate based on race, ethnicity, and gender, even when other factors such as education are similar (Hamilton et al. 2011). Whether a person is looking for a job, seeking a promotion, or considering a new line of work, race and ethnicity constrain individual choices and affect chances of success.

The purpose of this chapter is, first, to describe the workings of the labor market queue using data from the 2000 Decennial Census and the 2014 American Community Survey. It examines the outcomes of employer practices and worker efforts during this period before and after the Great Recession of 2008. The chapter updates a previous one on race and ethnicity in the labor market prior to the Great Recession (Spalter-Roth 2007). The recession resulted in substantially higher rates of unemployment and increasingly flat wages, while on-going processes including globalization, deregulation, technological innovation, growth of part-time and contract labor, and increased opposition to collective bargaining continued to grow. In addition, an increasingly diverse labor force that can compete with one another or be pitted against each other likewise continued to occur. With these processes came a growing gap between "good jobs and bad jobs" (Kalleberg 2011; Kalleberg et al. 2000; Weil 2014).

The major research question is whether this 14-year time-period, pre and post-recession, resulted in changes in the position in the queue, especially for racial, ethnic, and gender groupings. Did the relative positions for workers or jobs appear to change during this period or did positions in the queue remain unchanged? During this period were employers successful in restructuring labor market and occupation participation to meet their desires for a lower-wage, flexible workforce? How did workers attempt to stave off these changes or adapt to them? The chapter has two parts. The first describes the changes in the outcomes of the ranking and sorting process over time in terms of several key indicators, including employment and unemployment, occupational segregation, and earnings. The second part of the chapter attempts to understand how employer practices and worker strategies affect positions in the queue. Employer practices can include discrimination, restructuring firms, outsourcing or offshoring, emphasizing soft skills, and union-busting. Worker strategies can include increasing education and skills, using family or social connections, maintaining ethnic enclaves, using political or social pressures, and efforts at collective bargaining. Employers have much greater power in structuring the queue, yet workers do have strategies to try to obtain the jobs they want at wages, which are acceptable. Although this chapter updates an earlier one (Spalter-Roth 2007), it includes some of the literature from the 1980s and 1990s, when the analysis is still pertinent, as well as new literature. It ends with a summary and discussion of findings.

7.2 How It Works

The workers who go to the front of the queue versus workers that stay at the back is based largely on employers' views as to who is the best available employee and whether the most profit is made from hiring them. For example, employers may hire workers with H-1B visas rather than U.S. workers because they have needed skills and cost less (Fernandez and Castilla 2001; North 2011; Reskin 1998; Reskin and Roos 1990; Stainback and Tomaskovic-Devey 2012). These practices, occurring within firms, stratify workers of different races, ethnicities, and genders, workers with a wide variety of skills and credentials, and workers with differential access to information; and better or worse networking connections (Huffman and Cohen 2004; Hum 2000; Stainback and Tomaskovic-Devey 2012).

Research suggests that, as a result of the continuing shift from a manufacturing-based economy, the increases in deregulation, outsourcing, employers increasing prefer both cognitive skills and soft skills to physical skills (Holzer and Ihlanfeldt 1996; Moss and Tilly 1995; Murname, Willet, and Levy 1995). Further, the growth of contingent workers has resulted in the growth of "bad jobs" (Burtless 1990; Kalleberg 2011). Other desirable factors, from the employer's perspective, include compatibility, looks, ability to fit in as a team player, ability to socialize, manners, star power, and place of residence. All of these are mediated by race, ethnicity, and gender discrimination (Boushey and Cherry 2000; Conrad 2000; Feagin and Sikes 1994; Huffman and Cohen 2004; Kirschenman and Neckerman 1991; Moss and Tilly 1995; Tomaskovic-Devey 1993). In addition, employers often have the power to decide what counts as skills for a given job along with which skills they prefer. These choices can result in unequal working conditions, benefits, wages and opportunities (Appelbaum et al. 2006). Along with the decline of manufacturing, the regulatory environment had changed as the Reagan Administration, and now the Trump administration, push for deregulation and decline to support affirmative action. During the period covered by this chapter, the gap between white and black workers in terms of employment, unemployment, and occupational participation did not decrease. According to research by Stainback and Tomaskovic-Devey (2012), the increase of Hispanics in the labor market had the effect of increasing rather than decreasing this gap.

Within this changing environment, workers tried to get the best jobs they could and not to fall back in the queue. Relatively few adults have the option of not offering their labor to the market, although the offer can be refused. Resources from other family members may allow them to have some control over hours of work, if such flexibility is available from employers. The erosion of job privileges, control over work, and pay pushes a job lower down the queue while high rates of unemployment may make previously spurned jobs, including contract and part-time jobs, more desirable (Kalleberg 2011; Weil 2014). If jobs at the top vanish, then preferred groups can have "bumping rights" while those at the bottom are more likely to face unemployment (Conrad 2001; King 1992; Lichter and Oliver 2000; Reskin and Roos 1990; Waldinger 1996).

Often the ranking of people and jobs is a joint process. Jobs may lose prestige, pay, and autonomy, as Blacks, Hispanics, or immigrants fill jobs (Huffman and Cohen 2004). Nonetheless, particular groups may gain a niche in these less desirable jobs as information about job openings are passed through ethnic or racial networks (Bankston 2014; Hum 2000; Lim 2001; Waldinger 1996). Although skills are important in this process, some qualified workers are unemployed or have a "future of lousy jobs" (Burtless 1990) because they are not part of networks and never hear about the good jobs. Alternatively, some unqualified workers get good jobs, often because of familial or neighborhood contacts (DiTomaso 2013; O'Regan and Quigley 1993). Whites are the most likely to have contacts, although they frequently deny that they are hired on grounds other than merit (DiTomaso 2013). As we will see, between 2000 and 2014, blacks were twice as likely as whites to be unemployed, were segregated into fewer occupations, and paid less well, even though both black and white workers lost some desirable positions during this period. At the same, time both Hispanics and Asians have increased their labor force participation. In the past, the racial gap between blacks and whites narrows slightly in good times and increases slightly in bad times, but generally remains relatively invariant (Spriggs and Williams 2000). This relative invariance appears to be the case during the period we examine, although there was restructuring of the labor force.

7.3 Outcomes of the Queueing Process: Employment and the Division of Labor by Race, Ethnicity, and Gender

National employment statistics reflect the outcomes of the queuing process. These statistics show who is employed, who is unemployed, who works in what occupations, and who obtains what level of wages. These measures are surrogates for higher or lower status, greater or lesser control over their own and others' work, better or worse opportunities for upward mobility and job security, and higher or lower wages for different racial and ethnic groups (Spalter-Roth and Lowenthal 2005).

7.3.1 Labor Force Participation

In 2000, white men, age 16 and over, had the highest rate of labor force participation (including both employed and unemployed workers who were looking for jobs), followed by Asian men and Hispanic men (see Table 7.1). Black men had the lowest rate of labor force participation (lfp) of all men. Black women had a similar rate to black men. In all other cases, women had lower rates of labor force participation than men did, with Hispanic women having the lowest rate and Asian women the highest. White men also had the highest employment rate, with 68% in jobs during the reporting week. In strong contrast, only about half of black men had

jobs during the reporting period, with a 10% gap between their lfp and their employment rate. Black, white, and Asian women clustered at about 50%, with Hispanic women least likely to be employed. With the exception of white women (at 2.6%), white men's unemployment rate (at 3.3%) was the lowest. The unemployment rate of black men was, as it has been historically, more than twice that of white men. As was the case with white women, black women's unemployment rate was somewhat lower than that of their male same-race colleagues. Unemployment rates for Asians were higher than that of Hispanics in 2000. The basic pattern of the employment queue in 2000 showed that white men were at the top of the queue with Hispanic women and the bottom, although black men and black women closely followed Hispanic women.

By 2014, there were some significant changes in these patterns and some invariance. White men's lfp declined from 72.2 to 69.6%. During this period, the lfp rate of Hispanic men and Asian men increased so that their participation in the labor force was higher than that of white men. The lfp rate of Hispanic women increased as did that of black women. White women's lfp rate stayed relatively stable. Black men showed slight increases in labor force participation, but their rates were the lowest among men. Therefore, the pattern for black men remained relatively invariant during this period. By 2014, white men no longer had the highest rate of employment (at 64.2%), with the employment rate of Hispanic men about five points higher than that of white men.[1] Asian men's rate of employment was slightly lower than Hispanic men's, but higher than white men's lfp. Black men had the lowest employment rate with a 10% gap between their lfp and their employment rate. They remained at the bottom of the queue in terms of hiring for jobs, and as a result, they had the highest rate of unemployment, still double that of white men. All racial and ethnic groups of women had employment rates of about 55%,

---

[1] It should be noted that Hispanics can be white, and managers may perceive them as white.

Table 7.1 Labor force participation, employment, and unemployment rates, by race ethnicity, and sex, 2000 and 2014

| Race and ethnicity | Employment status for population aged 16 and over | | | | | |
| | In labor force | | Employed | | Unemployed | |
	2000	2014	2000	2014	2000	2014
Hispanic (all races)	61.4	68.8	55.2	61.4	5.7	7.4
Male	69.4	77.3	62.8	69.6	5.7	7.8
Female	53	60.1	47.2	53.2	5.6	7
White non-Hispanic	64.6	63.9	61.1	59.2	3.0	4.7
Male	72.2	69.6	68.0	64.2	3.3	4.8
Female	57.5	58.4	54.7	54.4	2.6	4.0
Black non-Hispanic	60.2	63.1	52.5	53.1	6.9	10
Male	60.9	62.8	52.5	51.9	7.3	10.9
Female	59.6	63.4	52.8	54.3	6.5	9.1
Asian or Pacific Islanders	66.2	66.3	57.7	61.5	7	4.8
Male	71.5	73.9	61.5	68.7	7.4	5.2
Female	60.9	59.6	53.8	55.3	6.6	4.3

Source US Census American Community Survey (ACS) 2010–2014 5 year averages and U.S. Census Bureau. 2000. "Profile of Selected Economic Characteristics." Census 2000, Summary File 4, DP-3

with black women's employment rates, slightly higher than black men's employment rate.

Unemployment is a key economic indicator showing that not everyone who wants to work can find a satisfactory job (see Table 7.1)[2]. The unemployment rate for all groups, except Asian men and women increased between 2000 and 2014, as a result of the Great Recession and a less than robust recovery. White women had the lowest rate of unemployment, closely followed by Asian women (at 4.3%) and Asian men (5.2%) had the lowest rate of unemployment among men, while black men had the highest rate. As we noted, other researchers have noted that when Hispanics join the labor force the difference between black and white workers increased (Stainback and Tomaskovic-Devey 2012).

These statistics indicate that, in a robust economy (in 2000), the supply of white and Asian workers may not meet employer demand, but the supply of Blacks and Hispanics who want to work outstripped the demand for these workers. The result was lower unemployment for whites and higher unemployment for Blacks, both nationally and in specific cities. For example, one analysis shows that the ratio of job applicants to job hires is significantly higher for blacks than for whites in Detroit (Farley et al. 2000). As noted, the roughly two-to-one ratio in unemployment rates between blacks and whites (for both men and women) has been constant throughout economic expansions and recessions, despite a shrinking gap in educational differences between the two groups. Unemployment gaps between whites and Hispanics have generally been smaller than between whites and blacks. Hispanics and blacks were also more likely than whites to be unemployed for longer periods. Black men, especially those with limited education, suffer higher rates of long-term joblessness than do white men with similar education (Lichter and Oliver 2000). Over the fourteen-year period covered by these data, we can see a

---

[2]The *labor force participation rate* represents the percentage of the adult population that is employed or actively seeking work. The *employment rate* is the percentage of the adult population that is employed, while the *unemployment rate* is the percentage of the adult population that is not working but is actively seeking work.

restructuring of the labor force in terms of lfp, employment, and unemployment. But, the differences between black and white men remained relatively invariant, and black men remained at the bottom of the queue.

7.3.2 Occupational Division of Labor

Occupational data are another indicator of the structure of the labor market and racial and ethnic disparities among women and men workers within occupations (see Table 7.2). Between 2000 and 2014, there were continuing changes in and noticeable restructuring of the occupational division of labor. In 2000, about one-third of white men and about one-fifth of Asian men and black men held managerial and professional jobs compared to one seventh of Hispanic men. Women of all races and ethnic groups were more likely to hold managerial and professional jobs when compared to their male counterparts, although at less prestigious, and lower paid positions. For example, by 2014 only 10% of women in professional and managerial occupations were employed in the relatively high paying computer and engineering jobs, compared to 44% of men (Bureau of Labor Statistics 2014). By 2014, there were losses for white men, but small gains for other groups, with Asians showing the greatest increases (although some of this change may be due to the re-categorization of Asians).

There was continuing restructuring in the production, transportation, and materials moving category. This restructuring began with job losses for white men going back to the 1960s. In 2000, about one-quarter of black, Hispanic, and Asian men worked in these industries, trailed by white men—who had previously lost a large share of relatively skilled blue- collar manufacturing jobs (26.1, 28.3, and 23.1%, respectively vs. 19.1%). Women, regardless of race or ethnicity held a small share of these jobs. White men were the least likely to hold service jobs, while black and Hispanic women were the most likely to be employed in service occupations (about 25% of each group).

Between 2000 and 2014, the data show restructuring in the occupational division of labor for men and for women. All race, ethnic, and gender categories had lost a substantial percentage of manufacturing jobs, as these industries continued to restructure. Black men still held the largest percentage of these jobs compared to the other groups. Asian men lost the largest share of these positions (from 23.1 down to 12.3%). Other occupations changed. Hispanic men were the most likely to hold jobs in construction and transportation, while black men held the lowest share of these jobs, these were previously jobs held by black or white men (Waldinger 1996). The percentage of service jobs increased for all groups of men, with white men showing the largest increase (from about 10.6 to 22.9%), but black men still had the highest employment rate among men in service jobs.

The portion of professional and managerial jobs decreased by about eight percentage points for white men, stayed relatively stable among black and Hispanic men (who were the least likely to be professional and managerial workers). Asian men saw the largest increase in this category of occupations among all categories of men, suggesting a possible preference by employers for what they consider the skills and temperament of Asian workers. Therefore, Asian men experience the greatest restructuring of the division of labor between professional and manufacturing jobs. These increases indicate the continued restructuring of men's work from blue collar to service.

Women, regardless of race and ethnic group, are distributed across a narrower array of occupations than are men, especially white men (Reskin and Padavic 1988; Padavic and Reskin 2002). White, black, and Hispanic women all had higher rates of participation in professional and managerial jobs than did their male compatriots —along there were significant differences among these groups of women with white women having the highest percentage among these three groups. As noted, they were in lower status and lower-paid jobs in this category. Asian women had the highest percentage of professional and managerial jobs, although they held a smaller

Table 7.2 Selected occupational data, by race, ethnicity, and sex, 2009 and 2014

Race and ethnicity	Selected occupations for employed civilian population aged 16 and over									
	Management professional and related		Service		Sales or office		Construction extraction or maintenance		Production transportation or materials moving	
	2000	2014	2000	2014	2000	2014	2000	2014	2000	2014
Hispanic (all races)	18.1	21.5	21.8	34.2	23.1	21.7	13.1	15.8	21.2	16.1
Male	14.6	15.8	19.0	26.4	14.8	14.6	21.9	26	26.1	21.1
Female	22.9	25.2	25.6	31.2	34.8	31.1	0.9	2.5	14.3	9.6
White non-Hispanic	35.6	39.6	13.4	32.6	27.0	24.7	9.8	9.6	13.6	10.7
Male	33.6	25.1	10.6	22.9	18.0	17.6	17.5	17.3	19.3	16.2
Female	38.0	42.3	16.5	41.4	37.5	35.4	0.7	1.2	6.9	5.1
Black non-Hispanic	25.2	30.4	22	38.4	27.3	25.1	6.5	5.9	18.6	15.1
Male	20.0	23.5	19.4	29.9	18.3	18.1	13.3	11.6	28.3	24.1
Female	29.7	34.1	24.2	28.0	34.8	30.8	0.8	1.0	10.4	8.3
Asian[a]	42.5	49.2	16.1	16.2	29.6	19.9	0.5	1.9	11.9	9.6
Male	44.0	49.2	19.8	14.2	18.0	17.4	17.2	6.7	23.1	12.5
Female	40.9	44.1	21.9	21.8	41.4	27.2	0.9	0.9	8.9	7.8

Source U.S. Bureau of labor Statistics Annual Report 2011–2015; US Census American Community Survey (ACS) 2010–2014 5 year averages and U.S. Census Bureau. 2000. "Profile of Selected Economic Characteristics." Census 2000, Summary File 4, DP-3
[a]It should be noted that between these years, the Bureau of Labor Statistics changed the definition of this category, and excluded Pacific Islanders and other small groups

percentage than did Asian men. They were significantly less likely to hold jobs in manufacturing, transportation, or construction and more likely to be employed as service workers. These patterns continued between 2000 and 2014. There were very large increases in the percentage of women in service work—facing what Burtless (1990) called "a future of lousy jobs." The share of women of all racial and ethnic groups in these jobs increased substantially during this period in areas such as food preparation, cleaning, and personal care, but there were major increases in the percentage of women in these lower-paid service jobs, categories. For example, black and Hispanic share of service jobs increased, especially in bottom rank of jobs such as food services. These occupations are often in work environments characterized by poor pay, few benefits, and little career mobility (Conrad 2000, 2001).

7.3.3 Weekly Earnings

Occupational segregation helps explain persistent wage gaps between whites and both blacks and Hispanics, especially between white men and black or Hispanic women (Boushey and Cherry 2000; Padavic and Reksin 2002). The wage gap has narrowed somewhat as blacks moved into a wider range of occupations in the 1960s and 1970s, boosted by affirmative action, equal employment opportunity laws, and higher education levels. The relative earnings of blacks stagnated in the 1980s, although wages did increase for blacks and Hispanics in the strong economy of the late 1990s (Holzer 2001; Reimers 1998). Other researchers found that when there is an increase in immigrants in the labor force, there is a decrease in wages, especially for low-paid workers, as a result of employer efforts to increase profits (Borjas 2014).

Although there were relative increases in wages in the 1990s, these increases did not continue in the 2000–2014 period. According to the Bureau of Labor Statistics (2014), the median wages for all groups of men declined by 6.8% between 2000 and 2014 (see Table 7.3). This change was not spread equally among all groups of men. The differences among race and ethnic groups of men reflect changes we have seen in the occupation division of labor where Asian men gained a larger share of managerial and profession jobs, while white men lost these jobs as well as manufacturing jobs, as did black men. Between 2000 and 2014, the median weekly earnings for white men were stagnant, declining by about 1.0%, while the median weekly earnings of black men declined by 2.0%. The ratio of black men's earnings to white men's earnings in 2014 was 75.7%; this difference was lower than it was in 2000. The winners during this period were Asian men whose median weekly earnings increased by almost 15%. The earnings of Hispanic men increased by 4.7%, although in 2014 as in 2000, although they were the lowest paid male workers.

In contrast to men, women's wages increased during this period, perhaps as a result of more pay equity in occupations, and the stagnation of male wages. Here again, however, the increases were not spread evenly among racial and ethnic groups. Among white women this increase was 6.2%. This increase was almost double of the

increase experienced by black women. By 2014, black women earned about 83% of what white women earned, smaller than the gap between black men and white men. The wage gap between black men and women (at 88.9%) was substantially smaller than that of white men and women, likely because of the shift by men into low-paid service work. As was the case for Asian men, Asian women's earnings increased more than any other group of women (by 10.6%). This increase was lower than the increase for Asian men but higher than all other groups of women. Hispanic women had the second largest increase in earnings (nearly 9.0%), but as with Hispanic men, they remained the lowest paid workers.

Taken together, these data reveal a stratified labor force with substantial differences in unemployment rates, occupational participation, and earnings in 2000 among racial, ethnic, and gender groups. These differences increased by 2014, with Asian men and women seeing comparatively large gains in professional and managerial positions.

7.4 Job Queue Processes: Employer Practices and Worker Strategies

In this next section, we examine the employer practices and worker strategies that lead to positions in the queue, understanding that

Table 7.3 Inflation—adjusted median usual weekly earnings, by race and Hispanic ethnicity and gender

Year	Total 16 and over	Hispanic, all races	White, non-Hispanic	Black, non-Hispanic	Asian/Pacific Islander
Men					
2000	$882	$574	991	$702	$942
2014	$876	$601	$901	$667	$1021
% change	−0.69	+4.7	−0.009	−2.1	+14.6
Women					
2000	$678	$503	$691	$590	$752
2014	$719	$548	$734	$611	$841
% change	+6.0	+8.9	+6.2	+3.5	+10.6

Source U.S. Department of Labor, Bureau of Labor Statistics Reports. 2014. Report 1058 *Highlights of Women's Earnings*, Inflation-adjusted median usual weekly earnings, by race and Hispanic or Latino ethnicity for fulltime wage and salary workers, 1979–2014

employers have more power in the sorting process.

7.4.1 Employer Practices

Many employers prefer white men for jobs that have high prestige, power over other workers, provide career ladders, higher earnings, and skill training (Appelbaum et al. 2006; Tomaskovic-Devey 1993; Stainback and Tomaskovic-Devey 2012). Yet, this preference appears to have decreased between 2000 and 2014, with Asian rather than white men having the best access to "good" jobs. This may be the result of a changing employer preference. Black men are over-represented in low wage jobs, especially in the service sector (Hamilton et al. 2011), as are most women. There is evidence that employers shun black men from inner cities for unskilled jobs and, instead choose to fill them with other demographic groups, including immigrants. This is most likely in cities with large or growing immigrant populations (Bankston 2014; Bean and Stevens 2003; Borjas 1998, 2014; Bound and Holzer 1993; Howell and Mueller 1997; Johnson et al. 2000; Waldinger 1996; Wilson 1996). These preferences are implemented through a variety of practices over time, starting with de jure segregation.

7.4.2 Employer Taste for Discrimination

What are employer preferences and practices that allow them to maintain a "taste for discrimination" (Becker 1971)? Becker predicts that competition in the market will wipe out discrimination because it is unprofitable have not come to pass. These preferences and practices range from the most coercive discrimination of *de jure* (legal) segregation to the everyday practices of de facto discrimination, such as occupational segregation, skill preferences, hiring procedures, and creation of hostile workplaces.

De Facto and De Jure Discrimination. Prior to the passage of the Civil Rights Act of 1964, there were widespread and blatant barriers and systematic and coercive sanctions to participation by Blacks in entire sets of occupations and firms. Market forces did not alleviate these barriers. Most blacks were denied access to opportunities and were not allowed to apply for certain positions or for jobs in certain firms (Darity and Mason 1998). Under Jim Crow laws, many workplaces were legally segregated (Jaynes and Williams 1989). The great majority of Americans agreed with the statement, "whites should have the first chance at any kind of job" (Bobo and Suh 2000). Hispanic, Asian, and Native American as well as black workers were excluded from many job opportunities. In the South, Jim Crow laws kept work places segregated and denied training or education that allowed access to these opportunities. Barriers were so deeply embedded and coercively sanctioned that the "Great Migration" to the north was a major pre–civil rights strategy to move out of a narrow band of marginal, ill-paying, degrading, and often-dangerous agricultural and private household service jobs (Jaynes and Williams 1989).

Although there were direct exclusionary laws, in most cases, occupational segregation was kept in place because of a powerful system of norms and practices, often internalized, but coercively sanctioned through violence and intimidation when violated (Jaynes and Williams 1989).

De Facto Segregation. With the passage of the 1964 Civil Rights Act, racially-based discrimination or "pure discrimination" became illegal (Darity and Mason 1998). The result was not full integration in the labor market, although segregation was not as great as in the periods of hyper-segregation (Stainback and Tomaskovic-Devey 2012). In a race-conscious society, employers may continue to use strategies that rank entire groups of workers in terms of their race and ethnic characteristics (Waldinger 1996). When black workers are hired, they are paid less, on average, and less likely to be hired or promoted into professional level jobs (Hamilton et al. 2011; Huffman and Cohen 2004).

A series of studies in Chicago, Atlanta, Detroit, Los Angeles, and Boston found that many employers will report racial preferences and are willing to admit that they discriminate against inner-city black males in hiring and promotion (Bobo and Suh 2000; Farley, Danzinger, and Holzer 2000; Holzer 1996: Kirschenman et al. 1995; Moss and Tilly 1995, 1997, 1996a, b). Widespread publicity emphasizing poor schools, drug use, crime, and welfare dependency shapes employers' perceptions of inner-city black workers and leads to discrimination (Neckerman and Kirschenman 1991). Many blacks live in racially segregated neighborhoods with high rates of unemployment, few social networks, and deep isolation (Massey and Denton 1993; Wilson 1996, 2015). Reports of high crime rates may make employers less willing to hire less-educated young black males overall (Kirschenman and Neckerman 1991). These stereotypes are reflected in the narratives of black workers who claim that they are the last hired and the first fired and that employers do not give them opportunity to prove that they can do more (Bonilla-Silva 2003).

Further, several studies provide evidence that color or skin shade plays a decisive role in determining economic outcomes, as we have seem with black/white differences among Hispanics. Where interviewers reported the skin tone of respondents, researchers found that dark-skinned blacks do worse on all social and economic dimensions (Seltzer and Smith 1991; Keith and Herring 1991). In a study done in greater Los Angeles, dark skinned black males had half the chance of finding employment than lighter-complexioned black males after controlling for schooling, age, and criminal record (Johnson et al. 2000). Likewise, studies using the 1979 National Chicano Survey report that Chicanos with lighter skin color and more European features have higher earnings, higher socioeconomic status, and face less in-market discrimination (Arce et al. 1987; Telles and Murguia 1990). Our own data (not shown) shows that black Hispanics are nearly twice as likely than white Hispanics to suffer unemployment, indicating a relationship similar to blacks and whites.

7.4.3 Restructuring

An extensive body of literature finds that organizations play a key role in generating and perpetuating inequality in employment outcomes (Castilla 2008). Based on employer decisions, three processes—(1) restructuring, (2) off shoring, and (3) out-sourcing to other U.S. companies have affected U.D. laborers especially those in the production trades. These three processes have had a significant effect on the placement of a group in the job queue (Norwood et al. 2006). Restructuring results from a decision to reshuffle and reorganize all, or part, of a business' internal production processes. This process can involve direct U.S. job losses, such as in the manufacturing and managerial occupations. Off-shoring can be part of the restructuring process. It arises from a decision to expand or transfer business operations or production activities outside of the United States. The job losses we see in certain occupations suggest that U.S. workers are losing jobs to foreign workers. Outsourcing can occur as the result of switching production and services to domestic firms that result in lower wage bills. Much of the restructuring literature focuses on the decline of manufacturing and its effects on race and ethnicity in the 1980s and 1990s. The global outsourcing of services (or offshoring) and the out-sourcing of jobs to firms with temporary labor forces has become (almost) commonplace in manufacturing (Kletzer 1998, 2005; Paul and Wooster 2010). The sharp decline in manufacturing in the United States and the movement of jobs "offshore" to cheaper workforces in the 1970s and 1980s, continuing today, has had racially differential consequences for blue-collar workers, precipitating a persistent wage gap between more and less educated men (Wilson 1996, 2015). Many relatively well-paying, unionized manufacturing jobs in the steel, auto, and durable goods industries were eliminated, due both to off-shoring, and out-sourcing, reducing job opportunities and relatively high wages for less educated men (Kalleberg et al.

1997; Kalleberg 2011). Between 1997 and 2002, the share of foreign-sourced goods in manufacturing almost doubled—from 12.4 to 22.1% and continues to do so (Burke et al. 2004). As we have seen one result of these processes appears to be occupational switching, often from better to poorer paying jobs with less stability and autonomy, and lower wages (Ebenstein et al. 2014).

White men without post-secondary education suffered the greatest wage losses in the recessionary period. But, as we have seen, black men were particularly hard hit by job losses increasing their unemployment rates, lowering their earnings, and, hence, their placement in the job queue. Hispanic men fared somewhat better in the wake of the industrial downturn, keeping a larger share of the remaining manufacturing jobs. In Chicago, for example, as service-oriented industries replaced manufacturing jobs, employment increased for Hispanic men with limited education or skills, but decreased for black men primarily as a result of employer preferences (Wilson 2015). Corporate downsizing and restructuring that started in the 1990s' economic boom, continued through the 2008 recession, and continues into the present. As we have seen, displacement and job losses among managerial and professional employees, as well as blue-collar workers were unevenly distributed by race, ethnicity, and gender. In January 2014, according to the Bureau of Labor Statistics, the reemployment rates for long-tenured displaced workers were lowest for black workers (about 55% were re-employed in contrast to Hispanics (65%) and whites (62%). Black men were least likely to regain jobs, because they were concentrated in routine manufacturing operatives jobs, which suffered the highest casualties during restructuring. In contrast, white men were the most likely group to be re-employed a year after displacement. Among Hispanics, Puerto Ricans endured a dramatic decline in economic well-being during the period of economic restructuring. These workers were vulnerable because of their concentration in Northeastern central cities that experienced intense economic dislocation, their overrepresentation in job sectors most adversely affected by such restructurings. Hispanic women were more likely than other groups to drop out of the labor force, as shown in Table 7.1. Educational and occupational advantages have not protected displaced workers against gender and racial inequities in re-employment after downsizing (Spalter-Roth and Deitch 1998).

In the United States, the shift away from manufacturing was accompanied by the shift to service work, as we saw. Although service work includes skills ranging from the brain surgeon to the hospital orderly, from the Wall Street broker to the Wal-Mart clerk, from the four-star chef to the short-order cook, in general, it is a lower-wage industry than manufacture. Although the United States is often described as a "post-industrial society," the majority of the work force is employed in relatively low-skilled jobs, as we have seen in Table 7.2. There are still beds to be made, floors to be swept, goods to be rung up (Waldinger 1996). Overall, the 2000–2015 period continued to see employer-generated restructuring of the occupational division of labor.

7.4.4 Preferences for Immigrant Labor

The loss of manufacturing jobs and the stagnation of wages, especially among black men, occurred at the same time as the largest surge in immigration occurred since the early part of the 20th century (Bean and Stevens 2003; Grodsky and Pager 2001). Many employers preferred to hire immigrants. They argued that immigrants have a stronger work ethic and have more "people skills" than native-born blacks (Moss and Tilly 1996b). According to some estimates the immigrant population raised to 42.4 million in 2014, although other estimates are substantially lower. In Chicago, for example, men of Mexican origin, who might be predicted to fare poorly given the increased rewards to education, in fact, enjoyed increases in employment rates compared to black men. Employers who hire immigrant workers are attempting to restructure the workforce in their favor in order to cut costs and obtain a pliable workforce that can be kept in line through threats of retaliation against those who attempt to defend their rights to earned wages, overtime, and decent conditions (North 2013; Smith and Cho 2013).

In contrast to resource-rich whites and Asians who may benefit from low-wage services of domestics and other service workers, blacks tend not benefit from immigration. First, most benefits from hiring immigrants are received by firms, and blacks own a relative small share of firms in the United States, and, second, blacks are more likely than whites and Asian-Americans to exhibit a relatively similar skills' distribution to immigrants. In New York City, for example, foreign-born workers substantially increased their share of employment in every black niche. During the 1980s service industries such as hotel and restaurants grew (Waldinger 1996). Immigrants were employed in the lowest-level jobs in these industries. Blacks, who were long excluded from getting skilled jobs in manufacturing industries such as the garment industry and "front of the house jobs" in service industries such as hotels, witnessed an erosion of their share of low-skilled jobs (Johnson and Oliver 1992). This declining share of jobs resulted from employer preferences for immigrant labor, and immigrants' abilities to use networks to gain some control over the dispersion of jobs (Waldinger 1996). More recently, Borgas et al. (2014) found that the employment rate of black men, and particularly of low-skilled black men, fell between 1960 and 2000. At the same time, their incarceration rate rose. The authors found a 10% immigration-induced increase in the supply of workers in a particular skill group, lowered the employment rate by 5.9% points, and increased the incarceration rate by 1.3% points. Other economists have found that Labor market competition from immigrants is most intense for natives with the lowest levels of education and varies significantly by geographic area (Card 2005) In short, employer recruitment of immigrant labor may have a negative effect for low skilled workers, especially black male workers, but evidence is still being collected for this contentious issue.

7.4.5 Union Busting and Opposition to Collective Bargaining

More than 30 years ago, then President Ronald Reagan threatened to fire nearly 13,000 air traffic controllers, members of the Professional Air Traffic Controllers Organization (PATCO) unless they called off their strike. The Reagan administration fired these federal workers, broke the union, and as a result, undermined the bargaining power of workers and their labor unions. The PATCO firings emboldened employers increased their strategies to eliminate unions and collective bargaining from the workplace (McCartin 2011). As a result, union density has decreased from its high of one third of the workforce to its current low of about nine percent in the private sector (Milkman 2004, 2014). Employer strategies to "bust" unions or prevent successful organizing efforts in the private sector include hiring union-busting consultants. Currently, between 70 and 80% of employers do this, by recruiting and supporting anti-union workers, sending letters to families of workers who might join unions, delaying union elections, holding meetings to discourage or threaten workers from joining, and firing union organizers. State and local elected officials have increased their efforts to decrease the collective power of public unions by efforts to encourage the passage of "right to work " state–wide laws For example in 2001, Oklahomans voted on the "right to work" law, joining 26 states (mainly in the South that lave these laws on the books. In 2015, Wisconsin (under Governor Scott Walker) public sector unions were busted and a right to work law was passed. The law bans labor contracts that require workers to pay union dues or representation fees. The law also makes it difficult for unions to negotiate solid contracts. Wal-Mart and other firms hope to use Oklahoma as a model for a renewed campaign to reduce the wages and benefits for workers nation-wide. In 2016, however, under the Obama administration, the Department of Labor issued a "Persuader" rule that would require employers to disclose the resources they spent dissuading workers from organizing (Hoffa 2016). This is a modest step to level the playing field, and to decrease the ability of employers to prevent collective bargaining. This rule will probably be cancelled under the Trump administration.

7.4.6 Employer Demands for Soft Skills

The changes in the organization of manufacturing to just-in-time, flexible production and the growth of the service industries that stress "customer satisfaction" resulted in increased emphasis on what some researchers have labeled as "soft skills." Soft skills are based on employers' desire for workers with particular attitudes and ways of interacting that, in employers' view, demonstrate enthusiasm, a positive work attitude, a lack of a "chip" on one's shoulder; including smiling, making eye contact, and not "talking back" (Moss and Tilly 1997, 1996a). Soft skills are highly subjective. Many employers rely on their "gut feelings" in selecting job applicants during hiring interviews. This usual business practice is likely to capture employers' feelings of who will fit in and with whom they are comfortable. When employees are selected for low-skilled jobs, black men are at a disadvantage because of a generalized fear of them and because their body language and interview skills do not reinforce notions of politeness, motivation, and enthusiasm (Kirschenman et al. 1995; Moss and Tilly 1996b). Negative views of black men's soft skills are lower in cities without other competing minority groups (in Detroit compared to Los Angeles), in firms outside the inner city, in larger firms, and in minority-owned firms (Farley et al. 2000; Moss and Tilly 1996a). For employers interviewed in studies of the desire for soft skills, black women are preferred to black men, because they are thought to work harder because they are considered to be the sole source of their families' support (Holzer and Ihlanfeldt 1996). Hispanic recruits are seen as trying to support families, as having a stronger work ethnic than blacks, and of complaining less (Moss and Tilly 1997). These findings indicate that the

demand for soft skills is associated with greater employer stereotyping and with more subjective methods of screening job applicants (Kirschenman et al. 1995). Yet, not all researchers agree that "soft skills" are entirely responsible for the lack of employment of black men. For example, research by Hamilton et al. (2011) finds that lacking neither hard skills nor soft skills provide convincing arguments for black males sorting into low-wage occupations. These authors suggest that discrimination provides a better explanation for why employers are less likely to hire black men.

7.4.7 Relying on Networks

Among widely accepted recruitment practices, social networks contribute to unequal access to employment and advancement opportunities in the queue for minority job seekers (Peterson et al. 2000; Reskin 1998). Word-of-mouth recruiting —where employers ask for recommendations from their current workers, from other employers, or from their own networks, is the most prevalent form of filling jobs (Reskin 1998). This form of recruiting usually reinforces the racial, ethnic, and gender composition of the workforce Access to desirable jobs can be constrained by exclusionary, racially segregated social circles, with some groups having access to information about positions due to their relations to employers DiTomaso 2013; Neckerman and Kirschenman 1991; Peterson et al. 2000). Other studies have found that organizational sponsorship is generally related to career success (Ng et al. 2005). For under-represented minorities, who have less access to such networks, meritocracy becomes more important than informal hiring. They have less information and are less likely to have someone at the firm who will vouch for them (Peterson et al. 2000). Most high-level managers are white men who feel most comfortable with those like themselves and seek compatriots from their professional and personal networks (Maume 1999). They are more likely to mentor such individuals and to provide more resources to train them. Mentoring is positively associated with career success. Several characteristics of networking appeared to be associated with career success, e.g. size of the advice network, range, emotional intensity, frequency of the contacts, and years acquainted. These mentoring/mentee relations are most likely to be same race, ethnic and gender groups (Savitz-Romer et al. 2009; Spalter-Roth et al. 2013). Employers who recruit and mentor those who are most like them probably have the least diverse workforces. In addition, employers also have networks among themselves such as serving on one another boards and participating in organizations for employers.

7.5 Worker Strategies

As employers are implementing the above-discussed ranking and sorting processes (Appelbaum et al. 2006), and, as a result, the share of jobs with benefits, such as tenure, stability, and opportunities, is declining (Kalleberg et al. 1997, 2011). In their turn, workers are also carrying out strategies to obtain and keep the best jobs in the queue that they can under the circumstances. Many workers struggle to gain access to "good jobs." Other workers attempt to keep better jobs for themselves and for their social groups. Workers employ various strategies to secure and retain stable jobs, gain promotions, and improve their standing in the job queue. Tactics include improving education and skills, using inherited contacts and networks, creating ethnic niches, bringing legal cases, and using collective bargaining techniques. Some of these approaches aggravate existing racial and ethnic inequalities in the workplace. For example, young, white job seekers benefit the most from family history and social connections, which give them access to employment networks and more prestigious jobs (DiTomaso 2013; Oliver and Shapiro 1995).

7.5.1 Getting More Education

The pursuit of human capital in the form of higher education degrees and credentials is a widely-used strategy to improve positions in the queue. This strategy is not equally available to all, nor is it a strategy that all groups benefit from equally (Bernstein 1995; Carnevale and Strohl 2013; Hamilton, Austin, and Darity 2011). Since the 1940s blacks have decreased the education gap between themselves and their white counterparts, especially at the high school level, although significant gaps still remain in the share of each graduating from college and gaining post-graduate education. The median years of education of these groups are now similar. However, the closing of the educational gap has not been reflected equally in the closing of the wage gap between blacks and whites, as we have seen in Table 7.3. A California study, which examined black and Hispanic as well as white youth, found absolute increases in the number of Blacks and Hispanics who graduated from high school, attended "some college," and were awarded bachelor's degrees compared to whites. Relative test scores also improved. Yet, more educationally qualified minority workers in their late 20s and early 30s find their wages were lower relative to those of comparably educated whites (Carnevale and Strohl 2013). These findings suggest that for blacks and Hispanics increased educational credentials mean increased earning power, but not when compared to whites or Asians. According to Wilson (2015) one of the reasons for this difference, however is the fact that blacks and Hispanics, on average, do not have the resources to attend the best high schools, colleges, and universities. Therefore, the higher education system plays an important role in the reproduction of white racial privilege (Carnevale and Strohl 2013), and gaining more education does not appear to benefit all workers equally.

7.5.2 Job Hoarding

The United States is frequently described as a meritocracy (Jencks and Phillips 1998). Yet, as noted, most people get their jobs through connections (Reskin 1998). Family background, family connections, and other ascribed characteristics are strong predictors of access to good jobs. Researchers have long known the power of white parents' education and a father's occupation in predicting a son's occupational prestige (Blau and Duncan 1967; Bowles and Gintis 2002). White Americans' greater ability to hoard jobs and pass along occupational status to their children is still true, where access to networks with better contacts increases the opportunity of obtaining better jobs, with greater pay, better benefits, and more job security, and greater ability to amass assets (Oliver and Shapiro 1995). This ability is especially true when the contacts are white and male (DiTomaso 2013; O'Regan and Quigley 1993). Resources in the form of information sharing, recommendations, and protection of jobs from the open market (DiTomaso 2013) based on social connections in neighborhoods, kinship circles, and schools are especially important in facilitating employment. Favors are granted through these networks. Whites more often identify employment opportunities through referrals, and these avenues are more likely to produce higher-paying positions. In contrast, blacks tend to pursue jobs by directly visiting prospective employers and submitting applications, a practice associated more often with lower-paying positions (Farley et al. 2000; Johnson et al. 2000). Blacks are less likely to be able to benefit from what have been called alumni effects or the intergeneration transmission of advantage of social resources (DiTomaso 2013; Oliver and Shapiro 1995; Tomaskovic-Devey 1993). As a result, whites gain racial advantage. Yet those whites who have access to contacts and networks tend not to see the results as discriminatory (DiTomaso 2013). To keep other workers from gaining access to their positions, general workplace harassment may occur including staring, dirty looks, belittling statements, ostracism, and ridicule (Roscigno et al. 2008).

7.5.3 Developing Ethnic Enclaves

As noted, immigrants may be preferred for certain jobs, based on skills, stereotypes of their characteristics, and their willingness to accept a lower wage. Individuals can be recommended by their co-ethnics including friends and relatives. The result can be the growth of ethnic niches that gain some control over the dispersal of jobs and protect jobs against outsiders (Bankston 2014; Waldinger 1996; Waldinger and Litcher 2003). Existing ethnic networks funnel newcomers into specialized economic activities, such as restaurants, laundries, taxi-driving, gardening, and construction. Enclaves appear to dominate a variety of industries including construction, meat- packing, textiles, and agricultural labor, depending on geographic area.

There is a consensus that while ethnic niches help co-ethnics find jobs, they often provide lower wages and constrain them from finding other jobs (Bankston 2014). For example, the rising growth of the Latino population in rural areas of the Midwest is due to the restructuring of the meatpacking and poultry-processing industries. As these industries sought to restructure and cut costs in the 1980s, plants increasingly made their way to rural communities, which continue to serve as magnets attracting Hispanics and other minorities in search of steady employment outside large urban centers (Rochín et al. 1998). More recently the meat packing industry appears to have replaced Hispanics with Somalis. Success in the queueing process involves finding a good niche, dominating it, and keeping resources "within the tribe" (Waldinger 1996; Darity et al. 1997). White ethnics have been especially successful at this effort, moving from niches at the bottom of the queue to positions at the top. Previous literature in sociology questions the outcomes of immigrants' participation in ethnic enclaves for their economic and social well-being. The "enclave thesis" speculates that immigrants benefit from working in ethnic enclaves, in the short run, yet research on the long-run effects of enclave participation on immigrants' economic outcomes is mixed about whether ethnic enclave effects are positive or negative in terms of wages and mobility (Xie and Gough 2011).

The distinctive history of blacks from slavery through ghettoization has limited their success in pursuing this strategy (Waldinger 1996). When sizeable numbers of blacks migrated north in the 1940s, white ethnics were already entrenched in many niches from low to high skill. By the 1970s, when whites, as well as manufacturing jobs, were exiting the cities, Black efforts to move up the ladder were only moderately successful. They established gains in the public sector, but not in other industries. As a result, they have no niches in lesser-skilled jobs and are largely detached from the private sector (Waldinger 1996). Efforts to decrease the size of the public sector through privatization have especially negative consequences for blacks. Efforts to use the tools of affirmative action to break into niches held by whites are objectionable to the majority of whites who emphasize that it constitutes unfair reparations and "reverse discrimination" against them (Bonilla-Silva 2003). Thus, blacks appear to be less successful at controlling jobs and occupations.

7.5.4 Collective Bargaining

Collective bargaining is another historic method for controlling the competition for jobs and improving their quality. Occupational unions strive for control over hiring through union shops, seniority rules, employee training, and union-run employment exchanges. The purpose of these strategies is to ensure a supply of better wage jobs by decreasing cut-throat competition among employers to hire at ever lower wages (Cobble 1993; Milkman 2004, 2014). For minority groups, union-controlled hiring and promotion procedures were often exclusionary. For example, in the construction industry, union locals often refused to accept blacks as members and many white workers refused to sponsor them, feeling that blacks would lower the status and the pay of the industry. Over time, there was an increased effort to overcome race, ethnic, and gender divisions (especially in newer unions in

service and public sectors). Although wage levels of white men were highest, union membership provided greater wage increases to black and Hispanic men and women and increased their job tenure (Spalter-Roth and Hartmann 1994). Currently, median earnings of non-union members were only 79% of earnings for union workers. In addition, higher rates of unionization correlate with higher rates of black employment (Moss and Tilly 1996a).

With the steep drop in union density (from 33.4% of the workforce in 1945 to 11.1% in 2016), efforts were made, especially in unions in the service sector and state and local governments to bring about a new labor movement. This movement partnered with community groups to improve worker's conditions, even if collective bargaining efforts did not succeed. There was an expectation that the new labor would be more diverse than the traditional labor movements, with greater diversity among union organizers and staff and more work with communities of color. For example, there was an effort to recruit organizers from Historically Black Colleges and Universities (Rooks 2004). Organizing efforts focused on mostly non-white communities and community organizations (see section on Political and Legal Strategies). Yet workers of color attracted to the new union movement found that race was still tangential to class. They also found anti-black feelings among the immigrants that unions were trying to organize. With limited strategies to decrease racism in the workplace, there was agreement among the new union organizers that the result was a lack of trust, and a lack of empowerment of women and organizers of color. Yet there was a feeling that through their efforts workers of color were empowered (Rooks 2004). Currently black workers are more likely to be union members than are white, Asian, or Hispanic workers (Department of Labor 2014).

7.5.5 Legal and Political Struggles

Both white ethnics and varying minority groups have used an array of tactics in the competition over positions in the queue. In New York City, for example, these tactics included mobilizing political power to either contest or reinforce the status quo of the civil service system; organizing strikes; using lawsuits—such as the NAACP efforts to decrease the white ethnic hold over fire-fighting jobs. Conflict and organized struggle have been especially crucial in African American efforts to open up white niches in manufacturing and municipal employment. Blacks or black-dominated social movements have been more likely than other non-white groups to use strategies such as suing under civil rights or equal opportunity laws, boycotts, and demonstrations (Waldinger 1996). Workers can sue employers based on of discriminatory job advertisements, recruitment, pay, layoffs, job classification, and promotions. Minority and women workers can obtain jobs and monetary damages (as a result of the 1991 Civil Rights Act) by filing charges with the Equal Employment Opportunity Commission. However, many cases are resolved either through conciliation or settlements because intentional discrimination is hard to prove. These laws had limited effects on the ways organizations went about recruiting, screening, and evaluating workers. In continuing their customary practices, establishments continued to exclude groups of workers from many lines of work (Reskin 1998). All of these struggles such as the fight for affirmative action encounter negative reactions and pushback (Leonard 1990).

A recent political organizing effort is the fight to increase the minimum wage to $15.00 per hour —a political demand aimed primarily at state and local governments. Janice Fine, a professor of labor relations at Rutgers noted that the strikes were a way for the labor movement to revamp its role after decades of declines in membership, interest and influence (2006).[3] This effort began in New York City in 2011 with Communities for Change (C for C) surveying mainly black and Hispanic low-income residents about affordable housing and other issues. Many of the respondents worked in fast-food. The size and scope of the

project exceeded C for C's capacity so they asked the Service Employees International Union (SEIU) for assistance in organizing the fast-food industry. SEIU responded by adding a Fight for $15 component to its own Fight for a Fair Economy campaign. Unions had reached a point where they realized that things were so bad that if there isn't a climate change for unions, the labor movement would fade away and thus coalitions with social movements and community groups are a pathway for change (Milkman 2014; Smith and Cho 2013).

From an initial meeting of some 40 workers in fall 2012, Fight for $15 swiftly expanded. A week after Thanksgiving, over 200 NYC fast-food workers walked off their jobs and took to the streets of New York to demand a $15.00 per hour minimum wage. With SEIU providing continuing financial and organizing support, demonstrations soon spread to Chicago, St Louis, Detroit, Milwaukee, and other cities. One year later, another one-day strike took place in more than 100 US cities. Two years later a December fast-food workers staged a one-day strike in 150 cities. On April 15, 2015, in over 200 cities across the country, an estimated 60,000 low-wage workers—including fast-food workers, home-care assistants, child-care aides, Wal-Mart workers, airport workers and adjunct professors —walked out on their jobs to protest their low wages and to demand a $15.00 per hour minimum wage in the United States.

Low-wage workers in conjunction with their union allies mounted or supported ballot initiatives at both the state and local levels. Largely as a result of Fight for $15, a major focus of union organizing tactics has shifted from the shop floor to the ballot box and city hall, and has become less a matter of union self-interest, but rather a matter of championing the interests of the workers as a whole.

7.6 Conclusions

In this chapter, the labor market is described as a set of queuing processes and practices in which employers' rank workers in terms of their views

[3]Fine (2006).

of who is likely to be productive, who they can pay the least, who will not complain about working conditions, who they know, and who is likely to fit in. Workers rank jobs in terms of wages, benefits, autonomy, and workplace conditions. These queues are neither gender neutral nor color blind, despite laws that prohibit deliberate discrimination.

Employers are likely to be white men, and as a result of their perceptions, they often rank workers by race, ethnicity, and gender different occupations and industries. During the period of 2000 through 2014, that included the Great Recession of 2008, employers used a variety of strategies to restructure the workforce to increase profits and control, decreasing higher paying production jobs and increasing lower-paying service jobs. As we have seen, not everyone who searched for a job has an equal opportunity to find one and to work in a wide range of positions, and unemployment rates increased during this time-period. Employers appeared to continue some groups to others, and, of course, were more powerful in pursuing their ends than were workers. For example, there was a greater increase in Asian men in professional and managerial jobs compared to other groups of men, although this change may also reflect changes in the measurement of the category. In trying to keep or improve their positions in the queue, workers such as blacks and Hispanics often completed against one another. In spite of changes in the structure of the labor market during this period, differences among blacks and whites remained largely invariant.

Black workers and Hispanic workers appeared to remain at the back of queues, despite some advances, with employers justifying their decisions, especially in the hiring of black workers, in terms of lack of proper attitudes, ability to fit in, or management potential. The relative lack of change in the positions relations among black and Hispanic worker's positions suggests that employer practices clearly outweigh worker strategies, especially because workers are not unified by race, ethnicity and immigrant status. Some worker strategies appear to be more successful than others and sometimes at the expense of other workers, for example ethnic enclaves, along with a preference for immigrant workers may have helped some workers at the expense of others. For example, Hispanic workers made gains in construction jobs. As DiTomaso's work shows (2013), white ethnics are likely to be successful at job hoarding, although their ability to do so may be less possible, with the continued decline in manufacturing. Black workers seem to be less successful at hoarding jobs or creating enclaves. Union density and the ability to bargain collectively has continued to decline, although unionized workers continue to have higher wages. Blacks have become the largest share of union workers and have become active in struggles to increase the minimum wage, during a period of the decline in manufacturing jobs and increase in service (such as health care positions). Yet, as we have seen, they remain twice as likely to be unemployed as whites.

Taken together, these data reveal a stratified labor queue with substantial differences in unemployment rates, occupational participation, and earnings. Between 2000 and 2014 there were some significant changes in positions in the queue while some stayed stagnant.

7.6.1 The Future

The ranking and sorting process occurs within a constantly changing economy. Changes occur as industries decline and grow; as employers search the globe for profits often in the form of cheaper, more flexible workforces; as workers migrate for better job opportunities, or attempt to take collective action. There are race, ethnic, and gender biases in these decisions.

What can we expect in the next decade? Social, economic, and political change is notoriously hard to predict. For example, will automation occur at an intensifying rate, displacing workers at all levels? Will union protections decline with the increase in "right to work" states? Will an even higher percentage of immigrants be deported, leaving gaps in the queue? Will wages decrease because of fewer jobs or increase as some groups of workers need to be replaced? Will cutbacks in social safety net programs (such as Medicaid) and worker protections (such as OSHA) render more workers too ill to work, so that they fall out of the queue? Will discrimination increase with the end of federal agencies such as the Office of Federal Contract Compliance? One thing is certain; none of these changes will be race or gender blind.

For example, many studies predict the impact of automation. A computer that dispenses expert radiology advice is just one example of how jobs currently done by highly trained white-collar workers can be automated, thanks to the advance of deep learning and other forms of artificial intelligence. The idea that manual work can be carried out by machines is already familiar; and now ever-smarter machines can perform tasks done by information workers, too (The Economist 2017). Industry spokesmen claim that the only impact of automation will be to get rid of repetitive jobs but will increase other sorts of jobs, yet provide little evidence for this claim. If there is a downturn in job growth, as a result of automation, and jobs at the top vanish, then preferred groups can have "bumping rights" while those at the bottom are more likely to face unemployment (King 1992; Lichter and Oliver 2000; Reskin and Roos 1990; Waldinger 1996). Yet industry spokesmen claim that automation will get rid of repetitive jobs. Other industry spokespeople have argued that automation and the gig economy go together (Uzialko 2017). Some predictions are especially ominous for workers, with dismal prospects for many types of jobs as powerful new technologies are increasingly adopted not only in manufacturing, clerical, and retail work, but in professions such as law, financial services, education and medicine (Rothman 2013).

In a capitalist economy with a meager safety net, adults need to work in order to survive. In the face of expected changes, which workers will be able to maintain their jobs? If jobs at the top of the queue vanish, then we would expect a general restructuring of jobs with those at the bottom will face a below-poverty living standard (King 1992; Lichter and Oliver 2000; Reskin and Roos 1990; Waldinger 1996). Efforts by right-wing conservatives to promote "race blind" policies and to ignore the effects of discrimination, is likely to continue under the current administration. The current polarization of the population, encouraged by the right wing and its presidential candidate, means that the cooperation among groups of workers does not seem likely, at least in the short-term future. Yet, there are some exceptions, such as the Fight for $15 which appears to be a multi-racial movement of people at the bottom of the queue. Future research should find that examining changes in the queueing process will be a useful mechanism for evaluating structural inequalities and their impact on workers.

Acknowledgements This first version of this chapter is based upon the working papers of 45 social scientists produced for a conference held by the American Sociological Association on "Race, Racism, and Race Relations: What Do We Know and What Do We Need to Know?" supported by generous grants from the Ford Foundation and the W.G. Kellogg Foundation. The authors have rewritten this chapter, using a broader time period, and the views presented in this chapter are solely the authors.

References

Appelbaum, E., Bernhardt, A., & Murnane, R. (2006). *Low-wage America: How employers are reshaping opportunity in the workplace.* New York: Russell Sage Foundation.

Arce, C. H., Murguia, E., & Frisbe, W. P. (1987). Phenotype and life chances among chicanos. *Hispanic Journal of Behavioral Studies, 9*(1), 19–33.

Bankston, C. L. (2014). *Immigrant networks and social change.* Malden, MA: Polity Press.

Bean, F. D., & Stevens, G. (2003). *America's newcomers and the dynamics of diversity.* New York: Russell Sage Foundation.

Becker, G. S. (1971). *A theory of discrimination* (2nd ed.). Chicago, IL: University of Chicago Press.

Bernstein, J. (1995). *Where's the payoff?: The gap between black academic progress and economic gains.* Washington, DC: Economic Policy Institute.

Blau, P. M., & Duncan, O. D. (1967). *The American occupational structure.* New York: The Free.

Bobo, L. D., & Suh, S. A. (2000). Surveying racial discrimination: Analyses from a multiethnic labor market. In L. D. Bobo, M. L. Oliver, J. H. Johnson Jr., & A. Valenzuela Jr. (Eds.), *Prismatic metropolis: Inequality in Los Angeles* (pp. 523–560). New York: Russell Sage Foundation.

Bonilla-Silva, E. (2003). *Racism without racists: Color-blind racism and the persistence of racial inequality in the United States.* Lanham, MD: Rowman & Littlefield Publishers, Inc.

Borjas, G. (1998). Do blacks gain or lose from immigration? In D. S. Hamermesh & F. D. Bean (Eds.), *Help or hindrance?: The economic implications of immigration for African Americans* (pp. 51–74). New York: Russell Sage Foundation.

Borjas, G. (2014). *Immigration economics.* Cambridge: Harvard University Press.

Bound, J., & Holzer, H. (1993). Industrial shifts, skills levels, and the labor market for white and black males. *Review of Economics and Statistics, 125*(3), 387–396.

Boushey, H., & Cherry, R. (2000). Exclusionary practices and glass-ceiling effects across regions: What does the current expansion tell us?". In R. Cherry & W. M. Rodgers III (Eds.), *Prosperity for all? The economic boom and African Americans* (pp. 160–187). New York: Russell Sage Foundation.

Bowles, S., & Gintis, H. (2002). The inheritance of inequality. *Journal of Economic Perspectives., 16,* 3–30.

Burke, J., Epstein, G., & Choi, M. (2004). *Rising foreign outsourcing and employment losses in U.S. manufacturing, 1987–2002.* Amherst: Political Economy Research Institute, University of Massachusetts.

Burtless, G. (1990). Earnings inequality over the business and demographic cycles. In G. Burtless (Ed.), *A future of lousy jobs?: The changing structure of U.S. wages.* Washington, DC: The Brookings Institution.

Card, D. (2005). *Is the new immigration really so bad?* Unpublished paper. Department of Economics, University of California, Berkeley.

Carnevale, A. P., & Strohl, J. (2013). *Separate & unequal: How higher education reinforces the intergenerational reproduction of white racial privilege.* Washington, DC: Center on Education and the Workforce, Georgetown Public Policy Institute.

Castilla, E. J. (2008). Gender, race, and meritocracy in organizational careers. *American Journal of Sociology, 113*(6), 1479–1526.

Cobble, D. (1993). Introduction: Remaking unions for the new majority. In D. S. Cobble (Ed.), *Women and unions: Forging a partnership* (pp. 3–23). Ithaca, NY: ILR Press.

Conrad, C. (2000). In good times and bad: Discrimination and unemployment. In R. Cherry & W. M. Rodgers III (Eds.), *Prosperity for all? The economic boom and African Americans* (pp. 208–213). New York: Russell Sage Foundation.

Conrad, C. (2001). Racial trends in labor market access and wages: Women. In N. J. Smelser, W. J. Wilson, & F. Mitchell (Eds.), *American becoming: Racial trends and their consequences* (pp. 124–151). Washington, DC: National Academy Press.

Darity, W. J., Dietrich, J., & Guilkey, D. K. (1997). Racial and ethnic inequality in the United States: A secular perspective. *American Economic Review, 87* (2), 301–305.

Darity, W. Jr., Guilkey, D., & Winfrey, W. (1996). Explaining differences in economic performance among racial and ethnic groups in the USA: the data examined. *American Journal of Economics and Sociology, 55*(4), 411–426

Darity, W., & Mason, P. L. (1998). *Evidence on discrimination in employment: Codes of color, codes of gender.* Unpublished working paper.

DiTomaso, N. (2013). *The American non-dilemma: Racial inequality without racisms.* New York: Russell Sage Foundation.

Ebenstein, A., Harrison, A., McMillan, M., & Phillips, S. (2014). Estimating the impact of trade and offshoring on American workers using the current population survey. *The Review of Economics and Statistics, 96* (4), 581–595.

Farley, R., Danzinger, S., & Holzer, H. (2000). *Detroit divided.* New York: Russell Sage Foundation.

Feagin, J. R., & Sikes, M. P. (1994). *Living with racism: The black middle-class experience.* Boston, MA: Beacon Press.

Fernandez, R. M., & Castilla, E. (2001). How much is that network worth? Social capital in employee referral networks. In N. Lin, K. Cook, & R. Burt (Eds.), *Social capital: Theory and research* (pp. 85–104). Chicago: Aldine de Gruyter.

Fernandez, R. M., Castilla, E., & Moore, P. (1998). Social capital at work: networks and hiring at a phone center. In *Conference Paper, Social networks and social capital: an international perspective.* Duke University, October 30–November 1.

Fine, J. (2006). *Worker centers: Organizing communities at the edge of the dream.* Cornell University Press ILR Imprint. http://www.cornellpress.cornell.edu.

Grodsky, E., & Pager, Devah. (2001). The structure of disadvantage: Individual and occupation determinants of the black-white wage gap. *The American Sociological Review., 33*(August), 542–567.

Hamilton, D., Austin, A., & Darity, W. D. Jr. (2011). *Whiter jobs, higher wages: Occupational segregation and the lower wages of white men.* Washington, DC: Economic Policy Institute Briefing Paper.

Hoffa, J. P. (2016). *DOL C\Rule change sheds light on anti-union tactics.* Huff Post Business. March 24, 2016.

Holzer, H. (1996). Why do small firms hire fewer blacks than large ones? Working paper. Institute for Research on Poverty.

Holzer, H. (2001). Racial differences in labor market outcomes among men. In N. J. Smelser, W. J. Wilson, & F. Mitchell (Eds.), *American becoming: Racial trends and their consequences* (pp. 98–123). Washington, DC: National Academy Press.

Holzer, H., & Ihlanfeldt, K. (1996). *Customer discrimination and employment outcomes of minorities.* Working paper. Institute for Research on Poverty.

Howell, D. R., & Mueller, E. J. (1997). *The effects of immigrants on African-Americans earnings: A jobs-level analysis of the New York City Labor Market, 1979–89.* Working paper no. 210. New York: The Jerome Levy Economics Institute.

Huffman, M. I., & Cohen, P. N. (2004). Racial wage inequality: Job segregation and devaluation across U. S. labor markets. *American Journal of Sociology, 109* (4), 902–936.

Hum, T. (2000). A protected niche? Immigrant ethnic economics and labor market segmentation. In L. D. Bobo, M. L. Oliver, J. H. Johnson Jr., & A. Valenzuela Jr. (Eds.), *Prismatic metropolis: Inequality in Los Angeles* (pp. 279–314). New York: Russell Sage Foundation.

Jaynes, G. D., & Williams, R. M., Jr. (1989). *A common destiny: Blacks and American society.* Washington, DC: National Academy Press.

Jencks, C., & Phillips, M. (1998). *The black-white test score gap.* Washington, DC: Brookings Institution.

Johnson, J. H., Jr., Farrell, W. C., Jr., & Stoloff, J. A. (2000). African American males in decline: A Los Angeles case study. In L. D. Bobo, M. L. Oliver, J. H. Johnson Jr., & A. Valenzuela Jr. (Eds.), *Prismatic metropolis: Inequality in Los Angeles* (pp. 315–337). New York: Russell Sage Foundation.

Johnson, J. H., Jr., & Oliver, M. L. (1992). Structural changes in the U.S. economy and black male joblessness: A reassessment. In G. E. Peterson & W. Vroman (Eds.), *Urban labor markets and job opportunity* (pp. 113–147). Washington, DC: Urban Institute Press.

Kalleberg, A. L. (2011). *Good jobs, bad jobs: The rise of polarized and precarious employment systems in the United States, 1970s–2000s.* New York: Russell Sage Foundation, American Sociological Association Rose Series in Sociology.

Kalleberg, A. L., Reskin, B. F., & Hudson, K. (2000). Bad jobs in America: Standard and nonstandard employment relations and job quality in the United States. *American Sociological Review, 65*(2), 256–278.

Keith, V. M., & Herring, C. (1991). Skin tone and stratification in the black community. *American Journal of Sociology, 97*, 760–778.

King, M. C. (1992). Occupational segregation by race and sex, 1940–1988. *Monthly Labor Review*, April, 1992.

Kirschenman, J., Moss, P., & Tilly, C. (1995). Employer screening methods and racial exclusion: Evidence from new in-depth interviews with employers. Russell Sage Foundation. http://epn.org/sage/rstikm.html.

Kirschenman, J., & Neckerman, K. M. (1991). 'We'd love to hire them but ...' The meaning of race for employers. In C. Jencks & P. Peterson (Eds.), *The urban underclass* (pp. 203–234). Washington, DC: Brookings Institution.

Kletzer, L. (1998). Job displacement. *Journal of Economic Perspectives, 12,* 115–136.

Kletzer, L. (2005). Globalization and job loss from manufacturing to services. *Economic Perspectives, 29,* 38–46.

Leonard, J. S. (1990). The impact of affirmative action regulation and equal employment law on black employment. *Journal of Economic Perspectives, 4,* 47–63.

Lichter, M. I., & Oliver, M. (2000). Racial differences in labor force participation and long-term joblessness among less-educated men. In L. D. Bobo, M. L. Oliver, J. H. Johnson Jr., & A. Valenzuela Jr. (Eds.), *Prismatic metropolis: Inequality in Los Angeles* (pp. 220–248). New York: Russell Sage Foundation.

Lim, N. (2001). On the back of blacks: Immigrants and the fortunes of African Americans. In R. Waldinger (Ed.), *Strangers at the gates: New immigrants in urban America* (pp. 186–227). Berkeley: University of California Press.

Massey, D. S., & Denton, N. A. (1993). *American apartheid: Segregation and the making of the underclass.* Cambridge: Harvard University Press.

Maume, D. J. (1999). Glass ceilings and glass escalators: Occupational segregation and race and sex differences in managerial promotions. *Work and Occupations, 26* (4), 483–509.

McCartin, J. A. (2011) The strike that busted unions. *The New York Times*, August 2, 2011.

Milkman, R. (2004). *Immigrant workers and the future of the I.S. labor movement.* New York: Russell Sage Foundation.

Milkman, R. (2014). *New labor in New York: Precarious workers and the labor movement.* Ithaca: Cornell University Press.

Moss, P., & Tilly, C. (1995). *Raised hurdles for black men: Evidence from interviews with employers.* New York: Russell Sage Foundation. Retrieved October 19, 2005. http://epn.org/sage/rstimo.html.

Moss, P., & Tilly, C. (1996a). *Informal hiring practices, racial exclusion, and public policy.* Prepared for presentation at the meetings of the Association of Public Policy and Management, Pittsburgh, PA, October 31–November 2, 1996.

Moss, Philip, & Tilly, Chris. (1996b). 'Soft' skills and race. *Work and Occupations, 23,* 252–276.

Moss, P., & Tilly, C. (1997). *Why opportunity isn't knocking: Racial inequality and the demand for labor.* Unpublished manuscript. Department of Regional Economic and Social Development, University of Massachusetts, Lowell, MA.

Murname, R. J., Willet, J. B., & Levy, F. (1995). The growing importance of cognitive skills in wage determination. *The Review of Economics and Statistics, 77*(2), 251–266.

Neckerman, K. M., & Kirschenman, J. (1991). Hiring strategies, racial bias, and inner-city workers. *Social Problems, 38*(4), 433–447.

Ng, T. W. H., Eby, L. T., Sorenson, K., & Feldman, D. C. (2005). Predictors of occupational success. *Personnel Psychology, 58*(2), 367–408.

North, D. (2011). *Employer proclaims he profits from H-1B workers.* Washington, DC: Center for Immigrant Studies.

North, D. (2013). *Motivation for hiring alien workers?.* Washington, DC: Center for Immigration Studies.

Norwood, J., Carson, C., Deese, M., Johnson, N. J., Reeder, F. S., & Rolph, J. E. (2006). *Off shoring. how big is it.* A Report of the Panel of the National Academy of Public Administration for the U.S. Congress and the Bureau of Economic Analysis. Washington, DC: The National Academy of Public Administration.

O'Regan, K. M., & Quigley, J. M. (1993). Family networks and youth access to jobs. *Journal of Urban Economics., 34,* 230–248.

Oliver, M. L., & Shapiro, T. M. (1995). *Black wealth/white wealth: A new perspective on racial inequality.* New York: Routledge.

Padavic, I., & Reskin, B. (2002). *Women and men at work* (2nd ed.). Thousand Oaks, CA: Pine Forge Press.

Parvez, Z. F. (2002). *Women, poverty, and welfare reform (Social activism fact sheets) Akron, OH: Sociologists for women in society.* Retrieved October 19, 2005. http://newmedia.colorado.edu/usocwomen/socialactivism/socialactivism.html.

Paul, D. L., & Wooster, R. B. (2010). An empirical analysis of motives for offshore outsourcing by U.S. firms. *The International Trade Journal, 24*(3), 298–320.

Peterson, T., Saporta, I., & Scidel, M.-D. L. (2000). Offering a job: Meritocracy and social networks. *The American Journal of Sociology, 106*(3), 763–816.

Reimers, C. (1998). Unskilled immigration and changes in the wage distribution of black, Mexican American, and non-Hispanic white male dropouts. In D. S. Hamermesh & F. D. Bean (Eds.), *Help or hindrance? The economic implications of immigration for African Americans* (pp. 107–148). New York: Russell Sage Foundation.

Reskin, B. F. (1998). *The realities of affirmative action in employment.* Washington, DC: American Sociological Association.

Reskin, B. F., & Padavic, I. A. (1988). Supervisors as gatekeepers: Male supervisors' response to women's integration in plant jobs. *Social Problems, 35,* 401–415.

Reskin, B. F., & Roos, P. (1990). *Job queues, gender queues.* Philadelphia: Temple University Press.

Rochín, R. I., Saenz, R., Hampton, S., & Calo, B. (1998). *Colonias and Chicano/a entrepreneurs in rural California.* JSRI research report #16. The Julian Samora Research Institute, Michigan State University, East Lansing, Michigan.

Rodgers, W., & Spriggs, W. E. (1996). What does the AFQT really measure: Race, wages, schooling and the AFQT score. *The Review of Black Political Economy (Spring),* 13–45.

Rooks, D. (2004). Sticking it out or packing it in? Organizer retention in the new labor movement. In R. Milkman & K.Voss (Eds.), *Rebuilding labor: Organizing and organizers in the new union movement* (pp. 194–224).

Roscigno, V. J., Hodson, R., & Lopez, S. H. (2008). Power, status, and abuse at work. *The Sociological Quarterly, 50*(1), 3–27.

Rothman, D. (2013). *How technology is destroying jobs?* MIT Technology Report. June 12, 2013. https://www.technologyreview.com/s/515926/how-technology-is-destroying-jobs/.

Savitz-Romer, M., Jager-Hyman, J., & Coles, A. (2009). *Removing roadblocks to rigor: Linking academic and social supports to ensure college readiness and success.* Washington, DC: Pathways to College Network, Institute for Higher Education Policy.

Seltzer, S., & Smith, R. C. (1991). Color differences in the Afro-American community and the differences they make. *Journal of Black Studies, 21*(3), 279–286.

Smith, R., & Cho, E. H. (2013). *Workers' rights on ice: How immigration reform can stop retaliation and save labor rights.* New York: National Employment Law Project.

Spalter-Roth, R. (2007). Race and ethnicity in the labor force: employer practices and worker strategies. In H. Vera & J. R. Feagin (Eds.), *Handbook of the sociology of racial and ethnic relations* (pp. 263–283). New York: Springer.

Spalter-Roth, R., & Deitch, C. (1998). '*I don't feel right-sized—I Feel out-of-work sized': The unequal effects of downsizing on women in the workforce.* Paper presented at the session on Employment Equality and Restructuring, co-sponsored by the Sex and Gender Section, for the 93rd Annual Meeting of the American Sociological Association, August 21–25, 1998.

Spalter-Roth, R., & Hartmann, H. I. (1994). What do unions do for women? In S. Friedman, R. W. Hurd, R. A. Oswald, & R. Seeber (Eds.), *Restoring the promise of american labor law.* New York: ILR Press.

Spalter-Roth, R., & Lowenthal, T. A. (2005). *Race, ethnicity, and the American labor market: What's at work.* Washington, DC: American Sociological Association Research Brief. Retrieved October 19, 2005. http://www.asanet.org/gallaries/default-file/RaceEthnicity_LaborMarket.pdf.

Spalter-Roth, R., Mayorova, O., Shin, J., & White, P. (2013). The impact of cross-race mentoring for "ideal" PhD careers in sociology. *Sociological Spectrum, 33*(6), 484–509.

Spriggs, W. E., & Williams, R. M. (2000). What do we need to explain about African American unemployment?". In R. Cherry & W. M. Rodgers III (Eds.), *Prosperity for all? The economic boom and African*

Americans (pp. 188–207). New York: Russell Sage Foundation.

Stainback, K., & Tomaskovic-Devey, D. (2012). *Documenting desegregation: Racial and gender segregation in private sector employment since the civil rights act*. New York: Russel Sage Foundation.

Telles, E. E., & Murguia, E. (1990). Phenotypic discrimination and income differences among Mexican Americans. *Social Science Quarterly, 71*(4), 682–694.

The Economist. (2017). *Artificial intelligence: The impact on jobs*. Retrieved May 23, 2017. http://www.economist.com/news/special-report/21700758-will-smarter-machines-cause-mass-unemployment-automation-and-anxiety.

Tomaskovic-Devey, D. (1993). *Gender and racial inequality at work: The sources and consequences of job segregation*. Ithaca, NY: ILR Press.

Tomaskovic-Devey, D. (2016). Southern sociological presidential address. *Social Currents, 1*(1), 51–73.

Uzialko, A. C. (2017). *Business news daily*. Retrieved May 26, 2017. http://www.businessnewsdaily.com/9939-business-automation-gig-economy-workers.html.

Waldinger, R. (1996). *Still the promised city?: African-Americans and new immigrants in postindustrial New York*. Cambridge, MA: Harvard University Press.

Waldinger, R., & Litcher, M. I. (2003). *How the other half works: Immigration and the social organization of labor*. Berkeley: University of California Press.

Weil, D. (2014). *The fissured workplace: Why has work become so bad?*. Cambridge: Harvard University Press.

Wilson, W. J. (1996). *When work disappears: The world of the new urban poor*. New York: Alfred A. Knopf, Inc.

Wilson, W. J. (2015). Reflections on the issue of race and class in 21st century America. *Issues in Race & Society, 3*(2), 11–26.

Xie, Y., & Gough, M. (2011). Enclaves and the earning of immigrants. *Demography, 48*(4), 1293–1315.

Racial and Ethnic Health Inequities: An Intersectional Approach

8

Lynn Weber, Ruth Enid Zambrana, M. Elizabeth Fore
and Deborah Parra-Medina

Contents

L. Weber (✉)
Department of Psychology and Women's and
Gender Studies Program, University of South
Carolina, Columbia, SC, USA
e-mail: WEBERL@mailbox.sc.edu

R. E. Zambrana
Department of Women's Studies, University of
Maryland, College Park, MD, USA
e-mail: rzambran@umd.edu

M. E. Fore
Department of Community and Public Health, Idaho
State University, Pocatello, ID, USA
e-mail: foremarg@isu.edu

D. Parra-Medina
Department of Mexican American and Latina/o
Studies, University of Texas at Austin, Austin, TX,
USA
e-mail: parramedina@austin.utexas.edu

Abstract

Nowhere is the severity and impact of racism on our nation and its people clearer and more profound than in the arena of health—where racism is literally a matter of life and death. Employing an intersectional lens, this essay addresses four aspects of the complex relationship between health and race, ethnicity, and other systems of inequality. First, we situate the national discourse on health care disparities in an historical and social movement context, followed by several ways that racial and ethnic differences in health are defined. Second, we provide an overview of data on differences in health and health care. Third, we examine dominant and critical models for explaining the differences, specifically comparing traditional biomedical approaches with intersectional social constructionist approaches. We conclude with proposed strategies to reduce and eliminate health inequities across race, ethnicity, gender, and social class.

8.1 Introduction

Nowhere is the severity and impact of racism on our nation and its people clearer and more profound than in the arena of health—where racism is literally a matter of life and death. Since the middle of the twentieth century, extensive population studies have repeatedly documented the lowered quality and length of life and restricted life chances of low-income and poor racial/ethnic groups in the U.S. and indeed of poor populations worldwide. Compared to the White majority in the U.S., racial and ethnic minorities, particularly African Americans, Native Americans, and Latino subgroups[1] (namely Mexican American, Puerto Rican and low-income immigrant Central American groups) are more likely to die in infancy and to have shorter life spans. Their lives are characterized by poorer health and lower quality of health care as well. They are more likely to live with the debilitating effects of chronic diseases (hypertension, diabetes, AIDS/HIV, asthma, liver disease, heart disease and to die of cardiovascular (heart) disease, stroke, and some cancers (Agency for Healthcare Research and Quality [AHRQ] 2014; Centers for Disease Control [CDC] 2004, 2015; Institute of Medicine [IOM] 2003). Racial/ethnic people also have greater exposure to environmental hazards

and to health-damaging social contexts (e.g., violence), less insurance coverage, less access to health care, and lower quality of care when they do have access.

This essay addresses four aspects of the complex relationship between health and race, ethnicity, and other intersecting systems of inequality. First, we situate the national discourse on health care disparities in an historical and social movement context, followed by several ways that racial and ethnic differences in health are defined. Second, we provide an overview of data on differences in health and health care. Third, we examine dominant and critical models for explaining the differences, specifically comparing traditional biomedical approaches with intersectional social constructionist approaches. Finally, we identify proposed strategies to reduce and eliminate health inequities across race, ethnicity, gender, and social class.

8.2 Racial/Ethnic Health Disparities and Inequities: Forces of Change and Definitions in National Discourse 1978–2020

Differences in rates of life and death and the quality of health care experiences are variously referred to as health inequalities, health inequities, and health disparities. U.S. government agencies, including the National Institutes of Health (NIH) and the Centers for Disease Control (CDC) as well as public health and social science practitioners, tend to view health disparities as

> … a chain of events signified by a difference in (1) environment, (2) access to, utilization of and quality of care, (3) health status, or (4) a particular health outcome that deserves scrutiny (Carter-Pokras and Baquet 2002: 427).

Whitehead (1992) developed a broader concept of health equity, which has been adopted by the European World Health Organization (EURO/WHO) and which defines health inequities as "…differences in health which are not only unnecessary and avoidable but, in addition,

[1]For the purposes of this article and consistent with federal standards for racial and ethnic data collection, we use the terms Hispanic and Latino interchangeably, especially by staying true to direct quotes and/or health data, in which Hispanic is almost always used in the collection of empirical data. Hispanics can be of any race or national origin group and represent about 22 countries. Most of the national health data has been collected on Mexican-origin and Puerto Ricans, the two largest Hispanic subgroups, with Cubans and other Central and South Americans included when possible.

are considered unfair and unjust" (429). She distinguishes between health inequalities that are more likely to be considered unavoidable and thus fair, such as natural biological variation or health damaging behavior that is freely chosen (such as recreational drug use) and health inequalities that are avoidable and thus unfair (such as exposure to unhealthy, stressful living and working conditions, inadequate access to essential health and other basic services, and health damaging behaviors where the degree of lifestyle choice is severely restricted.

The avoidability and unfairness of racial/ethnic health disparities—which are seen as serious consequences of a vast array of social determinants, including racism—have long fueled the movement to eliminate health inequities specifically and the civil rights movement more broadly. Nowhere has the connection between racial justice, human rights, and health been more clearly stated than when Fanny Lou Hamer rallied the civil rights movement saying that she and all Black people were "…sick and tired of being sick and tired."

From the early 1970s through the 1990s, eye-opening observations of inequity—by mainly racial/ethnic community and professional activists and advocates—produced a powerful force to reduce health inequity. The advocacy of grassroots activists (e.g., National Women's Health Network, National Black Women's Health Project, National Latina Health Organization), professional organizations (e.g., American Public Health Association, American Nurses Association), and policy-makers (e.g., Congressional Black, Hispanic, and Women's Caucuses) brought greater research, visibility, and action to the cause of eliminating health disparities (Aquirre-Molina et al. 2001; Morgen 2006; Ruzek 1999; Schulz and Mullings 2006).

Highlighting the multilayed efforts across government, private and non-governmental sectors to address health inequity in the U.S., Chart 8.1 provides a glimpse of major efforts to reduce health disparities and improve health equity in the United States for racial and ethnic minorities. The 17 reports listed in Chart 8.1 illustrate the plethora of efforts to eliminate or at least to reduce racial/ethnic health inequities over the last four decades.

Elimination of persistent health disparities became a major priority for national health agencies, politicians, health advocates, and researchers. One of the first initiatives was the 1978 OMB Directive 15 that mandated identifying racial and ethnic groups including Hispanics in the U.S. data collection sysytems (Zambrana and Carter-Pokras 2001). On February 21, 1998, President Clinton committed the nation to an ambitious goal: by the year 2010, eliminating disparities in six areas of health status that disproportionately affect racial and ethnic minority groups at all life stages—infant mortality, cancer screening and management, cardiovascular disease, diabetes, HIV/AIDS, and immunizations—while continuing the progress in improving the overall health of the American people.

In 2000, the NIH developed a strategic plan to reduce and eliminate health disparities and established a National Center on Minority Health and Health Disparities. By July 2002, over 2000 people attended the first "National Leadership Summit on Eliminating Racial and Ethnic Disparities in Health," which was sponsored by the Office of Minority Health, U.S. Dept. of Health and Human Services and is now an annual event. In 2003 IOM released the first ever report, *Unequal Treatment: Confronting Racial and Ethnic Disparities in Health Care*, that publicly acknowledged multiple non-medical factors as determinants of health outcomes (Smedley et al. 2002). By 2006, although the NIH research priorities and *Healthy People 2010* described eliminating racial, ethnic and gender health disparities and achieving health equity as top priorities, the Agency for Health care Research and Quality (AHRQ) had produced reports since 2003 that consistently showed racial/ethnic health disparities continuing unabated (AHRQ 2014). Two more recent reports on Women's Health USA (U.S. Department of Health and Human Services 2013) and Hispanic Health (CDC 2015) highlighted significant disparities between racial/ethnic women and White women and between Latinos and Non-Hispanic Whites

1978: OMB Directive 15 requires the National Health Interveiw Survey to collect information about Hispanic origin

1982-1984: The Hispanic Health and Nutrition Examination Survey (HHANES) collects data on the three largests Hispanic subgroups in the US (Mexican Americans, Cuban Americans, and Puerto Ricans)

1985: Department of Health and Human Services releases the Secretary's Tast Force Report on Black and Minority Health (Heckler Report)

1986: HHS creates the Office of Minority Health

1999: Intitute of Medicine report entitled "To Err is Human" leads to the development of the Agency for Healthcare Research and Quality

2000: Healthy People 2010, a national health promotion and disease prevention agenda, sets the elimination of health disparities as a goal

2000: Office of Minority Health releases National Standards for Culturally and Linguistically Appropriate Services (National CLAS Standards)

2001: Publication of *Health Issues in the Latino Community*

2002: First AHRQ National Healthcare Quality Report and National Healthcare Disparities Report

2004: Sullivan Commission on Diversity in the Healthcare Workforce releases "Missing Persons: Minorities in the Health Professions"

2010: Publication of *Health Issues in Latino Males*

2010 Women's health USA, Health Resources and Services Administration

2010: The Affordable Care Act (ACA) expands health care access and reauthorizes the Office of Minority Health

2011: HHS introduces the HHS Action Plan to Reduce Racial and Ethnic Health Disparities and the National Stakeholder Strategy for Achieving Health Equity

2013: The Office of Minority Health updates the National CLAS Standards

2014 Agency for Health Care Quality and Research, National Healthcare Quality and Disparities Report

2015: CDC Vital Signs: Hispanic Health Report

Chart 8.1 Landmark reports on race, ethnicity, gender and health

—24% more poorly controlled high blood pressure, 23% more obesity; 28% less colorectal screening, less cancer screening, and alarmingly high rates of diabetes and chronic liver disease. The recent 2014 Agency for Healthcare Research and Quality indicates that while insurance coverage improved substantially for Black and Hispanic adults, few health care disparities were reduced or eliminated. In sum, limited progress has been observed in decreasing racial/ethnic quality of care disparities through 2013, with more measures showing disparities worsening rather than improving for people in poor households. The data serve as a reminder that if national policy constraints on health care access and quality are left un-remedied, they will continue to produce staggering disparities and inequities.

The definition of health disparities has expanded over the last 35 years as new information has increased our understanding of the multiple factors associated with health outcomes beyond biological factors. Health inequity, health inequality, and heath disparity are all terms that have been used to describe differences in disease and death rates, yet there are subtle differences in the definition of each. Health inequality is any difference in health, no matter the underlying cause. Health inequity is a difference in health outcomes that is "systematic, avoidable, and unjust." Recent definitions of health disparities go further: The U.S. Department of Health and Human Services (USDHHS), the federal agency that governs all U.S. public health agencies, including the Centers for Disease Control and Prevention, the National Institutes of Health, and the Agency for Healthcare Research and Quality, defines health disparity as:

> …a particular type of health difference that is closely linked with social, economic, and/or environmental disadvantage. Health disparities adversely affect groups of people who have systematically experienced greater obstacles to health based on the racial or ethnic group; religion; socioeconomic status; gender; age; mental health; cognitive, sensory or physical disability; sexual orientation or gender identity; geographic location; or other characteristics historically linked to discrimination or exclusion.

The report also recognizes the stress of racism on physical and emotional health.

The changing definition of health disparities has been documented in *Healthy People*, a ten-year plan from the U.S. Department of Health and Human Services that sets goals, objectives, and accompanying benchmarks to improve the overall health of Americans. *Healthy People 2000* included the goal of reducing health disparities in various subpopulations, defined by race, ethnicity, gender, income, disability, and age (Office of Disease Prevention and Promotion 1990). With the release of *Healthy People 2010*, the goal was no longer to just reduce health

disparities but to eliminate them and expand subpopulations to include sexual orientation, education, and geographic location (USDHHS 2000). *Healthy People 2010* moved closer to the current definition of health disparities by describing the multidisciplinary approach needed to eliminate health inequity but had not yet defined the underlying causes of those differences. *Healthy People 2020* includes the current definition that builds upon previous reports and focuses on underlying causes of health disparities (USDHHS 2014). A goal of *Healthy People 2020* is to "…achieve health equity, eliminate disparities, and improve the health of all groups." Strong progress has been made in expanding and understanding social, political and psychosocial factors associated with prevention and management of health conditions in the U.S. But translating and applying the science to improve the health of the nation lags behind the research to understand the causes of the inequities.

8.3 Overview of Health Disparities in the U.S.

Race and ethnicity, social class, and socioeconomic status are life and death matters—they affect our quality of life, the kinds of diseases and conditions we live with, the kinds of health behaviors we engage in, how long we live, the likelihood that our children will live past infancy, our access to health care and the quality of care we receive. Below we present recent data summarizing racial and ethnic disparities in our nation's health on three key indicators: life expectancy, causes of death, and infant mortality. Next, we present data on the differences in the prevalence and mortality of three chronic conditions that contribute to heart disease and stroke, the first and fifth leading causes of death in the U. S.: hypertension, diabetes, and overweight/ obesity. We follow with data on the differences in cancer rates for breast cancer and cervical cancer, diseases that are diagnosed later among racial/ethnic women often resulting in premature death. And finally, we present differences in the use of tobacco which is associated with the top three causes of death among women—heart disease, cancer, and stroke (Martell et al. 2016).

Even though our social locations across multiple dimensions of social inequality shape the circumstances of life and death for all of us, there is not a one-to-one correspondence between every possible indicator of morbidity and mortality and racial ethnic subordinate status. Of the top 13 causes of death in 2013, for example, Whites had higher mortality rates than African Americans on 5 causes of death: chronic lower respiratory diseases, unintentional injuries, Alzheimer's disease, suicide, and alcohol induced deaths. The top 6 leading causes of death for Hispanics[2] are malignant neoplasms (cancer), diseases of the heart, cerebrovascular diseases, unintentional injuries, diabetes mellitus, and Alzheimer's.

Cancer is the leading cause of death among Latinos, with breast and cervical cancers the most common diagnoses (Penedo et al. 2016). These indicators on which dominant groups rank highest also provide insights into the different experiences of life and death for people in dominant and subordinate racial/ethnic, social class, and gender groups. White men, for example, are more likely to commit suicide than White women or racial/ethnic people, but these deaths have been associated with the shame and stress associated with *downward* social mobility (Kochanek et al. 2004). Likewise, White women are more likely to die from Alzheimer's disease than any other race-gender group—an indicator that is certainly related to the fact that they live longer than any other group (National Center for Health Statistics [NCHS] 2005; Kochanek et al. 2004).

Depression is one of the most prevalent mental health diagnoses in the United States: a 2011 CDC report found U.S. women to have a 20.2% diagnosis rate for major depression (NCHS 2012).: the prevalence of depression among African American women varies by data source and varies when socioeconomic factors are considered; though it appears that non-Hispanic Black (NHB) women experience depression at lower rates than White women but higher rates than NHB men (Banks and Kohn-Wood 2002). These rates are moderated by other social factors, including SES and education. U.S. Latinas have a 32.6% rate of depression, significantly higher than the rates for the general population; and Latino subgroup variation reveals even higher rates of depression among Puerto Ricans, 38% of whom reported high depressive symptoms, compared to 22% for Mexicans (Wasserthiel-Smoller et al. 2014).

Associations between depression, hypertension, and cardiovascular disease (CVD) are strong: among middle-aged U.S. adults, more than one half of those diagnosed with major depressive disorder would also report CVD comorbidities (González and Tarraf 2013) associated with increased functional impairment. Despite high rates of hypertension and depression for non-Hispanic Blacks and Latinos (prevalence of hypertension among Puerto Ricans is 32%) (Pabon-Nau et al. 2010), members of these populations are less likely to report receiving treatment for hypertension and depression compared to their non-Hispanic White counterparts (González and Tarraf 2013).

---

[2]Latino population health encompasses the health of 17.1% of the U.S. population, projected to become almost 50% by 2050. Almost 64.6% Mexican American and close to 9.5% Puerto Rican, it is a heterogeneous group comprised of multiple races, cultures, and histories and is the youngest, fastest growing racial/ethnic group in the United States. Geographically, two-thirds of Hispanics live in just five states: California, Texas, Florida, New York, and Illinois. As a result of residential segregation, Mexican Americans, Puerto Ricans and African Americans are the least likely to live in "neighborhoods of opportunity," determined by availability of sustainable employment, healthy environments, access to high-quality health care, adequate transportation, high quality child care, high-performing schools, and neighborhood safety. Acevedo-Garcia (2000), Clark et al. (2014), USGAO (1983) They are also more likely to live in dense urban neighborhoods and, for Mexican Americans, on the 2000 mile border, resulting in a higher likelihood of living near landfills and having greater exposure to environmental pollutants which are linked to chronic conditions such as asthma in Puerto Rican youth and which may contribute to cancer.

8.3.1 Population Health Indicators: Life Expectancy, Causes of Death, Infant Mortality

One challenge to understanding and eliminating health disparities is access to data that are disaggregated by racial and ethnic groups as well as by gender and socioeconomic status. We know, for example, that conditions of life, health, and other critical social indicators vary significantly for different Latino groups (Mexico, Puerto Rico, Cuba, Central/South America) (Zambrana 2011). Yet many government reports still do not present indicators disaggregated by these groups, and when they do, gender differences within groups are often not available. Data presented below represent the finest level of disaggregation available from each source.

Life Expectancy

Although women of all races live longer than men of the same race, overall African Americans live 3.6 fewer years than Whites (Table 8.1). For persons born in 2014, the life expectancy for non-Hispanic African American women was 78.1, while for White women it was 81.1 (NCHS 2016). Substantially shorter lives were expected for non-Hispanic African American men, who were projected to live an average of 4.5 fewer years than non-Hispanic White men and 9.1 fewer years than non-Hispanic White women (NCHS 2016). Although Hispanic men and women as a group have higher life expectancies than other groups, this difference masks wide variations in life expectancy among Hispanic subgroups. The incidence of and mortality from CVD, for example, vary among Latino subgroups and across geographical locations. Rates of smoking and obesity—two crucial risk factors for cancer and heart disease and leading causes of mortality for Latinos in the United States—

also vary across subgroups. Mexicans and Puerto Ricans are approximately twice as likely to die from diabetes as Whites. Mexicans are almost twice as likely to die from chronic liver disease and cirrhosis as Whites (NCHS 2012). A large cohort study of Latinos (SOL), currently underway and funded by NIH, is investigating cardiovascular disease (CVD) and other diseases and risk factors that lower the quality of life across subgroups (NIH/NHLB 2013).

CVD, for example, the leading cause of death and disease in the United States, is disproportionately experienced by racial/ethnic and low-income groups (American Heart Association (AHA) 2000). Biobehavioral research has consistently documented that physical inactivity, adverse dietary patterns, smoking, and obesity increase the risk of CVD (Johnson and Sempos 1995; Mokdad et al. 2004; Must et al. 1999). Population-wide surveillance data indicate that inactivity rates are particularly prevalent among women, older adults, adults with lower educational achievement, and racial/ethnic minorities. In recent years, physical inactivity has been a primary target for research and intervention to eliminate disparities in CVD because while race, gender, and social class are deemed to be "unmodifiable," physical inactivity is believed to be modifiable, a "true" proximal cause of disease and to hold great potential for reducing or preventing CVD and other chronic conditions (Johnson and Sempos 1995).

Causes of Death

Racial/ethnic minorities have higher mortality rates than Whites for 10 of 13 leading causes of death (see Table 8.2). Among 13 leading causes of death in 2013, the death rates for seven diseases—cancer, heart disease, stroke, diabetes, influenza and pneumonia, nephritis, homicide, and septicemia—were higher for African

Table 8.1 Life expectancy at birth by sex, race, and Hispanic origin, 2014

Race/ethnicity	Both sexes	Male	Female
White, not Hispanic	78.8	76.5	81.1
Black, not Hispanic	75.2	72.0	78.1
Hispanic	81.1	79.2	84.0

Source National Center for Health Statistics (NCHS) (2016)

Table 8.2 Age-adjusted[a] deaths per 100,000 population for selected causes by race and ethnicity, 2013

	Race				Ethnicity	
Top 13 overall causes	White	Black	American Indian or Alaska Native	Asian or Pacific Islander	Hispanic	Non-Hispanic
Malignant neoplasms	163.7	189.2	110.2	100.5	114.5	167.5
Diseases of the heart	168.2	210.4	120.6	92.8	121.2	173.9
Chronic lower respiratory diseases	44.8	29.5	30.8	13.6	18.7	44.1
Unintentional injuries	41.9	32.6	47.1	15.2	26.9	41.3
Cerebrovascular diseases	34.9	49.0	24.6	29.4	29.6	36.6
Alzheimer's disease	24.4	20.1	12.7	11.1	17.7	23.9
Diabetes mellitus	19.4	38.4	34.1	15.8	26.3	20.8
Influenza and pneumonia	15.8	16.7	15.0	15.0	13.2	16.1
Nephritis, nephrotic syndrome and nephrosis	12.1	25.0	11.4	8.1	11.1	13.3
Suicide	14.2	5.4	11.7	5.9	5.7	13.8
Homicide	3.1	17.8	5.3	1.5	4.5	5.3
Septicemia	10.1	18.3	10.2	5.0	8.4	10.9
Chronic liver disease and cirrhosis	10.7	7.3	24.8	3.3	14.0	9.7
Other overlapping causes						
Drug-induced deaths	16.4	10.2	13.2	2.5	7.3	16.0
Alcohol-induced deaths	8.7	6.0	26.8	1.8	9.0	8.1
Injury by firearms	9.6	17.2	7.4	2.4	5.4	11.3

[a]Age-adjusted rates control for differences in the age distribution of a population, thereby allowing comparison of disease or mortality rates between populations. Age-adjusted rates are the weighted average of the age-specific disease or death rates, where the weights are the proportion of the standard population in the corresponding age group
Source Xu et al. (2016)

Americans than for any other group. More African Americans, for example, die of diabetes mellitus, a health condition that is both a cause of death and a contributor to other causes of death, with a mortality rate that is almost twice that of the rate for Whites. African Americans are also five times more likely to die in homicides and two times more likely to die from firearms than Whites. American Indians/Alaska Natives have more alcohol induced deaths as well as deaths related to alcohol abuse—unintentional injuries and chronic liver disease and cirrhosis—than all other groups. With the exception of diabetes and chronic liver disease and cirrhosis, Hispanics

have lower death rates than non-Hispanics, but those rates vary significantly among subgroups with very different histories in the U.S.—Mexican, Puerto Rican, Cuban, South/Central American. And Asian/Pacific Islanders have the lowest morality rates of any race or ethnicity, largely because they have higher educational and income levels than non-Hispanic Whites (National Center for Health Statistics 2016).

Not only do the mortality rates differ among racial/ethnic groups, but the ten leading causes of death also differ. Three causes, homicide, septicemia, and chronic liver disease and cirrhosis, are listed in the top ten for only one race. African

Americans mortality rates resulting from homicide and septicemia are higher than those for other races/ethnicities. These conditions were ranked as the 8 and 9th, respectively, top causes of death for African Americans in 2013. American Indians/Alaska Natives die from chronic liver disease and cirrhosis at higher rates, with these conditions being the 5th leading cause of death for this population in 2013 (National Center for Health Statistics 2016).

Gender disparities in death rates exist for all racial/ethnic groups (Xu et al. 2016). Although alcohol-induced deaths are highest among American Indian/Alaska Natives, for example, the age-adjusted mortality rate (# deaths/100,000 population) for women is 18.3 and for men is 35.6, almost twice as high. Whites have the highest mortality rates for drug-induced deaths at 16.4 with men contributing to the higher rate at 20.0 deaths per 100,000. The most dramatic disparity is the death rate resulting from firearms. Firearm deaths, which killed 7697 African Americans in 2013, were more common among African American men than among African American women— 32.1 per 100,000 compared to 3.4 per 100,000.

Including both age and gender as variables in mortality rates illuminates the disparities that occur throughout the lifespan. Compared with other races/ethnicities, African Americans die at younger ages from chronic diseases, unintentional injuries and violence (Xu et al. 2016). Death rates (#/100,000) for all conditions for African American men and women are higher than rates for Whites in each 5-yr age group from birth to age 84. In 2013, the death rate from heart disease for African American men ages 55–64 was 430.0 but only 254.0 for White men. For African American women in the same age group, the death rate from heart disease was 213.0 but only 95.9 for White women. Not only were deaths from homicide higher among African American men than for any other group, but homicide is the number one cause of death for young African American men ages 15–34 at 66.6, nine times higher than for young White men at 7.1. Firearm-related injuries among African American men also differ by age with younger men aged 15–24 experiencing over four times more deaths (69.9) than Whites (16.0) (Xu et al. 2016).

Infant Mortality

Infant mortality rates are a second indicator of a healthy population and differ significantly across racial and ethnic groups. As shown in Table 8.3, non-Hispanic African American women have the highest infant mortality rate of any group (11.1) and more than double the rate among non-Hispanic White women (5.1) (NCHS 2016). Although Hispanics have infant mortality rates lower than that of non-Hispanic Whites, there are disparities among ethnic subgroups. Women of Puerto Rican descent have the highest infant mortality rate of 5.9 per 1000 live births compared to Cubans, who have the lowest infant mortality rate of any race/ethnicity at 3.0 per 1000 live births—reflecting their different histories in this country and related socioeconomic disparities (NCHS 2016).

Table 8.3 Infant mortality rates by race and Hispanic origin of mother, 2013

	Death rate per 1000 live births
White, non-Hispanic	5.1
Black or African American, non-Hispanic	11.1
American Indian or Alaska Native	7.6
Asian or Pacific Islander	4.1
Hispanic or Latina	5.0
Mexican	4.9
Puerto Rican	5.9
Cuban	3.0
Central and South American	4.3

Source National Center for Health Statistics (NCHS) (2016)

8.3.2 Chronic Conditions: Hypertension, Diabetes, Obesity/Overweight

Hypertension and Diabetes

Hypertension and diabetes, major risk factors for heart disease, stroke, and kidney failure, are more common among African Americans, Asian Americans, and Hispanics or Latinos. Further, non-Hispanic Black women and Hispanic women have higher rates of hypertension than their male counterparts.

The 2014 National Health and Nutrition Examination Survey (NHANES), which includes both interviews and physical examinations from a stratified random sample of the noninstitutionalized civilian population, includes age-adjusted prevalence data on chronic conditions, including hypertension, diabetes, and overweight/obesity (NCHS 2016). The 2014 NHANES data indicate that 44.0% of non-Hispanic Black women and 42.4% of non-Hispanic Black men either have high blood pressure and/or are taking anti-hypertensive medication, compared to 28.3% of non-Hispanic White women and 31.2% of non-Hispanic White men. Among Hispanics, 28.6% of all women and 29.4% of Mexican-origin women had hypertension compared to 27.7% of all men and 27.5% of Mexican origin men (NCHS 2016), Yet the Study of Latinos indicates that again, there are significant variations among subgroups: "...the percentages of participants with a history of hypertension were lowest among those of Mexican and South American backgrounds and highest among those of Cuban, Dominican, and Puerto Rican backgrounds" (NHLB 2013: 29). Two recent Women's Health Initiative analyses of hypertension among Hispanic women show an adverse cardiovascular risk profile as elder Hispanic women appear to be at high risk of hypertension.

NHANES data also indicate that both physician-diagnosed and undiagnosed diabetes are more common among non-Hispanic African Americans, non-Hispanic Asians, and Hispanics (NCHS 2016). In the 2014 NHANES survey, 18.0% of non-Hispanic African Americans and 16.3% of non-Hispanic Asians had physician-diagnosed or undiagnosed diabetes compared with 9.5% of Whites. When considering ethnicity, 16.8% of Hispanics overall and 18.0% of Mexican origin individuals had physician diagnosed or undiagnosed diabetes. Furthermore, among those with physician-diagnosed diabetes, poor glycemic control, defined as A1c >9, was more common in Hispanics at 29.8% and non-Hispanic Blacks at 23.9% compared to non-Hispanic Whites at 16.6% (NCHS 2016).

Obesity and Overweight

A recent CDC report shows that nearly one-third of the U.S. adult population is obese. The negative health consequences associated with the "obesity epidemic" are well-documented and present a significant impact upon public health. Among Hispanics in 50 states and the District of Columbia, the reported prevalence of obesity ranged from 21.0% (Maryland) to 36.7% (Tennessee) and was ≥30% in 11 states (Singh et al. 2013). The association of obesity with increased incidence of hypertension, hyperlipidemia, and diabetes, the most widely recognized cardiovascular disease (CVD) risk factors, signifies that obese individuals are particularly at risk of death from CVD and its sequelae (Arias et al. 2008). Yet despite the public health impact associated with increasing incidence in obesity and co-occurring health conditions, the exact causes of this phenomenon are still undetermined and yet to be fully examined in underserved, racial/ethnic communities (see Brennan et al. 2015).

Over the last 20 years, overweight [defined as a body mass index (BMI) of 25–29.9] and obesity (BMI >30) have increased dramatically and quickly in U.S. adults in every race/ethnic group, both genders, and all age groups (Kuczmarski and Flegal 2000; Mokad et al. 1999). From 1988 to 2014, the number of Americans who are overweight or obese has increased in all ages, races, and ethnicities, with the highest rates occurring in non-Hispanic African American women (NCHS 2016). Obesity, estimated to be the second leading cause of "preventable" death in the United States, is directly related to poor diet and physical inactivity and is a risk factor for a multitude of chronic diseases including heart disease, type 2 diabetes, stroke, gallbladder disease, osteoarthritis, and some cancers (endometrial, colon, and postmenopausal breast) (Must et al. 1999; NHLBI 2013). The 2011–2014 NHANES data indicate that 82.0% of non-Hispanic Black women and 69.6% of non-Hispanic Black men were overweight or obese compared to 63.5% of non-Hispanic White women and 73.7% of non-Hispanic White men. Among Hispanics, 82.7% of Hispanic men and 80.3% of women of Mexican origin were overweight/obese (NCHS 2016).

Cervical and Breast Cancer

Cervical cancer is more prevalent among Black women than among White women, with incidence rates of 8.7 and 6.9 per 100,000 population, respectively, and African American's survival rates are also lower (Howlader et al. 2016). Breast cancer data reveal more fully the complex effect of race, ethnicity, and social class on women's life experiences with these cancers. Cancer registry data collected between 2004 and 2013 indicate that African American women are less likely to be diagnosed with breast cancer than White women. And when they are diagnosed, the diagnosis occurs at a later stage in the disease, so they are much more likely to die from it (28.2 deaths per 100,000 vs. 20.3) (Howlader et al. 2016).

Cervical cancer incidence rates are higher for Hispanic women compared to non-Hispanic Whites. Hispanic women also experience a higher mortality rate for cervical cancer, which implicates both elevated incidence and lower detection rates. An investigation into cervical cancer disparities found an association between low socioeconomic status, limited English proficiency, and being foreign born; and disparities in Latina cervical cancer treatment and disparities. (Downs et al. 2008) Hispanic women living in U.S.-Mexico border states experience a higher incidence of cervical cancer, and foreign-born Hispanic women are 40% more likely to die of cervical cancer than their U.S.-born counterparts. Breast cancer has the greatest incidence among and is the leading cause of cancer death for Hispanic women. Though breast cancer incidence rates are lower for Hispanic women than for non-Hispanic White women, Hispanic women are more likely to be diagnosed at later stages with larger tumors and are 20% more likely to die of breast cancer than non-Hispanic white women (Haile et al. 2012).

Behavioral Health Risk: Smoking

Tobacco use is the major contributor in the three leading causes of death among women: heart disease, cancer, and stroke. Smoking increases the risk of a woman's dying of lung cancer by 12 times, dying of bronchitis and emphysema by 10 times, and triples the risk of dying of heart disease (CDC 1993). Not only correlated to race/ethnicity but also to socioeconomic status, smoking is more common among White women than African American women, with smoking rates being inversely related to education (NCHS 2005). Among non-Hispanic White women, 18.7% currently smoke compared to 14.4% of non-Hispanic African American women (NCHS 2016). Though these rates are similar, the most striking differences are across educational levels. For women of all races/ethnicities with at least a bachelor's degree, only 6.2% smoke, but 21.2% of women who do not have a high school diploma or GED smoke (NCHS 2016).

While smoking among Latinos overall is lower compared to Whites (10.7% and 16.6%, respectively), smoking is more common among Puerto Rican and Cuban males (28.5% and 19.8% respectively) (CDCP, 2018). Other data suggest even higher rates of smoking among Puerto Rican and Cuban men (34.7% and 31.1%, respectively) (Daviglus et al. 2012).

8.3.3 Disparities in Health Care: Access and Treatment

Latinos and African Americans are more likely to experience healthcare disparities and communication barriers. Access is often defined solely by access to health insurance, yet insurance is but one of many crucial factors influencing access to quality health care among Latinos (Carrillo et al. 2001). While health insurance status accounts for "primary access" to health care, insured Latinos still face barriers to care, including language and culture differences from their practitioners, long waiting times, and few after-hours care opportunities (Carrillo et al. 2001).

Multiple researchers report that racism and implicit bias contribute to inequalities in diagnosis and treatment for cardiovascular disease, diabetes, hypertension, chronic pain, and psychiatric disorders (Lewis et al. 2015; Burgess et al. 2008; Drwecki et al. 2011; Green et al. 2007; Moskowitz et al. 2012; Sabin and Greenwald 2012; Greer et al. 2014). In addition, poor patient-provider communication negatively affects patient satisfaction, adherence to treatment, and attitudes towards providers and provider decision-making (Sheppard et al. 2016; Burgess et al. 2008; Cooper et al. 2012; Martin et al. 2013).

Other organizational, systemic barriers within the health care system include:

> …few interpretation services and language-appropriate health education materials and signage; bureaucratic, complicated intake processes, long waiting times for appointments, and limited operating hours (including after-hours availability); and [locations] outside the community, making them difficult to reach via public transportation (Carrillo et al. 2001).

In 2009, about one third of Latinos, mainly Mexican Americans, lacked health insurance while in 2014 one quarter lacked health care insurance (Cohen and Martinez 2015). These data however do not present an accurate picture of subgroup access to health care. Cubans who are refugees have access to health care, for example, while Mexican origin groups are less likely to have access because of employment in the service and constructions industries and undocumented status, for some (see Zambrana

2011; Rodriguez et al. 2014 for a description of Latino populations) (Table 8.4).

Health Insurance: The Affordable Care Act

To address needs of the millions of Americans without access to affordable, quality healthcare, President Obama signed the Patient Protection and Affordable Care Act (ACA) in 2010, which included a four-year plan to implement comprehensive health insurance reforms for all Americans (2010). Key features of the plan aimed at improving disparities include increased access to affordable health insurance and mandatory health insurance coverage for essential health services. The ACA also includes expanding eligibility for Medicaid services in states that chose expansion and subsidies to low income individuals for buying private insurance through state-based health insurance exchanges or the Health Insurance Marketplace, established by U.S. Department of Health and Human Services. The ACA requires that all health insurance, both public and private, cover essential services, including preventive healthcare, hospitalizations, prescription drugs, and laboratory service (Patient Protection and Affordable Care Act 2010).

Although the ACA has resulted in a decrease in the number of Americans without health insurance, from 48.3 million in 2010 to 35.7 million in 2014, disparities in insurance status continue to affect racial and ethnic peoples at higher rates than Whites. In 2014 among adults under the age of 65, 28.3% of American Indians, 27.2% of Hispanics of Mexican descent, yet only 13.3% of Whites had no health insurance. Cost and eligibility requirements have continued to contribute to the number of uninsured. In a 2014 survey of low-income Americans, researchers

Table 8.4 Trends in uninsured status, all ages, 2009–2014

Year	Hispanic (%)	Non-Hispanic White (%)
2009	32.8	13.1
2010	31.9	13.7
2011	31.1	13.0
2012	30.4	12.7
2013	30.3	12.1
2014	25.2	9.8

Cohen and Martinez (2015)

reported that 48% of uninsured adults reported that cost continued to be a barrier to coverage (Kaiser Family Foundation 2015). And this problem is likely to worsen in the near future. Some insurance companies (e.g., Aetna, Humana) have recently pulled out of or greatly reduced their involvement in the health insurance exchanges, citing the costs of insuring the formerly uninsured because they are sicker than estimated at the beginning of the ACA (New York Times, August 16 2016).

The lack of universal expansion of Medicaid also has led to disparities in the number of uninsured. The ACA provided expanded Medicaid eligibility for individuals with incomes at or below 138% of poverty and subsidies for those with higher incomes (Patient Protection and Affordable Care Act 2010). The ACA did not provide provisions for individuals in states that did not expand Medicaid eligibility, leaving by January 2016 2.9 million uninsured people in the 19 states that did not expand Medicaid (Garfield and Damico 2016). These states have more low-income women and larger racial/ethnic minority populations. Among uninsured adults living in non-Medicaid expansion states who would qualify for Medicaid, 52% are women and 55% are non-Whites—23% Hispanics, 28% African American, and 4% "other" (Garfield and Damico 2016).

Because of limited income and lack of insurance, women and racial/ethnic minorities frequently do not seek healthcare. In 2014, 12.2% of women and 10.1% of men reported delaying or not receiving needed medical care because of costs, and 13.5% of women and 8.8% of men did not receive needed prescriptions. The percent of adults aged 18-64 who did not receive dental care in the past 12 months because of costs remains high, with those identifying as two or more races experiencing the most burden at 19.5%, followed by Hispanics at 17.4%, Blacks at 16.0%, and only 12.9% of Whites. In addition, data from the most recent NHANES, 2011–2012, reported that among low-income adults aged 45–64, 69.7% of African Americans, 45.7% of Latinos of Mexican origin, and 51.6% of Whites had untreated dental cavities.

8.4 Understanding the Social Contexts of Racial/Ethnic Health Disparities

Despite increased public awareness and outcry, intensified concern among researchers and government funding agencies, and a half century of funding of social science research on health inequalities, there is very little evidence that health disparities across race and ethnicity as well as class, and gender have abated (see Chart 8.1). The Annual Healthcare Disparities Report in 2012 concluded that overall "quality is improving, access is getting worse, and disparities are not improving." One reason for this stubborn persistence of racial and ethnic health disparities lies in the hegemony of biomedical conceptions of and approaches to health in the U.S.

Because it leaves out or only nominally considers the social forces and contexts that shape and actually *produce* health, the biomedical paradigm, with its narrow focus on disease, individual bodies, health care, and treatment in clinical settings, inadequately represents health (Weber 2006; Weber and Parra-Medina 2003; Koh et al. 2011; Weber and Castellow 2012; Krieger 2014). And even though biomedicine has responded to racial/ethnic and feminist scholars and grassroots activists about how race and gender affect the etiology, natural history, and treatment of disease by initiating changes in policy such as mandated inclusion of women and people of color in clinical trials, the clinical practice framework remains. That framework has also dominated social science research designed to broaden the biomedical model by examining psychosocial factors in the etiology of disease and race- and gender-related health practices in the use of medical services. But these models do not adequately represent health because they are closely tied to conceptions of health as located in individuals, their bodies, and their micro-level interactions while the underlying social dynamics that actually produce health and health inequality are left unexamined (Weber and Parra-Medina 2003; Braveman and Gottlieb 2014; Hankivsky et al. 2011; Koh 2011; Krieger 2014; White et al. 2012).

Even scholars working solidly within the positivist biomedical paradigm have identified its hegemony over the research and policy landscape as an obstacle to improving the nation's health and eliminating health disparities. Over a decade ago, the prestigious Institute of Medicine of the National Academies of Science, for example, recognized the need for new approaches to public health and health disparities. In a report, *The Future of the Public's Health in the Twenty-First Century* (2002), the Institute pointed to the dominance of the biomedical paradigm as a *cause* of the gap between U.S. health-related expenditures—at that time roughly 13% of our gross domestic product, more than any other industrialized nation—and our health status, which lagged behind that of many nations:

> The vast majority of health care spending, as much as 95% by some estimates, is directed toward medical care and biomedical research. However, there is strong evidence that behavior and environment are responsible for over 70 percent of avoidable mortality, and health care is just one of several determinants of health (IOM 2002, p. 2).

Since 2002, the costs of healthcare have only grown. In 2014, per capita national health expenditures were $9523, total national health expenditures totaled $3.0 trillion, and now 17.5% of our gross domestic product is consumed by health expenditures—the largest percentage of any nation—while our infant mortality rates place us 26th in the world (CDC 2014, 2016; Thorpe et al. 2007). That 95% of our spending is devoted to research in areas that—at best—account for less than 30% of avoidable deaths clearly speaks to the power of biomedicine in America. The social structures and physical environments that provide the contexts for illness, disease, and death are clearly much more potent determinants of disparities and useful sites for interventions to eliminate them.

To effectively address health disparities, we must answer the question of how race and racism get into our bodies. We cannot, however, even begin to answer the question without first understanding what race, ethnicity, and racism are and how they are produced, maintained, challenged, and changed. And as has been the case for over a century, a key question today centers on whether race and racism are social or biological constructs and whether racial/ethnic disparities in health are the result of "(a) innate genetic differences, (b) the biological impact of present and past histories of racial discrimination and economic deprivation, or (c) both" (Krieger 2005, 2015).

Race and Genes

In the last decade a centuries old debate over the biological and/or social construction of race, ethnicity and disease has been refueled by the Human Genome Project—a fifteen year, $3 billion project to catalog and to analyze the entire human genome—the repository of DNA building blocks. Spurred by new technological capacity, The Human Genome Project has become one of the highest scientific priorities of government—eclipsing all other contenders for research dollars and reshaping the fields of biology and medicine (Cook-Deegan 1994; Woliver 2002). Scientists working on health disparities in this area subscribe to the notion that race is a genetic construct and that understanding patterns of genes across racially defined populations could help to identify populations at risk for various diseases and illnesses and at some point enable medical practitioners to use the information in treatment (Fine 2005).

That genetics has become hegemonic within health science and has overwhelmed social science approaches in research funding is undeniable. Krieger (2005) reports that for the decade 1995–2004, the NIH and CDC awarded 21,956 new grants that were indexed in the CRISP database of all NIH grants with the term *genetics* (including 181 additionally indexed by *race*) and only 44 that were indexed with the terms *racism* or *racial discrimination*—a ratio of 500 to 1. We conducted the same search of the new grants indexed in *NIH Reporter,* which replaced CRISP for the following decade. Between 2006 and 2015 the NIH and CDC awarded 25,293 new grants indexed with the term *genetics* (including 818 additionally indexed by *race*—a fourfold increase) and 171 indexed with the terms *racism* or *racial discrimination*—also an increase, but still a ratio of 500 to 3.

This gross imbalance might not be so disturbing had social science and biological research not demonstrated that human beings share 99.9% of their DNA in common and that the vast majority of genetic variation (90–95%) occurs within, not across, human populations (Braun 2002; Lee et al. 2001). And although it is possible to classify geographically defined populations by DNA clusters, there is no evidence that race as defined by continent or ancestry is useful in determining causes of disease or in predicting individual diagnoses or responses to drugs (Cooper et al. 2003; Fine 2005; Roux 2012).

While genetic research has provided answers to questions about causes of some diseases and conditions and has offered promising keys to treatments, today there is little reason to see genetic research as an effective avenue for eliminating racial and ethnic, socioeconomic, or gender disparities in health. Perhaps more importantly, the dominance of the biomedical paradigm and its continuing fascination with genetics make it increasingly difficult to address the *social hierarchies* of race and ethnicity as well as class, gender, sexuality, and nation—hierarchies that are demonstrably more involved in producing different health outcomes (Clarke and Shim 2011; Kreiger 2014). By obscuring the social bases of health, the biomedical paradigm facilitates the shift of national resources away from the fundamentals of health and towards an over medicalized, highly technical, and socially unequal health-care system that increasingly works well only for the privileged few.

Beyond Genetics: Psychosocial and Biobehavioral Explanations for Health Disparities
The recent push to find genetic causes and solutions for race-based health disparities is just the latest in the long-standing biomedically driven search for health inequities in individuals' bodies. But the assumptions and epistemology of the biomedical paradigm extend beyond human biology and have shaped the ways that behavioral and social sciences have approached the study of health and health disparities. Most importantly, biobehavioral and psychosocial research on health disparities also assumes that health and health disparities are to be located in individuals but looks for psychological and behavioral correlates or 'antecedents' of health outcomes. The search is for causes of morbidity and mortality that rest in the thoughts/perceptions, emotions, actions, and social interactions of individuals.

Receiving the bulk of research funding allocated to the study of health and health disparities in the behavioral and social sciences, psychosocial and biobehavioral research that extends the biomedical model to incorporate more psychological and social traits has increased our knowledge of the disease process and supported behavioral interventions that work for individuals. This research has, for example, identified health-related behaviors (e.g., smoking, exercise, diet) and psychological and social characteristics and processes among individuals and/or as manifest in individuals (e.g., social supports, locus of control, faulty logic, self-esteem, stress of discrimination, perceptions of mastery and control) that have significant impacts on health and in some cases on health disparities (Lewis et al. 2015; Smedley and Syme 2000).

One of the reasons that biobehavioral and psychosocial research has had such an appeal to funders, researchers, and policy makers is that the factors identified as causes of poor health outcomes (e.g., exercise, diet, smoking) are deemed to be more amenable to intervention than the presumably less maleable historically embedded social structures of race and ethnicity as well as other intersecting inequalities—social class, socioeconomic status, and gender.

Research has similarly focused on identifying mediators between social inequalities and mental health. Some common intervening factors in mental health research on depression in women, for example, have been sense of control, resilience, stress, role overload, and social supports (Matthews et al. 1998; Pavalko and Woodbury 2000; Swanson et al. 1997). But even when these factors reduce or explain variance attributed to race, gender, class, socioeconomic status or other dimensions of inequality in particular depression indicators, and as in CVD-physical activity research, fundamental questions about how these systems of inequality are generated and maintained go unanswered because the dimensions are simply taken as "givens" in the research (Shim 2014).

Since research in this vein relies on individual level data and analyses, it cannot fully capture the group processes that define systems of social inequality. By ignoring the social processes that generate and sustain race, class, gender, and other dimensions of inequality, researchers cannot see beyond the "proximate causes" to challenge the "fundamental causes" of health disparities (Link and Phelan 2000; Phelan and Link 2015). Interventions generated out of psychosocial research are also unlikely to have a significant impact on *health disparities* because discoveries about intervening pathways or proximate causes of disease and illness get introduced into a social order hierarchically organized by race, ethnicity, class, socioeconomic status, and gender (Link and Phelan 1995, 1996, 2000; Ruzek 1999). As Williams (1997: 327) states of social inequality, "As long as the basic causal forces are in operation, the alteration of surface causes will give rise to new intervening mechanisms to maintain the same outcome."

Summarizing some of the reasons that the relationship between socioeconomic status and disease persists, Link and Phelan (2000:39) suggest that socioeconomic status "... embodies resources like knowledge, money, power, and prestige that can be used in different ways in different situations to avoid risks for disease and death" (Link and Phelan 1995, 1996; Phelan and Link 2015). When interventions are developed to address health disparities, new intervening pathways spring up to replace the ones that may have been reduced or eliminated.

8.4.1 The Sociology of Racial and Ethnic Health Disparities: Macro Structures and Intersections

Three promising directions in sociological research on health disparities aim

- to move health disparities research "upstream," beyond the narrow focus on the individual
- to complicate the notion of disparities as inequalities by examining race and ethnicity in the historic and contemporary context of other systems of social inequality with which they are closely intertwined—gender, social class, socioeconomic status, sexuality, nation (Bowleg 2012; Viruell-Fuentes et al. 2012).
- to promote interdisciplinary and community-engaged research to incorporate the resource context and the voices of the underserved or misserved (Mullins and Maddox 2015).

The calls to "move upstream" to understand the macro social structural contexts shaping health and to incorporate gender and socioeconomic status into health disparities research emerge from traditional social science which has been wedded in critical ways to the biomedical framework. Largely based on survey research where individuals are units of analysis, the research still typically aims to identify the intervening links between social inequalities and individual health—albeit while incorporating more dimensions and measures of social inequality. Statistical problems arising from inadequate sample sizes, however, often limit the ability of such research to actually investigate the ways that race, ethnicity, gender, and social class may interact with one another to produce health outcomes for communities or individuals (Weber and Parra-Medina 2003; Bowleg 2012). In short, adding new measures may not be enough to adequately assess the impact of socially structured inequalities on health. As Ruzek et al. (1997: 22) state, "Grafting psychosocial factors onto biomedical models may lead to incremental improvements in primary prevention, screening, and treatment, but these are not adequate substitutes for providing the prerequisites for health. Nor does such grafting even begin to address women's differences and the complexities of meeting their health needs."

Community-engaged research is an outgrowth of civil rights community advocates' insistence on being part of the change and of the research that claimed to seek solutions to community problems. They demanded that research solutions need community–engaged voices in order to enhance understanding of social determinants at the institutional and provider levels and to inform interventions to improve favorable outcomes. Unfortunately, only surface attention has been paid to this important methodological consideration and funding agencies continue to promote dominant culture research investigators who often include community groups as tokens. However, models exist and guidelines that could effectively contribute to reducing health inequalities in subordinated communities (Thomas et al. 2011; Giachello et al. 2003).

Feminist Intersectionality and Health Disparities One critical body of research that has the advantages of being centered both on the intersectional and interactive dynamics of multiple systems of social inequality and on the macro as well as micro power relationships that constitute them is feminist intersectional scholarship. Feminist intersectional scholarship emerged from the voices of African–American and other women of color whose social location at the intersections of multiple systems of oppression made any politic, practice, or scholarship that treats these systems as separate seem absurd (Crenshaw 1989; Zambrana 1987; Collins 2000a, b; Hankivsky 2014). Black women have spoken of this contradiction for a very long time. In a now classic speech delivered in 1851, Sojourner Truth described the contradictions between her life as an African American and the qualities presumed to be those of women when she declared "And ain't I a woman?" (Loewenberg and Bogin 1976: 235). The complexities and contradictions in Black women's lives that Sojourner Truth describes remain relevant, and understanding this "intersectionality" is today a primary concern of feminist scholars across disciplinary, thematic, and scholar-activist boundaries (Collins 2015).

Because it emerged from a very different scholarly and social-justice impulse than traditional biomedically-driven scholarship on health and health disparities, feminist intersectional scholarship is a good place to look for a fresh critical approach to health science generally and to health disparities research in specific. First, it arose among women of color inside and outside the academy—not from the centers of power in the legitimized halls of academe and government, where women of color's voices are still not well represented. Second, intersectional scholarship arose as a critique of mainstream scholarship and scholarly institutions and of the exclusionary practices of emerging interdisciplinary and critical movements, including women's studies and ethnic studies (e.g., see Baca Zinn and Dill 1996; Dill and Kohlman 2012; Dill and Zambrana 2009). Consequently, intersectional scholarship benefits from the ways that these critical scholarships opened up new intellectual spaces that allow for different approaches to knowledge and research. Third, it arose primarily to understand and to address the multiple dimensions of social inequity (e.g., class, race, ethnicity, nation, sexuality, and gender) manifest at both the macro level of institutions and the micro level of the individual experiences of people who live "at the intersections" of multiple inequities. Finally, feminist intersectional scholarship's focus is not narrowly on health but more globally on the constructions of hierarchies of privilege and power across all social institutions, including the economy, family, education, law, religion, media. As a result, inquiry is not framed by the traditional biomedical emphasis on individuals or individual bodies as units of analysis and as targets of concern.

As a consequence of this very different history and motivation for and approach to research, feminist intersectional scholarship raises critical questions that challenge some of the taken-for-granted assumptions in traditional health disparities research. (For a detailed comparison of these approaches see Hankivsy and Grace 2014; Hankivsky 2012; Morgen 2006; Weber 2006; Weber and Parra-Medina 2003; Weber and Castellow 2012). Intersectional theory argues that gender, race, ethnicity, sexuality, and class are mutually constitutive, intersect in the lived experiences of those who occupy and negotiate different social locations in systems of power in the health care system and in the larger society and that health inequities are produced by racism, gender inequality, and class relations (Morgen 2006: 398)

Although much intersectional research has centered on concerns such as the economy and labor, education, family, and sexuality, research by feminist health researchers problematizes and seeks to re-vision the social construction of health in a more complex and inclusive way (e.g., Clarke and Olesen 1999; Hankivsky 2014; Hankivsky et al. 2011; Shim 2014; Zambrana 2001). This scholarship

- expands our conception of health to incorporate a broad framework of social relations and institutions, not just diseases and disorders, and situates health in communities and families not simply in individual bodies
- sees power relationships, not just distributional differences, in resources as central to social inequity and health inequities
- simultaneously addresses the intersections of race and ethnicity with gender, class, socioeconomic status, sexuality, age, rural-urban residence, region and other markers of social inequity
- embraces interdisciplinarity and multiple methodologies
- centers research in the lives and perspectives of multiply oppressed groups, particularly women of color
- sees activism for social justice in health for all people as an integral part of the knowledge acquisition process (cf., Ruzek et al. 1997; Dhamoon and Hankivsky 2011; Luft and Ward 2009; Schulz and Mullings 2006; Weber 2006; Weber and Castellow 2012; Zambrana and Carter-Pokras 2001).

Opposing reports on health disparities generated 15 years ago reveal the strengths of an intersectional approach to health inequity: an Institute of Medicine (IOM) report, *Unequal Treatment: Confronting Racial and Ethnic Disparities in Health Care* (Smedley et al. 2002), published by the National Academy of Sciences, and a publication prepared for the National Colloquium on Black Women's Health, an event

and publication co-sponsored by the National Black Women's Health Project (NBWHP), the Congressional Black Caucus Health Brain Trust, and the U.S. Senate Black Legislative Staff Caucus (National Black Women's Health Project 2003). The IOM report approaches the question of health disparities from the positivist biomedical framework while the Colloquium on Black Women's Health takes a feminist intersectional approach.

Morgen (2006) notes three critical problems with the positivist biomedical paradigm in the IOM report. First, the report extracts race/ethnicity from the matrix of power relations that shape inequality in the United States, including gender and class. By defining the technique of statistically controlling for other inequalities as a standard for establishing the scientific validity of race and ethnic health disparities, "...the committee, by definition could not develop an intersectional analysis" (Morgen 2006) Second, the report reduces structural/systemic inequalities to individual-level problems of bias, stereotyping, and discriminatory behavior—an outcome ensured by its Congressional mandate to assess racial and ethnic differences in health care that *are not otherwise due to known factors such as access to care, e.g., the ability to pay or insurance coverage* (Smedley et al. 2002, p. 3, emphasis added). And third, in the dominant language of science and policy, it framed issues in a putatively objective, scientific manner that masks the human costs of injustice. By contrast, the NCBWH was organized "to explore issues impacting the unequal burdens in health, health care access, and quality of care borne by African American women" (National Black Women Health Project 2003: 8). When women of color are positioned at the center of the analysis, the structural forces generating inequities that shape their lives are apparent, and revealing their impact in human terms is a key mechanism for challenging health inequities and promoting justice.

The Social Contexts of Reproduction: An Example

Mullings and Wali (2001) in collaboration with other researchers, students, community organizations, activists and individuals undertook a multi-year, ethnographic, participatory action research study of the social contexts of reproduction in Central Harlem—specifically of the great disparity in infant mortality rates (more than double) between African American and White women of all classes (Mullings 2000; 2002; National Center for Health Statistics 2004; Schoendorf et al. 1992).

The researchers and community participants first grounded their observations in an extensive exploration of the economic, political, and demographic history of the place and of the ways that social groups and inequalities have shaped the current environment. Women's lives were explored in a variety of institutional settings to reveal the meaning of inequality in everyday life:

...the ways in which race, class, and gender structure differential access to such resources as employment, housing, recreation, health care, and consequently health, and the structure of constraints and choices within which people operate (Mullings 2002: 33).

Community participants were key players in virtually all aspects of the research—from defining the problem to using results and shaping their presentation to affect city health policies. By working closely with community members over four years, researchers became aware of the ways that ideological constraints (i.e., controlling images or negative stereotypes) both psychologically and materially produced stress in the everyday lives of the community members. For example, a *New York Times* article on poverty in Harlem during the time the researchers were involved in the community revealed that images of dilapidated buildings that were dirty and unclean served both to reinforce existing negative stereotypes of residents and to justify blaming them for the conditions of their housing. What was not apparent to the journalists—and thus to the readers—was that broken light bulbs had been reported to building supervisors, dirty walls had been scrubbed but sorely needed paint, and that residents had repeatedly advocated on behalf of their buildings by taking landlords to housing court.

As Mullings and Wali (2001: 54) state:

In addition to the exposures to specific stressors and chronic strain brought on by poor housing conditions, women in tenements and public housing developments also had to expend extensive time and effort to keep their homes safe and clean. The continual representations in the media (much of it inaccurate) of poor people's homes as dirty and unkempt added to their frustration and sense of discrimination.

By engaging in ongoing and close relationships with community members, researchers came to see what most traditional research approaches often miss: the ways that poor African American women resisted the negative controlling images that ultimately serve to justify further negative treatment and the neglect of communities of color. And the researchers were taught the value of presenting community strengths/assets in their presentations to others of descriptive data about the community (e.g., the percentage of residents *not* receiving welfare, *with* college or high school educations, *employed*—not simply the reverse).

In this specific community, researchers learned that the mechanisms through which stressors and strains affecting reproductive health are likely to be found in the struggle to find or to maintain adequate income and benefits and healthful resources such as adequate housing, nutrition, child care and a safe environment. They put forth the concept of the Sojourner Syndrome to represent the physical, psychological, and emotional toll that these struggles effect in the lives of Black women (Mullings and Wali 2001: 162). They describe the Sojourner Syndrome as the negative health effects that result from the beliefs and behavioral strategies that African American women devise to survive in an oppressive and discriminatory social system. The constant stress of trying to improve one's position in a hostile society can result in negative health consequences such as hypertension and infant mortality (Mullings 2000).

In this case study, we see that critical institutional and interpersonal power relationships shape the contexts of choices and options for racial/ethnic men and women—producing stresses and constraints on obtaining some relief. First, the conditions of work and gender dynamics in the family leave poor women under great stress with little time to rest and restore. Although the reasons for making particular choices are varied, they can be understood in the contexts of poor women's and men's lives and the power relationships within which they live. They lack options, choices, and control in the economic, familial, political and health arenas. They lack the power to set macro policies and precedents that will shape the contexts of their lives. And they lack the power to shape the public interpretation for their sexuality. So they are stigmatized as bad mothers or oversexualized men and blamed for jeopardizing the health of others or their unborn children and denied full access to society's valued resources.

8.5 Strategies to Reduce and Eliminate Health Disparities

When we move "upstream" to fully integrate macro-structural forces into our understanding of the causes of health and disease and take seriously the intersections of race and ethnicity with other dimensions of social inequity, as in feminist intersectional scholarship, then certain strategies for change follow, and the limits of traditional interventions are highlighted.

Over 15 years ago, Mullings and Wali (2001: 26) argued that national agencies and institutions —particularly those concerned with health and disease—typically portrayed poor and racial/ethnic communities as pathological, "sick" and "disorganized," and interpreted oppositional behaviors as "noncompliance," "dysfunctional," or "pathological." As a consequence, they argued a sentiment, reiterated recently (McGowan et al. 2016) that national health agencies and policy-makers

> …are frequently unwilling to accept results that point to long-term structural change. Research emphasizing dysfunctional cultural and individual behavior produce recommendations for 'manageable' interventions in the lives of subjects. On the other hand, research designed to illuminate the structures of oppression and the ways in which people resist them frequently points to the need for

large-scale societal changes in employment and access to shelter, education, and health care. Though these 'rights' are integral to the discourse of international human rights, state institutions are not generally prepared to tackle transformative social change.

As noted earlier, the language and approach in health agencies has changed considerably since that 2001 assessment. Yet a recent review of public health research focused on intersectoral collaborations—across health, education, housing, employment—to produce structural change suggests that such efforts have produced mixed results in terms of its impact on health inequities, and the authors largely faulted the methodological complexity of such studies and the necessary complexity of assessing their impact

> Context-specific, complex, and process-oriented approaches such as intersectoral action require similarly appropriate mechanisms for assessing impact (WHO 2010; Barten et al. 2007). The complexity of evaluating the impact of intersectoral action on the SDH to improve health equity calls for more rigorous approaches to evaluate intersectoral action along a continuum, taking into account intersectoral processes, and the implementation and health equity impacts of interventions. Long-term, large, controlled quantitative studies, as well as mixed-methods studies (which would take into account contextual factors) and well-designed qualitative studies involving the intended beneficiaries, are required to better understand the impact of intersectoral action on health equity. (Ndumbe-Eyoh and Moffat 2013)

Nevertheless, to consider long-term structural change in broad social systems is a daunting task (See also Bambra et al. 2010) but one that scholars, including intersectional scholars, operating from a social justice framework, see as essential to making any substantial headway on addressing health inequities (Hofrichter 2003; Hofrichter and Bhatia 2010). Otherwise, as has been repeatedly demonstrated, treatments and interventions get introduced into a hierarchical social system wherein those with substantial resources and power are better able to take advantage of them, and health hierarchies get reproduced even as the health status of some is improved. Further, since intersectional researchers take seriously the structural conditions shaping health inequities, they are much more sanguine about the prospects for "eliminating" health inequities in the forseeable future. But because of their overt social justice agenda, they may be even more committed to finding effective strategies to challenge and to reduce health inequities. Thus, it is not surprising that most intersectional scholars recognize the necessity of concerted political action as well as of forging alliances across the domains of many groups— policy makers, researchers working from multiple paradigms, grassroots activists, professional organizations, and most importantly, community groups—to bring about the kinds of change necessary to reduce health disparities (Bowleg 2012; Collins 2015; Ruzek 2004; Hankivsky et al. 2012; Morgen 2002, 2006; Schulz and Mullings 2006; Weber 2006).

As Mullings and Wali (2001) imply, a fundamental part of the process of addressing health disparities lies in reconceptualizing health as a characteristic of societies and a human right. Moving beyond narrow biomedical constructions, which largely view health as the absence of disease, intersectional scholars' views of health more closely align with the World Health Organization's (WHO) broader definition of health. WHO calls for a perspective on health that focuses on the prerequisites for health—what people need to make health possible—freedom from fear of war; equal opportunity for all; satisfaction of basic needs for food, water, and sanitation; education; decent housing; secure work and a useful role in society; and political will and public support (for a more detailed discussion, see CDCP 2018; World Health Organization 2011, 2012, 2013a, b). This broader view of health makes clear that providing the prerequisites for health can both eliminate health disparities and require significant systemic change at the macro-level of policies and practices both within and outside of health care systems.

The focus on macro-level systemic change also reminds us of the power relationships that shape access to the prerequisites for health and the inevitable conflicts across race, ethnicity, class, and gender that accompany efforts to shift power and resources in the direction of oppressed groups. In intersectional research, directly addressing conflicting interests by highlighting how the health of some is tied to the sickness of others becomes the preferred path to understanding and reducing disparities and to providing for the collective health of a nation and the global community.

In the work of the women's health movement over the last 35 years, feminist intersectional scholars have learned hard lessons about conflicting interests across race, class, and gender lines. In fact, many feminist intersectional scholars contend that knowledge about social inequality is itself gained in the collaborative process of acting to promote social justice (cf. Collins 1998, 2000b; Mies 1983, 1991). In advocating participatory action research, for example, Mies wrote (1983: 125): "Social change is the starting point of science, and in order to understand the content, form, and consequences of patriarchy, the researcher must be actively involved in the fight against it; one has to change something before it can be understood." The women's health movement has been a testing ground for interracial, multi-ethnic, cross-class, and sexually diverse efforts to bring about broad structural changes in our nation's health that benefit women across race, class, ethnic, and sexual lines. The lessons learned in the movement have been critical to developing intersectional theory as the complexity of these power relationships was revealed in efforts to change them (Morgen 2002).

The social movements of the Civil Rights Era have demonstrated both the possibility of change for justice and the long-range difficulty of sustaining and building on that change (cf., Mullings 2005; Morgen 2002, 2006; Naples 2003; Omi and Winant 1994; Ruzek and Becker 1999). One clear message that has emerged from intersectional scholars' understandings of this history and their own involvement in activist scholarship is that effective research and policy for the future —in health and other arenas—will depend on our ability to develop strong, principled alliances and coalitions (Collins 2000a; Ruzek 2004; Morgen 2002, 2006; Schulz and Mullings 2006; Naples

2003; Weber and Parra-Medina 2003; Weber 2006; Weber and Castellow 2012). In the conclusions of her book on the women's health movement, Sandra Morgen (2002, p. 236) looked to the future and calls for

> ...a movement that is politically sophisticated, racially and class inclusive, vibrant, adaptable, and willing to nourish alliances with other movements and organizations that envision a more just and equitable society.

Women's health organizations were better organized than ever to collaborate in the national health care reform process that culminated in the Patient Protection and Affordable Care Act of 2010. One particularly expansive and effective feminist alliance is Raising Women's Voices (RWV), a national initiative striving to bring women's voices to the fore of the health care policy-making process. Founded by the Avery Institute for Social Change, the National Women's Health Network, and the MergerWatch Project, RWV put forth in 2008 a vision of what we must do to attain inclusive, feminist health care reform:

- Provide affordable and available health care coverage
- Develop acute, preventative, chronic, and supportive health care services
- Eliminate health disparities based on race, ethnicity, gender, class, immigration status, disability, or sexuality through research, policy, and culturally competent services
- Develop a transparent and user-friendly health care system
- Provide the highest attainable health standard for women, families, and communities through a holistic, comprehensive approach that includes considering community as well as individual health.

RWV (2009) is well organized with an advisory board representing 28 diverse feminist organizations, including, for example, the National Asian Pacific American Women's Forum and Black Women for Reproductive Justice; 22 regional coordinators; and many partners, including the Feminist Majority Foundation, the CommonWealth Fund, Planned Parenthood, and the National Women's Law Center. Comprising feminist researchers, advocates, health providers, and a variety of organizations, RWV organizes and disseminates information to stakeholders involved in health care reform. It informs the public by highlighting areas of concern in reform and its implementation—budget cuts threatening the new Public Health and Prevention Funds, coverage of abortions, contraception, and preventive health care—and describes actions that individuals and groups can take to affect public policy. It publishes comprehensive review papers written in an accessible yet not simplistic manner, and through regional coordinators, it also arranges for public presentations and community meetings (RWV 2009, 2010a, b, 2016).

RWV's efforts were clearly important in helping to shape the legislation that ultimately included improved women's health services, Medicaid coverage for 16 million more people, extension until age 26 of health coverage for adult children on parents' insurance plans, eliminating gender rating (charging women more than men for the same policy), eliminating the possibility of denied coverage for preexisting conditions or lifetime limits on coverage, increased access to affordable health insurance, increased availability of screening and preventive services, expansion of community health centers, and increased funding for health disparities research (Kaiser Family Foundation 2015; RWV 2010b; Uttley et al. 2010).

At the same time, feminist aims were thwarted and even regressed in important areas: failure of a single-payer system or for a public insurance option to compete with for-profit insurance companies, increased restrictions on abortion coverage, denial of health care coverage for undocumented immigrants, and inclusion of a "conscience clause" that protects health providers or payers who oppose abortion but not those who provide this legal health service (RWV 2010a; Uttley et al. 2010). But despite the increased political opposition to "Obamacare" which has drowned out attention to efforts for significant health reform, these activist groups along with many others continue in their efforts to improve the health policy terrain for diverse groups of women, as well as their families and children (see RWV 2016).

If we hope to develop a more equitable and engaged scholarship and practice to eliminate health disparities, we must also promote a more inclusive intellectual landscape to support alliances, dialogue, and collaboration across intersectional, critical public health, and biomedically-derived paradigms. These coalitions will involve scholars with a justice agenda who may be working from different disciplinary approaches as well as community groups whose engagement is necessary to sharpen the critique of the status quo, to improve scholarship, and to identify paths to effective activism and change.

In conclusion, efforts to reduce and ultimately eliminate racial/ethnic, socioeconomic, class, gender, and sexual health inequalities will require a thorough understanding of the ways that these systems of social inequality are constructed both inside and outside of health. Social transformation efforts must focus on systems that shape the prerequisites for health, not simply on the treatments for illnesses and disease. And principled coalitions—including across multiple scholarly traditions aimed at promoting social justice—must be forged to shift the balance of power toward promoting and sustaining health for the entire population, not just for the privileged who have access to the conditions of health and health care.

References

Acevedo-Garcia, D. (2000). Residential segregation and the epidemiology of infectious diseases. *Social Science and Medicine, 51*(8), 1143–1161.

Agency for Healthcare Research and Quality (2014). *2014 national healthcare quality & disparities report*. Rockville, MD: Agency for Healthcare Research and Quality. Also available at http://www.ahrq.gov/research/findings/nhqrdr/nhqdr14/index.html.

American Heart Association (2000). *Heart and stroke statistical update: 1999*. Dallas, TX.

Aquirre-Molina, M., Molina, C., & Zambrana, R. E. (2001). *Health issues in the Latino community*. San Francisco: Jossey-Bass Publishers.

Arias, E., Schauman, W. S., Eschback, K., Sorlie, P. D., & Backlund, E. (2008). The validity of race and Hispanic origin reporting on death certificates in the U.S. *Vital Health Stat, 2*(148), 1–23.

Avery Institute for Social Change, MergerWatch Project of Community Catalyst, & National Women's Health Network. (2008). A women's vision for quality, affordable health care for all. In *Raising women's voices for the health care we need*. Retrieved May 24, 2010, from http://www.raisingwomensvoices.net/storage/pdf_files/RWV-Principles-4.07.08.pdf.

Baca Zinn, M., & Dill, B. T. (1996). Theorizing difference from multiracial feminism. *Feminist Studies, 22*(2), 321–333.

Bambra, C., Gibson, M., Sowden, A., Wright, K., Whitehead, M., & Petticrew, M. (2010). Tackling the wider social determinants of health and health inequalities: Evidence from systematic reviews. *Journal of Epidemiology and Community Health, 64*, 284–291.

Banks, K. H., & Kohn-Wood, L. P. (2002). Gender, ethnicity and depression: Intersectionality in mental health research with African American women. *Scholarship*. Paper 6, from http://digitalcommons.iwu.edu/psych_scholarship/6. Accessed January 10, 2016.

Barten, F., Mitlin, D., Mulholland, C., Hardoy, A., & Stern, R. (2007). Integrated approaches to address the social determinants of health for reducing health inequity. *Journal of Urban Health, 84*, i164–i173. https://doi.org/10.1007/s11524-007-9173-7.

Bowleg, L. (2012). The problem with the phrase *women and minorities*: Intersectionality—an important theoretical framework for public health. *American Journal of Public Health, 102*, 1267–1273. https://doi.org/10.2105/AJPH.2012.300750.

Braun, L. (2002). Race, ethnicity, and health: Can genetics, explain disparities? *Perspectives in Biological Medicine, 45*, 159–174.

Braveman, P., & Gottlieb, L. (2014). The social determinants of health: It's time to consider the causes of the causes. *Public Health Reports, 129*, 19–31.

Brennan, V. M., Kumanyika, S., & Zambrana, R. E. (2015). *Obesity interventions in underserved communities*. Baltimore, MD: Johns Hopkins University Press.

Burgess, D. J., Crowley-Matoka, M., Phelan, S., Dovidio, J. F., Kerns, R., Roth, C., Saha, S., van Ryn, M. (2008). Patient race and physicians' decisions to prescribe opioids for chronic low back pain. *Social Science & Medicine, 67*(11), 1852–1860.

Carrillo, J. E., Trevino, F. M., Betancourt, J. R., Coustasse, A. (2001). Latino access to health care: The role of insurance, managed care, and institutional barriers. In M. Aguirre-Molina, C. W. Molina, & R. E. Zambrana (Eds.), *Health issues in the Latino community*. San Francisco, CA: Jossey-Bass.

Carter-Pokras, O., & Baquet, C. (2002). What is a health disparity? *Public Health Reports, 117,* 426–434.

Centers for Disease Control and Prevention. (1993). Smoking-attributable mortality and years of potential life lost—United States, 1990. *MMWR, 42*(33), 645–648.

Centers for Disease Control and Prevention. (2004). *The burden of chronic diseases and their risk factors: National and state perspectives 2004.* Atlanta: U.S. Department of Health and Human Services.

Centers for Disease Control and Prevention (2014). International comparisons of infant mortality and related factors: United States and Europe. 2010, *National Vital Statistics Report, 63*(5).

Centers for Disease Control and Prevention (2015). Leading causes of death, prevalence of diseases and risk factors and use of health services among Hispanics in the United States, 2009–2013. *MMWR, 64.* Also available at http://www.cdc.gov/mmwr/pdf/wk/mm64e0505.pdf.

Centers for Disease Control and Prevention (CDC) (2015). *Vital signs: Hispanic health.* Atlanta, Georgia: U.S. Department of Health and Human Services, Center for Disease Control and Prevention. http://www.cdc.gov/vitalsigns/hispanic-health/. Accessed February 7, 2016.

Centers for Disease Control and Prevention (CDC) (2016). *HIV in the United States at a glance.* Atlanta, Georgia: U.S. Department of Health and Human Services, Center for Disease Control and Prevention. http://www.cdc.gov/hiv/statistics/overview/ataglance.html. Accessed August 4, 2016.

Centers for Disease Control and Prevention (CDC). (2018). Current cigarette smoking among adults—United States, 2016. *Morbidity and Mortality Weekly Report, 67*(2), 53–59. Accessed April 27, 2018.

Clarke, A., & Olesen, V. (Eds.). (1999). *Revisioning women, health, and healing: Feminist, cultural, and technoscience perspectives.* New York: Routledge.

Clark, L. P., Millet, D. B., & Marshall, J. D. (2014). National patterns in environmental injustice and inequality: Outdoor NO2 air pollution in the United States. *Plos One, 9*(4). https://doi.org/10.1371/journal.pone.0094431.

Clarke, A. E., & Shim, J. (2011). Medicalization and biomedicalization revisited: Technoscience and transformations of health, illness and American medicine. In *Handbook of the sociology of health, illness, and healing* (pp. 173–199). New York: Springer.

Cohen, F. A., & Martinez, M. E. (2015). Health Insurance Coverage: Early Release of Estimates from the National Health Interview Survey, 2014. Division of Health Interview Statistics, National Center for Health Statistics. Centers for Disease Control and Prevention. U.S. Department of Health and Human Services. Accessed from http://www.cdc.gov/nchs/data/nhis/earlyrelease/insur201506.pdf.

Collins, P. H. (1998). *Fighting words: Black women and the search for justice.* Minneapolis, MN: University of Minnesota Press.

Collins, P. H. (2000a). *Black feminist thought* (2nd ed.) New York: Routledge.

Collins, P. H. (2000b). Moving beyond gender: Intersectionality and scientific knowledge. In M. M. Ferree, J. Lorber, & B. Hess (Eds.), *Revisioning gender* (pp. 261–284). New York: Roman and Littlefield.

Collins, P. H. (2015). Intersectionality's definitional dilemmas. *Annual Review of Sociology, 41,* 1–20.

Cook-Deegan, R. (1994). *The gene wars: Science, politics, and the human genome.* New York: W. W. Norton.

Cooper, R. S., Kaufman, J. S., & Ward, R. (2003). Race and genomics. *New England Journal of Medicine, 348,* 1166–1170.

Cooper, L. A., Roter, D., Carson, K., Beach, M., Sabin, J., Greenwald, A. G. (2012). The associations of clinicians' implicit attitudes about race with medical visit communication and patient ratings of interpersonal care. *American Journal of Public Health,* Online:e1–e9.

Crenshaw, K. W. (1989). Demarginalizing the intersection of race and sex: A Black feminist critique of antidiscrimination doctrine, feminist theory and antiracist politics. *University of Chicago Legal Forum, 1989,* 138–167.

Daviglus, M. L., Talavera, G. A., Avilés-Santa, M. L., Allison, M., Cai, J., Criqui, M. H., ... & LaVange, L. (2012). Prevalence of major cardiovascular risk factors and cardiovascular diseases among Hispanic/Latino individuals of diverse backgrounds in the United States. *Journal of the American Medical Association, 308*(17), 1775–1784.

Dhamoon, R. K., & Hankivsky, O. (2011). Why the theory and practice of intersectionality matter to health research and policy. In O. Hankivsky (Ed.), *Health inequities in Canada: Intersectional frameworks and practices* (pp. 16–50). Vancouver: UBC Press.

Dill, B., & Zambrana, R. E. (2009). *Emerging intersections: Race, class, and gender in theory, policy, and practice.* New Brunswick, NJ: Rutgers University Press.

Dill, B., & Kohlman, M. H. (2012). Intersectionality: A transformative paradigm in feminist theory and social justice. In. S. N. Hesse-Biber (Ed.), *The handbook of feminist research: Theory and praxis* (2nd ed., pp. 154–174). Thousand Oaks, CA: Sage Publications.

Downs, L. S., Smith, J. S., Scarinci, I., Flowers, L., & Parham, G. (2008). The disparity of cervical cancer in diverse populations. *Gynecologic Oncology, 109*(2), S22–S30.

Drwecki, B. B., Moore, C. F., Ward, S. E., Prkachin, K. M. (2011). Reducing racial disparities in pain treatment: The role of empathy and perspective-taking. *Pain, 152*(5), 1001–1006.

Howlader, N. Noone, A. M. Krapcho, M. Miller, D. Bishop, K. Altekruse, S. F. Kosary, C. L. Yu, M. Ruhl, J. Tatalovich, Z. Mariotto, A. Lewis, D. R. Chen, H. S. Feuer, E. J. Cronin, K. A. (Eds.) (2016). SEER cancer statistics review, 1975–2013, National Cancer Institute. Bethesda, MD, http://seer.

cancer.gov/csr/1975_2013/, based on November 2015 SEER data submission, posted to the SEER web site, April 2016.

Fine, M. J. (2005). The role of race and genetics in health disparities research. *American Journal of Public Health, 95*(12), 2125–2128.

Garfield, R., & Damico, A. (2016). The coverage gap: Uninsured poor adults in states that do not expand Medicaid–An update (issue brief). Washington, DC., Kaiser Family Foundation, The Kaiser Commission on Medicaid and the Uninsured (January 21, 2016). Retrieved from http://kff.org/health-reform/issue-brief/the-coverage-gap-uninsured-poor-adults-in-states-that-do-not-expand-medicaid-an-update/.

Giachello, A. L., Arrom, J. O., Davis, M., Sayad, J. V., Ramirez, R., Nandi, C., Ramos, C. (2003). Reducing diabetes health disparities through community-based participatory action research: The Chicago southeast diabetes community action coalition. *Public Health Reports, 118*(4), 309–323.

González, H. M., & Tarraf, W. (2013). Comorbid cardiovascular disease and major depression among ethnic and racial groups in the United States. *International Psychogeriatrics, 25*(05), 833–841.

Green, A. R., Carney, D. R., Pallin, D. J., et al. (2007). Implicit bias among physicians and its prediction of thrombolysis decisions for black and white patients. *Journal of General Internal Medicine, 22*(9), 1231–1238.

Greer, T. M., Brondolo, E., Brown, P. (2014). Systemic racism moderates effects of provider racial biases on adherence to hypertension treatment for African Americans. *Health Psychology, 33*(1), 35–42.

Haile, R. W., John, E. M., Levine, A. J., Cortessis, V. K., Unger, J. B., Gonzales, M., & Bernstein, J. L. (2012). A review of cancer in US Hispanic populations. *Cancer Prevention Research, 5*(2), 150–163.

Hankivsky, O. (2012). Women's health, men's health, and gender and health: Implications of intersectionality. *Social Science and Medicine, 74*(11), 1712–1720.

Hankivsky, O. (2014). *Intersectionality 101.* Vancouver, BC: Institute for Intersectionality Research & Policy, Simon Fraser University.

Hankivsky, O., de Leeuw, S., Lee, J. A., Vissandjee, B., & Khanlou, A. (2011) Introduction: Purpose, overview, and contribution. In O. Hankivsky (Ed.), *Health inequities in Canada: Intersectional frameworks and practices* (pp. 1–15). Vancouver: UBC Press.

Hankivsky, O., Grace, D., Hunting, G., Ferlatte, O., Clark, N., Fridkin, A., Giesbrecht, M., Rudrum, S., & Laviolette, T. (2012). Intersectionality-based policy analysis. In O. Hankivsky (Ed.) *An intersectionality-based Polic analysis framework* (pp. 33–45). Vancouver, BC: Institute for Intersectionality Research & Policy, Simon Fraser University.

Hankivsky, O., & Grace, D. (2014). Understanding and emphasizing difference and intersectionality in multimethod and mixed methods research. In S. Hesse-Biber & R. Burke Johnson (Eds.), *The Oxford handbook of multimethod and mixed methods research inquiry* (pp. 110–126). Oxford: Oxford University Press.

Hofrichter, R. (2003). The politics of health inequities: Contested terrain. In R. Hofrichter (Ed.), *Health and social justice: Politics, ideology, and inequity in the distribution of disease* (pp. 1–56). San Francisco, CA: Jossey-Bass.

Hofrichter, R., & Bhatia, R. (2010). *Tackling health inequities through public health practice: Theory to action.* Oxford: Oxford University Press.

Institute of Medicine (IOM). (2002). Committee on assuring the health of the public in the 21st century. *The future of the public's health in the 21st century.* Washington, DC: National Academy of Sciences.

Institute of Medicine (IOM). (2003). *From neurons to neighborhoods: The science of early childhood development.* Washington, DC: National Academy of Sciences.

Johnson, C. L., & Sempos, C. T. (1995). Socioeconomic status and biomedical, lifestyle, and psychosocial risk factors for CVD: Selected US National data and trends. In *Report of the Conference on Socioeconomic Status and CVD Health and Disease, 6–7 Nov,* USDHHS-PHS-NIH-NHLBI.

Kaiser Family Foundation (2015). Kaiser Family Foundation, Kaiser Commission on Medicaid and the Uninsured (2015). *Key Facts about the Uninsured Population:* http://kff.org/uninsured/fact-sheet/key-facts-about-the-uninsured-population.

Kochanek, K. D., Murphy, S. L., Anderson, R. N., Scott, C. (2004). Deaths: Final Data for 2002. *National Vital Statistics Reports, 53*(5).

Koh, H. K. (2011). The ultimate measures of health. *Public Health Reports, 126*(Suppl 3), 14.

Koh, H. K., Piotrowski, J. J., Kumanyika, S., & Fielding, J. E. (2011). Healthy people a 2020 vision for the social determinants approach. *Health Education & Behavior, 38*(6), 551–557.

Krieger, N. (2005). Stormy weather: Race, gene expression, and the science of health disparities. *American Journal of Public Health, 95*(12), 2155–2160.

Krieger, N. (2014) Got theory? On the 21st c. CE rise of explicit use of epidemiologic theories of disease distribution: A review and ecosocial analysis. *Current Epidemiology Reports, 1*(1), 45–56.

Krieger, N. (2015). Got theory? On the 21st c, rise of explicit use of epidemiologic theories of disease distribution: A review and ecosocial analysis. *Current Epidemiology Reports, 1*(1), 45–56.

Kuczmarski, R. J., & Flegal, K. M. (2000). Criteria for definition of overweight in transition: Background and recommendations for the United States. *The American Journal of Clinical Nutrition, 72*(5), 1074–1081.

Lee, S. S., Mountain, J., & Koenig, B. A. (2001). The meanings of 'race' in the new genomics: Implications for health disparities research. *Yale Journal of Health Policy Law Ethics,* (1), 33–75.

Lewis, T. T., Cogburn, C. D., & Williams, D. R. (2015). Self-reported experiences of discrimination and health: Scientific advances, ongoing controversies, and emerging issues. *Annual Review of Clinical Psychology, 11*, 407–440.

Link, B. G., & Phelan, J. C. (1995). Social conditions as fundamental causes of disease. *Journal of Health and Social Behavior* (extra issue), 80–94.

Link, B. G., & Phelan, J. C. (1996). Understanding sociodemographic differences in health: The role of fundamental causes. *American Journal of Public Health, 86*, 471–473.

Link, B. G., & Phelan, J. C. (2000). Evaluating the fundamental cause explanation for social disparities in health. In C. Bird, P. Conrad, & A. M. Fremont (Eds.), *Handbook of medical sociology* (5th ed., pp. 33–46). Upper Saddle River, NJ: Prentice Hal.

Loewenberg, B., & Bogin, R. (1976). *Black women in nineteenth-century American life: Their words, their thoughts, their feelings.* University Park, PA: Pennsylvania State University.

Luft, R. E., & Ward, J. (2009). Toward an intersectionality just out of reach: Confronting challenges to intersectional practice. *Advances in Gender Research: Special Volume: Intersectionality, 13*, 9–37.

Martell, B. N., Garrett, B. E., & Caraballo, R. S. (2016). Disparities in adult cigarette smoking—United States, 2002–2005 and 2010–2013. MMWR *Morb Mortal Wkly Rep, 65*, 753–758. http://dx.doi.org/10.15585/mmwr.mm6530a1.

Martin, K., Roter, D., Beach, M., Carson, K., & Cooper, L. (2013). Physician communication behaviors and trust among black and white patients with hypertension. *Medical Care, 51*(2), 151–157. 7p. https://doi.org/10.1097/MLR.0b013e31827632a2.

Matthews, S., Hertzman, C., Ostry, A., & Power, C. (1998). Gender, work roles, and psychosocial work characteristics as determinants of health. *Social Science and Medicine, 46*, 1417–1424.

McGowan, A. K., Lee, M. M., Meneses, C. M., Perkins, J., & Youdelman, M. (2016). Civil rights Laws as tools to advance health in the twenty-first century. *Annual Review of Public Health, 37*, 185–204.

Mies, M. (1983). Towards a methodology for feminist research. In G. Bowles, & R. D. Klein (Eds.), *Theories of women's studies* (pp. 117–139). London: Routledge and Kegan Paul.

Mies, M. (1991). Women's research or feminist research? The debate surrounding feminist science and methodology. In J. Cook, & M. M. Fonow (Eds.), *Beyond methodology: Feminist scholarship as lived research* (pp. 60–84). Bloomington, IN: Indiana University Press.

Mokdad, A. H., Serdula, M. K., Dietz, W. H., Bowman, B. A., Marks, J. S., & Koplan, J. P. (1999). The spread of obesity epidemic in the United States, 1991–1998. *Journal of the American Medical Association, 282*, 1519–1522.

Mokdad, A. H., Marks, J. S., Stroup, D. F., & Gerberding, J. L. (2004). Actual causes of death in the United States, 2000. *Journal of the American Medical Association, 291*, 1238–1245.

Morgen, S. (2002). *Into our own hands: The women's health movement in the United States 1969–1990.* New Brunswick, NJ: Rutgers University Press.

Morgen, S. (2006). Movement grounded theory: Analysis of health inequities in the United States. In A. Schulz & L. Mullings (Eds.), *Race, class, gender and health* (pp. 394–423). San Francisco, CA: Jossey-Bass.

Moskowitz, G. B., Stone, J., Childs, A. (2012). Implicit stereotyping and medical decisions: Unconscious stereotype activation in practitioners' thoughts about African Americans. *American Journal of Public Health*, Online:e1–e6.

Mullings, L. (2000). African–American women making themselves: Notes on the role of Black feminist research. *Souls: A Critical Journal of Black Politics, Culture, and Society, 2*(4), 18–29.

Mullings, L. (2002) The Sojourner syndrome: Race, class, and gender in health and illness. *Voices* (December), 32–36.

Mullings, L. (2005). Interrogating racism: Toward an antiracist anthropology. *Annual Review of Anthropology, 34*, 667–693.

Mullings, L., & Wali, A. (2001). *Stress and resilience: The social context of reproduction in Central Harlem.* New York: Kluwer Academic.

Mullins, I., & Maddox, Y. T. (2015). Embarking on a science vision for health disparities research. *American Journal of Public Health, 105*(Suppl 13), S369–S371.

Must, A., Spadano, J., Coakley, E. H., Field, A. E., Colditz, G., & Dietz, W. H. (1999). The disease burden associated with overweight and obesity. *Journal of the American Medical Association, 282*, 1523–1529.

Naples, N. (2003). *Feminism and method: Ethnography, discourse analysis, and activist research.* New York: Taylor & Francis.

National Center for Health Statistics (2004). *Health, United States, 2004 with Chartbook on trends in the health of Americans.* Hyattsville, MD.

National Center for Health Statistics (2005). *Health, United States, 2005 with Chartbook on trends in the health of Americans.* Hyattsville, MD.

National Center for Health Statistics (NCHS). (2015). Health, United States, 2014: With special feature on adults aged 55–64. Hyattsville, MD.

National Center for Health Statistics (NCHS) (2016). *Health, United States, 2015: With special feature on racial and ethnic health disparities.* Hyattsville, MD.

National Institutes of Health and National Heart, Lung, and Blood Institute (2013). *Hispanic community health study: Study of Latinos (SOL) data book, a report to the communities.* U.S. Department of Health and Human Services, Public Health Services. http://www.nhlbi.nih.gov/files/docs/resources/NHLBI-HCHSSOL-English-508.pdf.

National Women's Health Project (2003). Congressional Black Caucus Health Brain Trust, and U.S. Senate Black Legislative Staff Caucus. *National Colloquium on Black Women's Health.* Washington, D.C.:

Congressional Black Caucus Health Brain Trust and U.S. Senate Black Legislative Staff Caucus, April 2003.

Ndumbe-Eyoh, S., & Moffat, H. (2013). Intersectoral action for health equity: A rapid systematic review. *BMC Public Health., 13,* 1056.

New York Times (2016). Obamacare will survive aetna's retreat. August 16, 2016. http://www.nytimes.com/2016/08/17/opinion/obamacare-will-survive-aetnas-retreat.html.

Office of Disease Prevention and Health Promotion (1990). Healthy people 2000. DHHS Publication No. (PHS 90-50212. Washington, DC: U.S. Government Printing Office.

Omi, M., & Winant, H. (1994). *Racial Formation in the United States from the 1960s to the 1990s.* New York: Routledge.

Pabon-Nau, L. P., Cohen, A., Meigs, J. B., & Grant, R. W. (2010). Hypertension and diabetes prevalence among U.S. Hispanics by country of origin: The national health interview survey 2000–2005. *Journal of General Internal Medicine, 25*(8), 847–852. https://doi.org/10.1007/s11606-010-1335-8.

Pavalko, E. K., & Woodbury, S. (2000). Social roles as process: Caregiving careers and women's health. *Journal of Health and Social Behavior, 41,* 91–105.

Penedo, F. J., Yanez, B., Castañeda, S. F., et al. (2016). Self-reported cancer prevalence among Hispanics in the US: Results from the Hispanic Community Health Study/Study of Latinos. *PLoS ONE.* https://doi.org/10.1371/journal.pone.0146268.

Phelan, J. C., & Link, B. G. (2015). Is Racism a fundamental cause of inequalities in health? *Annual Review of Sociology, 41,* 311–330.

Raising Women's Voices (RWV) (2009). *Raising women's voices for the healthcare we need.* http://www.raisingwomensvoices.net/. Retrieved June 28, 2010.

Raising Women's Voices (RWV) (2010a). Health reform and reproductive health: Positive and negative effects. In *Raising women's voices for the health care we need.* http://www.raisingwomensvoices.net/storage/RWV%200n%20Health%20Reform%20and%20Reproductive%20HealthFINAL3.30.10.pdf. Retrieved June 14, 2010.

Raising Women's Voices (RWV) (2010b). What health reform will do for women and families. In *Raising women's voices for the health care we need.* http://www.raisingwomensvoices.net/storage/pdf_files/RWVHealth%20reform%20benefits%20for%20women3.21.10.pdf. Retrieved June 14, 2010.

Raising Women's Voices (RWV) (2016). *Raising women's voices for the health care we need.* http://www.raisingwomensvoices.net.

Rodriguez, C. J., Allison, M., et al. (2014). Status of cardiovascular disease and stroke in Hispanics/Latinos in the United States: A science advisory from the American Heart Association. *Circulation, 130*(7), 593–625.

Roux, A. D. (2012). Conceptual approaches to the study of health disparities. *Annual Review of Public Health, 33,* 41–58.

Ruzek, S. (1999). Rethinking feminist ideologies and actions: Thoughts on the past and future of health reform. In A. Clarke & V. Olesen (Eds.), *Revisioning women, health, and healing: feminist, cultural, and technoscience perspectives* (pp. 303–323). New York: Routledge.

Ruzek, S. (2004). How might the women's health movement shape national agendas on women and aging? *Women's Health Issues, 14,* 112–114.

Ruzek, S., & Becker, J. (1999). The women's health movement in the U.S: From Grassroots activism to professional agendas. *Journal of American Medical Women's Association, 54*(1), 4–8.

Ruzek, S., Olesen, V., & Clarke, A. (Eds.). (1997). *Women's health: Complexities and differences.* Columbus, OH: Ohio State University Press.

Sabin, J. A., & Greenwald, A. G. (2012). The influence of implicit bias on treatment recommendations for 4 common pediatric conditions: Pain, urinary tract infection, attention deficit hyperactivity disorder, and asthma. *American Journal of Public Health, 102,* 988–995.

Schoendorf, K. C., et al. (1992). Mortality among infants of black as compared to white college-educated parents. *New England Journal of Medicine, 326,* 1522–1526.

Schulz, A. J., & Mullings, L. (Eds.). (2006). *Gender, race, class, and health: Intersectional approaches.* San Francisco, CA: Jossey-Bass.

Sheppard, V. B., Hurtado-de-Mendoza, A., & Talley, C. H. (2016). Reducing Racial disparities in breast cancer survivors' ratings of quality cancer care: The enduring impact of trust. *Journal for Healthcare Quality: Promoting Excellence in Healthcare, 38*(3), 143–163. 21p.

Shim, J. K. (2014). *Heart-sick: The politics of risk, inequality, and heart disease.* New York: NYU Press.

Singh, G. K., Rodriguez-Lainz, A., & Kogan, M. D. (2013). Immigrant health inequalities in the United States: Use of eight major national data systems. *The Scientific World Journal.*

Smedley, B. D., & Syme, S. L. (Eds.). (2000). *Institute of medicine report. Promoting health: Intervention strategies from social and behavioral research.* Washington, DC: National Academy Press.

Smedley, B. D., Stith, A. Y., & Nelson, A. R. (Eds.). (2002). *Institute of medicine report. Unequal treatment: Confronting racial and ethnic disparities in health care.* Washington, DC: National Academy Press.

Swanson, N. G., Piotrkowski, C. S., Keita, G. P., & Becker, A. B. (1997). Occupational stress and women's health. In S. J. Gallant, G. P. Keita, & R. Royak-Schaler (Eds.), *Health care for women: Psychological, social, and behavioral influences* (pp. 147–159). Washington, DC: American Psychological Association.

Thomas, S. B., Quinn, S. C., Butler, J., et al. (2011). Toward a fourth generation of disparities research to achieve health equity. *Annual Review of Public Health, 32,* 399–416.

Thorpe, K. E., Howard, D. H., & Galactionova, K. (2007). Difference in disease prevalence as a source of the U. S.–European health care spending gap. *Health Affairs, 26*(6), 678–686.

United States General Accounting Office (USGAO) (1983). Siting of hazardous waste landfills and their correlation with racial and economic status of surrounding communities.

U.S. Department of Health and Human Services. (2000). *Healthy people 2010: Understanding and improving health* (2nd ed.). Washington, DC: U.S. Government Printing Office.

U.S. Department of Health and Human Services (2014). *Healthy people 2020.* Retrieved from http://www.healthypeople.gov/.

Uttley, L., Avery, B., Alina, A., Pandit, E., & Pearson, C. (2010). Statement in response to the house of representatives votes in support of the patient protection and affordable care act and the health care and education affordability reconciliation act. In *Raising women's voices for the health care we need.* Retrieved May 24, 2010 from http://www.raisingwomensvoices. net/storage/pdf_files/RWV%20Statement.HCR% 20Bill%20Passage%203.21.10.pdf.

Viruell-Fuentes, E. A., Miranda, P. Y., & Abdulrahim, S. (2012). More than culture: Structural racism, intersectionality theory, and immigrant health. *Social Science and Medicine, 75*(12), 2099–2106. https://doi.org/10. 1016/j.socscimed.2011.12.037.

Wasserthiel-Smoller, S., Arredondo, E. M., et al. (2014). Depression, anxiety, antidepressant use, and cardiovascular disease among Hispanic men and women of different national backgrounds: Results from the hispanic community health study/study of Latinos. *Annals of Epidemiology, 24*(11), 822–830.

Weber, L. (2006). Reconstructing the landscape of health disparities research: Promoting dialogue and collaboration between the feminist intersectional and positivist biomedical traditions. In L. Mullings, & A. Schulz, (Eds.), *Race, class, gender and health* (pp. 21–59). San Francisco, CA: Jossey-Bass.

Weber, L., & Castellow, J. (2012). Feminist research and activism to promote health equity. In Sharlene Hesse-Biber (Ed.), *Handbook of feminist research: Theory and praxis* (2nd ed., p. 2012). Thousand Oaks, CA: Sage Publications.

Weber, L., & Parra-Medina, D. (2003). Intersectionality and women's health: Charting a path to eliminating health disparities. In V. Demos, & M. T. Segal (Eds.), *Advances in gender research: Gender perspectives on health and medicine* (pp. 181–230). Amsterdam: Elsevier.

White, K., Haas, J. S., & Williams, D. R. (2012). Elucidating the role of place in health care disparities: The example of racial/ethnic residential segregation. *Health Services Research, 47*(3pt2), 1278–1299.

Whitehead, M. (1992). The concepts and principles of equity and health. *International Journal of Health Services, 22,* 429–445.

Williams, D. R. (1997). Race and health: Basic questions, emerging directions. *Annals of Epidemiology, 7*(5), 322–333.

Woliver, L. (2002). *The political geographies of pregnancy.* Champaign, IL: University of Illinois Press.

World Health Organization (2011). *Rio political declaration on social determinants of health.* October 2011. Rio de Janeiro: WHO.

World Health Organization. (2012). *Environmental health inequalities in Europe. Assessment Report.* Copenhagen: WHO Regional Office for Europe.

World Health Organization. (2013a). *Handbook on health inequality monitoring with a special focus on low and middle-income countries.* Geneva: WHO.

World Health Organization. (2013b). *Health 2020: A European policy framework supporting action across government and society for health and well-being.* Copenhagen: WHO.

World Health Organization (WHO) (2010). Intersectoral action to tackle the social determinants of health and the role of evaluation 2010, Geneva: World Health Organization, Report of the first Meeting of the WHO Policy Maker Resource Group on Social Determinants of Health, Viña del Mar, Chile, pp. 27–29.

Xu, J. Q., Murphy, S. L., Kochanek, K. D., & Bastian, B. A. (2016). Deaths: Final data for 2013. *National Vital Statistics Reports, 64*(2).

Zambrana, R. E. (1987). A research agenda on issues affecting poor and minority women: A model for understanding their health needs. *Women and Health,* Winter, 137–160.

Zambrana, R. E. (2001). Improving access and quality for ethnic minority women: Panel discussion. *Women's Health Issues, 11*(4), 354–359.

Zambrana, R. E. (2011). *Latinos in American society.* Ithaca, NY: Cornell University Press.

Zambrana, R. E., & Carter-Pokras, O. (2001). Health data issues for Hispanics: Implications for public health research *Journal of Health Care for the Poor and Underserved, 12*(1), 20–34.

Militarism as a Racial Project

9

Victor Ray

Contents

Abstract

This paper argues that militarism is a "racial project" central to the social construction of race and the perpetuation of unequal race relations. Typical sociological research on race in the military is largely demographic in nature—reifying race as a social fact and often assuming the military decreases overt racial animus. In place of this perspective, I claim that the military should be seen as both benefiting from unequal race relations in the wider society and reinforcing those relations through military policy. Ultimately, scholars should focus on how the military influences broader patterns of racial inequality.

V. Ray (✉)
Department of Sociology, University of Tennessee, Knoxville, TN, USA
e-mail: vray3@utk.edu

On April 4, 1967 during a speech in Harlem's Riverside Church, Dr. Martin Luther King Jr. called the United States the "greatest purveyor of violence in the world today" (1967). Although Dr. King had long felt the Vietnam war was immoral, he was reluctant to make his opposition public (Branch 2007) fearing his stance against the war would harm the civil rights struggle. Pushed by young activists from the Student Nonviolent Coordinating Committee (SNCC), who were appalled by war's brutality and its connection to domestic racial oppression (Carmichael and Thelwell 2003), Dr. King was moved to argue that the nation must move "Beyond Vietnam." If not, the nation would fail to overcome the "giant triplets of racism, extreme materialism, and militarism" (King 1967) that distorted democracy.

Dr. King's critique of the United States' militarism has become a rallying cry for the anti-war left, who highlight the parallels between Dr. King's era and our own. What draws less attention from analysts and activists is Dr. King's highlighting the link between colonial violence abroad and domestic "racial projects." (Omi and Winant 2015). Dr. King states:

> We were taking the black young men who had been crippled by our society and sending them eight thousand miles away to guarantee liberties in Southeast Asia which they had not found in southwest Georgia and East Harlem. So we have been repeatedly faced with the cruel irony of watching Negro and white boys on TV screens as they kill and die together for a nation that has been unable to seat them together in the same schools. So we watch them in brutal solidarity burning the huts of a poor village, but we realize that they would hardly live on the same block in Chicago.

Inverting the domestic racial order, explicit inter-personal racism among U.S. soldiers—central to the social organization of almost every aspect of daily life in America—receded during acts of violence against a colonized enemy. Strangely, this "brutal solidarity," minimizing the racial animosity central to the organization of daily life in the context of the United States, is premised upon an equally racialized suppression of anti-colonial struggle. Shifting our focus in Dr. King's essay from his indictment of the U. S.'s violence to the connection between military violence and racialization—or the construction of race through the organization of violence—explicitly ties the effects of U.S. militarism at home and abroad to what Omi and Winant call a racial project. According to Omi and Winant, racial projects are attempts to "shape the ways in which human identities and social structures are racially signified, and the reciprocal ways that racial meaning becomes embedded in social structures." (2015, 13). Although many scholars have shown the connection between colonial violence and race-making (Fanon 1963; Go 2004; Hirschman 1986), few recognize militarism itself as a "racial project" deeply implicated in domestic racial policy. Scholarship on race and the military tends to view race in a reductive manner, as a simple demographic variable (Zuberi 2001), or focus on how the military reduces the most explicit forms of racial animus (Moskos and Butler 1997).

In this chapter, I argue that militarization has served as an important and neglected site in the domestic construction of race. The threat of force is a determinative part of the structural base (Bonilla-Silva 1997) from which races are socially constructed. Using "racial formation theory" (Omi and Winant 2015) and the "racialized social system" (Bonilla-Silva 1997) framework, I show that militarization has been central in the production of structures of racial exclusion. I begin with a brief review of the demographics of the military, showing how military policies rely upon racialized social relations. Racialized opportunities—both within the military and in the civilian sphere—have expanded or contracted in response to militarism. I then show how scholarship from the U.S. black radical tradition provides a counterpoint to mainstream theorizing about race in the military. Military veterans have often been at the center of social movements for greater inclusion, as their experiences in the military are channeled into civilian activism. Thus, militarism shapes racial realities well beyond the immediate context of the "race relations" (Steinberg 2007) paradigm under which the military is typically studied.

9.1 Representing Race in the Military

The military is one of the most integrated institutions in the United States. Seeing race as a resource, the military recognizes that the appearance of calm race relations provides real benefits for recruiting, force readiness, and international legitimacy. Like businesses who have adopted the policy of using race to increase market-share through niche targeting (Skrentny 2013), the military manages racial difference to bolster public relations. Unlike civilian institutions, which have undermined Affirmative Action policies (Embrick 2011; Moore and Bell 2011) the military still relies on strong racial preferences, including quotas ensuring proportional representation and promotion criteria designed to lessen well-known racial evaluation biases. Good race relations are "mission critical"—central to the military's ability to function as a cohesive fighting unit (Leach 2004). The claim that militarism is a racial project mean military policy influences larger meanings and actions surrounding race and racism. That is, military policy and racial ideology co-evolve as the institution adapts to changing cultural norms. Integration and the color-blind application of rules have long been official military policy, yet in practice these rules are often applied in ways that reinforce racial inequality.

Military policies aimed at increasing minority representation, from one perspective, have been highly successful. People of color are over-represented in all branches of the military, with a particularly high concentration in the Army (Armor and Gilroy 2009). Since at least Moskos and Butler's (1997) *All You Can Be,* the dominant scholarly explanation for the overrepresentation of people of color in the military was that the military had lessened racial inequality to such a degree that it was a much better choice for upwardly mobile people of color. According to this narrative, long-standing exclusion from mainstream avenues for employment and wealth accumulation have created deep racial inequalities. These inequalities, coupled with the well-documented levels of discrimination in the civilian labor market—which influence even the most highly educated people of color—create a situation where nonwhites are searching for a mobility avenue where they can compete on near-equal footing. In this narrative, the military provides a respite from labor market discrimination.

The military's stated commitment to nondiscrimination have contributed to the overrepresentation of people of color in the military. Since the inception of the "All-Volunteer Force" (AVF) in the 1970s, black representation has fluctuated, but has never fallen below population proportions. Concerns about black over-representation are tied to ideological concerns surrounding democratic representation. According to Janowitz (1983), the military should be comprised of "citizen soldiers" who see military service as an essential requirement of citizenship. Thus, differential treatment based on race is a betrayal of democratic ideals. More practically, such an imbalance burdens people of color who are excluded from the benefits of full citizenship. Ultimately, military sociologists have long highlighted how the structure of the military mitigates against some forms of racial inequality by equalizing income across ranks and providing universal healthcare. As scholars have noted, the military is the United States' only "socialist meritocracy" (Lundquist 2008).

Several recent scholars have claimed that black service has advanced the cause of racial equality. For instance, Christopher Parker, (2009) argues that black service was indeed rewarded by an extension of membership in the larger political community. He claims that military service has played a valuable symbolic role in the black community, representing "membership in the national political community" (2009, 67). However, the nature of the military as a racial project becomes clear through this distorted inclusion. While it may, in some instances, be true that service has provided blacks a marginal level of political inclusion, this tells us little about why white inclusion in the political community is automatic, or why blacks must buy this inclusion by bargaining their lives. Further, the promised inclusion stemming from service that Parker (2009) argues for is undermined by his own scholarship, which points out that black soldiers returning from wars have repeatedly experienced repressive measures, such as exclusion from the franchise and in some cases, riots targeting black soldiers (2009).

However, the claim that the military greatly reduces racial inequality is at odds with the large body of sociological research on the reproduction of racialized relations generally. Nearly every civilian domain that sociologists study is rife with racial inequality (Reskin 2012). Variously described as "systemic racism" (Elias and Feagin 2016), "institutional racism" (Ture and Hamilton 1967), or a "racialized social system" (Bonilla-Silva 1997), scholars have long shown that racism is an intricate and foundational element of American race relations. For instance In their review of the literature on race in the military, Burk and Espinoza (2012) call into question the long-standing representation of the military as a panacea for racism. Surveying a large body of literature, they show that black soldiers move up the ranks more slowly than their white counterparts and are more likely to face military discipline—including the death penalty (Burk and Espinoza 2012). Seeing the military as part of a racial project expands the narrow, individualistic frames typically used to account for racial inequality in the military. Rather, it sees the military as a racial structure with implications for the domestic racial order.

9.2 Racial Formation and the Military

In their seminal text on the creation and transformation of racial structures, *Racial Formation in the United States* (2015) Michael Omi and Howard Winant outline a theoretical history of race relations that questions static, essentialist notions of race. First, racial formation theory replaces biologically reductionist notions of race with an understanding of racial categories as historical processes that are "created, inhabited, transformed, and destroyed" (1994, 55). Racial categories are unstable and politically contested. Race is not a simple correlation between skin tone and category, but rather a political tool that arose under European colonial expansion and has been tied to sub- and super-ordination from the start (Omi and Winant 2015; Elias and Feagin 2015). Different races were not discovered, they were created; European economic and military expansion were central to their invention and maintenance (Mills 1997). Military power—both domestically and abroad—has been central to the construction and maintenance of racial difference.

Second, racial formation theory sees racial categories arising out of conflicting "racial projects." Racial projects attempt to connect ideas about race to social structures—influencing the social "organization of bodies" (i.e. segregation and attendant racial hierarchies). Racial projects are always conflict-ridden, and they combine both discursive elements ("black is beautiful," or "no one is illegal"), with attempts at institutionalization. Once a racial project becomes institutionalized, it provides (or denies) resources, which can further the groups' relative position.

The final element in the racial formation paradigm is agency. Racial group power is not over-determined through an already existing racial structure. Rather, the racial terrain is contested by interested actors, albeit with startlingly different levels of racialized power. In the U.S. case, Omi and Winant argue that white racial projects are institutionalized at the level of the "racial state," and imply that white racial interests have guided policy since the country's inception (see also Feagin 2000). Bonilla-Silva's (1997) "racialized social system" framework adds an important addendum to Omi and Winant. Although racial formation theory is an advance over the largely undertheorized approach to race dominant in much military sociology, the theory's conceptualization of racial projects as largely *overt* and *conscious* may miss much about the way the modern military structures racial relations. According to Bonilla-Silva (2010), theories that focus largely on overt racial behavior miss how the institutionalization of racial interests in the post-civil rights era has progressed in largely non-racial guise. The "racialized social systems" (Bonilla-Silva 1997) framework argues that in societies partially structured by racial inequality, institutions and ideologies arise that reproduce, however unintentionally, the racialized nature of the social order. The military—consistently ranked among the most respected institutions in the United States—has an outsize voice in debates about race and equal opportunity.

In the thirty years since Omi and Winant (1994) first proposed their theory, it has been subject to many critiques. Perhaps the most frequently applied critique is that these authors focus too much attention on the racial projects of the "racial state" and individuals (Feagin and Elias 2013). In response to this critique, a body of scholarship has recently begun to show how organizations such as the military can also influence the trajectory of racial inequality. Joyce

Bell (2014) has shown how the incorporation of Black Power activists transformed social work by institutionalizing the pro-black ideology of the movement. Similarly, Mora (2014) argues that the inclusion of the Latino category on the census occurred because a diverse set of organizational racial projects coalesced around a shared set of interests. Stakeholders pressured the state to recognize shared "racial" group interest—as official recognition brought with it some advantages including access to grants (Mora 2014, 203).

Militarism, as a racial project, has also played a large role in the domestic allocation of racial inequality. As a cultural and political project, U. S. militarism—as a cultural and political force—has shaped patterns of acceptance for racial minorities in a number of ways. Civilian labor market discrimination has led to the consistent over-representation of people in the military. Similarly, reverence for the military has spillover effects that influence racialized interactions for those who may have never served. Such as when valorization of the military is used to silence civilian claims of inequality. Although the military is the enforcement arm of the racial state, organizational pressures within the military may undermine—or deepen—racial inequality more broadly. But as Dr. King points out, the "brutal solidarity" of military service may undermine some of the more notable markers of domestic racial inequality.

9.3 The Black Radical Tradition and the Military

Although both racial formation theory (Omi and Winant 2015) and the racialized social systems (Bonilla-Silva 1997) approach were developed to explain racial phenomena in the post-civil rights era, the seeds of both theories have long been implicit in the black radical tradition. This tradition has had a mixed relationship to the U.S.'s long project of militarism, as leaders in this tradition have seen militarism both as an avenue for potential black inclusion with the benefits of full citizenship or as tied, as Dr. King's quote above

points out, to a larger project of racialized violence linking blacks at home to destruction abroad. Frederick Douglass argued that black participation in the military during the Civil War would lead to greater post-war inclusion and citizenship benefits.

At some points in his long intellectual journey, W. E. B. Du Bois also claimed service could earn blacks the benefits of citizenship. Du Bois, in an apparent bid to convince blacks to close ranks around the first World War, writes, "*first* your country, *then* your rights" (in Parker 2009). This call from Du Bois in the pages of *Crisis* asks Blacks to put aside their grievances and breaks with his usual structural analysis in favor of a view that sees "your country" as not centrally implicated in the racial order of the day. That is, full membership in a country cannot be analytically separated from rights.

Although Du Bois' writing at times supported military service as an avenue for black advancement, his more radical writings eschewed this approach. In his essay, *The Souls of White Folks*, Du Bois (2012 [1920]) presages Dr. King's connection of warfare abroad and exploitation at home. Linking European militarism to the project of global white supremacy, Du Bois argued that the entire basis of the First World War was "primarily the jealous and avaricious struggle for the largest share in exploiting the darker races" (1920, 35). In this critique, Du Bois provides a startlingly different explanation for how Blacks in the U.S. relate to U.S. militarism. Rather than gaining "their rights," this vision of colonial expansion as a global racial project sees the U.S. as a central player in structuring racial domination worldwide. This is the critique that later black radicals such as Stokely Carmichael (Kwame Ture) picked up in their critiques of U.S. militarism and its relation to racial progress at home and abroad. Arguing that "no Africans had any business fighting America's wars. Period. And that was even more true when they were clear-cut imperialist wars like Vietnam" (Carmichael and Thelwell 2003), the Student Non-Violent Coordinating Committee (SNCC) broke with leaders that saw military service as the path to greater racial incorporation. Further, SNCC, through their radical activism, pushed other black leaders, such as Dr. King, to come out strongly against the war in Vietnam.

In addition to providing a critique of the military as a racial project, Du Bois' (Du Bois 1935) magisterial *Black Reconstruction in America* provides a political outline of how a strategy of massive non-violence provides a better path to racial incorporation for people of color in the U.S. Du Bois (1935) points out that blacks served in the Civil War, but points to the non-violent resistance of their general strike in the South as the primary reason the war ended. Du Bois claims that this strike involved up to half a million people, crippling the South's ability to maintain its troops and even statehood, "without their labor, the south would starve" (1935, 80). Contra the narrative of Black progress that sees militarism as a path to inclusion, Du Bois provides an example of how passive resistance bought blacks' freedom.

This brief historical review of Black leaders' thoughts on militarism shows that military participation has been variously seen as a path to full citizenship or a part of the U.S.'s global racial project. During the Civil War and the Civil Rights Movement, a second strain of Black radical thought showed that non-violence was also an effective tool against the military apparatus. In the case of the Civil War, the massive resistance of the slaves' general strike proved the deciding factor in achieving Black freedom. Although there is some ambivalence, it is possible to trace a thread of resistance to militarism from black leaders across the course of the 20th century (Bonilla-Silva et al. 2015). Black citizenship has been premised upon what Hartman calls, "the capacity to kill and the willingness to die" (Hartman 1997, 154). Thus, opposition to militarism has been grounded in the realization that even the willingness to die hasn't brought full citizenship for African Americans. I now move to a discussion of the modern military as a racial project, examining how current scholarship suffers through ignoring the insights of the black radical tradition.

9.4 Making Race in the Modern Military

Sociologists have long recognized that "through warfare and militarization, "societies reorder themselves, both in opposition to an outside enemy and internally" in accordance with purported social needs (Modell and Haggerty 1991, 206). Conservatives who have long seen service as an assimilation tactic inculcating mainstream values (Lutz 2007) confuse contact with the lessening of racialized power. The creation of the all-volunteer force was such a transformation, as it altered the relationship between racial inequality and enlistment. According to Richard J. Whalen, a former Nixon campaign staffer, the so-called "all-volunteer" force (AVF) was designed to contain and control the political backlash against the draft following the Vietnam War, which Whalen helped to engineer. Cynically, the architects of the all-volunteer army combined "political expediency and libertarian idealism" and found the minimum amount of money necessary to buy off the lower classes and "create a de facto all-volunteer army." This policy heavily influenced the Iraq and Afghanistan conflicts, with the *New York Times* in 2003 claiming that "America's 1.4 million-strong military seems to resemble the makeup of a two-year commuter or trade school." In the racialized social system perspective (Bonilla-Silva 1997), the AVF is racial in its effects because the burdens of service fall disproportionately on people of color. Since the post-Vietnam War inception of the AVF, the U. S. military has, among other strategies, marketed itself as an avenue for social mobility. The military has claimed that it can teach skills transferrable to the civilian labor market and offers post-service educational funding for those who qualify. In line with these claims, sociological research on race in the military tends to highlight the social benefits veterans receive from service. Particularly for women and minorities (and women who are minorities), overrepresentation of blacks and women of color in the military (Segal and Segal 2004) is the result of self-selection into an institution that provides a buffer against discrimination. Some claim this buffer helps to provide opportunities for advancement absent in the general labor market. Implicitly, these authors see the racial function the military is serving as they argue that black overrepresentation is partially a response to exclusion in the civilian labor market.

The creation of the AVF, while facially neutral, has placed an oversized burden on Blacks in the military, as they are represented in the ranks at nearly double their population proportions (Segal and Segal 2004). Looking at these figures outside of their proper context of racial discrimination in the civilian labor market is disingenuous and creates the illusion that Black participation in the military is a choice made free from racialized constraints.

Furthermore, the focus of much sociological research on service alone obscures a number of racialized post-service outcomes that have long-term effects on well-being. For instance, it is well documented that blacks were excluded from many post-service opportunities such as the G. I. Bill's education benefits (Katznelson 2005). It has also been argued that the exclusion from education and housing benefits both created the largest wealth transfer to whites in U.S. history and that it provided a path of ethnic incorporation for groups such as Jews (Brodkin 2004). In addition to post-service economic exclusion—a continuity since Du Bois—there is some evidence that service affects mental health differentially. Further, although it is a hotly debated finding, research also indicates that combat exposure has effects that are exacerbated by racial stratification, influencing long-term psychological outcomes (Kulka et al. 1990; Beals et al. 2002), and that Black and Hispanic vets specifically have higher long-term post-combat rates of PTSD (Modell and Haggerty 1991). This strain of research argues that minorities who have been subject to racialized abuse at home have a harder time dissociating from the humanity of their combatants. This relative inability to dehumanize the object of attack can manifest itself in long-term post-service psychological decline.

Ultimately, seeing militarism as part of a larger racial project allows us to examine the relationship between the military and broader race relations. Further, movements such as large neo-Nazis, who are joining the military to get training can be seen as not a historical aberration but rather as a continuation of militarism being used to alter race relations. Further, it allows us to see incidents such as the torture carried out at Abu Ghraib as not divorced from U.S. policy but, as Roberts (2008) points out, a continuation of tactics developed at home on a racialized prison population. Similarly, the synergistic relationship between the military persecutions of people of color abroad and at home has also resulted in the transfer of counter-insurgency weapons and technology from foreign battlefields to urban communities (Davis 2006). Current sociological theory is up to the task of analyzing militarism as a holistic facet of a racialized system affecting many areas of social life. Unfortunately, current sociological analysis of militarism typically atomizes its effects, allowing the illusion of Black progress to be hidden in the broader context of Black exploitation.

References

Armor, D. J., & Gilroy, C. L. (2009). Changing minority representation in the U.S. Military. *Armed Forces & Society, 36*(2), 223–246.

Beals, J., Manson, S. M., Shore, J. H., Friedman, M. J., Ashcraft, M., Fairbank, J. A., & Schlenger, W. E. (2002). The prevalence of post-traumatic stress disorder among American Indian Vietnam veterans: Disparities and context. *Journal of Trauma Stress, 15*, 89–97.

Bell, J. M. (2014). *The black power movement and American social work.* New York: Columbia University Press.

Bonilla-Silva, E. (1997). Rethinking racism: Toward a structural interpretation. *American Sociological Review, 62*(3), 465–480.

Bonilla-Silva, E. (2010). *Racism without racists: Color-blind racism and the persistence of racial inequality in the United States.* Third Edit. Lanham, Boulder, New York, Toronto, Plymouth, UK: Rownman & Littlefield.

Bonilla-Silva, E., Seamster, L., & Ray, V. (2015). Unpacking the imperialist Knapsack: White privilege and imperialism in Obama's America. In B. Bergo &

T. Nicholls (Eds.), *"I don't see color": Personal and critical perspectives on white privilege* (pp. 146–166). University Park: Pennsylvania State University Press.

Brodkin, K. (2004). How the jews became white and what that says about race in America. New York. Rutgers University Press.

Burk, J., & Espinoza, E. (2012). Race relations within the US Military. *Annual Review of Sociology, 38*(1), 401–422.

Carmichael, S., & Thelwell, M. (2003). *Ready for revolution: The life and struggles of Stokely Carmichael (Kwame Ture)*.

Davis, M. (2006). *City of quartz: Excavating the future in Los Angeles* (New Edition).

Du Bois, W. E. B. (1935). *Black reconstruction in America, 1860–1880*. New York: The Free Press.

Du Bois, W.E.B. 2012 [1920]. *The Souls of White Folk. in Darkwater: Voices From Within the Veil*. New York: Dover Publications.

Elias, S., & Feagin, J. R. (2016). *Racial theories in social science: A systemic racism critique*. New York: Routledge.

Embrick, D. G. (2011). The diversity ideology in the business world: A new oppression for a new age. *Critical Sociology, 37*(5), 541–556.

Elias, S., & Feagin, J. (2015). *Racial Theories in the Social Sciences: A Systemic Racism Critique*. New York: Routledge.

Fanon, F. (1963). *The wretched of the earth*. New York: Grove/Atlantic.

Feagin, J. (2000). *Racist America*. New York: Routledge.

Feagin, J., & Elias, S. (2013). Rethinking racial formation theory: A systemic racism critique. *Ethnic and Racial Studies, 36*(6), 931–960.

Go, J. (2004). 'Racism' and colonialism: Meanings of difference and ruling practices in America's Pacific Empire. *Qualitative Sociology, 27*(1), 35–58.

Hartman, S.V. (1997). *Scenes of subjection: Terror, slavery, and self-making in nineteenth-century America*.

Hirschman, C. (1986). The making of race in Colonial Malaya: Political economy and racial ideology. *Sociological Forum, 1*(2), 330–361.

Janowitz, Morris. (1983). The Reconstruction of Patriorism. Chicago: The Univeristy of Chicago Press.

Katznelson, I. (2005). *When affirmative action was white: An untold history of racial inequality in twentieth-century America*.

King Jr, M. L. (1967). Beyond Vietnam: A time to break silence. *speech, Riverside Church, New York, NY, April 4*.

Kulka, R. A., Schlenger, W. E., Fairbank, J. A., Hough, R. L., Jordan, B. K., Marmar, C. R., & Weiss, D. S. (1990). *Trauma and the Vietnam War generation: Report of findings from the National Vietnam Veterans Readjustment Study*. New York: Brunner/Mazel .

Leach, B. W. (2004). Race as mission critical: The occupational need rationale in military affirmative action and beyond. *The Yale Law Journal, 113*(5), 1093–1141.

Lundquist, J. H. (2008). Ethnic and gender stratification in the military: The effect of a Meritocratic Institution. *American Sociological Review, 73*(3), 477–496.

Lutz, C. (2007). Grunt Lit: The participant-observers of empire. *American Ethnologist, 34*(2), 322–328.

Mills, C. W. (1997). *The racial contract*. First. Ithica and London: Cornell University Press.

Modell, J., & Haggerty, T. (1991). The social impact of war. *Annual Review of Sociology, 17*(1), 205–224.

Moore, W. L., & Bell, J. M. (2011). Maneuvers of whiteness: 'Diversity' as a mechanism of retrenchment in the affirmative action discourse. *Critical Sociology, 37*(5), 597–613.

Mora, G. C. (2014). Cross-field effects and ethnic classification The Institutionalization of Hispanic Panethnicity, 1965–1990. *American Sociological Review, 79*(2), 183–210.

Moskos, C., & Butler, J. S. (1997). *All that we can be: Black leadership and racial integration the army way*. New York: Basic Books.

Omi, M., & Winant, H. (1994). *Racial formation in the United States: From the 1960s to the 1990s*. Second. New York, NY: Routledge.

Omi, M., & Winant, H. (2015). *Racial Formation in the United States. Third Edition*. New York: Routledge.

Parker, C. S. (2009). *Fighting for democracy: Black veterans and the struggle against white supremacy in the Postwar South*. Princeton and Oxford: Princeton University Press.

Reskin, B. (2012). The race discrimination system. *Annual Review of Sociology, 38*(1), 17–35.

Roberts, D. (2008). Torture and the biopolitics of race. *University of Miami Law Review, 62*(2), 229.

Segal, D.R., & Segal, M.W. (2004). *America's military population*.

Skrentny, J. D. (2013). *After civil rights: Racial realism in the new American workplace*. Princeton and Oxford: Princeton University Press.

Steinberg, S. (2007). *Race relations: A critique*. Stanford: Standford University Press.

Ture, K., & Hamilton, C. V. (1967). *Black power: The politics of liberation*. New York: Random House.

Zuberi, T. (2001). *Thicker than blood: How racial statistics lie*. Minneapolis: University of Minessota Press.

Part III

Politics and Economics of Conflict and Change: Rationalization of Racial and Ethnic Hierarchy

Racial Democracy, Multiculturalism, and Inequality

10

Peter Kivisto and Andrey Rezaev

Contents

Abstract

The simplest answer to the question of what a racial democracy would look like is that it would be a society in which racial differences at the level of identity carried with them no race-specific inequalities. The value of the idea of racial democracy is that, by serving as an ideal type, it simultaneously provides a tool of analysis to assess whether or not the racial barriers to equal citizenship have been overcome and a political goal. More specifically, the idea of racial democracy is intended as a concrete concept that can be used to assess the state of democracy in the nation. Those who have been historically disenfranchised and more recently ignored by policy makers and the public alike function as miner's canaries. They test the atmosphere of the civil sphere to see if democracy can survive. One of its virtues is that it can provide a comparative frame of reference, allowing us to assess the extent to which identity politics remain tied to redistributive politics, and thus measuring the distance we still have to travel to achieve a just, multicultural, and egalitarian social order.

P. Kivisto (✉)
Department of Sociology, Augustana College, Rock Island, IL, USA
e-mail: peterkivisto@augustana.edu

A. Rezaev
St. Petersburg State University, Petersburg, Russia
e-mail: a.rezaev@spbu.ru

© Springer International Publishing AG, part of Springer Nature 2018
P. Batur and J. R. Feagin (eds.), *Handbook of the Sociology of Racial and Ethnic Relations*,
Handbooks of Sociology and Social Research, https://doi.org/10.1007/978-3-319-76757-4_10

10.1   Introduction

The nation-building projects in the modern world, whether they are nations located at the world system's core or periphery, entail coming to terms with ethnic and racial heterogeneity. For scholars, it is necessary to examine carefully the historically contingent processes at play in the construction of what Spickard (2005) calls "ethnic systems," Omi and Winant (1986) refer to as "racial formations," and Feagin (2013) describes as "white racial frames." Whatever the language that one might prefer, the common thread linking them is the understanding, as Spickard (2005: 2) puts it, that *"race is about power, and it is written on the body."* In this chapter, we will argue that, as applied to the United States, the idea—indeed, the ideal—of a racial democracy can be a valuable analytic tool in understanding the implications of Spickard's statement. Insofar as this is the case, what is being proposed herein is the importation of a term from Latin America to the US, ironically perhaps because in its earliest articulations it was intended to differentiate the racial dynamics of Brazil in particular and other Latin American nations in general from the US. Simply put, a racial democracy can be defined for our purposes as a racially diverse nation that is not characterized by racial inequality. As such, the term can be seen as a social justice metric, not as explicit social policy.

Central to any discussion of democracy is citizenship, for it is by virtue of being a citizen that people are accorded membership in a polity that entails an admixture of rights and obligations. It is as citizens that they are in a position to make claims on the political system. In making this case we will explore two distinct but nonetheless interrelated matters. The first involves the question of who is to be included among the ranks of citizens and the reverse side of the coin, who is to be excluded. The second involves the matter of the terms or the modes of inclusion. Although there is considerable overlap between these two topics, it is also true that, both in terms of public discourse and scholarly agendas, the first received substantially more attention

until about 1970, while with the rise of multiculturalism thereafter the second has become a major theme (Kivisto 2005).

As such, the first topic requires a look to the past, while the second more explicitly and evidently concerns the present and its implications for the future. This examination of the past is not intended to offer anything resembling a comprehensive historical overview of the processes of exclusion or the movements aimed at advancing the cause of expanding inclusion. Rather its purpose is to indicate in what ways inclusion in the former sense of the term remains an unrealized goal and to understand the relevance of inclusion for the emergence of multiculturalism as a new mode of societal incorporation.

The democratic cultures that shaped the nation of Western Europe and North America, certainly by the eighteenth century, revived and redefined the idea of citizenship. This involved at the philosophical level inheriting and embracing elements of citizenship's ancient origins in the Greek city-state and in the Roman Empire, while at the same time at the political level repudiating and replacing the autocratic model of subjecthood that characterized the feudal era with the idea of the citizen as an active agent in political decision-making. It also held out the conviction that the status of the citizen *qua* citizen was an equal to all other citizens in spite of inequalities of wealth. At its core, despite nation-specific variations, the citizen was seen as an independent or free person engaged in the process of self-rule (Kivisto and Faist 2007). Skinner (1998: 74) describes the system of self-rule as one, "in which the sole power of making laws remains with the people or their accredited representatives, and in which all individual members of the body politic—rulers and citizens alike—remain equally subject to whatever laws they choose to impose on themselves." Kerber (1997: 34) concurs with this definition while stressing: "'Citizen' is an equalizing word. It carries with it the activism of Aristotle's definition—one who rules and is ruled in turn."

The role of citizen came to constitute the central mode of belonging to the nation. It is thus implicated in the construction of modern conceptions of nationality. For this reason, the distinction between citizens and noncitizens, those who were for one reason or another excluded from full membership as citizens in these societies, served as a significant and consequential differential mark of identity. It spoke to who could and who could not take part in the ongoing process of self-rule. The idea of full membership is crucial here insofar as while in some instances it was possible to distinguish the citizen from the alien, in other instances the distinction is not quite so clear, as the idea of denizens attests.

What does the idea of full membership suggest? Likewise, what do we mean when we speak about second-class citizens? In other words, what do these adjectives tell us about those individuals who are in some ways members of a nation-state, but lack something possessed by those for whom these adjectives are not attached to their citizenship status? This can be answered by considering one of the three crucial features that characterize the democratic political process. The three are: (1) the right to participate in the public sphere; (2) limitations on the power of government over the individual; and (3) a system based on the rule of law. The second two elements speak to the framework in which citizens participate in the democratic process as equals. Those who do not possess full membership, but are regarded as second-class citizens are permanent residents of the nation who do not have the right to participate in the political process as equals. Such individuals are not permitted to vote, to engage in policy making, to run for elective office, and the like. They possess formal, but not substantive, citizenship. Although their identities may be different from aliens, they share much in common insofar as both are denied certain fundamental rights that accrue to those possessing full membership in the society (Marshall 1964).

10.2 The Dialectic of Inclusion and Exclusion

The principal fault lines used to define the boundaries of inclusion versus exclusion have historically been based on three major social divisions: class, gender, and race. And, indeed, though much has changed, these divisions remain salient—and indeed tend to be intersecting. During the formative period of these fledging democracies, the privileged white, property-owning male citizens were intent on disqualifying a majority of the nation's residents from citizenship rights. Confronted with a disjunction between the egalitarian ideals of democratic theory and the desire to exclude from full societal membership certain categories of persons who did not share their class, gender, or racial identities, they responded by erecting ideological justifications for exclusionary policies that resulted in, to borrow the language of Parkin (1979: 44–73), "social closure as exclusion." For their part, the white working class, women, and nonwhites responded, always in difficult circumstances and with varying degrees of success, by creating social movements aimed at acquiring the political voice that had been denied them.

Race and gender constituted the two most significant limitations inscribed on the universalistic values of Enlightenment thinkers. This was evident in the varied social constructions of nation-specific definitions of citizenship during the eighteenth and nineteenth centuries. Although there was a universal character to citizenship status for all who possessed it, the general tendency was to deny membership to certain categories of people not only based on certain moral defects or defects of character (criminals and the insane), but on the ascribed identities of race and gender. Thus the universal citizen was invariably a circumscribed identity insofar as it was only available to white males. As Glenn (2002: 21) has pointed out, the argument for constructing this boundary rested to large extent on the public-private and the independent-dependent dichotomies. Both loomed large in the rationales for the exclusion of women from the ranks of citizens. In the case of race, the public-private was less evident, while the idea of independence-dependence was central.

This could be seen in countries such as Germany that historically operated with a *jus sanguinis* conception of national identity. Underpinning this exclusionary policy was the racist belief that various non-German ethnic groups were incapable of the independence required of citizens. While useful as manual laborers, they were not capable of participating in collective self-rule. Such a conception shaped Germany from the founding of the modern state in 1871 until a new citizenship law was passed in 1999, thereby ending the one of Europe's most exclusionary citizenship policies (Kivisto 2002: 169). While in effect, the previous law prevented those who entered Germany due to labor shortages from becoming citizens, whether they be Slavs working in East German agriculture a century ago, or Turks and Yugoslavs doing the nation's dirty, difficult, and dangerous work today. Germany was clearly not alone among the ethnonational civic regimes, but it did serve as a paradigmatic instance of this particular type.

One can find a parallel resistance to inclusionary policies in other societies that did not embrace an explicitly ethnonational definition of national identity, defining nationalism in civic rather than ethnic terms. For example, although the republican ideals of France ought to have made that nation far more open to absorbing diverse peoples into its ranks, provided they embraced the ideals of the republic, in practice France's civic nationalism was far from universal in its willingness to accept the racial other (Brubaker 1992; for a recent comparison, see Alba and Foner 2015). One could see a similar racial exclusion in operation in settler societies. Australia, due to its status as part of the British Empire, at first viewed those eligible for citizenship as being limited only to British subjects. This was transformed into a whites-only policy until the 1960s, after which time the nation became more receptive to redefining who was

eligible for citizenship. Henceforth, the battle pitting those advocating an open society versus those promoting a restrictive version of national identity increasingly took place over immigration policy (Kivisto 2002: 109–112, 2016). In the end labor shortages became sufficiently acute that economic considerations won out over the opposition of cultural conservatives. Coincident with changes in naturalization policies regarding immigrants was a change in the relationship of the state to Aboriginal peoples who had long been excluded from citizenship. Originally treated as wards of the state, it was not until the passage of the 1948 National and Citizenship Act that all Aboriginals were defined as citizens, and only after a 1967 referendum were they granted the right to vote in federal elections.

Thus, racial exclusion shaped citizenship regimes widely. However, nowhere was its impact more consequential than in the United States, and for that reason this particular case is of unique importance in understanding racial exclusion. Shklar (1991) is not alone in arguing that the existence of chattel slavery in a presumably democratic nation more than anything else shaped the ways Americans thought about race and racial exclusion Shklar writes that she had not "forgotten how ungenerous and bigoted immigration and naturalization policies have often been, but [she argues] their effects and defects pale before the history of slavery and its impact upon our public attitudes" (Shklar 1991: 14). Indeed, the way that blacks were defined vis-à-vis the issue of citizenship served to frame the way that other groups defined as racially distinct were located in the scheme of things, as will be seen below in surveying the history of immigrant groups seeking citizenship.

Between independence and the immediate aftermath of the Civil War, the United States operated with a rather ill-defined conception of national independence. The states possessed considerable latitude in determining both who was and who was not eligible for citizenship, but also in defining the precise rights accruing to citizens. However, the Constitution did divide the nation's population into three categories: those defined as "the people," who were presumably candidates for citizenship; Indians, who were viewed as permanent aliens residing within the nation because they were members of tribal governments that had relations to the United States similar to the relations with foreign nations; and finally "others" referred to black slaves. In this scenario, Indians as members of various tribes and black slaves were treated as ineligible to become citizens. Feagin (2006: 279) points out that enshrined in the US Constitution were provisions that insured that democracy was not available to all peoples and nowhere in the document was there "recognition of the humanity or rights of" African slaves.

However, there were ambiguities contained in this formulation, not the least of which had to do with the status of free people of color. Particularly in the wake of the American Revolution, when as Bailyn (1967: 60) put it, a "contagion of liberty" swept the new republic (Wilentz 2005), free blacks pressed for the right to become citizens. Glenn (2002: 32–33) has described their situation during the latter part of the eighteenth century as follows:

> More generally, blacks, especially free blacks, had fewer explicit restrictions on their rights at the beginning of the [nineteenth] century than by mid-century. Indeed, there was a brief period after the Revolution when some blacks were able to realize in a small way the status and rights of citizens. Blacks themselves had seized the initiative during the Revolution, taking advantage of the upheaval to escape from bondage. ...In sum, though far from enjoying equality, for the first quarter-century after the Revolution free blacks were conceded to be citizens of a sort, and in many states could vote on the same terms as whites.

During this period, an extremely small minority of blacks, who were not only free people of color but also owned property, managed to achieve a second-class version of citizenship. But as Glenn (2002) and Wilentz (2005) have noted, even this limited access to citizenship eroded as the nation got closer to the Civil War. It was only in the aftermath of the war that blacks were formally accorded the rights to citizenship. In 1865, the passage of the Thirteenth Amendment abolished slavery, while in the following year the Fourteenth Amendment granted

citizenship to all blacks and required equal treatment of all citizens under both federal and state laws, and the Fifteenth Amendment forbade denying the right to vote on the basis of race.

During Reconstruction, African Americans vigorously asserted their new political status. In the first place, they voted. But more than going to the polls, they entered the political process by running for office at the local, state, and federal levels. Numerous blacks were elected to various prominent positions, serving in various southern states as lieutenant governors, secretaries of state, state treasurers, and related high-ranking positions, while at the national level blacks were elected to both the Houses of Congress (Foner 1988).

However, by the mid-1870s the federal government withdrew from its active engagement in the reconstruction of the South (where over 90% of blacks resided), thereby allowing whites in the region to reassert their supremacy. Emerging in the latter part of the nineteenth century and extending until the civil rights movement succeeded in dismantling it in the 1960s, the Jim Crow era entailed two interrelated features: domination and segregation. Scholars debate about whether the laws passed in the southern states merely codified the existing pattern of race relations or amounted to a significant structural change (Glenn 2002: 113).

Whatever the case, the result was the perpetuation of a caste system within a class society. While the impact of Jim Crow laws operated at all levels—cultural, economic, and political—we look here solely at the political consequences. Opposed to the political power of blacks, yet due to the Fifteenth Amendment unable to simply legally prohibit all blacks from voting, states sought to employ a variety of criteria whose sole purpose it was to disenfranchise blacks. The two most widely used means for accomplishing this task were literacy tests and the poll tax.

The legislated basis of white supremacy was backed up by the threat of extra-legal violence at the hands of a number of terrorist organizations. Lynching became a pervasive feature of southern life, serving as a constant form of intimidation of blacks. Although precise figures on the actual number of lynchings do not exist, one reliable source, the Tuskegee Institute, reported that 4730 people were lynched between 1882 and the dawn of the civil rights movement in 1951. Another type of collective violence directed against blacks was the riot, whereby whites attacked blacks and their property—often burning homes and businesses to the ground (Glenn 2002: 109–110; Litwack 1998: 284–298). The peak of much of this activity occurred between 1890 and 1920, and the intended results were achieved. The percentage of blacks that were eligible to vote declined dramatically throughout the South. Thus, by the first decade of the twentieth century only six percent of blacks could vote in Mississippi, while the figures were four percent in Georgia and one percent in Louisiana (Glenn 2002: 112).

When blacks began to migrate to the North, beginning around World War I and again during and after World War II, they did so not only for economic reasons, but for political reasons as well. In effect, when they moved to what for a short time they called the Promised Land (until they discovered the northern version of racism), they were both economic migrants and political refugees. This situation would characterize the situation for blacks until the 1960s.

The civil rights movement constituted a watershed moment in the history of black-white relations. In particular, the passage of the Voting Rights Act of 1965 signaled a new effort on the part of the federal government to insure that blacks in the South would no longer be denied the franchise. As an indication of the positive impact of this legislation, 68.4% of African Americans have registered to vote since its passage. However, forces opposed to the expansion of voting rights won a major victory in 2013 in the Supreme Court's *Shelby County, Alabama v. Holder* decision, which considerably weakened this civil rights tool (Arnwine and Johnson-Blanco 2013). Indeed, voter suppression has become a major issue in numerous states. Moreover, policies of mass incarceration, that Michelle Alexander (2010) has aptly characterized as "the new Jim Crow" combine with

policies of felon disenfranchisement that deprive approximately 5.4 million offenders of the right to vote (Manza and Uggen 2008). Given that blacks are disproportionately imprisoned, the intent of such legislation can be construed as the same as that of literacy tests and poll taxes.

Other people of color confronted barriers to inclusion. Thus, because they continued to be viewed as members of alien tribal nations, Native Americans did not acquire the right to citizenship until passage of the Indian Citizenship Act in 1924. However, the majority of non-black people of color were immigrants, and for that reason the barriers they confronted were shaped chiefly by immigration and naturalization laws. Actually, as we shall see below, the phrase people of color, a contemporary expression, can be ironically applied to immigrants from the late nineteenth and early twentieth centuries whose progeny have over the passage of time "become white" (Roediger 1991, 2005). Newcomers were needed as the demand for labor in an industrial economy could not be met by the native-born alone. At the same time, intense opposition to the entry of certain groups of people emerged, or if they were to be admitted as temporary workers, nativists were adamant in their opposition to granting them citizenship. In this regard, the United States is similar to other immigrant receiving nations in the Americas in its willingness to implement racist policies in the interest of "culling the masses" (Fitzgerald and Cook-Martín 2014; see also Zolberg 2006).

Tichenor (2002) has pointed out that four collective actors have historically shaped immigration and naturalization policies. Two have favored liberal laws and two have historically supported restrictive ones. Promoters of a liberal approach include business interests seeking labor recruits and cultural cosmopolitans. Those embracing restrictive laws included organized labor opposed to what they perceived to be a competitive threat by foreign workers who were presumed to undercut existing wage levels and cultural conservatives. What has made coalitions among natural allies over this issue vexing is that business and cultural conservatives tend to be aligned with the Republican Party, while labor and cultural cosmopolitans tend to be

Democratic Party stalwarts. Thus, effective coalitions required cross-party alliances. This situation shaped the politics of immigration control from the nineteenth century until recently when organized labor (though not necessarily the rank-and-file) changed its stance and become an active advocate of new immigrants, whom they see as key to union growth.

In terms of immigration control, Asians were singled out earliest. More specifically, with the passage of the Chinese Exclusion Act of 1882, the Chinese were the first group to be denied admission to the United States. The Gentleman's Agreement of 1907 was designed to place strict limits on the number of Japanese that could enter the country. However, this was merely the beginning of a far more aggressive campaign of immigration restriction that arose during a period of heretofore unprecedented immigration.

Asians were not alone in being singled out, as increased attention was directed at the larger components of the new immigrants who originated from nations in Southern and Eastern Europe. As a variety of piecemeal laws passed around the turn of the century attests, nativists feared the newcomers for a variety of reasons. They were seen as a threat to the culture, advocates of political radicalism, morally and intellectually inferior, inclined to pauperism, and bearers of disease (Daniels 2004: 27–58; Zolberg 2006). The zenith of opposition to mass immigration occurred with the passage of the National Origins Act in 1924, which set admission quotas of 2% of the number of persons of a nationality as reflected in the 1890 census. In so doing, the law was intentionally structured along lines that privileged Western and Northern Europeans at the expense of other groups. The result was to in effect end mass immigration to the nation for the next four decades.

Naturalization laws likewise were shaped along racial lines. The earliest law, the Naturalization Act of 1790, defined those persons eligible to become citizens through a process of naturalization as limited to "free white persons" (Glenn 2002: 24). In the wake of the Civil War and the passage of the Fourteenth Amendment, the definition of who qualified for naturalization

was redefined to include in addition to free persons of color, "persons of African nativity or African decent." Subsequently, as Lyman (1993: 380) notes, both the Chinese and Japanese were denied the right to become citizens. Such would be the case for the Chinese from 1882 until 1943, when the exigencies of a world war would prompt the government to permit its Chinese allies' residents in the United States to naturalize. In the case of the Japanese, this would not occur until 1952, well after the cessation of hostilities.

Within this framework, where whites and blacks could naturalize but the two main immigrant groups from Asia could not, members of many groups found themselves located in an ambiguous situation. The law called for discerning what it meant to be non-white but not black. Actually, a number of both Chinese and Japanese immigrants raised this question in the courts. Thus in 1878 Chinese immigrant Ah Yup, who was identified in the court brief as a member of the Mongolian race, petitioned to become a citizen. His petition was rejected. The rationale offered by the court was that neither "in popular language, in literature, nor in scientific nomenclature, do we ordinarily, if ever, find the words 'white person' used in a sense so comprehensive as to include an individual of the Mongolian race" (quoted in Lyman 1991: 204). In a 1922 Supreme Court case, a Japanese immigrant named Takao Ozawa claimed that anthropological evidence indicated that the Japanese were Caucasian and thus they ought to be considered eligible for citizenship. His argument, too, was rejected (Lyman 1991: 206–208).

This set the stage for numerous other groups to seek to be declared white in order to be accepted into the "white republic" (Saxton 1990). Thus, as Lyman (1991) has chronicled, among the groups declared ineligible for citizenship were the Burmese, Koreans, Hawaiians, Arabs, and East Indians, while others such as Armenians and Syrians were declared to be white and therefore were permitted to become naturalized citizens. Race as it was deployed in some of these cases was linked to religion (thus, the designation Hindoo contained both religious and racial connotations) or politics. One of the more interesting instances of the latter occurred when sixteen Finnish immigrants in northern Minnesota were denied their first citizenship papers on the grounds that Finns were Mongolians. This rejection took place in 1908, in the immediate aftermath of a bitter strike by iron miners on the Mesabi Range. The Finns singled out in this way were all activists in the Finnish Socialist Federation, and thus their involvement in what was described in court papers as an "East Asian philosophy" was meant to imply that their political views were reflective of their racial origins. This was a somewhat hard sell given that there was a growing sentiment that European-origin immigrants were white. In fact, the case was soon thereafter thrown out, with the District Court judge concluding that although the ancient Finns had indeed been Mongols, nonetheless they had over the course of history mixed sufficiently with Teutonic peoples to be considered white (Kivisto and Leinonen 2011).

Over the course of the twentieth century scientific racism progressively lost influence, with World War II serving as a watershed. The Nazi experience gave what was once respectable a bad name. However, this did not mean that racism simply evaporated; rather it persisted, albeit in different guises. Thus, the Immigration and Naturalization Act of 1952 not only reaffirmed the national quota system of the 1924 National Origins Act but added new reasons for exclusion based on political ideology and sexual orientation. At the same time, the Jim Crow system, despite challenges, remained intact. It took a powerful civil rights movement in the 1950s and 1960s to finally dismantle that racial formation (Omi and Winant 1986).

As the nation entered into the post-civil rights era, race and class began to intersect in new ways, making possible the expansion of a black middle class no longer rooted in the segregated black community. At the same time, however, it left behind in those communities the poor, or what Wilson (2004) described as "the truly disadvantaged." Thus, while one sector of black America came to acquire the various forms of capital—financial, social, and human—that permitted civic involvements as something other

than second-class citizens, the other sector remained marginalized. High levels of persistent inequality intruded on their prospects of casting off the exclusionary legacy of Jim Crow. When Barack Obama became the nation's first black President in 2008, it constituted a major achievement. At the same time, as was more evident by the time of his re-election campaign, he has confronted an increasingly polarized nation in which his opponents included not only colorblind racists, but also those whose racism was of the unvarnished variety (Alexander and Jaworsky 2014).

It was in the heat of the civil right struggle that a new immigration law, the Hart-Celler Act (1965), was passed. Its liberal sponsors sought to end the racist character of existing law by abolishing the national quotas system. Although its sponsors downplayed the significance of the law, and in particular its potential for creating a new period of mass migration, it is quite clear that the law was intended to open the nation's doors once again. In this it succeeded; indeed, the US is now in a migratory wave that is having as significant an impact on American society as the preceding wave did.

In terms of the ethnic composition of the nation, the consequence of the current migratory wave is that the Latino and Asian populations have grown significantly. Indeed, as the 2010 census revealed, Latinos constituted 16% of the population, making them the largest racial minority. The nation is now considerably more diverse—ethnically, religiously, and linguistically—than it was in 1965. This has alarmed contemporary nativists. Thus, Huntington (2004: 181, 184) bemoaned not only the presence of large numbers of immigrants, but also their presumed unwillingness to assimilate—opting instead for multiculturalism.

This represents a serious misreading of present realities: it misrepresents the immigrants themselves (and one might add that it also misrepresents other minority groups—including ethnonational minorities and indigenous peoples), and it misinterprets the ways that contemporary liberal democracies are experimenting with novel modes of incorporating diversity

(Kivisto 2005). In particular, it misconstrues multiculturalism. It is to this topic that we now turn. What follows is predicated on the conviction that modern industrial nations have until recently relied on a limited number of modes of incorporating heretofore marginalized groups that have tended to rely on the expectation that incorporation occurs at the individual, and not at the group level. Multiculturalism, in both practice and theory, is a recent mode of incorporation that challenges this assumption. In the process, it informs current discourses on the relationship between inclusion and citizenship.

10.3 Multiculturalism as a Mode of Inclusion

Multiculturalism has generated during the past two decades a veritable cottage industry of scholarly and popular publications, primarily but not solely focusing on the advanced industrial nations of the globe. It has been widely used in various ways during this time, including in the depiction of interethnic relations, the defense of group rights, as a valorization of difference, and as a rationale for new state policies of incorporation. It has also generated intense ideological debates. Two decades ago Nathan Glazer (1997) proclaimed that "we are all multiculturalists now," and others have argued that however fitfully and fraught with conflict and unease, the world's liberal democracies have imbibed what might be seen as a multicultural sensibility, even if it has not been translated into official policies or explicit endorsements of multiculturalism (Kivisto 2012; see also Modood 2013; Kymlicka 2015). This view has been challenged by those who contend that the multicultural moment is over as state policy, social practice, and perhaps as theoretical construct as well (Ash 2012; see also Barry 2001; Joppke 2001; Joppke 2005; Tiryakian 2004). However, while there is clear evidence of a backlash to multiculturalism, analyses reveal that in terms of concrete policies and practices, there is little evidence of the retreat of multiculturalism—though the term itself is not

always used to describe such policies and practices (Vertovec and Wessendorf 2010).

Although the United States did not become an officially state-sanctioned multicultural society, due to a number of causal variables, it increasingly came to exhibit a multicultural sensibility. What made the US case distinctive (as noted in the preceding section) was the emergence of a civil rights movement from within the black community—a movement created by the offspring of slaves. This movement originally pressed for equality and integration, but a more militant Black Power phase would question the desirability of the latter.

Criticism of Anglo-conformity as the appropriate model of incorporation into American society grew from the 1960s onwards, when it was challenged by both second and third generation white ethnics from Southern and Eastern Europe and by the rise of Black Nationalism. The Red Power and Chicano movements would also play roles in critiquing it. Even without multicultural legislation, the federal government, paralleling the attitudes of the general public, was increasingly willing to tolerate and even support manifestations of symbolic ethnicity (the proactive role of the federal government became especially evident with the passage of the Ethnic Heritage Studies Act in 1972).

However, multiculturalism was not merely advanced symbolically. Rather, it took more substantive form in policies that came to constitute "the minority rights revolution," which Skrentny (2002: 4) depicts as rising very quickly during the 1960s as a result of a congeries of "federal legislation, presidential executive orders, bureaucratic rulings, and court decisions that established nondiscrimination rights." The minority rights revolution was generally not equated with multiculturalism, though the parallels to policies elsewhere that were so designated is quite clear. A distinctive feature of these efforts, Skrentny (2002: 4) went on to note, was that they "targeted groups of Americans understood as disadvantaged but not defined by socioeconomic class." In so doing, they reframed what it meant to belong in America—to "be" an

American—by claiming that groups previously located on the societal periphery ought to be relocated in the center.

Two particular policies stand out as being of singular importance: affirmative action and bilingual education. At least from the perspective of state intent—however difficult it is to specify state intentionality—these policies resemble those enacted in Australia insofar as the focus is on individual members of disadvantaged groups, and not the groups themselves. Thus, the legislative purpose of affirmative action was to assist minority individuals to obtain university admission, employment slots, and business ownership opportunities through a variety of administrative devices. In other words, its purpose was defined as assisting individual upward social mobility. Likewise, the Bilingual Education Act of 1968 was conceived as assisting individual immigrants —chiefly Latinos and Asians—in making the transition from their native languages to English language proficiency. Lawmakers did not see the act as designed to protect or preserve native languages over time. Perhaps the only significant exception to this focus on minority individual rights was the gerrymandering of electoral districts to enhance the likelihood of increasing minority membership in Congress.

Multiculturalism in practice has meant that at the same time that differences were to be not only tolerated but valorized, there was also an expectation that such an approach would serve the interests of the state insofar as it simultaneously constitutes what Alexander (2006: 450–457) calls a "mode of incorporation." As these experiences and that of some other advanced industrial nations indicates, the logic of such an approach is predicated on the assumption that multiculturalism threatens neither the core values of liberal democratic societies nor the incorporation of ethnically marginalized groups—both "multinational" and "polyethnic" ethnics, to use Kymlicka's (1995: 17) terminology.

If there is a lesson to be learned from existing practice-related formulations of multiculturalism, it is that they are designed to serve a dual purpose. On the one hand, they are a response to the demands on the part of marginalized ethnic groups for collective rather than merely individualistic solutions to inequality and exclusion. In other words, they are responses to the claims-making efforts of mobilized groups for recognition and/or redistribution (Kivisto 2012; see also, Young 1990; Parekh 2000; Kymlicka 2001: 152–176; Sciortino 2003). Kivisto (2012: 8–14) identifies five types of political claims: exemption, accommodation, preservation, redress, and inclusion. Voluntary immigrants can avail themselves of the first two types, while other groups can appeal to all five types. At the same time, both the state and the public often engage in making counter-claims. At least from the perspective of decision-makers, policy-formulators, and most of the political advocates of some version of group rights, a major goal is to bring heretofore-marginalized groups into the societal mainstream. Moreover, as Alexander and Smelser (1999: 14–15) observe, "Although the radical multicultural position advocated by many spokespersons for minority groups seems to contradict [the sense of] connectivity, the actual political and social movements advocating multiculturalism consistently employ a civil-society discourse." In other words, multiculturalism in a racial democracy constitutes a "mode of incorporation" that is characterized by a particular type of civic participation. Indeed, this is what Kivisto meant by the politics of inclusion.

It should be noted that this is not the way multiculturalism is construed by many commentators. Critics of multiculturalism seldom consider the possibility that it constitutes a mode of democratic inclusion. Such critics are varied and can be found across the political spectrum, though those on the political right are more inclined to be hostile to multiculturalism both as an ideal and as social policy. The arguments of those opposed to multiculturalism fall into several broad categories. The first argument is that multiculturalism is divisive and as such threatens national unity. This was the thesis advanced by Schlesinger, advocate for the "vital center," in his highly influential *The Disuniting of America* (1992). The left's concerns with multiculturalism is that one of the unintended consequences of the promotion of a politics of recognition (Taylor 1992) is that in the process a politics of redistribution is ignored or placed on the back burner (Fraser 1995).

In recent years, there is evidence of a growing awareness on the part of multiculturalism's advocates that it is necessary to move beyond these and related polemics and to similarly move past the philosophical controversies surrounding multiculturalism in its varied forms (see for example Benhabib 2002; Gutmann 2003; Habermas 1998), ranging from, to use the distinction employed by Appiah (2005: 73–79), "hard pluralism" (e.g., Iris Marion Young and John Gray) to "soft pluralism" (e.g., Will Kymlicka and Joseph Raz), if a convincing conceptual framework for multiculturalism is to emerge. Two strands of a sociologically-informed approach have emerged, one focusing on multiculturalism as a macro-level process (Alexander 2006) and the other as practices entailing claims-making that is amenable to analysis at the micro- and mezzo-levels (Kivisto 2012). Part of the task at hand is to weave together these two theoretical strands.

10.4 Racial Democracy and Redistribution

Much of the scholarly conversation on multiculturalism to date has focused on the issue of recognition. While this is an essential component of multiculturalism, it represents only one side of the coin, the other being redistribution. In other words, the concerns of those on the left such as Nancy Fraser are valid, but to so conclude is not to reject the politics of recognition. Instead, the task at hand is to integrate such a politics with a politics of redistribution, which has been the hallmark of the traditional left. The argument offered herein is that the idea of racial democracy offers a conceptual handle for linking recognition and redistribution.

To make such a claim requires offering an account of what racial democracy means. As is the case with most concepts used in the social sciences, it has a history. Racial democracy was first developed as an explanatory device to depict race relations in Brazil by anthropologist Gilberto Freyre, who in *Master and Slave* (1963a [1933]) and its sequels, *The Mansions and the Shanties* (1963b [1936]) and *Order and Progress* (1970 [1959]) sought to distinguish the situation in his nation from the *Herrenvolk* democracy of the United States. In part, he painted an idyllic portrait of the Brazilian past where white masters lived in close proximity to and in general harmony with the vast slave population. Racial interdependency, high rates of miscegenation, and the greater ease by which Brazilian slaves could obtain their freedom signaled for Freyre factors contributing to the conclusion that Anglo-American racism was a virtual impossibility in the Brazilian context.

Winant (2001: 226–228) contends that Freyre was chiefly responsible for providing the nation with a myth of national origins, one that "abandoned in part the previously taken-for-granted superiority of whiteness and the principles of racial hierarchy, substituting for these a new racial nationalism that vindicated and glorified miscegenation and hybridization." In his formulation, what emerged in Brazil's relatively relaxed racial climate was the so-called "new man (sic) of the tropics." Racial democracy, thus, constituted a form of assimilation predicated on the creolization of the population—in effect a racial melting pot (Degler 1986; Hoetink 1971; Pierson 1942).

In both scholarly and popular form, the idea of racial democracy took root, not only in Brazil, but throughout Latin American and Caribbean nations with similar colonial histories to that of Brazil, resulting in what some have referred to as Iberian exceptionalism, which attributes the presumed racial egalitarianism of this part of the Americas to three factors. This include the fact that Spain and Portugal lived under Moorish rule, that Catholics were more willing than Protestants to view the racial other as having a soul, and the demographic reality of small numbers of single male colonizers entering into sexual and emotional contacts with indigenous women (Peña et al. 2004).

Critical race theorists have made the argument that Brazil and similar nations cannot accurately be described as racial democracies, contending that the concept is a myth, and a pernicious one at that (Guimarães 2001; Hanchard 1994; Twine 1998; Warren 2002; Winant 1999, 2001). One part of the critique focuses on a historical question about the nature of the Spanish and Portuguese pasts, challenging the racial democracy perspective, which viewed these pasts as essentially benign. The reality, critical race theorists point out, is that all of the colonizers of the Americas were brutal, the only significant differences being in regard to the varying degrees of brutality. In comparative terms, it is not clear whether the Iberians were the least brutal. It is clear, however, that they were brutal. The second part of the critique calls attention to the fact that darker-skinned people are far from equal in these nations. They are economically disadvantaged and prevented from entering the centers of power. In short, as Spickard (2005) would put it, their oppression and marginalization is inscribed on their bodies. The third prong of the critique of the myth of racial democracy is that it is pernicious insofar as it stymied the development of social movements aimed at redressing oppression and marginalization. The claim of critical race theorists is that the myth succeeded in denying, in Winant's (2001: 228) words, "both black difference and black inequality." In other words, it served as an ideological mask that, in the name of national unity, has affected what amounts to censorship about existing racial disparities, with the result being that antiracist struggles have been to large extent thwarted (Twine 1998; Hanchard 1994).

These criticisms of the myth are accurate because the evidence is clear that "skin color is a central axis of social stratification" in several Latin American countries (Telles 2014: 3). A growing recognition of this reality has emerged in Brazil and other nations of the region, which has led to a multicultural turn. Telles (2014: 2) has observed that, "Today most Latin American countries have constitutionally declared themselves multiculturalist." To the extent that this is true, it is now possible to engage in a reconsideration of what is meant by racial democracy. Recently, Bailey (2004) has pointed out that there is a growing consensus among scholars that earlier criticisms have been overly critical. Thus, Fry (2000) and Sheriff (2001) have argued that the concept of racial democracy functions in Brazilian society less as an ideology and more as an ideal by which to measure and judge present reality. Bailey's research has lent support to this position by providing empirical evidence for the idea that ordinary Brazilians do not share the elite ideology of a racial democratic paradise, but instead are acutely aware of the existence of racial inequality and racism. For them, racial democracy serves as the basis of a counter-hegemonic critique of the existing racial formation. This perspective constitutes what can be viewed as the "racial commonsense" of most Brazilians (Bailey 2004: 729), which shapes how they come to engage in egalitarian claims making in what they perceive to be an unequal world shaped to a significant extent along racial lines (Guidry 2003). In this sense, racial democracy comes to constitute a useful concept in the arsenal of race and ethnic studies scholars. It can serve as a framework for constructing a metrics to adjudicate the extent to which any particular ethnically heterogeneous society can be construed as sufficiently egalitarian to be a genuine democracy. The role of sociology is to provide the metrics, while the task of political philosophy is to provide the arguments for what constitutes a just and egalitarian democratic society. The following section reviews existing levels of inequality in the United States and their deleterious consequences, which are viewed as impediments to achieving a genuine racial democracy.

10.5 Racial Inequality in the Age of Obama

This article cannot provide the metrics, but rather can only call attention to the sorts of issues involved in linking levels of inequality to critiques of existing liberal democratic regimes. In so doing, such an enterprise is inextricably linked to a progressive politics. The traditional political fault line that divides left and right speaks to widely divergent views about the appropriateness of seeking to construct an egalitarian society. The left, in its various forms, has promoted equality. From this side of the political divide, a truly just society must be an egalitarian one. This point has been driven home in recent publications that have received widespread attention, among which are books by Piketty (2014) and Atkinson (2015). In contrast, the right contends that inequality is not only natural and therefore inevitable, but also often proves to be beneficial. If in the past, the right justified inequality in religious terms, appealing to the idea of God's hierarchal order in which all people had their appropriate place, today they are more likely to appeal to the ideology of meritocracy. Infrequently this takes on a biological essentialism, as with the authors of *The Bell Curve* (Herrnstein and Murray 1994). In most instances, there is a distinctly psychological and cultural cast to the argument. Thus, conservatives justify the inequality of privilege on the basis of certain individuals' presumed value to society and on such imputed personal attributes as diligence, possessing a strong work ethic, intelligence, competitiveness, and so forth. From this ideological perspective, the poor are poor due to character defects and subcultural flaws. Inequality can actually serve them well insofar as it succeeds in goading them to change their profligate ways.

In the current epoch of global capitalism defined by neoliberal economic policies, the pursuit of equality has for several decades not been on the political agenda. Indeed, it has not been a centerpiece of mainstream political action since the demise of the Great Society (leaving aside for this discussion the shortcomings and the bad faith of liberal politics during that era). Instead, policies have been promoted that allow markets to operate increasingly free from the intervention of the state. Markets are seen as generators of wealth, and any intrusion into the "natural" functioning of markets is criticized for stifling economic growth. Thus, the welfare state is seen as an impediment to growth and for this

reason efforts to reduce its size and scope have been vigorously pursued. The logic of this strategy is based on the assumption that when those at the top are permitted to increase their wealth, the impact of their increased wealth benefits not only them, but the rest of society as well, as added wealth trickles down throughout the class structure. In such a scenario, levels of inequality may increase, but everyone is better off for it. Therefore, according to exponents of neoliberalism, any attempt to implement redistributive policies that are designed to reduce existing levels of inequality ought to be rejected.

The problem with this argument is that it is based on ideology rather than empirical evidence or a clearly articulated moral vision about what a just and fair society would look like. It fails to adequately account for the wide range of negative impacts of inequality on individuals and communities. It also fails to account for the fact that once in place, inequality tends to be perpetuated—becoming what Tilly (1998) referred to as "durable inequality." As he pointed out, such inequality speaks less to ideas of meritocracy or the functionally beneficial character of inequality, and more to the capacity of those with power, wealth, and privilege to effect strategies of closure that prevents those who are lower on the social ladder from climbing up the rungs.

Sociology and the related social sciences have long-established research agendas devoted to the analysis of social problems. The focus of much of this work is on either the consequences of specific problems for those individuals most adversely impacted by them or for the society at large. However, insufficient attention has been devoted to linking social problems to the functioning of a liberal democracy and to the capacity of all citizens to function as equals in the democratic process of self-rule.

10.5.1 Income and Wealth Inequality

A substantial body of research has established that the US is the advanced industrial nation with the highest level of inequality, and the racial divide has been exacerbated by the 2008 recession. This is evident in the most commonly used yardsticks to measure inequality: income and wealth distribution. In terms of the former, in 2014 the median income for Asian households was $74,297, $60,256 for non-Hispanic white households, $42,491 for Hispanic households, and $35,398 for African American households (DeNavas-Walt and Proctor 2015: 7). This picture is complicated by the fact that there are growing levels of inequality within each of these groups (Leicht 2016). Turning to the poor, whereas 10.1% of non-Hispanic whites were living at or below the poverty line in 2014, 12.0% of Asians, 23.6% of Hispanics, and 26.2% of blacks lived in poverty (DeNavas-Walt and Proctor 2015: 12–14).

Wealth is more difficult to measure than income. Landmark studies appearing near the end of the past century reveal that wealth is distributed along racial lines in an even more skewed manner than income. Thus, while a quarter of white households possessed no wealth or negative wealth during the 1990s, 61% of black and 54% of Hispanic households fit into this category. While 38% of white households lacked the financial assets to survive for three months at the poverty line, as many as 73% of Hispanic households and 80% of black households lived in this precarious financial position (Oliver and Shapiro 1997: 86–87). Viewed another way, the median white household possessed $7000 in net financial assets, in contrast to the zero assets held by the median black household. The median white household had over eight times the net worth of the median black household (Mishel, Bernstein, and Boushey 2003: 284).

Post-recession data reveal the following data about the median net worth of households in 2009: $113,149 for whites, $78,066 for Asians, $6325 for Latinos, and $5677 for blacks (Kochhar et al. 2011). The immediate loses sustained across all racial groups, as a consequence of the recession were deep and also differentiated along racial lines, with whites losing smaller percentages of their wealth than other racial groups. The subprime mortgage crisis, for example, hit minorities especially hard.

Even considering only middle class households, whether it is defined by income, college education, or white-collar occupation, black households possess less than their middle-class white counterparts. Near the end of the past century, blacks owned only 35% of the net worth of white households in the first definition, 23% by the second, and 15% by the third. In terms of financial assets—that which can help prevent financial disaster in extenuating circumstances—middle-class black households had no net financial assets whatsoever if one excludes home equity and vehicle ownership (Oliver and Shapiro 1997: 94). This meant that the average black middle class family had to rely almost entirely on income alone to maintain its middle class standard of living, and could not withstand a single financial obstacle without it becoming a potential financial catastrophe.

More recent data reveals that this general picture has not changed in the past two decades. Indeed, blacks in the 40–59th income percentile have less than 35% of the median wealth of their white counterparts. The figure improves for the 60–79th percentile, rising to nearly 55%. It declines to under 50% for the 80–89th percentile, and plunges dramatically for the 90–100th percentile to under 25% (Bruenig 2013).

10.5.2   The Consequences of Inequality

Considerable attention has been devoted to teasing out the consequences of inequality, which serve as a necessary empirical grounding for assessing the constraints on equal opportunity, which in turn impact the ability to enter the public sphere in the role of citizen on equal terms with other members of the polity. The assumption of liberal democracies is that an equal opportunity society is one that provides the means by which disadvantaged citizens are provide the tools to do so. In order to assess whether or not a society has succeeded in making equal opportunity a reality, there are a variety of quality of life measures one can turn to. For instance, Coverdill et al. (2011) demonstrate that

African Americans experience a lower quality of life compared to whites on five measures: marital happiness, overall happiness, health status, trust, and satisfaction with finances. While the gap between whites and blacks has been reduced over the past three decades for the first four measures, it has remained unchanged for finances. Latino perceptions reveal a lower quality of life compared to non-Latinos.

The physical health consequences of inequality also reveal significant racially-based disparities. Regardless of the exact measurement used, low-income and poor health is strongly linked. For example, impoverished African Americans endure disproportionately high incidences of hypertension, heart problems, diabetes and its complications, and sudden infant death syndrome (Mullahy and Wolfe 2001: 284). Cancer among males, sickle-cell anemia, tuberculosis, arteriosclerosis, and AIDs also

affect significantly higher percentages of blacks than whites (Mead et al. 2008; for early findings, see Pearson 1994). Life expectancy is another factor that varies by race. Geronimus, et al. (2001) found that the life expectancy of a black male living in urban poverty is 42 years, three decades short of the national average. In this instance, the interplay of race and class is at work, for overall the black-white gap has been reduced to 3.7 years—75.3 years for all blacks versus 79.0 for all whites in 2011, according to the Center for Disease Control.

Health-related disparities are linked to the lack of adequate access to affordable and quality health care. In 2003, 15.6% of the population was without health coverage, amounting to 45 million people. This trend has a disproportionate impact on racial minorities. For example, nearly one third of Latinos had no health coverage (DeNavas-Walt, Proctor, and Mills 2004: 14–15; see also Feagin and McKinney 2003: 180–210). Since the passage of the Patient Protection and Affordable Care Act (better known as Obamacare) in 2010, as the number of Americans without insurance has declined, racial disparities have also been reduced, but not eliminated (Levins 2015).

Food insecurity is another problem that strikes racial minorities harder than the general population. Thus, while 14.5% all households is defined as food insecure, the figure for whites is 11.2%, for Latinos 23.3%, while it is 24.6% for African Americans (RTI International 2014). Making matters worse, food costs more for the urban poor than for the general population. Many chain stores, where customers find the lowest prices, are not located in or near urban poor neighborhoods, which have become food deserts. Because many poor people do not own cars or have access to adequate public transportation, residents often have little choice but to shop at closer, but more expensive, non-chain stores. These stores carry a far smaller selection of certain types of food, particularly fresh produce, meat, and dairy products.

Turning to housing, discrimination based on race remains an endemic problem long after the civil rights movement, which, combined with a shortage of decent and affordable housing, is responsible for the concentration of poverty in select geographic areas (Lichter, Parisi, and Taquino 2012). While some of the most overt forms of housing discrimination are far less in evidence since the 1960s, new and more subtle modes of discrimination persist, many of them difficult to detect. For example, housing audits have demonstrated that housing agents show blacks fewer housing units than whites, particularly if those units are located in predominantly white neighborhoods. In addition, redlining practices and discriminatory lending policies result is blacks being denied housing loans at a higher rate than whites (Marcuse 2005).

What is the result of geographic segregation by race? A body of evidence shows that while highly educated black communities can truly uphold a "separate but equal" status with socio-economically similar white communities, poorer and less educated blacks experience neighborhood conditions inferior to other impoverished populations to due to their relative concentration in urban inner city settings. This is particularly evident in those neighborhoods characterized by hypersegregation (Massey and

Denton 1993). Police protection, firefighting, sanitation services, and similar municipal services are invariably of poorer quality in such neighborhoods. Children have fewer places to play and an even smaller number of safe recreation areas (Evans and Kantrowitz 2002). More youth in these neighborhoods drop out of school, have decreased childhood IQ scores, and become pregnant as teenagers (Boardman and Saint Onge 2005). Those who live in impoverished and racially segregated neighborhoods (especially African Americans and to a lesser degree Latinos) suffer from significantly higher mortality rates, including infant mortality rates (Leclere et al. 1997). Wilson (2000) has stressed the emergence since deindustrialization took hold of "jobless ghettoes," which are plagued by crime, prostitution, drug trafficking, and gang activity. Often, potential employers do not welcome individuals raised in these locales, in part due to discrimination, but also in part due to the underdevelopment of skills in these communities; this inability to find work, thus, reinforces and thus perpetuates disadvantage.

Racial inequality results in vast educational inequalities, which are rooted in two interconnected factors: unequal funding for schools and discrimination. School funding is based significantly on local property taxes, which means that schools located in areas populated primarily with lower class households are going to have substantially smaller budgets than schools in middle or upper class districts. However, this inequality is exacerbated in inner cities, where lower class youth and racial minorities are concentrated.

A half-century after *Brown v. Board of Education of Topeka,* American schools have undergone a process of resegregation. In a study conducted by Harvard's Civil Rights Project, the researchers have determined that the gains made in the 1960s and 1970s have eroded, and particularly in the 1990s the rate of resegregation has increased dramatically. By the beginning of this century, 70% of black students attended schools that contained predominantly minority student populations, while Latinos have also experienced increasing levels of educational segregation (Orfield 2004). The

result is that minority students, particularly poorer ones, increasingly attend public schools that are inferior to those of their white counterparts. One recent study, however, has concluded that by 2009 there is evidence of a modest reintegration of schools (Stroub and Richards 2013).

Minority students lag behind whites in terms of educational achievement. At the beginning of this century, a smaller percentage of blacks and Latinos enrolled in colleges and universities than whites; in 2000, 39% of 18- to 24-year old whites were enrolled, 31% of blacks, and 22% of Latinos (Hoffman et al. 2003: 93). Since then, the enrollment gap has narrowed. However, that is not true of graduation rates (Casselman 2014). The percentage of degrees earned by blacks and Latinos indicates that they are underrepresented in terms of achieving bachelor and master degrees as well as doctorates, while whites are slightly overrepresented and Asians significantly overrepresented (U.S. Department of Education 2012). Given that education has a direct effect on the development of human capital, which in turn plays a central role in securing quality positions in the job market, there is ample evidence to indicate that the nations' school system fails to provide genuinely equal educational opportunities, thereby serving to reinforce existing inequalities rather than contributing to overcoming them.

Discrepancies in the possession of social capital perpetuate inequality by deterring upward mobility for those at the bottom of the social structure while simultaneously facilitating if for those already near the top. While social capital is important to the attainment of socioeconomic status, its benefits are distributed highly inequitably by race. Since individuals tend to maintain social networks with others of similar characteristics, the networks of members of the disadvantaged racial minorities tend to consist of individuals from within the group with similar SES profiles. These connections tend not only to be lacking in the number of beneficial resources for socioeconomic advancement, but also lack the diversity of resources that are available to those of higher SES (Lin 2000).

Portes (1998) observes that all too frequently for inner city residents, social networks do not reach outside of the inner city, and therefore their knowledge of and ability to obtain good jobs is severely limited. Furthermore, since inner city residents tend to be more transitory, social ties within these locales tend to be more tenuous and less extensive. Blacks and to a somewhat lesser extent Latinos have less extensive networks than whites. Since blacks often reside in segregated neighborhoods, their social networks are restricted to other blacks, which is not advantageous in an economy dominated by whites. Even in the middle and upper classes, blacks often have relatively few weak ties to white networks, instead forming strong ties among themselves (Lin 2000). These differences play out in explicit ways, such as when a person seeking a job begins to turn to people she knows. Simply stated, blacks social networks are such that they do not work to their advantage in terms of entering the economic mainstream.

As this survey indicated, racial inequality remains a pervasive feature of American society over a half century after the civil rights movement ended. One can point to some gains during the Obama administration, particularly in the area of health insurance coverage, but working with an opposition party in the thrall of right-wing populism has made more robust changes impossible. Inequality takes many different guises, impacting racial minorities in all facets of their lives. Moreover, there is a durable character to this inequality that suggests it cannot be remedied without a concerted effort to address its structural underpinning. Insofar as this is the case, it is clear that the US falls far short of being a racial democracy.

10.6 What Would a Racial Democracy Look like?

Perhaps the simplest answer to the question of what a racial democracy would look like is that it would be a society in which racial differences at the level of identity carried with them no race-specific inequalities. In other words, such a society would be predicated on racial difference *and* racial equality. Being a citizen is not cost free. Full citizenship requires investments of resources, specifically financial capital, human capital, and social capital. Those without adequate resources to enter the public sphere as a relative equal of others find themselves marginalized and incapable of genuinely engaging in the ongoing process of self-rule. Despite the progressive move to becoming a more inclusive society since the founding of the republic, the preceding survey of racial inequality reveals that the legacy of exclusion and oppression continues to adversely impact the lives of blacks and Latinos who confront the impacts of the durable inequalities that the nation has not yet remedied (Feagin and Vera 1995).

The value of the idea of racial democracy is that, by serving as an ideal type, it simultaneously provides a tool of analysis to assess whether or not the racial barriers to equal citizenship have been overcome and a political goal. It is a constructive antidote to the pervasive desire to treat the US as a colorblind society, the trope widely favored by political conservatives and by sectors of the liberal community. Proponents of a colorblind ideology have come into prominence since the end of the civil rights movement, deflecting questions about the continuing impact of racism by seeking to account for racial inequalities by turning to non-racial explanations. The result, as Bonilla-Silva (2003) describes it, is a new form of racism, "without racists."

More specifically, the idea of racial democracy is intended as a concrete concept that can be used to assess the state of democracy in the nation. Those who have been historically disenfranchised and more recently ignored by policy makers and the public alike function, to borrow from Guinier and Torres (2002), as miner's canaries. They test the atmosphere of the public sphere to see if democracy can survive. One of its virtues is that it can provide a comparative frame of reference, allowing us to assess the extent to which identity politics remain tied to redistributive politics, and thus measuring the distance we still have to travel to achieve a just, multicultural, and egalitarian social order.

References

Alba, R., & Foner, N. (2015). *Strangers no more: Immigration and the challenges of integration in North America and Western Europe.* Princeton, NJ: Princeton University Press.

Alexander, J. C. (2006). *The Civil Sphere.* New York: Oxford University Press.

Alexander, M. (2010). *The new jim crow: Mass incarceration in the age of colorblindness.* New York: The New Press.

Alexander, J. C., & Jaworsky, B. N. (2014). *Obama Power.* Cambridge: Polity Press.

Alexander, J. C., & Smelser, N. J. (1999). Introduction: The ideological discourse of cultural discontent. In N. J. Smelser & J. C. Alexander (Eds.), *Diversity and its discontents: Cultural conflict and common ground in contemporary american society* (pp. 3–18). Princeton, NJ: Princeton University Press.

Appiah, K. A. (2005). *The ethics of identity.* Princeton, NJ: Princeton University Press.

Arnwine, B., & Johnson-Blanco, M. (2013, October 24). Voting rights at the crossroads. Economic Policy Institute.

Ash, T. G. (2012). Freedom & diversity: A liberal pentagon for living together. *New York Review of Books, 59*(18), 33–36.

Atkinson, A. B. (2015). *Inequality what can be done?.* Cambridge, MA: Harvard University Press.

Bailey, S. (2004). Group dominance and the myth of racial democracy: Antiracism attitudes in Brazil. *American Sociological Review, 69*(5), 728–747.

Bailyn, B. (1967). *The ideological origins of the American revolution.* Cambridge, MA: The Belknap Press of Harvard University Press.

Barry, B. (2001). *Culture and equality.* Cambridge, UK: Polity Press.

Benhabib, S. (2002). *The claims of culture: Equality and diversity in a global era.* Princeton, NJ: Princeton University Press.

Boardman, J. D., & Saint Onge, J. M. (2005). Neighborhoods and adolescent development. *Child Youth Environment, 15*(1), 138–164.

Bonilla-Silva, E. (2003). *Racism without racists: Color-Blind racism and the persistence of racial inequality in the United States.* Lanham, MD: Rowman and Littlefield.

Brubaker, R. (1992). *Citizenship and nationhood in France and Germany.* Cambridge, MA: Harvard University Press.

Bruenig, M. (2013). Middle-Class blacks and whites have vastly different fortunes. *Prospect,* August 30.

Casselman, B. (2014). Race gap narrows in college enrollment, but not in graduation. http://fivethirtyeight.com/features/race-gap-narrows-in-enrollment-but-not-in-graduation.

Coverdill, J. E., López, C. A., & Petrie, M. A. (2011). Race, ethnicity, and the quality of life in America, 1972–2008. *Social Forces, 89*(3), 783–805.

Daniels, R. (2004). *Guarding the golden gate: American immigration policy and Immigrants since 1882.* New York: Hill and Wang.

Degler, C. (1986). *Neither black nor white: Slavery and race relations in Brazil and the United States.* Madison: University of Wisconsin Press.

DeNavas-Walt, C., & Proctor, B. D. (2015). *Income and poverty in the United States: 2014.* U.S. Census Bureau, Current Population Reports, P60-252. Washington, DC: Government Printing Office.

DeNavas, C., Proctor, B. D., & Mills, R. J. (2004). Income, poverty, and health insurance coverage in the United States, 2003. U.S. Census Bureau. Current Population Report (pp. 20–226). Washington, DC: Government Printing Office.

Evans, G. W., & Kantrowitz, E. (2002). Socioeconomic status and health: The potential role of environmental risk exposure. *Annual Review of Public Health, 23,* 303–331.

Feagin, J. R. (2006). *Systemic racism: A theory of oppression.* New York: Routledge.

Feagin, J. R. (2013). *The white racial frame: Centuries of racial framing and counter-framing* (2nd ed.). New York: Routledge.

Feagin, J. R., & McKinney, K. D. (2003). *The many costs of racism.* Lanham, MD: Rowman and Littlefield.

Feagin, J. R., & Vera, H. (1995). *White racism: The basics.* New York: Routledge.

Fitzgerald, D. S., & Cook-Martín, D. (2014). *Culling the masses: The democratic origins of racist immigration policies in the Americas.* Cambridge, MA: Harvard University Press.

Foner, E. (1988). *Reconstruction: America's unfinished revolution, 1863–1877.* New York: Harper and Row.

Fraser, N. (1995). From redistribution to recognition? Dilemmas of justice in a postsocialist age. *New Left Review, 212*(August/September), 68–93.

Freyre, G. (1963a [1933]). *The masters and the slaves.* New York: Alfred A. Knopf.

Freyre, G. (1963b [1936]). *The mansions and the shanties.* New York: Alfred A. Knopf.

Freyre, G. (1970 [1959]). *Order and progress.* New York: Alfred A. Knopf.

Fry, P. (2000). Politics, nationality, and the meanings of 'race' in Brazil. *Daedalus, 129,* 83–118.

Geronimus, A. T., Bound, J., Waidmann, T. A., Colen, C. G., & Steffick, D. (2001). Inequality in life expectancy, functional status, and active life expectancy across selected black and white populations in the United States. *Demography, 38*(2), 227–251.

Glazer, N. (1997). *We are all multiculturalists now.* Cambridge, MA: Harvard University Press.

Glenn, E. N. (2002). *Unequal freedom: How race and gender shaped American citizenship and labor.* Cambridge, MA: Harvard University Press.

Guidry, J. (2003). Being equal in an unequal world: Citizenship, common sense, and social movements in Brazil. Unpublished manuscript.

Guimarães, A. S. (2001). The misadventures of nonracialism in Brazil. In C. Hamilton, L. Huntley, N. Alexander, A. Guinarães, & W. James (Eds.), *Beyond racism: Race and inequality in Brazil, South Africa, and the United States* (pp. 157–185). Boulder, CO: Lynne Rienner Publishers.

Guinier, L., & Torres, G. (2002). *The miner's canary: Enlisting race, resisting power, transforming democracy.* Cambridge, MA: Harvard University Press.

Gutmann, A. (2003). *Identity in democracy.* Princeton, NJ: Princeton University Press.

Habermas, J. (1998). *The inclusion of the other.* Cambridge, UK: Polity Press.

Hanchard, M. G. (1994). *Orpheus and power: The movimento Negro of Rio de Janeiro and Sao Paulo, Brazil, 1945–1988.* Princeton, NJ: Princeton University Press.

Herrnstein, R. J., & Murray, C. (1994). *The bell curve: Intelligence and class structure in American life.* New York: The Free Press.

Hoetink, H. (1971). *Caribbean race relations: A study of two variants.* New York: Oxford University Press.

Hoffman, K., Charmaine, L., & Thomas D. S. (2003). *Status and trends in the education of blacks.* Report No. NECS-2003-034. Washington, DC: National Center for Educational Statistics.

Huntington, S. (2004). *Who are we? The challenges to America's national identity.* New York: Simon and Schuster.

Joppke, C. (2001). Multicultural citizenship: A critique. Archives of *European Sociology, XLII*(2), 431–477.

Joppke, C. (2005). *Selecting by origin: Ethnic migration in the liberal state.* Cambridge, MA: Harvard University Press.

Kerber, L. (1997). The meanings of citizenship. *Dissent, 44*(Fall), 33–37.

Kivisto, P. (2002). *Multiculturalism in a global society.* Malden, MA: Blackwell Publishing.

Kivisto, P. (Ed.). (2005). *Incorporating diversity: Rethinking assimilation in a multicultural age.* Boulder, CO: Paradigm Publishers.

Kivisto, P. (2012). We really are all multiculturalists now. *The Sociological Quarterly, 53*(1), 1–24.

Kivisto, P. (Ed.). (2016). *National identity in an age of migration: The US experience.* London: Routledge.

Kivisto, P., & Faist, T. (2007). *Citizenship: Discourse, theory, and transnational prospects.* Malden, MA: Blackwell Publishing.

Kivisto, P., & Leinonen, J. (2011). Representing race: Ongoing uncertainties about finish American racial identity. *Journal of American Ethnic History, 31*(1), 11–33.

Kochhar, R., Fry, R., & Taylor, P. (2011). *Wealth gaps rise to record highs between white, blacks, and hispanics.* Washington, DC: Pew Research Center.

Kymlicka, W. (1995). *Multicultural citizenship.* New York: Oxford University Press.

Kymlicka, W. (2001). *Politics in the vernacular: Nationalism, multiculturalism, and citizenship.* New York: Oxford University Press.

Kymlicka, W. (2015). Solidarity in diverse societies: Beyond neoliberal multiculturalism and welfare chauvinism. *Comparative Migration Studies, 3*(17), 1–19. https://doi.org/10.1186/s40878-015-0017-4.

LeClere, F. B., Rogers, R. G., & Peters, K. D. (1997). Ethnicity and mortality in the United States: Individual and community correlates. *Social Forces, 76*(1), 169–198.

Leicht, K. (2016). Getting serious about inequality. *The Sociological Quarterly, 57*(2), 211–231.

Levins, H. (2015). The ACA's impact on minority health insurance disparities. http://ldihealtheconomist.com/he0000107.shtml.

Lichter, D. T., Parisi, D., & Taquino, M. C. (2012). The geography of exclusion: Race, segregation, and concentrated poverty. *Social Problems, 59*(3), 364–388.

Lin, N. (2000). Inequality in social capital. *Contemporary Sociology, 29,* 785–795.

Litwack, L. (1998). *Trouble in mind: Black southerners in the age of Jim Crow.* New York: Alfred A. Knopf.

Lyman, S. M. (1991). The race question and liberalism: Casuistries in American constitutional law. *International Journal of Politics, Culture, and Society, 5*(2), 183–247.

Lyman, S. M. (1993). Marginalizing the self: A study of citizenship, color, and ethnoracial identity in American society. *Symbolic Interaction, 16*(4), 379–393.

Manza, J., & Uggen, C. (2008). *Locked out: Felon disenfranchisement and American democracy.* New York: Oxford University Press.

Marcuse, P. (2005). Enclaves yes, ghettos no: Segregation and the state. In D. P. Varady (Ed.), *Desegregating the city: Ghettos, enclaves, and inequality* (pp. 15–30). Albany: State University of New York Press.

Marshall, T. H. (1964). *Class, citizenship, and social development.* Garden City, NY: Doubleday.

Massey, D. S., & Denton, N. A. (1993). *American apartheid: Segregation and the making of the underclass.* Cambridge, MA: Harvard University Press.

Mead, H., Cartwright-Smith, L., Jones, K., Ramos, C., Woods, K., & Siegel, B. (2008). *Racial and ethnic disparities in W. Y. Healthcare: A Chartbook.* The Commonwealth Fund, publication 1111. www.commonwealthfund.org.

Mishel, L., Bernstein, J., & Boushey, H. (2003). *The state of working America.* Ithaca, NY: Cornell University Press.

Modood, T. (2013). *Multiculturalism: A civic idea.* Cambridge: Polity Press.

Mullahy, J., & Barbara, L. W. (2001). Health policies for the non-elderly poor. In S. H. Danziger & R. H. Haveman (Eds.), *Understanding Poverty* (pp. 278–313). New York: Russell Sage Foundation.

Oliver, M. L., & Shapiro, T. M. (1997). *Black wealth/white wealth: A new perspective on racial inequality.* New York: Routledge.

Omi, M., & Winant, H. (1986). *Racial formation in the United States: From the 1960s to the 1980s.* New York: Routledge and Kegan Paul.

Orfield, G. (2004). *Brown at 50: King's dream or Plessy's nightmare?* Cambridge, MA: The Civil Right Project, Harvard University Press.

Parekh, B. (2000). *Rethinking multiculturalism: Cultural diversity and political theory.* Cambridge, MA: Harvard University Press.

Parkin, F. (1979). *Marxism and class theory: A bourgeois critique.* New York: Columbia University Press.

Pearson, D. (1994). The black man health issues and implications for clinical practice. *Journal of Black Studies, 25*(1), 81–98.

Peña, Y., Sidanius, J., & Sawyer, M. (2004). 'Racial democracy' in the Americas: A Latin and U.S. comparison. *Journal of Cross-Cultural Psychology, 35*(6), 749–762.

Pierson, D. (1942). *Negroes in Brazil: A study of race contact in Bahia.* Chicago: University of Chicago Press.

Piketty, T. (2014). *Capital in the twenty-first century.* Cambridge, MA: The Belknap Press of Harvard University Press.

Portes, A. (1998). Social capital: Its origins and applications in modern sociology. *Annual Review of Sociology, 24*, 1–24.

Roediger, D. (1991). *The wages of whiteness: Race and the making of the American working class.* London: Verso.

Roediger, D. (2005). *Working toward whiteness: How America's immigrants became white, the strange journey from ellis Island to the suburbs.* New York: Basic Books.

RTI International. (2014, July 24). Current and prospective scope of hunger and food security in America: A review of current research.

Saxton, A. (1990). *The rise and fall of the white republic: Class, politics, and culture in the nineteenth-century America.* London: Verso.

Schlesinger, A., Jr. (1992). *The disuniting of America: Reflections on a multicultural society.* New York: W. W. Norton.

Sheriff, R. (2001). *Dreaming equality: Color, race, and racism in urban Brazil.* New Brunswick, NJ: Rutgers University Press.

Shklar, J. N. (1991). *American citizenship: The quest for inclusion.* Cambridge: MA: Harvard University Press.

Skinner, Q. (1998). *Liberty before liberalism.* Cambridge, UK: Cambridge University Press.

Skrenty, J. D. (2002). *The minority rights revolution.* Cambridge, MA: The Belknap Press of Harvard University Press.

Spickard, P. (2005). Race and nation, identity and power: Thinking comparatively about ethnic systems. In P. Spickard (Ed.), *Race and nation: Ethnic systems in the modern world* (pp. 1–29). New York: Routledge.

Stroub, K. J., & Richards, M. P. (2013). From resegregation to reintegration: Trends in the racial/ethnic segregation of metropolitan public schools, 1993–2009. *American Educational Research Journal, 50*(3), 497–531.

Taylor, C. (1992). With commentary by Amy Gutmann, Steve C. Rockefeller, Michael Walzer, and Susan Wolf. *Multiculturalism and the politics of recognition.* Princeton, NJ: Princeton University Press.

Telles, E. (2014). *Pigmentocracies: Ethnicity, race, and color in Latin America.* Chapel Hill: The University of North Carolina Press.

Tichenor, D. J. (2002). *Dividing lines: The politics of immigration control in America.* Princeton, NJ: Princeton University Press.

Tilly, C. (1998). *Durable inequality.* Berkeley: University of California Press.

Tiryakian, E. A. (2004). Assessing multiculturalism theoretically: E Pluribus Unum, Sic et Non. In J. Rex & G. Singh (Eds.), *Governance in multicultural societies* (pp. 1–18). Burlington, VT: Ashgate.

Twine, F. W. (1998). *Racism in a racial democracy: The maintenance of white supremacy in Brazil.* New Brunswick, NJ: Rutgers University Press.

U.S. Department of Education. (2012). *Degrees conferred by sex and race.* http://nces.ed.gov/fastfacts.display.asp?id=72.

Vertovec, S., & Wessendorf, S. (Eds.). (2010). *The multiculturalism backlash: European discourses, policies, and practices.* London: Routledge.

Warren, J. (2002). *Racial revolutions: Antiracism and Indian resurgence in Brazil.* Durham, NC: Duke University Press.

Wilentz, S. (2005). *The rise of American democracy: Jefferson to Lincoln.* New York: W. W. Norton.

Wilson, W. J. (2000). Jobless Ghettos: The social implications of the disappearance of work in segregated neighborhoods. In R. Marshall (Ed.), *Back to shared prosperity: The growing inequality of wealth and income in America* (pp. 85–94). Armonk, NY: M. E. Sharpe.

Wilson, W. J. (2004). *The truly disadvantaged: The inner city, the underclass, and public policy.* Chicago: University of Chicago Press.

Winant, H. (1999). Racial democracy and racial identity: Comparing the United States and Brazil. In M. Hanchard (Ed.), *Racial politics in contemporary Brazil* (pp. 98–115). Durham, NC: Duke University Press.

Winant, H. (2001). *The world is a Ghetto: Race and democracy since World War II*. New York: Basic Books.

Young, I. M. (1990). *Justice and the politics of difference*. Princeton, NJ: Princeton University Press.

Zolberg, A. R. (2006). *A nation by design: Immigration policy in the fashioning of America*. Cambridge, MA and New York: Harvard University and Russell Sage Foundation.

The Diversity of Diversity Education

11

Amir Marvasti, Karyn McKinney and Brad Pinter

Contents

Abstract

This chapter approaches diversity as contextually defined and institutionally embedded. We argue that diversity is not one thing or one set of preferred, universal practices, rather it is a fluid concept defined and enacted for the institutional purpose at hand. Through this approach, we address the disappointment sometimes expressed by those who hold a purist view (i.e., the oft heard complaint that such and such is not "true diversity"). We locate the cause of such disillusionments in part in the failure of diversity educators to actively engage and promote the fluidity of the concept and its many applications. We suggest the way out of this conundrum is to deconstruct the purist view and instead to found diversity practices based on more tangible local organizational objectives.

A. Marvasti (✉)
Department of Sociology, Penn State Altoona,
Altoona, PA, USA
e-mail: abm11@psu.edu

K. McKinney
Department of Sociology and Women's, Gender and
Sexuality Studies, Penn State University, Altoona,
PA, USA
e-mail: kdm12@psu.edu

B. Pinter
Department of Psychology, Penn State University,
Altoona, PA, USA
e-mail: tbp1@psu.edu

11.1 Introduction

Throughout the United States "businesses spend from $200 million to $300 million a year on diversity training" (Vedantam 2008). Such training is offered through increasing professionalized entities that train and certify "diversity educators." For example, the website of a leading

© Springer International Publishing AG, part of Springer Nature 2018
P. Batur and J. R. Feagin (eds.), *Handbook of the Sociology of Racial and Ethnic Relations*,
Handbooks of Sociology and Social Research, https://doi.org/10.1007/978-3-319-76757-4_11

diversity training company (Diversity Training University International, DTUI) promises high income to the diversity educators enrolled in its programs:

> It is estimated that the majority of diversity trainers do not receive compensation at their deserved rate. I see it this way. Most trainers do not have adequate training. It is hard to make a living if you do not know what is needed to look like a professional. Your profit depends on your expertise. Trained organizational development specialists receive top dollar for their services. Diversity training is a special area of organizational development. This means diversity trainers should receive as much as $5000 to $7500 per day, $1500 to $4500 per half day, or $125-$180 per hour. Anyone making less than these prices is underpaid. Chief Diversity Officers and Vice Presidents of Diversity & Inclusion have six-figure salaries. (Source: http://dtui.com/bec_tr_courses.html)

Indeed, in recent years, diversity programs and their training workshops have proliferated and become a common of feature of formal organizations. However, it is often unclear what "diversity" refers to and what particular goals it aims to achieve. At best, the particular meaning and application of diversity tends to vary from one setting to another. For instance, in a particular business setting, "diversity" may be equated with a simple count of the number of employees with differing ethnicities or religious preferences and be accompanied by a target for some minimal level of representation of each group to satisfy external regulations, whereas in another realm, "diversity" may instead focus on recruiting multiplicity of backgrounds with the goal to elevate discourse or innovation. Rather than seeing these variations as diversions from the "true" meaning of diversity, we take the position that diversity education is practiced across many "provinces of meaning" (Schutz 1945) with varying goals and consequences. In the following sections, we discuss two dominant diversity education domains. We argue that recognizing the many variations in the use and application of diversity education will be beneficial to diversity educators and other practitioners, regardless of their particular objectives.

11.2 Diversity Education as Progressive Social Change

The most common, and somewhat taken-for-granted, view of diversity education is that it improves the status of under-represented groups in the workplace. The ideal scenario for diversity education is that it works as promised to fulfill its noble goals, which explicitly or implicitly are stated as creating a harmonious and less prejudiced workplace/community/society. The notion that diversity training and experiences are a safeguard against discrimination in the workplace is partly based on the psychological literature that suggests that by eradicating prejudice, one can reduce discriminatory behavior.

It should be noted that in popular discourse the terms "prejudice," "stereotype," and "discrimination" are used interchangeably, but in fact from a social science standpoint they refer to different concepts. As Susan Fiske notes, "stereotypes [are] the cognitive component, prejudice [is] the affective component, and discrimination [is] the behavioral component of (group) category-based responses" (1998: 372). Fiske also cites research by Dovidio et al. based on a meta analysis of twenty-three studies that shows "prejudices predict discrimination far better than stereotypes" (1996: 372). Indeed, the eminent sociologist Robert Merton argued decades ago that the relationship between prejudice and discrimination is itself not always direct or one-to-one (1949, original, reprinted 2012). For example, a person could be prejudiced and not practice discrimination; conversely, a person could practice discrimination without being prejudiced. The relationship between attitudes and behavior is discussed later in the chapter.

In the following section, we assess the idealized view of diversity education in terms of its claims about changing biased attitudes and curbing discriminatory behavior, and consider the possibility that the promotion of diversity education as means of ending discrimination may be unrealistic.

11.2.1 Changing Attitudes

Numerous studies have investigated the potential for diversity interventions to change biased attitudes. In a typical example, Chang (2002) assessed explicit racial attitudes of students who were finishing a University course on diversity with another group of students who were just beginning the course. Results showed less bias held by the former group compared to the latter. Similarly, Hussey et al. (2010) found positive attitude change for students enrolled in a "diversity-infused" undergraduate social psychology course compared to a standard course. In contrast, other studies, such as by Henderson-King and Kaleta (2000), find less support for the efficacy of diversity education, arguing that, at most, diversity education acts as a buffer against developing additional negative attitudes.

While there is support for the short-term value of diversity education, it is less certain whether such change has lasting effects. This is in part due to methodological limitations of typical research strategies used to study attitude change (e.g., heavy use of cross-sectional comparisons based on self-report). Further, the larger literature on attitude change suggests several additional barriers to lasting change. One such barrier is implicit attitudes, which are "introspectively unidentified (or inaccurately identified) traces of past experience that mediate favorable or unfavorable feeling, thought, or action toward social objects" (Greenwald and Banaji 1995: 8). Implicit attitudes appear to form in early childhood (Dunham et al. 2008) and persist into adulthood.

Further, despite otherwise good intentions, implicit prejudicial attitudes can undermine social interactions. For example, McConnell and Leibold (2001) demonstrated that biased implicit attitudes for white participants were associated with more negative social interactions with a black experimenter. Against such ingrained attitudes, it may be unrealistic to expect short-term attitude change to have lasting effects. Consistent with this possibility, Lai, Hoffman, and Nosek (2013) summarized the current state of knowledge on this question thusly: "In sum, the existing literature provides solid evidence for implicit

prejudice malleability, but little and mixed evidence for 'long-term' implicit prejudice change" (p. 322). Part of the difficulty in producing change may be a product of the way in which the mind structures information. Researchers have long documented how stereotype-inconsistent information—such as that which may be featured in diversity education programs—may be relegated to a separate mental category that serves to preserve existing mental structures. This process, known as subtyping (Weber and Crocker 1983), as well as other, similar information processing tendencies may make it difficult to change prejudicial attitudes.

11.2.2 Curbing Discriminatory Behavior

Whereas the previous section focused on the possibility of changing attitudes, in this section we discuss the possibility of changing behavior. Because, if diversity education is to be effective, surely it must engage more than the mind; it must also affect behavior. Since LaPiere's (1934) seminal observation of attitude-behavior inconsistency related to a Chinese couple traveling the U.S., social scientists have been acutely aware of the difficulties involved in predicting behavior from attitudes. Many factors can serve to undermine consistency, including (to name just a few) nature of the attitude (explicit or implicit), a person's motivations, relevance or importance of the attitude, elaboration of the attitude, and the ability to access and act upon the attitude.

Further, changing cultural values make it increasingly less likely that people will display discriminatory behavior in public. Researchers have suggested that this change in opinion has been accompanied by a change in the expression of prejudice to less blatant forms (see, for example, Bonilla-Silva 2003). For instance, Gaertner and Dovidio (1986) proposed a theory of aversive racism, which posits that aspirational egalitarian beliefs are in conflict with ordinary prejudicial feelings, leaving people uncomfortable and avoidant of different others.

Besides intrapersonal processes, researchers have observed the deleterious effects of competition on prejudicial attitudes and discriminatory behavior. The best known example, Realistic Group Conflict Theory (Campbell 1965) suggests that competition over scarce resources (e.g., jobs) exacerbates perceived group-based differences. From this brief review, it would seem overly optimistic that short-term diversity education should be thought of as a panacea for prejudicial attitudes or discriminatory behavior.

11.3 Diversity Education as Maintaining the Status Quo

In this section, we consider a more cynical interpretation of diversity education. Specifically, we examine the possibility that far from eradicating inequalities, diversity education schemes may be supporting the status quo.

11.3.1 Self-serving Organizational Goals

From a practical standpoint diversity training can be useful in organizational settings in at least two ways. First, some in the field of management have suggested that diversity is good for increasing company profits (see, for example, Andrevski et al. 2010). The idea that diversity in the workplace should not be pursued as an end to itself but for the good of the company (and its profits in particular) is well illustrated in the following story about a diversity expert published in a business journal.

> When Stephen Lowisz was growing up in metro Detroit, his dad was "one of the most racist sons of a gun you'll ever meet," he said. And he didn't know much better. … Today, he is a diversity consultant and CEO of Qualigence International, a Livonia-based recruiting and research firm with more than 60 employees and $5.5 million in annual revenue. … Diversity, he tells his clients, is not about doing the right thing or creating set-asides; it's about building a business filled with the best and brightest talent so your firm can compete globally. (Haimerl 2013)

Notice that in this context, what matters is the direct link between diversity and corporate profit. Another argument often made in favor of the "business case" for diversity is that companies and businesses with a visibly "diverse" set of employees are more able to attract a similarly diverse and potentially larger customer base, resulting in increased revenues.

Another practical, though somewhat cynical, function of diversity is simply to allow organizations to comply with government regulations, and more specifically to help workers and their employers avoid race or gender discrimination lawsuits. As Kalev et al. put it,

> There are reasons to believe that employers adopt antidiscrimination measures as window dressing, to inoculate themselves against liability, or to improve morale rather than to increase managerial diversity. (2006: 610)

Interestingly, while organizational leaders may embrace diversity as a matter of legal necessity, they may at the same believe that it is fundamentally counterproductive. For example, a recent study shows that in organizational settings some "observers hold schemas that link racial diversity with expectations of increased interpersonal friction and conflict among team members" and are thus less likely to assign resources to diverse teams within their firms (Lount et al. 2015, p. 1359).

11.3.2 Disguising and Perpetuating Inequality

An even more cynical view of diversity suggests that it can in fact be used in a more systematic and subversive fashion to disguise underlying racism. This view of diversity relates to a body of growing research on the more subtle expression of racism. Specifically, a number of scholars have pointed out that today racism is less blatant than in the past. It is often characterized by a denial that racism exists, coupled with a corresponding belief that any lingering racial inequality is the fault of members of the groups experiencing it (Bobo and Smith 1998;

Bonilla-Silva 2003). Researchers have found empirical evidence of this modern (or "laissez-faire") racism. For example, Karyn McKinney, in *Being White*, found that most young whites do not express open hostility or prejudice, but instead believe that racism is over and thus it is whites who are now experiencing the effects of racial inequality (2005). Thus context is important in untangling the meaning of race talk, because racism may be hidden beneath language that sounds like it is progressive (Marvasti and McKinney 2007).

In *Racism Without Racists* (2003), Eduardo Bonilla-Silva demonstrates that racism can and does exist without clearly identifiable "racists," and in fact, those he identifies as holding progressive ideas about race subscribe to many of the color-blind ideas about race that less progressive whites do. Further, Bonilla-Silva shows how context matters in the use of race talk. Whites use coded race talk as "rhetorical shields" to appear to be less racist. Especially for younger whites, this coded race talk establishes the ideology of color-blindness through which they can make claims of racial tolerance. Bonilla-Silva also points out that because race talk is highly emotional, when discussing race, whites often become incoherent and engage in digressions. They may also use diminutives, playing down the degree to which they disagree with racially progressive policies and ideologies.

Thus, in his work, Bonilla-Silva shows how context matters in race talk. Similarly, Picca and Feagin show how race talk differs by context. In the "front-stage," or multiracial environments, very different racial discourse is used by whites than in the "back-stage," or all-white environments (2007). It is impossible to understand the meaning of coded race language without observing how it is used. Although the rhetoric of race is less overtly racist than it has been in the past, racial inequality persists because of the ideologies hidden behind much of the current "diversity tolerant" language.

Similarly, Wingfield and Feagin explore how racial inequality still exists even when we are presumably in a "post-racial" U.S., evidenced for many in the presidency of Barack Obama. They demonstrate how the framing of the U.S. as post-racial relies on the same kind of colorblind rhetoric that Bonilla-Silva uncovers (2010).

In recent work, researchers contrast idealized discourses of diversity with the reality of inequality in the United States. They find that far from being a basis for progressive change, common uses of the term "diversity" can obscure racial inequality. In Marvasti and McKinney's (2011) study, for many of their respondents, "diversity" implies assimilation to a white normative culture. Indeed, for at least one-third of Marvasti and McKinney's respondents, diversity meant "oneness," "equality," or even "color-blindness." In another study, respondents obviously conflate the meanings of "multiculturalism" and "assimilation" (George 2005). In Bell and Hartmann's (2007) research, even for respondents who recognize a definition of diversity that implies the inclusion of multiple cultures, diversity is often defined overly broadly, in effect making "diversity" about everything, and thus about nothing. Overall, Bell and Hartmann find evidence that it is not only possible, but is in fact common, for respondents to speak positively about "diversity" while ignoring or denying lingering structural inequality based on race (2007). It is this usage of the word "diversity" that has become institutionalized, and thus has a place as a dominant racial discourse, as what Bell and Hartmann call "happy talk" in U.S. culture (2007).

Others have similarly found that discourses of diversity have come to be used to hide lingering racial and ethnic inequality. In one study, Ellen C. Berrey found that diversity language on college campuses may sometimes increase inclusion. However, even when it does, it often has the counter-effect of downplaying racial inequality while discounting the experiences of students of color (Berrey 2011). Other research suggests that indeed the language of diversity has been subsumed under the ideology of color-blindness and diversity talk serves as a tool to maintain inequality (Moore and Bell 2011). Indeed, several empirical studies show how by setting aside discussions of discrimination and inequality, diversity talk in organizations can make anti-affirmative action arguments by whites appear to be racially neutral (Collins 2011b; Moore and Bell 2011).

In a study of Fortune 1000 corporate managers, David Embrick found that these corporate leaders do employ a language of diversity (2011). However, when they discuss diversity in their companies, they most often leave out explicit discussions of race and gender altogether. Further, they are eager to discuss their companies' efforts toward "promoting diversity," but when asked to discuss particular programs used to do so, they are unable to recount specific policies and practices (Embrick 2011).

Sharon Collins found in her study of the labor market that "diversity" in organizations refers to activities that are meant to signify "corporate good will" (2011a). In fulfilling this purpose, practices deemed as supportive of diversity might actually hide underlying bias in the organization. She also suggests that diversity discourse, and the very definition of diversity itself, is purposely kept flexible in organizations so that it can work to protect business as usual in the organization. As such, diversity talk serves as a "proxy" for racial progress (Collins 2011a).

11.4 Diversity Education as Institutionally Embedded Practice

Central to our argument is the realization that diversity education signifies many things and is used for many purposes depending on the context or the specific organizational need. Specifically, in understanding the role of diversity education, we are aided by the works of Alfred Schutz (1945) and his concepts of "pragmatic motives" and "provinces of meaning."

First, "pragmatic motives" as a concept helps us understand that actions, or practice, in everyday life is purposeful; actions are intended to carry out a specific act, not just fulfill some metaphysical ideal. As Schutz puts it,

> The world of everyday life is the scene and also the object of our actions and interactions. We have to dominate it and we have to change it in order to

realize the purposes which we pursue within it among our fellow-men. Thus, we work and operate not only within but upon the world. ... In this sense it may be correctly said that a pragmatic motive governs our natural attitude toward the world of daily life. World, in this sense, is something that we have to modify by our actions or that modifies our actions. (1945: 534)

Second, "provinces of meaning" (1945: 551) points to the fact that everyday life is made up of multiple realities in which experiences take on their meaning or significance. While these worlds are interrelated, each is governed by slightly different set of rules:

> the world of dreams, of imageries and phantasms, especially the world of art, the world of religious experience, the world of scientific contemplation, the play world of the child, and the world of the insane – are finite provinces of meaning. ... This means that ... all of them have a peculiar cognitive style ... each of these finite provinces of meaning may receive a specific accent of reality. (1945: 553)

Together these concepts help explain the confusion and frustration expressed by many about positive diversity talk and its failure to achieve its "true" goals. The problem with diversity education, as a province of meaning, is that for some it represents a universal language that travels across the many worlds of reality. As we have shown, this idea is not compatible with the multi-faceted reality of diversity education, which is in fact used for many purposes and across many provinces of meaning.

The point is that the infinite variations in which ideas can be expressed makes it impossible to police language and constantly channel it in the "appropriate" direction. As Schutz reminds us, "It is the meaning of the experience and not the ontological structure of the object, which constitutes reality" (Schutz 1945: 551). Applied to the realm of diversity education, this means that it is the interpretive framework (Gubrium and Holstein 1998) of an inter-group exchange that informs what the participants mean by particular words and actions—such exchanges are not uniformly dictated by the preferred or idealized policies. The only way in which diversity education would work as a set of universally true practices is for speakers and listeners to exist in a cultural sphere where sarcasm and irony do not exist. Following Schutz, this would require a unified and singular province of meaning where everyone agrees (willingly or by force) to use certain words and ideas in a fixed way across time and place. This very idea, of course, is the antithesis of diversity and more akin to totalitarianism.

11.5 The Future of Diversity Education

In this chapter we made the case that diversity is not one thing but many things to the extent that it is used to serve divergent institutional purposes. In some ways, diversity amounts to a social theory whose popularity and application varies over time and across settings. The more pragmatic version of diversity will likely endure in one form or another as it has become institutionally embedded and useful for a variety or organizational purposes. However, its particular meaning and rhetoric will likely change in response to societal changes and internal bureaucratic demands.

For example, it appears that "diversity" is exceedingly accompanied with the terms "inclusion" and "inclusivity.". This transformation of the language of diversity is evident in an exemplary report from Brown University titled "Pathways to Diversity and Inclusion: An Action Plan for Brown University." The report specifically states:

> To achieve our goals as a university, we must embrace both diversity and inclusion. It would be an empty victory to achieve one without the other. Absent diversity, an inclusive campus may become a homogeneous intellectual echo chamber that cannot teach individuals how to learn from, or communicate and collaborate with, people different from themselves. Absent inclusion, a diverse campus may generate misunderstandings and feelings of invisibility, fragmentation, frustration, and even anger that stem from the unproductive clash of people who bring different worldviews, experiences, and concepts of identity to campus but who do not often interact/engage with one another on campus. (Pathways to Diversity 2016, p. 1)

Here diversity without some sense of inclusion and togetherness is devalued and even identified as a source of unnecessary conflict or "unproductive of clash of people."

Similarly, Elon University's housing initiative echoes this trend where students are assigned to housing units that resemble "neighborhoods" (Residence Life 2017). The goal is to create "communities [that] bring together diverse groups of students with common interests" (Brown 2016). Interestingly, Elon University includes a position for "Associate Provost for Inclusive Community" who is charged with "supporting people of many backgrounds, cultures, beliefs and perspectives, and providing an enhanced focus on learning around difference and efforts to create a welcoming campus climate for all" (Townsend 2012).

While coupling inclusion with diversity is gaining momentum, the underlying problem of defining and operationalizing the concept is no closer at hand. A recent *Harvard Business Review Digital Articles* article states "without inclusion there's often a diversity backlash" but goes on to point out: " It's easy to measure diversity: It's a simple matter of headcount. But quantifying feelings of inclusion can be dicey" (Sherbin and Rashid 2017, p. 3). We maintain both concepts, diversity and inclusion, are equally difficult to measure and implement.

Returning to diversity education, the field seems to betheoretically under-developed. While it may be true that the underlying causes of prejudice are similar in many cases, and so are the daily experiences of disadvantaged groups, the particular needs of disadvantaged groups are not the same. In some ways, the next phase in the evolution of diversity training should involve: (1) the development of more rigorous assessment tools to measure and improve the effectiveness of diversity programs, (2) explicit, locally relevant, and tangible goals that could be tracked over time, and (3) the realization that different resources and strategies may be needed to meet the needs of different populations. This type of flexibility and data-driven policy is consistent with an organizationally embedded (Gubrium and Holstein 1993) view of diversity.

References

Andrevski, G., Richard, O. C., Ferrier, W. J., & Shaw, D. S. (2010). Managerial racial diversity, competitive aggressiveness and firm performance: A moderated mediation model. In *Academy of Management Annual Meeting Proceedings*.

Bell, J., & Hartmann, D. (2007). Diversity in everyday discourse: The cultural ambiguities and consequences of "happy talk." *American Sociological Review*, 895–914.

Berrey, E. C. (2011). Why diversity became orthodox in higher education and how it changed the meaning of race on campus. *Critical Sociology, 37*(5), 573–596.

Bobo, L., & Smith, R. (1998). From Jim Crow racism to laissez-faire racism: The transformation of racial attitudes. In W. Katkin, N. Landsmen, & A. Tyree (Eds.), *Beyond pluralism*. Urbana, IL: University of Illinois Press.

Bonilla-Silva, E. (2003). *Racism without racists: Color-blind racism and the persistence of racial inequality in the United States*. Lanham, Maryland: Rowman and Littlefield.

Brown, S. (2016). At Elon, living differently together. *The Chronicle of Higher Education*. http://www.chronicle.com.ezaccess.libraries.psu.edu/article/At-Elon-Living-Differently/236439?cid=cp38. Retrieved July 30, 2017.

Campbell, D. T. (1965). *Ethnocentric and other altruistic motives* (pp. 283–311). Lincoln, NE: University of Nebraska Press.

Chang, M. J. (2002). The impact of an undergraduate diversity course requirementon students' racial views and attitudes. *Journal of General Education, 51*(1), 21–42.

Collins, S. M. (2011a). Diversity in the post affirmative action labor market: A proxy for racial progress? *Critical Sociology, 37*(5), 521–540.

Collins, S. M. (2011b). From affirmative action to diversity: Erasing inequality from organizational responsibility. *Critical Sociology, 37*(5), 517–520.

Dunham, Y., Baron, A. S., & Banaji, M. R. (2008). The development of implicit intergroup cognition. *Trends in Cognitive Sciences, 12*(7), 248–253.

Embrick, D. G. (2011). The diversity ideology in the business world: A new oppression for a new age. *Critical Sociology, 37*(5), 541–556.

Fiske, S. T. (1998). Stereotyping, prejudice, and discrimination. In D. T. Gilbert, S. T. Fiske, & G. Lindzey (Eds.), *Handbook of social psychology* (4th ed., Vol. 2, pp. 357–411). New York: McGraw-Hill.

Gaertner, S. L., & Dovidio, J. F. (1986). The aversive form of racism. In J. F. Dovidio & S. L. Gaertner (Eds.), *Prejudice, discrimination, and racism* (pp. 61–90). Orlando, FL: Academic Press.

George, D.F. (2005). Unity through diversity? Assimilation, multiculturalism and the debate over what it means to be American. Unpublished doctoral dissertation. University of North Texas.

Greenwald, A. G., & Banaji, M. R. (1995). Implicit social cognition: Attitudes, self-esteem, and stereotypes. *Psychological Review, 102*, 4–27.

Gubrium, J. F., & Holstein, J. A. (1993). Family discourse, organizational embeddedness, and local enactment. *Journal of Family Issues, 14*(1), 66–81.

Gubrium, J., & Holstein, J. (1998). Narrative practice and the coherence of personal stories. *The Sociological Quarterly, 39*(1), 163–187.

Haimerl, A. (2013). Experts: Bottom line … diversity is good for business. *Crain's Detroit Business*. November 3. http://www.crainsdetroit.com/article/20131103/NEWS/311039934/experts-bottom-line-diversity-is-good-for-business. Retrieved August 30, 2014.

Henderson-King, D., & Kaleta, A. (2000). *The Journal of Higher Education, 71*(2), 142–164.

Hussey, H. D., Fleck, B. K. B., & Warner, R. M. (2010). Reducing student prejudice in diversity-infused core psychology classes. *College Teaching, 58*(3), 85–92.

Kalev, A., Dobbin, F., & Kelley, E. (2006). Best practices or best guesses? Assessing the efficacy of corporate affirmative action and diversity policies. *American Sociological Review, 71*, 589–617.

Lai, C. K., Hoffman, K. M., & Nosek, B. A. (2013). Reducing implicit prejudice. *Social and Personality Psychology Compass, 7*(5), 315–330.

LaPiere, R. T. (1934). Attitudes vs actions. *Social Forces, 13*, 230–237.

Lount, R. L., Sheldon, O. J., Rink, F., & Phillips, K. W. (2015). Biased perceptions of racially diverse teams and their consequences for resource support. *Organization Science, 26*(5), 1351–1364. https://doi.org/10.1287/orsc.2015.0994.

Marvasti, A. B., & McKinney, K. D. (2007). The work of making race invisible. (Amir Marvasti & Karyn McKinney) 2007. In J., Feagin, & H. Vera (Eds.), *Racial and ethnic relations handbook*. Boston: Kluwer Press.

Marvasti, A. B., & McKinney, K. D. (2011). Does diversity mean assimilation? *Critical Sociology, 37*(5), 631–650.

McConnell, A. R., & Leibold, J. M. (2001). Relations among the implicit association test, discriminatory behavior, and explicit measures of racial attitudes. *Journal of Experimental Social Psychology, 37*, 435–442.

McKinney, K. D. (2005). *Being white: Stories of race and racism*. New York: Routledge.

Merton, R. K. (2012) (original 1949). Discrimination and the American creed. In C. Gallagher (Ed.), *Rethinking the color line: Readings in race and ethnicity*. New York: McGraw Hill.

Moore, W. L., & Bell, J. M. (2011). Maneuvers of whiteness: Diversity as a mechanism of retrenchment in the affirmative action discourse. *Critical Sociology, 37*(5), 597–613.

Pathways to diversity and inclusion: An action plan for Brown University. (2016). http://brown.edu/web/documents/diversity/actionplan/diap-full.pdf. Retrieved July 30, 2017.

Picca, L. H., & Feagin, J. R. (2007). *Two-faced racism: Whites in the backstage and frontstage*. New York: Routledge.

Residence Life. (2017). http://www.elon.edu/e-web/students/residence_life/residential-campus/living-learning-communities.xhtml. Retrieved July 30, 2017.

Schutz, A. (1945). On multiple realities. *Philosophy and Phenomenological Research, 5*(4), 533–576.

Sherbin, L., & Rashid, R. (2017). Diversity doesn't stick without inclusion. *Harvard Business Review Digital Articles*, 2–5. https://hbr.org/2017/02/diversity-doesnt-stick-without-inclusion. Retrieved July 30, 2017.

Townsend, E. (2012). Brooke Barnett named interim associate. provost. http://www.elon.edu/E-Net/Article/63656. Retrieved July 30, 2017.

Vedantam, S. (2008). Most diversity training ineffective, study finds. Washington Post. January 20. http://www.washingtonpost.com/wp-dyn/content/article/2008/01/19/AR2008011901899_pf.html. Retrieved August 30, 2014.

Weber, R., & Crocker, J. (1983). Cognitive processes in the revision of stereotypic beliefs. *Journal of Personality and Social Psychology, 45*(5), 961–977.

Wingfield, A. H., & Feagin, J. R. (2010). *Yes we can? White racial framing and the 2008 presidential campaign*. New York: Routledge.

The Reality and Impact of Legal Segregation in the United States

12

Ruth Thompson-Miller and Joe R. Feagin

Contents

R. Thompson-Miller (✉)
Department of Sociology, University of Dayton,
Dayton, OH, USA
e-mail: rthompsonmiller1@udayton.edu

J. R. Feagin
Department of Sociology, Texas A&M University,
College Station, TX, USA
e-mail: feagin@tamu.edu

Abstract

In this article, we cover the history of Jim Crow, how African Americans were bound by laws of segregation and experienced racial violence on a daily basis, there was always resistance. Ultimately, the Civil Rights Movement was instrumental in ending the formal laws of segregation. The informal practices

© Springer International Publishing AG, part of Springer Nature 2018   203
P. Batur and J. R. Feagin (eds.), *Handbook of the Sociology of Racial and Ethnic Relations*,
Handbooks of Sociology and Social Research, https://doi.org/10.1007/978-3-319-76757-4_12

have taken longer to end; indeed, they have not yet ended. White challenges to the ending of legal segregation prevented African Americans from enjoying a full actual end to the realities of blatant segregation for years after the anti-segregation laws were passed. Moreover, the psychological, long-term impact on older, currently living, African Americans who experienced the tyranny of legal segregation is apparent in their painful narratives which will be incorporated into this article.

12.1 Introduction

In this article, we will discuss the social system of legal segregation (Jim Crow). We cover the history of Jim Crow, how it began, and the legal foundation on which it was formulated. We will incorporate voices of African Americans, which will shed light on the daily experiences of African Americans who lived through Jim Crow. We will discuss the racial etiquette that was demanded and enforced by whites, and performed and adhered to by African Americans. All institutions, including the educational system, were bound by the laws of legal segregation. Central to the system of legal segregation was the use of racial violence through lynchings, rapes, and property loss, especially at the hands of groups like the Ku Klux Klan (Wang 1999; McDevitt et al. 2002). Even though African Americans were bound by laws of segregation and experienced racial violence on a daily basis, there was always resistance. Some organizations that spearheaded collective resistance were the black church, the NAACP, and other private organizations. Everyday citizens who wanted to see an end to the oppressive system also engaged in the resistance to legal segregation. Ultimately, the Civil Rights Movement was instrumental in ending the formal laws of segregation. The informal practices have taken longer to end; indeed, they have not yet ended. White challenges to the ending of legal segregation prevented African Americans from enjoying a full actual end to the realities of blatant segregation for years after the anti-segregation laws were passed (Chafe 2001). Moreover, the psychological, long-term impact on older, currently living, African Americans who experienced the tyranny of legal segregation is apparent in their painful narratives which will be incorporated into this article.

12.2 The Black Codes

This article focuses on the era of legal segregation. However, it's important to give some historical framework as to how legal segregation became such an intricate and longstanding set of practices in the United States. The social system of legal segregation (Jim Crow) began in 1870s and ended in the 1960s. Prior to the 1896 Supreme Court decision, *Plessy vs Ferguson*, the case which resulted in Court approval of the formal laws of legal segregation, there were similar laws known as Black Codes. Generated after the Civil War, and similar in effects to the just-ended institution of slavery, the Black Codes helped to create and enforce a system of racial inequality and servitude for technically freed African Americans. After the Civil War, ex-Confederate officers and officeholders who led most southern legislatures spearheaded the passing of statutes whose impact resembled slavery. "The measures controlled nearly every aspect of black life, with whites allowed to employ draconian remedies against recalcitrant blacks. These laws soon became known simply as the Black Codes" (Packard 2002: 42).

In 1865, President Andrew Johnson supported the Black Codes, which were a near-slavery system intended to force African Americans to work without benefit of significant payments. Segregation of railroad cars and many facilities spread, especially after 1870. "[The] Florida legislature went a step further the same year by forbidding whites to use cars set apart for use of Negroes, as well as excluding Negroes from cars reserved for whites" (Woodward 1974: 23). The Codes generally prohibited African Americans from voting, attending public schools, and being admitted into public hospitals, as well as prohibiting African Americans from utilizing public facilities such as hotels, parks, and public transportation. Public facilities were segregated. The Black Codes encouraged whites to take the law into their own hands and physically attack nonconforming "free" blacks and to pressure them to work in arrangements that provided little or no payments (Feagin 2000). The ending of the Black Codes in 1866 did not bring the oppression to an end, for the everyday social control dating back to slavery continued in the form of an extensive racial etiquette, which we discuss later. The ending of Black Codes was but a short reprieve for African Americans, because within a few years the laws of legal segregation were implemented in the southern and border states. They would last for decades, indeed until the late 1960s.

12.3 The Implementation of Legal Segregation Laws

Researcher Smythe (1948) has emphasized how the concept of Jim Crow seems to have first appeared as such in Cincinnati, Ohio in 1832, and also how it developed into a term synonymous with "racial accommodation." Individuals in positions of power utilized Jim Crow to systematically segregate human beings by racial groups. And the concept was soon incorporated into many aspects of legal and social science thinking. It operated as a system of racial inequality and degradation for African Americans (Folmsbee 1949; Packard 2002).

There were attempts by African Americans to fight against the laws of legal segregation, often before they were officially implemented. There were numerous challenges to segregated public schools years before Brown v. Board of Education ended up in the Supreme Court in 1954. Peter Irons notes that the first challenge to segregated public schools began in "1849 with a lawsuit filed in Boston by Benjamin Roberts, after his five-year-old daughter, Sarah, was turned away from the primary school nearest her home on the ground of her being a colored person" (2002: p. ix). The court decided it was best that she continue to attend a segregated school. This Massachusetts Supreme Court decision

preceded the landmark 1896 U.S. Supreme Court case of Homer Plessy, a Black man who refused to sit in the legally required "colored" section on a train. The decision in *Plessy vs Ferguson* paved the way for widespread legal segregation by affirming that separate facilities for blacks and whites could be "separate but equal." This legal fiction increasingly included racially segregated public schools, other public facilities, and many other aspects of public life. The U.S. Constitution and federal court decisions created contemporary forms of the racist institutions that are still functioning today (Thompson-Miller et al. 2014).

Legal segregation (Jim Crow) was a social system that Southern (and border state) whites utilized after the abolishment of slavery. The primary function was to continue the social system of servitude, the racial caste hierarchy, and the economic control of African Americans. The social system was at base controlled through the use of overt and implied racial violence. Even though the 1968 Civil Rights Act, nearly 40 years ago, finally outlawed the official segregation system its reality and impact continue. The personal narratives of older African Americans that we collected and that will be quoted later in this article indicate that the emotional, economic, and social ramifications of the experience are still greatly felt (Faulkner 1982; Feagin and Sikes 1994).

As early as 1866, some southern states began enacting some formal segregation laws. By the 1880s extensive Jim Crow segregation could be seen in Florida, Tennessee, Texas, Mississippi, and Georgia, and soon spread across all southern and border states. More than one hundred years after the end of the Civil War, until the late 1960s, African Americans lived under a system of official second-class citizenship—formally in all and border southern states, and informally in most northern states. Van Woodward notes, "[In] the summer of 1956 the legislatures of Florida, North Carolina, and Virginia were called into special sessions to consider bills designed to tighten segregation laws" (1974: 162). The laws, written and unwritten in the South, kept African Americans subjugated in a system that governed every aspect of their social, political, and economic life. The legal system of Jim Crow prohibited voting and access to public facilities including public transportation; and it legalized an unfair penal system. "With its 'WHITES ONLY' and 'COLORED ONLY' signs, posted above railroad waiting rooms, bathrooms, and drinking fountains, the Jim Crow system inflicted daily humiliations on blacks of both sexes and all ages" (Irons 2002: 12; Feagin and McKinney 2003).

12.4   The Interview Data

The personal life narratives that we reference here are part of a research project that has been ongoing for several years. Nearly 100 elderly African Americans in the Southeast and Southwest have recently been interviewed about their experiences during the long era of legal segregation. Most interviews took place in the participant's home. On average, each interview lasted approximately one to two hours. We interviewed the participants utilizing a carefully crafted interview schedule. We chose questions for the interview schedule after review of the relevant social science literatures.

The narratives in this article are a representation of what elderly African Americans actually lived through in their everyday lives during legal segregation. We collected many accounts of encounters with whites, which took place in both public and private spaces, throughout the years of legal segregation. Historically, there are many misconceptions and contradictions about the everyday practices and interactions between African Americans and whites during legal segregation. The narratives of these elderly African Americans shed significant light on some of those misconceptions.

12.5   Racial Etiquette

The racial etiquette of legal segregation was a system used to control and dictate the physical, psychological, and social interactions between whites and blacks. Stetson Kennedy describes racial etiquette as "a compulsory ritual denoting first- and second-class citizenship. It has more

than psychological and social significance; it's serving also the basic economic and political purpose of facilitating the exploitation of non-whites by whites, collectively and individually" (1959: 206). The social practices of racial etiquette included removing or tipping your hat for whites, moving off the sidewalk when whites walked by, addressing whites (young and old) as sir, madam, or the like. Also, this meant never speaking up for your rights or "being uppity." According to our respondents and other studies, instances where whites views blacks as acting "uppity" included speaking too well, living in a home that whites deemed as nice, wearing nice clothes, and owning a nice automobile (Kennedy 1959; Johnson 1943; Litwick 1979; Tolnay and Beck 1992).

The practice of racial etiquette allowed ordinary whites, young and old, to inflict racial oppression on African Americans. Law enforcement agents and high-ranking officials enforced the racial etiquette of Jim Crow as if it were written into the laws of the U.S. Constitution. What incident would incite white violence changed depending on the day, the person, and the state; violence was often unpredictable. According to Jerrold Packard, racial violence would be inflicted upon African Americans for behavior that was perceived as being disrespectful, for "reckless eyeballing," or for the purpose of sending a message of "stay in your place" to the black community (2002). No one was immune to witnessing the violence of segregation. "In Georgia, Martin Luther King Sr. … witnessed drunken white men beat a black man to death for being 'sassy.' …The victim's 'sassiness' consisted of refusing the demand of the white men that he hand over his paycheck" (Litwick 1999: 13). In the South, whites used racial etiquette in many instances to justify inflicting individual or collective racial terror on African Americans.

12.6   Jim Crow Education

Frequently, in the rural areas of the South the majority of African Americans worked as sharecroppers or tenant farmers on the land of white people. The white owner (or overseer) often expected slave-like labor from the black families. Children were often allowed to attend school for only a few months of the year, that is, when the crops didn't need to be picked. Parents often taught their children to conceal their schooling from the white owner. The act of keeping a child from an education is, in effect, an act of racial violence against the child and his or her community.

The public schools during legal segregation were, "separate and unequal." Many of the segregated schools that African American children attended were held in community churches and private homes. The salaries that African American teachers received were typically a fraction of what white teachers received. Parents were often forced to purchase the books, school supplies, and other essential needs for their children. In some instances, children didn't have desks and chairs to sit on (Irons 2002). African American children usually attended schools that were overcrowded and often resembled a "windowless log cabin," while white students typically attended schools that were "beautiful red and white brick buildings" (Brundage 2005: 141–142).

12.7 The Centrality of Racial Violence

During legal segregation, much racial violence was legitimized and essential to the routine operation of legal segregation. The violence that whites inflicted on African Americans was not seen as deviant, but legal or customary (Bufacchi 2005). The violence of segregation often took the form of mob beatings, rapes, house and church burnings, and lynchings. All such actions, moreover, took place within a well-institutionalized framework of racial oppression. This framework generally shaped, indeed frequently mandated, the array of violent actions by whites. Whites attacking African Americans did not need to be immediately motivated by racial prejudice, but could act because of group pressures to conform within an institutionally racist system with already-defined racial targets

(Jackman 2002; Blee 2005; Feagin 2006). "Some white folks go so far as to take offence (and action) against nonwhites whom they consider to be 'acting uppity' or 'putting on airs.' Some Negroes having built for themselves a fine house, have refrained from painting the exterior, in order not to antagonize whites in the community whose homes are not so fine. A large automobile can also prove a liability in some sections" (Kennedy 1959: 207).

12.8 Lynchings

Whites' regular use of lynching as a brutal technique brought death to thousands of African American men, women, and children. Several thousand African Americans have been put to death by lynchings since the beginning of legal segregation (Ginzburg 1962; Dray 2003). Calculations indicate "on the average, a black man, woman, or child was murdered nearly once a week between 1882 and 1930 by a hate-driven white mob" (Tolnay and Beck 1995: ix). Not surprisingly, virtually all older African Americans have seen or heard about local whites collectively engaging in lynchings that targeted African Americans defined as breaking with white custom or law. Social science research has shown that African Americans can be psychologically affected by lynchings, without ever witnessing one (Eyerman 2001; Brown et al. 2000; Kelly 2005). White mob lynchings of African American men, women, and children were common during legal segregation, as we see in this elderly respondent's painful recollection:

> There was a man, a black man. He was a janitor, he cleaned up the place, and he went and told this white man that was so mean to me. ...That he didn't have to treat me the way he was treating me. He [the white man] took and pushed me over one of the tables...he [black man] got tired of him doing that, before I know it he leaned back and hit that white man and beat him up. It scared me so bad because I didn't know what he [the white man] was going to do to him. When the police come, he [the white man] had almost beat him to death. You know. So anyways, my parents raised enough money to get him out of jail. [Pauses, then starts to cry], somebody back then, you could go up and

down the highway and see the Black boy hanging from the tree, and he was dead. They killed him on the tree. ...I didn't think that I could live to see somebody beat somebody like that man did and not [have anyone] do anything about it. [Cries harder]... the white man, they took hot water, they boiled that water, and they put him in the water, and cooked him. How could somebody treat somebody, a human being, and just threw them in the pot, they had a big ol' pot they use to make soap out of it. And they just throw them in there [the pot]. Whenever you use to do stuff, you were dead. You couldn't do anything, you had to just stand there and watch them do him like that, and every time his head would come up like that, they pushed him right down in the pot. God brought us through all of that, he sure did. He brought us, God made for that person down there to die that day. When we got down there we pray, and we ask God to forgive him, because they didn't know what they was doing. It didn't help his family to see him tortured down there...it was a black pot, a cast iron...they rejoiced. Can you believe that they [whites] rejoiced about what they did to him in the black pot, they rejoiced.

The vivid details of an African American man being boiled in a pot, while his family watched, epitomized the atrocities of violence during legal segregation. Racial violence is a collective act by a white mob, and it inflicts psychological trauma on individuals who witnessed it and heard about it. Clearly, this respondent's frequent crying during the interview demonstrates the extreme psychological distress (Krieger et al. 2005).

During legal segregation African Americans commonly believed that many whites actually enjoyed lynching, mutilating, or otherwise hurting them. During legal segregation, some whites were photographed smiling, rejoicing, and celebrating in front of burned and mutilated bodies of African Americans as they hung from trees. Historically, one of the misconceptions is that the Ku Klux Klan committed thousands of lynchings. However, James Allen, John Lewis, Leon Litwick, and Hilton Als dispel this misconception with nearly 100 photographed images of burned, lynched, and mutilated bodies of African Americans. Litwick states, "The photographs stretch our credulity, even numb our minds and senses to the full extent of the horror, but they must be examined if we are to understand how normal men and women could live with, participate in, and defend such

atrocities, even reinterpret them so they would not see themselves or be perceived as less than civilized. The men and women who tortured, dismembered, and murdered in this fashion understood perfectly well what they were doing and thought of themselves as perfectly normal human beings. Few had any ethical qualms about their actions" (2000: 34).

12.9   Rape

During the era of legal segregation, recurring sexual assaults against African American women were common knowledge in the white and African American communities. Historically, the research of social scientists has generally failed to document thoroughly these frequent assaults on African American women by white men. That research is more likely to focus on the frequent allegations of rape of white women by black men. However, a more common problem historically lies in the fact that African American families regularly faced the raping or otherwise sexual threats against their young daughters, mothers, and sons by white men, including those with local power and influence (Feagin 2006: ix–x, 74–81).

One of our respondents in her late seventies recalls a family story of rape:
In later years, my mother and her sisters would never tell us anything but I have. ...a cousin, I called her Aunt Bell, but she was really a cousin. ...She told me, that this white prostitute across the street, Ms. Ann, my Auntie Celeste worked for her and she was over there working one day and this [white] man, that owned a store a block up the street, came to see Ms. Ann. ...He was married. Ms. Ann wasn't there, he raped my Aunt and my Aunt got pregnant and when she got pregnant she told them [her family] what happened, she told them that he had raped her that day and they went to talk to him, and you know what they did? They made *her* leave town. They said you have to send her out of town, and my Aunt said that is what they did to Blacks. The white men would rape the Black girls, and if the Black girls got pregnant the families would have to send them out of town to have the babies, and the like, so that's what happened in that situation in the family...She would tell me other families it happened to, in [names town]. ... Our family wasn't one that told a lot of things.

You see, they wanted to hide everything that's what they wanted to do. My mother or my aunt would never have told me about you know her situation they would have gone to their grave. Because I remember when Aunt Bell told me mama knew she was talking about something and then Aunt Bell told me, later on she told me [my mama said to her], "You shouldn't have been telling them all of that" So they didn't want you to know what happened.

The psychological injury to the woman is apparent, and the female members of the family intended to take the story of this violent rape to their graves. The rape, the resulting pregnancy, and the subsequent departure of this young woman from her hometown reveal an all too common story of legal segregation. According to the respondent, the young woman apparently did not tell her family about the rape until she realized she was pregnant. During legal segregation, African American victims of rape often suffered alone or in silence (Burke 1991). This respondent's family was not alone, for "white men would rape the Black girls, and if the Black girls got pregnant the families would have to send them out of town." Unfortunately, for black women the responses from white society to their sexual assaults were not outrage, concern, or criminal punishment for perpetrators. White men were virtually never held responsible for raping black women. "Paramour rights are the unwritten antebellum law declaring a white man's right to take a black woman as his paramour, whether she is married or not" (Ellis and Ellis 2003: xv). This is an aspect of segregation which assisted white men in their abuse of African American women, and it included the inability of black men to do anything to protect black women.

12.10 Racial Expulsion: Property Loss

Successful and educated African Americans citizens, "all too often, paid a heavy price" if they expected to hold on to their material gains. Those who had the most to lose financially typically internalized the practices of racial etiquette even more. The more an African American acquired

economically, the more they deferred to whites to stay in their good graces and to alleviate the possibilities of repercussions because of their accomplishments (Litwack 1999: 321). Tolnay and Beck note that "poor whites lynched poor African Americans because they represented a threat to their well-being" (Tolnay and Beck 1995: 72). And Africans Americans were chased off their land and out of the south.

A retired nurse recalls how her aunt was living in a home that whites deemed to be nice and how that leads to collective, physical violent actions:

My aunt came here to visit us and they set the house on fire and they burned him [cousin] up in the house, when he tried to get out the window, they pushed him back in the house. They just nasty and mean. … Black people, weren't suppose to live in no, really nice area like that. She was living on this lake, and they wanted it and, and they probably knew that, she was here in [names town], and, so they went there and he was, cause they left him home by himself. My cousin, he was a young man. …And they just burned…the house down and burnt him up in the house. She left that place. She didn't want nothing else to happen. …They know who did it, but wasn't nothing they can do about it. All the white people, they stuck together. …Back in the forties. Just like Rosewood. They burned him alive.

Collective white jealousy made the hope of attaining the American housing dream dangerous and in some cases impossible. With sadness in her voice and tears in her eyes, she describes how white jealousy turned her family's housing dream into a deadly sequence of events. This is not an isolated incident, for several respondents shared similar stories of how, if whites wanted a property, they would assault or kill to get it. For example, Rosewood was an African American town in Florida. It was destroyed in the 1930s by a white mob that killed numerous black residents. An undocumented, but doubtless huge number of African Americans throughout the South and border states suffered great physical and material injury, including death, with no official or media reporting. Unfortunately, it was a common occurrence during legal segregation for African Americans to lose lives, property, and family members to racial violence at the hands of whites (McDevitt et al. 2002). The actual number of lost lives, property, and families remain undocumented and uncompensated, to the present day.

A man in his late fifties recalls stories of African Americans losing their land and lives to whites: "My grandmother said, 'At one time a lot of blacks owned the land that is now owned by whites and that they were forced to sell their land.' Those who did not sell lost their lives. Or the land was taken from them by means of taxation and indebtedness that they had incurred and they weren't aware that they were incurring. …Some of them were killed to take the land; they [whites] killed some of them to take the land" (Thompson-Miller et al. 2014). During the era of legal segregation, the land of African Americans was stolen by whites through an array of techniques.

12.11 Resistance to Legal Segregation

Even though active resistance usually sparked further violent attacks by white individuals or mobs, some African American men, women, and children did periodically engage in confrontational resistance. A prominent religious leader, now in his eighties, speaks to the importance of constant and confrontational resistance, especially to desegregate the schools:

> You had to do that! You had to do that! In order to change the system you had to do that! You had to test it. You had to make them show their real color. …If you didn't keep protesting the system, [change] never would have happened and some of us just decided that, we were going to test the system. It was dangerous to do it but we did it. Yeah. We did it. …Schools were segregated. We wrote the school board and told them to consider integrating the schools. If they didn't integrate the schools we were gonna file a suit. As time went on, we decided to file a suit. I went to several parents and told them we had to file a suit. I told them we had to have a particular child. All of them said, "NO!" My younger daughter was at [names school] at that time. I said to her," We got to use a name on the lawsuit to file the suit. Don't tell your mother about it but would you agree to do this?" She said, "Yes."

Especially in the 1950s and 1960s, African Americans like this respondent and his child actively resisted legal segregation and pressed the larger African American community to resist collectively. They showed that they were fighters, demonstrating great courage and agency in resisting segregation in spite of the threat of violence. Black churches and the National Association for the Advancement of Colored People (NAACP), among other black organization, were instrumental in organizing collective resistance against the brutal laws of legal segregation.

In 1954 the landmark decision in the *Brown* case officially overturned the infamous "separate but equal" doctrine of the *Plessy vs Ferguson* decision. *Brown* was based on the tireless work of Black men, women and children, including members of the NAACP. African Americans and their white allies challenged legal segregation in public schools, at great personal risk to themselves and their families. Eventually, the Supreme Court decided that legal segregation violated the U.S. Constitution. African American men and women who were involved in the civil rights movement were inspired by the *Brown* decision (Patterson 2001). With the support of liberal whites, African Americans began to fight harder for their civil rights in hope that all legal segregation would finally come to an end. After *Brown*, they organized sit-ins, boycotts, and demonstrations to end legal segregation. "The civil rights movement was heroic. …it inspired even higher expectations that *Brown* had in 1954" (Patterson 2001: xxi). Derrick Bell affirms this point, "*Brown* was the primary force and provided a vital inspirational spark in the post-World War II civil rights movement. Defenders maintain *Brown* served as an important encouragement for the Montgomery bus boycotters, and that it served as a key symbol of cultural advancement for the nation" (2004: 130).

12.12 Long Term Effects of Racial Violence—"Segregation Stress Syndrome"

Although the Civil Rights Movement began the long, yet successful fight, to end legal segregation, the long-term affects of years of racial violence took its toll on the lives, wealth, and psyche of African Americans. The research on this impact, and applying the idea of Post-traumatic Stress Disorder to their experiences, mostly remains to be done. Yet, the preliminary findings indicate a positive correlation exists in frequency and degree of PTSD and African Americans (Allen 1996: 210; Christopoulos 2002; Myers et al. 2000; Gray 1987). Researchers Terry Mills and Clara Edwards give an assessment of the effects of childhood traumatic experiences like the incidents that occurred during segregation: "The present cohort of older black Americans experienced very stressful life events and warlike trauma" (2002: 273–304).

We have introduced the idea of a "segregation stress syndrome"–which encompasses the chronic and enduring stress of, as well as the extremely painful responses to, official segregation that are indicated in the interviews of the elderly African Americans who participated in our research project (on the use of "PTSD" for Black responses to current racism, see Williams and Williams-Morris 2000; Feagin 2006). Some of the symptoms of "segregation stress syndrome" are physical, such as crying, sweating, and increased anxiety. The syndrome has some psychological components such as the sufferer avoiding situations, individuals, or objects that remind him or her of the traumatic racial events. In addition, the syndrome often includes some denial, for instance, not personally associating with the traumatic event, stating that it happened to someone else, and emotionally distancing oneself from the pain. Survivors of traumatic experiences, similar to the events that occurred regularly during legal segregation, sometimes have problems feeling comfortable and trusting individuals who remind them of their perpetrators (Bryant-Davis and Ocampo 2005: 488; Pizarro et al. 2006; Kessler et al. 1999). The victims of the racialized rape and assault of legal segregation often experience depression, anger, anxiety, or fear, just some of the symptoms of "segregation stress syndrome."

We have here shown from the interviews just a few of the many instances of psychological impact on our respondents, those who suffered the pain and long-term consequences of the racial violence that occurred during legal segregation.

12.13   Conclusion

In this article, we have documented some aspects of the history of legal segregation, using in part the life narratives of older African Americans who lived through that extreme apartheid system. We have discussed the extreme racial etiquette and racial violence that was used to enforce such social practices. Racial violence that was central to legal segregation included thousands of lynchings, hundreds of thousands of rapes, much loss of life, and much loss of property, all at the hands of whites. Historically, African Americans frequently resisted legal segregation through non-violent civil disobedience organized in Black churches and the NAACP.

Legal segregation ended, officially, less than 40 years ago with emergence of the Civil Rights Movement and the passage of major civil rights laws, the last in 1968. For the most part, African Americans are no longer worried about individual and organized acts of random racial violence such as rape and lynching. However, the deeper reality is that the racially violent experience of legal segregation did profoundly affect and shape the lives of older African Americans in collective and individualized ways, to the present day. How much the participants were affected is evident in the poignant and emotional ways in which they have shared their life narratives. African Americans found creative ways to counter the everyday customs and laws of legal segregation. They developed strategies such as deference, obedience, and avoidance. Presently, elderly African Americans are passing the strategies that they learned from their parents on to their children and grandchildren. However, in spite of everything African Americans endured during legal segregation, some have lived to tell what such oppressive life was like for them.

References

Allen, I. M. (1996). PTSD among African Americans. In A. Marsella, M. Friedman, E. Gerrity, & R. Scurfield (Eds.), *Ethnocultural aspects of posttraumatic stress disorder: Issues, research, and clinical applications* (pp. 209–238). Washington, DC: American Psychiatric Association.

Allen, J., Lewis, J., Litwack., & Als, H. (2000). *Without sanctuary: Lynching photography in America.* Santa Fe, New Mexico: Twin Palms Publishers.

Bell, D. (2004). *Silent covenants: Brown v. board of education and the unfulfilled hopes for racial reform.* New York: Oxford University Press.

Blee, K. M. (2005). Racial violence in the United States. *Ethnic and Racial Studies, 28,* 599–619.

Brown v. (1954). Board of education of Topeka, 347 U.S. 483, 495.

Brown, T. N., Williams, D. R., Jackson, J. S., Torres, M., Sellers, S. L., & Brown, K. T. (2000). Being black and feeling blue: The mental consequences of racial discrimination. *Race and Society, 29*(2), 117–131.

Brundage, F. W. (2005). *The Southern past: A clash of race and memory.* Cambridge, Massachusetts: The Belknap Press of Harvard University Press.

Bryant-Davis, T., & Ocampo, C. (2005). Racist incident-based trauma. *The Counseling Psychologist, 33*(4), 479–500.

Bufacchi, V. (2005). Two concepts of violence. *Political Studies Review, 3,* 193–204.

Burke, P. J. (1991). Identity processes and social stress. *American Sociological Review, 56,* 836–849.

Chafe, W. H. (2001). *Remembering Jim Crow.* New York: New Press.

Christopoulos, V. P. (2002). *The relationship between exposure to violence and posttraumatic stress disorder symptoms in inner city youth* (Ph.D. dissertation). Department of Psychology, Pace University, New York.

Dray, P. (2003). *At the hands of persons unknown: The lynching of Black America.* New York: The Modern Day Library.

Ellis, A. E., & Ellis, L. C. (2003). *The trial of ruby Mccollum.* Indiana: First Books Library.

Eyerman, R. (2001). *Cultural trauma: Slavery and the formation of African American Identity.* New York: Cambridge University Press.

Faulkner, A. O. (1982). *When I was comin' up: An oral history of aged blacks.* Connecticut: Shoe String Press.

Feagin, J. R. (2000). *Racist America.* New York: Routledge.

Feagin, J. R. (2006). *Systemic racism: A theory of oppression.* New York: Routledge.

Feagin, J. R., & McKinney, K. D. (2003). *The many costs of racism.* New York: Rowman and Littlefield Publishers.

Feagin, J. R., & Sikes, M. P. (1994). *Living With Racism.* Beacon Press: MA, Boston.

Folmsbee, S. J. (1949). The origin of the first Jim Crow law. *The Journal of Southern History, 15,* 235–247.

Ginzburg, R. (1962). *100 Years of Lynchings.* Baltimore, Maryland: Black Classic Press.

Gray, J. A. (1987). *The psychology of fear and stress.* New York: Cambridge University Press.

Irons, P. (2002). *Jim Crow's children: The broken promise of the brown decision.* New York: Penguin Group.

Jackman, M. (2002). Violence in social life. *Annual Review of Sociology, 28,* 387–415.

Johnson, C. (1943). *Backgrounds to patterns of Negro segregation.* New York: Harper and Row.

Kelly, B. D. (2005). Structural violence and schizophrenia. *Social Science and Medicine, 61,* 721–730.

Kennedy, S. (1959). *Jim Crow guide to the U.S.A.* London: Camelot Press.

Kessler, R. C., Mickelson, K. D., & Williams, D. R. (1999). The prevalence, distribution, and mental health correlates of perceived discrimination in the United States. *Journal of Health and Social Behavior, 40,* 208–230.

Krieger, N., Smith, K., Naishadham, D., Hartman, C., & Barbeau, E. M. (2005). Experiences of discrimination: Validity and reliability of a self-report measure for Population health research on racism and health. *Social Science and Medicine, 61,* 1576–1596.

Litwick, L. F. (1979). Been in the storm so long: The aftermath of slavery. New York: Vintage Books.

Litwick, L. F. (1999). *Trouble in mind.* New York: Random House.

Mason-Schrock, D. (1996). Transsexuals' narrative construction of the 'true self'. *Social Psychology Quarterly, 3,* 176–192.

McDevitt, J., Levin, J., & Bennett, S. (2002). Hate crime offenders. *Journal of Social Issues, 58,* 303–318.

Mills, T. L., & Edwards, C. (2002). A critical review of research on the mental health status of older African Americans. *The Journal of Aging and Society, 22,* 273–304.

Myers, M. A., & Thompson, V. L. S. (2000). The impact of violence exposure on African American youth in context. *Youth & Society, 32,* 253–267.

Packard, J. (2002). *American nightmare: The history of Jim Crow.* New York: St. Martin's Press.

Patterson, J. T. (2001). *Brown V. Board of education: A civil rights milestone and it's troubled legacy.* New York: Oxford University Press.

Pizarro, J., Silver, R. C., & Prause, J. (2006). Physical and mental health costs of traumatic war experiences among civil war veterans. *Archives of General Psychiatry, 63,* 193–200.

Plessy v. Ferguson. (1896). 163 U.S. 537.

Smythe, H. H. (1948). The concept of Jim Crow. *Social Forces, 27,* 45–48.

Thompson-Miller, R., Feagin, J. R., & Picca, L. (2014). *Jim Crow's legacy: The lasting impact of segregation.* New York: Rowman and Littlefield Publishers.

Tolnay, S. E., & Beck, E. M. (1992). Racial violence and black migration in the American South, 1910–1930. *American Sociological Review, 57,* 103–116.

Tolnay, S. E. & Beck, E. M. (1995). *A festival of violence: An analysis of Southern Lynchings,* 1882–1890. Chicago: University of Illinois Press.

Wang, L. (1999). The complexities of 'hate.' *The Ohio State Law Journal, 60,*799–900.

Williams, D. R., & Williams-Morris, R. (2000). Racism and mental health: The African American experience. *Ethnicity & Health, 5,* 243–268.

Woodward, V. C. (1974). *The strange career of Jim Crow.* New York: Oxford University Press.

United Statesians: The Nationalism of Empire

13

Melanie E. L. Bush

Contents

For a full exploration of the subject matter explored in this chapter, see Bush and Bush (2015). *Tensions in the American Dream: Rhetoric, Reverie or Reality.*

M. E. L. Bush (✉)
Department of Sociology, Adelphi University,
Garden City, NY, USA
e-mail: bush@adelphi.edu

Abstract

Events of the 21st century have led to heightened contestation about the meaning and parameters of U.S. nationalism, patriotism, and loyalty. At a time when questioning and dissent are viewed as matters of social responsibility among some and as criminal acts by others, when the U.S. issues travel bans for several majority-Muslim countries and immigrants who have contributed significantly to the nation are increasingly subject to deportation, we can easily say that "notions of nation", who "belongs" and the very character of the U.S. are in transition. What functions do nationalism, patriotism, and citizenship serve in a nation founded and built upon the presumption of empire? With this question in mind, this chapter explores this history within the context of the emergence of coloniality and the modern world system and examines its contemporary expression.

13.1 Introduction

Events at the turn of the 21st century have led to heightened contestation about the meaning and parameters of U.S. nationalism, patriotism, and loyalty. At a time when the phrase "Support the Troops" signifies interpretations both of sending more soldiers to war and bringing home those already in combat, when questioning and dissent are viewed as matters of social responsibility among at least some public officials and as criminal acts by others, when this "nation of immigrants" spawns a new generation of "minute-men" to defend national borders, when countries issue travel advisories about visiting the U.S. and we can easily say that "notions of nation", who "belongs" and the very character of the U.S. are in transition. Was the United States ever a veritable multicultural union? Can it be?[1] Does claiming national allegiance provide a vantage point from which to stand for peace, justice, and equality (Nussbaum 1996,

136) or does it divide us within and from people of other nations? What functions do nationalism, patriotism, and citizenship serve in today's interconnected world in a nation founded and built upon the presumption of empire?

With these questions in mind, this chapter addresses the origins and development of the U.S. nation and empire within the context of the emergence of coloniality and the modern world system; the national founding principles and their lived reality; the belief in U.S. exceptionalism and the creation of patriotism; the meaning of "belonging"; the "American"[2] Dream and the portrait of a "nation of immigrants."

13.2 "America" the Beautiful: The Origins and Development of a Nation and Empire

Is the United States a meritocracy-how frequently does hard work lead to success? Do those who work at the hardest jobs with the longest hours reap the greatest rewards? Portrayed as the perfect democracy, what are the origin and development myths of this nation and empire?[3] Bacon's Rebellion, the Declaration of Independence,[4] the Constitution, institution of slavery, legislations such the Dred Scott decision, People v. Hall, the Treaty of Guadalupe Hidalgo, Jim Crow, and the ruling in Brown v. The Board Education provide markers in the history of how nation, white supremacy, and empire have been intrinsically linked in the development of the U.S. nation. Each of these signifies a moment or an event that established, that reproduced the racial order in the context of

---

[1]The 2016 election campaign brings this question to the forefront of national conversation. Candidate Donald Trump calls to close borders with a variety of restrictions for particular populations such as Mexicans and Muslims. One answer can be found in Rick Tyler's campaign for Congress in Tennessee to "Make America White Again". http://ricktylerforcongress.com/2016/06/07/the-billboard-strategy/.

[2]For a discussion critical of the use of "American" as equated with the United States, see page 301.

[3]Elizabeth Martinez speaks of the origin narratives that every society creates "to explain that society to itself and the world with a set of mythologized stories and symbols." She explores the "American" origin narrative in detail (1996) and attributes this labeling to Roxanne Dunbar Ortiz.

[4]Horne's (2014), provides evidence that contrary to popular rhetoric; the founding fathers' motivation for breaking from England was primarily to protect the institution of slavery.

the United States. The story of "America is entrenched with and built upon numerous presumptions of exceptionalism and superiority. From the early years of European conquest, enslavement, and expansion, "nation" has been equated with a white racial portrait, contradicting earlier notions of enlightenment, common unity, and belonging in the U.S. Did "all" ever mean ALL, did "men" ever mean "human," and did "equal" ever really mean equal opportunity, treatment or outcome?[5] Indeed, "for two-thirds of U.S. history, the majority of the domestic population was not eligible for full U.S. citizenship because of their race, original nationality, lack of property, or gender" (Bush and Bush 2015, 5).

The equation (of nation, white supremacy, and Eurocentrism) was the foundational justification for trespass, genocide, domination, exploitation, and entitlements to land, labor, and wealth. As the colonies and then the nation were created, struggles occurred about whose interests would be served, and who could claim what rights. The nation and its laws were established (however contested) with ideas about who would be protected. Subsequently in the 19th and 20th centuries, the demand made of European immigrants was to become like "us," like it or not, but for peoples from other parts of the globe it was that you will never be like "us" (Smedley 1993, 32). The case was built about who belonged and who did not, who was "same" and who was "different," "civil," and "savage"-who could own land, who could read, who could be in charge of and exploit other people's labor and who could not. These questions were resolved in the naturalized hierarchies of race, language, culture, and gender and through an ambiguous concept of national belonging, whereby core values such as "democracy," "equality," "freedom," and "justice" were evoked on behalf of "all" and implemented on behalf of "some." Much of this hierarchy and these presumptions remain intact in the second decade of the twenty-first century articulations about the economy, prison system, political arena and everyday life. As Michelle Alexander, legal scholar states in a recent article about what is needed at this moment in time,

> This nation was founded on the idea that some lives don't matter. Freedom and justice for some, not all. That's the foundation. Yes, progress has been made in some respects, but it hasn't come easy. There's an unfinished revolution waiting to be won.[6]

The question is whether this revolution is national or global, institutional or systemic, collective or individual or all simultaneously.

Patriotism in this context has demanded unquestioning loyalty, presumed European superiority, and the equation of might and right. This ideology of nation has disallowed discussion of the structuring of society and put forth an elusive notion of national identity evoked as needed to enlist complicity with the whims of the dominant elite. The question of who belongs and the corresponding entitlements vacillates between tangible notions of naturalization and citizenship, unambiguous birthright, and the ambiguous notion that being "American" corresponds to a particular belief system. Election year discourse in 2016 demonstrates continued contestation about what being "American" means with unambiguous rhetoric demanding complicity and conformity with white racial and male-centered norms.

The controversy over belonging and inclusion was embedded in the Declaration of Independence. The early years of the U.S. nation as described by William J. Wilson, in 1860, "… they the white people and they alone, find its boundaries too circumscribed for their greedy grasp. Possessing acres by the millions, yet they would elbow us and all others off of what we possess, to give them room for what they cannot occupy" (Roediger 1998, 65); Frederick Douglass in his famous speech, "What to the Slave Is Your Fourth of July?" (Douglass 1970, 349); and Jacobs (1861) in her discussion of the annual practice of "muster," a time when armed whites terrorized the enslaved population in anticipation

---

[5]For an excellent engagement of this question see: http://www.truth-out.org/opinion/item/36684-three-comforting-myths-about-the-declaration-of-independence.

[6]https://medium.com/embrace-race/something-more-is-required-of-us-now-what-58e8ec2885b8#.3utv444x5.

of revolts. She suggests that this institution served to unite whites across class lines (Roediger 1998, 336); by so doing, it also defined the parameters of citizenship.

These examples of the centering and privileging of the white European experience have been endemic "not just a by-product of white supremacy but an imperative of racial domination" (Roediger 1998, 6). The new nation of the United States was built using the labor of Africans, Chinese, exploiting the land and natural resources of indigenous peoples and Mexican territories, simultaneously excluding most of these groups from citizenship and the benefits of "belonging." Despite entering as "not quite white", immigrants from Europe in the 19th century were ultimately integrated into the expanding industrial economy where there was opportunity for upward mobility. Through this economic assignment, and the policies and programs of the early 20th century that provided further opportunities and supports for upward mobility such as the G. I. Bill and FHA loans, they were enlisted in a pan-ethnic racial "club" and "became party to strategies of social closure that maintained others' exclusion" (Waldinger 2001, 20).

National identification in the United States has always been inherently tied to racial status and citizenship and citizenship, even as articulated in the French revolution was both inclusive and exclusive and contradictory in both theory and practice. In *Tensions in the American Dream: Rhetoric, Reverie or Reality*, Bush and Bush argue that it is precisely this dynamic that underlies the contemporary historical crisis.

The reason for this disjuncture between rhetoric and reality is simple: Historical capitalism requires social inequality, though social stability is best served by public perception of equality of opportunity *and* the existence of real opportunity for upward mobility, at least for *some*. But upward opportunity for *all* would place a great deal of pressure on employers to pay higher wages. In a competitive economic system, employers of wage labor seek to impose some restraints on the pressure to pay higher wages.... inequality is a fundamental reality of the modern world-system, as has been the case for every known historical system... particular to historical capitalism is that

equality and democracy have been proclaimed as its objective, and indeed as its achievement.... (2015, 5–6)

The initial emergence of the notion of European racial superiority and racial exploitation corresponded to the appearance of the modern world system and coloniality in the long 16th century (Cox 1948, 322). While contact and interaction across geographically distinct populations occurred during earlier times, there is no evidence of race prejudice even in the Hellenistic empire, which had extended further into Africa than any other European empire (Cox 1948, 322; Grosfoguel 2013). The 16th century was "a historic watershed in global relations between Black and white people" and states that neither racial slavery nor systemic white racism existed prior to this, although color prejudice was present in some places (Drake 1987, xxiii).

While interethnic interactions endure a long history, in the past they did not necessarily reflect inevitable conflict, competition, or struggle (Smedley 1998, 690). Identities were constructed by a wide range of characteristics including, but not limited to, place of birth, language, kinship, religion, or occupation. They were generally context-specific and malleable up to the 17th century (Smedley 1998, 691, 2). Up to the 17th century, Blackness was not a stigma, nor was race essentialized in the way that it later came to be (Harrison 1998, 620, 621). In an extremely important article, "The Structure of Knowledge in Westernized Universities Epistemic Racism/ Sexism and the Four Genocides/Epistemicides of the Long 16th Century", Ramon Grosfoguel describes the critical events that mark this historical moment (2013). These catastrophes lay the ground for the structuring of relations between peoples and the racist and sexist ideologies and rationales that were to be considered valid from this point, throughout modernity from the colonial period forward. This became a global and naturalized organization of power in the modern world system. We see the evidence in contemporary times. He explains what happened and how.

With the emergence of the world capitalist system, the colonial exploration of the globe, and the beginning of the European trade of Africans in parts of the "new" world, racial notions were used to justify the subordination and exploitation of large numbers of people who formed a labor pool for building settlements and agricultural cultivation. During the earliest period in the development of capitalism, "The white man had no conception of himself as being capable of developing the superior culture of the world-the concept 'white man' had not yet its significant social definition-the Anglo-Saxon, the modern master race, was then not even in the picture" (Cox 1948, 327). Racial dynamics, however, quickly developed within the context of the expansion of capitalism and colonial settlements. This process initially took the form of a European center with Euro-dominated colonies. The link between national development under capitalism and white supremacy was forged at this time.

Ultimately, the British settler colony in North America evolved into the United States, which then became the new center (Drake 1987). A vivid example of the process of racial development was the fateful Bacon's Rebellion in 1676 in Virginia, which established early boundaries distinguishing Africans, Europeans, and native peoples (Zinn 1995, 37–59). This event is generally portrayed solely as a response to common exploitation and oppression, as African and European bond-laborers rebelled to demand an end to servitude. However, another key component of this struggle was an orchestrated attempt by the dominant elites to drive a wedge between these groups and the native population. Any combination of these forces was a tremendous threat to the white planters, whose wealth was great compared to that of the general white population. Poor Europeans had much more in common with enslaved Africans, and a potential alliance could have been disastrous for those in power. "In the early years of slavery, especially, before racism as a way of thinking was firmly ingrained, while white indentured servants were often treated as badly as Black slaves, there was a possibility of cooperation" (Zinn 1995, 37). The plantation bourgeoisie

responded to the threat of coalition by offering European laborers a variety of previously denied benefits, such as amnesty for those who rebelled, corn, cash, and muskets for those finishing their servitude, the right to bear arms, and the opportunity to join slave patrol militias and receive monetary awards.

> They constituted the police patrol who could ride with planters, and now and then exercise unlimited force upon recalcitrant or runaway slaves; and then, too, there was always a chance that they themselves might also become planters by saving money, by investment, by the power of good luck; the only heaven that attracted them was the life of the great Southern planter. (Du Bois 1979, 27)

This may be viewed as the nation's first "affirmative action" policy (Harrison 1998, 621). These actions were taken to quell this potentially dangerous alliance and as a means for control. Racism on the part of poor whites became a practical matter (Zinn 1995, 56). The explicit use of race as a justification for white supremacy was implemented as a tool to divide and conquer and framed the development of nation from the very beginning. Prior to this period, there was little advantage and therefore little motivation for poor whites to ally themselves with the ruling powers. At this time, though, they were accorded "social, psychological and political advantages" calculated to alienate them from their fellow African bondsmen (Morgan 1975, 331–333, 344; Du Bois 1979, 700). Racism was implemented as a means of control to establish and then maintain the structure of social organization in the "new" world. Racial domination became encoded in the process of nation-state building for the United States as "Blacks were sold out to encourage white unity and nationalist loyalty to the state" (Marx 1998, 267). Slavery, therefore, played a critical role in providing a justification for the unification of whites racially as a nation (Marx 1998, 267), a pattern that continues to impact national identity, notions of whiteness, and formulations of race in society today. Whites were told that their whiteness rendered them "superior," and to maintain this status they needed to place their allegiances with those in power who had the resources and could divvy up benefits.

"During America's colonial era the ideal of white identity was male, English, Protestant, and privileged. Over time this ideal evolved into free, white, male, Christian, propertied and franchised. These characteristics developed into a norm that subsequently became synonymous with American." (Davis 2005, 155, citing Babb 1998). This identity was also intertwined with notions of freedom, thereby reinforcing the relationship between whiteness and Americanness (Davis 2005, 155). "There were perfectly strategic reasons to allow the identity of American to evolve in opposition to blackness-exploitation, appropriation and subordination of Blacks and Black labor" (Davis 2005, 156).

While particularly applied as a black-white polarization, this ideological formulation of race was also flexible. A stigma of racial inferiority could be invoked as needed to maintain divisions and enforce a social hierarchy. For example, during the mid-19th century, Chinese workers were used as the primary labor force in building California's railroads. Their subsequent brutalization, subjugation, and exclusion were framed overwhelmingly in racial terms (Smedley 1993, 268). This stigma was similarly applied to native and Mexican peoples who were characterized as savages, unfit to own and govern their land "coincidentally" at the time that those lands were desired by the wealthy elite justified by the narrative of manifest destiny. The "Trail of Tears" and the annexation of one third of Mexican land are brutal testaments to this history of internal colonization, land appropriation, and genocide. That political discourse in the second decade of the twenty-first century asserts that Mexicans should go back to where they came from sheds light on the irony that it is indeed Europeans who are on land not their own.

Throughout the 18th and the early 19th centuries, the formation and consolidation of working-class whiteness (Roediger 1999, 14) and "American" identity were founded not just on economic exploitation but also on racial folklore (Du Bois 1970). Du Bois describes this dynamic eloquently:

It must be remembered that the white group of laborers, while they received a low wage, were compensated in part by a sort of public and psychological wage. They were given public deference and titles of courtesy because they were white. They were admitted freely with all classes of white people to public functions, public parks, and the best schools. The police were drawn from their ranks, and the courts, dependent upon their votes, treated them with such leniency as to encourage lawlessness. Their vote selected public officials and while this had small effect upon the economic situation, it had great effect upon their personal treatment and the deference shown them. (Du Bois 1979, 700, 701)

During this period, various theoretical trends emerged in the social and biological sciences to further justify this ordering of the world. "These models created a new form of social identity as the concept of 'race' developed as a way to rationalize the conquest and brutal treatment of native populations and the institution of slavery" (Smedley 1998, 697). Another dimension was the emergence of "American English" during the early part of the 19th century.

When the new nation formed, British culture was still dominant, and it was not yet clear what it meant to be American. (Noah) Webster thought it was vital to shake off "foreign manners" and build an independent national culture. ... Webster's political purpose in writing his dictionaries was promoting national unity. ... He believed that a "federal language" could be a "band of national union." (Cohen 2006)

This perspective played a significant role in the much later emergence of the "English-only" movement and the depiction of those speaking languages other than English as less "American" and worthy despite the fact that the United States does not have an officially declared language. By the mid-19th century this arbitrary ranking of peoples and racial ideology had diffused around much of the world (Smedley 1998, 695), which reinforced the emerging notions of who was "American." A vivid example of this was the 1903 "World's Fair" where being "American" and being "white" were explicitly viewed as superior in stark contrast to the ancestors and inhabitants of the colonized world of those considered lesser beings, for example, Filipinos and Africans.[7]

The end of the 19th century and first half of the 20th were marked by two significant U.S. Supreme Court decisions concerning the Fourteenth Amendment,[8] signifying important shifts in the racial order within the United States (Baker 1998, 2). In 1896, Plessy v. Ferguson codified the practice of "separate but equal," and in 1954, the Brown v. Board of Education ruling overturned it.

> The social context from which turn-of-the-century constructs of race emerged-industrialization, poll taxes, public lynching, unsafe working conditions, and Jim Crow segregation-at the same time gave rise to a professional anthropology that espoused racial inferiority and, as a consequence, supported and validated the status quo. (Baker 1998, 3)

While Baker is speaking of anthropology, much of his critique also applies to other scholarly disciplines and state policy as well. The legitimacy of the racial order was validated by westernized forms of knowledge (Grosfoguel 2013) and inscribed in "science" and social practices that reinforced and reproduced the concepts of race, hierarchy, and nation to the benefit of few and detriment of many. Simultaneously, many of the symbolic representations now referred to as the epitome of US patriotism emerged.

Like the idea of the American Dream and democracy, the American flag has come to symbolize the elevated status of the United States in the global order. The flag's symbolic meaning has been traced initially to the period after the First Reconstruction and through World War I (O'Leary 1999, 7–9) with many legal and political struggles over the definitions of loyal or disloyal citizens. During the period from 1870 to 1920, there was disagreement and conflict over which icons, heroes, events, and identities

constituted the national memory and the historical narrative. The "Pledge of Allegiance" was written in 1891; the "Star-Spangled Banner" was taken as the national anthem in 1931 with points of contradiction and ambivalence about American ideals throughout (O'Leary 1999). Francis Scott Key himself was a white supremacist, slave owner and firm defender of the institution of slavery.[9]

The turn of the 20th century marked a period of contestation about who was to be designated "white," as a huge influx of immigrants from Europe and other parts of the globe tested the boundaries of citizenry and racial identity. Paralleling the pace of immigration at the end of the century, the first decade of the 20th century witnessed the largest number of immigrants (8.8 million) admitted into the United States (Kraly and Miyares 2001, 47). The vast majority (92%) of these people originated from Europe. During the last decade of the 20th century, 7.6 million people immigrated to the United States: from Europe, 17.4%; from Asia, 38.9%; from North America, 33.4%; from South America, 6.6%; from Africa, 4.0%; and from Oceania, 0.7% (Kraly and Miyares 2001, 49).

At issue during both periods, was the question of how they would be integrated and racially designated in U.S. society. The nation's expanding industries needed labor; mass immigration made cheap labor easily available. Immigrants were exploited but also "used as an instrument for more effective exploitation of others, whether native or immigrant. For this reason, immigrant workers were sometimes compelled to put aside their ethnic loyalties" (Steinberg 2001, 38). African, Asian, and Mexican workers were used as low-paid labor source for the least skilled jobs and sectors and established the infrastructure for industrialization and modernization. European immigrants worked primarily within the modern industrial sector that strategically provided them with opportunities for upward mobility (Blauner 1972, 62). This reality challenges the popular

---

[7]A thorough exploration of this can be found in the California Newsreel Film "Race: The Power of an Illusion (2003), Part II: The Stories We Tell". http://www.newsreel.org/nav/title.asp?tc=CN0149.

[8]The Fourteenth Amendment "enshrined in the Constitution the ideas of birthright citizenship and equal rights for all Americans" (Foner 1998, 105).

[9]http://www.huffingtonpost.com/jefferson-morley/francis-scott-key_b_1645878;.html http://www.alternet.org/culture/o-say-can-you-see.

notion that "all Americans 'start at the bottom'" and work their way up the ladder. The racial labor principle designated a different bottom for different groups (Blauner 1972, 62, 63). The slogan "nation of immigrants" therefore describes most predominantly the European experience despite the fact that Jews, Italians, and Irish were not fully accepted as whites.

During this period Du Bois significantly contributed to a paradigm shift in the social sciences toward recognition of the connection between race and the concept of culture, united in an understanding of economics and politics (Baker 1998, 107–110). He described race as a social relationship, integral to capitalism, and the ultimate paradox of democracy constructed to reinforce and reproduce patterns of systemic inequality (Du Bois 1986 (1903), 372). "Back of the problem of race and color, lies a greater problem which both obscures and implements it: and that is the fact that so many civilized persons are willing to live in comfort even if the price of this is poverty, ignorance, and disease of the majority of their fellowmen: That to maintain this privilege men have waged war until today" (Du Bois 1953, xiv). Race and nation have always been intrinsically linked in the trajectory of the U.S. nation.

During the first half of the 20th century, an ethnicity-based paradigm was often used to understand social relations in the United States emerging as an extension of challenges made to biologistic and social Darwinist conceptions of race (Omi and Winant 1994, 12). Ethnicity was offered as a description of group formation that focused on culture and descent rather than biology and on the process of migration and the adaptation of immigrants in the United States. In 1913, Robert Park of the University of Chicago, a leading theorist within this group, asserted that by their second generation, Poles, Lithuanians, and Norwegians were indistinguishable from native-born Americans (Schaefer 1995, 111). Park projected that ethnicity would dissolve as immigrants assimilated into society reflecting a pattern of integration into U.S. society, which he labeled the "race relations cycle." This involved stages of contact, accommodation, assimilation, and amalgamation achieved through intermarriage (Steinberg 2001, 47). Park considered all modern nationalities to be a mixture of several groups. According to this idea, ethnicity was expected to disappear into a new American culture.

This period marked a new stage in the consolidation of whiteness in the United States as a racialized category such that European Americans were transformed into a panethnicity that represented the distancing of individuals from their national origin, heritage, and language, and being grouped as "white" (Alba 1990, 312) and American. Hence, too, white classification was clearly linked to national identity.

Two books in particular drew attention to the primacy of race within U.S. society and signaled a paradigm shift from the belief in biological to cultural explanations of racial difference. In *Man's Most Dangerous Myth: The Fallacy of Race* (1945), M. F. Ashley Montagu, a physical anthropologist, asserted:

> The idea of "race" was not so much the deliberate creation of a caste seeking to defend its privileges against what was regarded as an inferior social caste as it was the strategic elaboration of erroneous notions, which had long been held by many slaveholders. What was once a social difference was now turned into a biological difference, which would serve, it was hoped, to justify and maintain the social difference. (1945, 20)

Gunnar Myrdal's *American Dilemma* (1944) put forth a call for racial democratization, emphasizing the need for the assimilation of African Americans:

> If America in actual practice could show the world a progressive trend by which the Negro finally became integrated into modern democracy, all mankind would be given faith again-it would have reason to believe that peace, progress and order are feasible. America is free to choose whether the Negro shall remain her liability or become her opportunity. (Myrdal 1964, 1021–1022)[10]

---

[10]W. E. B. Du Bois originally came up with the idea for this comprehensive study of race relations; however, his proposal was turned down. Subsequently the General Education Board (GEB)-connected Carnegie Corporation decided to fund Myrdal and not Du Bois with the implicit explanation that, despite his expertise, Du Bois was too involved with the subject (Donate et al. 2002, 227).

Here again, the racial order was embedded into the question of national identity. Myrdal's study became "the blueprint for state-based racial reform in the postwar era, strongly influencing debates about segregation and the runner-up to the Brown decision" (Winant 2001, 158). His suggestion that racism revealed a contradiction between American ideals and practice was considered a major advance at the time it was written. It later became apparent that this work marked a shift in emphasis from a biological to cultural focus still evident today (Steinberg 2001, 265). Less discussed was how his work illuminated tensions within the prevailing image of nation. How would the United States reconcile the embeddedness of white supremacy in its structure with the rhetoric of democracy and justice? (Bush and Bush 2015).

In *Beyond the Melting Pot* (1963), Glazer and Moynihan asserted that immigrant groups do not "melt" into U.S. society but are transformed into new social forms based on political interests rather than on culture or heritage (Omi and Winant 1994, 18). New communities were unlike each other and unlike those from where they migrated. Moynihan and Glazer argued that the United States had developed a pluralist model that acknowledged differences but emphasized cooperation. By the 1970s, they spoke of ethnicity as a social category that allowed contemporary forms of group expression based on distinctiveness and, in turn, provided an opening to demand rights based on the group's character and self-perceived needs (Glazer and Moynihan 1975, 3). Ethnicity was presented in the abstract, decontextualized from the historical and structural implications of embedded hierarchies. *Beyond the Melting Pot* examined five ethnic groups in New York City and implied (sometimes explicitly) that the American commitment to progress and achievement was justly and equally apportioned. The book asserted that inherent cultural norms, ideology, and values led to the success and progress of one group but not another. Structural relations of the social system were neither considered nor deemed significant in their analysis (Mullings 1978, 11). National identity was normalized and centered in the experience of European immigrants whose upward mobility was deemed the outcome of their particular cultures and values as opposed to social policies that paved the way for their integration into mainstream white society. National identification came much more fluidly to those who reaped the benefits of "belonging."

Moynihan and Glazer equated the histories and rationalized the social inequities of Jewish, Italian, and Irish immigrants ("ethnics"), Puerto Ricans, and African Americans. While the concept of the "undeserving poor" had long been established, deriving from period of early capitalism when pauperism was the fate of large number of people who forfeited their land and were displaced to the city, it was during the period of the 1960s that the concept of the "culture of poverty" emerged. In formulating this framework, Oscar Lewis compared groups of people who are poor, and whom he characterized as having negative traits, values, and norms, to those who were poor but do not appear to have such negative attributes. He wrote: "The culture or subculture of poverty comes into being in a variety of historical contexts. Most commonly it develops when a stratified social and economic system is breaking down or is being replaced by another, as in the case of the transition from feudalism to capitalism or during the industrial revolution" (Lewis 1961, xxv). Lewis elsewhere states that the causes and consequences of poverty are a direct result of the total social system, in particular, industrial capitalism (Lewis 1969, 190–191). He asserts that the structure of society is the most important factor in the perpetuation of poverty. Lewis's description of the characteristics of what he called the "culture of poverty" included a high degree of family disintegration, disorganization, resignation, and fatalism. Unfortunately, his work was used as a justification to blame individuals and groups exhibiting these characteristics and to justify inequality through an explanation of the inherent cultural weakness of the poor (Lewis 1969, 191) rather than as a means to critique the system within which these characteristics appear.

This (mis)interpretation of Lewis's work parallels the underlying assumptions, particularly about the weakness of the African American culture, in Moynihan and Glazer's writings (1963) as indicated above and in Moynihan's later writings (1965) about a "tangle of pathology" characterizing Black families as having negative, self-perpetuating values. These theories bolstered popular rhetoric that continued to emphasize the superiority of whites and white (ethnic) culture and the inferiority of African Americans and Latinos in particular. This period also brought the development of the narrative of Asians as "model minorities" despite the stark segmentation in economic circumstances within different communities as well as the brutal history of tentative belonging experienced by this group as symbolized by the internment of Japanese Americans during World War II. With the increasing predominance of discourse depicting the United States as a meritocracy, the culture-of-poverty framework provided an explanation for why certain groups received benefits such as access to better jobs, education, higher incomes, and more wealth and why others did not.

The dynamics shaping mainstream discourse from the late 1960s to the mid-1970s were complex. Many groups and individuals were calling for a new vision of society based on social equality and justice for all and concern for the common good. This led to the characterization of this period as a "Second Reconstruction." The prevalence of the culture-of-poverty frame-work reflected a conservative influence that sought to command the parameters of thinking about the poor in an attempt to limit the power of a vision of society concerned with the common good, so well-articulated by many popular movements of this period (Di Leonardo 1999, 59; Steinberg 1999, 222). The ruling elite was clear about what was at stake should structural factors responsible for the unequal organization of society become revealed.[11] The image

of the United States as the land of opportunity and locus of democracy epitomized what would be vulnerable. As options expanded for white ethnics, allowing for significant upward mobility, justifications were needed to explain persistent inequality evident relative to all other groups.

During the late 1960s, "momentum built within white ethnic neighborhoods to the extent that their concerns and grievances demanded the attention of the society at large" (Ryan 1973, 1).

> Partly it [was] a consequence of the growing discontent among white ethnics with their socio-economic position in America, partly it was one facet of the broader movement toward self- definition on behalf of many groups within American society. ... It is in part a reaction to the social and political upheavals of the 1960s compounded by the inflationary economic spirals which followed. (Ryan 1973, 1)

The white ethnic position accepted the civil rights demand for outlawing discrimination, but not if it called for proactive or affirmative measures (Glazer and Moynihan 1963, 17; Omi and Winant 1994, 19). This perspective asserted that, "through hard work, patience and delayed gratification, etc. Blacks could carve out their own rightful place in American society" (Omi and Winant 1994, 19) and thereby echoed the culture-of-poverty argument from the perspective of white panethnicity. Ethnic identification by whites was constituted in a form of "white backlash" against the social programs that were set up as part of or as a result of the Civil Rights Act (1964), Voters Rights Act (1965), Immigration Act (1965), War on Poverty, and the Welfare Rights and nationalist movements of the 1960s. White ethnics (partially funded by the government as Heritage Societies) asserted that they too, suffered, and should be the recipients of social programs to address inequality in the United States.

Rather than the disappearance of ethnicity, there was resurgence and a demand for the recognition and acceptance of white ethnic groups as a political force. It is ironic that, although the antipoverty and civil rights programs and policies were portrayed as benefiting Blacks and Latinos exclusively, in fact, many

---

[11]Gil Scott-Heron describes this period, "Civil rights, women's rights, gay rights; it's all wrong. Call in the cavalry to disrupt this perception of freedom gone wild. First one wants freedom, then the whole damn world wants freedom" (Scott-Heron 1992). I owe thanks to Roderick D. Bush, professor of sociology, St. John's University, for a clarifying discussion on this topic, 5 January 2002.

white ethnics (particularly women) also bene-fited. For example, 75% of students initially admitted through the Open Admission Policy in the City University of New York were white ethnics who were the first in their family to attend college (Ryan 1973, 164; Lavin et al. 1979, 69). Information such as this was muted in the public arena as the "new ethnicity" move-ment took strong stands against such programs and demanded resources for their own groups. Emphasis was placed on ethnicity as the primary classification for discussing groups as carriers of culture.

These ideas then influenced the discourse about rights, equality, democracy, community self-definition, and resistance. By the mid-1970s, Moynihan and Glazer had reevaluated some of their own earlier thinking and put forth what is known as a "bootstraps model" (Omi and Winant 1994, 21). While this model recognized the injustice of slavery and racism, it articulated the idea that successes and failures of specific groups are a result of different norms that they brought to bear in dealing with circumstances they faced. Little else is deemed relevant, including the economic climate, the reigning ideological stance of benign neglect, or the existing social structures within which all groups exist (Omi and Winant 1994, 22). Black, Latino, and Asian ethnic or national categories are not viewed as notable (e.g., whether someone's family is from Haiti or Ethiopia; Peru or the Dominican Republic; China or India), whereas a white ethnic classification is considered significant (Omi and Winant 1994, 22). Ethnicity generally asserts an upward dis-tinction in status, whereas race signifies a downward distinction since whiteness is assumed to be "natural," and not "raced." By this time, national identity was very much infused with the presumptions of European belonging and marginalization of everyone else. "… English-men used science, literature and culture to transform themselves into Americans, and to fabricate a past that enabled them to emerge as the only people with a legacy, a culture and a history" (Davis 2005, 153).[12]

In *Ethnic Dilemma, 1964–1982,* Nathan Gla-zer writes that while the 1960s legislation intended to lead us to a colorblind society, it actually increased color consciousness in the United States and forced institutions to pay an increasingly high level of attention to race and ethnicity (Glazer 1983, 3). His writings signaled another political shift to the right and a further attack on measures intended to equalize resour-ces such as through school integration, affirma-tive action, and various social welfare programs. This trend has continued throughout the past two decades, with continuing consolidation of the conservative agenda articulated, for example, by the Project for a New American Century and polarization of wealth worldwide. The founda-tion and legitimacy of more recent waves of anti-immigration legislations throughout the country emanates from this ideological perspec-tive. The U.S. nation should be protected for those who "belong," especially its wealth. The painful irony is that for many immigrants, par-ticularly those from Latin and South America, their journeys have been precipitated by U.S. intervention and destabilization within their nations of origin (Gonzalez 2000). Similarly, the existence of minutemen established "to bring attention to the national crisis of illegal immi-gration" as "our nation was founded as a nation governed by the 'rule of law', not by the whims of mobs of ILLEGAL aliens who endlessly stream across U.S. borders"[13] provides harsh reminder of the hypocrisy in protecting Mexican land from Mexicans.

Theoretical notions of the culture of poverty have remained a central part of public discourse. In the 1990s this concept was utilized in attacks on the public sector and debates about welfare and higher education. Issues of standards and merit have been raised without the language of race yet implying cultural deficits of Black and Latino communities and implicitly presuming white superiority. Another explanation for group differences that reemerged during the 1970s is the concept of ethnicity. While previously

---

[12]Davis references Babb (1998).

[13]http://www.minutemanproject.com/ and http://www.minutemanproject.com/AboutMMP.html.

employed in discussions about the process of assimilation, this notion had not been consolidated as an explanation for differences in social position between "white ethnics" and people of color. This marked the emergence of oblique coding of race in literature, media, and discourse, allowing racialized policies and practices to function without the bluntness of explicit language. After all, who would argue against upholding "standards" for education or measures to make our communities "safe," or disagree with the need for "family values"?

This section briefly provided an overview of the history and development of the United States as a nation with identity firmly rooted in the European experience. The next explores the founding principles and their lived incarnations.

13.3 Democracy, Equality, Freedom and the Lived Experience of the U.S. Founding Principles

Deeply rooted in the concept of American identity is the notion of uniquely democratic values, idealized principles of freedom, equality and individualism and the belief that nowhere around the globe do people care so much about justice.[14] Popular discourse conveys implicit belief s and contradictory interpretation of these ideals. For example, democracy is often taken to mean very ordinary things for example being able to "say what you want to say, when you want to say it"[15] yet recent evidence of governmental surveillance outside legal constraints lays this commonplace "truth" to rest. Similarly a *New York Times* article posed, "Is Freedom Just Another Word for Many Things to Buy? That Depends on Your Class Status" (Schwartz et al. 2006, 14). For millions of people in the U.S. without health

insurance, jobs, or housing, freedom means being free to be sick, unemployed, or homeless.

The United States is believed to be unique-built on a democratic foundation and supported with inspirational mottos such as "all men are created equal" and "for the people, by the people." The *New York Times* asserts that "American Idealism … has always existed in a paradoxical linkage with greed, an alarming tolerance for social injustices and the racial blindness that allowed the same mind that shaped the Declaration of Independence to condone slavery" (Editorial, 31 December 1999).

Founded as it was by people fleeing religious and political persecution, the Bill of Rights explicitly stands for freedom of speech, including the right to dissent. Meanwhile such rights have been parceled out to those considered "deserving," in contrast to those who are not, throughout U.S. history. "'Us versus them' thinking easily becomes a general call for American supremacy, the humiliation of 'the other'" (Nussbaum 2001, 11). After September 11th, many who called for historical analysis were labeled seditious anti-American traitors.

In *An American Dilemma*, Gunnar Myrdal articulated the moral contradiction whereby the United States ideology professes an allegiance to democratic and egalitarian ideals while allowing the reality of racial discrimination to exist within its boundaries (1964[1944]). This contradiction points to the answer as to who is considered deserving, who counts, who belongs, who is visible, who matters, through whose eyes is policy set. The very issue of whose lives matter has become part of the national consciousness after the murder of Trayvon Martin and the emergence of the Black Lives Matter movement. Despite rhetoric of post-racialism, the blatant disregard for Black life continues to occur in plain view, and without consequence. Tax rebates to the rich that occur simultaneously with budget cuts to education, health, and welfare. While white supremacy is not the only factor operating, because the concentrations of whites and people of color correspond to the spectrum of economic well-being or lack thereof, these policies clearly demonstrate the racial order and

---

[14]In an interesting examination of "American Values," Gerda Lerner explores the dyads of equality and racism; open access versus elitism; federalism versus imperialism; individualism versus community; pluralism versus nativism, among others (1997, 74–92).

[15]Jacob, white male (Bush 2004, 113).

how it is embedded in the national policy.[16] Furthermore, because the overwhelming majority of whites in the United States deny the existence of racial inequality and uphold the idea that we live in a meritocracy, it is they who support the status quo notions about nation and empire, by accepting dominant explanations for poverty as being culturally based rather than structural and systemic. A Pew Research Center study in 2016 about Black and white views on race and inequality found that,

> …black and white adults have widely different perceptions about what life is like for blacks in the U.S. For example, by large margins, blacks are more likely than whites to say black people are treated less fairly in the workplace (a difference of 42 percentage points), when applying for a loan or mortgage (41 points), in dealing with the police (34 points), in the courts (32 points), in stores or restaurants (28 points), and when voting in elections (23 points). By a margin of at least 20% points, blacks are also more likely than whites to say racial discrimination (70% vs. 36%), lower quality schools (75% vs. 53%) and lack of jobs (66% vs. 45%) are major reasons that blacks may have a harder time getting ahead than whites.[17]

Simultaneously due to the dramatic and growing polarization of wealth throughout the last decades of the 20th century, the population at large has become increasingly aware of big business's control. However, it is a moment of tension as many people have been persuaded that inequality is inevitable even as they feel uneasy about that narrative because of their own personal experiences. This issue is thoroughly explored in *Tensions in the American Dream* (Bush and Bush 2015). Movements for equality, representation, and justice are viewed as clamoring for power, and will ultimately lead to the demise of unity and the "republic."[18]

Immigration patterns are portrayed as proof that the United States is "God blessed" (why else would everyone want to come here) and rarely is the question of how wealth accumulated in this part of the world discussed. The "hidden" history of imperialism is not part of the national psyche despite over 100 interventions in the last century.[19] In *Harvest of Empire,* Juan Gonzalez writes of the complicity of the United States in the generation of immigrants by supporting reactionary political regimes and protecting corporate interests that displace small farmers, but this story is never part of discussions of migration. The question "why" people migrate is not addressed in mainstream discourse-only that "America" is the place to be.

There exists a presumption that having a political structure presumably elected by the populous and a system of "checks" and "balances" in the governmental organization ensures democratic process and representation. However, when the class interests of both the "checks" and the "balances" are similar, there actually can be no real accountability to the population at large. Additionally, in recent elections both in 2008 and 2012 (aside from the issue of alleged election fraud), roughly 40% of the eligible population did not vote, of those who voted, just 51% supported the winning candidate.[20] In 2012, 53% of the voting age population voted overall.[21] In the 2000 presidential election, 38% of U.S. voting age citizens who had not completed high school voting compared to 77% of those with a bachelor's degree or higher (Livingston et al. 2003, VI). Interestingly in 2012, "For the first time ever, the black voter turnout rate in a presidential election exceeded the white voter turnout rate— 66.2% versus 64.1%."[22]

---

[16]Other observations of the difference between the ideal and the practice of democracy in the United States appear in the works of, for example, Frederick Douglass, Anna Julia Cooper, and David Walker (Blassingame 1982; Wiltse 1965; Lemert and Bhan 1998).

[17]http://www.pewsocialtrends.org/2016/06/27/on-views-of-race-and-inequality-blacks-and-whites-are-worlds-apart/.

[18]This is similar to the trend articulated in the bestseller by Bloom (1987) in which he decries the decline of American common values.

[19]For a partial list of U.S. military interventions from 1890 to 1999, including approximately 100 incidents, see Grossman (2003).

[20]United States Election Project (2004). http://www.cnn.com/election/2012/results/race/president/.

[21]http://www.pewresearch.org/fact-tank/2015/05/06/u-s-voter-turnout-trails-most-developed-countries/.

[22]http://www.pewresearch.org/fact-tank/2013/05/08/six-take-aways-from-the-census-bureaus-voting-report/.

In contrast,

> [O]ne in fifty adults has currently or permanently lost the ability to vote because of a felony conviction … The racial impact of ex-felon disenfranchisement … is truly astonishing. In Alabama and Florida 31% of all black men are permanently disenfranchised. In five other states- Iowa, Mississippi, New Mexico, Virginia and Wyoming-the number is one in four. … In effect, the Voting Rights Act of 1965 which guaranteed millions of African Americans the right to the electoral franchise is gradually being repealed by state restrictions on ex-felons from voting. A people who are imprisoned in disproportionately higher numbers, and then systematically denied the right to vote, can in no way claim to live under a democracy." (Marable 2002)

Also significant is that over half of the members of Congress are millionaires, which has very concrete impacts on their decision-making.[23] "Congress not only seems more responsive to policy desires of the very rich, but increasingly they are the very rich," said Josh Bivens, director of research at the Economic Policy Institute, a liberal Washington-based research group that focuses on income inequity and poverty. "They probably know far fewer people cut off by the failure to extend unemployment benefits, and that makes them less sensitive to just how much damage that cutoff is going to cause."[24]

Race plays a continuing and significant role in shaping the odds of being a millionaire for anyone in the U.S. Economists examined the possibilities, based on age, education and race and found that people face very different chances, even if the same age and educational achievement. Race stood out as the key factor that elevates or depresses the odds. For example, "a black graduate-degree holder has just about the same odds of being a millionaire as a white person who only completed high school."[25]

Additionally, when decisions where being made about sending troops to Iraq, only one member of Congress had a child in the service there,[26] and during the following period, fewer than a dozen members of Congress had children in the military anywhere (Dickinson 2005). That trend continues, with only 1% of Congress and of graduates from elite schools serving (Roth-Douquet and Schaeffer 2006.) Very few have had military experience themselves.[27] There are also significant racial disparities between the % of people in the armed forces compared to the civilian population. African-Americans, who are roughly 13% of the population overall, account for 22% of the armed forces. "The Defense Department acknowledges that recruits are drawn primarily from families in the middle and lower-middle socioeconomic strata" (Dickinson 2005). It then comes as little surprise that the policies the government endorses do not generally correspond to the needs, concerns, and dreams of the average American despite the demand for national allegiance even from those people who are rendered "disposable." Government policies resulting in massive displacement of people from the Gulf Region serve as a vivid and painful example.

That the general public knows so little about the structure and status of nations, peoples, and societies outside the United States further reinforces the sense of exceptionalism.[28] This imparts the sense of being special, different, and the need to protect the treasured commodity of "American" democracy and benevolent image of the United States: The government directs, the police protect, the schools educate, and individuals are responsible for the course of their lives. If one is not successful it is due to lack of motivation or hard work, an explanation reminiscent of the culture-of-poverty framework so often called upon to justify the disproportionate

---

[23] http://www.nytimes.com/2014/01/10/us/politics/more-than-half-the-members-of-congress-are-millionaires-analysis-finds.html.

[24] Ibid.

[25] http://www.bloomberg.com/features/2016-millionaire-odds/.

[26] Mitchell (2003) Media General News Service, Few lawmakers have children in military. http://www.nytimes.com/2003/03/22/us/a-nation-at-war-children-of-lawmakers-senators-sons-in-war-an-army-of-one.html.

[27] See: http://www.pewresearch.org/fact-tank/2013/09/04/members-of-congress-have-little-direct-military-experience/.

[28] See Schwalbe, Michael (2002) "The Costs of American Privilege." *Counterpunch.* http://www.counterpunch.org/2002/10/04/the-costs-of-american-privilege/October 4.

concentrations of poverty within certain populations, in particular communities of color. Another explanation points to differing abilities: "Not everybody is created equal. You can't ask everybody on the street what they think about something, and then implement that idea. Not everybody is as smart as everybody else. Not everybody has the same opportunities. Everybody feels equal, but not everybody is."[29]

We are told that people are in positions of power there because they're smarter (or better educated) than the rest of us. Why can't we involve everyone in the important decisions-isn't that the definition of democracy? Connections are drawn between economic, social, and political power, but explanations of the evolution of various patterns remain individualized. Are "they" in positions of power for the benefit of society or for themselves? How did they get there anyway? There is ambivalence and uncertainty about the origin of the nation and the ideals associated with U.S. exceptionalism:

> The idea of America had good intentions, but it left a lot of people out who were not WASPs. The founding fathers thought they were doing something revolutionary and good but they were not. Their intentions were good, like the Constitution and the formation of democracy. Opportunity is there but everybody can't achieve it. Yet there is that potential.[30]

> I don't think it was at all a democracy. Not one bit, when you think about it, what was the first thing they did when they came here? They killed all the natives and abused the slaves! What was the country built on? It was built on slavery, and that's not democratic at all. You don't have slaves now, or if you do, they're called below-minimum-wage workers. It's more democratic now; you don't have slaves.[31]

Many people do acknowledge inequality, however there is considerable ambivalence about its source. Lack of success is considered individual failure. Ambiguity about whether the ideals of the U.S. nation have been actualized perpetuates the exceptionalism, patriotism, and nationalism but also provides an opportunity to question the status quo. The ignorance of and uncertainty about structural responsibility reinforces mainstream narratives about the ways that the "American" society is superior, but they simultaneously function as openings because-as the statements above demonstrate incongruencies create opportunities to discuss ways that the ideals are, in fact, realities and myths simultaneously.

This contradictory nature of the character of the U.S. nation underlies notions of "American" identity. When it comes to perceptions about whether as a society, the United States has achieved equality particularly between whites and Blacks, a recent study the Pew Research Center found that 36% of white versus 88% of Blacks say that "racial discrimination is a major reason why black people in our country may have a harder time getting ahead than whites."[32] In terms of treatment in the workplace, 22% of whites and 64% of Blacks say "Blacks in the U.S. are treated less fairly than whites". In relation to how blacks are treated when voting in elections, 74% of whites versus 53% of Blacks say they are treated equally. In terms of treatment by the police, 41% of whites and 14% of Blacks say they are treated equally.[33]

However, Blacks continue to lag behind significantly in many or most categories. Median income for whites is $71,300 versus $41,300 for Blacks; "the median net worth of households headed by whites was roughly 13 times that of black households ($144,200 for whites compared with $11,200 for blacks)".[34] Perceptions of equality by whites are indeed misperceptions (Morin 2001, A1; Freeman 2001, C3). These mistaken beliefs lead to political positions that oppose measures to equalize opportunity that have significant implications for addressing historical patterns for if one does not believe that inequality exists, why support actions aimed at making things more fair? This certainly has

---

[29]Sam, white male (Bush 2004, 115).

[30]Shalom, white male (Ibid.).

[31]Catherine, white female (Op. Cit.).

[32]http://www.pewsocialtrends.org/interactives/state-of-race-in-america/.

[33]http://www.pewsocialtrends.org/2016/06/27/on-views-of-race-and-inequality-blacks-and-whites-are-worlds-apart/.

[34]Ibid.

implications for the group experience of belonging or marginalization as combined with culture-of-poverty rhetoric establishes who really matters in this society.

In an analysis of the "White Fairness Understanding Gap" Paul Street cites six factors that he feels contribute to these misunderstandings. These include an American educational curriculum notoriously conservative on questions of social, racial, and economic justice; the lack of exposure of whites to the everyday realities of African Americans; media distortions that exaggerate affluence among Blacks; neighborhood and school segregation; pragmatic reasons for denying structural causes for inequality; and the general weakness of the political left such that progressive politics is viewed as a zero-sum game (2001, 9) with advances made by one group detracting from those of another. In contrast to the national self-portrait and generous, concerned with freedom, equality and democracy, the lived reality evidences deep divides. The narrative of nationhood and exceptionalism places the blame for poverty on those who are poor; of those who are poor, communities of color receive the brunt not just of the beliefs about lazy individuals but of generalized profiling that designates whole groups as unworthy.[35]

In national surveys approximately 17% of respondents indicate they believe in Black genetic inferiority. That comprises 34 million white Americans, approximately the size of the entire U.S. Black population (Wise 2000)-quite a sizable number, not to be dismissed. However, this perspective does not seem unusual in an environment in which President Francis Lawrence of Rutgers University in 1995 could state that he supported affirmative action because disadvantaged Blacks didn't have the "genetic, hereditary background" to score well on tests (www.Tolerance.org 2001) and in which *The Bell Curve* could become a bestseller.

While most people agree that there is unequal treatment of different groups, they still often say that everyone can be assimilated. This infers that people can be assimilated but only unequally. Assimilation is viewed as an assumed and accessible goal for anyone who tries hard enough. If this is not true, then what would that say about the image of U.S. society? Clear distinctions are made between those who believe all people should be given a fair chance to succeed and those who believe that if people don't have equal access to resources, measures should be taken to equalize opportunity.[36] While many people may be willing to acknowledge specific inequalities or injustices, viewing them as a systemic problem is less acceptable. People may agree in principle with universal equality, but they worry that measures to equalize resources inevitably lead to having to give something up oneself.

"Our society generally worships the symbols of authority, and power. We applaud those who are wealthy, and despise the poor. Individuals are all too often judged by their market value, rather than by their character as human beings" (Marable 2002). While the ideal of equality is generally supported, measures to level opportunities are viewed as benefiting people of color and discriminating against whites. Significantly fewer people are willing to support proactive measures, perhaps because they fear it means having to give something up. Struggles about multiculturalism and diversity can distract people from talking about structures of inequality that keep patterns and structures of racialization in place all over the world.

"Ours is a society that routinely generates destitution-and then, perversely, relieves its conscience by vilifying the destitute" (Ehrenreich 2002, 9). If people are ideologically prepared with an understanding of economic forces and how they influence politics, they may be more willing to understand race as a smokescreen for the elites who manipulate whites into believing that Blacks are to blame.[37]

---

[35]See Appendix I for Table 13.1: Beliefs about Factors Contributing to Racial Inequality (Bush 2004, 183).

[36]See Appendix III Table 13.3: Evaluation of Equal Opportunity (Bush 2004, 209).

[37]Thanks to Dr. Donald Robotham for a clarifying discussion about this topic on 4 December 2000.

13.4 What Is an "American"? The System and Its Symbols

Who IS an American? Someone born in the United States ... a citizen ... someone who believes in the "American" dream? Canadians? Mexicans? Ambiguity about what it means to be "American" and how you become one and/or a citizen allows underlying constructs race to both reinforce structured inequality. For most people of European descent there is no question about what it means to be "American"; they just "are." Similar to being white, being American and a U. S. citizen is an assumed state of being from which all "others" depart. This status can be bestowed by birth, through inheritance or naturalization, by association, or through a belief system, but it can also be retracted, especially for people of color.

Discrimination against the Arab American population, many of whom were born in the United States, testifies to their vulnerability, regardless of their place of birth or citizenship. A political cartoon that circulated soon after the events of September 11 showed one man, who appeared to be white, angrily shaking his finger at a man who appeared to be Arab and saying, "Go back to where you where you were born." To this, the man asks, "Chicago?" Support for Donald Trump with his calls to establish a database of all Muslims in the U.S., his depiction of Mexicans as criminals and rapists, justifying plans to close the borders is a further testament to contested contemporary notions of who "belongs". Similarly, during the fall of 2001, this issue became acutely visible when, for example, the Federal Bureau of Investigation summoned hundreds of men with Arab surnames for interviews about terrorism. The government justified this blatant racial profiling in the name of "homeland security."[38]

One might wonder why the government has not rounded up microbiologists, given significant evidence that multiple envelopes of anthrax were sent to various individuals by an American microbiologist (Blackhurst 2001). If the reasoning is that perpetrators of mass murder should be swiftly and summarily executed, why not call upon tobacco industry executives? (Williams 2001, 11) Or, one can certainly raise question about non-combatant deaths by drone strikes, with estimates from 200 to more than 900 between 2009 and 2015.[39]

Black incorporation is difficult because the dominant culture relies on a narrow conception of who is and can be 'American'. Black people are considered unfit for membership because cultural representations of American identity have been shaped and defined as not-Black ... American identity is directly associated with (and defined as white)" (Davis 2005, 154). "The value-laden identities of American and Black are crucial mechanisms in the apparatus of white supremacy, and are used relentlessly to maintain white cultural hegemony in America using "science" and attitudes to produce and reproduce systemic white hegemony (Davis 2005, 154).

This ambiguous and value-laden nature of being "American" means that the label may refer to someone with citizenship, nationality, residency or a quality related to a sense of belonging or even "... a belief system; it's the way you act and think toward other people. It's not where you're from or where you're born."[40] In this way the meaning of being American shifts between something tangible (naturalization and citizenship), something unambiguous (bestowed by birth), something ambiguous (a belief system), and something transitory (a combination of any of these).[41] Even whites who say they never

---

[38]This is reminiscent of the period when Japanese Americans were rounded up and place in internment camps.

[39]http://www.huffingtonpost.com/entry/drone-strikes_us_5776b00ce4b04164640fded9?utm_medium=email&utm_campaign=Politics%20070116&utm_content=Politics%20070116 + CID_bad79a0d14a6ba63c7fe5f14c1394ac5&utm_source=Email%20marketing%20software&utm_term=US%20Killed%20Up%20To%20116%20Civilians%20In%20Drone%20Strikes%20Outside%20War%20Zones%20White%20House%20Says.

[40]Keri, Black female (Bush 2004, 107).

[41]Martinez writes, "Today's origin myth and the resulting definition of national identity make for an intellectual prison where it is dangerous to ask big questions, moral questions, about this society's superiority; where

think about being American expect a range of privileges as part and parcel of their birthright, including the "psychological wage" of a belief that "we are the 'best'" and the material goods that accompany being located in the homeland of the world elite. "[The United States] has no collective identity except as the best, the greatest country, superior to all others and the acknowledged model for the world" (Hobsbawm 2003, B8).

It was found that foreign-born whites (68.3%) believe that the United States can be multicultural and American significantly more than foreign-born Blacks (42.9%).[42] This may reflect the racialized experience of foreign-born Blacks being classified first and foremost as Black while foreign-born whites feel that their ability to assimilate is not hampered by how they are racially identified. Notions of loyalty are defined by symbols "foisted in the face of generations by the media at the behest of large business and religious leaders."[43]

Another extremely important aspect of this discussion is the way that the label "American" is commonly equated with being of the United States, rather than the continent. *The Concise Oxford English Dictionary* provides the following definitions:

> adj. relating to or characteristic of the United States. • relating to the continents of America; n. a native or inhabitant of the United States. a native or inhabitant of any of the countries of North, South, or Central America.[44]

This popular practice intrinsically racializes who is and is not included, thereby projecting "American" with white image. Elizabeth Martinez, author, points out that the concepts of "America" and "Las Americas" are rendered irrelevant and nonexistent as the United States has defined these terms solely in relation to

itself.[45] There have been calls for U.S. national identity to be redefined for example as "United Statesian"; however, this, too, is a contested label as other nations also have "united states" or "America" as part of their official name (e.g., Estados Unidos Mexicanos).[46] Also at issue are distinctions drawn between nation (generally understood as a cultural designation), state (political), and country (combination of the people and its governing bodies).[47]

In "Don't Call This Country 'America': How the Name Was Hijacked and Why It Matters Today More than Ever,"[48] Martinez discusses the relationship between the appropriation of this label and the U.S. history and worldview. She argues that while there are more than 20 countries within the continents of North and South America, it is the policy of manifest destiny to deny their existence, thereby equating "American" with someone of European descent. "In most U.S. eyes, the norm for American remains white-whether we admit it or not ... In unthinking self-defense, we unite with a name that reflects a worldview both imperialist and racist" (Martinez 2003, 3). This articulates a presumption of U.S. dominance such that there is no consideration of a broader "American" world.

The mystification of the term "American" and its equation with someone from the United States, specifically of European descent, reinforce patterns of structured inequality by naturalizing these two concepts as one and the same. Toni Morrison explains that the conflation of

---

other-wise decent people are trapped in a desire not to feel guilty, which the necessitates self-deception. ... When together we cease equating whiteness with 'Americanness,' a new day can dawn" (1996, 24).

[42]Bush (2004, 108).

[43]Correspondence with Abednigo Ndlovu, Johannesburg, South Africa, January 20, 2006.

[44]"American" *adj.,* (2004). Adelphi University (WALDO). alicat.adelphi.edu:80/views/ENTRY.html?subview=Main&entry=t23.el621.

[45]Martinez speaks of this when she says "If ever there was a time for people in this white-dominated super-power to reject its racist contempt for 20 other American countries that happen to be of color, it is right now as Bush charges from one racist war to another" (2003, 69–72).

[46]Various blogs and websites debate this issue. Wikipedia includes an extensive discussion of the label "American," a narrative of contested origins and a section entitled "Seeking alternate names" including entries such as "Nacirema" and "Washingtonian." http://en.wikipedia.org/wiki/Use_of_the_word_American#The_alternatives.

[47]http://en.wikipedia.org/wiki/Country.

[48]Unpublished manuscript by Elizabeth (Betita) Martinez, "Don't Call This Country 'America': How the Name Was Hijacked and Why It Matters Today More Than Ever." San Francisco, Calif. (circulated via e-mail, February 2003).

national and racial identity is particular to the United States. She says, "Deep within the word 'American' is its association with race. To identify someone as a South African is to say very little; we need the adjective 'white' or 'black' or 'colored' to make our meaning clear. In this country it is quite the reverse. American means white" (1992, 47). This points to the uncertainty that many people have about the racial and national nature of American identity and raises issues of homogeneity, assimilation, Eurocentrism, and incorporation into mainstream society. This equation of being American with being from the United States speaks to the centering and naturalization of whiteness, for this question does not arise for foreign-born whites. Simultaneously, the question of belonging emerges for U.S.-born people of African descent. "In the eyes of this particular white person our identity as 'black' supplanted either of our identities as U.C. students and rendered us merely black-not customers, not students, not 'Americans.'"[49] Davis argues that Du Bois' formulation of "double-consciousness is actually "assessment of American citizenship" and cites Robert Staples' assertion that "being human-also American-seems beyond the pale of consideration for people of African-descent."[50] A report issued in 2012 notes that "every 28 h every 28 h someone inside the United States, employed or protected by the U.S. government kills a Black child, woman or man."[51] This reality is described as "'Operation Ghetto Storm,' a perpetual war to invade, occupy and pacify Black communities—much like the U.S. invades and occupies the Middle East."[52]

In contrast, for people of European descent national pride is often presumed, regardless of an individual's conscious awareness of his or her identity:

I consider myself to be an American. I was born in America; my parents were born in America. I think my grandparents were born in America, but I have Irish, German, and Dutch heritage. I love this country and that means a lot to me. Sometimes I'm amazed at myself when I hear, like, "God Bless America" or "The Star Spangled Banner." I get emotional, and I think, wow, God blessed this country.[53]

What does it means to say "God blessed this country" when there are as many gods as there are religions, and when most of the world's people do not subscribe to a religion that believes in a Judeo-Christian "God"?[54] Why bless our country (5% of the global population) and not someone else's? This notion reinforces national pride and presumes superiority and specialness.

These passages offer conflicting portraits of whether, in order to be a "real American," you must uphold a certain ideology or feel a national pride, or whether it's enough to be born here or immigrate to the United States. It is unclear whether to claim American identity, one must "pledge allegiance to the flag," show loyalty to symbols, and speak English. In light of changing demographics in the United States, this is particularly important as, for example, in 1996, 35% of public school students in New York City spoke a language other than English at home (Tell 1999). What determines someone's identity and status, as well as self-determined roles versus those set by state and legal systems? Does national identity necessarily mean citizenship; what does national loyalty require? It appears to depend on whether one has the power to assert judgment. Being white, one is generally provided options to be patriotic and nationalistic, or not, and to decide the terms on which one's identities

---

[49]Davis (2005). In this article, Dr. Davis examines "the meaning of the term 'American'" and the way in which whiteness has become equated with 'American-ness' in the United States.

[50]Davis, 2005, pages 149–150, draws from Staples (1993).

[51]http://www.operationghettostorm.org/.

[52]Ibid.

---

[53]Mara, white female (Bush 2004, 110).

[54]In an article entitled "Oh, Gods;" Toby Lester (2002, 41) points out that new religions are born all the time. He quotes ... David B. Barrett, author of the World Christian Encyclopedia: "We have identified nine thousand and nine hundred distinct and separate religions in the world, increasing by two or three new religions every day". Further-more, 67% of the world's people are non-Christian (www.adherents.com2003).

are negotiated. You can decide to think about being American, or not. You can choose one identity, one day, and another on a different day. A person of color, however, as described above, does not have that privilege. One's identity is selected for you, like an arranged marriage with legal mandate not to speak out politically.

Another way that this dynamic is expressed is in the way that people of European descent much more frequently consider themselves to be American than any other group. Research done for the *Everyday Forms of Whiteness* (*Breaking the Code of Good Intentions*), found that 83.8% of U.S.-born people of European descent consider themselves to be American, versus 58.1% of U.S.-born Blacks (2004, 112). Referring to Du Bois' writings about double-consciousness, Leniece Davis says, "Du Bois begins to understand how racial difference separated blacks and whites and served as the basis of black exclusion from full and equal participation in American society. The focus on racial difference(s) thwarts blacks' efforts to wholly claim and assume the identity of American. As such, black people become estranged from their identity of American" (2005, 150) expressed as "though I was and am an American, I didn't have what most Americans feel-that unique sense of belonging" (Gilmore 2002, 27).

Similarly, foreign-born Blacks identify themselves as "American" significantly less than any other group (Bush 2004, 112). These data suggest evidence of the racialization of the foreign-born experience such that foreign-born whites are more easily assimilated into U.S. society than foreign-born Blacks. The national organization "Public Agenda" recently conducted an extensive survey on immigrants in America. They found that 42% chose "I have become an American" and 41% took a middle position: "I act like an American outside, but at home I keep my own culture and traditions " (Farkas et al. 2003, 30). "The Pew Hispanic Center found that among Latino youth the percent identifying as American ranges from 3% (first generation immigrants), to 33% (second generation), to 50% (third generation and higher). It is significant that two-thirds of Latinos

aged 16–25 are U.S. born.[55] "Asked whether they think of themselves first as an American or first as a Muslim, a 47% plurality of U.S. Muslims say they consider themselves Muslims first; 28% say they think of themselves first as Americans. In May 2006, when U.S. Christians were asked a parallel question, 42% said they think of themselves as Christians first, while 48% said they are Americans first."[56] (See the Appendix for 2009 survey responses "I Consider Myself to be an American" and How Often Do You Think about Your National Identity? Bush 2011).

Ideology also plays a role in decisions about identity. Heightened after September 11, questioning U.S. foreign policy has come to be viewed as an attack on "America" as the mainstream explanation was that the individuals involved are jealous of "our freedoms." This line of thinking presumes the experience of middle- and upper-class whites who are protected from the everyday affronts that both class and racial inequality invoke including an economic draft that leads to the overwhelming majority of the military drawing from the lower socioeconomic strata with a concentration from communities of color. Similarly, the justification for random interrogation of Arab Americans is framed as "I have nothing to hide, why they should?" However, this perspective epitomizes the experience of individuals who have never been "the persistent object of suspect profiling, never been harassed, never been stigmatized just for the way they look" (Williams 2001, 11).

13.4.1 Patriotism

Referring to one's self as "American" and believing that God Blessed America" provides a

---

[55]Pew Hispanic Center, "Graphic: Latino Youths Optimistic But Beset by Problems," http://pewhispanic.org/reports/report.php?ReportID=118. Accessed May 10, 2010.

[56]Pew Research Center 2007. Muslim Americans: Middle Class and Mostly Mainstream. May 22, 2007. http://www.people-press.org/2007/05/22/muslim-americans-middle-class-and-mostly-mainstream/.

sense of elevated status in relationship to the rest of the world. Immanuel Wallerstein discusses God's unequal blessings and how the United States has always defined itself, measured by the yardstick of the world: "We are better; we were better; we shall be better" (2001). This identity confers elevated standing to those who hold it, regardless of class position, gender, or skin color, as whiteness does. At the same time, as discussed previously, distinctions are made between images of "true Americans" and people of status made questionable by the ambiguous borders and margins at which they are positioned. Thus all native-born Blacks, Latinos, and Asians hold tentative status as Americans, depending on circumstance. Additional distinctions are made between generations, linguistically, and within both immigrant and native-born populations.

U.S. national identity thus functions as one of many axes from which to understand the imposition of patterns of dominance and subordination on different groups within the U.S. population, at times to contradict and in other circumstances to enhance the status of its holder. Narratives about the United States as a global peacekeeper portray its citizens as "nice guys" (white). This imagery was exemplified in a comment made by a firefighter, as reported in November 2001, on CNN. He said, "We in the United States take care of everyone all over the world and this is what we get?"[57]

In fact, the concept of being American has held distinctive meanings for different people at various times in history, just as patriotism has been evoked simultaneously to make the case for inclusion and exclusion, unity and dissent, and both military sacrifice and conscientious objection. In this way, the United States has two somewhat contradictory traditions (Scott 2003, 4.1) currently being contested in public discourse. Benedictine Sister Joan Chittister, OSB, writes in her weekly column in the *National Catholic Reporter,* "The world wants to know who we really are-international menace or mighty hero?" (2003).

Patriotism is often a rallying cry for national unity and maintaining the social order-a demand placed particularly on those who benefit most tentatively due to their vulnerable status in society. The phrase "if you aren't with us, then you are against us" draws lines of demarcation, the "Pledge of Allegiance" seals commitment to nation and to God so there are no questions of one's loyalty or the divine function. The "Star-Spangled Banner" firmly roots this allegiance in military images of right and might and white given that the history of the U.S. nation corresponds to the transition from the British Empire to that of the United States, orchestrated through military and ideological interventions.

Like the American Dream and democracy, the American flag has come to symbolize the elevated status of the United States in the global order. In *To Die for: The Paradox of American Patriotism,* Cecilia Elizabeth O'Leary traces the development of the flag's symbolic meaning to the period after the First Reconstruction and through World War I (1999, 7–9). She documents the legal and political struggles over the definitions of loyal or disloyal citizens. She says that during this period (1870–1920) there was disagreement and conflict over which icons, heroes, events, and identities would constitute the national memory and the historical narrative.

Many of the symbols and rituals of patriotism that we now assume as having always existed actually came into being within the last century. The "Pledge of Allegiance" was written in 1891; the "Star-Spangled Banner" was taken as the national anthem in 1931. O'Leary traces the points of contestation, contradiction, and ambivalence about American ideals and their everyday manifestations. She ultimately speaks of the contradictions of U.S. nationalism, as did Immanuel Wallerstein when he insisted that we reckon with national traditions of both patriotism and resistance (Wallerstein 2001). It is a challenge that many have recently faced-that is, how to understand contradictory patterns without essentializing either trend. This is the challenge, for if we acknowledge the agency of ordinary people in the United States and around the world, and build a movement recognizing the

---

[57]CNN News (2001).

contradictions of nation and empire recognize contradictions, we have the ability to change this history.

Overall this raises the question of the purpose and function of nationalism. In his famous work, *Imagined Communities,* Benedict Anderson locates the rise of "nations" as corresponding to the development of industrial capitalism, a historically contextualized concept and asserts that once the printing press opened the possibilities of communication across territories, it became necessary to consolidate identity within communities. What it has come to mean is very different.

13.5 The "American" Dream[58]

While data on the diminishing standard of living, reports of massive layoffs, and challenges faced in receiving adequate schooling and health care are readily available in mainstream media, there still exists a widespread belief that the "Dream" is achievable if you work for it. After September 11, 2001, media coverage occasionally noted concerns about the unequal distribution of funds raised for families of the deceased (Barstow and Henriques 2001, Al) and differentials in the severance packages of people who lost jobs.[59] These long-standing economic disparities have become increasingly difficult to explain and justify.

The ideal of the American Dream has been depicted routinely in the media throughout the second half of the 20th century and forms the foundation of what life in "this great country" is all about. That immigrants can arrive penniless and in time will get rich saturates everyday discourse. This idea is a central pillar of the ideology of U.S. society (Hochschild 1995). For many, this was the case. The post-World War II era of rapid industrial growth and U.S. hegemony around the globe brought much, to many. However, for African Americans, Latinos, and Native Americans, this dream was never a reality. After immigration laws changed in 1965, increasing numbers of people came to the United States, just when deindus-trialization began to occur. The most prominent explanations for why these groups were not upwardly mobile drew increasingly from a culture-of-poverty framework.

Central tenets of the "Dream" revolve around the achievement of success in the forms of high income, a prestigious job, and economic security (Hochschild 1995, 15). The idea that this is an achievable goal for all has been built into what it means to be an American. Consider President Bill Clinton's speech in 1993 to the Democratic Leadership Council: The American Dream that we were all raised on is a simple but powerful one-if you work hard and play by the rules, you should be given a chance to go as far as your God-given abilities will take you" (Hochschild 1995, 18). This raises many questions about for example educational and socioeconomic inequalities that provide different foundation s for different communities. In addition, what are "God-given" abilities in a world shaped by white supremacy?

However, over the last several decades the wealth and income gap has significantly grown. From 1960 to 2006, the wealth ratio of the top and bottom 20% went from 1:30 to 1:75. Average annual compensation of the top 100 chief executives went from 30 to 1000 times the pay of the average worker (Moyers 2006). This means that in 2007, the share of income of families of the top 10% was 49.7%; the top 1% earned 23.5% of all income (Saez 2009, 3). Paralleling this increased polarization of wealth, imagery

---

[58]A photo essay of contemporary views about the concept of the American Dream can be found by Ian Brown, "American Dreams." The New York Times. Sunday Review July 3, 2016. 5 and online.

[59]In one estimate, each firefighter's family received almost $1 million, whereas families of people who were not unionized or were undocumented stood to receive little, if anything. Comparisons of the severance packages of people who lost jobs as a result of this tragedy also reveal great disparities. On the one hand, the severance package for the outgoing executive director of the Massachusetts Port Authority was reported at $175,000, the airlines bailout was cited at $15 billion, and the overall economic stimulus package is essentially a giant corporate tax break, whereas laid-off employees of the Hotel Employees and Restaurant Employees International Union and various airlines were reported to have received little or nothing in the form of unemployment benefits (Jackson 2001, A23).

about the American Dream shifted from a small house, with a white picket fence and a two-car garage, two kids, a dog, and a cat, to the lifestyle of the most affluent as portrayed on shows such as "Dallas," "L.A. Law," and "Beverly Hills 90,210" (Roper Survey Organization 1993, 86; Crispell 1994, BI).

Media in the United States does sometimes reports on poverty rampant throughout the world, yet the realities of the stratification within the United States are rarely shown. The "united we stand" slogan and "we are all in this together against the enemy" rhetoric function to obviate internal tensions and differences and to further promote the notion that America is the "greatest country in the world," with more modernity, more technology, more efficiency, more liberty, more culture, and more democracy than any-where else. This notion, deeply ingrained in the American psyche, signals that

> We are more civilized than the rest of the world. ... We represent the highest aspirations of everyone. ... We are the leader of the free world, because we are the freest country in the world, and others look to us for leadership, for holding high the banner of freedom, of civilization. ... The Twin Towers are a perfect metaphor. They signaled unlimited aspira-tions; they signaled techno-logical achievement; they signaled a beacon to the world. (Wallerstein 2001)

At a time when the United States' decline as a hegemonic power looms large on the horizon, we need as a nation to reconsider the belief in our solitary greatness, engage our "closest friends and allies," and accept that they, too, have ideals and interests (Wallerstein 2001). The substance of the American Dream, as even a far-fetched ideal, has been shaken, even among some patri-ots who most vigorously defend its possibility. The events of 2001 and after propelled a coming to terms with the realities experienced by the everyday American. Increasing lines at the unemploy-ment offices and greater numbers at soup kitchens and homeless shelters are just the beginning. Such trends are compounded by the expanded privatization of all aspects of social services, to such an extent that schools, medical facilities, and policing, for example, have increasingly become domains for profit-bearing as opposed to being services delivered for the public good.

Jennifer Hochschild, professor of politics and public affairs at Princeton University, states, "The political culture of the United States is largely shaped by a set of views in which the American Dream is prominent, and by a set of institutions that make it even more prominent than views alone could do" (1995, 37). There is a persistent divergence of opinion about possibili-ties in the future for equal rights between Blacks and whites, 43% of Blacks and 11% of whites say that the country will not make the needed changes.[60]

Hochschild's study parallels studies by *The Washington Post* and the National Opinion Research Center about perceptions of the current status of equality in society, in which whites consistently state that they believe discrimination is lessening, and Blacks report the persistent reality of racial inequality in their lives. Paul Street, Research Director of the Chicago Urban League, describes it as the "White Fairness Understanding Gap" (2001, 9–11). These data are critical to an understanding of the viability of the American Dream, in the way that different populations perceive the dream as a myth or a reality. If, as a nation, all people cannot count on freedom, justice, equality, and opportunity, then the ideology that holds these ideals as the explanation for American's specialness is undermined. For whites, race usefully explains why the dream is no longer attainable. Hochs-child explains the connection this way:

> Something is wrong with the American Dream, and the problem is associated with Blacks (and immigrants) in some way. Identifying what is wrong and how Blacks are implicated in it is a difficult and thankless task for which they receive almost no institutional support. It is far easier to cling to the Dream, insist that it really works, and find someone to blame for the lacunae. (1995, 69)

---

[60]http://www.pewsocialtrends.org/2016/06/27/on-views-of-race-and-inequality-blacks-and-whites-are-worlds-apart/st_2016-06-27_race-inequality-overview-01/.

Foreign-born whites appear to believe significantly more than any other group that the United States is a land of equal opportunity for all people.[61] This pattern appears to be a consequence of their racialized experience, where similar to previous European immigrants, they have been provided opportunities to improve their standard of living, more than the U.S.-born communities of color (e.g., access to various social services under the guise of assisting political refugees). It also seems to indicate that the U.S.-born whites are experiencing the economic pressures of the recent decades and feel less certain about their own futures. In summarizing participants' perspectives in the research conducted for *Tensions in the American Dream*, Bush and Bush explain:

> ...those we spoke with had already thought about many of the issues we raised. While some felt certain about their own beliefs, many expressed uncertainty or confusion about how to make sense of commonly referred to explanations that did not really explain either their life challenges or good fortunes. Many appeared to be rethinking some of the assumptions on which they had built their lives thus far. (2015, 146)

They found there are many factors contributing to this including a heightened distrust of politicians, the political process, greater numbers of immigrants with multiple national allegiances, increased detachment from religion, intensified economic challenges and feelings of vulnerability in the workplaces, through foreclosures and debt of all sorts including for students. Extraordinarily problematic responses for example to Hurricane Katrina, abuse and torture in Abu Ghraib, and the wars in Iraq and Afghanistan, with massive loss of life to the citizens of those countries and to people in the United States, have come into the public view. The lack of substantive explanations for these situations appears to lead both to people holding on firmly to the traditional narratives, and to a greater degree of questioning (Bush and Bush 2015, 148).

The American Dream appears to inspire pride and hopefulness, yet when whites face economic pressures, rather than looking toward structural explanations for their troubles, they tend to blame individuals and groups. For example, in discussions about the difficulty in financing education, racially designated scholarships are often targeted as the problem despite the reality that this perception is significantly exaggerated (Bush 2004, 100). Rather than viewing minority assistance as a means to address historical patterns, they are characterized as perpetuating inequality by advantaging students of color.

Herein lay several ways of thinking that reinforce and reproduce mainstream discourse and structures about rights, belonging, and nation. The "American Dream" is achievable with hard work, and lack of effort is the cause of failure. Americans are superior; to be truly American one needs to be of European descent. The process of racialization and its consequent negative impact (subordination) and positive impact (privileging) are illusive. They are implicit but unspoken within notions of identity, opportunity, and equality. Resistance is viewed as anti-American and ungrateful, and it's better not to acknowledge the underlying historical factors that have led to the betterment of living conditions in the United States in contrast to those of other people around the world.

Simultaneously, popular notions of democracy, the American experience, and the "Dream" provide several openings for heightened awareness. The profound and righteous ideals and idealism embodied in notions of freedom, equality, justice, and democracy provide the basis for a vision of a better world. Inconsistencies and incongruities in application of these principles, when acknowledged, provide opportunities to analyze and understand how mainstream discourse about the realities of U.S. national history and present-day positioning is strictly regulated to maintain the status quo. Economic downturns put pressure on whites, who either turn to the dominant explanations about who is to blame or can be more open to a deeper analysis from the perspective of the majority rather than the elite.

---

[61] See Appendix IV for Table 13.4: The United States Is a Land of Equal Opportunity for All People (Bush 2004, 122).

13.6 Nation and Empire

The ideals of American democracy, which have influenced liberal democracies around the world, rely crucially on the notion of consent as the basis of citizenship. What makes someone an American is that he or she agrees to be one. … By raising their hands and taking the pledge of citizenship, immigrants formally enact the consent upon which our political system depends; yet which native-born citizens only tacitly affirm. Postel (2001, A12)

Notions of what it means to be American, of democracy, and of birthright are deeply implicated in the foundation of our society. People came to the United States for a multitude of reasons and circumstances, and their experiences, once arrived, varied. The concept "the United States, a nation of immigrants" disguises the unequal status of various groups in how they arrived, what they experienced when they arrived, or how their lands and peoples were "incorporated" as part of the U.S. nation. "A nation of immigrants" presumes a European experience, where choice is the primary factor in migration. This portrait also renders invisi-ble the very real transnational experience of many immigrants to the United States during the second half of the 20th century where ties are maintained actively with their homelands, whether through the flow of funds, care of children, or their intermittent stays in both loca-tions. Their migration represents very different experiences of allegiance and strategic sur-vival than the early generations of European immigrants (or for that matter evens the recent migrants from Eastern Europe). For this group, being "American," patriotism, and national allegiance have a much more fluid character.

Bonnie Honig, author of *Democracy and the Foreigner* (2001), argues that while democracies need immigrants, "[We're] nervous about what they are going to do to our democracy. We criminalize alien populations, bar them from political activity; marginalize them in terms of the labor force. We practice xenophobia and xenophilia at the same time" (quoted in Postel 2001, A12). While what Honig asserts is cer-tainly true, she does not account for the differ-ential experiences of immigrants upon their arrival to the United States. Why is it that a boat of refugees from one country is allowed entry, while another is turned away? Additionally, "Malcolm X argued that in the process of Americanizing, European immigrants acquire a sense of whiteness and [an understanding of] white supremacy" (Roediger 1994, 187). Fur-thermore, providing commentary about the racialized nature of the Americanization process, he asserted that the first English word immigrants learn upon arrival to the U.S. is "nigger," (Haley and Malcolm 1965, 399) as the racialized nature of U.S. society bears down upon them.

Foreign-born whites often view the United States as the land of opportunity, an idea likely shaped before they arrived, as part of Cold War ideology. They tend toward a perspective in direct opposition to what they were told by their gov-ernments (Soviet and post-Soviet.) Upon arrival, the treatment they receive reinforces their beliefs as they absorb a "Horatio Alger" narrative that inverted communist ideology in relationship to a capitalist perspective. That is, everything that was bad about their prior lives would now be good, in "America." They arrive with a worldview that established freedom as a U.S. phenomenon and, as both the narrative and the statistics below indicate, they defend this image. Their experience as white immigrants has meant they have generally fared well, for example, in educational achievement, with slightly fewer high school diplomas but higher levels of college accomplished.[62] However, as they come to feel the impact of the increasing polarization of wealth and power under the reign of global capitalism, they may find themselves in more dire circumstances and seek explanations for the difficulties they face.[63]

In contrast to the highly transnational and transmigrant nature of immigrants from the African, Latin, and Asian diasporas, the

---

[62]Interestingly, of the U.S.-born whites, only one third of those who were born in New York City had completed a bachelor's degree, as compared to three quarters of those who had moved to the city from elsewhere in the United States (Mollenkopf et al. 2001).

[63]Personal communication with Professor Donald Robotham, The Graduate School and University Center of the City University of New York (1 December 2000).

experience of Eastern European immigrants tends to root them in their new surroundings, where they feel welcome. Annelise Orleck, associate professor of history at Dartmouth College, reports that among the Soviet Jews she studied, most do not return home for visits. They say that everyone they know is in the United States. Orleck quotes one woman as saying, "America is my country, not Russia. I have no one left there to worry about" (2001, 135).

Regardless of their foreign-born status, European immigrants are treated as whites, providing them with an incentive to ascribe to racialized beliefs about the culture of poverty. Their defense of the structure as fair and equitable denies discrimination expressed in racialized patterns of assimilation or rejection. This process is evident as social services and the ever-present and useful "benefit of the doubt" are available to white immigrants but not to those from the African, Asian, or Latino diasporas. In the case of Amadou Diallo, the four police officers and the jury saw him as a Black man first, which led to his murder and the officers' acquittals. The wallet in Amadou's hands "became" (i.e., was assumed to be) a gun. Had Diallo been Russian, would this image transformation have occurred?[64]

There is an irony to the perceptions of foreign-born whites, as the civil rights movement laid the foundation for the liberalization of immigration policy in the 1960s. These statistics indicate, however, that foreign-born whites are unlikely to support measures to eradicate structural causes for racial inequality. In other words, once arrived, foreign-born whites assume the dominant position, rather than recognizing where support came from to increase their opportunities and, in turn, supporting opportunities for better conditions and access for other groups.[65]

The immigrant status of foreign-born whites lets them more easily assimilate into a white-dominant society, so perhaps they do not see the challenge in integrating their ethnic or national background into their identity as Americans. Foreign-born Blacks sometimes note that their racial identity became an issue only after they arrived in the United States. "Black immigrants face a unique set of social circumstances upon entering our borders ... The term 'cross-pressures' [names] the contradictory circumstances that mark the West Indian experi-ence in the United States" (Bashi 1999, 890). One factor is that they come from societies in which they form majorities and which urge them to downplay race, and their experience in the United States provides opportunities for upward mobility but simultaneously immerses them in a society in which race is a key structuring principle (Bashi 1999, 891).

Another aspect of the question about whether the United States can be multicultural and have a unified national identity is examined in a discussion of Du Bois' writings. Many African Americans would "find it undesirable to subordinate their blackness to Americanness or American-ness to their blackness as a means of creating a unified individuality ... Instead they desire the unity of the two ... The practice of exclusion makes black people feel that they are not recognized as truly American" (Davis 2005, 151).

13.6.1 National Identity

The dynamic whereby resistance is racialized posits that people in the United States have

---

[64]This event occurred on 4 February 1999 in the Bronx. New York. Four police officers, searching for someone who had committed a rape, came upon Mr. Diallo in the vestibule of his home. They testified that he reached for a gun, which then in their minds justified shooting 41 bullets, 19 of which entered his body. It was later discovered that Mr. Diallo was reaching for his wallet to provide identification. Mayor Rudolph Giuliani characterized attention to this incident as "obsessive media concern" and "frenzy" (Barry 1999). Massive protests against police brutality and racism followed, for it was widely recognized that, had Diallo been white, the shooting was highly unlikely to have occurred. (See Bush, 2011).

[65]From an illuminating discussion with Dr. Leith Mullings, CUNY Graduate School, 21 September 2001. This is a complex issue; for a fuller examination, see (Bobo 2000, 186–202; Smith and Seltzer 2000; Steinberg 1995, 190–192; Gallicchio 2000).

freedom of speech, yet it depends on who says what as to whether that freedom is justifi-able or not. Critical discourse is aggressively marginalized and implied to be criminal or crazy.

The perspectives of foreign-born whites are clearly distinct from that of those born in the United States; they tend to defend the system, whereas U.S.-born whites defend the symbols. Whether this is the result of having had a U.S. education or of having been exposed to the influence of mass media is not clear. Both groups articulate a willingness to identify with ideals in contrast to hesitancy about committing to action and structural explanations. They seem to be able to say one thing yet do another; diversity should be embraced, but "not in my backyard."

The media present us with images project a common experience, implicitly "white." When diverse images are presented, they generally portray Blacks who assimilated (such as on "The Cosby Show," "The Jeffersons," or "The Fresh Prince of Bel-Air") or interracial friendships in a way that camouflages or denies racial inequality and undermines our abil-ity to analyze significant and dramatic structural and systemic patterns. Images of people "getting along" lead one to conclude that there must no longer be a "race problem" ("The Hughleys," "White Men Can't Jump," "Regarding Henry") (DeMott 1998). There are posi-tive aspects to these shows, which offer a hopeful vision and a less stereotyped view of different groups of people, though the negative impact significantly defuses the idea that something needs to be done. Portraits of sameness imply that race is a set of interpersonal relations, focusing attention on individuals and away from institutional inequality.[66]

The rendering invisible of structural patterns allows symbolic representations of what being American means to dominate. Hence, patriotism and nationalism, with implicitly racialized ideo-logical underpinnings, need not always be artic-ulated. They can be called upon, at moments such as those after September 11, to impose the presumptions and draw the lines between who is and who is not a trustworthy, loyal, and "true" American. This truth is painfully evident in the study, "Fatal Shootings By US Police Officers in 2015: A Bird's Eye View," was conducted by criminal justice researchers from the University of Louisville and the University of South Car-olina. ... Black men accounted for about 40% of the unarmed people fatally shot by police and, when adjusted by population, were seven times as likely as unarmed white men to die from police gunfire ... falsely perceiving blacks to be a greater threat than non-blacks to their safety.... Black individuals shot and killed by police were less likely to have been attacking police officers than the white individuals fatally shot by police ..."[67] Actor Jesse Williams presentation at the 2016 BET awards eloquently points to the stark distinction in the ways that Blacks and whites are treated by law enforcement and chal-lenges the notion that significant progress has been made. He says,

> ...police somehow manage to deescalate, disarm and not kill white people everyday... yesterday would have been young Tamir Rice's 14th birth-day so I don't want to hear anymore about how far we've come when paid public servants can pull a drive-by on 12 year old playing alone in the park in broad daylight, killing him on television and then going home to make a sandwich. Tell Rekia Boyd how it's so much better than it is to live in 2012 than it is to live in 1612 or 1712.[68]

The melting pot and assimilation and pre-sumed upward mobility narratives avert attention from a broad understanding of economic and social forces that structure the everyday experi-ences of the majority of people worldwide. "Normal" is presented using criteria that few even white Americans experience. Individual circumstances are decontextualized; the respon-sibility for being poor is placed firmly on the shoulders of those viewed as "too lazy" to work hard enough to achieve upward mobility. Mis-representations and lies are perpetrated outright. So for example, despite the mainstream narrative

---

[66]For an excellent analysis of implicitly racial messages in media, see DeMott 1998 [1995].

[67]https://www.washingtonpost.com/graphics/national/police-shootings-2016/.

[68]http://time.com/4383516/jesse-williams-bet-speech-transcript/.

about the limitless possibilities of upward mobility in the United States, "…people in the United States actually have less upward mobility than people in other industrialized nations: Germans are 1.5 times more mobile, Canadians nearly 2.5 times more mobile, and the Danish 3 times more mobile."[69] Similarly "studies show that people in the United States dramatically underestimate levels of wealth inequality in the United States. They tend to believe that there is a much higher degree of equality and appear to prefer the existence of such equality. A recent national study indicates that people in the United States prefer to live in a country more like Sweden than the United States, with ideal wealth distributions that are far more equal than they estimate those in the United States to be" (Ariely 2011 as referenced in Bush and Bush 2015, 128).

The naturalization of both whiteness and American identity hide the processes of privileging. Whites tend to assume that everyone has access to the same resources and receive the same treatment as they do-that there is a common "American" experience. However, even people of color born in the United States are often not considered truly "American." In recent years, someone of Arab descent may be challenged in his or her claim to an American identity as were many Japanese Americans interned in concentration camps during the early 1940s. That "God blessed America" as opposed to any other nation also expresses this "Americentrism. "That the borders and definitions of being "white" and being "American" have changed over time, and continue to do so, provide examples of how these identities bestow status differentially, depending on the circumstance.

13.7 Conclusion

The notion of race is and has been historically crafted, manipulated, reinforced, reproduced, and rearticulated to justify the presumed superiority of people of European descent and to distract

attention from the social arrangement that concentrates power and wealth in a very small percentage of the world's population. The heightened instability of U.S. hegemony within the world capitalist system over the last two decades and the consequent vulnerability of western and white supremacy materially impact poor, working- and middle-class people in concrete and everyday ways.

During times when ordinary people experience political and economic insecurity, ideology plays a critical role in shaping how they understand and interpret what they feel and where they place blame. Since the events of fall 2001, the structures of power have become more visible than they had been since the 1960s. Political leaders moved aggressively to dictate the terms of these interpretations, looking to justify the current social organization and their power within it. We have been told we are not at war with Islam, Muslims, Arabs, Afghanistan, or the Iraqi people, yet who is profiled, and who is bombed? Would the public reaction be the same if the suspects were British, French, or German?

Many educators and activists struggled to bring to light the history of the United States' foreign and economic policies that form the backdrop for events such as September 11th, invasions into Afghanistan, Iraq and Latin America. Such policies enabled, for example, continuous interventions in the affairs of sovereign nations over the last 100 years, recent support for Islamic fundamentalists, and economic partnerships between the Bush and the bin Laden and Hussein families.[70]

Simultaneously, political and media leaders assert narratives about freedom and justice that cloak the economic self-interest of the most powerful in language such as that "What is good for corporations, is good for us all" and "Either you are with 'us' (good), or with the 'terrorists' (evil)." They ostentatiously exclaim their own right to power in plain view. A McCarthy-era type of repression has emerged, attempting to

---

[69]See Pew Charitable Trusts 2007, 9 as quoted in (Bush and Bush 2015, 128).

[70]For details, see International A.N.S.W.E.R. (Act Now to Stop War & End Racism), (www.IntemationANSWER. org; Hatfield (2001); and Helmore (2003).

conceal the facts and implications of these events and aiming to squelch dissent.[71] The contradictions of this dominant worldview have been exposed, though not often explicitly articulated. More people died from bombings in Afghanistan than on September 11 (Herold 2001), and it appears that during that time more U.S. soldiers were killed by "friendly fire" than enemy fire.[72]

At a memorial service for those who died at the World Trade Center, Rudolph Giuliani, heading one of the most racist New York City mayoral administrations in history, was seen singing "We Shall Overcome" with Oprah Winfrey at his side. The slogan "United We Stand" reinforces mainstream narratives about our having achieved equality for all people, dismisses the systemic racialized structuring of our society and of the world-system (which, if anything, has been heightened by recent events), and stigmatizes and marginalizes voices that challenge patterns of inequality in the United States and throughout the world.

Since then public debate about the meaning of patriotism surfaced. U.S. flags became increasingly visible, and choosing to wear or fly one became a measure of one's loyalty. The meaning of being American was actively contested, and the reality of war loomed heavily in the hearts and minds of many people. Rigid notions of identity and the interpretation of history left little room for dialogue. The demand for us to "choose sides" between "good" and "evil" made it difficult to discuss alternative perspectives, as voicing dissent became grounds for suspicion, resulting in the silencing evident not only in the lives of ordinary people but also in the halls of Congress. The heroes portrayed in the media were overwhelmingly white firefighters and policemen. Raising the question of how this employment pattern came into existence and how it is perpetuated is deemed unacceptable, for it sheds light on the deeply stratified (apartheid-like) labor structure that is supposed to remain "hidden," as if we should pretend it does not exist.

Assumptions about national identity and its symbols are present even when not explicit. It is also clear that the dearth of open engagement in society about the meaning of concepts such as democracy, freedom, peace, and justice has real consequences because, during such periods, underlying and concealed presumptions determine what people do. Significantly increased political polarization along ideological lines represents this lack of engagement and increasing segregation racially, economically, and ideologically. The consequences for democratic process are significant.[73]

In reflecting on changes in the beliefs of ordinary people in the U.S. between the first and second edition of *Everyday Forms of Whiteness: Understanding Race in a "Post-Racial World*, Bush says:

> There is certainly a broad sense that there is some sort of problem with the way society is organized though most people are not so sure what that problem exactly is. The dynamics of racial antagonisms have somewhat changed such that the "black-white" polarity is less prominent, primarily evident in discourse that continues to specifically pathologize and criminalize the black experience. Negative stereotyping particularly of Latino immigrants, and anyone of Arab, Muslim or Middle Eastern descent has increased. These ideological frames are widespread and increasingly adhered to by all racial groups and the public at large. Race has become more focused on "immigration," "terrorism," identity and as a proxy for poverty despite the realities faced by most all people in the United States. These have been historically present in the discourse about race, but have become primary points of reference.

There is a need for deeper understanding of global and local concerns as individuals, as a society, as a nation, and as members of the broadest, all-encompassing community of humanity in the 21st century. It is in this context that the questions of nation, national pride, and empire must be analyzed. Why would qualities of cooperation and caring being presented as

---

[71]A recent campaign has called for "intellectual diversity" legislation to reign in what they perceive to be a liberal bias in academia (Horowitz 2004; Fish 2004).

[72]More U.S. soldiers have been killed in Iraq since the war was declared "over" than during the formal battle.

[73]http://www.people-press.org/2014/06/12/political-polarization-in-the-american-public/.

"American" as opposed to "human" nature? Is it true that only "Americans" can lay claim to generosity, democratic ideals, the striving for freedom, and the passion for equality?

Hope ultimately resides in our ability to conceive of ourselves as members of a global society, rather than as "Americans"-all the while taking responsibility for the actions taken in "our" name, and with our taxes. This is similar to considering oneself as part of the human community, positioned and allied with the world's majority, yet recognizing the social reali-ties of racism. Therein lie the particular responsibilities of whites who benefit from the presumption of white superiority.

Martin Luther King Jr. in his (1967) speech said war is a nightmare "for the victims of our nation and for those it calls the enemy." Speaking out against war was the "privilege and the burden of all of us who deem ourselves bound by allegiances and loyalties which are broader and deeper than nationalism, and which go beyond our nation's self-defined goals and positions" (Cohen 1996, vii–viii). The nationalism of those in positions of dominance, like whiteness, is a fabrication with real social consequence constructed solely to bestow value upon its owners. It is, as the "Race Traitors" describe whiteness, like royalty-an identity propped up to render some people more worthy and righteous than others (Ignatiev and Garvey 1996).

After 9/11 President Bush announced "Freedom itself is under attack." Our antagonists, he went on, "hate our freedoms, our freedom of religion, our freedom of speech, our freedom to assemble and disagree with each other." But as Eric Foner articulates,

> Freedom is the trump card of political discourse, invoked as often to silence debate as to invigorate it. ... Calling our past a history of freedom for everybody makes it impossible to discuss seriously the numerous instances when groups of Americans have been denied freedom, or the ways in which some Americans today enjoy a great deal more freedom than others. (Foner 2003)

We are told not to criticize or to look at history-that's mixing apples and oranges. "Osama bin Laden and Islamic fundamentalism are the problem." The United States repre-sents goodness, generosity, democracy, superiority and freedom, so "they" (whoever "they" are) must personify evil.

> Is not nationalism that devotion to a flag, an anthem, a boundary so fierce it engenders mass murder-one of the great evils of our time, along with racism, along with religious hatred? These ways of thinking-cultivated, nurtured, indoctrinated from childhood on-have been useful to those in power and deadly for those out of power ... in a nation like ours-huge, possessing thou-sands of weapons of mass destruction-what might have been harmless pride becomes an arrogant nationalism dangerous to others and to ourselves. (Zinn 2005)

If not now, when is the time to push back against the false, historically constructed narratives that increase the violence and harm being done to more and more people? When is it time to act?

NOTE: Portions of this chapter draw from previous writing in Bush, Melanie E. L. 2011. *Everyday Forms of Whiteness: Understanding Race in a "Post-Racial" World.* Second edition of 2004. *Breaking the Code of Good Intentions: Everyday Forms of Whiteness.* Lanham, MD: Rowman and Littlefield Publishers, Inc., and 2002. "American Identity and the Mechanisms of Everyday Whiteness." *Socialism and Democracy.* New York: The Research Group on Socialism and Democracy.

Appendix I

See Table 13.1.

Table 13.1 Beliefs about the factors contributing to racial inequality[a]

	Not at all (%)	Moderately (%)	A lot (%)
How much do you think the following factors contribute to the average lower incomes and poorer housing of blacks?			
Low IQ	48.8	33.7	17.5
Lack of motivation	21.2	5.9	32.8
Historic inequality	20.3	41.0	38.7
Discrimination	10.5	46.3	43.3
How much do you believe discrimination contributes?			
Latinos	8.3	43.8	45.8
Asians	7.7	38.5	43.6
U.S.-born blacks	0.0	48.8	48.8
Foreign-born blacks	0.0	19.1	71.4
U.S.-born whites	11.8	54.4	29.4
Foreign-born whites	19.5	57.3	18.3
How much do you believe historic inequality contributes?			
Latinos	20.8	41.7	35.4
Asians	7.7	38.5	46.2
U.S.-born blacks	7.0	32.6	55.8
Foreign-born blacks	11.1	25.4	55.6
U.S.-born whites	25.7	43.4	26.6
Foreign-born whites	26.8	42.7	25.6

[a]Bush (2004, 183)

Appendix II

See Table 13.2.

Table 13.2 Assimilation and equal treatment[a]

	Disagree (%)	Moderately agree (%)	Agree (%)
All People, regardless of color, can be assimilated into U.S. Mainstream Society			
	16.1	41.1	42.8
People of color are treated equally to whites when applying for jobs and housing and being approached by the police			
Overall	69.9	21.1	8.9
Latinos	85.4	6.3	8.3
Asians	66.7	23.1	10.3
U.S.-born blacks	83.7	14.0	2.3
Foreign-born blacks	93.7	4.8	1.6
U.S.-born whites	59.6	30.2	9.6
Foreign-born whites	41.5	36.6	19.5

[a]Bush (2004, 187)

Appendix III

See Table 13.3.

Table 13.3 Evaluation of equal opportunity[a]

Disagree (%)	Moderately agree (%)	Agree (%)
All People, regardless of class status, race, or ethnicity, should be given a fair chance to succeed		
2.4	4.6	92.9
If people don't have equal access to resources, measures should be taken to equalize opportunity		
6.2	22.4	71.4

[a]Bush (2004, 209)

Appendix IV

See Table 13.4.

Table 13.4 The United States is a land of equal opportunity for all people[a]

	Disagree (%)	Moderately agree (%)	Agree (%)
Overall	28.0	43.0	29.0
Latinos	27.1	52.1	20.8
Asians	23.1	48.7	28.2
U.S.-born blacks	41.9	39.5	18.6
Foreign-born blacks	36.5	46.0	15.9
U.S.-born whites	25.0	42.7	32.4
Foreign-born whites	15.9	35.4	48.8

[a]Bush (2004, 122)

Appendix V

See Table 13.5a–c.

Table 13.5a Consider myself to be an American[a] (Data from 2004 edition)

	Disagree (%)	Moderately agree (%)	Agree (%)
Overall	21.8	28.3	49.9
Latinos	33.3	29.2	37.5
Asians	30.8	38.5	30.9
U.S.-born blacks	4.7	34.9	30.9
Foreign-born blacks	47.6	38.1	12.7
U.S.-born whites	2.9	12.5	83.8
Foreign-born whites	32.9	37.8	29.3

Table 13.5b I consider myself to be an American (Data from 2011 edition)

	Strongly disagree (%)	Disagree (%)	Agree (%)	Strongly agree (%)	Don't know (%)
Overall	4.8	14.3	53.3	20.0	7.6
Latinos	0.0	14.3	57.1	14.3	14.3
Asians	0.0	20.0	40.0	13.3	26.7
Blacks	3.6	21.4	50.0	17.9	7.1
Whites	7.0	9.3	58.1	18.6	7.0
Indigenous	0.0	50.0	50.0	0.0	0.0
Multi or bi-racial	0.0	15.4	38.5	46.2	0.0

Table 13.5c How often do you think about your national identity? (Data from 2011 edition)

	Never (%)	Occasionally (%)	Once a month (%)	Once a week (%)	Daily (%)
Overall	8.6	47.6	11.4	17.1	15.2
Latinos	7.1	50.0	14.3	21.4	7.1
Asians	13.3	53.3	13.3	6.7	13.3
Blacks	3.6	57.1	3.6	17.9	17.9
Whites	7.0	48.8	11.6	20.9	11.6
Indigenous	0.0	50.0	0.0	50.0	0.0
Multi or bi-racial	7.7	46.2	7.7	23.1	15.4

[a]Bush (2011, 103), Bush (2004, 112)

References

Alba, R. D. (1990). *Ethnic identity: The transformation of white America*. New Haven, CT: Yale University Press.

Babb, V. (1998). *Whiteness visible: The meaning of whiteness in American literature and culture*. New York: New York University Press.

Baker, Lee. (1998). *From savage to negro: Anthropology and the construction of race, 1896–1954*. Berkeley: University of California Press.

Barstow, D., & Henriques, D. B. (2001, December 2). Gifts to rescuers divide survivors. *New York Times*, A1.

Bashi, V. (1999). Review of crosscurrents: West Indian immigrants and race by Milton Vickerman. *American Journal of Sociology*, 890–892.

Blackhurst, C. (2001, 21 October). Anthrax. Attacks now being linked to U.S. right-wing cranks. Online at http://news.independent.Co.uk/world/Americas/story.jsp?story=l00635.

Blassingame, J. (ed.). (1982). *The frederick douglass papers*. New Haven, CT: Yale University Press.

Blauner, B. (1972). *Racial oppression in America*. New York: Harper & Row.

Bloom, A. (1987). *The closing of the American mind*. New York: Simon & Schuster.

Bobo, L. D. (2000). Reclaiming a Du Boisian perspective on racial attitudes. *Annals of the American Academy of Political and Social Science, 568*, 186–202 (March).

Bush, R. D. (1999). *We are not what we seem: Black nationalism and class struggle in the American century*. New York: New York University Press.

Bush, R. D. (2009). *The end of white world supremacy: Black internationalism and the problem of the color line*. Philadelphia, PA: Temple University Press.

Bush, Melanie E. L. (2011). *Everyday forms of Whiteness: Understanding race in a "post-racial" world* (2nd ed., 2004). *Breaking the code of good intentions: Everyday forms of whiteness*. Lanham, MD: Rowman and Littlefield Publishers, Inc.

Bush, M. E. L., & Bush, R. D. (2015). *Tensions in the American dream: rhetoric, reverie or reality*. Philadelphia, PA: Temple University Press.

California Newsreel Film. (2003). *Race: The Power of an Illusion*. http://www.newsreel.org/nav/title.asp?tc=CNO149.

Catherine S., & Angus S. (Eds.). (2004). *The concise Oxford English Dictionary*. Oxford University Press. *Oxford Reference Online*. February 2006. http://0-www.ox.fordreference.com.

Chittister, S. J. (2003, July 15). I give up: What is Americanism? From where I stand. *National Catholic Reporter, 1*(16). Online at http://nationalcatholicreporter.org/fwis/pc071503.htm. Accessed July 15, 2003.

CNN News. (2001, November 29). 7:00 a.m.

Cohen, J. (Ed.). (1996). *For love of country: Debating the limits of patriotism*. Boston: Beacon Press.

Cohen, A. (2006, February 12). According to webster: One man's attempt to define 'America'. *The New York Times* (Editorial Observer). Online at http://www.nytimes.com.

Cox, O. C. (1948). *Caste, class & race: A study in social dynamics*. New York: Monthly Review Press.

Crispell, D. (1994, October 21). We don't need much to have it all. *Wall Street Journal*, B1.

Dan, B. (1999). Giuliani says diallo shooting coverage skewed poll. *New York Times*. On the web, 17 March. http://www.nytimes.com.

Davis, L. T. (2005). Stranger in mine own house: Double-consciousness and American citizenship. *National Political Science Review*, 149.

DeMott, B. (1998 [1995]). *The trouble with friendship: Why Americans can't think straight about race*. New Haven, CT.: Yale University Press.

Dickinson, T. (2005). The return of the draft. *Rolling Stone*. 27 January.

DiLeonardo, M. (1999). 'Why can't they be like our grandparents?' and other racial fairy tales. In R. Adolph Jr. (Ed.), *Without justice for all: The new liberalism and our retreat from racial equality*. Boulder, CO: Westview Press.

Donate, G. A., Robin, C., Satow, R., & Vitale, A. (2002). *People, power and politics*. Boston: Pearson Custom Publishing.

Douglass, F. (1970 [1855]). *My bondage and my freedom*. Chicago: Johnson Publishing Company.

Drake, S. C. (1987). *Black folk here and there: An essay in history and anthropology* (Vol. 1). Los Angeles: University of California Center for Afro American Studies.

Du Bois, W. E. B. (1953, 1961). *The souls of black folk: Essays and sketches*. Greenwich, CT: A Fawcett Premier Book.

Du Bois, W. E. B. (1970 [1940]). *Dusk of dawn: An essay toward and autobiography of a race concept*. New York: Schocken Books.

Du Bois, W. E. B. (1979 [1936]). *Black reconstruction in America: 1860–1880*. West Hanover, MA: Atheneum Publishers.

Du Bois, W. E. B. (1986 [1903]). The souls of black folk. In H. Nathan (Eds.), *W. E. B. Du Bois: Writings* (pp. 358–547). New York: Library of America.

Ehrenreich, B. (2002, January 20). Hobo heaven. *Review of down and out, on the road*. In K. L. Kusmer (Ed.), *New York Times Book Review*.

Farkas, S., Duffett, A., Johnson, J. Moye, L., & Vine, J. (2003, Summer). Now that I'm here: What America's immigrants have to say about life in the U.S. Today. *American Educator*, 28–36.

Fish, S. (2004, February 13). 'Intellectual diversity': The trojan horse of a dark design. *Chronicle of Higher Education*. http://chronicle.com/free/v50/i23/23b01301.htm. Accessed February 19, 2004.

Foner, E. (1998, 1990). *The story of American freedom*. New York: W.W. Norton.

Foner, E. (2003, Spring). Rethinking American history in a post 9/11 world. *Liberal Education, 89*(2).

Freeman, G. (2001, July 15). Misperceptions may be holding back race relations. *St. Louis Post-Dispatch Inc.* Five Star Lift Edition, C3.

Gallicchio, M. (2000). *The African American encounter with Japan and China: Black internationalism in Asia, 1895–1945*. Chapel Hill: University of North Carolina Press.

Gilmore, B. (2002). Stand by the man: Black America and the dilemma of patriotism. *The Progressive, 66*(l), 24–27.

Glazer, N. (1983). *Ethnic Dilemmas 1964–1982*. Cambridge, MA: Harvard University Press.

Glazer, N., & Moynihan, D. P. (1963). *Beyond the melting pot, the negroes, puerto ricans, jews, Italians and Irish of New York City*. Cambridge: Massachusetts Institute of Technology.

Glazer, N., & Moynihan, D. P. (1975). *Ethnicity: Theory and experience*. Cambridge: Harvard University Press.

Gonzalez, Juan. (2000). *Harvest of empire: A history of latinos in America*. New York: Penguin.

Grosfoguel, R. (2013, Fall). The structure of knowledge in westernized universities Epistemic racism/sexism and the four genocides/epistemicides of the long 16th century. *Human Architecture: Journal of the Sociology of Self-Knowledge, XI*(1), 73–90.

Grossman, Z. (2001, September 20). *A century of U.S. military interventions: From wounded knee to Afghanistan Znet*. Online at www.zmagorg/crisescurevts/interventions.htm. Accessed July 7, 2003.

Haley, A., & Malcolm, X. (1965). *The autobiography of Malcolm X*. New York: Ballantine Books.

Harrison, F. (1998). Introduction: Expanding the discourse on 'race.' *American Antluvpologist, 100*(3), 609–631.

Hatfield, J. (2001, July 3). Why would Osama bin Laden want to Kill Dubya, his former business partner? *Online Journal*. Online at www.onlinejournal.com/Special_Reports/Hatfield-R-091901/hatfield-r-091901.html. Accessed August 2, 2003.

Helmore, E. (2003, March 30). Oscar winner Michael Moore targets Bush and bin Laden. Published by the Observer/UK. *Common Dreams News Center*. Online at www.commondreams.org/headlines03/0330-06.htm. Accessed September 28, 2003.

Herold, M. W. (2001). *A dossier on civilian victims of United States aerial bombing of Afghanistan: A comprehensive accounting*. Online at www.cursor.org/stories/civilian_deaths.htm. Accessed January 20, 2002.

Hobsbawm, E. (2003, July 4). Only in America. *The Chronicle of Higher Education*, B7–B9.

Hochschild, J. L. (1995). *Facing up to the American dream: Race, class and the soul of the nation*. Princeton, NJ: Princeton University Press.

Honig, B. (2001). *Democracy and the foreigner*. Princeton, NJ: Princeton University Press.

Horne, G. (2014). *The counter-revolution of 1776*. New York: New York University Press.

Horowitz, D. (2004, February 13). In defense of intellectual diversity. *Chronicle of Higher Education*. http://chronicle.com/free/v50/i23/23b01201.htm. Accessed February 19, 2004.

Ignatiev, N., & John, G., (Eds.). (1996). *Race traitor*. New York: Routledge.

International Institute for Democracy and Electoral Assistance. (n.d.). *Turnout in the world-country by country performance*. Online at http://idea.int/vt/survey/voter_turnout_pop2.cfm. Accessed July 7, 2003.

International Institute for Democracy and Electoral Assistance. (n.d.). *United States voter turnout from 1945 to Date*. Online at http://idea.int/vt/country_view.cfm. Accessed July 7, 2003.

Jackson, D. Z. (2001, October 31). Buckingham 's lucrative landing: United we stand, except at the unemployment line. *Boston Globe*, A23.

Jacobs, H. (1861). *Incidents in the Life of a Slave Girl*. Source: "North American Slave Narratives, Beginnings to 1920" at the "Documenting the American South" website of The University of North Carolina at Chapel Hill (pp. 265–275). http://docsouth.unc.edu.

King, Jr., M. L. (1967, April 4). Beyond Vietnam. Speech delivered at riverside church. Accessible at http://www.commondreams.org/views04/0115-13.htm.

Kraly, E. P., & Miyares, I. (2001). Immigration to New York: Policy, population and patterns. In N. Foner (Ed.), *New immigrants in New York.* New York: Columbia University Press.

Lavin, D. E., Richard, D. A., & Silberstein, R. A. (1979). Ethnic groups in the city University of New York. *Harvard Educational Review, 49*(1), 53–92.

Lemert, C., & Bhan, E. (1998). *The voice of Anna Julia cooper.* New York: Rowman & Littlefield.

Lerner, G. (1997). *Why history matters: Life and thought.* New York: Oxford University Press.

Lester, T. (2002, February). Oh, Gods! *Atlantic Monthly,* 37–45.

Lewis, O. (1961). *The children of sanchez: Autobiography of a Mexican family.* New York: Random House.

Lewis, O. (1969). Author's response to culture and poverty: Critique and counter-proposals. *Current Anthropology, 10*(2–3), 189–192.

Livingston, A., Wirt, J., Choy, S., Provasnik, S., Rooney, P., Sen A., & Tobin, R. (2003). The condition of education 2003. National Center for Education Statistics. U.S Department of Education. Institute of Education Sciences NCES, 2003–2067.

Marable, M. (2002, July 25). *Abolishing American apartheid, root and branch.* Presentation at the Symposium on Racism in San Francisco.

Martinez, E. (1996, December). Reinventing 'America.' *Z Magazine,* 20–25.

Martinez, E. (2003, July–August). Don't call this country 'America': How the name was hijacked and why it matters today more than ever. *Z Magazine,* 69–72.

Marx, A. (1998). *Making race and nation: A comparison of South Africa, The United States and Brazil.* New York: Cambridge University Press.

Mitchell, K. B. (2003, November 16). *Members of congress with children in Iraq.* Footnote Fahrenheit. Media General News Service. http://www.newsaic.com/f91Jchap7-8.html.

Mollenkopf, J., John K., & Mary W. (2001). *Chutes and ladders: Educational attainment among young second generation and native New Yorkers. In The Center for Urban Research: City University of New York.* Paper presented at the ICMEC Conference on New Immigrants in New York City. CUNY Graduate Center, November.

Montagu, A. M. F. (1945). *Man's most dangerous myth: The fallacy of race.* New York: Columbia University Press.

Morgan, E. S. (1975). *American slavery, American freedom: The ordeal of colonial Virginia.* New York: W. W. Norton.

Morin, R. (2001, July 11). Misperceptions cloud whites view of blacks. *Washington Post.* Final edition, AI.

Morrison, T. (1992). *Playing in the dark: Whiteness and the literary imagination.* New York: Vintage Books.

Moyers, B. (2006, February 24). *Restoring the public trust.* http://TomPaine.com.

Moynihan, D. P. (1965). *The negro family: The case for national action.* Washington: U.S. Department of Labor.

Mullings, L. (1978). Ethnicity and stratification in the urban United States. *Annals of the New York Academy of Sciences, 318,* 10–22.

Myrdal, G. (1964). *An American Dilemma.* (Vols. 1 and 2). New York: McGraw-Hill (1944). *New York Times.* (1999 Editorial). The Journey to 2000. 31 December, A20.

Nussbaum, M. (1996). Reply. In J. Cohen (Ed.), *For love of country: Debating the limits of patriotism.* Boston: Beacon Press.

Nussbaum, M. (2001, December 17). Can patriotism be compassionate? *The Nation,* 11.

O'Leary, C. E. (1999). *To die for: The paradox of American patriotism.* Princeton, NJ: Princeton University Press.

Omi, M., & Winant, H. (1994). *Racial formation in the United States.* New York: Routledge.

Orleck, A. (2001). Soviet jews: The city's newest immigrants. In N. Foner (Ed.), *New immigrants in New York.* New York: Columbia University Press.

Postel, D. (2001, December 7). Outsiders in America. *Chronicle of higher education,* A12.

Roediger, D. R. (1994). *Toward the abolition of whiteness: Essays on race, politics and working class history.* New York: Verso.

Roediger, D. R. (1998). *Black on white: Black writers on what it means to be white.* New York: Schocken Books.

Roediger, D. R. (1999 [1991]). *The wages of whiteness: Race and the making of the American working class* (1st ed.). New York: Verso.

Roper Survey Organization. (1993, May–June). How we classify ourselves. *American Enterprise,* 87.

Roth-Douquet, K. Schaeffer, F. (2006). AWOL: The unexcused absence of America's upper classes from military service—and how it hurts our country. Harper Collins.

Ryan, J. (1973). *White ethnics: Their life in working class America.* Englewood Cliffs, NJ: Prentice-Hall.

Saez, E. (2009) *Striking it Richer: The Evolution of top incomes in the United States* (Update with 2007 Estimates). Pathways, August 5, 2009. http://elsa.berkeley.edu/~saez/saez-UStopincomes-2007.pdf

Schaefer, R. T. (1995). *Race and ethnicity in the United States.* New York: Harper-Collins College Publishers.

Schwartz, B., Markus H. R. & Snibbe, A. C. (2006, February 26). Is freedom just another word for many things to buy? That depends on your class status. *New York Times Magazine,* 14–15.

Scott, J. (2003, July 6). The changing face of patriotism. *New York Times Week in Review,* 1.

Scott-Heron, G. (1992). *'B' movie. Reflections..* Compact Disc: Bertelsmann Music Group Company.

Smedley, A. (1993). *Race in North America.* San Francisco: Westview Press Inc.

Smedley, A. (1998). 'Race' and construction of human identity. *American Anthropologist, 100*(3), 690–702.

Smith, R. C., & Seltzer, R. (2000). *Contemporary controversies and the American racial divide*. Oxford: Rowman & Littlefield.

Staples, R. (1993). The illusion of racial equality. In G. Early (Ed.), *Lure and loathing: Essays on race, identity and the ambivalence of assimilation*. New York: Penguin Books.

Steinberg, S. (1995). *Turning back: The retreat from racial justice in American thought and policy*. Boston: Beacon Press.

Steinberg, S. (1999). Occupational apartheid in America: Race, labor market segmentation and affirmative action. In R. Adolph Jr. (Ed.), *Without justice for all: The new liberalism and our retreat from racial equality*. Boulder, CO: Westview Press.

Steinberg, S. (2001). *The ethnic myth: Race, ethnicity and class in America*. Boston: Beacon Press.

Street, P. (2001, October). The white fairness understanding gap. *Z Magazine*, 9–11.

Tell, S. (1999). E-mail to the Mult-cul@ubvm.cc.buffalo.edu list, July.

Tolerance.org. (2001). *Hate in the news. Hate Goes to School*. www.tolerance.org/news/article_hate.jsp?id=3I2. Accessed November 24, 2001.

United States Election Project. (2004). *Voting-Age and Voting-Eligible Population Estimates and Voter Turnout*. http://elections.gmu.edu/Voter_Turnout_2004.htm.. Accessed December 10, 2005.

Waldinger, R. (2001). Rethinking 'race'. *Ethnicities, 1*(l), 19–21.

Wallerstein, I. (2001, December 5). *America and the world: The twin towers as metaphor*. Presentation at the Charles R. Lawrence II Memorial Lecture, Brooklyn College. Online at www.binghamton.edu/fbc/iwbkln02.htm. Accessed December 10, 2001.

Williams, P. J. (2001, December 10). Disorder in the court. *The Nation*, 11.

Wiltse, C. M. (1965). *David Walker's appeal*. New York: Hill & Wang.

Winant, H. (2001). *The world is a ghetto: Race and democracy since World War II*. New York: Basic Books.

Wise, T. (2000, December 4). Everyday racism, white liberals and the limits of tolerance. *LiP Magazine*. www.lipmagazine.org.articles/featwise_11.htm.

Zinn, H. (1995). *A People's history of the United States 1492-Present*. New York: Harper Perennial.

Zinn, H. (2005, May 20). *The scourge of nationalism*. http://www.commondreams.org/views05/0516-29.htm.

Part IV

From a Global Perspective: Colonial Legacies, and Post-colonial Realities

A Dialectical Understanding of the Vulnerability of International Migrants

14

Jorge A. Bustamante

Contents

This paper consists of five parts. The first presents the issues brought by President Trump ever since his electoral campaign that affects in many senses the life of people who have lived at the two sides of the US-Mexico border. The empirical reality of close to 20 million human beings interacting across that international border justifies calling it a region. That has a history of interdependence and resilience. The latter is defined for the purpose of this chapter, as the ability of the border population (so defined as the inhabitants of the US-Mexico Border Region) to overcome the problems of this international vicinity.

The second part alludes to another issue highlighted by Donald Trump that goes beyond the geographical confines of the US-Mexico border as a region. This implies entering into the complexities of the issues related to immigration. This requires an upgrading to the abstraction level, from the bombastic rhetoric of Donald Trump to this work's theoretical approach, aiming to provide an analytical model that explains the relationship between international migrations and human rights. For this purpose a diagram of the dialectical processes resulting in the vulnerability of migrants was designed to summarize this analytical model. Part three. consists of an historical analysis of the rise and dynamics of a bilaterally shaped phenomenon of labor migration from Mexico to the United States. Part four. consists of some analysis of the political and social implications of

J. A. Bustamante (✉)
Department of Sociology, University of Notre Dame, Notre Dame, IN, USA
e-mail: Jorge.A.Bustamante.1@nd.edu

© Springer International Publishing AG, part of Springer Nature 2018
P. Batur and J. R. Feagin (eds.), *Handbook of the Sociology of Racial and Ethnic Relations*,
Handbooks of Sociology and Social Research, https://doi.org/10.1007/978-3-319-76757-4_14

the US immigration changes announced by President Trump.

14.1 Part I. It All Began at the Border

If there is a geographical area that has been particularly affected by the events of September 11, 2001, then the international border between Mexico and the United States stands out first. It is understandable that a country that enters in a state of war after been attacked in its own territory with enormous loses, for the first time in its history, reacts by closing its international borders. Deriving concomitantly, there were changes to the immigration phenomenon. A first dimension of change is that from the geographical vicinity between two countries of contrasting development and cultures to another that suffered the effects from a shift in U.S. immigration perspectives. That change in perspectives emerged from one based on labor and economics to another based on national security. The immediate U.S. reaction to close its doors has become gradually replaced with stricter controls over whatever crosses its borders. Nevertheless, the fact remains; border life is not what it used to be before September 11th. In the short run, new controls had slowed down crossing the border for every item. Along the border, optimists thought that in the long run, and for the most part, things would gradually return to what it was before that tragedy of 9/11. Others more realistically thought that for a long while, life at the border would never be the same.

An intense interaction of almost 20 million people from both sides of the U.S.-Mexico Border Region has made their lives, under many circumstances, conceived as if the border did not exist. That has been the case among the ways of life for plenty of families around the region. For the planning of weddings, birthdays, family reunions and religious ceremonies, the border had been more virtual than real. This was reversed from a virtual border to a real one after that September 11th. The population around this region was then forced to act under higher awareness about what it meant for their feelings to cross an international border. New perspectives brought by 9/11 made border population realize that by crossing the border they were entering into grounds where institutions, the laws and the governments addressed them with virtual, and not so virtual, verbal interaction, reminding them that there is a line that marks the beginning and the end of two different nations. After that 9/11, one of the effects of what happened at the border was that people living along the border were confronted with an increase in the number of authorities where they were reminded that the border makes a difference. Their own identities were then filtered through acts of awareness, about what side of the border they really belong to. People from the U.S.-Mexico Border Region might continue to have a lot of things in common with those of the other side but they are more frequently reminded that it is not the same whether they are within the Southern or Northern side of the border. The border might be changing from being something that unites to something that divides.

Perhaps that is the nature of an inherent relation between sovereignty and the nation's borders. After 9/11, ensuring that its international borders were protected regardless of how good the relations were with its neighboring countries is understandable to the United States. Taking care of the integrity of the national sovereignty is certainly not something that a country could delegate to a neighboring country. This is similar to saying that there is nothing more internal or domestic, than taking care of one's own borders. In this sense, an international border cannot be the same during conditions of war than during conditions of peace. People's lives along the border had almost adjusted to changes brought by 9/11 when Donald Trump came to the scene speaking loudly about building a bigger wall between the United States and Mexico. Ever since the beginning of his electoral campaign he used a language that sounded as if Mexicans and Mexico belonged to an enemy country. This represented a remarkable change from what the geographical vicinity meant for border population before that 9–11.

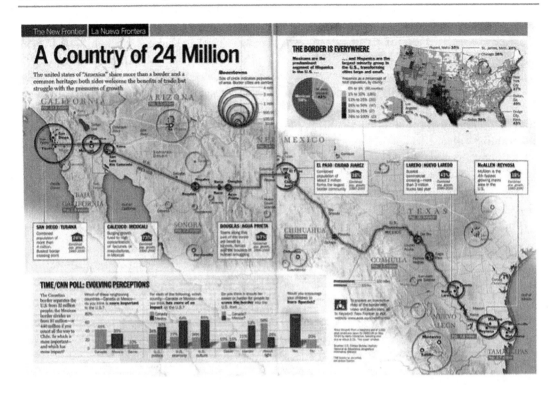

In *Time* magazine's June 11th, 2002 edition (Vol. 152. Num. 23) there was a lengthy coverage about the US-Mexico Border Region. The main thesis of that unusually broad media coverage portrayed this region as place of convergence for the best economic growth opportunities that the globalization and trilateral processes had ever brought. *Time* magazine writers in that issue portrayed very optimistic scenarios based on the realities according to a thriving process of integration throughout all three North American Free Trade Agreement (NAFTA) economies, particularly economic realities between Mexico and the United States, and even more particularly at the border region we share. Those optimistic scenarios were some of the many casualties of the 9/11 terrorist attack. Yet, such scenario changed with the appearance of Donald Trump even as vital needs at the border have not changed. Those living on the two sides of the border still have to eat, to provide for their families, seeking the cooperation from their other side's neighbors for the common tasks that geography has imposed on them. For Mexicans their vicinity with the United States had meant that there would be times when its vicinity is an opportunity, and times when it would become a problem. The latter appeared attached to mistreatment and/or discrimination. This region's population had always seen an enormous challenge for good neighboring. Some times, it had been met by acts of solidarity such as, when the borderline river (Rio Bravo for Mexico; Rio Grande for the U.S.) bursts its banks inundating border settlements of the two sides. Some other times, such as those with President Trump's anti Mexican rhetoric, when Mexicans have felt treated as an enemy country. Even so, the fact remains: neither side will ever be able to change geography.

14.2 Part II. A Dialectical Relation Between International Migrations and Human Rights

The basic premise of this analysis is that a social process exists in people's interactions between the two countries that resulting in conditions of **vulnerability**[1] of international migrants as subjects of human rights.

This diagram entitled "Dialectics of Migrants' Vulnerability," depicts this social process, which implies; (1) a socio-legal inclusiveness that arises out of a dialectical process between two legal notions of **sovereignty** and, (2) the social construction of conditions of vulnerability for international migrants, who are mobilized across international borders by the dynamics of the

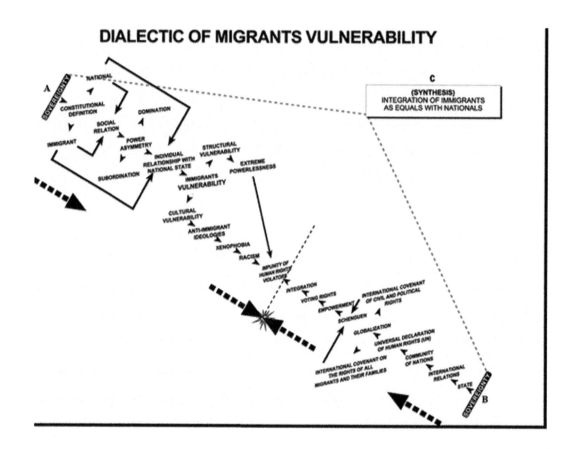

DIALECTIC OF MIGRANTS VULNERABILITY

---

[1]This social construct refers to a condition of powerlessness. It precedes the "labeling" understood as an act of power over *vulnerable* people.

international relations arising from the **globalization**[2] of international markets.

This diagram conveys a theoretical framework of a socio-legal inclusiveness. It addresses an apparent contradiction between a notion of international migration and a notion of human rights. The first is generally understood as partially corresponding to the sovereign right of a country of destination, as far as it implies the right of a country to determine who can enter its borders and who cannot. On the other hand, a notion of human rights derived from the UN Universal Declaration of Human Rights, which implies rights for all human beings, regardless of national origin. To the extent that countries of destination of international migrations decide to accept as their sovereign rule to protect the human rights of all people regardless of their migratory status. Accordingly, that sovereign decision implies a self-imposed limitation, if not an apparent contradiction, between that exercise of a sovereign right in two opposite directions. This work's diagram is suggested to analyze that apparent contradiction by means of dialectics, in George Hegel's terms, as an analytical tool.

Three assumptions provide its understanding. First, the dialectical relations between the two acts of sovereignty, and acts emerging in between, correspond to a social process. Second, this a social process corresponding to two different times in history, in which a set of

contradictions have origin from two opposite acts of sovereignty; Third, the evolution implied in each side of the diagram is relatively independent from each other, except that both evolutions are moved by the international relations implied in the concept of **globalization**. The notion of a clash between the evolutions of the two sides of the diagram implies a growing process of maturity and a dynamism that reaches its maximum force as confronted by another force of an opposite sign. In other words, this work analyzes the clash between vulnerability of migrants depicted on one side of the diagram, and **empowerment** of migrants on the opposite side. Behind this notion of a dialectical clash is the assumption that there is a point of maximum vulnerability of the migrants that characterizes the impunity of those who violate their human rights. That impunity stops, at the point of encounter with an opposite force. That force comes from the empowerment of the migrants. This empowerment has been evolving as a result of pressures coming from the international community or what is known as globalization. An illustration of this process and this outcome is the granting of voting rights to legal immigrants in local elections, as it has occurred in several nation States within the European Union.

Following the model proposed by Hegel's dialectics, the clash between a thesis and its antithesis gives way to a synthesis. This is understood by Hegel as consisting of elements from the two colliding forces. This is the way **integration** (as explained below) is understood in the diagram as (C) or, as the dialectical synthesis of (A) and (B).

The main actors of the social process implied in the diagram are, (a) the immigrants (indistinctly understood as foreigners) as they are nationals of a country of origin; (b) the officials of the nation/State of their immigration; (c) the nationals of a country of destination.

This social process begins when a country of destination, exercising its sovereignty, decides to include in its constitution a distinction between nationals and foreigners, by establishing a definition of who is one and who is the other. This act of sovereignty, identified in the diagram as (A),

---

[2]Malcolm Waters' comments on Giddens' definition, quoted above, help to clarify the meaning of globalization implied in the diagram: "This definition usefully introduces explicit notions of time and space into the argument. It emphasizes locality and thus territoriality and by this means stresses that the process of globalization is not merely or even mainly about such grand, center-stage activities as corporate mega-mergers and world political forums but about the autonomizations of local life worlds. Globalization, then, implies localization, a concept that is connected with Giddens' other notions of relativization and reflexivity. The latter imply that the residents of a local area will increasingly come to want to make conscious decisions about which values and amenities they want to stress in their communities and that these decisions will increasingly be referenced against global scapes. Localization implies a reflexive reconstruction of community in the face of the dehumanizing implications of rationalizing and commodifying." (Waters 1995)

enters into a long term process that ends up in an apparent contradiction—defined in the diagram as dialectically opposed—to another act of sovereignty. This is when a sovereign decision is made by a country of destination to commit itself to respect and protect an international standard of human rights, regardless of the national origin and migratory status of individuals. Then, constitutionally remaking that international standard into a **law of the land**; therefore, becoming (B) in the diagram. As such, the latter is in contradiction with (A) which preceded it.

That decision to make a constitutional distinction between nationals, on the one hand, and immigrants as foreigners, on the other, implies the emergence of a basis for a social relation between those acting under the constitutionally defined role as nationals, and those acting under the constitutionally (by default) defined role as foreigners. These two exercises of sovereignty depicted at each of the extremes in the diagram as dialectically opposed, become interrelated in the practice of international relations arising from the phenomenon of globalization.[3] Thus, the "thesis" in this dialectical process *à la Hegel* is A), and the "antithesis" is (B). Further below in this work the "synthesis", namely **integration**,[4] will be identified in the diagram as (C).

Problems of power and authority in the past of human societies have confronted the source, or locus, of authority, which has moved from God, to the State, to the people. The definition of sovereignty[5] has been based chronologically on these three sources. At their origin in medieval times, under the doctrine of Christian unity, the concepts of "sovereignty" and "sovereign" were one and the same, except for the semantic distinction between an attribute and the subject of its enactment.

The diagram starts from the Hegelian notion of dialectics, which is not to be confused with that of *dialectical materialism,* coined by Hegel's rebellious student Carl Marx, after he had criticized Hegel's dialectic as one that should be *standing on its head* which made it necessary to *turn it right side up again.* He claimed to have done just that by creating his "*historical materialism*" equated to "dialectical materialism". The present rendering of Hegel's dialectics has nothing to do with Marx's "correction" of his mentor's philosophy of history. Here, Hegel's dialectics should be viewed as a social process. One that is taking place between two opposite exercises of sovereignty, each with different objectives and opposed to each other as a *thesis* opposes an *antithesis,* out of which a *synthesis* emerges. Implicit in this use of dialectics as a tool of analysis is the inclusiveness of two cognitive domains, namely, law and sociology. One is of a legal or normative nature and the other of a social empirical nature. The bridge between the two dimensions is implied in the passage from a norm—an *ideal construct*—into actual human behavior, in the empirical context of social relations. The diagram assumes such inclusiveness in alluding to a social process in which the main actors are those defined constitutionally, as

---

[3]For the purposes of this paper, Anthony Giddens definition is the most fitting. "Globalization can … be defined as the intensification of worldwide social relations, which link distant localities in such a way that local happenings are shaped by events occurring many miles away and vice versa. This is a dialectical process because such local happenings may move in an obverse direction from the very distant relations that shape them. Local transformation is as much part of globalization as the lateral extension of social connections of time and space." (Giddens 1990).

[4]There are two contrasting notions of *integration.* One, predominant in the United States, derives from the studies of Robert Ezra Park, whose followers, according to Michael Haas, have argued "that differences between ethnic groups are a function of attitudes of prejudice" (Haas 1992: p. 61). This thesis assumes that such differences can be removed through intense interethnic interactions, which could lead to a color-blind society. About this assumption, Haas comments: "There are at least four flaws in integrationism. First, it is a theory of assimilation. The closer an ethnic group resembled the dominant culture, the more it would be "tolerated" and

ultimately "accepted" and "admitted" to equal status…" The other notion of integration, predominant in Western Europe, is more recent. This is epitomized by the Schengen Agreement, binding for member states of the European Union, where integration means equal rights for nationals and foreigners. The latter notion is the one adopted in this article.

[5]For an in-depth analysis of the historical context in which the notion of *sovereignty* has evolved, see Bartelson (1995).

nationals on the one hand and, those defined legally and socially, as foreigners or immigrants. The main feature of this inclusiveness is the dialectical dynamic, which is energized by the international relations of globalization, and that is the relational context for emerging conditions under which the vulnerability of international migrants comes into being. This vulnerability is understood here as a condition of powerlessness; given that an international migrant is socially placed in a position of inferiority *vis-à-vis* the nationals by an act of power of the nation/State of his/her immigration. This act of power implies an act of discrimination against "non nationals", derived from the constitutional distinction between "nationals" and "non nationals.

By establishing this dichotomized definition, the constitution of a country of destination is establishing a criterion for a social asymmetry between nationals and foreigners. Regardless of how consciously this is done, such constitutional distinction is transferred to the context of an empirical social relation between actors who assume their roles, claiming the authority of the constitution. Then, the asymmetry of power implied in the constitutional distinction becomes enacted as a power differential in the empirical reality of the social relation between nationals and an immigrant/foreigner. To the extent that an unequal power is implied in such constitutional distinction between nationals and foreigners; distinctive access to the social forces of society allows for the rise and development of anti immigrant ideologies or social constructions, of which implementation justifies, reinforces and promotes the power differentials originally assigned to the constitutional distinction. The rise of anti immigrant ideologies is a direct result of the power differentials derived from the asymmetry of power established by that constitutional distinction. A social outcome of such power differentials is a pattern of discrimination against immigrants. This is particularly evident in the labor relations of Mexican immigrants in the United States where employers tend to be US nationals and workers are Mexican immigrants. The labor relations between them are best

illustrated by the case of the California economy. Mexican immigrants make more than 90% of the total of the labor force employed in the agricultural production of that State; agricultural production equal to one third of the total of the US agricultural production, according to the NAWS survey conducted under the auspices of the US Department of Labor which results were published in 1994.

In such labor market study, one finds empirical evidence to substantiate the existence and operation of a power structure where the basic social relations of nationals (US employers) and immigrants are a social characteristic of the national system of agricultural production in the United States. This is what could be inferred from the following paragraph taken from the conclusive remarks of a research report published by the US Secretary of Labor in 1994.

> In effect, migrant workers so necessary for the success of the labor intensive U.S. agricultural system, subsidize that very system with their own and their family's indigence. The system functions to transfer costs to workers who are left with income so marginal that, for the most part, only newcomers and those with no other options are willing to work on our nation's farms. (U.S. Department of Labor 1994)

These remarks deriving from a scientific research, give empirical support to the notion of a power asymmetry between migrant workers and their employers in California. They illustrate the strength of a US demand of immigrant's labor; also showing the degree of vulnerability as subjects of human and labor rights imposed on migrant workers to whom costs of agricultural production are transferred in order for the US agricultural system to function.

The fact that the publication of these research findings, from which the above quotation comes, took place before the appearance of California's Proposition 187 (explained below), illustrates the dynamics of a social process on its way to a growing impunity for the violators of immigrant's human rights, which is assumed in the diagram. At some point, such impunity, as suggested in this work, is stopped by the empowerment of the immigrants. The apparent contradiction between international migrations and human rights requires some additional discussion about its historical context.

For this work, evolution of the asymmetry of power is an assumption deriving from the constitutional distinction between nationals and foreigners. That evolution follows similar paths that have followed other socially constructed "distinctions", out of which discriminatory behavior against a social group has been subjectively justified. That has been the case of racism, sexism, homophobia and xenophobia.

Integration *a la* European Union, becomes a true Hegelian synthesis of the dialectical opposition in the diagram between (A) and (B). Such a synthesis implies the elimination of inequalities that characterize the social relations between nationals and foreigners. By the time an evolution of A) is confronted with its opposite B), the result (synthesis) of that confrontation depicted in the diagram, is a new stage of human rights different, but shaped with elements of the previous stages. That given case is one where previous inequalities between nationals and foreigners have been erased. The new out coming product generated by the dialectical relations between (A) and (B), is **integration**. This new stage implies, that human rights may be no longer different between nationals and foreigners. Such was one of the accomplishments of the Schengen Agreements.

There seems to be a distance of light years between the empowerment of migrants that one can derive from legislation, such as that recommended by the Schengen Agreements, and enacted by countries such as Spain, The Netherlands, Denmark, to grant voting rights to immigrants in local elections, and, the conditions of vulnerability of migrants such as those implied by President Trump's threats against all US immigrants in general and Mexican immigrants in particular. However, when one takes into account the time it took for European countries to evolve from the "Treaty of Rome" in 1957 to the Schengen Agreements regarding "voting rights" to immigrants, one could hypothesize about immigrant's rights having possibly a better future

than that ominous one anticipated at the beginning of the new US administration in 2017. That is the hypothesis behind the dialectics of vulnerability implicit in the diagram.

A recount of the dialectical contradiction between (A) and (B) includes the notion that all nation states have the sovereign right to define who is a national and who is a foreigner, as well as the sovereign right to control their borders. In both cases, the implication is to define the frontier between the essential inner and outer components of a nation. Most democratic nations have these rights written in their constitutions. Although such legitimate distinctions, in most of the cases, do not explicitly place the foreigner[6] in a subordinate position *vis-à-vis* the national, when they interact socially within the receiving country, the duality (national-foreigner) is, nevertheless, very often transformed; or better said, socially constructed, into an object of a de facto discrimination against foreigners by nationals. As Robert Miles[7] widely discusses, this distinction is implicit at the origin of all kinds of discriminatory practices against foreigners, at personal, group, and institutional level. This implies a power structure wherein nationals are more likely to occupy dominant positions *vis-à-vis* foreigners. In this, sort of a metamorphosis from the normative to the social lays the **virtual** contradiction between **immigration** and **human rights**. In reality, there is no contradiction. The sovereign right that is implicit in the definition of each concept respectively is of the same legal nature. These concepts imply two different instances of an exercise of sovereignty, in two different times in the history of a country of destination. These two exercises of sovereignty are dialectically opposed. Such a dialectical opposition was generated from the dynamics of international relations implied in the process of **globalization**. As international migrations are a consequence of globalization, the international

---

[6]The terms "foreigner" and "immigrant" are used interchangeably in this article.

[7]For a discussion of the dominant/subordinate relation of nationals/immigrants assumed in most recipient countries, see Robert Miles, *op. cit.* (particularly in reference to what he calls the problem of "Euro-racism"), pp. 207–215.

community acquires an acting role in the evolution implied in each side of the diagram. In order to justify the abstraction level for this acting role, every analyst requires looking to the history of specific international relations between countries of origin and destination to focus at the micro cosmos of the social relations between the international migrant and a national of the country of his or her destination. The following section is an attempt to penetrate analytically in such a micro cosmos.

Having defined *vulnerability* as a condition imposed on immigrants, the following graph depicts yearly variations of such conditions distinguished by the routes migrants follow in their trans migration journey from the southern border of Mexico to its northern border with the United States.

This work's findings are summarized into the following:

(1) Caution should be observed before generalizing about the status of Mexican immigration to the United States. This graph shows until 2016, immigration from Mexico had not diminished, let alone stopped. This immigration following the Pacific route (red line) shows an increase from 2015 to 2016. The opposite is true about the route of the Gulf of Mexico.

(2) Graph´s blue line refers to immigrants entering the US from Mexico by plane. Their migration flow has been relatively stable except for the earliest and latest years; probably due to US labor market variations.

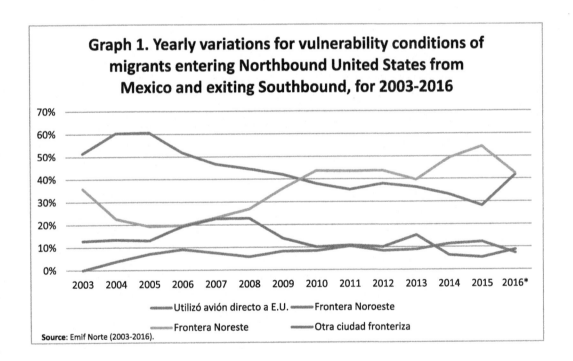

Graph 1. Yearly variations for vulnerability conditions of migrants entering Northbound United States from Mexico and exiting Southbound, for 2003-2016

Legend: Utilizó avión directo a E.U. — Frontera Noroeste — Frontera Noreste — Otra ciudad fronteriza

Source: Emif Norte (2003-2016).

These are people with higher income and education than those above.

(3) Purple line refers to a residual category of immigrants' border crossers through Mexican border cities other than those at the two extremes.

14.3 Part III. The Historical Context of Mexican Immigration to the United States

Before September 11 it seemed like the governments of Mexico and the United States were closer than ever before to an agreement on the question of migration. This raises a common sense question, how come it has taken so long? It is only logical that a bilateral agreement is the path to follow for a bilateral problem that is caused by factors located at the two sides of the border.

Accepting that Mexican immigration to the United States is a bilateral phenomenon, there is a contrasting level of public concern about it in the United States as compared to Mexico. For example, even when, other than occasional signs of public indignation when the media reports on a Mexican migrant that has been hurt or killed by a US Border Patrol agent, there has hardly been enough debate about the causes and consequences of this phenomenon in Mexico. For instance, the legislative proposal sponsored, years ago, in a bipartisan fashion by Senators Kennedy and MacCain that was left, and pending for approval by the death of Senator Edward Kennedy, included for the first time a principle of bilateral negotiation regarding the questions of US immigration from Mexico. These have always been viewed unilaterally by the United States.

At the time of the Kennedy MacCain proposal there were about 10 million Mexican immigrants in the United States who send close to 20 billion Dollars in remittances to the Mexican economy. At the time of the last review of this Chapter (January of 2017) there was an estimate of close to 20 million Mexican nationals residing on a permanent basis in the United States who were sending remittances to Mexico for 27 billion US Dollars at the end of 2016. (February 24, 2017)

There is not enough historical awareness about certain elements that have made such a rational option of a bilateral agreement so difficult to reach by the two governments. It is certainly not because such an option has escaped the minds of the leaders of the two nations[8] There is not enough awareness in Mexico of the extent to which certain laws pertaining to the legal context of labor relations in the United States have been in the way. For instance, the famous Wagner Labor Act of 1935. This Law established the legal frame within which labor relations were to be conducted in the United States. This law was good news for the industrial workers but bad news for the farm workers. They were not included in the new legal frame under which labor rights were granted to industrial workers. The important point is that such labor legislation excluded farm workers from the legal definition of an "employee" for whom the rights of this law were granted (See, 29 U.S.C. Section 151 sec 152(3)). This Law was amended by the Taft-Hartley Labor Act passed by the U.S. Congress in 1947 an then amended by the Landrum-Griffing Act which was passed by Congress 1n 1959, but the original exclusion of agricultural workers from the right to organize and bargain collectively through representatives of their own choice, remain unchanged. This in fact signified a discrimination against farm workers from the legal basis upon which industrial workers were to be treated by US employers. Behind this *de jure* discrimination was the development of a structural context of asymmetry of power between farm workers and their employers in the United States. The understanding of such an asymmetry of power lies behind the understanding of why it has been so difficult for the United States and Mexico to reach an agreement on the migration question.

As demonstrated in the classic study of the bracero program made by Dr. Ernesto Galarza in his book, *Merchants of Labor; A*

---

[8]Olloqui (2001).

History of the Bracero Program, published in 1964, the bracero agreements were thought to be a rational solution to the migrant workers question by the political leaders of the two countries. But, eloquently explained by Dr. Galarza, far from being a rational solution for the migrant workers, the bracero agreements became an instrument at the service of the US growers. The US agribusiness used the bracero agreements to legitimize and perpetuate the conditions of exploitation under which the Mexican migrant workers were treated in the United States.[9] This was what Texans, including President Bush, learned in their up bringing. That Mexican "braceros" were good for agribusiness. There had been little wonder why President Bush thought that Mexican temporary workers were good for the US national interests. That being the reason why he was proposing a temporary workers or a "guest workers" program as a solution to the migratory question. Except that at that point in time it would not be through a bilateral agreement but through unilateral decision by the US Congress.

The statement here about the old "bracero agreements" is not to suggest that the same peasants were treated any better in Mexico. The post war years were a time when peasants as a social class were increasingly abandoned by the Mexican government and by Mexico's emergent middle and upper classes, in the context of a dramatic change in the nation.[10] At the middle of the Twentieth Century, Mexico changed from being a country based on an agrarian society to a country based on a new urban society that had its economic base on industry and services.

For many years the notion within the Mexican government was that the bracero agreements were a model to be followed to regulate the migratory situation. This notion derived from the reading of the written terms of the first bracero agreement signed by the two governments in 1942. Indeed, the written texts of that first

agreement spoke of vary favorable conditions for the Mexican migrant workers.[11] There was, however an enormous distance between the written text and the reality. Ernesto Galarza tried very hard to convince the Mexican government at the end of the second World War, as one can read in his memoranda to the President of Mexico, found in the Mexico's National Archives by researcher Jaime Velez Storey and partially published with John Mraz.[12] Through a series of articles published by the prestigious journal *El Trimestre Economico* in the Nineteen-fifties, Galarza tried to persuade the Mexican government that the words of the first bracero agreement were something substantially different than the reality lived in the United States by the Mexican migrant workers[13]. The asymmetry of power between them and their U.S. employers determined the abysmal difference between the words and the reality of the bracero agreement.[14] The history of such an asymmetry of power derived from a historical context in which the United States government persuaded an initially reluctant Mexican government under the presidency of Manuel Avila Camacho (1942–1946), to sign the first bracero agreement negotiated and approved by Mexico under the geopolitical conditions in which the United States entered the Second World War.[15] The Mexican government was not in the position to challenge the emergent power of the United States. I have argued elsewhere that the asymmetry of power between the migrant workers and their U.S. employers was rooted in the asymmetry of power between the governments of the United States and Mexico.[16]

The realities of that asymmetry of power were reflected in the racism about the Mexican immigrants expressed at the highest circles of the U.S. government ever since the beginning of the 20th Century. John Nance Garner, who was U.S. Vice President years later, once said: "The

---

[9]Galarza, Ernesto, List of migrant workers' complaints included in a Memorandum prepared for the president of Mexico cited by Mraz and Storey (1996).

[10]Torres (1979).

[11]Olloqui, Opus cit. p. 12.

[12]Mraz and Velez-Storey, Opus cit. p. 49, Footnote 25.

[13]Galarza Ernesto, El trimestre Economico.

[14]Galarza, *Merchants of Labor*.

[15]Ojeda-Gomez (1971).

[16]Bustamante (1992).

Mexican race as inferior and undesirable as U.S. citizens as they are, should not worry any one because they are **genetically determined** with a **homing pigeon** instinct of ever return to where they came from".[17] The Mexican government did not have the power, nor the will to protect its people against such an anti-Mexican ideological statements. Nor to set the record straight that what the United States was referring as an immigration policy was in reality a U.S. labor policy.

It was early in the twentieth century when the United States developed a basic ambivalence about the presence of immigrants from Mexico. That is, an ambivalence between wanting the immigrants as cheap labor but not wanting them as members of the American society.[18] This has been an ambivalence that is seldom discussed in the United States; no matter how politically important the issue of immigration—let alone undocumented immigration- has become in the decision making process determining the laws of the land in the U.S. Congress. That basic ambivalence has blinded Americans from seeing the objective realities of a U.S. labor demand which shape the Mexican undocumented immigration phenomenon as the result of a process of interaction with the factors that produce

---

[17]This, and other equally racist arguments can be found in, U.S. Congress (1929).

[18]US social scientists in charge of the assessing of conditions of immigration to the United States were suggesting as early as 1910 an immigration policy toward Mexico that would encourage the importation of labor power without the burden of increasing immigration with the following words: "The progress of the Mexican children in the Los Angeles schools is below the average and they leave school early. A large percentage of the native born can not speak the English language. Because of their stron attachment to their native land, low intelligence, illiteracy, migratory life, and the possibility of their residence here being discontinued, few become citizens of the United States... In so far as Mexican laborers come into contact with natives or European immigrants they are looked upon as inferiors... Thus it is evident that in the case of the Mexican he is less desirable as a citizen than as a laborer. The permanent additions to the population however, are much smaller than the number who immigrate for work. U.S. Senate, U.S. Immigration Commission (Dillingham Commission) Reports. Vol. 1, pp. 690–691.

emigration from Mexico as the labor supply for such U.S. labor demands. It is not lack of information what explains that blindness about how Mexican immigrants are wanted so badly in the United States. The same year that "Proposition 187",—the most anti-Mexican anti-immigrant law in the history of the U.S.-Mexico relations (this is elaborated ahead)—, was voted in favor by two thirds of Califonia's electorate, showing how deeply rooted was the hate against Mexicans in that State, the findings of a scientific study published by the U.S. Department of Labor was not only recognizing the U.S. undocumented immigrant's labor demands but empirically defining their function in U.S. agriculture as "a subsidy" to the U.S. economy.

The findings of the scientific report from which a paragraph was quoted above, was published in the midst of a widely publicized propaganda to vote in favor of "prop. 187", as a part of the reelection campaign of then Governor Pete Wilson. Those findings were virtually non existent both, for the proponents of Proposition 187, nor for the two thirds of the electorate of California who voted in favor in the elections of November of 1994. Six months after the publication of that research report by the US Department of Labor, Proposition 167 emerged.

The story of how Pete Wilson supported Proposition 187, resorting to Californians' anti-Mexican prejudices for his political interests of reelection, is going to be told one day as an emulation of the almost successful George Wallace's campaign to be nominated as the presidential candidate of the Democratic Party still heralded by the words of his inaugural speech as a governor of Alabama in 1963: "*Segregation now! Segregation tomorrow! Segregation for ever!*" Pete Wilson was less dramatic in his use of racist ideologies for political purposes, but no less inclined to appeal to anti-Mexican prejudices than in his time Wallace was in his appeal to anti-Black's.

The contradiction between Pete Wilson's ideological basis for his support of "Proposition 187" and the US Labor Department's conclusive paragraph quoted above, could not be more apparent. The quoted paragraph refers to published empirical evidence of the extent immigrant undocumented labor is not only wanted, but needed, in California. This is in stark contradiction to Pete Wilson statements saying that the presence of such labor force in California is the cause of a "suffering of personal injury and damage". Myths based on prejudices and racial hate. Such myths were then enough basis to criminalize a whole ethnic group (the Latino)—that is ideologically identifiable in California by the color of their skin—, as the most apparent basis to *a priori* "**know**" the migratory status of a person, so as to justify his or her denunciation to the immigration authorities.

The above references to Pete Wilson's anti immigrant reasoning are relevant now that President Trump has issued "executive orders" against immigrants thirty years later, with the same ideological basis, except that "proposition 187" was later on declared unconstitutional by US federal courts.

The criminalization of those who appear being illegal aliens by ethnic profile, implied in the proposition 187 in California, did not disappear after it was declared unconstitutional by a federal court decision. Some of the same proponents of Proposition 187 in California ten years ago, were behind "Proposition 200" in Arizona and more recently, behind the legislation known as the Real ID law sponsored by congressman James Sensenbrenner of Wisconsin. This led to the legislative proposal HR-3447 which was approved by the House and is (as of March of 2006), pending of approval by the US Senate. Bill HR-4437 includes some of the most xenophobic elements of Proposition 187, with some additions, such an empowerment of any police in the United States to arrest and expel from the United States, any individual who look suspicious of being an illegal alien and upgrading the criminalization of undocumented entries to the United States from a misdemeanor to a felony. The latter surfacing recently as a virtual replica of the former thus, showing the persistence of both the anti-Mexican ideologies and the ambivalence of many Americans about the presence of the Mexican immigrants in the United States.

14.3.1 Ideologies in México

The question of Mexican emigration to the United States has not being free of ideologies in Mexico. This was the case of what I have called elsewhere the ideology of the "escape valve"[19]. In a social context in Mexico where the majority of the population at the beginning of the Second World War consisted of very poor farm workers, they were viewed downwardly by upper income social classes. So, by the time the United States government put pressure on the Mexican government to sign the first of the "Bracero agreements" in 1942, as a way to supply the labor force needed by the United States at the time of the labor shortages produced by the War effort, the recruitment of the temporary workers made under the terms of the bilateral agreement consisted basically of peasants from that virtual underclass sector of the Mexican society. By the time the War ended, there was an increasing gap between the interest of the Mexican peasants and the interest of the Mexican government. This was particularly the case under the administration of president Miguel Aleman (1946–1952).[20] Such a gap explained the beginning of the notion that the emigration of Mexican peasants to the United States was an "escape valve". Under this notion, the emigration of Mexican migrant workers to the United States was seen in Mexico as a sort of solution to the pressures both, real and potential, derived from the increasing abandonment of the Mexican government of an increasingly impoverished peasants. There was an inverse relation between the support the government gave to a new social class of industrial entrepreneurs who led the beginning of the economic growth of industry, and the abandonment of the countryside both, by the government and by the Mexican civil society. Behind the "push factors" of the emigration from Mexico to the United States, were Mexico's lack of capabilities to achieve modernization through an industrial development, without abandoning its agricultural sector and its farm workers. Mexico as a nation became enchanted with the illusion of

---

[19]Bustamante (2002).
[20]Garcia-Cantu (1978). See also, Bortz (1992).

modernization by turning its back to its past of an agriculture based society.

Emigration from Mexico to the United States became an "escape valve" that was viewed by the Mexican elites as necessary to alleviate the pressures and the costs of the abandonment of peasant's social class. That notion of emigration to the United States as an "escape valve" became a predominant ideology of the Mexican Government about emigration to the United States. Such an ideology obscured the realities of exploitation and rampant violations of human and labor rights of the Mexican immigrants in that country throughout the "bracero period" (1942–1964).

The decade of the 50s were the years when the Mexican Government found that there was no political cost in doing nothing for the Mexican migrant workers in the United States. This marked the context in which the Mexican government tried very hard to cover up the conditions under which the Mexican migrant workers were treated in the United States. I had an argument with a Mexican Consul in a U.S. border state right after I posed as an undocumented immigrant in 1971, as part of the research for my doctoral dissertation, after he flatly denied there were Mexican undocumented immigrants in the United States. I had to refer to him my "participant observation" recent experience. When I asked him how come he had to lie to me denying the existence of what I just had witnessed, he reluctantly proposed that if I give him my word that I will never reveal his name, he let me read a "circular" (an internal memo), from the Ministry of Foreign Affairs of Mexico, where an instruction to all Mexican Consuls in the United States was very clear, not to expressively recognize, nor to make any statement alluding to the illegal presence of Mexican immigrants in the United States. Before 1964 and years after, the Mexican Government had as a top priority to persuade the US government of the renewal of the Bracero agreements. This interest was an important factor that explained why the Mexican government was so complacent about the impunity with which frequent incidents of violations of human and labor rights of Mexican immigrants were taking

place mostly in Texas and California. Before 1964 the Mexican government was too busy lobbying for renewed versions of the bracero agreement with an increasing indifference about the distance between the written terms of these agreements and the realities lived by the Mexican migrant workers.

That indifference compunded by an increasing corruption as a way of life at all levels of the Mexican government and, by the political control over the Mexican peasantry through the Confederación Nacional Campesina (CNC), which proved over the years to be a very efficient mechanisms of manipulation of the PRI's "peasants' sector" through a mixture of populism and corruption which gave shape to the rise of "caciques", a sort of regional bosses, who ruled the country side of Mexico by a combination of patriarchal protection to supporters and an iron hand, full of impunity, to handle opponents. This way the PRI ruled most of Mexico from 1929 until the year 2000.

The works of Ernesto Galarza explained the conditions under which it became functional for the two sides; on the one hand, for the interest of the Mexican government of maintaining an "escape valve" of Mexican emigration of an increasingly impoverished, unemployed, uneducated, unorganized underclass of Mexicans and, on the other hand, an interest of U.S. agribusiness in maintaining a source of cheap labor.[21] This explains why at the end of the last bracero agreement in 1964 the Texas and California's growers associations, and the Mexican government, became the most persistent proponents of the renewal of the bracero programs.

The ideology of the "escape valve" inhibited the Mexican government from defending or actually protecting the Mexican migrants in the United States, other than through rhetorical references. Far from being a solution to the problems associated to migration between the two countries, the bracero agreements became concomitant to the rise of the undocumented migration. As it was documented in Julian Samora's book *Los Mojados, The Wetback*

---

[21]Galarza (1970).

Story published in 1972, by the time of the end of the last of the bracero agreements in 1964, there were more Mexicans crossing as undocumented immigrants than the number of "braceros" contracted through the bilateral agreements at the pick of their numbers.

The absence of a political cost for the Mexican government for doing nothing for the Mexican migrants in the United States was not independent of the Mexican civil society's general indifference about their plight.

After several years of studing that difference a hypothesis was suggested in earlier works that such an indifference was not unrelated to a generally unrecognized Mexican racism. It was not until the "Chiapas rebellion" of 1994 that the question of Mexican racism, virtually "came out of the closet", from a deeply entrenched part of the Mexican culture. The Mexican migrants have been viewed by the Mexican middle and upper social classes as something distant from them. As if the plight of the Mexican migrants about the constant violations of their human and labor rights in the United States and in Mexico was something virtually happening in a different planet, or something that was happening to people with whom the middle and upper classes of Mexico had nothing to do. It was certainly not racism in any pure form. The disdain of the Mexican middle and upper social classes about the problems of the Mexican migrants in the United States had elements of classism. That is, a social distance felt by the middle and upper classes away from the peasants of Mexico. This explains why the plight of the Mexican migrant workers was never taken to the streets by any Mexican organization, particularly by any one of those who claim to protect or defend the interest of the Mexican poor or the Mexican peasants. It has not been until very recently that public institutions such as the Mexican Catholic Church have expressed concern and have begun to support few programs in defense of the Mexican migrants. For many decades the main institutions representing the Mexican civil society, namely the Churches, the unions, the political parties or students organizations, did no more than rhetorical references when an incident of abuse of the

human rights of the migrants reach the mass media and then, reflecting more anti-American sentiments than sincere concerns for the migrants.

This long time indifference of the Mexican civil society about the plight of the Mexican migrants has not been sufficiently studied. It remains as a gross incongruence. The dependence that the national economy of Mexico has had of the remittances of US dollars made by the migrant workers in the United States had no congruence with the rampant indifference of the Mexican middle and upper classes about the problems of the migrant workers in the United States. Only exports of Mexican oil, have produced more income of US dollars per year for the Mexican economy, than the close to twenty billion dollars that the Central Bank of Mexico has estimated as the total of remittances from the United States for the year 2004–2005.[22] There is not enough consciousness in Mexico of what would be the social consequence of an exhaustion or even a diminishing of migrant workers' remittances from the United States. It is very likely that the remittances from Mexican migrants in the United States are financing the absence of a violent break of the social order in México.

Returning to the years of the bracero program, a paradox should be noted. The end of the bracero programs was basically due to the pressures exerted by the AFL-CIO.[23] Through several decades the AFL-CIO was one of the most important anti-immigrant forces in the United States.[24] Not only were they successful in ending the bracero programs, but also they were the principal proponents of anti-immigrant legislation for decades.[25] That ended on February 17, of 1999 when the Executive Committee of the AFL-CIO in a meeting in New Orleans, made a 180-degree change of course. From then on, the AFL-CIO has become the most vocal proponent

---

[22]Craig (1971).

[23]Olloqui, Opus cit. p. 17.

[24]Mexico, Secretaria del Trabajo y Previsión Social (STPS) (1964).

[25]Garcia (1980).

of a "blanket amnesty" to undocumented immigrants. To be sure this change was not an act of nature. Behind it, was the surging of a new *Latino* leadership arriving to the upper echelons of the AFL-CIO.[26] These new leaders, among them Linda Chavez-Thompson, AFL_CIO's Executive Vice President, Ana Avendaño and Eliseo Medina, conveyed the message to the top that an inclusion of undocumented immigrants in the rank and file of the AFL-CIO, not only would bring a new source of union fees but a new dimension of international involvement and political clout to an otherwise weakening political strength of the AFL-CIO. In a statement published on February 28 by the news agency Reuters it was announced the rejection of the AFL-CIO of the "guest workers" proposals under discussion in the US Congress. Linda Chavez-Thompson was quoted as saying: "To embrace the expansion of temporary guest worker programs is to embrace the creation of an undemocratic, two-tiered society". This was probably related to a close watching of the demographic trends of the Latino population in various circles of the American life.

14.4 The Years of the "Silent Invasion"

An important factor in the absence of a bilateral agreement on the migratory phenomena between Mexico and the United States has been the distance between the predominant definitions of this phenomenon in the governmental circles of the two countries respectively, as well as within the political elites and, the predominant views of the public opinion about the presence of undocumented immigrants from Mexico within the United States. From the first economic recession of the 20th Century in the United States in 1907, to all the subsequent ones until the present, a pattern has always appeared basically consisting of the following sequence, (a) the rise of unemployment rates and other signs of a recession

catch the public attention; (b) politicians make an association between the rise of unemployment and the presence of the immigrant workers; (c) there is a social construction of immigrant workers as "escape goats" of the recession; (d) politicians then propose anti-immigrant measures as a solution to the economic crisis; (e) the vulnerability of immigrants as subjects of human rights increases together with the impunity of the abusers; (f) the economic recession subsides; (g) that is followed by an end of the anti-immigrant furor.

The recession that came as the result of the oil cartel action taken by OPEC countries in 1974 was not an exception to such a pattern. Those were the years when General Leonard Chapman was appointed as Commissioner of U.S. Immigration and Naturalization Service (INS). He coined the phrase of a "silent invasion" in reference to the presence of undocumented immigrants from Mexico.[27] He gave testimony to various US congressional committees speaking about estimates of 20 million undocumented immigrants from Mexico. It was only after the end of his tenure as Commissioner of INS, that his successor, Leonel Castillo, lowered previous estimates to 3 million. The enormous difference in the estimates that two successive commissioners of the INS presented to US congressional committees made evident the extent to which previous estimates had been a fabrication made to substantiate the notion of a "silent invasion" with some base numbers of ideological origin to the political construction of the Mexican immigrant as an "escape goat". It was under General Chapman that the rise of anti-immigrant sentiments in the United States crystallized in a definition of a phenomenon of Mexican immigration to the United States as a crime related phenomena. This became a predominant definition in the United States government circles where there was a consensus to reject any recognition of the existence of a demand of the labor force of the undocumented immigrant, particularly in the agricultural production of California and

---

[26]U.S. Congress (1926), U.S. Senate (1953) and Taylor (1981).

[27]This was confirmed in a letter from the AFL-CIO representative in México City.

Texas.[28] There was a social construction of the Mexican undocumented immigrants as criminals that led to the notion in the United States that the only solution to a "problem" defined as one of criminal nature, was either a police or a military type of solution.[29] This notion was concomitant to another notion claiming the only solution to the "Mexican illegal question" had to be unilateral.[30]

Such a position of the United States prompted a delayed reaction of the Mexican government during the presidency of Carlos Salinas de Gortari (1988–1994) expressing opposition to what was termed an unfair and unjustified "criminalization" of the undocumented immigrant from Mexico. Through the Secretary of Foreign Affairs, Fernando Solana, the Mexican government came out with a contrasting definition of the undocumented immigration from Mexico to the United States as derived from a de facto international labor market.

The Mexican reaction defining the phenomena of undocumented immigration of Mexicans in the United States as basically a labor phenomena, contradicted the predominant definition of the same phenomena in the United States governmental circles. The net result of this contradiction between the predominant definitions in the two governments about the same migratory phenomenon was a status quo. Although, the position of the Mexican government during the ninety's was never beyond the confinements of the rhetoric.

President Ernesto Zedillo (1994–2000) saw, that whatever degrees of freedom he had in negotiating with the United States, they were crippled very early in his administration by the Mexican economic crisis of 1994. This not only provoked a drastic devaluation of the Mexican Peso but also, a close call for the forfeiture of the Mexican foreign debt. A collapse was avoided thanks to President Bill Clinton's decision to bail out the Mexican government by a loan of 20 billion dollars.

President Zedillo owed so much politically to president Clinton that he couldn't find room for any criticism in spite of the deaths of Mexican migrants due to the beginning of the "Operation Gatekeeper" in 1994. This was designed not to stop, as one would expect from an immigration law enforcement agency, but to deflect the route of entry's of undocumented immigrants from Mexico into the United States toward areas away from the visibility of urban eyes like those of San Diegans. As it was recognized by the chief of the border patrols in a written testimony to a U.S. Congressional Committee, the design of "Operation Gatekeeper" was made under the assumption that undocumented immigrants were going to get discouraged by the risk of death presented by the areas of crossing where the migrants were diverted to.[31] These were mountainous terrain East from San Diego, or the deep irrigation channels, such as the All American Canal, or the inhospitable desert areas between California and Arizona, where soon enough the number of migrants deaths begun to climb. Risks of dehydration in the desert lands or hypothermia during the winter months or drowning in the irrigation channels, did not discouraged the inflow of undocumented immigrants, they caused their death in stead. As it is shown by the increase in the number of deaths of migrants presented in the following maps:

---

[28]U.S. House of Representatives (1975).

[29]Meissner, Doris (Hearings).

[30]Bustamante (1983).

[31]Senator Simpson (quotation).

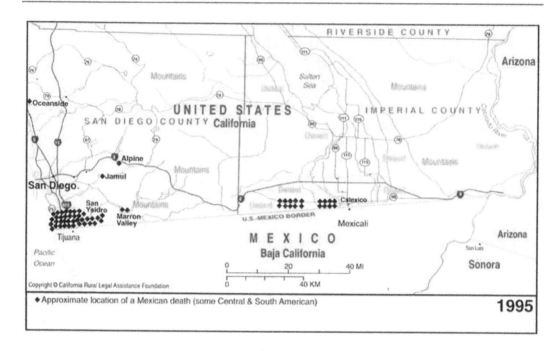

♦ Approximate location of a Mexican death (some Central & South American)

1995

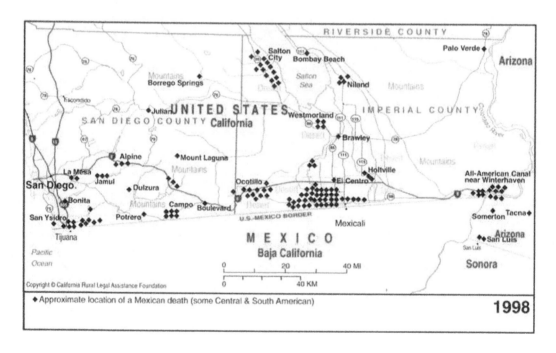

♦ Approximate location of a Mexican death (some Central & South American)

1998

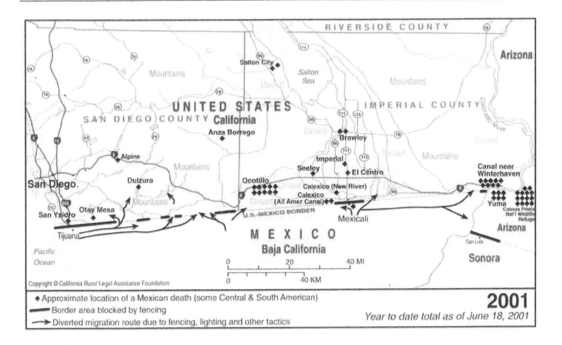

Very soon after the starting of "Operation Gatekeeper" in 1994 the number of migrants dying in the area where "Operation Gatekeeper" was put into effect, showed clearly that the assumption based on which "Operation Gatekeeper" was designed, was wrong. This was a conclusion reached by a report of the GAO of the U.S. Congress after conducting an investigation of the extent to which the "Operation Gatekeeper" had reached it's stated objectives.[32] What really happened with the immigration flows of undocumented immigrants from Mexico was not a diminishing of the volumes of their flow to the United States but a change of places of entry toward the west from the traditional areas through San Diego. In that process, the number of deaths of migrants had been climbing at a rate of more than one migrant killed per day as an average, in the area covered by "Operation Gatekeeper". Some non governmental organizations such as the Rural Legal Foundation of California and the American Civil Liberties Union of San Diego and Imperial Counties, criticized their own government for the violation of human rights that this operation implied as they alleged, it's implementation was in violation of the Charter on Human Rights of the Pan American Union. No Mexican institution, let alone the Mexican government, reacted in solidarity to such a criticism made by American NGO's and by American citizens. In fact, when President Zedillo was invited by governor Gray Davis to visit California in May of 1998, he declared to the Spanish Daily *La Opinion*, on the verge of his visit to California, that the deaths of the migrants were neither a responsibility of the United States nor that of Mexico.

14.4.1   The Present and the Future

These and many other things changed with the emergence of the political leadership of Vicente Fox. He was able to correctly interpret a general feeling of Mexicans being fed up with the ruling of the PRI, which had been in power for the last 71 years. Vicente Fox ran a political campaign for the election of president of Mexico based on a promise about change, particularly a

---

[32]U.S. Border Patrol, "Border Patrol Strategic Plan 1994 and Beyond" Prepared testimony for a Congressional Hearings, see, www.stopgatekeeper.com.

change from corruption in the practice of government.[33] As a governor of the State of Guanajuato and as a prosperous rancher in that State, he was familiar with the phenomena of emigration of Mexicans to the United States. Guanajuato is one of the Mexican provinces with an oldest tradition of emigration of its people to the United States. Comparably speaking, Guanajuato had a high concentration of population at the beginning of the 20th Century, when the U.S. Congress decided to appropriate some monies to fund the recruitment of Mexican workers. The First World War had stopped the influx of immigrants from Europe. Blacks had gone North from the Deep South to substitute European immigrants in the lowest paid occupations. The conditions of the War had produced a massive need for agricultural production for exports. It had produced also some labor shortages, particularly in Texas and California. The first anti immigrant laws of the United States had succeeded in expelling the Chinese first, and then the Japanese and then the Philippines in the wake of the "Asian bared zone". This created a sort of a vacuum of cheap labor, the sensitivity of which was taken to Washington by some Congressman of California who, after the first economic recession of the 20th Century in 1907, argued in the US Congress that, the Mexicans should be sought after as immigrant workers for which purpose public monies should be appropriated. The idea was approved and recruiters were sent south to Mexico. The U.S. Congressional records tell the story. Congressman from California argued that the "Mexican race" was physically fitted for stoop labor because they were shorter, closer to the ground, as opposed to the white race who was born for stand up work thus, fitted for the industrial production.[34] Racist ideologies of white supremacy had penetrated the ivory towers of U.S. academia at the turn of the Century. Ideas of white supremacy were incorporated in the main stream of U.S. social science.[35]

Published in, "*Problemas Agricolas e Industriales de Mexico*", Mexico, 1958, Vol. 10, pp. 15

---

[33]U.S. General Accounting Office, Report to Congressional Committees (2001).

[34]Quoted in Feagin (1999). Chand, Opus cit., p. 264.

[35]Feagin, Opus cit. p. 385.

Published in, *"Problemas Agricolas e Industriales de Mexico"*, Mexico, 1958, Vol. 10, pp. 33

Published in, *"Problemas Agricolas e Industriales de Mexico"*, Mexico, 1958, Vol. 10, pp. 65

American recruiters were sent South to Mexico with the goal of attracting Mexican workers to fill the vacuums of cheap labor left with the immigration restrictions against immigrants from Asia. U.S. labor recruiters could not find concentrations of people in Mexico right across the border. Some of the actually most populated cities of the Mexican Northern Border, like Tijuana, Baja California, where this work's author is resident, didn't exist as urban settlements at the beginning of the 20th Century. So, U.S. labor recruiters had to go farther south until they found higher concentrations of population. That is why they reached Guanajuato thus, introducing what soon became a tradition in that State, namely, to emigrate to the United States in search for higher wages.

Vicente Fox, as a governor of Guanajuato, was very much aware of the importance of remittances in Dollars from the United States by the Mexican migrant workers. So, in his political campaign for the Mexican presidency he called migrant workers "heroes" acknowledging for the first time by a Mexican president, the importance of migrant workers remittances in the Mexican balance of payments, which in the year 2004 represented more than 13 billion Dollars per year —currently 20 billion—, according to *Banco de México's* estimates, making these remittances of U.S. Dollars within the top sources of revenues for the Mexican economy. Calling migrants "heroes" was quite a change from the ideology that saw migrants as an "escape valve".

There is one aspect of ethics in the discussion of US immigration that is rarely discussed. That is the moral responsibility that derives from the U.S. immigrant's labor demand, which existence was scientifically demonstrated by the study conducted by the U.S. Department of Labor; and based on data from the National Agricultural Workers Survey quoted above. Two points could be argued from the fact that there is a U.S. demand of the labor force of undocumented immigrants, unilaterally produced by Americans. Firs, that if there is a labor demand originated endogenously by an American source, namely, U.S. employers, there is a co-responsibility of the United States and México, in the shaping of the immigration phenomenon from México. That labor force of the undocumented immigrant is as needed in the United States as it is real in a **de facto** U.S.-Mexico international labor market. Next, if one accepts the assumption that such a demand interacts with the factors producing in Mexico the supply of the labor force for that market, such inherent bilateral nature of that labor market makes the shaping of the migratory phenomenon as bilaterally caused. For this reason, whatever solution to the US immigration from Mexico, it should be bilaterally approached. That alludes to the format that the study and the eventual solution of problems related to the migratory phenomenon should take. There is a moral principle arising from the reality of the U.S. labor demand of Mexican immigrants. That moral principle is one of responsibility deriving from the role such a labor demand plays in the bilateral shaping of the migratory phenomenon. In fact, the right enunciation of such a responsibility is one of a co-responsibility shared by the two nations

involved in such a **de facto** international labor market, namely, that of Mexico and the United States. As member nations of the United Nations Organization the juridical nature of that responsibility should be congruent and guided by the Universal Declaration of Human Rights. This is the reasoning that should substitute the irrationality of xenophobia, violence, unilateralism and all other factors that contribute to the vulnerability of migrants as subjects of human and labor rights.

In order to better understand the bilateral nature of the responsibility as this was defined above, a further elaboration on the Mexican politics will be added.

Vicente Fox visited the United States and Canada in August of 2000, after his electoral victory that made him President of Mexico. During such a visit he surprised many Mexicans when he said that the deaths of migrants at the border would be "intolerable" in his administration. He also surprised the United States with his audacious proposals of an open border for Mexican migrants after sufficient closing of the wage gaps between the United States and Mexico. The idea was not accepted in the highest circles of the US government but it certainly made Americans think about it. Fox's proposals on migrant labor had the legitimacy of a "democracy bonus" that had come from an electoral victory under the most free elections in the history of Mexico. The image of Vicente Fox as a champion of democracy, after having been in his past a regional director of Coca-Cola for Mexico and Central America, was not difficult to be swallowed by the American media. Fox came to the United States as president elect, free of the strings attached to previous negotiations led by President Zedillo. Soon enough it became clear that Fox had a powerful American allay, George W. Bush, also a former rancher, who became President of The United States almost at the same time than Vicente Fox.

None of the U.S. presidents before George W. Bush, including his father, had deviated from the notion that the "illegal aliens" were criminals. This is why the different position taken by

President Bush during his visit with Vicente Fox at his ranch in Guanajuato, represented such a significant change of U.S. immigration policies. On that moment and for the first time, Bush's speech included recognition, of a U.S. labor demands as a factor that shaped the phenomena of immigration of Mexicans to the United States. His speech included also references to the human and labor rights of the Mexican immigrants in the United States and, perhaps the most important change, he mentioned a need to negotiate a bilateral solution to the immigration question. The most serious obstacle for a bilateral agreement on the migrant question had been removed. A very efficient diplomacy under Fox's Secretary of Foreign Affairs, Jorge G. Castañeda, in preparation of this presidential meeting in Guanajuato, was probably an important factor towards such change in the U.S. perspective, from blatant unilateralism to a proposal of a bilateral approach through negotiations. Before this change happened there was an irreconcilable contrast between the predominant definition in the United States of the presence of undocumented immigrants from Mexico as a crime related phenomena. One that can only be solved by a police or military type of solution that could only come unilaterally and, on the other hand, the predominant definition in Mexico of the same phenomena as one of labor nature, shaped by the factors that create a U.S. labor demand, in interaction with the factors that create a Mexican labor supply. A power asymmetry between the governments of the two countries had maintained a *status quo* of that contradiction for more than thirty years; which, ever since the years of General Leonard Chapman appointed as high commissioner of then, U.S. INS, and who had coined the term of "silent invasion", permeating the U.S. political culture as reflected by references to the Mexican immigration in the U.S. mass media.

Under that ideological environment, the abuses of human and labor rights against the Mexican immigrants came to the surface through mass media reports, showing the conditions of impunity, under which U.S. law enforcers of various levels, from the local to the federal, were involved in incidents of violence against Mexican immigrants with no consequences.[36] These were years when extreme cases of exploitation were reported by U.S. media, such as one who provoked legal action with charges of slavery against a U.S. employer.

The Mexican government was incapable of doing anything concrete against the increasing vulnerability of Mexicans in the United States. During the decades of the 70s, 80s and, 90s the most important source of legal protection of Mexican immigrants came from Mexican American organizations in the United States, such as Mexican American Legal Defense and Educational Fund (MALDEF), National Council of la Raza, League of United Latin American Citizens (LULAC) and, GI-Forum, in addition to numerous community organizations in California, Texas, Colorado and New Mexico.

The legal support and the protection of the human rights of the Mexican migrants were not coming from Mexico during these three decades. As demonstrated by the litigation of *Brown v. Texas Board of Education*, there were lawyers hired and paid by Mexican American organizations who were concerned for the vulnerability of Mexican migrants as subjects of human and labor rights. Such was the case where a federal court in Houston declared unconstitutional to exclude the Mexican children of undocumented immigrants from public schools. The author was an expert witness in that trial which represented an important victory for the immigrants after fair recognition that the majority of them pay taxes

---

[36]*Los Angeles Times* published a series of reports from April 22 to April 24, 1993, including the following text: "Some agents complain that commanders place so much emphasis on amassing drug seizures—thus impressing top brass and law makers in Washington—that supervisors turn a blind eye to evidence of wrongdoing by agents .... Management will let you do whatever you need to do to get the job done to stop drug smuggling. Said Thomas A. Watson a five years Nogales veteran who was fired this month for complicity in the cover-up of a fellow agent's fatal shooting of a suspected trafficker. Drugs are what the chief wanted. Drugs made the head lines .... Many agents admit that they prefer drug duty—waiting in remote annyons with automatic weapons to waylay traffickers along backcountry trails—to the more prosaic task of apprehending illegal immigrants" April 23, 1993, p. A26.

and social security while they work in the United States.

The role of Mexican Americans in the protection of the human and labor rights of Mexican immigrants has not been sufficiently recognized in Mexico, except for the award "*Aguila Azteca*", which is the highest award granted by the Mexican government to non-nationals for services rendered to Mexicans. This award was received by Antonia Hernandez, president of MALDEF, Julian Samora, professor of the University of Notre Dame and Blandina Cardenas, civil rights activist and scholar from Texas.

There was however, a gradual change from rhetoric only, to a more than symbolic action, during the administration of Carlos Salinas de Gortari, where the Mexican government reinforced consular protection. Political appointees were sent to occupy some of the most important Mexican Consular General offices in the United States. This change also meant a change from rhetoric to action in the performance of Mexican consuls. This was expressed in a more conspicuous and closer contact between the new Mexican consuls and the local communities of Mexican origin in the cities of Los Angeles, San Diego, Chicago, Houston, and San Antonio. These changes were taking place at the same time that predominance of self-denominations among people of Mexican origin were changing from Mexican Americans to Chicanos, to Hispanics to Latinos.

By the time Vicente Fox was elected as president of Mexico the "Latino vote", had surfaced in the political scene of the United States as a political force to be reckon with. The close victory of Ms. Loretta Sanchez over her republican opponent in 1996 in the District that includes Orange County in California, was a clear indication of the difference that the vote of former Mexican undocumented immigrants could make, after they had become US citizens. That election, in what use to be a strong hold of the Republican Party showed a pattern: the majority of Mexican undocumented immigrants who became U.S. legal residents and then, U.S. citizens, joined the Democratic Party.

President Fox has shown a particular sensitivity for the U.S. minority of Mexican origin population, referred by themselves and by others in the United States as "Latinos". The fact that more than two thirds of them are descendants of Mexican nationals has led President Fox to explicitly include them as a part of the Mexican population to whom he is supposed to serve as President of Mexico. Arguably this is not a very orthodox view, if one takes into account that the majority of Latinos are U.S. citizens, Fox however, has contributed to the blurring of national identities which begun in the preceding *sexenio* (six-year term administration of Mexican presidents) with the constitutional reform in Mexico that instituted a virtual "double nationality". In fact, this was a constitutional reform which established that the Mexican nationality will be considered in Mexico as permanent, regardless of the acquisition of other nationalities by Mexicans. If a Mexican citizen gains another country's citizenship, he or she can no longer use his or her citizen's rights, particularly the right to vote in Mexican elections, unless he expressively resigns the other country's acquired citizenship. This reform on Mexican nationality left untouched the constitutional rules for Mexican citizenship. Thus, there can be a dual nationality but not a dual citizenship for Mexicans. This distinction is confusing in the United States where it is common to equate nationality with citizenship. This is not the case in Mexico. There, nationality implies certain patrimonial rights given in exclusivity to Mexican nationals by the Mexican Constitution, such as the right to own property within the zone of 50 km parallel to Mexican borders and 100 km parallel to Mexican coastal lines. (Article 27 of the Mexican Constitution). Contributing to that confusion, particularly in the United States, president Fox's insistence, in fact an expressive promise, of granting voting rights to Mexican citizens who reside outside of Mexico in presidential elections. This is currently a controversial issue in Mexico, after the establishment of a cumbersome system of absentee ballots by a certificate mail, failed to produced more than one percent of fully registered voters out of an estimated potential number of 400 thousand expected to cast their votes in the following Mexico's presidential election on July 2 of 2006. The controversy about the vote of Mexicans abroad starts from the fact that there are more Mexican citizens residing on a permanent basis in the United States (close to 20 million), that is, more than in any other Mexican province except for the Federal District (the Mexico City Metropolitan Area). These numbers are associated to the hypothesis that a presidential election would turn out to be decided by those living outside of the country. In fact, there was a very poor preparation for the implementation of the constitutional reform that established the right to vote for Mexicans abroad. Neither of the proponents of the right to vote for Mexicans abroad, including President Fox, never addressed, for instance, the fact that the right to vote was to be exercised in another country, therefore, in violation of the legal principle of international law against the extraterritoriality of the law; nor, the fact that there are U.S. laws which require a license issued by the U.S. federal government to conduct political activities for other countries within the United States territory, with penalties of fines or prison for violators, nor provided solution to how Mexican electoral campaigns in the United States could escape from being subjected to U.S.' own electoral laws, particularly for the electoral propaganda, financing and conducting of an electoral campaign. Even worst: Which country's judicial system will eventually decide on final procedural voting controversies? Could it be that the U.S. Supreme Court of Justice could decide who will be the president of Mexico? These and many other questions remained to be answered in Mexico and in the United States, way before the rules for the implementation of such a right to vote for Mexicans abroad allows for its actual exercise.

The September 11 events only exacerbated those difficulties for these and many other matters pertaining to the bilateral relations between Mexico and the United States.

President Fox might well had been ahead of his time. The fact is that he proceeded as if there was no difference between what was and what might have been. At the very beginning of his administration he created a cabinet level position for Dr. Juan Hernandez, a U.S. citizen of Mexican origin (a Latino himself), in charge of matters of "Mexicans abroad". The creation of such a high level office was a good idea. Its creation corresponded to the importance that the ever growing population of Mexican nationals, Mexican citizens and U.S. citizens of Mexican origin living in the United States should have in the Mexican decision making process. However, the replacement of Juan Hernandez by the creation of a new Institute of Mexicans abroad, resulted in the establishment of certain distance between President Fox and the migrant's every day lives. Not that he was ever very close to them, but Juan Hernandez used to serve as an efficient bridge of communication between the President of Mexico and the migrants' experiences in the United States. It could be said that President Fox's personal involvement with those who he used to call "heroes" during his electoral campaign, had fallen, from weak, to almost rhetorical. Other aspect where the rhetorical supersedes the factual in the Fox administration, is in regard to the respect of human rights of immigrants from Central America. The reality is that there are as serious violations of human rights of Central Americans in México as there are of Mexicans in the United States. Notably, however, a sort of a catch 22 for the Mexican government. On the one hand, it is criticized at home and abroad for being too lenient for the border controls of people and drugs on its Southern Border, the majority of both ending up entering the United States, and on the other, it is criticized for human rights violations in trying to do so. Mexican law enforcement authorities seem to be overwhelmed by the violence of the gang members of *Mara Salvatrucha* in its Southern Border. The fact of the matter is that, in contrast to the United States, which has not ratified the UN Convention for the Protection of all Migrant Workers and their Families, México has done so, therefore, it has to abide by it. This UN Convention entered into effect in 2003. Thus, according to the Mexican Constitution it is "The Law of the Land" in México, as it is the most comprehensive UN standard for the human and labor rights of all migrants. Importantly, this distinction should lead to an understanding about the difference, pointed out earlier in the paper, between the vulnerability of migrants while in their country of origin and their vulnerability once they have entered another country. In the first case, questions of the vulnerability of migrants tend to be considered as "domestic," or of an internal nature, because the rights violated are of an endogenous origin; therefore, a matter to be handled internally by the judicial system of the country of origin of the migrants, whereas in the case of the vulnerability of international migrants, the rights violated are of an exogenous origin. This gives its related matters an international character since the questions related to them are supposed to be dealt by the international community. This is important when there is a territorial overlap between the violations of rights of internal migrants derived from the Mexican laws and the violation of the rights of international migrants such as the case of immigrants from Central American countries in the Mexican Southern Border Region, derived from the above mentioned UN convention.

Returning to the immigration issue in the United States, some comments should be made about the options that appear to be more salient in the bilateral negotiations as they were publicly known before the events of September 11. There are two conflicting notions in the United States about how to solve the migratory question with Mexico. Two contentious parties could not have represented that conflict more acutely than, one the one hand, the AFL-CIO promoting a "blanket amnesty" for all undocumented immigrants and, on the other, the California and the Texas growers associations promoting a "guest workers program". Both have respectively important allies. The respective promotions could not be more contradictory. The AFL-CIO side is adamantly opposed to the "guest workers program" claiming that it will be a mechanism of perpetuation of the exploitation of migrant workers as they were by the old "bracero agreements". On the side of the growers, in words of former

Senator Phil Gramm of Texas, amnesty will pass "over my cold dead body"—he said. On the AFL-CIO side, there were in full support, of a wide regularization of all undocumented immigrants. This is the position of all Latino organizations of national memberships. The grower's side had the support of President Bush and the wealthiest and more conservative side of the Republican Party, with the exception of the group of legislators headed by Congressman James Sensenbrenner of the Republican Party who were adamantly opposed to any "amnesty" measures or anything which favors undocumented immigrants. This powerful group of legislators were to the right of President Bush in matters of immigration.

The general indifference in Mexico about the migrant workers' plight has prevented a more significant participation of the Mexican political parties in a public debate about the mentioned options for a U.S.-Mexico agreement on migrant workers. In fact, there has not been a comparable debate in Mexico about these or other options on the subject in spite of president's Fox unprecedented attention to their plight. There were however important implications for the Mexican migrants. The option that would have been more convenient for the average Mexican migrant worker was what ever came closely to the "amnesty", a term not accepted by the Mexican government, because it alluded to a pardon granted to criminals by the executive branch of government. There has been some confusion in the United States with the terms "legalization" or "regularization." In reality the three terms, amnesty, legalization and regularization mean the same, in there sought after consequences; namely, making the "documented" to become "undocumented." This means, the "empowerment" that is brought to the undocumented when he or she becomes documented. That is, a non restrictive access to the protection of the law such as the police or the court system in the United States, without taking the risk of being deported.

This "empowerment" has not taken place before, with previous temporary migrant U.S. visas program, particularly with the old bracero programs, as in this work was argued before. The main reason has been, that none of the temporary visa programs (H1, H2, H2A, H2B etc.) have significantly modified the asymmetry of power between the migrant worker and his or her U.S. employer. To the extent that amnesty related options could have led to U.S. citizenship and full voting rights, such options could have indeed signified "empowerment" in the sense implied in the diagram, which means a way out of the conditions of vulnerability attached to be an undocumented immigrant. This is not the kind of migrants' empowerment the U.S. growers would be interested in pursuing, basically because it would reduce the asymmetry of power between them and the migrant workers which conditions the cost of labor imposed to the latter.

Notwithstanding the greater benefit for migrants that could be derived from a "legalization" or an amnesty related option, the reality was that this had been the least likely option being palatable for U.S. legislators. In fact, President Bush had stated that he was not going to support this option.

Geopolitics between Mexico and the United States have never been so overlapping as they are today and as they will continue to be in the near and not so near future. If there is one factor even more important than NAFTA for such a future, this would be the Latino vote.

With the exception of California's gubernatorial election of 2004, when Arnold Schwarzenegger was elected, previous elections in California have shown the political cost that Republican candidates could suffer by supporting anti-immigrant measures. Both the elections of 1996 and, more clearly the election of 1998 showed how the Latino vote of California punished the candidates of the Republican Party by giving the victory to Democrats, such as governor Gray Davis and Lieutenant Governor Cruz Bustamante.

The emergence of the Latino vote in California was the result of a paradox derived from the reelection campaign of Pete Wilson in 1994, which was based in the support of Proposition 187. Reference by its proponents of extending the limitations established for the undocumented immigrants to all "aliens", that is to say, to all Mexicans in California including those with a U. S. visa of legal residence, instilled a serious fear in all of Mexican origin population in the State, including U.S. citizens. This reminded many Latinos the anti Mexican campaign in the Thirties when U.S. citizens of Mexican origin were expelled from California back to Mexico, as documented by Hoffman in the United States and Carreras de Velazco in México.[37] The paradox was, that a bill ("Proposition 187") which was intended against the Mexican undocumented immigrants, produced a "fear of God" among the Mexican origin population of California. Those among them who were U.S. citizens, went to the following elections in California, ready to vote against all candidates of the Republican Party which political platform had included strong anti-immigrant language ever since the Republican Party's convention where president's Bush's father was elected candidate, to the present.

Public debate on Proposition 187 was marked by the court's main argument in its first, and again, in its final decision about its unconstitutionality, namely, its violation of the "supremacy clause" (immigration matters are of the exclusive jurisdiction of the federal government). This was perhaps the main reason why there has not been an in-depth discussion of Proposition 187's basic premises. This work argues that Proposition 187 was based on biased perceptions, tainted by racist and xenophobic ideologies; and that its basic provisions represent instances of "institutional racism" against people of Mexican origin, identified as such by the color of their skin. This bias has persisted in all the subsequent anti-immigrant legislative projects such as the "Law 200" in Arizona, the "Real ID Law" sponsored by Congressman James Sensenbrenner and the subsequent HR-4437 also sponsored by Sensenbrenner, which was approved by the House of Representatives. Furthermore, this work argues that all of these legislative projects are a reflection of the conditions of "vulnerability" in which an ethnic

---

[37]The two best studies on the massive expulsion of Mexicans during the years of the Great Depression are, by de Velazco (1974) and Hoffman (1974).

minority of Mexican origin in general, and Mexican immigrants in particular, have lived in the United States as subjects of human rights. The most relevant empirical evidence that supports the argument of an ideological bias against undocumented immigrants is summarized by the conclusive remarks quoted above from the US Labor Department Study published in 1994.

14.5   2001

The Mexican immigrant labor is not only necessary for a return to business as usual in the United States, it is necessary for the recovery of the US economy. President Bush heard voices from his own party, i.e. Senator MacCain, and certainly from the other party, speaking about the need to rationalize what so far has been a **de facto** labor market between Mexico and the United States. One where the US demands for immigrant labor is as real as the supply of it.

It was said before that there basically were two factors in the return of the bilateral relations to where they had been before September 11. As one factor, the before mention about shared bilateral **de facto** labor market. The other is of a different nature. It is the "Latino vote". As this is growing as a dire consequence of demography, it is bound to be of a crucial importance for the US presidential election, particularly in the States of California and Texas that might determine who the next president will be. The 2005 California elections left an important lesson. The "Latino vote" is not impartial to immigration policies. They vote in favor of proponents of pro-immigrant measures and they vote against the proponents of anti-immigrant measures. That explains the voting pattern against the candidates and programs of the Republican Party in California, including the blatant defeat of all the amendments proposed by Governor Schwarzenegger, as they were voted in the November of 2005 elections, a defeat due basically to the Latino vote. It is true that Latinos have had a history of low voting records but it is also true that those ethnic differences tend to disappear when controlled by education levels.

As Latinos are improving in their education levels, they will be voting in greater numbers. Thus, presidential candidates of the two parties are going to try hard to obtain the Latino vote in the whole United Sates and this factor will work in favor of the return of both governments to the table of negotiations for a bilateral agreement on the immigrant labor question.

14.6   A Synthetical Conclusion

This paper has implied a navigation from the abstract level of dialectics to the concrete level of migrant deaths at the border. The fact of the matter is that the international migration from México to the United States is a human phenomenon with too many facets, therefore difficult to explain. Here, an effort has been made to cover just a few of them by focusing on its contradictions. This corresponds to an old analytical suggestion used by a number of philosophers ever since the dialogues of Plato, who went beyond Socrates' recommendation to postpone the study of dialectics until the age of thirty. For Hegel as for Plato, dialectic moves in the realm of truth and ideas. The synthesis of *thesis* and *antithesis* results in a more complete truth. The German philosopher George Hegel view dialectic as an avenue to respond to the challenge of explaining history. Looking at the contradictions between the *material* and the *ideal,* was a first step in Hegel's dialectics as a method of analysis. There is no further claim of a Hegelian analysis here, than what it corresponds to the basic epistemological premise of his dialectical approach to the understanding of history.

After many years of doing empirical research on the migrations from Mexico to the United States, it has become increasingly clear that international labor migrations touch on every aspect of the social, economic and cultural elements of the development of a nation, both of its origin and its destination. As the world seems to shrink with the rise of new technologies of communication, the mobilization of people crossing borders in multiple directions makes migrations an ever growing phenomenon impossible of being disassociated to what it is understood in this paper as "the process of globalization" (see Footnote 33). In the sense of this understanding, arises the question of the human rights of the migrants. Its dialectical analysis is suggested by the apparent contradiction between the universality of a notion of human rights that does not accept distinctions of national origins and a notion on international migrations that can not be disentangled with the sovereign right of a country to make distinctions between nationals and foreigners. When this question is analytically separated in its two elements, as this paper postulates, it becomes apparent that in between lies a process, social in nature, because it derives from the social relations between "nationals" and "immigrants" as so defined by most Constitutions. From this basic premise derives a complex development in which the conditions of migrants vulnerability emerge and is reinforced by the rise of anti immigrant ideologies including prejudices and racism. The dynamics that get started on each end of the diagram, enter in a collision course where the force from one end (impunity of violators of immigrant's rights), clashes against the force coming from the opposite end (empowerment-voting rights) giving place to something anew, a synthesis, conceptualized as the "integration" of immigrants to the receiving nation. This integration is more a hypothesis than a reality, particularly in the case of the immigration from México to the United States. A historical perspective was included in order to analyze some salient aspects of the social process of a **de facto** international labor market in which context that immigration phenomenon takes place. An emphasis is placed in the bilateral nature of the phenomenon. One that is caused by factors located at the two sides of the U.S.-Mexico border, for which a solution to problems related to it, can only come from a bilaterally shaped agreement. An analysis was presented of some of the factors that have prevented such an agreement. Some of US proposals for US immigration policies in 2006 were analyzed and Mexican politics about the labor emigration from Mexico to the United States were discussed.

Acknowledgements I want to thank Jorge Bustamante de la Mora, who provided invaluable research and editing work for this chapter.

References

Bartelson, J. (1995). *A genealogy of sovereignty.* Cambridge: University Press.

Bortz, J. (1992). The effect of Mexico's post-war industrialization on the U.S.-Mexico price and wage comparison. In J. A. Bustamante, C. W. Reynolds, & R. A. Hinojosa-Ojeda (Eds.), *U.S.-Mexico relations; Labor market interdependence* (p. 228). Stanford, CA: University of Stanford Press.

Bustamante, J. A. (1983). Mexican migration: The political dynamics of perceptions. In: C. W. Reynolds & C. Tello (Eds.), *U.S.-Mexico relations: Economy and social aspects.* Stanford, CA: University of Stanford Press.

Bustamante, J. A. (1992). Interdependence, undocumented migration and national security. In, J. A. Bustamante, et al. (Eds.), *U.S. Mexico relations; Labor market interdependence* (p. 28). Stanford, CA: Stanford University Press.

Bustamante, J. A. (2002). *International migrations and human rights* (p. 39). México: Instituto de Investigaciones Jurídicas, Universidad Nacional Autónoma de México (UNAM).

Craig, R. B. (1971). *The Bracero program. Interest groups and foreign policy.* Austin, TX: University of Texas Press.

de Velazco, M. C. (1974). *Los Mexicanos que devolvió la crisis 1929–1932.* Mexico, DF: Secretaria de Relaciones Exteriores, Dirección General de Archivo.

Feagin, J. R. (1999). *Racial and ethnic relations* (6th ed., p. 301). Upper Saddle River, NJ: Prentice Hall.

Galarza, E. (1970). *Spiders in the house and workers in the fields.* Notre Dame: University of Notre Dame Press.

Garcia, J. R. (1980). *Operation wetback: The mass deportation of Mexican undocumented workers in 1954.* Westport: Greenwood Press.

Garcia-Cantu, G. (1978). Politica Exterior y Braceros 1838–1946. In *Utopias Mexicanas.* Mexico, DF: Fondo de Cultura Económica.

Giddens, A. (1990). *The consequences of modernity* (p. 64). Stanford: Stanford University Press.

Haas, P. M. (1992). Epistemic Communities and International Policy Coordination. In *International Organization, Knowledge, Power and International Policy Coordination* Vol. 46, No. 1, (PP. 1–35). The MIT Press.

Hoffman, A. (1974). *Unwanted Mexican-Americans in the great depression: Repatriation pressures, 1929–1939.* Tucson: Arizona, University of Arizaon Press.

Mexico, Secretaria del Trabajo y Previsión Social (STPS). (1964). *Los Braceros.* Mexico, DF: STPS.

Mraz, J., & Storey, J. V. (1996). *Uprooted: Braceros in the Hermanos Mayo Lens* (pp. 47–49). Houston, TX: University of Houston, Arte Publico Press.

Ojeda-Gomez, M. (1971). Estudio de un caso de decisión política: El programa norteamericano de importación de braceros. In *Extremos de México*. Mexico DF: El Colegio de México.

Olloqui, J. J. (Ed.). (2001). *Estudios en torno a la Migración* (pp. 7–19). México, DF: UNAM.

Taylor, P. S. (1981). *Labor on the land: Colected writings, 1930–1970*. New York, NY: Arno Press.

Torres, B. (1979). Historia de la revolución Mexicana VII. In *México en la Segunda Guerra mundial. Período 1940–1952* (Vol. 19). Mexico, DF: El Colegio de México.

U.S. Congress. (1926). *Hearings before the committee on immigration and naturalization*. Washington, DC: U. S. Government Printing Office.

U.S. Congress. (1929). House committee on immigration and naturalization. In *Seasonal agricultural laborers from Mexico, 69th congress, 1st session* (pp. 6–62).

U.S. Department of Labor. (1994). *Migrant farmworkers: Pursuing security in an unstable market*. Research report no. 5 (p. 40). Office of Program Economics, May, 1994.

U.S. General Accounting Office, Report to Congressional Committees. (2001). *INS' Southwest border strategy; Resource and impact issues remain after seven years* (p. 24). Washington, DC: U.S. Government Printing Office.

U.S. House of Representatives. (1975). Report no. 94-506, p. 5.

U.S. Senate. (1953). *Subcommittee of the senate committee on the judiciary. S1917. Appropriations hearings*.

Waters, M. (1995). *Globalization* (pp. 4–5). London: Routledge.

Research Literature on Haitian Americans: Trends and Outlook

Yanick St. Jean

Contents

Interviews with Haitian Americans in the past decade reveal acute understanding that immigrants, having left their native soil, continue to benefit the homeland. Though the respondents don't use the word, transnationalism and its value are precisely what these respondents are thinking and living.

This chapter updates an earlier review of selected research literature published between 1996 and 2006 on Americans of Haitian origin. The earlier review highlighted major trends in that literature, particularly to research targeting Caribbean groups separately. The current version selectively adds to this literature, starting with an attempt at defining the Caribbean origins of these Americans, origins generally ignored by American social scientists (see Portes et al. 1997).

15.1   The Caribbean

There has been no general framework for studying the Caribbean region as a whole. Instead of scholarly analysis, the Caribbean is identified with stereotypes and media sensationalism. When one thinks of the Caribbean, the mass of greater and lesser Antilles immediately comes to mind. But some definitions push boundaries beyond traditional expectations. For instance, Scher (2010: 1) points out that "in many compendia of the 'world's people' the Caribbean is absent, generally subsumed under Latin America." For Sidney Mintz, the Caribbean is a "socio-cultural continuum, one that might include those New World slave and plantation societies from Brazil to Louisiana" (Scher 2010: 1). Clawson (2012: 8) doubts the existence of Latin America as other than "cultural entity." And if cultural heritage is what binds together Latin America, then "with the exception of Cuba, the Dominican Republic, and Puerto Rico,

Y. St. Jean (✉)
Department of Sociology, Northwest Arkansas
Community College, Bentonville, AR, USA
e-mail: ystjean@nwacc.edu

© Springer International Publishing AG, part of Springer Nature 2018
P. Batur and J. R. Feagin (eds.), *Handbook of the Sociology of Racial and Ethnic Relations*,
Handbooks of Sociology and Social Research, https://doi.org/10.1007/978-3-319-76757-4_15

traditional Hispanic values are largely missing from many of the Caribbean Island [thus,] most scholars do not consider them a part of Latin America (Clawson 2012: 9). Hillsman and D'Agostino's designation of the Caribbean includes not only greater and lesser Antilles, which they term *insular*, but also the *circum-Caribbean*, "typically Caribbean enclaves in the Atlantic Ocean and on the South American and Central American coasts (2003: 10). They incorporate parts of the United States by attaching Miami and South Florida and suggesting Miami as capital of the Caribbean.

Questioning the existence of Latin America beyond cultural entity eliminates the non-Hispanic Caribbean (including French- and Kreyol-speaking Haiti). On the other hand, expanding the Caribbean beyond traditional boundaries of Greater and Lesser Antilles includes Haiti and beyond. If South Florida and Miami have become part of the Caribbean, why not New York, Boston, Toronto, Montréal, and other major cities with large concentrations of Caribbean immigrants? Should not the Caribbean extend to these cities as well?

15.1.1 Tropical Paradise and Other Stereotypes

The Caribbean region (however defined) is stereotyped as a tropical paradise. The stereotype extends to sunny beaches, waterfalls, palm, coconut, and mango trees, flora, architecture, meringue, reggae, salsa, carnivals, friendly people (Hillsman and D'Agostino 2003). For those who can afford the adventure, these islands are a perfect getaway from harsh winters and American obsessions with time and structure.

Moreover, the Caribbean itself has contributed to the well-known story of paradise. Writes Derek Walcott (cited in Scher 2010: 2): "Sadly, to sell itself, the Caribbean encourages the delights of mindlessness, of brilliant vacuity, as a place to flee not only winter but the seriousness that comes only out of culture with four seasons. So how can there be a people there, in the true sense of the world?" Also real are the dark stories

of "black magic, midnight rites and sacrifice or a land of perpetual sensuality: the sorcery of seduction" (Scher 2010: 2). These narratives of beauty encouraging tourism, mixed with counter-narratives of black magic, turn the Caribbean into what may be described as an 'attractive devilry'!

Popular images of the region obscure important contributions made to the world. Blurred are reactions of the world to political and ideological movements in the region. Blurred is the bravery of Caribbean populations as they worked to free themselves from exploitation, including colonialism and slavery. Blurred is the global impact of Caribbean literature and artistic production. The United States intervened more here than anywhere else in the world, attesting to the strategic importance of the region. As accomplishments like these are forgotten, stereotypes prevail. Increasingly, however, an inter-reliant world calls for researchers to reject these stereotypes and turn minds and methods to study the real Caribbean (Hillsman and D'Agostino 2003).

Media stereotypes are a common problem of Caribbean nations, especially Haiti. Caribbean cultures are misunderstood and sensationalized by emphasis on the region's political and economic difficulties and problems of immigration and drugs (consistent with the 'beautiful yet devilish' narratives). Ignored "are the valiant Caribbean efforts to define uniquely Caribbean identities and create autonomous institutions" (Hillsman and D'Agostino 2003: 9).

Yet there is no general framework to explain the Caribbean. Current analyses focus on one nation at a time. Admittedly the single case study can help identify particular cultural and other regional patterns. This emphasizes differences and neglects what these nations as a region have in common.

15.1.2 The Single Case Study

Emile Durkheim would propose a holistic view of the region, since the whole is not merely the sum of its parts. However, focusing on this regional whole does not (should not) preclude studying the unique contributions of each part to Caribbean unity. Thus, it is possible to begin to develop a paradigm for the entire region, by isolating first the particularities of nations. This places any residue (the common side) into focus and can help situate that difference in the dynamics of nations.

A good illustration of a comparative approach is Sidney Mintz's description of seven features of houses and yards in the Caribbean. He argues that these features stem from "the experience of slavery and the plantation system" (Scher 2010: 21). Comparing two single cases, Dominican and Puerto Rican, George Duany (2010: 106) found "transnational migrants face different, often conflicting, definitions of their racial identity in the sending and receiving societies … confirm [ing] the socially constructed nature of racial classification systems." Similarly, whether Vodou, or Santeria, Orisha, Caribbean religions are hybrids of African and European (Scher 2010: 185). Another example is D'Agostino's chapter "on Caribbean politics", where he describes similarities in Caribbean political systems, and demonstrates this by exploring separately those of Puerto-Rico, Cuba, Dominican Republic, Jamaica, Grenada, and Haiti (2003: 91–119 passim). Only after this single-case exploration does he conclude that "[d]espite … divergent origins and structures, political systems throughout the Caribbean have much in common. All have been influenced by the legacies of colonialism, slavery, economic exploitation and dependence, external domination, and elite-dominated exclusionary rule" (2003: 124). Thus "[w]hatever focus we choose to describe the culture of the Caribbean, none of it makes much sense without contextualizing the emergence of these societies within the historical conditions that brought these people, in a certain way, to this place" (Scher 2010: 2).

Portes et al. (1997: 1564) also employ the single-case approach. In the *Urban Caribbean*, they stress "the political and economic differences between Costa Rica, Haiti, Guatemala, the Dominican Republic, and Jamaica in order to assess the importance of common findings" (see Schefner 1998).

Haiti and Americans of Haitian origin, like the rest of the Caribbean, are neglected by mainstream American social scientists. In this review article, I isolate some key literature on Haitian Americans, looking for trends and for insight into not only Haitian Americans but also their connections to the homeland and Caribbean.

15.2 Haitians in the United States: A Single-Case Study

While the whole Caribbean region shares with Haiti the general experience of colonialism and slavery, the uniquely Haitian experience can be differentiated from that of regional sister states. Haiti and the Dominican Republic share Hispaniola, the second largest island of the Antilles. Haiti (formerly St. Domingue) was France's richest colony in the late 1700s, status that earned her the title *La Perle des Antilles* (The Pearl of the Antilles). On January 1, 1804, after a successful slave revolt against France that started in 1791, Haiti became the first black country (and only the second country in the Western hemisphere after the United States) to become independent (Hillsman and D'Agostino 2003; see also, Pamphile 2001; Zéphir 2004). François Dominique Toussaint L'Ouverture (1743–1803), leader of the Haitian revolution, was a former slave of the Bréda plantation. Gaou Guinou, Toussaint's grandfather, who was sold to the Comte of Bréda, came from a West African tribe (Herskovits 1941). This successful revolt is a unique historical event of which Haitians are very proud. So is the rest of the Caribbean (see Zacaïr 2010); and so is the African world (Hillsman and D'Agostino 2003). The King of Allada (in the west African country of Bénin) celebrates Toussaint L'Ouverture once a year with a Vodou festival. Overlooking the location of this festival is a giant statue of this son of Dahomeyan royalty.

The successful defeat of Napoleon's troops by the enslaved—followed by Haitian independence —is an example of extraordinary resilience. Haitians took freedom and social justice matters into their own hands. But regardless of historical magnitude, what makes Haiti unique is not limited to the successful revolution. Under President Aléxandre Pétion, Haiti aided Simon Bolivar in the movement in South America (especially Venezuela) toward independence from Spain and from slavery (see Nicholls 1996: 46).

However, Haiti is unique in other less edifying ways. Of the entire Caribbean region, she became notorious as the origin of the AIDS epidemic early on, when it was known as a killer. Haitians, along with homosexuals, hemophiliacs and heroin addicts (the *four H's* as they were called) were placed by the Centers for Disease Control, in a high-risk category for AIDS (see for example, St. Jean 1984, 1996). Moreover, while Cuban refugees have been given political asylum in the United States, Haitians, labelled economic refugees, are returned to the country of origin. The differential treatment of Haitian immigrants is described in the following example:

A woman who was pregnant and ill among the Haitians had been allowed to remain in the United States but had been separated from her young children, who were sent back to Haiti. This revelation led to a public outcry and the eventual decision to unite the two children with their mother in the United States. [Yet] when little Elian was discovered off the Florida coast, the reaction of people in the United States was to embrace this child (Dawkins 2000: 120).

Even immigration incarceration is unequal for, as elsewhere, Cubans and Haitians are not subject to the same treatment (Simon 1998). Negative stereotypes and representations of Haiti are common (Dubois 1996).

Both fame and infamy then, have meanings and consequences for Haiti, Haitians, Haitian Americans, the Caribbean region as a whole, and the world; consequently, these experiences must be studied within their larger contexts. For example, what are the consequences of discrimination against Haitian migration to the neighborhood Caribbean, including the Bahamas,

Brazil, Guadeloupe and Dominican Republic? Though not as horrendous as the 1937 Parsley massacre and other extreme racist, anti-Haitian manifestations on the east side of Hispaniola, violence against Haitian migrants is common in the Caribbean (see Zacaïr 2010: 2, 3).

In many ways, the Haitian and Haitian-American situations are unlike the rest of the Caribbean. The extent and reasons for this discrimination require further study. Why, for example, were the infamous CDC classifications unique to Haitians? Discrimination against Haiti occurs in other international areas. Comparisons of the specifics of the Haitian experience such as language, religion, colonization contribute to clearer understanding of the complex yet interdependent Caribbean region. For this reason, researchers must consider the single-case study of Haiti and Haitian Americans.

The Haitian people have historically been deprived and abused. Never has there been a period of stability and social change when the general population would expect its government to provide the resources necessary to enhance social and economic growth, and yet it is a distinct history and culture which sustains and connects all Haitians to one another (Pierce and Elisme 1997: 52).

15.3 Haitian American Experience and Research Literature

Haitian Americans are "people living in the United States whose origins are the island of Haiti" (on the definition of Haitian-American see, for example, Charles et al. 1998; Catanese 1999: 86–123). In a compilation of stories about the 2010 earthquake (*goudougoudou* as Haitians refer to it), Edwidge Danticat (2011a, b: 14) points out that "migration is such an integral part of the Haitian experience that those living outside of the country were once designated as part of a 'tenth department,' and an ideological auxiliary to Haiti's first geographical nine" (see also Glick Shiller and Fouron 2001: 12). It may be one of several reasons why Haitians in the United States prefer the appellation 'Haitian-Americans' which links them to "home."

Sociological Abstracts is an international catalog of key publications in sociology. A search of these abstracts for materials on Haitian Americans published in the past two decades produced few peer-reviewed articles, book chapters, and book reviews, as was the case for 1996–2006. This sparsity may be due to varied definitions of "Haitian-American" and the inclusion of this category in the literature focusing on "African Americans," "Black-Americans," or even found among *The Other African Americans* (see Shaw-Taylor and Tuch 2007). I explore sources beyond *Sociological Abstracts* for this updated review.

Major topics in the available literature on Haitian Americans include the second generation of immigrants, trans-nationalism networks, identity and citizenship, the diaspora of people, of religions, the long-term impact of the AIDS stigmatization, and ethnic disparity in writings on the Caribbean (see Hillsman and D'Agostino 2003, especially pages 229–235). Many writings on Haiti and Haitian issues likely useful to researchers may not be listed in these *Abstracts*. Included are many articles on health issues, slave revolutions, and the African Diaspora. Writings about slavery comprise the significant Haitian Revolution, its profound effect on the Americas, and the role of the extraordinary leader Toussaint L'Ouverture in the defeat of Napoleon's troops (William-Myers 1996). There is a general focus on the second generation. There is new emphasis on alcohol abuse and other adolescent issues, post-earthquake problems of adaptation in the new society, and identity formation (for example, see Doucet 2014). Of interest, too, is what seems new attention to violence against women, and women empowerment. Buchanan et al.'s (2010) study of the population with Haitian ancestry in the United States is notable.

A consistent trend is the link between local and global aspects of immigrant life. I select strategically among major trends in the literature on diaspora and transnationalism.

Trans-nationality typifies Caribbean Americans. Trans-nationality (or long-distance nationalism) means that an immigrant group lives simultaneously in different nation-states. This global flow leads to the formation of enclaves abroad and links families into two nations. Trans-nationality has consequences for the transfer of funds and goods sent to families in the homeland to supply basic necessities (Hillsman and D'Agostino 2003; Glick-Schiller and Fouron 2001). Haitian Americans share this transnational experience with other Americans from the Caribbean.

An insider look into Haitian-American life, and a good starting place for this research, is Flore Zéphir's *The Haitian Americans*. An observer of the Haitian diaspora, Zéphir defines diaspora as "continuity between the land of origin and the land of resettlement … interconnectedness between events at home and the sociopolitical reality of this country" (2004: 10).

Though Zéphir writes about Haitian-American life, depictions of pre-migratory and post-migratory experiences link her volume to the issue of Caribbean and Caribbean American trans-nationalism. Haitian Americans experience continuity between land of origin and land of resettlement. Moreover, there is a collective memory of place, of socialization, of experience, and of institutions. Geographical 'boundaries' are irrelevant.

Zéphir begins with a review of the history and policies of immigration in the United States and the reasons Haitian-Americans immigrate: prosperity and happiness. However, this explanation is not complete without travelling to the old place of memory or sending context. Knowledge of the glorious Haitian past is necessary to understand the Haitian diaspora. Other topics include Catholicism, Vodou, the Haitian economy, Duvalier/post Duvalier years, as well as political and economic nightmares pushing Haitians out of their country and pulling them into the United States. There are also discussions of prejudice and discrimination in the United States. On page 19 of *The Haitian Americans* is a telling photograph with the following inscription: "Haitian boat people intercepted and 'inspected' on October 29, 2002, by police officers wearing masks." Immediately I associated this picture with a Haitian respondent I interviewed in the early 1980s. He reported seeking treatment at a

Florida hospital. Although he had no symptoms of AIDS, once he identified himself as Haitian, he was met by hospital personnel in masks and gloves (St. Jean 1984).

> In their new environment, Haitian Americans established ethnic communities:
> Haitians have managed to visibly re-create the cultural habits of their homeland.... Haitian immigrants' notion of ethnicity is shaped, on the one hand, by values directly inherited from the homeland and, on the other, by the realities of the American context. As such, Haitian ethnicity is transnational (Zéphir 2004: 117).

Zéphir's earlier *Haitian Immigrants in Black America: A Sociolinguistic Portrait* (1996) discusses "the process of identity formation among Haitian immigrants in the U.S." These writings show the Haitian American identity complex, hybrid and transnational, neither the old Haitian identity, nor an American. Instead, it represents a mix of old and new: Haitian-American identity. Haitian Americans share the transnational nature of identity with other Caribbean Americans. What follows describes some forms of transnationalism reported in the literature of the past decades.

15.3.1 Generations and Transnationalism

First- and second-generation Haitian Americans differ in many ways. The first-generation is characterized by "racial pride and a sense of belonging to a nation" (Zéphir 2004: 119). They want to retain their identity, for "'l'haïtien sait son chez lui, et il connait ses racines" (Haitians know their proper home and they know their roots) (2004: 121). First generation Haitians speak French and *Kreyol*.[1] Spoken by 100% of Haitians, Kreyol is a mark of ethnicity. Educated Haitians of the first generation speak French, which marks a higher social class. The French literary heritage comes in for study, along with Haitian authors such as Jacques Roumain, Jean Price-Mars, the more recent Danny Laférrière a Haitian-Canadian elected to the French Academy

in 2013, and Lilas Desquiron. Zéphir lists many noted Haitian American writers, among them novelists Marjorie Valbrun, Marie St. Fleur, Fred Séraphin, and Edwidge Danticat (see Zéphir 2014: 151–171).

Another characteristic of this first generation is their distancing from native African Americans (Pamphile 2001; Zéphir 1996, 2004). Although Haitian Americans see themselves as Black (Zéphir 2004), their sense of blackness is linked to Haitian history through Africa and not to the black experience in the United States" (Zéphir 2004: 127). There is an exception to this attitude: "[O]ne can witness the high level of interactions between Haitian American and African American leaders in the struggle for racial equality" (Zéphir 2004: 128). This first generation of Haitian Americans is different from the next. The literature deals more often with the second generation.

> The second-generation ... do not speak English with an accent (or the same heavy accent as the parents) and have a great deal of familiarity with the American way. Because of these characteristics, they are certainly not overtly distinguishable from American Blacks. In consequence, second-generation Haitian immigrants seem to have more ethnic options at their disposal than do the parents (Zéphir 2004: 130).

A transnational perspective takes account of history in and of the country of origin. "[T]ransnational relations form a significant part of second-generation identities, particularly for Haitian Americans" (Levitt and Waters 2002). The theme of trans-nationalism is consistent in the literature. Since the first generation generally distances itself from African-Americans, we would expect this attitude also from the second generation. But this is not generally the case.

Research by Feagin and Dirks (2005) demonstrates that whites, especially white students, tend to classify Haitian Americans with African-Americans, Native Americans, Asian Indian Americans as non-white. Haitian Americans place themselves in the non-white category with other groups traditionally viewed as non-white. However, first-generation Haitians see themselves as a separate *ethnic* group from

---

[1] I use the Haitian spelling.

African-Americans. While a segment of the second-generation may deny haitianness (see, for example, Zéphir 2004; Stepick and Swartz 1998), others from that generation display strong to weaker haitianness. They know themselves to be black and are proud of their racial identity. Still, they are likely to see themselves as a separate group from African-Americans, primarily due to historical, cultural, and experiential factors, despite perceptions of the host society.

Given that transnational relations significantly shape the identities of the second generation, how are Haitian Americans affected by these relations? One telling example is the reaction of the second generation to the AIDS labeling of Haitians.

> Many of the Haitian young people who took to the streets of New York to protest against the stigma of the AIDS label began supporting transnational projects to rebuild Haiti. The second-generation in Haiti meanwhile learned to look to the diaspora for the political power to change Haiti.... Youngsters in Haiti, faced with the barriers of class, color, gender discrimination, political turmoil, and the lack of economic opportunity, saw migration to the United States and Haitian diaspora as the hope for both themselves and Haiti (Glick-Schiller and Fouron 1998: 197).

Thus, from the United States, the second generation turn eyes to Haiti, while from Haiti, that generation looks to the diaspora-reference group. The second generation in Haiti and the United States "share a claim to a Haitian homeland and nostalgia for a Haiti that never was, binding them across national borders and across generations" (Glick-Shiller and Fouron 1998: 198). Clearly, this claim to the Haitian land has meaning for the political and nation-building future of Haiti.

Transnationalism also means increased flow of remittances from the diaspora to the homeland. One scholar discussed the implications of these funds for the sending country (Itzigsohn 2000). These economic and nation-building benefits could be observed at the beginning of the administration of Jean-Bertrand Aristide, the deposed president of Haiti, when

> Links between the diaspora and the Haitian government constituted an important source of funds and personnel. After the coup of 1991, the unity of individuals in the diaspora and those remaining in Haiti strengthened, particularly in the form of leadership in US Haitian organizations.... It is concluded that the ideology of transnational nations-state has become a powerful resource for immigrant-sending countries to develop a new rhetoric of national independence (Glick-Schiller and Fouron 1998).

Transnationalism, an important source of remitted funds for Haitian families, also increases Haiti's gross national product (GNP) and may reduce the popular media stereotypes of Haiti: "poorest country of the Western Hemisphere." While economic poverty is indeed rampant in Haiti, the media avoid discussions of its background: colonization, the early extraction of resources from Hispaniola and, after independence, isolation that led to the disintegration of infrastructures and political instability. The ransom Haiti paid to France for independence and diplomatic recognition precipitated Haiti's economic collapse. The United States has repeatedly intervened in Haitian affairs since the 1804 independence (for example 1915–1934 and 1994–1996). Haitian scholar, Patrick Bellegarde-Smith (2004: 18, 106, 129, 144) highlights "Haiti's cheap labor and proximity to the U.S. market [as] great advantages for U.S. firms while "[f]or Haiti itself, … the combination of cheap labor, changing land uses, and increased importation of foodstuffs may prove debilitating." These and other reasons for Haiti's being labeled "poorest" are not part of the American understanding of Haiti. By contributing to economic well-being and nation building, transnationalism can also improve the media image of that nation.

Through trans-nationalism, the second-generation seems to hold the key to the economic and political future of Haiti. Second-generation Haitian Americans figure prominently in the literature of the past decades. The spirit of the Haitian revolution is alive in this generation wishing to reclaim the land of their Haitian forbearers.

> As the Haitian community matures and as a second and third generations come of age, perhaps they will be seen as less alien and more American. After all, America is a permanently unfinished society,

where the new and old always blend to produce a much larger and better nation, one out of many, "the varied carols of America" (Zéphir 2004: 149).

This transnational perspective on the Haitian experience is a major theme in articles published since 1996. To understand Haitian Americans, one must first understand their past in the country of origin, their present in the receiving country, current interrelations and interactions with the sending country, and the transnational nature of their identities. Zéphir interprets Haitian American life from a Haitian-American point of view. A more profound understanding of the Haitian diaspora with its double consciousness will require many more such voices from within.

15.3.2 Citizenship and Trans-nationalism

Trans-nationalism impacts citizenship. Diasporic citizenship "is a set of practices that a person is engaged in, and a set of rights acquired or appropriated, that cross nation-state boundaries and that indicate membership in at least two nation states" (Laguerre 1998: 90). Haitian American scholar Michel Laguerre presents a range of perspectives on international migration and introduces the concept of *Diasporic citizenship*. One example of Diasporic citizenship is the virtually unknown Haitian American involvement in Plessy v. Ferguson. Most of those who brought the case to the Supreme Court were Haitian Americans continuing the fight for equality that started the Haitian revolution (Laguerre 1998).

Diaspora and *citizenship* have different meanings:

> Diaspora means displacement and reattachment. It refers to rerootedness, that is living in another state, and implies transnationality in its relations with the homeland. ... Diaspora ... is a mechanism that expands the space of the nation beyond the borders of the state. ... By diaspora, we refer to individual immigrants or communities outside the legal or recognized boundaries of the state or the homeland, but inside the reterritorialized space of the dispersed nation (Laguerre 1998: 8).

Improved means of communications facilitate social contacts between homeland and hostland.

> When a member of the Haitian Diasporic community in New York City calls a family member still in Haiti to advise her how she should vote in the Haitian elections on the basis of information garnered in New York, the social distance is small in comparison with the geographical distance that separates the callers (Laguerre 1998: 9).

The new immigration requires new terminology. While diaspora means activity, citizenship is fixed within a nation. Thus, needed is a concept of citizenship that reflects more accurately "movement" in Diaspora.

According to Laguerre, Haitian Americans "escape complete minoritization since the link with the homeland allows one to enjoy the majority status one cannot exercise in the adopted country" (Laguerre 1998: 192; Pedraza 1999: 380). This majority status might influence the strong haitianness of some Haitian Americans which can promote distance from African-Americans. This idea deserves further research.

15.3.3 Religion and Transnationalism

Religion is traditionally neglected by sociologists. Mooney's work is important, given the meaning of religion for new immigrants (Leonard et al. 2005; Ebaugh and Chafetz 2000) and the relationship between social ties, social capital, and religion. These ideas about the meaning and benefits of religion are also consistent with trends in the literature on Haitian Americans. Transnational religion (especially Catholicism) produces social capital for Haitian immigrants in Miami, Montréal, and Paris. "Social capital is access to valuable resources attained by virtue of membership in social networks." Religious institutions influence their members' social networks. Assimilation and segmented assimilation theories should be modified to take into account the impact of religious beliefs and religious institutions in the social advancement of their members (Mooney 2013).

Is it possible to relate the idea of reciprocity to trans-nationalism? A study comparing the helping behavior of Haitians, Christian funda-mentalists, and gang members suggest that they share the belief that "what goes around comes around" (Shaw 2008). Reciprocity can be linked to Mooney's work on religion, because building social networks and capital may well depend on reciprocity. However, I am not so sure why the comparison of these groups brings to mind the earlier Haitian classification of Haitians with hemophiliacs, heroin addicts, and homosexuals (three H's) as high risk groups for AIDS. This discussion does not offer a transnational per-spective and, for that reason, is somewhat dif-ferent from trends observed so far in the literature. But, it is possible to stretch this idea and imagine the consequences of reciprocity that takes a transnational character.

Religious life (perhaps reciprocity also) is transnational. It is necessary to understand how immigrants interact with the religious culture (s) of the sending country. Following is an interesting account of religious trans-nationalism.

> Fet Viej Mirak on East 115th Street is a religious event whose meaning also spans New York and Haiti. But rather than substituting the New York feast for the one they left at Sodo, Haitians add the Harlem location as another possible site of spiritual work. In this way, East 115th Street is opened up as one more site in the expanding "religioscape" of transnational Haitian religious culture. During the pilgrimage for Notre Dame du Mont Carmel in New York, the Haitian population reterritorializes spiritual practice, reinscribing sacred space onto their new landscape of settlement (McAlister 1998: 155).

Here again is an expansion of the homeland to the United States. The diaspora establishes social networks. These networks potentially increase social capital (Mooney), reciprocity (Shaw), and economic capital.

> The pilgrimage to Mont Carmel in East Harlem expands their saint's influence in the Haitian world. Haitians in the diaspora reached out to Mont Carmel and Ezili Dantò, both nationalist divinities, extending prayers for family and friends throughout the diaspora and in Haiti. By sending the feast by the thousands, the New York Haitian population has collectively placed the Church of our Lady of Mount Carmel on an invisible com-munity map. In stepping onto the public state of the Catholic feast, they orient themselves within

the shifting "ethnoscape" of New York City. They make sense of the confusing complexity of the ethnic landscape by locating the church as a center of spiritual power where they will be welcome (McAlister 1998: 154).[2]

Turner (2006: 131–132) explains the impor-tance of the work of Zora Neal Hurston "for understanding the profound and enduring con-nection between Haitian and New Orleans Vodou," as well as connections between these religious traditions and the New Orleans Jazz and Heritage Festival. The formation of diasporic ethnic communities reinforces a sense of being part of a majority, even if only symbolic. Transnational religious phenomena are appar-ently common also among Latin Americans:

> When national populations spread through migra-tion to new localities, they bring their divinities with them, re-territorializing their religious prac-tices. The supernatural world assents, and comes to bear up communities in transition (p. 154) .... Religious sites in the United States become added that the American landscape; they multiply, rather than replace, spiritual centers of the home country (McAlister 1998: 125).

The fluidity of the concept of trans-nationalism makes it difficult to study. But it represents the immigrant experience better than such concepts as assimilation and multiculturalism, which seem static (on assimilation and multiculturalism, see Alba 1999). Trans-nationalism views immigra-tion as a continuous process involving both the present and the past. Yet, Alba (1999) predicts also that

> The concepts assimilation and multiculturalism are likely to figure importantly in the American future. Assimilation has been the predominant pattern among the descendants of earlier immigrants, as we now recognize in retrospect; and it is likely to be a highly prevalent one among the descendants of contemporary immigrants, though not as para-mount as it has been.... Assimilation does not require absolute extinction of the difference, in other words (Alba 1999: 21).

---

[2]"Ezili is the deity of love, wealth, motherhood. In her manifestation as Ezili Dantò, she is dark-skinned, strong, and courageous and is often assimilated with the Catholic Mater Salvatoris" (see Bellegarde-Smith and Michel 2006: 95–96).

15.3.4 Health and Trans-Nationalism

Consistent with the transnational phenomenon, Haitians use "a combination of biomedical healthcare services and traditional practices" (Folden 2003: 67). In matters of health, as elsewhere, transnationalism breads hybridity, linking place of origin to new home. They combine their new worldview with the old.

Transnationalism means that health professionals need to understand the Haitian view, especially the role of the supernatural in Haitian's understanding of mental health and illness (Desrosiers 2002). Different healthcare beliefs and options derive from ethnic differences. For example, Haitian Americans, African Americans, and Jamaicans have different approaches to health care based upon national origins (Orezzolli 2000).

Trans-nationalism means that events in the homeland affect immigrants in the host nation. One study shows that the early AIDS classification of Haitians influenced Haitian women in the United States in their social relationships (Santana and Dancy 2000). Early on in the United States, Haitians were classified as carriers of AIDS, regardless of the length of their residence in the United States. Several decades after this classification, Haitian-American women still felt the stigma that followed them in the receiving country.

Service utilization

A study of the use of social services by Haitian immigrants in South Florida finds that many qualified Haitians do not use government services to the poor even though they qualify. Moreover, persons who share "households with unqualified persons are less likely to access services than are other qualified immigrants and are more likely to experience hardships that impede their ability to find stable employment" (Kretsedemas 2003). This Haitian American phenomenon may be partially explained by religious capital. Catholic and other churches could be helping these immigrants (see Mooney 2013). Haitian immigrants may have established strong religious and social networks that produce social capital. However, cultural factors of pride and dignity may explain this lack of enrollment.

15.3.5 Other Topics

This analysis of literature on Haitian Americans is far from exhaustive. Other topics include racism and stereotypes (Dubois 1996); new models of fatherhood (Bibb and Casimir 1996); and ethnicities and families (Auerbach et al. 1997). Education is a vitally important issue. Making the curriculum relevant to immigrant students requires a transnational perspective (McIntyre et al. 2001; Désir 2007). Whatever issue is addressed, the explanation goes back to transnationalism. *Immigrant Faiths* (2005) offers a transnational perspective on immigrant religion with a chapter on Haitians. It observes a growing complexity in studying new immigrants, and the need to frame these groups and their religious lives in the context of hybridity and diaspora. Many recent publications are focusing on the impact on Haitian Americans of the devastating 2010 earthquake (see for example Allen et al. 2012). Trans-nationalism or "long-distance nationalism" continues to guide the literature on Haitian Americans.

15.4 Conclusions

What makes Haitian Americans unique can also help isolate characteristics that tie them to the broader Caribbean and to other Americans of Caribbean origin. While the Caribbean region is not the sum of its parts, each nation contributes its uniqueness to the region. Isolating the unique eventually advances the explanation of the region and its immigrant population in the United States.

As a story of a single island nation contributes to the story of the Caribbean, individual life stories also contribute to the story of a society. While the details of each story may vary, these stories are similar in many ways. They weave patterns that can blur differences. So, to know one immigrant story is to know another. The "similarities" in these stories tell the story of the society that produced these immigrants. To recognize the interaction of parts is to practice imaginative sociology.

In *A Very Haitian Story*, the noted Haitian American author Danticat (2004) writes a narrative of immigration. The title itself illustrates the imaginative sociology, for even as the story is Danticat's own, it points to a very Haitian pattern. The story is about Danticat's uncle's experience with United States immigration authorities.

> When immigration officials at Miami international Airport ask my uncle how long he would be staying, he explained that they [he and his son] would be killed if he returned to Haiti and that he and Maxo [his son] wanted asylum. They were arrested and taken to the Krome Detention Center, where, my uncle told his lawyer three days later, the medicine he brought with him from Haiti—a combination of both herbal and prescription medicines for an inflamed prostate and high blood pressure—was taken away from him. Twenty-four hours later, still in custody, he died at the nearby hospital.
>
> [W]hile the American government just reviewed, for the fourth time, another 18-month term of the temporary protected status granted to approximately 85,000 Hondurans and Nicaraguans after hurricane Mitch in 1998, it will not give the same status of 20,000 Haitians living here. It denies Haitians this status even though the interim government in Haiti (with the backing of both Democratic and Republican officials in the United States) appealed for the measure to give Haiti time to stabilize its security system and recover from a severe housing shortage resulting from the ravages of [hurricane] Jeanne.

Danticat's uncle's story is shared by many a Haitian American. While the details are different, there is a core. In the country of origin some experiences push; in the receiving country there is also the perception that immigrants are not pulled but, instead, pushed away, according to Danticat, by the American government's fear of mass migration from Haiti.

The experience of her uncle affected Danticat. To leave out that story, which originates in the country of origin and continues in the host, would disrupt the continuity of history and place in the transnational experience. However, that story represents an ideal-type story of Caribbean immigrants. "If you are an immigrant New York, there are some things you inevitably share.... You probably left behind someone you love in the country of your birth," writes Danticat (2004: 1). She imagines the United States before immigrating from Haiti. "When we fantasized, we saw ourselves walking the penny-gilded streets and buying all the candies we could stuff into ourselves. Eventually we grew to embrace the idea that New York was where we were meant to be, as soon as the all-powerful gatekeepers saw fit to let us in" (Danticat 2004: 1). Danticat's fantasy is likely the American dream of pre-migratory Caribbean Americans. This idea deserves further research.

Danticat's family story illustrates the idea of transnationalism that permeates the literature of the past decades. Another illustration is "Georges Woke Up Laughing" (2001) where the authors paint the Haitian experience of trans-nationalism from a personal standpoint (Fouron and Glick-Schiller 2002). An interesting and very useful research would be a compilation of life stories of Haitian Americans, especially those who have achieved economic and/or educational success in the United States. Stories of the contributions of these successful individuals rarely appear in the literature on Haitian Americans or in the media. Such research might reveal patterns in the struggles that have contributed to their success. For example, what differentiates Haitian Americans such as Rejin Leys, Vladimir Cybil Charlier, Edouard Duval-Carrié, Wyclef Jean, Edwidge Danticat, countless other Haitian American physicians, scholars and other professionals? What have they contributed to the United States? Have their life experiences been different from others? I found a glaring absence of this topic from the literature that I reviewed.[3]

---

[3]*Special Collections* at the University of Miami Library, Coral Gables, Florida, has several oral histories of renowned Haitian Americans. Go to http://merrick.library.miami.edu/specialCollections/asm0085/; title: *Haitian Diaspora Oral History Collection*: University of Miami Special Collections. http://proust.library.miami.edu/findingaids/index.php?p=collections/findingaid&id=1246; *Jean Mapou Papers* are found also in Special

Transnationalism is closely related to the idea of collective memory, even though more than memory is involved. It links communities and interactions in two or more nations. "Memory [which] needs continuous feeding from collective sources is sustained by social and moral props. Just like God needs us, so memory needs others" (Schwartz 1992).

Collective memory can be seen in the second generation's hope for reclaiming old country. If the younger Haitian Americans do so, it would begin fulfilling the promise of Toussaint L'Ouverture during his capture by the French. Toussaint who died in 1803 predicted:

> En me reversant, on n'a abattu que le tronc de l'arbre de la liberté des nègres. Celui-ci repoussera par les racines, parce qu'elles sont profondes et nombreuses (In overthrowing me, you have only cut down the trunk of the tree of liberty. It will grow again for its roots are deep and numerous). The second and third generations may be some of many roots of this tree of liberty.

If trends toward trans-nationalism continue, the volume of insightful writings by Haitian American and Caribbean American authors can also be expected to increase. The writings of Michel Laguerre and Flore Zéphir about the Haitian and Haitian American experience contain depth rarely seen in the writings of American social scientists about Haitian Americans issues. Laguerre and Zéphir write from outside in, but also inside out. The American sociological literature on Haitian Americans needs this "inside out" perspective. Multidisciplinary research using personal and traditional stories deepen understanding of Haiti and Haitian Americans. And as one Haitian American scholar puts it, "Haiti needs new narratives" (Ulysse 2015).

This transnational literature will continue to focus on later generations. Since transnationalism can involve more than two nation-states, it will complicate the study of Haitian Americans and other Americans of Caribbean origin. Fluency in

local languages will be needed to access the transnational character of immigrant experience. So Haitian-American studies will increasingly be produced by Haitian American authors, researchers, and translators. Insider studies with a focus on difference will provide a comparative approach and encourage development of a paradigm to explain the experience of other Caribbean Americans.

The transnational phenomenon means that concepts like assimilation and multiculturalism, though probably here to stay (see Alba 1999), will decrease in importance. Though integral to the transnational phenomenon, assimilation and multiculturalism may be displaced by such concepts as collective memory, ethnogenesis, or hybridity, that more fully represent the transnational character of the Haitian American.

Transnationalism may reduce interactions with other ethnic groups within the United States, given the immigrants' closeness to the homeland, and interactions between the homeland and host land. Likewise, transnationalism may slow the assimilation of new immigrants, particularly in terms of learning the English language.

Haitian Americans are not leaving. Diversity is here to stay, and Alba (1999: 22) suggests:

> As long as contemporary immigration continues at a robust level, it will expand and reinforce diversity even if assimilation is a major pattern among second- and third-generation individuals.... [D]iversity is sustained by aggregate processes—especially high levels of immigration and the resulting communities and infrastructures.

This new, transnational approach to studying ethnic communities parallels the increased diversity of the American population. This presents exciting though challenging opportunities for researchers. As Alba predicts, "racial and ethnic stratification is... part of the bedrock of the American social structure, and there is little prospect that this fact will be altered substantially in the foreseeable future." But, too, I suggest, as ethnic communities see themselves part of a majority elsewhere, ethnic stratification in the United States will have a different impact upon these groups. As part of a transnational majority, immigrants will have a powerful effect on the

Collections, University of Miami Libraries, Miami, Florida. The *Archival Collections* include the *Haitian Women of Miami (FANM) records*, donated by Marlène Bastien, Executive Director of Haitian Women of Miami.

host-land's ethnic stratification. These ideas, too, need further research.

For Haitian immigrants, transnationalism is not a new phenomenon. Whether symbolically or in fact, Haitian American have lived simultaneously in their home land and host society.

It's a matter of [whether] you want to stay home and perish or whatever, and be hungry not have a future, or you want to seek a life where it will be better for you. But with the hope that maybe you can return home waiting to bring … back or to open up opportunities for all those who can't leave. I want as many Haitians here as possible. Yes, I do. As many… If for any reason, the more the more there are here, the better it is for Haiti two ways. Those people's misery is alleviated, number one. And number two, by them being here they can surreptitiously provide some help to the mother country, to Haiti. So as many as possible…. As many Haitians that we can have here the better it is for Haiti.[4]

References

Alba, R. (1999). Immigration and the American realities of assimilation and multiculturalism. *Sociological Forum, 14*, 3–25.

Allen, A., Marcelin, L. H., Schmitz, S., Hausmann, V., & Schultz, J. M. (2012). Earthquake impact on Miami Haitian Americans. *Journal of Loss and Trauma, 17*, 337–349.

Auerbach, C., Silverstein, L. B., & Zizi, M. J. (1997). The evolving structure of fatherhood among Haitian Americans. *Journal of African American Men, 2*, 59–85.

Bellegarde-Smith, P. (2004). *Haiti: The breached citadel*. Ontario: Canadian's Scholars' Press Inc.

Bellegarde-Smith, P., & Michel, C. (2006). *Haitian Vodou: Spirit, myth and reality*. Bloomington: University Press of Indiana.

Bibb, A., & Casimir, G. J. (1996). Haitian families. In M. McGoldrick, J. Giordano, & J. K. Pearce (Eds.), *Ethnicity and families* (pp. 97–111). New York: Guilford.

Buchanan, A. B., Albert, N. G., Beaulieu, D. (2010). *The population with Haitian ancestry in the United States*. U.S. Bureau of Census.

Catanese, A. V. (1999). *Haitians migration and Diaspora*. Boulder, USA: Westview Press.

Charles, C., Fjellman, S. M., Glick, N. B., Stepick, A., & Zephir, F. (1998). *Haitian Americans*. Conn: Human Relations Area Files NK07.

Clawson, D. (2012). *Latin America and the Caribbean*. N.Y.: Oxford.

Danticat, E. (2004). A very Haitian story. *The New York Times*, Editorial Desk, Section A: 23.

Danticat, E. (2011a). *Haiti Noir*. NY: Akashic Books.

Danticat, E. (2011b). *Create dangerously*. New Jersey: Princeton University Press.

Dawkins, M. P. (2000). Rethinking U.S. immigration policy. *Black Issues. Higher Education, 17*, 120.

Désir, C. (2007). Understanding the sending context of Haitian immigrant students. *Journal of Haitian Studies, 13*(2), 73–93.

Desrosiers, A. (2002). Treating patients. *American Journal of Psychotherapy, 56*, 508–522.

Doucet, F. (2014). Panoply: Haitian and Haitian American youth crafting identities in US schools. *Trotter Review, 22*(1), 7–32.

Dubois, L. (1996). A spoonful of blood: Haitians, racism and AIDS. *Science and Culture, 6*, 7–43.

Ebaugh, H. R., & Chafetz, J. S. (2000). *Religion and the new immigrants: Continuities and adaptations in immigrant congregations*. Latham, MD: AltaMira Press.

Feagin, J., & Dirks, D. (2005). *Who is white? College students' assessments of key US racial and ethnic groups*. Charlotte, NC: Southern Sociological Society (SSS).

Folden, S. (2003). Health seeking behaviors of Haitian families for their school aged children. *Journal of Cultural Diversity, 10*, 62–68.

Fouron, G., & Glick-Schiller, N. (2002). The generation of identity: Redefining the second generation within a transnational social field. In P. Levitt & M. C. Waters (Eds.), *The changing face of home: The transnational lives of the second generation* (pp. 168–208). New York: Russell Sage Foundation.

Glick Schiller, N., & Fouron, G. (1998). Transnational Lives and National Identities: the identity politics of Haitian immigrants. In P. Smith & L. E. Guarnizo (Eds.), *Transnationalism from Below* (pp. 130–161). New Brunswick: Transaction Publishers.

Glick-Schiller, N., & Fouron, G. E. (2001). *George woke up laughing: Long-distance nationalism and the search for home*. Durham, NC: Duke University Press.

Herskovits, M. (1941). *The myth of the Negro Past*. Boston: Beacon.

Hillsman, R. S., & D'Agostino, T. J. (2003). *Understanding the contemporary Caribbean*. Boulder, CO: Lynne Reinner.

Itzigsohn, J. (2000). Immigration and the boundaries of citizenship: The Institutions of Immigrants' Political Transnationalism. *International Migration Review, 34*, 1126–1154.

Kretsedemas, P. (2003). Immigrant households and hardships after welfare reform: A case study of the Miami-Dade Haitian Community. *International Journal of Social Welfare, 122*, 314–325.

Laguerre, M. (1998). *Diasporic citizenship: Haitian Americans in transnational America*. New York: St. Martin's.

---

[4]Remarks by Haitian Americans interviewed in 2004.

Leonard, K., Stepick, A., Vasquez, M., & Holdaway, J. (2005). *Immigrant faiths*. Latham, MD: AltaMira Press.

Levitt, P. & Waters, M. C. (Eds.) (2002). *The Changing Face of Home*. New York: Russell Sage Foundation.

McAlister, E. M. (1998). The Madonna of 115th street revisited: Vodou and Haitian Catholicism in the age of transnationalism. In S. Warner & J. G. Wittner (Eds.), *Gathering in Diaspora* (pp. 123–160). Philadelphia: Temple University Press.

McIntyre, E., Rosebery, A., & Gonzalez, N. (Eds.). (2001). *Classroom diversity*. Portsmouth, NH: Heinemann.

Mooney, M. A. (2013). Religion as a context of reception: The case of Haitian immigrants in Miami, Montreal and Paris. *International Migration, 51*(3), 99–113.

Nicholls, D. (1996). *From Dessalines to Duvalier*. New Brunswick: Rutgers University Press.

Orezzolli, Max. C.E. (2000). Health beliefs and health care options of disparate black communities in the United States. *Dissertation Abstracts International, 61* (6), 2476-A, December.

Pamphile, Léon Dénius. (2001). *Haitians and African Americans*. Gainesville: University of Florida Press.

Pedraza, S. (1999). Assimilation or Diasporic Citizenship? *Contemporary Sociology, 28*, 377–381.

Pierce, W. J., & Eslime, E. (1997). Understanding and working with Haitian immigrant families. In P. M. Brown & J. Shalett (Eds.), *Cross-cultural practice with couples and families* (pp. 49–65). New York: Haworth Press.

Portes, A., Dore-Cabral, C., & Landold, P. (1997). *The urban Caribbean*. Baltimore: Johns Hopkins University Press.

Santana, M.-A., & Dancy, B. L. (2000). The stigma of being named AIDS carriers on Haitian-American women. *Health Care for Women International, 21*, 161–171.

Schefner, J. (1998). The urban Caribbean: Transitions in the new global economy. *Social Forces, 76*, 1564–1566.

Scher, P. W. (2010). Introduction: The Caribbean perspective. In P.W. Scher (ed.) *Perspectives on the Caribbean*. U.S.A.: Wiley-Blackwell.

Schwartz, B. (1992). Introduction. In L. A. Coser (Ed.), *On collective memory* (pp. 1–34). Chicago: The University of Chicago Press.

Shaw, E. (2008). Fictive Kin and Helping Behavior. *Sociation Today, 6*(2), 1–31.

Shaw-Taylor, Y., & Tuch, S. A. (2007). *The other African Americans*. Lanham, USA: Rowman and Littlefield.

Simon, J. (1998). Refugees in a carceral age: The rebirth of immigration prisons in the United States. *Public Culture, 10*, 577–607.

St. Jean, Y. (1984). *Case analysis of Haitians with AIDS*. Unpublished Master's Thesis. University of Texas at El Paso.

St. Jean, Y. (1996). American attitudes towards Haitians: AIDS as Stigma. In D. Sciulli (Ed.), *Normative social action* (pp. 153–164). Greenwich, T: JAI Press.

Stepick, A., & Swartz, D. F. (1998). *Pride against prejudice: Haitians in the United States*. Boston: Allyn Bacon.

Turner, R. B. (2006). The Haiti-New Orleans Vodou Connection: Zora Neale Hurston as initiate-observer. In C. Michel & P. Bellegarde-Smith (Eds.), *Vodou in Haitian life and culture* (pp. 117–134). New York: Palgrave MacMillan.

Ulysse, G. A. (2015). *Why Haiti needs new narratives*. Middletown, CT: Wesleyan University Press.

William-Myers, A. J. (1996). Slavery, rebellion, and revolution in the Americas: A historiographical scenario on the theses of Genovese and others. *Journal of Black Studies, 26*, 381–400.

Zacaïr, P. (2010). *Haiti and the Haitian Diaspora in the Wider Caribbean*. Gainesville: University of Florida Press.

Zéphir, F. (1996). *Haitian immigrants in Black America*. Westport, CT: Bergin and Garvey.

Zéphir, F. (2004). *The Haitian Americans*. Westport, CT: Greenwood.

"At Least We Don't Have Trump": Canadian Racism's Systemic Character—A Countersystem Perspective

16

Kimberley Ducey

Contents

16.1 Introduction

""Raise your hand if you're a marginalized person who has been victimized by the age-old white Canadian proverb "At least we don't have Trump.""[1] Suggestive of an enduring white Canadian myth, the preceding line appeared in the aptly titled article, "Trump is the New 'We Didn't Have Slavery' for White Canadians." Challenging the long-standing myth that white

[1]Nyangweso (2017).

K. Ducey (✉)
Department of Sociology, The University of Winnipeg, Winnipeg, MB, Canada
e-mail: k.ducey@uwinnipeg.ca

folks in Canada have always been more enlightened on racial issues than white folks in the U.S., the author of the piece, African Canadian Sharon Nyangweso, further observed:

Donald Trump's presidency has been traumatizing for people of colour, immigrants, women, LGBTQ+ folks and the poor. White Canadians however, have benefited from yet another American benchmark to measure themselves against. For as long as America has it's well documented, relatively publicized history of slavery, oppression and genocide, Canada thrives. Not only do these smears on American history polish the shine on Canadian morality, it serves as a tool to silence non-white people in Canada. America's disease allows white Canadians to be ignorant. As far back as the late 1800s when Canada had a state-mandated policy of starving Indigenous folks into reservations and submission, white Canadians still held themselves on a moral

© Springer International Publishing AG, part of Springer Nature 2018
P. Batur and J. R. Feagin (eds.), *Handbook of the Sociology of Racial and Ethnic Relations*,
Handbooks of Sociology and Social Research, https://doi.org/10.1007/978-3-319-76757-4_16

platform above America. … [However, for] every stop and frisk America has, Canada has a Black man carded. For every Black woman and girl missing and silenced in America, Canada has a missing or murdered Indigenous woman. For every Japanese family torn apart by the American government during World War Two, there is a Canadian family in the West with clear memories of a head tax placed on them for being Chinese. For every Indigenous Water Warrior at Standing Rock, there is an Indigenous activist fighting a pipeline in Canada. For every American travel ban, there will be a Canadian immigration prison fighting human rights abuses claims. Canada's history with people of colour is as soiled as America's. But America has always been the louder, more obnoxious cousin that Canada can point out to distract from its own demons.[2]

Systemic racism is alive and well in Canada. Indeed, in many ways it has long resembled systemic racism in the U.S., including via countless exploitative and discriminatory practices by whites, by virtue of white power and privilege that are institutionalized in a racial hierarchy, through the perpetuation of strategic material and other resource inequalities by white-controlled and well-institutionalized societal reproduction apparatuses, and through a myriad of racial prejudices, stereotypes, images, emotions, interpretations, and narratives, which are designed to justify and maintain white racial domination and white virtuousness.[3]

Systemic racism flourishes north of the U.S. border as seen in a recent mass shooting at a Québec mosque by a white male who espoused right-wing ideologies, including support for President Trump and far-right French politician Marine Le Pen *to* swastikas and racial epithets popping-up across the country *to* the necessity of providing emergency hijab kits to Muslim women on a Canadian campus after they had their head coverings pulled off *to* Canada's recent year-long 150th birthday celebrations that erased

the history of Indigenous Peoples[4] who called this land "home" for at least 15,000 years.

Drawing on Canadian examples, including empirical data from an ethnographic study I conducted, I document and analyze *white* racism. Specifically, I apply U.S. sociologist Joe R. Feagin's *systemic racism theory* to the Canadian context. Because important concepts of systemic racism theory underpin the chapter, I begin with a brief introduction to some of Feagin's key ideas. I next move to a brief description of four instances when racism's systemic character was officially recognized by the highest levels of Canadian leadership, including in a 2016 human rights tribunal judgement, a 2012 landmark court case on racial profiling, a 1998 declaration of systemic racism by the Canadian Bar Association, and in findings from a 1996 royal commission on Indigenous Peoples. I next briefly examine instances of white racial framing and counter-framing in Canadian history. In the final section of the chapter, I argue that white racial framing shaped the thoughts and actions of elite white women who governed a low-income housing project that was the subject of an ethnography I conducted. Moreover, I contend that black residents routinely responded to white racial framing with counter-framing, effectively challenging the white racial frame.

---

[2]Ibid.

[3]Feagin and Feagin (1978), Feagin and Vera (1995), Feagin (2010, 2014).

---

[4]Aboriginal Peoples was the proper collective noun for First Nations, Inuit, and Métis for some time in Canada, even being widely adopted by national groups and the federal government. The distinction was even made legal in 1982 when the *Constitution Act* came into being in Canada. Recently, the federal Canadian government—under the leadership of Liberal Prime Minister Justin Trudeau—adopted Indigenous Peoples and its legal ramifications. By recognizing First Nations, Inuit, and Metis as Indigenous Peoples, the Canadian government acknowledges their internationally legal right to offer or withhold consent to development under the U.N. Declaration of the Rights of Indigenous Peoples, which Canada endorsed with conditions under Trudeau's predecessor, Conservative Prime Minister Stephen Harper. I use the term Indigenous Peoples whenever possible out of respect for Indigenous Peoples and the U.N. Declaration of the Rights of Indigenous Peoples.

16.2 Definitions

Mainstream social analysts researching racism make extensive use of concepts like *bigotry*, *individual discrimination*, *intolerance*, *prejudice*, and *stereotyping*. Notwithstanding the potential value of such concepts, examining racism through such optics privileges individualistic analyses over systemic ones. In contrast, concepts like *systemic racism*, the *WRF*, and the *counter-frames* of People of Color and Indigenous Peoples are essential to Feagin's systemic racism theory and to my analysis here. Indeed, Feagin has long expounded on the limits and limitations of relying on individualistic conceptions when undertaking studies of racism.

16.2.1 Systemic Racism

As Feagin has long maintained, *systemic racism* is a manifestation of deep-seated white Eurocentrism; of racially oppressive institutions conceived and fashioned by an elite (most of whom are white men), who have done much harm to the globe, especially to People of Color and Indigenous cultures; and of racial ordering that privileges white folks above People of Color and Indigenous Peoples.

Systemic racism in Canada, as elsewhere, depends on racialized power relations with deep historic links to social systems such as settler-colonialism and genocide. These social systems were fashioned by an elite who have ruled Canada for more than 150 years and who have persistently promoted and upheld *white* racialized beliefs and customs. As Feagin has long argued, *systemic* racism is thus tantamount to *white* racism.

16.2.2 White Racial Framing Versus Counter-Framing

A key facet and device of systemic racism is what Feagin terms *white racial framing*. Routinely saturated with an age-old white male Eurocentrism, white racial framing thus gives rise to prevailing descriptions and constructions of social reality from the almost exclusive standpoint of elite white men. The WRF—for which white racial framing serves as the scaffold—is a meta-structure that cultivates and strengthens thinking and conduct, as well as social structures, systems, and organizations, which concur with the racial-group interests of *all* whites.

In contrast, the negative effects of the WRF on People of Color and Indigenous Peoples have long necessitated enormous expenditure by those oppressed to not only withstand the oppression, but to develop important *counter-framing* and dynamic tactics for fighting back. With their anti-oppression interpretations of the socio-racial organization of society, People of Color and Indigenous Peoples have long resisted dominant and status quo narratives of white racial framing. For example, antiracist counter-framing that denies white European assertions of cultural superiority have been avowed by Indigenous Peoples during the entire span of European meddling in and domination of North America. Indigenous Peoples, for example, have vehemently resisted white colonization of both lands and minds, including European ideals of Christianity, sedentary living, agriculture, and education.[5]

16.2.3 Systemic Racism Theory

Distinct from conventional race theory, *systemic racism theory* moves beyond staples such as racial group comparisons and racial attitudes, to tackle *institutionalized racism*, including white folks' responsibility for systemic racism. Systemic racism theory is especially attentive to insights from People of Color and Indigenous Peoples, who have historically been excluded from and have existed on the margins of Canadian academia and the larger society.

Following in the footsteps of Feagin, systemic racism theorists endeavor to provide explanations for *white* racism's configurations and processes, including its prevailing WRF. As *countersystem*

---

[5]Feagin (2014), p. 278.

analysts, systemic racism theorists consistently counter a sundry of white-framed methods, theories, and concepts that have long dominated conventional social science in Canada and beyond.[6]

16.3 Recognizing Racism's Systemic Character at the Highest Levels of Leadership

16.3.1 2016 Canadian Human Rights Tribunal

An illustration of the recognition of racism's systemic character is the 2016 Canadian Human Rights Tribunal's judgment, which found that discriminatory policies of the government's Indigenous Affairs Department—whose responsibilities are to First Nations, Inuit, and Métis Peoples—led to protracted underfunding that injured thousands of Indigenous children. Specifically, it was concluded that the Canadian government discriminated against children living on reserves in its funding of child welfare services. The quasi-judicial body issued its findings nine years after the *Assembly of First Nations* and *The First Nations Child and Family Caring Society of Canada* issued formal grievances against the federal government for failing to provide children on reserves with the same level of services provided to children elsewhere in Canada.[7] The official ruling read as follows: "The panel acknowledges the suffering of those … children and families who are or have been denied an equitable opportunity to remain together or to be reunited in a timely manner."[8]

The ruling took nearly nine years in large part because of resistance from the then-ruling federal Conservative government. These mostly white affluent men, who still make-up the majority of the Canada's political elite, attempted to have the case thrown out on technicalities no less than

eight times.[9] Such pushback ensued, despite the fact that children living on reserves were deprived of essential health and social services, whilst their birth families were purposefully dispossessed of monies that would allow the children to remain with them instead of being placed in foster care. Clearly then, as the Commissioners ruled, the mostly white male Canadian government preserved "the historical disadvantage and trauma suffered by aboriginal people, in particular as a result of the Residential Schools system."[10]

16.3.2 2012 Landmark Court Case on Racial Profiling

Another instance of the acknowledgment of racism's systemic character came four years earlier when Joel Debellefeuille, a black businessman residing in a suburb of Montréal, Québec, won a landmark court case on racial profiling. He sought legal redress for being incessantly profiled while driving a new BMW. On one occasion, white police officers grew especially suspicious because they believed that a black man could not have a Québécois name like Debellefeuille. The car was registered to a Mr. Joel Debellefeuille and for the white police officers, the black man driving the new BMW could not possibility be him. And so, they concluded that the car must be stolen. Debellefeuille would have to endure three court cases before the landmark ruling.[11]

The trial judge issued a strong admonition of the racial stereotypes and cultural bias that led white police officers to think that a black man could not have a Québécois-sounding surname. "To believe wrongly or by ignorance that the family name "Debellefeuille" could not be the

---

[6]Ibid.

[7]Kirkup (2017).

[8]Ibid.

[9]In 2011, approximately 350,620 people lived on reserves in Canada, nearly all of whom claimed some form of "Aboriginal identity." While reserves are governed by the *Indian Act*, residence on a reserve is governed by the Minister of *Indigenous and Northern Affairs Canada* and band councils. For more, see Historica Canada (2017).

[10]Galloway (2017).

[11]Sam (2017).

last name of a person with black skin only denotes a flagrant lack of knowledge of Québec society," the judge wrote. The judge also determined that Debellefeuille's constitutional rights to equality and to protection against arbitrary detention, both of which are protected by the *Canadian Charter of Rights and Freedoms*, were infringed upon.[12]

Debellefeuille himself publicly remarked: "It has been a long and expensive three-year battle against racial profiling and for the protection of my constitutional and civil rights. … My fight is not just about me or my family, but it is for all Black and other racialized people in this city and province who are too often the target of police racism and who cannot afford to fight all the way."[13]

16.3.3 1998 Canadian Bar Association

Another instance of an official admission of racism's systemic character came much earlier, in 1998, when the Canadian Bar Association unequivocally declared that the Canadian Judiciary did not reflect Canadian society. Sadly, nearly 20 years after the original 1998 declaration, fewer than 20 of Canada's 2000 federal judges were black; while a majority of black judges worked exclusively in the province of Ontario.[14]

16.3.4 1996 Royal Commission Report on Aboriginal Peoples

Earlier still, recognition of racism's systemic character was seen at the highest levels of Canadian leadership via the *1996 Royal Commission Report on Aboriginal Peoples*, which explored the relationship between Aboriginal Peoples, the Government of Canada, Indian and

Northern Affairs Canada, and the culture of Canada as a whole. The Commission concluded that Aboriginal Peoples are being "pushed … to the edge of economic, cultural and political extinction."[15] Members of the Commission, including several high-profile Indigenous jurists, traveled to numerous Indigenous communities to conduct interviews, concluding:

> Canada is widely thought to be one of the best countries in which to live. … Yet, within Canada's borders, there are two realities. Most Canadians enjoy adequate food and shelter, clean water, public safety, protection from abject poverty, access to responsive medical and social services, and the good health that results from these things. Aboriginal people are more likely to face inadequate nutrition, substandard housing and sanitation, unemployment and poverty, discrimination and racism, violence, inappropriate or absent services, and subsequent high rates of physical, social and emotional illness, injury, disability and premature death. The gap separating Aboriginal from non-Aboriginal people in terms of quality of life as defined by the World Health Organization remains stubbornly wide.[16]

As these examples reveal, *white* racism against racialized people and Indigenous Peoples is a central part of the larger reality and normalcy of systemic racism in Canada.

16.4 More White Racial Framing and Counter-Framing

16.4.1 White Racial Framing Revisited: Historica Canada's Version of Events

Feagin's WRF sheds much light on how systemic racism actually operates. It presents a vantage-point from which white oppressors have long viewed Canada and the world. In this racial framing, as Feagin explains, whites combine racial stereotypes (the verbal-cognitive aspect), metaphors and interpretive concepts (the deeper cognitive aspect), images (the strong visual

---

[12]Center for Research-Action on Race Relations (2017).
[13]Ibid.
[14]See Footnote 11.

[15]1996 Royal Commission (2017).
[16]Ibid; Otway (2002).

aspect), emotions (feelings), narratives (historical myths), and repetitive inclinations to discriminatory action. The frame reinforces and grows out of the material reality of racial oppression.[17]

The WRF contains not only negative stereotypes, images, metaphors, narratives, and emotions concerning People of Color and Indigenous Peoples, it contains positive stereotypes, images, metaphors, narratives, and emotions, extolling the virtues of white folks.[18]

Illustrations commending righteous whites are routinely seen in Historica Canada's Heritage Minutes, a series of one-minute vignettes appearing on Canadian television since 1991, which dramatize purported critical moments in the country's history. The majority of individuals profiled in these clips have been white men. Only three black men were profiled as of 2017, including baseball great Jackie Robinson in a vignette to his 1946 inaugural game with the Montréal Royals (a Brooklyn Dodgers' farm team). The Robinson piece conveniently erases the systemic racism he faced at the hands of white Canadians. In Historica Canada's version of history, white Montréal baseball fans and initially reluctant white teammates are effortlessly won over by Robinson's athletic prowess. White fans excitedly chant, "Jackie, Jackie, Jackie." The vignette ends with the words, "Record numbers of cheering Montréalers helped Jackie Robinson break baseball's colour bar that year. And he never forgot the city that launched his journey to baseball's hall of fame." Note how "race" is made minimal in the successful performances of Robinson in a way negated and removed from daily racial struggles. The vignette also expediently obscures that the vilest forms of systemic racism, segregation, and discrimination were still acceptable, even legal, and practiced throughout Canada in 1946, the year Robinson played his inaugural game with the Montréal Royals. In fact, that very same year Viola Desmond refused to leave a whites only section in a Nova Scotia movie cinema and was subsequently punished for violating racial segregation under

the guise of a petty tax violation. 70 years later Desmond became the second black woman featured in a Heritage Minute vignette.[19] Even more recently she was chosen to be the first Canadian woman to appear on the front of a banknote, the ten dollar bill.[20]

Before Desmond was honored with a Heritage Minute in 2016, the only other vignette to feature a black female as a central character was entitled, *Underground Railroad*. In the clip "Liza," who makes it safely to Canada ahead of her father, who was also formerly enslaved, appears hysterical as she anticipates his arrival via the Underground Railroad.[21] Arguably it is the unnamed white woman in the vignette, who soothes and pursues "Liza" down a busy street, that is the heroine of the piece. She is sophisticated and a pillar of strength and dignity; whereas, "Liza" is unsophisticated and frail.[22] White racially framed renderings of the Underground Railroad are brimming with narratives of poor illiterate fugitives who were naturally indebted to righteous white Canadians for taking them in. Historica Canada's version of events falls within this tradition. That mostly white "conductors" helped nameless blacks to freedom is largely embellished however. As U.S. historian Henry Louis Gates, Jr. explains, the Underground Railroad was primarily "run by free Northern African Americans, especially in its earliest years, most notably the great Philadelphian William Still. He operated with assistance of white abolitionists, many of whom were Quakers."[23]

16.4.2 Counter-Framing Revisited: Black Women Counter-Framers

As we have seen, Feagin adopted the terminology *counter-frame* to denote a countering-white-racial-oppression frame developed by various

---

[17]Feagin (2013).

[18]Feagin (2010).

[19]Driedger (2017).

[20]Kohut (2017).

[21]Annett (2017).

[22]Ibid.

[23]Gates (2017).

racialized groups. He suggests that such counter-frames are typically, though not exclusively, developed by People of Color and Indigenous Peoples as a way of making sense of persistent racial disparities. Feagin contends that while it is important to acknowledge that white racial framing helps legitimize systemic racism, it is also essential to understand counter-framing.

While most whites seldom acknowledge white racism's systemic character, and regularly perpetuate the WRF, throughout the course of Canadian history racialized people have challenged systemic racism and the stereotypes and exclusionary patterns that accompany the dominant frame. A few of these irrefutable contributions are fairly recognizable, such as the anti-slavery movement in the 1800s and the human rights struggles in the 1960s and 1970s. An individual example of Canadian counter-framing is the story of Mary Ann Shadd Cary. White racism was a life-long target of Shadd Cary's condemnation. She joined a generation of black women counter-framers who were stirred to action by "women at the podium, speaking before [unrestrained] audiences, editing newspapers, penning tracts and letters to the editor, organizing for church conferences, operating social and benevolent societies, and honing their skills in literary societies."[24]

Shadd Cary criticized cyclical racial oppression by elite and non-elite white men and women. She thus exposed the façade that is central to the WRF—i.e. superior white virtuousness. Canadian feminism is generally regarded as having begun with the white women's literary guild in 1876. Nevertheless, two decades earlier, Shadd Cary was running the *Provincial Freeman* (1853–1859), a newspaper in Ontario, which regularly countered the WRF. For example, there is her 1854 decision to reproduce Harriet Beecher Stowe's speech that pressed white women to become abolitionists.[25]

Other black women, such as Mary Bibb and Amelia Freeman, also founded women's literary and mutual improvement clubs in the early 1850s. Since they were black, they too were judged by the dominant framers as *not* representative of *all* women. Indeed, they were deemed inferior to white women.[26]

Recognizing black women's literary accomplishments as counter-framing is essential because black resistance to *white* racism not only includes open conflict with the dominant group, but more indirect struggles too, and with black women at the centre of those struggles. Moreover, the activism of Shadd Cary, Bibb and Freeman remind us that elite white women have played an active role in the preservation of the WRF.

16.5 Racialized (M)others: Gilmore House

16.5.1 The Gilmore House Ethnography

Gilmore House was established to assist lone mothers pursuing full-time post-secondary studies by offering them a much sought-after subsidized housing unit. The project was funded by government subsidies and donations. Once accepted, following a thorough screening process, mothers and their children moved into an apartment, but not before the mother signed the *Social Contract*. The agreement firmly monitored and controlled residents' everyday lives, including via the notorious "no man rule," limitations on the duration female guests might visit, submission of end-of-semester transcripts, tendering of yearly tax returns, and when applicable, presenting to the elite all information on impending legal and psychiatric issues.

I lately concluded a four-year ethnography of Gilmore House, including field work and interviews with residents and the elite who governed the project. The governing agents, who were mostly white affluent middle-aged women, clearly had a preferred resident profile and selected new tenants accordingly. White

---

[24]Jones (2007).
[25]Jane (1999).

[26]Archives of Ontario (2017), Shadd (2017).

applicants were highly desired; black applicants were not. Formal and informal eligibility controls mostly denied black women entry to the project, whilst black residents residing in Gilmore House faced daily white racial framing at the hands of the elite who oversaw the project. Black residents were routinely constructed, for example, as "more likely to abuse the program" (words of an elite). They were consistently framed as "more interested in furthering their families than their education" (words of an elite), even though empirical data arising from my study and the project's own historical records proved otherwise. For a project that prided itself on helping lone mothers in full-time post-secondary studies by giving them a subsidized housing unit, even an alleged interest in furthering one's family as opposed to one's education, was deemed the "ultimate sin" (a common phrase uttered by the elite).

16.5.2 A Tale of Two Gilmore House Residents

White residents routinely explained to me that the elite white women running Gilmore House "bent rules" (their words) for them. Regarding *full-tim*e enrollment in a post-secondary institution, for example, a white resident explained: "I had to drop a class, which would put me in part-time status. I really wanted to drop because I didn't want to bring down my GPA. … It was an Internet course, and I wasn't on top of it. I spoke to [an elite] about it. She said I could just make it up this semester, which I really appreciated and I could then drop it."

Meanwhile, a black resident's decision to drop a course was framed by the same Gilmore House official as violating one of the fundamental rules of the project—i.e. helping lone mothers in *full-time* post-secondary studies. Accordingly, her request was formally discussed during a meeting of the Board of Directors, which was not part of the process the white resident faced. In this instance, unlike the white resident, the request to drop the course had nothing to do with concerns over a GPA.

The black resident's written "Statement of Appeal," which the white resident was not required to submit, included excruciating facts that led to a frantic attempt to drop the course and thus a need to fall to part-time status. The black resident described lectures at her university wherein her mostly white classmates and white professor habitually made derogatory comments about black immigrants.

Similar to the black students that scholar Sharon Fries-Britt interviewed, who spoke about being shunned by both white and non-black racial minority students on campuses, the resident described persistent rejection.[27] In the black resident's written "Statement of Appeal," she made clear that fellow students openly claimed that blacks received unfair opportunities on the basis of skin color, including preferential grading. In the words of the resident: "I am being harassed. … I have tried hard to rise above it and tell myself, "They don't mean me. They don't mean me. They don't mean me."" As if comments regarding preferential grading were not painful enough, the white male professor discussed affirmative action in similar terms, claiming he had unduly lost out to black candidates for various academic positions.

Via email correspondence, the resident shared with me what she told the Gilmore House elite after it was suggested that she ought to confront her fellow students and the professor, rather than drop the course.

> I'm personally hesitant to confront them in class because there are a lot of statements they make that require people to actually take the initiative to find out why these stereotypes exist, and requires knowledge of politics. For someone like me, I could easily refute all of their statements but not in simplified ways. … These people want oversimplified answers to complicated issues and it just doesn't work that way. I don't know. I'm just feeling jaded about the whole thing. I feel like people are going to use anything I say as an excuse to continue their racism. It's something I've thought about a lot growing up because the most ignorant people I've ever met demand all answers to social issues be simple, and [they] tend to gravitate toward ideologies that use the most oversimplified arguments possible to explain social ills.

---

[27]Fries-Britt (1998).

Notwithstanding the black resident's request to drop the course and remain in Gilmore House, and despite falling to part-time status, when the (all white and female) Board of Directors discussed the case there was little mention of race or racism. Their focus was the resident's violation of Gilmore House's *Social Contract*—the aforementioned set of obligations which are part of the rental lease. Even when claiming revulsion at and intolerance for discrimination, white officials kept the discussion focused on the *Social Contract*.[28] To borrow the words of scholar Pearl M. Rosenberg: "[A]ll the labor it takes NOT to see [race] and to NOT mention it [was] impressive."[29]

The Board of Directors ultimately decided that the black resident would be in violation of the *Social Contract* if she dropped to part-time status. She thus remained in the course. The resident capitulated out of fear of being asked to leave Gilmore House. When I asked a Director of the Board why the rules could not be bent in her case, she claimed that the rules were never bent. She further explained that "to bend the rules would be like opening Pandora's box" and others might also "misuse the program." Clearly, this was not a concern when it came to the white resident who dropped the Internet course, or other white residents I interviewed over the course of four years who were regularly part-time students. In contrast, in four years, I encountered only one black resident who was a part-time student.

16.5.3 (White Elites) Save the Welfare Queen, (Black Residents) Dethrone the Welfare Queen

While in the estimation of the elite who governed Gilmore House, all residents were in need of moral regulation by virtue of being poor lone mothers, there is an abundance of empirical data to suggest that they judged black residents far more harshly, and generally assumed them to be *more* problematic and *less* deserving of the project's perks than white residents. Foundational to this belief was the *welfare queen myth*. Welfare queen is a designation that first emerged in the 1970s to admonish poor women—typically blacks and Latinas—for their purportedly inferior mothering, wayward sexuality, and for their independence from men.[30]

During informal events, meetings, and gatherings that I attended during the course of my ethnographic study, including at the homes of the elite, the image of the welfare queen routinely surfaced. Officials openly complained that "too many black women are applying to the program" (words of an elite). As previously mentioned, black residents's subordinate value was explained in terms of the expectation that they were less likely than white residents to complete their education, which notably was not backed-up by the program's historical records.

The presence of "too many black residents" (words of an elite) was also said to undermine the legitimacy of the program in the eyes of (the mostly white male) donors. In particular, aforementioned concerns that black residents were more likely to "further their families" than "further their education" (words of an elite) were continually cited.

In propagating the welfare queen myth, the white officials were clearly operating out of the WRF. As sociologist Patricia Hill Collins has shown, this bias goes all the way back to European colonialism and U.S. slavery (1870–1914). Both systems of oppression were partly justified by claims that blacks were primitive and animalistic, with ravenous sexual appetites.[31] Black women were positioned as sexually available, likened to promiscuous wild animals, and largely unable to protest. White women, on the other hand, were deemed asexual, beautiful, chaste, and biologically superior.[32]

---

[28]For other studies that show this is a tendency black students face, see Fries-Britt and Turner (2001), Smedley et al. (1993).

[29]Rosenberg (2004), p. 260. Caps in original.

[30]Boris (2007), p. 599.

[31]Lewis (2007), pp. 24–28.

[32]Collins (2005b).

Constructing black residents as primarily interested in producing babies rather than producing post-secondary diplomas is connected to this racist legacy and to contemporary portrayals of black women as sexually available and as over-breeders.[33] Recent scholarship suggests that such discourse continues to construct black women as chronically promiscuous,[34] while black men are cast as degenerate, hypersexual, and carnal.[35] The historical construction of white women as more sexually innocent than black women lived on in the Gilmore House doctrine, even though *all* residents were expected to be sexual and thus, in the view of the elite who ran the program, this had to be controlled.[36]

In the elite's framing of white residents as opposed to black residents, there sits an interesting demonstration of Feagin's systemic racism theory. Recall that the WRF includes racialized images, ideologies, emotions, and narratives that justify and effect racial oppression. In other words, the WRF does not merely include racial stereotypes and prejudices. For Gilmore House officials, the WRF frame comprised a deep-seated *pro-white* subframe (an affirmative positioning of white lone mothers) and *anti-others* frames (an adverse positioning of black lone mothers). This pro-white subframe—the center of the WRF—forcefully emphasized white superiority, righteousness, and moral goodness. Another clear example of this central accent on virtuous whites is seen in the elite's reframing of black applicants who left Gilmore House having completed their education. Their time in Gilmore House was positively reframed, purportedly resulting from the elite having imparted in them superior (READ: white) ways of mothering and studying.

---

[33]Collins (1986, 1990, 2005a).

[34]Collins, *Black Sexual Politics*; McGruder (2009).

[35]Collins, *Black Sexual Politics*; Coad (2008), Rahimi and Liston (2009).

[36]Breines (1992); For an interesting study concerning sexual politics, the sexual revolution, the portrayal of female sexual innocence in 1960s American film and changing female roles, see: Macpherson (2004), pp. 175–185.

16.5.4   (Un)sayable Assumptions of Race and Financial Responsibility: Residents' Meetings

Interview data is replete with testimonials illuminating *all* residents' awareness of the negative ways in which their financial struggles were constructed by economically privileged Gilmore House officials. Poor-bashing was a common complaint amongst all residents. However, owing to those who administered the project, the deep-seated *pro-white* subframe and *anti-others* frames gave advantage once more to white residents, even if both groups were poor-bashed. Take for example late rental payments. The differential treatment of black residents was agonizingly apparent. The lengthy field-note that follows, transcribed during and immediately after the monthly *Meeting of Residents*, documents white racial framing by the official who chaired the meeting.[37]

> The Director is a Bohemian-styled white woman in her early 50s. … She wears a fur vest and carries a regal purse into the meeting. I just heard her tell one of the white residents that she just had her closet papered [Note to self: Wall papered?] that afternoon. … As the meeting unfolds, she seems to intentionally direct comments towards certain mothers, the only two black women present. … She keeps looking at them every time she mentions the penalties for late rent. … To my private horror, at one point she points to these two women. … As she points her finger at each of them individually, right arm and hand stretched out, she says, "You and you" and proceeds to publicly chastise them. … I wonder if others notice that the women being singled out are black *and* they are the only two black women present.

Directly after the meeting, the white Director seemed to corroborate the assumptions in my field-note, suggesting that specific mothers, both of whom were black even though the Director never mentioned this point, have "attitude problems" and "need an attitude adjustment." At one point the Director exactly uttered those iniquitous words, "I'm not prejudiced but," before asking if

---

[37]For a discussion of the public humiliation black women face in public places, see: Feagin (1991), p. 101, 107.

I also noticed "the belligerence of those specific [black] women." Her preamble, "I'm not prejudiced but" was proceeded by the customary wavering and awkward moments that sometimes accompanies such statements. She seemed to inadvertently confirm that the residents' skin tones was foremost on her mind. Two days after the meeting, when I was speaking to one of the black women about this particular incident, she embarrassingly remarked, "Now I can say I have been racially profiled everywhere." In due course, she resisted by withdrawing from community responsibilities (e.g. refused to attend the subsequent mandatory *Meeting of Residents*). She explained:

> I don't even bother responding to [the Director] anymore because I know that she clearly has her head so far up her own ass that she has no desire to listen to what a woman of color – me – has to say. ... She angrily tried to respond to something I said a few meetings ago. ... I won't bother to go to this next meeting. ... She's more concerned about being right. ... Also the casual way she said "retarded" [during the last meeting] was absolutely appalling. But I've met plenty of white women just like her in my time and I'm really just tired of it. So I was glad that [another black resident] at least tried to speak up.

16.5.5 White Privilege, White Residents

While it is true that all Gilmore House residents interviewed described poor-bashing by the project's officials, there were important differences concerning the experiences of white and black residents. Psychologist Phyllis Wentworth's study of post-secondary students effectively captures this point, arguably shedding light on why white officials handled the aforementioned case of the white resident who wished to drop the Internet course so differently to the case of the black resident who wished to also drop a course.[38]

All of Wentworth's participants were white, female, older than average college age, and from working-class families. While their families

expected them to graduate from high school and immediately get married and/or obtain paid employment, which they did, they eventually became the first members of their families to attend college. Some of the women were victims of violent domestic relationships and/or faced other obstacles prior to enrolling in college. Nevertheless, akin to the white women living in Gilmore House, the whites in Wentworth's study experienced what they described as "second chances," "bending of rules," "flukes," "chance," "luck," or "good fortune" in overcoming difficulties, including obtaining apartments without a security deposit, avoiding reference checks when it came to employment opportunities, and support from an endless array of powerful and enthusiastic mentors. Neither Wentworth's white respondents or my white respondents contemplated the possibility that being white had worked to their advantage.[39]

Wentworth's study and my ethnography demonstrate that in spite of the difficult circumstances some white women face, white privilege still functions. Simply put, their lives may be difficult, but their lives are not difficult because they are white. Of course, this is not meant to suggest whites do not need or deserve assistance. It simply means that they benefit from being white, even as they endure poor-bashing, sexism, and other oppressions. Black residents, on the other hand, had to contend with gendered racism on top of poor-bashing, sexism, and other oppressions.

16.6 Conclusion

As the chapter illustrates, white racism is acutely affixed to the fabric of Canadian society. It is staunchly institutionalized, organizationally secure, and historically resolute. It substantially shapes Canadian society via macro-level institutions and structures and the micro and meso social order.

To make sense out of the experiences of Canadians of color and Indigenous Peoples, we must continuously accent the role of whites,

---

[38]Wentworth (1994).

[39]Ibid.

particularly elite whites, as the originators, enforcers, and remodelers of *white* racism. Since the country's creation, white men have been the most socially, politically, and economically influential racial group, as well as the group with the most socioeconomic resources, whilst, Canadians of color and Indigenous Peoples have long faced enormous disadvantages relative to whites. The ubiquity of systemic racism should put to rest the idea that racial oppression is dying or an aberration from a Canadian democratic norm. Racism is systemic and reflected in all major Canadian institutions.

Feagin's systemic racism theory has much to offer Canadian scholars interested in accurately understanding Canadian racism and advocating for genuine democracy and social justice. With his focus on how whites as a racial group have played the primary role in creating and shaping inegalitarian, hierarchical, and unjust relationships among racial groups, Feagin's work has the potential to provide new insights into Canadian racism. And while Feagin has skillfully shown that in the U.S. these racially oppressive conditions have regularly generated counter-framing that assertively resists the dominant WRF and systemic racism, his theory applies exceptionally well to Canada too.

References

1996 Royal Commission. (2017). Report of the Royal Commission on Aboriginal People (1996). *Christian Aboriginal Infrastructure Developments.* http://caid.ca/RepRoyCommAborigPple.html, March 12, 2017.

Abu-Jamal, M., & Davis, A. Y. (2014). Alternatives to the present system of capitalist injustice. *The Feminist Wire.* January 20, 2014. http://thefeministwire.com/2014/01/alternatives-to-the-present-system-of-capitalist-injustice/. Accessed February 28, 2015.

Albo, G. (2007). Neoliberalism and Canada's ruling class. *Monthly Review.* July 4, 2007. http://mrzine.monthlyreview.org/2007/albo070407.html.

Annett, E. (2017). Black history month in 60 seconds: Canada's Rosa Parks gets her due in new heritage minute. *Globe and Mail.* August 26, 2016. http://www.theglobeandmail.com/arts/film/black-history-month-how-do-heritage-minutes-stack-up-on-diversity/article28505721/. Accessed March 12, 2017.

Archives of Ontario. (2017). *The provincial freeman.* https://web.archive.org/web/20120126000215/ http://www.archives.gov.on.ca/english/archival-records/interloan/provincial-freeman.aspx. Accessed March 12, 2017.

Associated Press. (2015). *Dutch Santa Claus sidekick 'Black Pete' is a negative stereotype, court rules.* July 03, 2014. http://mashable.com/2014/07/03/black-pete/. Accessed February 28, 2015.

Bell, D. A. (1980). Brown v. Board of Education and the interest-convergence dilemma. *Harvard Law Review, 93,* 518–534.

Bell, D. (2005). *Silent covenants: Brown v. the Board of Education and the unfulfilled hopes for racial reform.* New York, NY: Oxford University Press.

Bell, D. (2008). *Race, racism, and American law* (6th ed.). New York, NY: Aspen Publishers.

Bonilla-Silva, E. (2001). *White supremacy and racism in the post civil rights era.* Boulder, CO: Lynne Rienner.

Boris, E. (2007). On cowboys and welfare queens: Independence, dependence and interdependence at home and abroad. *Journal of American Studies, 41*(3). https://doi.org/10.1017/s002187580700401x.

Breines, W. (1992). *Young, white, and miserable: Growing up female in the fifties.* Boston, MA: Beacon Press.

Brodie, Janine. (2002). The great undoing: State formation, gender politics, and social policy in Canada. In Catherine Kingfisher (Ed.), *Western welfare in decline.* Philadelphia, PA: University of Pennsylvania Press.

Camus, R. (2011). *Le grand Remplacement, Suivi de Discours d'orange.*

Center for Research-Action on Race Relations. (2017). *A landmark court decision on racial profiling: Joel Debellefeuille won his case against Longeuil Police.* Center for Research-Action on Race Relations. September 27, 2012. http://www.crarr.org/?q=fr/node/19465. Accessed December 19, 2017.

Cornell University Law School. (2017). "Civil Rights Cases," 109 U.S. 3, Decided: October 16th, 1883, *Legal Information Institute.* https://www.law.cornell.edu/supremecourt/text/109/3. Accessed March 12, 2017.

Chou, R. S., & Feagin, J. R. (2015). *The myth of the model minority: Asian Americans facing racism* (2nd ed.). New York: Paradigm-Routledge.

Coad, D. (2008). *The meterosexual: Gender, sexuality, and sport.* Albany, NY: SUNY Press.

Collins, Patricia Hill. (1986). Learning from the outsider within: The sociological significance of black feminist thought. *Social Problems, 33*(6), 14–32. https://doi.org/10.1525/sp.1986.33.6.03a00020.

Collins, P. H. (1990). *Black feminist thought: Knowledge, consciousness, and the politics of empowerment.* New York, NY: Routledge.

Collins, P. H. (2005a). Black public intellectuals: From Du Bois to the present. *Contexts, 4*(4), 22–27. https://doi.org/10.1525/ctx.2005.4.4.22.

Collins, P. H. (2005b). *Black sexual politics: African Americans, gender and the new racism*. New York, NY: Routledge.

Daniels, J. (2015). Two-faced racism at the secret service. *RacismReview.com*. May 12, 2008. http://www.racismreview.com/blog/2008/05/12/two-faced-racism-at-the-secret-service/. Accessed March 7, 2015.

DeVega, C. (2015). 20 things I learned about racism when i dared to talk about ISIS and the Lynchings of Black Americans. *We Are Respectable Negroes*. http://www.chaunceydevega.com/2015/02/20-things-i-learned-about-racism-when-i.html. Accessed February 28, 2015.

Driedger, L. (2017). Prejudice and discrimination in Canada. *Historica Canada*. February 10, 2011. http://www.thecanadianencyclopedia.ca/en/article/prejudice-and-discrimination/. Accessed March 12, 2017.

Du Bois, W. E. B. (2003 [1920]). *Darkwater: Voices from within the Veil*. New York: Humanity Books.

Feagin, J. R. (1991) The continuing significance of race: Antiblack discrimination in public places. *American Sociological Review, 56*(1). http://www.jstor.org.proxy2.lib.umanitoba.ca/stable/2095676.

Feagin, J. R. (2006). *Systemic racism: A theory of oppression*. New York, NY: Routledge.

Feagin, J. R. (2010) *The white racial frame: Centuries of racial framing and counter-framing*. New York: Routledge.

Feagin, J. R. (2013). *The white racial frame: Centuries of racial framing and counter-framing* (2nd ed.). New York: Routledge.

Feagin, J. R. (2014). *Racist America: Roots, current realities, and future reparations* (3rd ed.). New York: Routledge.

Feagin, J. R. (2016). *How blacks built America: Labor, culture, freedom, and democracy*. New York, NY: Routledge.

Feagin, J. R., & Barnett, B. M. (2004). Success and failure: How systemic racism trumped the *Brown V. Board of Education* Decision. *University of Illinois Law Review*, 1099–1130.

Feagin, J. R., & Elias, S. (2013). Rethinking racial formation theory: A systemic racism critique. *Ethnic and Racial Studies, 136*, 931–961.

Feagin, J. R., & Feagin, C. B. (1978). *Discrimination American style: Institutional racism and sexism*. Englewood Cliffs, NJ: Prentice Hall.

Feagin, J. R., & Feagin, C. B. (2011). *Race and ethnic relations, census update* (9th ed.). New York: Pearson.

Feagin, J. R., & O'Brien, E. (2004). *White men on race: Power, privilege, and the shaping of cultural consciousness*. Boston, MA: Beacon Press.

Feagin, J. R., & Vera, H. (1995). *White racism: The basics*. New York: Routledge.

FindLaw. (1883). *U.S. Supreme Court Case. Civil Rights Cases, 109 U.S. 3*. http://caselaw.lp.findlaw.com/scripts/getcase.pl?court=US&vol=109&invol=3.

Finkielkraut, A. (2013). *L'identité Malheureuse*. Paris, FR: Editions Stock.

Frankenberg, R. (1993). *White women, race matters: The social construction of whiteness*. Minneapolis, MN: University of Minnesota Press.

Fries-Britt, S. (1998). Moving beyond black achiever isolation: Experiences of gifted black collegians. *Journal of Higher Education, 69*(5), 556–576. http://www.jstor.org.proxy2.lib.umanitoba.ca/stable/2649110.

Fries-Britt, S., & Griffin, K. (2007). The black box: How high-achieving blacks resist stereotypes about Black Americans. *Journal of College Student Development, 48*(5). https://doi.org/10.1353/csd.2007.0048.

Fries-Britt, S., & Turner, B. (2001). Facing stereotypes: A case study of black students on a white campus. *Journal of College Student Development, 42*(5), 420–429.

Galloway, G. (2017). Ottawa to overhaul welfare provisions on first nations reserves. *Globe and Mail*. January 26, 2016. http://www.theglobeandmail.com/news/politics/indigenous-children-on-reserves-face-discrimination-from-ottawa-tribunal-rules/article28392603/. Accessed March 12, 2017.

Gates, H. L., Jr. (2017). Who really ran the underground railroad? *African Americans: Many rivers to cross (PBS)*. http://www.pbs.org/wnet/african-americans-many-rivers-to-cross/history/who-really-ran-the-underground-railroad/. Accessed March 12, 2017.

Gilmore, P., Smith, D. M., & Kairaiuak, A. L. (2004). Resisting diversity: An alaskan case of institutional struggle. In M. Fine, L. Weis, L. C. Powell, & L. Mun (Eds.), Wong *off white: Readings on race, power & society*. New York, NY: Routledge.

Gilroy, P. (1993). *The Black Atlantic: Modernity and double consciousness*. New York: Verso.

Historica Canada. (2017). *Reserves*. http://www.thecanadianencyclopedia.ca/en/article/aboriginal-reserves/ Accessed March 12, 2017.

Jane, R. (1999). *Mary Ann Shadd Cary: The black press and protest in the nineteenth century* (p. 91). Bloomington: Indiana University Press.

Jefferson, T. (2015). *Notes on the State of Virginia*. http://avalon.law.yale.edu/18th_century/jeffvir.asp. Accessed February 28, 2015.

Jones, M. S. (2007). *All bound up together: The woman question in African American public life, 1830–1900* (p. 88). Chapel Hill, NC: University of North Caroline Press.

Kirkup, K. (2017). Canadian human rights tribunal: Government discriminated against children on reserves. *HuffPost*. January 26, 2016. http://www.huffingtonpost.ca/2016/01/26/tribunal-to-rule-if-government-discriminated-against-first-nations-children_n_9075992.html. Accessed December 19, 2017.

Kohut, T. (2017). Who is Viola Desmond? The First Canadian woman to grace front of banknote. *Global News*, December 8, 2016. http://globalnews.ca/news/3114370/viola-desmond-first-woman-canadian-banknote/. Accessed March 12, 2017.

Lewis, L. (2007). Contesting the dangerous sexuality of black male youth. In G. Herdt & C. Howe (Eds.), *21st century sexualities: Contemporary issues in health, education, and rights*. New York, NY: Routledge.

Liptak, A. (2013). Supreme court invalidates key part of voting rights act. *The New York Times*. http://www.nytimes.com/2013/06/26/us/supreme-court-ruling.html?_r=0. Accessed February 28, 2015.

Macpherson, P. (2004). The revolution of little girls. In M. Fine, L. Weis, L. C. Powell, & L. Mun Wong (Eds.), *Off white: Readings on race, power & society*. New York, NY: Routledge.

Manitoba Human Rights Commission. (2017). *Human Rights Adjudicator Finds Employees Forced to Tolerate Poisoned Work Environment*. April 29, 2016. http://www.manitobahumanrights.ca/publications/news_releases/2016_04_29.html. Accessed March 12, 2017.

McCarthy, T. (2015). Ferguson Report's Racist Obama Email: 'What Black Man Holds a Steady Job for Four Years.' *The Guardian*. March 03, 2015. http://www.theguardian.com/us-news/2015/mar/03/ferguson-report-obama-email-black-man-steady-job. Accessed March 7, 2015.

McGruder, K. (2009). Black sexuality in the U.S.: Presentations as non-normative. *Journal of African American Studies, 13*(3), 251–262. https://doi.org/10.1007/s12111-008-9070-5.

Miles, R. (1989). *Racism*. London: Routledge.

Mirchandani, K., & Chan, W. (2007). *Criminalizing race, criminalizing poverty. welfare fraud enforcement in Canada*. Winnipeg, MB: Fernwood Publishing.

Nyangweso, S. (2017). Trump is the New 'We Didn't Have Slavery' for White Canadians. *Rabble.ca*. December 19, 2017. http://rabble.ca/news/2017/12/trump-new-we-didnt-have-slavery-white-canadians. Accessed December 19, 2017.

Omi, M., & Winant, H. (1994). *Racial formation in the United States: From the 1960s to the 1990s* (2nd ed.). New York: Routledge.

Otway, L. (2002). Aboriginal women's health and healing on the plains. In P. Douaud & B. Dawson (Eds.), *Plain speaking: Essays on aboriginal peoples and the prairie*. Regina, SK: The Canadian Plains Research.

Picca, L. H., & Feagin, J. R. (2007). *Two-faced racism: Whites in the backstage and frontstage*. New York: Routledge.

Rahimi, R., & Liston, D. (2009). What does she expect when she dresses like that? Teacher interpretation of emerging adolescent female sexuality. *Educational Studies, 45*(6), 512–533. https://doi.org/10.1080/00131940903311362.

Redekop, B. (2017). Employer must award 3 employees $20 K each in sexual harassment case. *Winnipeg Free Press*. April 29, 2016. http://www.winnipegfreepress.com/local/employer-must-award-3-employees-20k-each-in-sexual-harassment-case-377578461.html. Accessed March 12, 2017.

Robertson, H.-J. (1999). Poor logic and poor children. *Phi Delta Kappan, 80*(7). http://www.jstor.org/stable/20439503.

Rosenberg, P. M. (2004). Color blindness in teacher education: An optical delusion. In M. Fine, L. Weis, L. P. Pruitt, & A. Burns (Eds.), *Off white. Readings on power, privilege, and resistance*. New York, NY: Routledge.

Royster, D. A. (2003). *Race and the invisible hand: How white networks exclude black men from blue-collar jobs*. Berkeley, CA: University of California Press.

Sam, Y. (2017). Quebec human rights commission must recognize systemic racism. *Huffington Post*. May 11, 2016. http://www.huffingtonpost.ca/yvonne-sam/quebec-systemic-racism_b_9904016.html. Accessed March 12, 2017.

Sarrazin, T. (2012) *Deutschland schafft sich ab*. Verlagsgruppe Random House.

Shadd, A. (2017). Mary Ann Shadd Cary: Abolitionist. *Library and Archives of Canada*. http://www.collectionscanada.gc.ca/northern-star/033005-2201-e.html. Accessed March 12, 2017.

Smedley, B. D., Myers, H. F., & Harrell, S. P. (1993). Minority status stresses and the college adjustment of ethnic minority freshman. *Journal of Higher Education, 64*(4), 434–452.

Tremonti, A. M. (2017). Yes, Canada, anti-black racism lives here: Journalist Desmond Cole. *The Current (CBC)*. http://www.cbc.ca/radio/thecurrent/the-current-for-march-9-2017-1.4015605/yescanada-anti-black-racism-lives-here-journalist-desmond-cole-1.4015609. Accessed March 12, 2017.

Ture, K., Carmichael, S., & Hamilton, C. (1967). *Black power*. New York, NY: Random House Vintage.

UNICEF Germany. (2014). *UNICEF: Werbung durch Herabwürdigung*. http://www.derbraunemob.info/unicef-werbung-durch-herabwurdigung/. Accessed February 28, 2015.

Walker, D. (1965). *Appeal to the Coloured Citizens of the World, with an introduction by Charles M*. Wiltse. New York: Hill and Wang.

Walsh, S. C., Brigham, S. M., & Wang, Y. (2011). Internationally educated female teachers in the neoliberal context: Their labour market and teacher certification experiences in Canada. *Teaching and Teacher Education, 27*(3). https://doi.org/10.1016/jtate.2010.11.004.

Wentworth, P. A. (1994). *The identity development of non-traditionally aged first-generation women college students: An exploratory study* (Master's Thesis). Department of Psychology and Education, Mount Holyoke College, South Hadley, MA.

Wingfield, A. H., & Feagin, J. R. (2010). *Yes we can?: White racial framing and the 2008 presidential Campaign*. New York, NY: Routledge.

Wright, C. (2000). Nowhere at home: Gender, race and the making of anti-immigration discourse in Canada. *Atlantis, 24*(2).

Heart of Violence: Global Racism, War, and Genocide

17

Pinar Batur

Contents

W. E. B. Du Bois pointed out that the expansion of capitalism and growth of global racism made the color line the problem of the 20th century. Even though the struggle against the global line of racial inequality also grew, the problem of the 21st century is the intensification of racial inequality manifested as war and genocide. The last century was marred by racial hate and killings, but, "genocide" came to be understood as "the coordinated plan of different actions aiming at the destruction of essential foundations of the life of national groups with the aim of annihilating the groups themselves" (Totten et al.

1997: xxiii). As Israel Charny warned, "there needs to be a growing consensus on the part of human beings and organized society that penetrates the very basis of human culture, that mass killing is unacceptable to civilized peoples. Otherwise, the prevailing momentum of historical experience will continue for generation after generation that genocide is a phenomenon of nature, like other disasters. This view of the inevitability of genocide as an almost natural event will continue to justify it in the sense of convincing people that nothing can be done (Totten et al. 1997: xxxix). War and genocide are horrid, and taking them for granted is racist. In the 21st century, our problem is not only seeing them as natural and inevitable, but even worse: not even seeing, not even noticing, but ignoring war, mass killings and genocide. Such act and thought, fueled by global racism, reveal that racial

P. Batur (✉)
Department of Sociology and the Program in Environmental Studies, Vassar College, Poughkeepsie, NY, USA
e-mail: pibatur@vassar.edu

© Springer International Publishing AG, part of Springer Nature 2018
P. Batur and J. R. Feagin (eds.), *Handbook of the Sociology of Racial and Ethnic Relations*,
Handbooks of Sociology and Social Research, https://doi.org/10.1007/978-3-319-76757-4_17

inequality has advanced from the establishment of racial hierarchy and institutionalization of segregation, to the confinement and exclusion, and elimination of those considered inferior through genocide. In this trajectory, global racism manifests genocide. However, this is not inevitable. This article, by examining global racism since 2000, the new century, explores the new terms of exclusion and the path to permanent war and genocide as pivotal to defining global anti-racist confrontation as a way to struggle against racism, the struggle of the 21st century.

17.1 Global Racism in the Age of "Unending Wars"

Racist legitimization of inequality has changed from presupposed biological inferiority to assumed cultural subordination, political dependency or economic marginality, to define new terms of the impossibility of coexistence, much less equality. The Jim Crow racism of biological inferiority is now being replaced with a new and modern racism (Baker 1981; Ansell 1997), with "culture war" as the key to justify difference, hierarchy, and oppression. The ideology of "culture war" is becoming embedded in institutions, defining the workings of organizations, and is now defended by individuals who argue that they are not "racist," but are not blind to the inherent differences between African-Americans/Arabs/Chinese or whomever, and "us." "Us" as a concept defines the power of a group to distinguish itself and to assign a superior value to its institutions, revealing that affinity with "them" will be harmful to its existence (Hunter 1992; Buchanan 2002).

How can we conceptualize this shift to examine what has changed over the past century and what has remained the same in a racist society? Joe Feagin examines this question with a theory of systemic racism to explore the societal complexity of interconnected elements supporting the longevity and adaptability of racism. He sees that systemic racism persists due to a "white racial frame," defining and maintaining an "organized set of racialized ideas, stereotypes, emotions, and inclinations to discriminate" (Feagin 2006: 25). The white racial frame arranges the routine operation of racist institutions, which enables social and economic reproduction and amendment of racial privilege. This frame defines the political and economic bases of cultural and historical legitimization. Central to systemic racism is the focus on actors, real people, who benefit, oppress, and are oppressed by its power. People of color, globally, feel the material consequences of this system physically, emotionally, socially, and economically in their continual subordination. Whites also experience its consequences as benefits that often allow them to move through life and up social and economic hierarchies with ease and without challenge. White people, then, play an important role in systemic racism in that they are inherently implicated in it. As systemic racism continues to position white actors in powerful roles, including at the forefront of racial discourse, people of color face what seem like insurmountable obstacles to making their voices heard and working against it. Therein lies the true power of systemic racism: self-reinforcement and the preclusion of the conditions of possibility for its eradication.

While the white racial frame is one of the components of systemic racism, it is attached to other terms of racial oppression to forge systemic coherency. It has altered over time from slavery to segregation to racial oppression, and since the collapse of the Soviet Union, the white racial frame emphasizes intensification of "culture war," or "clash of civilizations" to legitimate the racist oppression of domination, exclusion, war and genocide. The concept of "culture war" emerged to define opposing ideas in America regarding privacy, censorship, citizenship rights and secularism, but it has been globalized through conflicts over immigration, nuclear power and the "war on terrorism." Its discourse and action articulate to flood the racial space of systemic racism.

Racism is a process of defining and building communities and societies based on racialized hierarchy of power. The expansion of capitalism cast new formulas of divisions and oppositions, fostering inequality even while integrating all previous forms of oppressive hierarchical arrangements as long as they bolstered the need to maintain the structure and form of capitalist arrangements (Batur-VanderLippe 1996). In this context, white racial frame, defining the terms of racist systems of oppression, enabled the globalization of racial space through the articulation of capitalism (Du Bois 1942; Winant 1994). The key to understanding this expansion is comprehension of the synergistic relationship between racist systems of oppression and the capitalist system of exploitation. Taken separately, these two systems would be unable to create such oppression independently. But the synergy between them is devastating. In the age of industrial capitalism, this synergy manifested imperialism and colonialism. In the age of advanced capitalism, it is war and genocide. The capitalist system, by enabling and maintaining the connection between everyday life and the global, buttresses the processes of racial oppression, and synergy between racial oppression and capitalist exploitation begets violence. Etienne Balibar points out that the connection between everyday life and the global is established through thought, making global racism a way of thinking, enabling connections of "words with objects and words with images in order to create concepts" (Balibar 1994: 200). Yet, global racism is not only an articulation of thought, but also a way of knowing and acting, framed by both everyday and global experiences. Synergy between capitalism and racism as systems of oppression enables this perpetuation and destruction on the global level.

As capitalism expanded and adapted to the particularities of spatial and temporal variables, global racism became part of its legitimization and accommodation, first in terms of colonialist arrangements. In colonized and colonizing lands, global racism has been perpetuated through racial ideologies and discriminatory practices under capitalism by the creation and recreation of connections among memory, knowledge, institutions and construction of the future in thought and action. What makes racism global are the bridges connecting the particularities of everyday racist experiences to the universality of racist concepts and actions, maintained globally by myriad forms of prejudice, discrimination, and violence (Balibar and Wallerstein 1991; Batur-VanderLippe and Feagin 1999; Batur 2006). Under colonialism, colonizing and colonized societies were antagonistic opposites. Since colonizing society portrayed the colonized "other," as the adversary and challenger of the "the ideal self," not only identification, but segregation and containment were essential to racist policies. The terms of exclusion were set by institutions that fostered and maintained segregation, but the intensity of exclusion, and redundancy became more apparent in the age of advanced capitalism, as an extension of post-colonial discipline. The exclusionary measures, when tested, led to war, and genocide. Although, more often than not, genocide was perpetrated and fostered by the post-colonial institutions, rather than colonizing forces, the colonial identification of the "inferior other led to segregation, then exclusion, then war and genocide. Violence glued them together into a seamless continuity.

Violence is integral to understanding global racism. Fanon (1963), in exploring colonial oppression, discusses how divisions created or reinforced by colonialism guarantee the perpetuation, and escalation, of violence for both the colonizer and colonized. Racial differentiations, cemented through the colonial relationship, are integral to the aggregation of violence during and after colonialism: "Manichaeism [division of the universe into opposites of good and evil] goes to its logical conclusion and dehumanizes" (Fanon 1963: 42). Within this dehumanizing framework, Fanon argues that the violence resulting from the destruction of everyday life, sense of self and imagination under colonialism continues to infest the post-colonial existence by integrating colonized land into the violent destruction of a new "geography of hunger" and exploitation (Fanon 1963: 96). The "geography of hunger" marks the context and space in which oppression and exploitation continues. The historical maps drawn by colonialism now demarcate the boundaries of post-colonial arrangements. The white racial frame restructures this space to fit the imagery of symbolic racism, modifying it to fit the television screen, or making the evidence of the necessity of the politics of exclusion, and the violence of war and genocide, palatable enough for the front page of newspapers spread out next to the morning breakfast cereal. Two examples of this "geography of hunger and exploitation" are Iraq and New Orleans.

17.2 Iraq and New Orleans: The Dark Hearts of the Post-colonial World

In Joseph Conrad's *Heart of Darkness*, Marlow says "The conquest of the earth, which mostly means the taking it away from those who have a different complexion or slightly flatter noses than ourselves, is not a pretty thing when you look into it too much," because one sees the "conquerors, and for that you want only brute force—nothing to boast of when you have it, since your strength is just an accident arising from the weakness of others.... It was just a robbery with violence, aggravated murder on a great scale, and men going at it blind—as is very proper for those who tackle a darkness" (Conrad 1989: 31–32). Such darkness hides moral uncertainty, greed and violence, and obscures all awareness of racist intentions, such as Western involvement with Iraq. This involvement is racist: not just now, but from the beginning of British colonial domination, to the first Gulf War, to now. The "liberation of Iraq" from the barbaric "other" and the establishment of the British mandate in the 1920s, had the purpose of controlling the oil around Mosul, which required stability to foster investment and to insure profits. To subdue the Kurdish and other minorities, including nomadic Arab populations, the British, together with handpicked Iraqi elites, made liberal use of the newly developed technology of airplanes to bomb, gas and terrorize the people. During World War I, the RAF asked for permission to experiment with chemical weapons against what they called "recalcitrant" Arabs. Winston Churchill, then the Lord of the

Admiralty, replied "I do not understand the squeamishness about the use of gas.... I am strongly in favor of using poisonous gas against uncivilized tribes.... It is not necessary to use only the most deadly gases.... Gases could be used which would cause great inconvenience, and would spread a lively terror and yet leave no serious permanent effect on most of those affected." Churchill argued that chemical weapons are the application of western science to modern warfare. "We can not under any circumstances acquiesce in the nonutilization of any weapons which are available to procure a speedy termination of the disorder which prevails on the frontier" (Lichtman 1995: 519). Sixty years later, following the gas attack on Kurds in the town of Halabca, the Iraqi Defense Minister told reporters that "it is legitimate for any people to defend themselves with whatever means available," and that the state's use of chemical weapons was an "internal issue" (Marshall 1988).

Following the 1990–91 Gulf War, UN sanctions against Iraq remained in place, ostensibly to force Saddam Hussein to comply with demands to open the country up to weapons inspectors in search of nuclear, biological and chemical weapons. Claiming that the Iraqi regime was obstructing inspections in order to resurrect its WMD program, the Bush and Clinton administrations pressured the Security Council into tightening sanctions, to prevent importation of a long list of banned and "dual-use" materials such as chlorine, which could be used for water treatment or chemical weapons. While the sanctions' only impact on the regime was to strengthen Saddam Hussein's grip, the UN eventually conceded that more than 600,000 Iraqis, mostly children and elderly, had died from lack of proper hygiene and medicine. Bill Clinton's Secretary of State, Madeline Albright, when confronted by a Congressional panel, replied that "we find these numbers acceptable." Clinton and George W. Bush maintained that the deaths were the fault of Saddam Hussein, which made them a domestic political matter.

War in Iraq continues since the armed invasion in 2003, but who remembers the "shock and awe" campaign of the U.S. and British armies? In the aftermath of invasion, in addition to political devastation, economic destruction, sectarian fighting, and cultural annihilation, Iraq citizens are left to fight with the environmental damage of the war. These damages stemmed from three different locations and complemented each other. The first is the damage due to destruction of industrial and military sites, oil installations, and cities in Iraq, leaving behind a lethal cocktail of heavy metals, and all kinds of chemical contaminants without Iraqi means to remediate the sites, now or in the near future. Second, the lethal chemical weapon and radiation residues left by depleted uranium projectiles used by allied forces, which total between 290 and 800 tons. The decontamination will require at least the removal of soil from all sites. The third area of destruction is in the fragile biodiversity of Iraq, which had already suffered from the effects of intensive agriculture and oil economy. Ecodiversity is one of the best indicators of the health of the region, and a key issue in lives of human and non-human beings (McLaren and Willmore 2003). All three of these types of destruction often went unnoticed under the rhetoric of preventing the development and transfer of "weapons of mass destruction" to "terrorists," which enabled further oppression and destruction of the region without the possibility of peace and reconciliation.

But racism, war and genocide are never internal issues, because violence requires participants and collaborators. In the context of global racism, collaboration is legitimized by the white racial discourse of "just oppression." "Just oppression" is a racist belief in domination and compliance, to take it for granted that something like human dignity no longer matters, and therefore we can overlook abuse, violence and destruction by blaming the "other," or people of color, or in this case, Arabs or Iraqis, for the cumulative destruction. But it is impossible to utilize the white racial frame that justifies oppression, without the concept of "technical rationality." Richard Lichtman points out the importance of the "technocratic ideology of liberal modernism," which is central to "technical rationality" (Lichtman 1995; Marcuse 1998). The technocratic ideology of liberal modernism has a tendency to concentrate on ends, without assigning an ultimate value to the means or the consequences. It confronts what it sees as disorder and inefficiency, with seemingly neutral morality and no impact on the everyday, or the future. And it serves the double standard of responding when the un-technical, irrational "other" threatens rational, scientific "us," but not when the "other" threatens "another," as was the case with the Iraqi gas attacks on Kurds; or blame can be shifted to the "other," as with the killing by sanctions, or destruction of New Orleans, and to the people who were unable to leave New Orleans before and after the storm.

On Friday, August 26, 2005, a state of emergency was declared in Louisiana and the Gulf Coast states as Hurricane Katrina approached. The governors of the Gulf Coast states also asked George Bush to declare a federal state of emergency, especially for Louisiana. As Katrina threatened, the local newspapers forecast that the levees wouldn't hold, and Mayor Ray Nagin, announced that "we are facing the storm most of us have feared," then issued orders for the mandatory evacuation of New Orleans (Russell 2005). That evening, while water began to top the levees, approximately 30,000 people gathered at the Superdome with an estimated 36 h worth of food and clean water. By Monday the 29th, Katrina made landfall, and the Bush administration was notified of the levee breech. In fact, 28 government agencies reported that the New Orleans levees breached, leaving most of the city under water (Jordan 2006). These documents later became a point of departure to question whether or not the government moved to rescue the storm victims when the levees broke. George W. Bush repeatedly said, "I don't think anybody anticipated the breach of the levees," but documents later showed that FEMA officials discussed the possibility of such a breach in a briefing for George W. Bush. In fact, on March 1, 2006, news surfaced that nineteen hours before the arrival of Katrina, the Bush administration was notified by top hurricane experts of their fear for massive loss of life due to levee failure. As the levees failed that morning, George Bush was visiting senior citizens in

Arizona to promote Medicare drug benefits, and went to bed without acknowledging governor Blanco's plea: "Mr. President we need your help, we need everything you got" (Thomas 2005).

On Tuesday, August 30th, while the nation's newspapers showed George Bush playing guitar with singer Mark Willis, the navy ship *Baatan* was in the Gulf of Mexico. It had a 600 bed hospital available, along with helicopters and doctors, was loaded with food, and could produce approximately 100,000 gallons of potable water a day. Captain Tyson said "We are ready." But they were never called (Hedges 2005). By now Reuters reported 80,000 people were stranded in the city, as Bush continued to claim, "no one expected the levees to break." On September 1st, Michael Brown, the head of FEMA, said on national television that they had just learned that evacuees were at the New Orleans Convention Center. It was not before September 3rd and 4th that 25,000 hungry, thirsty, sunburned, and sick human beings were evacuated. Some by choice, and some without consent, were bused to Houston and other cities (CNN 2005).

As evacuees gathered at the Houston Astrodome, Barbara Bush, George Bush's mother, observed "So many people in the arena are, you know, underprivileged anyway, so this, this is working well for them" (APM 2005). Meanwhile, New Orleans City Councilman Oliver Thomas told CBS News "People are too afraid of black people to go in and save them." Rumors of shootings, looting, riots, and thieves made people afraid to save or take in people conceptualized as diseased, dirty, violent thugs and thieves. A black woman told CBS News "If we were lucky, we would have died" (CBS 2005). The Congressional Black Caucus, Black Leadership Forum, Urban League, and the NAACP, held news conferences and charged that the administration's slow response was due to most of the victims' being black and poor. As Jesse Jackson said in an interview, "We have an amazing tolerance for black pain." (CNN 2005) According to reports, more people died from starvation and heat than from drowning caused by Hurricane Katrina in New Orleans (CBS 2005).

But, this was not the first time for such events. In 1927, with heavy rains upriver threatening to flood New Orleans, a consensus of politically enfranchised whites emerged calling for the destruction of a downstream levee to avert the flood risk to New Orleans. The St. Bernard parish area was chosen purportedly because its residents were "regarded by city dwellers as backward or even 'primitive'" (Gomez 2000: 110). The 1927 Mississippi Flood was one of America's major natural disasters, but the bigger disaster occurred due to Jim Crow discrimination, segregation and violence. Ninety percent of the flood victims were black. The flood left over six hundred thousand people homeless. The basic policy embraced by the US Army Corps of Engineers, the National Guard, and State and Federal Agencies was to create segregated refugee camps and establish forced labor camps for black flood victims. There were one hundred and fifty four camps, and camps were patrolled by armed, mostly white National Guardsmen. One of the largest camps held 13,000 blacks, and they were ordered by armed white guardsmen to work on the levees. As a result, many blacks lost their lives when the levees broke, while others lost their belongings, because they did not have the time or means to make preparations. In refugee camps, tents, beds, clothing and food were given to whites. And while whites ate at sheltered tables, blacks stood or sat on the ground and ate without utensils. When blacks died their bodies were slit, loaded with sand and dumped in the river. The flood trash from white neighborhoods was gathered and dumped into black neighborhoods. Blacks were only allowed to leave the camps when their previous employer came to claim them. Relief supplies were given to the employer, which most employers used as provisions to run their businesses, and paid them as salary to their labor force. In addition, during this period the number of lynchings increased dramatically (Evans 2006: 6–9).

This callous disregard for black lives contrasted sharply with the tremendous capital expenditure devoted to saving muskrats. This small game brought trappers "5.1 million" in 1924–25. Boats were sent to rescue the muskrats, as "trappers and conservation agents transported thousands of rats to higher ground." And, rafts were floated into the river "allowing the animals to feed, take shelter, and give birth as they recuperated" from the trauma of the flood (Gomez 2000: 110–118).

17.3 Shades of Darkness: Islam, Muslims and the "Clash of Civilizations"

Albert Memmi argued that "We have no idea what the colonized would have been without colonization, but we certainly see what happened as a result of it" (Memmi 1965: 114). Beginning from 2000, in this new century, events surrounding Iraq and Katrina provide three critical points regarding global racism. The first one is that segregation, exclusion, and genocide are closely related and facilitated by institutions employing the white racial frame to legitimize their ideologies and actions. The second one is the continuation of violence, either sporadically or systematically, with single-minded determination from segregation, to exclusion, to genocide. The third point is that legitimization and justification of violence is embedded in the resignation that global racism will not alter its course, and there is no way to challenge global racism. Together these three points facilitate the base for war and genocide.

In 1993, in the aftermath of the collapse of the Soviet Union, Samuel P. Huntington racialized the future of global conflict by declaring that "the clash of civilizations will dominate global politics" (Huntington 1993: 22). He declared that the fault line will be drawn by crisis and bloodshed. Huntington's end of ideology meant the West is now expected to confront the Confucian-Islamic "other." Huntington intoned "Islam has bloody borders," and he expected the West to develop cooperation among Christian brethren, while limiting the military strength of the "Confucian-Islamic" civilizations, by exploiting the conflicts within them. When the walls of communism fell, a new enemy was found in Islam, and loathing and fear of Islam exploded

with September 11th. The new color line means "we hate them not because of what they do, but because of who they are and what they believe in." The vehement denial of racism, and the fervent assertion of democratic equality in the West, are matched by detestation and anger towards Muslims, who are not European, not Western, and therefore not civilized. Since the context of "different" and "inferior" has become not just a function of race or gender, but of culture and ideology, it has become another instrument of belief and the self-righteous racism of American expansionism and "new imperialism." The assumed superiority of the West has become the new "White Man's Burden," to expand and to recreate the world in an American image. The rationalization of this expansion, albeit to "protect our freedoms and our way of life" or "to combat terrorism," is fueled by racist ideology, obscured in the darkness behind the façade of inalienable rights of the West to defend civilization against enemies in global culture wars.

At the turn of the 20th century, the "Terrible Turk" was the image that summarized the enemy of Europe, and the antagonism towards the hegemony of the Ottoman Empire, stretching from Europe to the Middle East, and across North Africa. Perpetuation of this imagery in American foreign policy exhibited how capitalism met with orientalist constructs in the white racial frame of the western mind (VanderLippe 1999). Orientalism is based on the conceptualization of the "Oriental" other—Eastern, Islamic societies as static, irrational, savage, fanatical and inferior to the peaceful, rational, scientific "Occidental" Europe and the West (Said 1979). This is an elastic construct, proving useful to describe whatever is considered the latest treat to Western economic expansion, political and cultural hegemony, and global domination for exploitation and absorption.

Post-Enlightenment Europe and later America used this iconography to define basic racist assumptions regarding their uncontestable right to impose political and economic dominance globally. When the Soviet Union existed as an opposing power, the orientalist vision of the 20th century shifted from the image of the "Terrible Turk" to that of the "Barbaric Russian Bear." In this context, orientalist thought then, as now, set the terms of exclusion. It racialized exclusion to define the terms of racial privilege and superiority. By focusing on ideology, orientalism recreated the superior race, even though there was no "race." It equated the hegemony of Western civilization with the "right ideological and cultural framework." It segued into war and annihilation and genocide, and continued to foster and aid the recreation of racial hatred of others with the collapse of the Soviet "other." Orientalism's global racist ideology reformed in the 1990s with Muslims and Islamic culture as the "inferior other." Seeing Muslims as opponents of Christian civilization is not new, going back to the Crusades, but the elasticity and reframing of this exclusion is evident in recent debates regarding Islam in the west, one raised by the Pope and the other by the President of the United States.

Against the background of the latest Iraq War, attacks in the name of Islam, racist attacks on Muslims in Europe and the US, and detention of Muslims without trial in secret prisons, Pope Benedict XVI gave a speech in September 2006 at Regensburg University in Germany. He quoted a 14th century Byzantine Emperor who said "show me just what Muhammad brought that was new, and there you will find things only evil and inhuman, such as his command to spread by the sword the faith he preached." In addition, the Pope discussed the concept of Jihad, which he defined as Islamic "holy war," and said "violence in the name of religion was contrary to God's nature and to reason." He also called for dialogue between cultures and religions (Fisher 2006b). While some Muslims found the Pope's speech "regrettable," it also caused a spark of angry protests against the Pope's "ill informed and bigoted" comments, and voices were raised to demand an apology (Fisher 2006a). Some argue that the Pope was ordering a new crusade, for Christian civilization to conquer terrible and savage Islam. When Benedict apologized, organizations and parliaments demanded a retraction and apology from the Pope and the Vatican (Lee 2006). Yet, when the Pope apologized, it came as a second insult, because in his apology he said "I'm deeply sorry for the reaction in some countries to a few passages of my address at the University of Regensburg, which were considered offensive to the sensibilities of Muslims" (Reuters 2006). In other words, he is sorry that Muslims are intolerant to the point of fanaticism. In the racialized world, Pope Benedict's apology came as an effort to show justification for his speech—he was not apologizing for being insulting, but rather saying that he was sorry that "Muslim" violence had proved his point. In stark contrast, Pope Francis advocated understanding between the religious communities and peaceful coexistence. Though orientalism and the white racial frame are hard for intellectuals to shift, Pope Francis, and those who talk about racial hatred and exclusion, themselves often become target of racist legitimization.

White racial frame lives on. Like Samuel Huntington, Bernard Lewis was looking for Armageddon in his *Wall Street Journal* article warning that August 22, 2006 was the 27th of the month of Rajab in the Islamic calendar, and is considered a holy day, when Muhammad was taken to heaven and returned. For Muslims, this day is a day of rejoicing and celebration. But for Lewis, Professor Emeritus at Princeton, "this might well be deemed an appropriate date for the apocalyptic ending of Israel and if necessary, of the world" (Lewis 2006). He cautions that "it is far from certain that [the President of Iran] Mr. Ahmadinejad plans any such cataclysmic events for August 22nd, but it would be wise to bear the possibility in mind." Lewis argues that Muslims, unlike others, seek self-destruction in order to reach heaven faster. For Lewis, Muslims in this mindset don't see the idea of "Mutually Assured Destruction" as a constraint but rather as "an inducement" (Lewis 2006). Lewis, like Pope Benedict, views Islam as the apocalyptic destroyer of civilization, and claims that reactions against orientalist, racist visions such as his actually prove the validity of his position. Lewis's assertions run parallel with many political figures, such as President George Bush. In response to the alleged plot to blow up British airliners, Bush claimed "this nation is at war with Islamic fascists who will use any means to destroy those of us who love freedom, to hurt our nation" (TurkishPress.com. 2006; Beck 2006). Bush argued that "the fight against terrorism is the ideological struggle of the 21st century" and he compared it to the 20th century's fight against fascism, Nazism and communism. Even though "Islamo-fascist" has for sometime been a buzzword for Bill O'Reilly, Rush Limbaugh and Sean Hannity on the talkshow circuit, when the President of the United States used it, it drew reactions world-wide. Considering that since 2001, Bush had a tendency to equate the "war on terrorism" with "crusade," this new rhetoric equates ideology with religion and reinforces the worldview of a war of civilizations. As Bush said "…we still aren't completely safe, because there are people that still plot and people who want to harm us for what we believe in" (CNN 2006). Now, two decades into the new century, "Islam" has become synonymous with "terror," making every believer a suspect, and every Muslim a terrorist sympathizer. The rampant Islamophobia of the 2016 presidential campaign was peppered by the discussion of a "Muslim ban," "Muslim terrorists" versus "friendly Muslims" and "terrorist states." One of the candidates promised to keep all Muslims out of the U.S. until "they are vetted strongly," while the other was known with her unwavering support of the PATRIOT ACT, and the so-called "counter-radicalization policy" which links Islamic devotion to terrorist involvement as an ongoing "War on Terror."

Exclusion in physical space is only matched by exclusion in the imagination, and radicalized exclusion has an internal logic leading to the annihilation of the excluded. Annihilation, in this sense, is not only designed to maintain the terms of racial inequality, both ideologically and physically, but is institutionalized with the vocabulary of self-protection. Even though the terms of exclusion are never complete, genocide is the definitive point in the exclusionary racial ideology, and such is the logic of the outcome of the exclusionary process, that it can conclude only in ultimate domination. War and genocide take place with compliant efficiency to serve the

global racist ideology with dizzying frequency. The 21st century opened up with genocide, in Darfur.

17.4 The Role of Willful Ignorance in Global Racism: War or Genocide?

On September 22, 2006, Kofi Annan, Secretary-General of the United Nations, addressed the 5520th meeting of the Security Council, to condemn the escalation of violence in Darfur, Sudan. Against the Darfur Peace Agreement of May 5, 2006, the Sudan Liberation Army and government forces had resumed fighting. Nearly 3,000,000 displaced people were in need of emergency international aid for food, shelter and medical treatment, and the fighting was making it difficult for humanitarian workers to reach them. Council members were united in their belief that the situation was unacceptable, and that Darfur was "at the brink of total collapse," touching what some have called "the Rwanda threshold" with killings and rapes this time even targeting international and humanitarian workers (UN 2006).

The Darfur conflict was escalated by two different groups: the Sudan Liberation Army, and the Justice & Equality Movement, fighting with Sudanese Army units and Janjaweed militia units. As a result of this bloodshed, approximately 2–3 million people have been displaced, and 70–100 thousand people have died. One of the major questions regarding Darfur has been whether or not the conflict should be termed "genocide," under the terms of the Genocide Convention. Some argued that after all, the fight is between two "armies" that are both killing civilians—so what is new? It is a civil war. Basically, government-backed Sudanese Muslim Arabs are exerting domination over Christian and Muslim Blacks, and Animists, farmers, herders and nomads.

The complexity of events in Darfur stems from layers of conflict. The first is between the government and the rebels who are angered by the political and economic marginalization of southern Sudan. The second is the conflict between the northern, Arab-dominated government, and Christian, nomadic peoples in the south, going back to decolonization of Sudan by the British in 1956. Since 1983 this conflict has directly or indirectly claimed 2,000,000 lives. The third level of conflict is a split within Darfur, between Black farmers and Arab "nomadic livestock herders" (Straus 2005). The fighting has been sporadic, but almost all of it centers around oil extracted from southern Sudan, and piped through a new 1000 mile pipeline to tankers on the Red Sea (Salopek 2003). For example, the Nubas are victims of this complex conflict. The Nuba Mountains, bordering Sudan's oil pipeline, are at the frontline of conflict. The Nuba speak Arabic, and about half are Muslim, half are Christian, although many still keep faith in animist customs. When the Nuba joined the Sudan Liberation Army, government forces pushed them up into the mountains, where they could no longer grow food. And when the government banned humanitarian airlifts, the Nuba starved, and many of them, especially children, have died (Lange 2003).

Two issues, related to one another, emerge from this complexity: whether or not Darfur represents a case of war or genocide; and how to calculate the massive numbers of victims. Both of these questions are based on debates regarding how long death on this scale has been occurring in Sudan; how to count nomadic peoples and villagers who have fallen victim to this conflict; how to calculate victims while some have died, but others have fled to neighboring countries, and still others have suffered and perished from related malnutrition, hunger, disease, and poor settlement conditions. The key to the debate on the first issue, which began around March 2004, is whether or not these events were internal skirmishes, thus not warranting international action. In July 2004, the US House of Representatives unanimously passed a resolution labeling the events "genocide" (Straus 2005). The resolution called on the Bush administration to act according to the Genocide Convention, therefore encouraging it to act even if the UN Security Council failed to act. Secretary of State

Colin Powell insisted that calling the Darfur Genocide "genocide" would not change US policy towards Sudan. But he did commission an in-depth study on whether or not the events in Darfur merited the term "genocide" on the international level. The US was not alone, as Canadian, British and EU officials, along with Kofi Annan, continued to call Darfur "a massive violation of human rights," not genocide (Straus 2005). Meanwhile Human Rights Watch called Darfur "ethnic cleansing" and argued that it symbolized "forced removal of an ethnic group," not annihilation. And because of the various crises, and the nearly 20 year duration of the conflict, Kofi Annan also appointed a UN commission to determine if genocide has occurred in Darfur. All these debates came to a halt when US Secretary of State, Colin Powell, agreed that genocide, not war was taking place in Darfur (Straus 2005; Smith 2005). This declaration brought a new conundrum: if and what kind of international intervention was justified to stop the violence? A peace accord was signed in May, 2005 between the government and opposition forces, but to what end? The African Union sent 7000 peacekeepers to monitor the refugee camps, but the very small size of the force and the vastness of the county hampered their effectiveness. Unfortunately, they also ran out of money and time in September 2006 (Andisheh 2006). This time we knew that genocide would continue in Darfur. In 2008, the UN stated that it might have under-estimated the death toll by 50%, and later, *Lancet* declared that 80% of the deaths were due to illness (Degomme and Gupa-Sapir 2010). The total number of the people who lost their lives to the conflict and are still dying from it are debatable and unknown.

17.5 The Challenge of Being Antiracist in the Face of the Violence of Global Racism

The synergy between capitalism and racism creates a process, a continuous chain of cross-cultural and cumulative actions and interactions, setting the terms of oppression globally. This synergy emanates violence. Accepting global racism as an absolute product of this synergy will reinforce the tendency to imagine global racism as a never-ending inevitability, forging the belief that either it is here to stay or it will erode of its own volition. The debate regarding the number of victims or whether or not Darfur fits in the definition of "genocide" is an example of how the technical rationality of technocratic ideology of liberal modernism reveals this synergy. In this context, how can anti-racist theory and praxis challenge global racism, which is integrated into everyday life globally in the 21st century? Global racism permeates economic, political, social and cultural production, distribution and consumption; racial violence that once built colonial empires is now essential to the technocratic ideology of liberal modernism of the capitalist state. How can one challenge and destroy its white racial frame? How can we do more than just watch genocidal acts, and be silent? The response is constant struggle, and constant struggle is the key to challenging racism in the 21st century.

The necessity of antiracist praxis demands that global racism cannot be understood without understanding the struggle against its oppression and violence. Opposing and resisting racism globally requires exposing and confronting the complex synergy of global racism and capitalism. Since actions and ideologies tie the universal to the particular in the context of global racism, praxis is integral to the particularities of the everyday struggle against racism to sustain the global antiracist struggle at the universal level. Such struggle requires understanding of global racism as an axiom in the paradigm of oppression, as antiracism must be conceptualized as a domain assumption in the confrontation of the dominant paradigm that accommodates and perpetuates systems of oppression. Struggle is also a continuum, with a cumulative and humanizing synergy of its own.

In April 1942, Du Bois came to Vassar College, and subsequently went to Yale University to give school-wide talks and debate with students. In these two speeches, directed to the academy, he explored the global color line, and internal and external imperialist racial oppression in "The Future of Africa in America," and "The Future of Europe in Africa" (Aptheker 1985: 173–184, 184–198). In the midst of the Second World War, Du Bois pointed out that "with all our tumult and shouting rage against Hitler, we are perfectly aware that his race philosophy and methods are but extreme development and application of our own save that he is drawing his race lines in somewhat different places". He argued that oppression is linked globally. Thus, tying global racism to the struggle against it requires conceptualizing antiracism as a reflexive understanding of global racism in order to produce and reproduce thought, knowledge and action, uniting all levels and forms of struggle against systems of domination and oppression; linking struggle against racism to confrontation with class differentiation, sexism, and homophobia. A further challenge comes with integrating the unified thought and action of the struggles against oppression at the universal level into the experience of everyday life in its particularities. For example, as Du Bois pointed out "democracy cannot have a rebirth in the world unless it firmly establishes itself in America" (1985: 183). To explore global racism and its centrality to oppression, Du Bois pointed out the need to study the dynamics of its perpetuation, but how to connect the everyday and the global to reframe antiracist thought and action?

Looking at the context in which Du Bois gave these speeches provides a window to this connection. On February 19, 1942, President Franklin Roosevelt ordered Japanese Americans, and immigrants of Japanese descent to be exiled to concentration camps, then called "relocation centers." On April 9th, just a few days before Du Bois's visit to Vassar College, US troops surrendered to the Japanese on the Bataan Peninsula in the Philippines. When Du Bois came to Vassar, he not only gave a campus speech, but also an interview to the student newspaper, *Vassar Miscellany News*, known as "the Misc." In this interview, Du Bois pointed out that Vassar College, then known as a girls' school, was very fortunate to have Black students, but he challenged Vassar College to admit 100 Black students, which would be approximately 10% of its student body.

While Du Bois was on the campus, the college was celebrating "Founder's Day," a day of community celebration, sports, and leisure activities. According to the newspaper, one of the activities was to heave darts at a caricature of a presumed Japanese head. The organizing committee thought that this activity, called "Slap a Jap," would encourage purchase of War Savings Stamps by students. The following day, it is interesting to note, the editorial board of the college paper condemned this activity, even though students who sponsored it had said this kind of advertising was taking place all over the country and "the Japs probably did worse things." Editors responded with a statement that acknowledged Du Bois's speech, and his position regarding American democracy. They argued that "the vast majority of people follow their leader in their thinking, and the leader in this case is race prejudice and hatred.... Perhaps it is impossible really to practice democracy, or isn't this a test case?" (Kent and Heilner 1942: 2). The universality of the principles of equality and particularity of hate and destruction provide an understanding into the white racial frame, and the dynamics of perpetuation of racist connections. Not only are bigotry, discrimination and violence tied, but also anti-racist thought and action are cumulative and connected. When Vassar students recently joined in a reading of Du Bois's speech on the campus, taking turns to read a paragraph at a time, they were confronted with how "fresh" it is after 60 years, and how poignant it is that every time we read it out loud, there is violence in the world to which the speech still applies.

The purpose of reading an antiracist speech out loud is not to memorialize resistance to racism, but to remind us of the cumulative effect of praxis. The only reason to understand global racism is to devise antiracist strategies to develop an understanding of antiracist theory and praxis that is not reactionary, but is progressive, proactive, responsive and reflective. As Du Bois

argued "not only [has] this got to be overthrown, but the means of its overthrowing is a firm conviction on the part of white America that a change in the present organization of his world is best for the world. And that only by recognition and conviction, and action following such conviction, can the world come to a place where it recognizes human beings as essentially equal and works toward the actual equality which may be accomplished" (Aptheker 1985: 184).

Global racism, as a theoretical construct, focuses on the interconnectedness of racist thought and action globally, yielding a broader understanding. White racial frame provides for the global racist paradigm. But, global racism also facilitates a theoretical base to reconceptualize that racism and antiracism connect temporally, and spatially on a global level. As capitalism and global racism change, antiracist praxis must change. Since capitalism fragments, antiracist praxis must be reconceptualized to insist on unity of struggle. The complexity of antiracist praxis stems from the challenge of establishing coalitions with other thought and action against systems of oppression. The totality of oppression necessitates unified challenge. The further confrontation comes from bridging spatial and temporal gaps in our conceptualization of antiracist struggle to reinforce the understanding that local struggles are about global resistance, and past struggles illuminate future praxis. In this context, understanding racism in Iraq becomes a way to confront racism in America. An antiracist framework demands that this time we act against everyday racism in school and in the office, and against genocide in Darfur, Rwanda and Chechnya, and all forms of cumulative mass destruction globally. But first we need to know, and know how racism is connected globally, from Iraq to New Orleans to Darfur to Kosovo to Chechnya. Saturation of global racism on the everyday and global level requires antiracist praxis to be integrated into everyday life to confront issues of the everyday and global consistently. Antiracist praxis should be conceptualized, actualized, and integrated into everyday life sometimes even without the benefit of "beloved communities," organization, or resources. What gives antiracist praxis coherency is the goal of eradicating racism locally and globally, and understanding that the only way to eradicate racism locally is to fight to eradicate racism globally (Batur-VanderLippe 1999). When thousands are buried in mass graves in Iraq or Darfur, the silence that frames the foreign policy of the United States also serves to maintain domestic policies that allow inadequate inner city schools for people of color, discrimination and harassment in the work place, and segregated neighborhoods. The white racial frame it contains also frames New Orleans. If shouts are not heard against genocide in Bosnia, Rwanda, Darfur, there will be no powerful opposition to the Prison-Industrial Complex for people of color, the AIDS epidemic, environmental racism, or absence of housing and health care policies.

On April 4, 1967, Martin Luther King delivered a speech at a meeting of Concerned Clergy and Laity at Riverside Church in New York City to argue that "a time comes when silence is betrayal" in regards to Vietnam. He called for speaking out against the war and violence "as the enemy of poor" worldwide: "Some of us who have already begun to break the silence of the night have found that the calling to speak is often a vocation of agony, but we must speak. We must speak with all the humility that is appropriate to our limited vision, but we must speak." He was speaking against the global racism which limits the integrity, cripples communities, and destroys nations, and how it connects through violence. "We were taking the black young men who had been crippled by our society and sending them eight thousand miles away to guarantee liberties in Southeast Asia which they had not found in Georgia or Harlem. So we have been repeatedly faced with the cruel irony of watching Negro and white boys on TV screens as they kill and die together for a nation that has been unable to seat them together in the same schools. So we watch them in brutal solidarity burning the huts of a poor village, but we realize that they would never live on the same block in Detroit." King, at that time, called for action by surpassing indecision: "Now let us rededicate

ourselves to the long and bitter—but beautiful— struggle for a new world…. The choice is ours, and though we might prefer it otherwise we must choose in this crucial moment of human history" (King 1967).

Since 2013, *#Black Lives Matter* brought antiracist activism to the forefront in the United States, protesting brutal killings of black people at the hands of law enforcement, racial profiling, racial targeting, police brutality in Black communities and racial inequality, discrimination and injustice. Black Lives Matter! is no less than wanting the total transformation of American Society. It means to end grotesque levels of overt and covert racism, and it means re-building America on the basis of antiracism. It means that the fight that began with anti-slavery has not ended, but just started to transfer the economics, politics and culture of oppression. And Black Lives Matter! In the future, this movement will teach generations of anti-racist activists how to participate in the dynamics of discourse on antiracism and how to voice dissent, and the dimensions of the role of dissent in society. #Black Lives Matter will provide a counter-frame for white racial frame and it promises to provide a framework for choice for action, then and now, to seize this force to challenge all instrumentalities of domination, violence, destruction, war and genocide. But we need to remember: we are that force, and the struggle continues.

References

Andisheh, N. (2006). Don't panic! *Weekly Planet, 18*(40), 16.

Ansell, A. (1997). *New right, new racism: Race and reaction in the United States and Great Britain*. New York: New York University Press.

APM News Agency. (2005). September 5, 2005.

Aptheker, H. (1985). *Against racism: Unpublished essays, papers, addresses, 1887–1961, by W. E. B. Du Bois*. Amherst: University of Massachusetts Press.

Baker, M. (1981). *New racism*. London: Junction Books.

Balibar, E. (1994). *Masses, classes, ideas: Studies on politics and philosophy before and after Marx*. New York: Routledge.

Balibar, E., & Wallerstein, I. (1991). *Race, nation, class: Ambiguous identities*. London: Verso.

Batur, P. (2006). Just a link in the chain: Global racism and the concept of "blackness" in Russia. In S. L. Myers & B. P. Corrie (Eds.), *Racial and ethnic economic inequality: An international perspective* (pp. 5–14). New York: Peter Lang.

Batur-VanderLippe, P. (1996). Colonialism and post-colonialism: Global expansion of racism. In J. Feagin & C. Feagin (Eds.), *Racial and ethnic relations* (5th ed.). New York: Prentice-Hall.

Batur-VanderLippe, P. (1999). Centering on global racism and antiracism: From everyday life to global complexity. *Sociological Spectrum, 19*, 467–484.

Batur-VanderLippe, P., & Feagin, J. (1999). Racial and ethnic inequality and struggle from colonial era to the present: Drawing the global color line. In P. Batur-Vander & J. Feagin (Eds.), *The global color line: Racial and ethnic inequality and struggle from a global perspective*. Conn.: JAI Press.

Beck, A. (2006). US muslims bristle at bush term 'Islamic fascists'. *Reuters*. August 10, 2006. http://today.reuters.com/news/articlenews.aspx?type=domesticNews&storyID=2006-08-10. September 30, 2006.

Buchanan, P. (2002). *A republic, not an empire: Reclaiming America's destiny*. New York: Regnery Books.

CBS News. (2005). Race an issue in Katrina response. September 3, 2005. http://www.cbsnews.com/stories/2005/09/03/katrina/printable814623.shtml. September 28, 2006.

CNN. (2005). *CNN Reports: Katrina state of emergency*. Kansas City: Andrews McMeel Publishing.

CNN.com. (2006). Bush: U.S. at war with 'Islamic fascists. http://cnn.worldnews.printthis.clickability.com/pt/cpt?action=cpt&title=CNN.com+-+Bush. September 30, 2006.

Conrad, J. (1989). *Heart of darkness*. London: Penguin Books.

Degomme, O., & Gupa-Sapir, D. (2010). Patterns of mortality rates in Darfur conflict. *Lancet, 375*(9711), 294–300.

Du Bois, W. E. B. (1942). *Against racism* by Herbert Aptheker (Eds.). Cambridge: University of Massachusetts Press.

Evans, D. (2006). High water everywhere: Blues and gospel commentary on the 1927 Mississippi river flood. In Robert Springer (Ed.), *Nobody knows where the blues come from: Lyrics and history* (pp. 3–75). Jackson: University Press of Mississippi.

Fanon, F. (1963). *The wretched of the earth*. New York: Grove Press.

Feagin, J. R. (2006). *Systemic racism: A theory of oppression*. New York: Routledge.

Fisher, I. (2006a). Muslim leaders assail pope's speech on Islam. *New York Times*. September 14, 2006. http://www.nytimes.com/2006/09/14/world/europe/15papalcnd.html?pagewanted=print. September 18, 2006.

Fisher, I. (2006b). Pope assails secularism, adding note on jihad. *New York Times*. September 13, 2006. http://www.nytimes.com/2006/09/13/world/europe/13pope.html. September 18, 2006.

Gomez, G. M. (2000). Perspective, power, and priorities: New Orleans and the Mississippi river flood of 1927. In E. Craig (Ed.), *Transforming New Orleans and its environs* (pp. 109–120). Pittsburgh: University of Pittsburgh Press.

Hedges, S. J. (2005). Navy ship nearby underused. *Chicago Tribune*. September 4, 2005.

Hunter, J. D. (1992). *Culture wars: Struggle to define America*. New York: Basic Books.

Huntington, S. P. (1993). The clash of civilizations? *Foreign Affairs, 72*, 22–49.

Jordan, L. J. (2006). 28 government agencies reported levee breech. *Boston Globe* (AP). February 9, 2006.

Kent, J., & Heilner, M. (1942). Letter to the editor. *Vassar Miscellany News*. April 26, 1942, p. 2.

King, M. L. (1967). *Speech against the war*. New York, Riverside Church. http://www.informationclearinghouse.info/article2564.htm.

Lange, K. E. (2003). The Nuba: Still standing. *National Geographic*. February 2, 2003.

Lee, V. (2006). Local outrage over Pope's muslim remarks: Many surprised and angry. *ABC News*. September 15, 2006. http://abclocal.go.com/kgo/story?section=local&id=4567154&ft=print. September 18, 2006.

Lewis, B. (2006). August 22. *Wall Street Journal*, August 8, 2006, p. A10. http://online.wsj.com/article/SB115500154638829470-search.html?KEYWORDS=bernard+lewis&COLLECTION=wsjie/6month. September 22, 2006.

Lichtman, R. (1995). Gulf war: Participation in modernity. In Antonio Callari et al. (Eds.), *Marxism in postmodern age: Confronting the new world order*. New York: The Guilford Press.

Marcuse, H. (1998). *Technology, war and fascism*. New York: Routledge.

Marshall, E. (1988). Chemical genocide in Iraq? *Science, 241*, 1752.

McLaren, D., & Wilmore, I. (2003). The environmental damage of war in Iraq. *Guardian*. January 18, 2003.

Memmi, A. (1965). *The colonizer and the colonized*. Boston: Beacon Press.

Reuters. (2006). Pope sorry about muslim reaction, urges dialogue. *New York Times*, September 17, 2006. http://www.nytimes.com/2006/09/17/world/europe/17pope.ready.html. September 18, 2006.

Russell, G. (2005). Forecaster fear levees won't hold Katrina. *Times-Pucayne*, August 28, 2005, p. 1.

Said, E. (1979). *Orientalism*. New York: Vintage.

Salopek, P. (2003). Shattered sudan. *National Geographic*. February 2, 2003.

Smith, C. E., & Pipa, T. (2005). The politics of genocide: U.S. rhetoric vs. inaction in Darfur, 7 April–26 September 2004. *Kennedy School Review, 6*, 131–141.

Straus, S. (2005). Darfur and the genocide debate. *Foreign Affairs, 84*(1), 123–133.

Thomas, E. (2005). How bush blew it. *Newsweek*, September 19, 2005.

Totten, et al. (1997). *A century of genocide*. New York: Routledge.

UN Security Council. (2006). SC8823/5520. September 11, 2006.

TurkishPress.com. (2006). *Bush zeroes in on 'Islamic fascism'*. September 30, 2006. http://www. turkishpress.com/nw.asp?s=u&i=060902164310. o1bdm7qi&t=Bush+zeroes+i. September 30, 2006.

VanderLippe, J. (1999). Racism and the making of American foreign policy: The 'Terrible Turk' as icon and metaphor. In P. Batur-VanderLippe & J. Feagin (Eds.), *The global color line: Racial and ethnic inequality and struggle from a global perspective* (pp. 47–63). Stamford, CT: JAI Press.

Winant, H. (1994). *Racial conditions*. Minneapolis: University of Minneapolis Press.

Part V

Recent Debates: Our Voices will be Heard!

"What Hides in Comparison"

18

Carlos Alamo-Pastrana

Contents

On Wednesday, September 20, 2018, Maria—a category four hurricane—made landfall on Puerto Rico. The strongest hurricane to hit the island since 1932, Maria caused widespread devastation including catastrophic damage to Puerto Rico's weakened power grid and water supply.[1] More than a century of colonial policies and financial mismanagement by local elites were responsible for Puerto Rico's more than $72 billion dollar debt that made it nearly impossible for the island to secure funding to address its deteriorating infrastructure. One year earlier, the United States Congress passed the Management and Economic Stability Act of 2016 to address the island's increasingly bleak financial outlook. Without consulting Puerto Rican voters, President Barack Obama appointed the Financial Oversight and Management Board as a part of this legislation, to oversee the development and implementation of various austerity measures supposedly meant to bring the island back from the financial precipice. It is an understatement to say that the Puerto Rico was already on the proverbial ropes before hurricane Maria struck.

And as if the fiscal and humanitarian crisis could not get any worst, President Donald Trump and the rest of the federal government moved at a painstakingly irresponsible pace. Activists, celebrities, and journalists pounced on the forty-fifth president. One particular discursive

---

[1] Puerto Rico barely avoided another major hurricane two weeks earlier when Hurricane Irma passed just north of the big island. Despite not making direct landfall, Hurricane Irma still severely weakened the island's infrastructure. As of this writing, the majority of residents on the island remain without potable running water and electricity more than one month after Hurricane Maria.

Parts of this article also appear in Alamo-Pastrana (2016).

C. Alamo-Pastrana (✉)
Department of Sociology, Vassar College,
Poughkeepsie, NY, USA
e-mail: caalamo@vassar.edu

© Springer International Publishing AG, part of Springer Nature 2018
P. Batur and J. R. Feagin (eds.), *Handbook of the Sociology of Racial and Ethnic Relations*,
Handbooks of Sociology and Social Research, https://doi.org/10.1007/978-3-319-76757-4_18

method ran rampant across all these criticisms in the hours and days following hurricane Maria. Specifically, the criticisms lobbied at the president and his administration from across the political spectrum engaged in comparative interpretive strategies to make sense of the disaster in Puerto Rico. These comparative musings focused on two major topics: the ways in which hurricane Maria and its response was or was not like hurricane Katrina–the hurricane that twelve year earlier destroyed New Orleans and other parts of the Gulf region. Rolling Stone's Tim Dickinson for example noted that "Trump's callous response to [Puerto Rico's] calamity has made Bush's infamous Katrina response—sharing a birthday cake with Sen. John McCain as New Orleans drowned in 2005—seem statesmanlike by comparison."[2] At his first press conference in Puerto Rico Trump himself could not help but rate his performance relative to the disaster in Katrina years earlier. Looking to sanction the irresponsibly slow response of his administration, Trump pivoted: "[I]f you look at a *real catastrophe* like Katrina, and you look at the tremendous—hundred and hundred and hundreds of people that died. And you look at what happened here with really a storm that was totally overpowering. Nobody's ever seen anything like this. And what is your death count at this point, 17?"[3] Trump's comparative rationale used to understand catastrophes spiraled to the grotesque.

While Trump pontificated about "real catastrophes" many still fumed about his administration's negligence. Many others attributed this abandonment to Trump's obsession with the protests against police brutality occurring in the National Football League (NFL). Even members from Trump's own party took part in these comparative critiques of Trump. Republican strategist Steve Schmidt demanded in a tweet that Trump move away from "all the hubbub about N. F.L. football players." Schmidt suggested that Trump should instead "focus on Puerto Rico, focus on priorities."[4] But the majority of this

comparative wrath against the administration's inaction came from political moderates and democrats. Tracking Trump's tweets about the NFL relative to his tweets about Puerto Rico, The Washington Post's Philip Blum concluded: "Trump tweets more about the NFL than Puerto Rico because he is more interested in talking about the NFL than talking about Puerto Rico." Puerto Rican pop star Marc Anthony fumed at Trump: "Mr. President shut the fuck up about the NFL. Do something about our people in need in #PuertoRico. We are American citizens too."[5] Representative José Serrano, the highest-ranking Puerto Rican in Congress, similarly demanded: "The 3.4 million American citizens residing on the island—many of whom live in poverty—deserve more attention than the NFL."[6]

Anthony and Serrano are not wrong nor or they alone in their critique of the different ways Puerto Ricans experience colonial paternalism and the ways in which they are socially abandoned by the U.S. empire. In fact, Anthony and Serrano's assertions are rooted in the deeper colonial history of the island whereby proponents and opponents of empire, statehood, and independence have forcibly pressed their political positions through the use of comparative logics. This is true of Puerto Rican nationalists and abolitionists fighting against Spanish imperialism in the 19th century as it is of celebrities and politicians in Puerto Rico today.[7] And it is equally true of white nativists in the United States at the turn of the 20th century who opposed the annexation of Puerto Rico through the use of comparative racial logics as it is of the

---

[2]Dickinson (2017).

[3]Quoted in Blake (2017).

[4]Tracy (2017).

[5]Anthony, Marc. Available at: https://twitter.com/marcanthony/status/912428240387678208?lang=en. For more examples see: Oh (2017).

[6]Illis and Rafael (2017).

[7]For more on the relationship between abolitionism and independence in 19th century Puerto Rico see for example: de Hostos, Eugenio Maria de. [1954 (1873)] and; Segundo Ruiz Belvis, José Julián Acosta and Francisco Mariano Quiñones. 1969 (1867). Proyecto para la Abolicíon de la Esclavitud. San Juan: Instituto de Cultura Puertorriqueña.

emergence of the "alt right" that culminated with Trump's election in 2016.[8]

But the statements made by Anthony and the others are also emblematic of the ways in which comparison functions as both a method and as a politic. Put differently, comparative method exhaustively saturates the ways in which we think about and study empire and colonialism. This chapter considers the continued reliance on comparative method and the ways in which some of its basic premises are naturalized as everyday epistemology. We might assume disciplinary uses of comparison are devoid of subjective decisions and that they can work around historical relations of power. However, this chapter illustrates how comparative method takes these relations of power for granted in its use of variables that are not value free. Instead, these comparative ideas and rationale are rooted in deeper histories of exclusion that help shape varying political projects ensnared in comparative methods. Comparative method, nonetheless, is easily accepted as a method given its accessibility and adaptability to varying audiences.

This chapter begins with an analysis of the ways in which comparative method and analysis conceal particular knowledge formations especially with respect to race, gender, ability, and sexuality even as it presents itself as a rational, neutral, and a uniquely revelatory research tool. Such an approach camouflages the ways in which comparative instantiations have always been a part of U.S. liberalism and the construction of white supremacy. More specifically, the unrelenting use of comparison as a methodological and ideological tool across the political spectrum both naturalizes *and* dulls it analytic usefulness.

Focusing on political cartoons used in the United States and Puerto Rico throughout the twentieth century, the latter half of the article demonstrates that these methodological limits are not confined to conservative knowledge projects but are part of larger racial regimes that are complimented and naturalized by minority nationalisms that reinscribe hegemonic exclusions in an effort to gain legitimacy from the state. Taken together, this chapter demonstrates the ways in which comparison is deployed as a methodological tool that scaffolds both (white) (neo)colonialist projects as well as presumed revolutionary nationalisms.

The chapter closes with a consideration of new interventions that attempt to grapple with the history of comparative method. Admittedly the desire to outline new methodological interventions that attempt to resist the lure of comparative logics is in and of itself saturated and haunted by comparative logics. American Studies scholar Lisa Cacho teaches us that part of the problem with ascribing value to people and or ideas is that it necessarily requires an implicit or explicit devaluation of another subject or idea. The epistemic legacy of comparison has helped secure its own hegemonic standing as a defining feature of our analytic landscape that is all encompassing and difficult to break from. More simply, comparison only begets more comparison. Nonetheless, Cacho contends that "examining how 'value' and its normative criteria are naturalized and universalized enables us to uncover and unsettle the heteropatriarchal, legal, and neoliberal investments that dominant and oppositional discourses share in rendering the value of nonnormativity illegible".[9] As such, the final section of this chapter briefly explores some of the emergent scholarly and methodological approaches such as *dislocations* and *imbrication* that move away from the limited and obscuring tendencies of comparative method.[10] Dislocation and imbrication offer new avenues for disentangling and moving beyond comparisons that support conservative and reactionary knowledge projects.

---

[8]On the annexation of Puerto Rico see Centro Journal: "1898–1998." Vol. X, No. 1 & 2; Fall 1998.

[9]Cacho (2012, pp. 149).

[10]See for example: Alamo-Pastrana (2016), Lowe (2015), Seigel (2009) and Ferguson (2001).

18.1 Hegemonic Comparative Method and White Supremacy

Comparative method has a deep and extensive tradition within the social sciences. Comparative method typically locates its origins within some of the canonical figures in sociology including Karl Marx, Friedrich Engels, and especially Max Weber.[11] Though typically excluded from the sociological canon, W.E.B. Dubois's early work especially the *The Souls of Black Folk* (1903) is also worth considering as a classic example of the comparative study of race. Du Bois's historical and deeply personal text powerfully documents the social and psychologically damaging terror produced by the effects of racism in the United States.[12] Sociologist Mathew Lange defines comparative method as the:

> diverse methods used in the social sciences that offer insight through cross-case comparison. For this, they compare the characteristics of different cases and highlight similarities and differences between them. Comparative methods are usually used to explore causes that are common among a set of cases. They are commonly used in all social scientific disciplines[13]

Comparative method traditionally pursues an analysis that seeks to highlight causal factors that explain macro and micro sociological phenomena across and *through* multiple cases.

Max Weber's "ideal type" is among the central theoretical and methodological concepts within comparative analysis. According to Weber, an ideal type is "the one-sided *accentuation* of one or more points of view" into "*concrete individual* phenomena which are arranged according to those one-sidedly emphasized viewpoints into a unified *analytical* construct."[14] As analytic constructions in their most extreme form, ideal types are comparative reference points used to generate knowledge about differences and similarities between seemingly distinct social formations.

The universalist and essentialist tendencies implicit within ideal types as unified analytic constructs, however, make them susceptible to exclusionary epistemological configurations. Even more, comparative method often deals with the external deviations that reside outside traditional formations by simply integrating the excluded a new ideal type into the original analysis. This reductionist tendency, however, does not question the foundational validity of the initial categories. As sociologist Gurminder Bhambra accurately notes, "new (comparative) conceptualizations are placed alongside existing ones in a multiplication—rather than reconstruction—of theoretical constructs and presented as if they have no implications for previous formulations."[15] The creation of new ideal types alongside older categories of analysis represents a broader pluralist impulse that presupposes the fulfillment of the promise of liberalism and perfection of the nation-state through the accumulation and incorporation of difference. Universal ideal types presuppose the inclusion of new ideal types that naturalizes them and renders them difficult to challenge. This effort conceals the ways in which ideal types in and of themselves are the products of uneven power and social relationships.

For example, Bhambra notes that Weber conceptualized Germany, his reference point for much of his comparative and theoretical work, in ethnic terms and specifically in relation to and against Polish people. Even more, Weber conveniently downplays Germany's place as an imperial power and its role in his own formulations of the nation-state. The nation-state, according to Weber, is shaped by (forced) cultural homogeneity and the people's "shared political destinies and struggles" including

---

[11]Though not sociologists, the work of economist and philosopher Adam Smith (The Wealth of Nations, 1776) and political scientist Alexis de Toqueville (Democracy in America, 1835) are especially pertinent here.

[12]Morris's recent book on the life of Du Bois (Morris 2015) is worth a special mention here. In addition to demonstrating Du Bois's foundational contributions to the field of sociology, Morris's groundbreaking study also traces the personal and reciprocal intellectual confluences between Du Bois and fellow comparative sociologist Max Weber.

[13]Lange (2013, pp. 19).

[14]Weber (1949).

[15]Bhambra (2016).

imperialism and colonial expansion. "The failure to address the history of the German state directly and to theorize imperialism explicitly as an aspect of what is otherwise presented as the nation-state," concludes Bhambra, "has formatively shaped contemporary comparative historical sociology."[16]

The implicit value-free narrative of methodological improvement through inclusion within comparative analysis cannot be separated from the Eurocentric desire within sociology as a field to secure its standing through the use of scientific method as an objective value-free field of study. Understood this way, the deviations and other social formations outside the central and unquestioned categories of analysis such as the nation-state of comparative method are *disciplined* as sociological typologies. This Eurocentric academic impulse is also linked to the desire to discipline colonial, racial, and non-normative subjects in and of themselves so as to configure the nation-state in homogenous terms. The dissimilarities observed by ideal types, confirms Ethnic Studies scholar Lisa Lowe, are deviations that "institutionaliz[e] difference as a modern apparatus for apprehending and disciplining otherness."[17] These deviations require discipline because they constitute social formations that threaten hegemonic racial, gender, class, etc. orders.[18]

However, thinking of comparative method as simply the institutionalization of difference that is limited to methodological categories organized for sociological research does not fully capture why the method is so troubling. A significant part of its risk is attributable to how easy it is to replicate as *public* method and logic in order to produce broad generalizations about a plethora of social phenomena. The capacity to replicate comparative method as a *form* of analysis makes the method easily adaptable as a both a rhetorical and argumentative tool beyond the confines of sociology as a discipline. It is ironic that even as comparative logic literally produces social

difference with uneven outcomes for different groups, it remains among the most accessible types of sociological methods that allows people of diverse educational backgrounds to use various types information and evidence to informally organize and contrast data to produce popular knowledge.

In the case of Puerto Rico, comparative deviations created by ideal types have been used in varying ways to rationalize imperialist imperatives. As a colony of Spain beginning in 1493 and then invaded by the United States in 1898 during the Spanish-American War, Puerto Rican history is shaped exclusively within a backdrop of colonialism and imperialist expansion. Comparative logics shaped the extensive history of imperialist endeavors on the island and conditioned the ways in which varying groups on the island have responded. In the case of the United States, American officials have historically approached Puerto Rican racial difference as a non-normative social formation in need of colonial discipline. Using white patriarchal normativity as their comparative ideal type, American academics and government officials who opposed <u>and</u> favored American colonial expansion constructed Puerto Rico's colonial subjects as deviant, non-normative, and Black (yet another ideal type).[19]

Even before the United States invaded the island in 1898 during the Spanish-American War, popular depictions characterized Puerto Rico as a social problem inhabited by Black children where American institutions and the spirit of democracy could not flourish.[20] For example, Victor Gilliam's 1899 popular political cartoon illustrates the racialized and infantile depictions of the conquered colonial subjects of the Spanish American War of 1898 including Puerto Rico, Hawaii, the Philippines, Samoa, and

---

[16]*Ibid*, 341–343.

[17]Lowe no. 3 (2005).

[18]Hong and Ferguson (2011).

[19]See for example Guerra (1998), Findlay (1999), and Briggs (2002).

[20]Alamo, Carlos. Seams of Empire, 6–7. Political cartoons appearing before and after the Spanish American War are just one example of this. For a collection of some examples of these political cartoons see Centro Journal, 1998.

Cuba (Fig. 18.1). Titled after Rudyard Kipling's poem, "The White Man's Burden" the political cartoon depicts Uncle Sam struggling to carry his colonial subjects in a doko-like basket towards civilization. The symbolic boulders depict the impediments to civilization including superstition, vice, and ignorance.

The comparative strand here positions civilization (understood as White, Christian, and rational) against the barbarism (understood as non-White, culturally backwards, and non-Christian) associated with the colonies. These negative characteristics and traits, however, were also configured onto the racialized bodies of colonized populations in diverging ways. More specifically, they have been compared both against White patriarchal heteronormativity as well as against the various internal and external colonial racial groups found within the U.S. racial regime.[21] Taking its use of comparative logics further, the comic presents an image of competing imperialisms. Gilliam positions Uncle Sam behind and against his British equivalent, John Bull. Burdened by his own basket, John Bull is further along than Uncle Sam, whose subjects proximity to Blackness has left them near the bottom stuck in their own 'barbabrism' and 'oppression.' John Bull's colonial subjects, meanwhile, appear closer to the precipice of civilization. But the political cartoon also hints at the elusive promise of civilization (i.e. whiteness) given the repeated ways in which anti-normative behaviors such as vice and ignorance are repeated in the cartoon.

Proponents of imperialist wars were not alone in their use of such comparative logics. Under the guise of normative morality and constitutionality, opponents of the war grounded their opposition in Eurocentric positions that illustrated the cultural and racial deviations of colonial subjects that the United States would have to contend with. Meant as a critique of American expansionism, former vice-president of the Anti-Imperialist League and Stanford Chancellor David Starr Jordan simultaneously weighed the institutional and racial consequences that would come with the new territories. "Our question is not what we shall do with Cuba, Porto Rico and the Philippines," but rather, queried Jordan, "it is what these prizes will do to us."[22]

Diverging from those favoring expansion and contrary to the way in which traditional internal others had also been constituted as social problems in the U.S. racial regime, Jordan cautioned against the financial and social burdens that Puerto Rico's new colonial subjects brought to the nation.

> Wherever we have inferior and dependent races within our borders to-day, we have a political problem—'the Negro problem,' 'the Chinese problem,' 'the Indian problem.' These problems we slowly solve. Industrial training and industrial pride make a man of the Negro. Industrial interests may even make a man of the Chinaman, and the Indian disappears as our civilization touches him. But in the tropics such problems are perennial and insoluble ...[23]

The comparative interpretation of non-normative, racial, and colonial formations as social problems were a constitutive strategy that helped to define and secure white supremacy in 19th century America. The historical exclusions promoted by white supremacy prove that the United States has never been an egalitarian nation-state. According to sociologist Moon Kie Jung, the United States is more accurately an "empire-state" organized through comparative and legally sanctioned differentiations related to the elusive acquisitions of property, whiteness, and citizenship.[24]

Understood in this way, comparative method's *production* and disciplining of difference is not incompatible with the project of modern liberalism and promise of universal rights. Rather, ideal types organized as categories about race, gender, nation-states, sexuality, and religion were constitutive elements of liberalism. The creation of these categories helped to delineate

---

[21]See also Sebring (2015).

[22]Jordan, David Starr. Imperial Democracy. New York: Garland, 1972; pp. 5.

[23]Ibid, 32.

[24]Jung (2011), edited by Moon Kie-Jung, João Costa Vargas, and Eduardo Bonilla Silva. Stanford: Stanford University Press. pp. 2–3; 9.

Fig. 18.1 "The White Man's Burden (Apologies to Rudyard Kipling)" by Victor Gilliam, *Judge Magazine*, April 1, 1899

the boundaries and limits of white patriarchal normativity but also identified the terms under which empire and colonial expansion were necessary.[25]

18.2 Comparison and Minority Nationalisms

The capacity of comparative method to generate knowledge that facilitates the institutionalization of difference is grounds enough to consider its banishment as a methodological intervention.[26] But it is equally a constituent feature counter-hegemonic knowledge formation as well. Emergent scholarship from multidisciplinary fields including Women's Studies, Queer Studies, and American Studies have articulated the seductive and inescapable ways in which comparative logics are

embedded even within seemingly progressive movements. The majority of these critiques of comparative method have emerged from what can be loosely identified as the subfields of Queer of Color Critique and Women of Color Feminisms.[27]

In his study of the intimate relationship between canonical sociology and African American literature, sociologist and American Studies scholar Roderick Ferguson, for example, demonstrates the ways in which the (heteropatriarchal) nation state *and* revolutionary nationalisms sought to discipline and incorporate Black and queer non-normative subjects within the larger project of liberal capitalism that instantiates normativity and social value. Ferguson leans heavily on Marx's work in *The German Ideology* and *Economic and Philosophic Manuscripts*. In the latter Marx equates the ways in which industrial labor is alienated as comparatively similar to the ways in which a prostitute sells her own body and labor. Popular understandings of prostitution such as unrestrained

[25]Lisa Lowe, The Intimacies of Four Continents, pp. 7–14.

[26]For more on the banishment of comparative method see Micol Seigel's, Uneven Encounters.

[27]Hong and Ferguson, Strange Affinities.

sexual desire, sexual pathology, etc., made by radicals, according to Ferguson, are seen as indicative of capitalism's moral and social failings and man's feminization under capital. "Rather than embodying heteropatriarchal ideal," contends Ferguson, "the prostitute was a figure of nonheteronormativity, excluded from the presumed security of heteropatriarchal boundaries."[28] Accordingly, heteropatriarchy engrained itself as a defining feature of Marxist comparative logics.

In these ways, conservative *and* seemingly revolutionary projects comparatively utilize non-normative subjects to universalize heteropatriarchy and the heternormative subject. Ethnic studies scholar Lisa Cacho contends that such comparative traps are not surprising. Rather, they demonstrate the ways in which Whiteness and heteronormativity, two defining features of American citizenship, shape how we attribute and deny value to others and ourselves. These racialized and gendered ideas about legality and value are made readable through an inescapable and interdependent web of comparative analytics that permeate dominant *and* oppositional groups including minority nationalisms.

One such example in Puerto Rico is the Movimiento Pro-Independencia (MPI), which emerged in 1959 and proclaimed itself a part of the "vanguard" of the Puerto Rican Left. The majority of MPI members were former members of the traditional and culturally conservative Puerto Rican Independence Party (PIP) that sought political legitimacy through participation in the colonial electoral process. Members of the newly formed MPI accused the PIP lacking political militancy and being susceptible to co-optation from some of the island's traditional parties especially the Partído Popular Democratico which, at that point, had been in power for almost twenty years and enjoyed support from the U.S. colonial establishment and American corporations. In contrast, the MPI version of anticolonial struggle encompassed the integration of various revolutionary models found in

Southeast Asia, Africa, and most especially the 1959 Cuban revolution.[29]

Established by defectors from the PIP, including Juan Marí Bras, the MPI organized students, women, and workers. Juan Marí Bras, the MPI's leader, consolidated his group's membership through the incorporation of various threads of earlier local and internationalist radicalism. These leftist political strands included Marxist socialism, electoral boycotts, strategic violent confrontations, and a larger cultural approach that included its own newspaper *Claridad*. This ideological flexibility helped the party unite the deteriorating Puerto Rican Left and created a more concerted nationalist front. Broadening the MPI's political and ideological approaches allowed Marí Bras to also forge new relationships and exchanges with African American activists in the late 1960s. One such example included the invitation of Stokely Carmichael, chair of the Student Nonviolent Coordinating Committee, to speak at the University of Puerto Rico in the summer of 1967.

Juan Mari Bras and *Claridad*'s editorial staff pressed the connections between anti-Black racism in the continental United States, empire, and the consequences of the plebiscite in a political cartoon that appeared in the paper a week and-a-half before Carmichael's visit to the island. In the July 16, 1967 *Claridad* edition, a small political cartoon in the top right corner of the political commentary section depicts what appears to be a Black Puerto Rican being shoved by a hand holding a palm tree into the arms of four hooded and robed members of the Klu Klux Klan (Fig. 18.2).

One of the Klansmen also holds part of a rope in a noose as he and his fellow Klansmen quickly descend upon the Black Puerto Rican being pushed forward. In fact, the 1950s and 1960s marked a period of significant growth for the Klan as a socially and state sanctioned form of terror meant to undermine the demands and claims of the larger U.S. Civil Rights movement.

---

[28]Roderick Ferguson, Aberrations in Black. pp. 8–10.

[29]For Juan Marí Bras's take on the MPI's separation from the PIP see, "La Salida del P.I.P.," in Claridad, May 7, 1966; pp. 4.

Fig. 18.2 "Statehood Security" Claridad. July 16, 1967. Estadidad Seguridad," Claridad. July 16, 1967. University of Puerto Rico, Río Piedras: Coleccíon puertorriqueña

According to the Southern Poverty Law Center, after a period of decline in the 1930s and 1940s, Klan membership is estimated to have jumped up between 35,000 and 50,000 members in the 1960s.[30]

The growth in Klan membership precipitated a corresponding growth in racial violence against African Americans throughout the country and especially in the South including the murders of civil rights activists and educators.[31] The Civil Rights movement and the racial violence experienced by African Americans in the U.S. South emerged important themes in *Claridad*'s pages during the plebiscite campaign meant to make readers aware of the potential consequences of

statehood and the island's continued colonial relationship. A July 2, 1967 piece by *independentista* and political scientist Manuel Maldonado Denis, for example, described the recent conviction and sentencing of Muhammad Ali (Cassius Clay) for refusing to make himself available for induction into the United States Army. Maldonado Denis compares Ali's refusal with the refusal by Puerto Rican youth of the military draft (*servicio military obligatorio*). The article is also accompanied by of an image of police attacking Black student protestors in Texas as well as Otis Noel Pruitt's disturbing photo of the 1935 lynching of Bert Moore and Dooley Morton near Columbus, Mississippi. Moore and Morton were both accused of attacking two white women and were attacked and murdered by a mob before local police could arrest them. Taken together, the article draws linkages between the police and militarized violence and occupation (internal colonialism) experienced in Black neighborhoods in the United States and the neocolonial occupation found across the globe in places such as Vietnam and Puerto Rico.

An earlier June 25, 1967 edition of *Claridad* also incorporated the use of photographic images

---

[30]Staff of the Klanwatch Project of the Southern Poverty Law Center, Ku Klux Klan: A History of Racism and Violence. Montgomery: Southern Poverty Law Center. pp. 25.

[31]Examples include the murders of Willie Edwards (1957), Addie Mae Collins, Denise McNair, Carole Robertson Cynthia Wesley (1963), Henry Hezekiah Dee, Charles Eddie Moore, James Chaney, Andrew Goodman, Michael Schwer, Lt. Colonel Lemuel Penn (1964), Viola Gregg Liuzzo (1965), Vernon Dahmer, Ben Chester White (1966). *Ibid*, 29–33.

of lynching. This time, *Claridad* used the even more recognized August 7, 1930 Lawrence Beitler photo of the lynching of Thomas Shipp and Abram Smith in Marion, Indiana. Like Moore and Morton in Mississippi, Shipp Smith, and James Cameron (who escaped the mob) were accused of murdering a white factory worker and sexually assaulting his girlfriend, Mary Ball. Like so many other instances before, Ball recanted her original story of having been raped by anyone only after the lynching of Shipp and Smith. Anti-lynching activist and intellectual Ida B. Wells noted as early as 1895 that lynching did not intend to procure the protection and security of white femininity. Instead, lynching as a form of racial violence operated as an unsubstantiated hypocritical ruse used by the dominant racial order to help secure white patriarchy and wealth during moments of social and economic transformation.[32]

The *Claridad* photo of Ship and Smith's murder is accompanied with the caption: "The greatest legacy that Mr. Ferré promises us: Blacks lynched in Alabama by the racist Ku Klux Klan."[33] Here the connections between statehood and the threat of racial violence against Puerto Ricans are made explicit. The photo and caption are immediately followed by the poems *Lynch* and *Las Aguilas* (The Eagles) from acclaimed Afro-Cuban poet Nicolás Guillén. *Lynch* briefly tells of the horrors of lynching that it describes as a three-hooved beast with a whip-like tail that feeds on brutalized Black bodies. As mentioned earlier, the ways in which Puerto Ricans have been historically racialized as non-normative and Black colonial subjects as well as the larger history of racial violence against African Americans, Mexicans, and Asians in the United States understandably substantiates and legitimizes the

connections being made in the pages of *Claridad.*

Nonetheless, the methodological comparison meant to attain larger connections of racial solidarity reduces a deeper reading of the political cartoon. The cartoon raises a number of significant questions about race, culture, and politics that are overlooked at first glance. To begin, one must ask to whom does the white hand pushing the Black subject in the July 16, 1967 cartoon belong to? It could be argued that the use of the palm tree is meant for comedic effect and is simply meant to reference the prevalence of palm trees found throughout the island. In other words, the palm tree is a signifier for Puerto Rico more generally that enables readers of the cartoon to understand that the Black subject is being pushed away from the island and towards the Klan that is ready to lynch him.

It is more likely, however, that the use of a palm tree is an intentional political choice by the unidentified artist. Given the context of the earlier editions of *Claridad* and the political moment, the palm tree is a direct reference to the image selected by Ferre and his faction of *estadistas unidos* to represent the statehood option on the ballot of the plebiscite set to take place one week later on July 23, 1967 (Fig. 18.3).

One month after the plebiscite Ferre and others in the group selected the palm tree as the official symbol of their newly formed *Partido Nuevo Progresista* (PNP).[34] Understood in this way, the use of the palm tree helps to frame the white hand of a statehood supporter pushing the Black Puerto Rican toward their doom.

There is evidence that supports the theory of the emerging PNP leadership as a predominantly white and entrepreneurial class of elites that modeled their political behaviors and economic interests after U.S. elites. Antonio Ferre, Ferre's father and a Cuban immigrant, founded the steelwork Puerto Rico Iron Works in 1918 and that his son Luis later inherited. Ferre's familial ties to Cuba are important for understanding Luis

---

[32]Wells, Ida B. A Red Record: Tabulated Statistics and Alleged Causes of Lynchings in the United States, 1892–1894. Chicago: Donahue & Henneberry, 1895. See also Lengermann and Niebrugge-Brantley, The Women Founders, pp. 149–184.

[33]*La mejor herecia que nos promete Mr. Ferré: Negros linchados en Alabama por racistas del Ku Klux Klan.* Claridad, June 25, 1967, p. 8.

[34]Although the *Partido Nuevo Progresista* formed in August 1967, one month after the plebiscite, it did not officially register as a political party until January 1968.

Fig. 18.3 Sample Plebiscite Ballot, 1968. Palm Tree as a "Vote for Statehood". Plebiscitaria (1967)

Ferre's push for statehood at this particular moment given the victory of Fidel Castro and the Cuban Revolution in 1959. As sociologists Rafael Bernabe and César Ayala note, the success of the Cuban Revolution and the emergence of an increasingly radicalized Left in Puerto Rico "enhanced the statehooders' insecurities and their desire for protection through association with the United States."[35]

However, these kinds of insecurities cut across the political spectrum. If statehooders were necessarily insecure about their relationship with the United States given the emergent political alternatives being proposed by the Latin American Left, so to were *independentistas* insecure about the viability of their political project. This is most evident in the political cartoons use of a (Black) Puerto Rican as the central subject/victim in the text. Even as the cartoon aims to show how Puerto Ricans are racialized as Black and subjected to racial violence the cartoon also employs the use of Blackface. The use of Blackface minstrelsy in the United States often represented contradictory middle-class anxieties and fears of racialized others as well as a classic form of cultural appropriation that helped define the ambiguous and ever-shifting terrain of American citizenship.[36]

As cultural critic on Puerto Rican blackface Yeidy Rivero notes, while the Latin American tradition of blackface also expressed contradictory meanings, its use in popular culture often symbolized a nationalist and anticolonial form political satire that nonetheless reaffirmed hege-

---

[35]Ayala and Bernabe (2007, pp. 226).

[36]See for example Lott (1993).

monic whiteness.[37] Thought about in the context of its use in the pages of *Claridad*, it is feasible to see the subject being pushed forward as White Puerto Rican in Blackface being led to a lynching. More specifically, the predominantly white leadership of the 1960s Puerto Rican left is obscured by the political appropriation and mobilization of Blackface. Sandwiching the anticolonial project of *Claridad* between two representative symbols of assimilation and White supremacy ultimately renders the whiteness of the MPI's own leadership invisible and leaves the varying manifestations of hegemonic whiteness in Puerto Rico and across the Americas unexamined.

18.3 Emergent Methodological Interventions

New and promising methods from multidisciplinary fields such as Women's Studies, American Studies, Queer Theory, and Latin American Studies have worked to expose the concealments of comparison by tracing and highlighting the ways in which various subjects are framed as illegible by the normative and neoliberal investments of comparative method. American Studies scholars Grace Kyungwon Hong and Roderick Ferguson locate major components of this trend to the fields of women of color feminism and queer of color critique. "Women of color feminism and queer of color critique," contend Hong and Ferguson, "reveal the ways in which racialized communities are not homogenous but instead have always been policed and preserved the difference between those who are able to conform to categories of normativity, respectability, and value, and those who are forcibly excluded from such categories."[38] Further, cultural historian Micol Seigel contends that comparative history is about more than the

organization of dual categories and critique. Rather, it is a political project that itself produces the subjects, concepts and difference (race) that will be used in the construction of knowledge about people. Accordingly, Seigel argues that we should consider comparative method not simply as a method of analysis but rather a subject worthy of analysis in its own right.[39]

Transnational method is one method that attempts to think through the shortcomings of comparative method highlighted above. Shaped in part by feminist and queer knowledge formations, transnational method is meant to highlight the violence of neoliberal economic policies that create the "crises of place" or what Seigel and fellow historian David Sartorius term "dislocations."[40] Dislocation, they argue, permits a "reformulation of transnational method, shading its nation-bound referent and multiplying its metaphors of movement." The emphasis on movement allows for a reframing of the concept of dislocation that also helps to track the migration and the ways in which we banish and exile certain populations even as these subjects forge new relationships and solidarities. This version of transnational method allows for a continuous accounting of marginalized groups and their cultural practices in ways that do not privilege one space over another while still accounting for the structural relationships present across multiple spaces and categories.

Racial imbrication is another recent methodological and theoretical term that refuses comparative readings of race that reproduce exclusionary practices through reductionism.[41] In architecture or botany, imbrication describes the arrangement of tiles, roof shingles, leaves, or

---

[37]Rivero locates the emergence of this cultural formation to Cuba's 19th century *Bufo* theatre that was later adopted by Puerto Rican playwrights. Rivero (2004). See also, Rivero (2005).

[38]Hong and Ferguson, Strange Affinities, pp. 2.

[39]Seigel (2005).

[40]Seigel and Sartotius, for example, place their concept of dislocation in conversation with late queer of color critique theorist José Muñoz Esteban's concept of disidentification. For more on the relationship between post colonial feminisms and transnational method see Dawn Rae Davis's, "Unmirroring pedagogies: Teaching with Intersectional and Transnational Methods in the Women and Gender Studies Classroom," in Feminist Formations, vol. 22, no. 1; pp. 136–162.

[41]Alamo-Pastrana, Seams of Empire.

flower pedals so that their outer edges overlap with one another.[42] Alamo-Pastrana argues that racial imbrication occurs at the *structured* meeting points and within the relational stories about race found at the margins of racial regimes.

But racial imbrication resists romantic readings of the relational exchanges. In imbrication, a part of the subject of study is necessarily hidden from view at the point of overlap. Unless these points of imbrication are exposed through duress, they must be actively sought out and assessed. Not to do so risks that the social haunting will remain unaccounted for even as it repeats itself in the same observable pattern. The concept of imbrication therefore elucidates the contradictory ideas and social formations produced at the political edges of racial regimes but it also exposes what the margins themselves conceal from view.

Racial imbrication can be understood and deployed in two interrelated ways. As a methodological tool, it enables researchers to make specific linkages about varying and diverse racial regimes. Accordingly, racial imbrication directs scholars to the unexpected, yet structured, points of overlap among seemingly diverse points of racial difference. As a sociological method, racial imbrication also asks researchers to consider which parts of their analysis explicitly or implicitly conceal ideas or subjects. Imbrication, as method, demands that these areas of convergence be rigorously questioned and analyzed. If used properly as methodological tools, transnational method and racial imbrication offers researchers possibilities to excavate the potential gaps or exclusions created by traditional comparative projects.

Returning to the critiques of President Trump and his administration in Puerto Rico following hurricane Maria that I began this chapter with are instructive in this regard. While the critiques are not incorrect they do, nonetheless, miss the mark. In the case of comparing hurricanes Katrina and Maria we should consider what gets lost in these comparisons. Critiquing Trump's desire to compare the differing death tolls between the two disasters the Washington Post's Aaron Blake noted: "comparing death tolls is a dicey decision for a few reasons. The first is that it's just… yucky."[43] But it is more than yucky. Specifically, the comparison between the two hurricanes is inherently meant to add more value to one of the disasters over the other and thus devalue the different populations impacted by both natural disasters.

This is especially problematic since it triangulates the predominantly Black city of New Orleans against Puerto Rico and in relation to an invisible and overarching structure rooted in White supremacy. Similar to the political cartoons of the 19th century, the comparison seeks to pit different marginalized populations against one another in an effort to secure social value within the national imaginary. Even more, it reduces a deeper conversation about the multiracial and colonial histories of these spaces and groups as ordered within the U.S. racial regimes to a conversation about which disaster garnered more or less attention.

As noted above, dislocations and imbrication are about more than the structured connections between groups, nations, or racial regimes. They both also seek to understand and contest racial regimes. Transnational and imbricative methodological practices help to imagine new class, racial, national and gendered arrangements. Here we should consider the desire to tell the U.S. president to "shut the fuck up about the NFL" and focus on hurricane relief efforts and what it means with respect to our inability to hold and nurture the intimate relationship between these two stories and what they tell us about the ways in which African Americans and Puerto Ricans are simultaneously dislocated from the national imaginary.

The protests in the NFL began specifically as a direct challenge to the state sanctioned violence

---

[42]I first encountered "imbrication" in Lisa Lowe's essay "Insufficient Difference," in which she notes that imbrication and other terms such as encounters, entanglements, and intimacies can help us "excavate what has been suppressed under the rubric of difference Lowe, "Insufficient Difference," 412. See also, Hong and Ferguson, Strange Affinities.

[43]Blake, Aaron, "Trump Just favorably compared…".

perpetrated by police and directed towards African Americans. This effort effectively mobilized and worked alongside varying social groups and organizations to bring this issue to the forefront of public discourse and to challenge the practices of local and state police departments. Instead of silencing such conversations, a more nuanced critique would hold the issue of police brutality alongside the ways in which Puerto Ricans are similarly policed across spaces in the diaspora and in major metropolitan centers such as New York, Chicago, and Philadelphia. It could also tell us about the 2008 Civil Rights Division of the Department of Justice's investigation of the Puerto Rico Police Department (PRPD) and how significant parts of this investigation focused on the ways in which the PRPD discriminated against Black Puerto Ricans and/or other national groups especially Dominicans and Haitians that have migrated to the island or have lived there for multiple generations.

These issues should not be explicitly separated from a discussion about natural disasters and their impact on marginalized and colonized groups. Instead, they should be brought together to tell the complicated, and at times contradictory, ways in which they produce structural racism or what geographer Ruth Wilson Gilmore defines as the "state sanctioned group differentiated vulnerability to premature death" of marginal groups within the U.S. empire state.[44] Reckoning with the ways comparative discourses contribute to and activate the structural limits and outcomes that limit the material and social life chances of some groups requires the kinds of possibilities provided by new methodological interventions. Hegemony deploys its power in diverse and complex ways. Sociologists and other intellectuals must get better at tracing the imbricative contours of domination and the types of dislocations it creates. We should avoid the seduction of simplistic and insufficient comparative narratives that, in the end, serve to reinscribe the work of hegemony.

---

[44]Gilmore (2007).

Acknowledgements I would like to thank Pinar Batur, Merida Rua, William Hoynes for their valuable feedback and suggestions.

References

Alamo-Pastrana, C. (2016). *Seams of empire: Race and radicalism in Puerto Rico and the United States*. Gainesville: University Press of Florida.

Anthony, Marc. Twitter Post. 25 Sept 2017, 2:26 PM. https://twitter.com/marcanthony/status/912428240387678208?lang=en.

Ayala, C. J., & Bernabe, R. (2007). *Puerto Rico in the American century: A history since 1898*. The University of North Carolina Press.

Belvis, S. R., José J. A., & Francisco M. Q. [1969 (1867)]. *Proyecto para la Abolicíon de la Esclavitud*. San Juan: Instituto de Cultura Puertorriqueña.

Bhambra, G. (2016). Comparative historical sociology and the state: Problems of method. *Cultural Sociology, 10*(3), 340.

Blake, A. (2017). Trump Just favorably compared Puerto Rico's death toll to Katrina. *Washington Post*, 3 Oct 2017.

Bras, J. M. (1966). "La Salida del P.I.P." *Claridad*. Colleccion puertottiqueña; University of Puerto Rico, Rio Piedras. 7 May 1966.

Briggs, L. (2002). *Reproducing empire: Race, sex, science, and U.S. Imperialism in Puerto Rico*. Berkeley: Universty of California Press.

Cacho, L. (2012). *Social death: Racialized rightlessness and the criminalization of the unprotected*. New York: New York University Press.

Davis, D. R. (2010). Unmirroring pedagogies: Teaching with intersectional and transnational methods in the women and gender studies classroom. *Feminist Formations, 22*(1), 136–162.

de Hostos, E. M. [1954 (1873)]. *Obras Completas: España y America*. Paris: Ediciones Literarias y Artísticas.

de Tocqueville, A. (1935). *Democracy in America*.

Dickinson, T. (2017). How Puerto Rico is becoming Trump's Katrina. *Rolling Stone*, 26 Sept 2017.

Ferguson, R. (2001). *Aberrations in black: Toward a queer of color critique* (pp. 8–10). Minneapolis: University of Minnesota Press.

Findlay, E. J. (1999). *Imposing Decency: The politics of sexuality and race in Puerto Rico, 1870–1920*. Durham: Duke University Press.

Gilliam, V. (1899). The white man's burden (apologies to Kipling). The Ohio State University, The Billy Ireland Cartoon Library & Museum, Collection SPEC.CGA. CGA.

Gilmore, R. (2007). *Golden Gulag: Prisons, surplus, crisis, and opposition in globalizing California*. Berkeley: University of California Press.

Guerra, L. (1998). *Popular expression and national identity in Puerto Rico: The struggle for self, community, and nation*. Florida: University Press of Florida.

Hong, K. G., & Ferguson, R. (2011). *Strange affinities: The gender and sexual politics of comparative racialization*. Durham: Duke University Press.

Illis, M., & Rafael, B. (2017). Dems Trash Trump for NFL focus as Puerto Rico reels. *The Hill*, 25 Sept 2017. http://thehill.com/homenews/administration/352359-dems-bash-trump-for-nfl-focus-as-puerto-rico-reels

Jordan, D. S. (1899). *Imperial democracy*. New York: D. Appleton and Company.

Jung, M.-K. (2011). Constituting the U.S. empire-state and white supremacy. in *State of white supremacy*, 2–3 and 9. Stanford, California: Stanford University Press.

Lange, M. (2013). *Comparative historical methods*. London: Sage.

Lott, E. (1993). *Love and theft: Blackface minstrelsy and the American working class*. Oxford: Oxford University Press.

Lowe, L. (2005). Insufficient Difference. *Ethnicities, 5,* 410.

Lowe, L. (2015). *The intimacies of four continents* (pp. 7–14). Durham: Duke University Press.

Morris, A. (2015). *The scholar denied: W.E.B. DuBois and the birth of modern sociology*. Oakland: University of California Press.

Oh, I. (2017). Trump keeps tweeting about NFL protests while largely ignoring Puerto Rico. *in Mother Jones*, 25 Sept 2017.

Plebiscitaria, J. E. (1967). *Manual de instrucciones para el uso de los funcionarios de la Junta de Colegio para la votacion del plebiscito de 1967*. Río Piedras: University of Puerto Rico. Coleccion puertorriqueña, 23 July 1967.

Rivero, Y. (2004). Caribbean Negritos: Ramón Rivero, blackface, and "Black" Voice in Puerto Rico. *Television and New Media, 5*(2), 316–317.

Rivero, Y. (2005). *Tuning out blackness: Race and nation in the history of Puerto Rican television*. Durham: Duke University Press.

Sebring, J. (2015). Civilization & Barbarism: 'The white man's burden' (1898–1902). *The Asia Pacific Journal* (6 July 2015).

Seigel, M. (2005). Beyond compare: Comparative method after the transnational turn. in *Radical History Review*, no. 91 (Winter 2005): 62–90.

Seigel, M. (2009). *Uneven encounters: Making race and nation in Brazil and the United States*. Durham: Duke University Press.

Smith, A. (1776). *The wealth of nations*. Edinburgh: Turnbull and Spears Staff of the Klanwatch Project of the Southern Poverty Law Center. *Ku Klux Klan: A History of Racism and Violence* 25. Montgomery: Southern Poverty Law Center.

Tracy, A. (2017). Is the Crisis in Puerto Rico becoming Trump's Katrina. *Vanity Fair*, 25 Sept 2017.

Comparative Method, 2. Durham: Duke University Press.

Unidentified Artist. (1967). *La mejor herecia que nos promete Mr. Ferré: Negros linchados en Alabama por racistas del Ku Klux Klan*. Claridad. Coleccion puertorriqueña; University of Puerto Rico, Rio Piedras 25 June 1967.

Weber, M. (1949). Objectivity in social science and social policy. In E. Shils (Eds.), *Max Weber on the methodology of the social sciences* (pp. 49–112). Glencoe: Free Press.

Wells-Barnett, I. B. (1895). *A red record: Tabulated statistics and alleged causes of lynching in the United States*.

Race and Food: Agricultural Resistance in U.S. History

19

Isaac Sohn Leslie and Monica M. White

Contents

19.1 Introduction: Racism and Resistance in U.S. Food Systems

The U.S. has never solved the most fundamental problem for societal survival: how to provide healthy, affordable food to the people without exploiting laborers and destroying the earth. The genocide, land-grabbing, and slavery that oppres-

sed people of color in the past continue to fuel capitalist industrial agriculture today, which relies on new forms of racist exploitation to feed the privileged and malnourish the rest. The history of U.S. agriculture also contains another less-told story—one where farmers of color have resisted systemic oppression, and used agriculture to build what White (2018) calls Collective Agency and Community Resilience (CACR). Today, the Alternative Food Movement (AFM) is redesigning food systems to be healthier for people and the environment. At the same time, however, the AFM is reproducing racialized inequities: with predominantly white organizational leadership, their approaches to food justice often minimally engage communities of color, at best, and often silence the voices of those who are food insecure. In response to this glaring inequality, the Food Justice Movement (FJM) demands that food movements prioritize social justice for producers and consumers.

I. S. Leslie (✉)
Department of Sociology, University of Wisconsin-Madison, Madison, WI, USA
e-mail: ileslie2@wisc.edu

M. M. White
Nelson Institute for Environmental Studies and the Department of Community and Environmental Sociology, University of Wisconsin-Madison, Madison, WI, USA
e-mail: mmwhite3@wisc.edu

© Springer International Publishing AG, part of Springer Nature 2018
P. Batur and J. R. Feagin (eds.), *Handbook of the Sociology of Racial and Ethnic Relations*, Handbooks of Sociology and Social Research, https://doi.org/10.1007/978-3-319-76757-4_19

As these movements build new agricultural and community models to confront existential issues such as food security, climate change, and social justice, it is crucial we learn from the rich history of path-breaking agriculturalists of color.[1]

Critical to understanding agricultural resistance is the context of the current food system's failure to adequately feed many people of color. In 2013, 14% of U.S. households were food insecure, meaning that poverty and inequality limited their ability to have "consistent access to sufficient, safe, and nutritious food to maintain a healthy and active life" (Ayazi and Elsheikh 2015: 38). About ten percent of white households are food insecure, compared to 24% of Latinx,[2] 26% of Black, and 23% of Native American households (Ayazi and Elsheikh 2015: 37). The numbers are startlingly higher for those who are also LGBTQ+; 36% of Latinx, 37% of Black, and 55% of Native American LGBTQ+ (compared to 23% of white LGBTQ+) people do not have enough money for food (Gates 2014: 5).[3] Food insecurity is not only a matter of poverty. A long history of discriminatory policies has fueled residential segregation and supermarket flight from certain areas. Many call these places "food deserts," an offensive term to some,[4] which are areas in communities of color that have little

or no access to affordable, healthy food (Barker et al. 2012; Walker et al. 2010). At the same time, some urban communities of color, which previously had independent food stores that provided affordable, culturally appropriate food, are being gentrified and independent stores are being replaced by supermarket chains like Whole Foods, which lack both affordability and culturally appropriate food (Anguelovski 2015).

To interpret prominent examples of the ways that farmers[5] have resisted racial oppression throughout U.S. history and in today's AFM, we use White's (2018) theoretical framework of Collective Agency and Community Resilience (CACR). White developed CACR to analyze historical Black agricultural resistance and to inform the contemporary FJM and urban agriculture movement. Leslie (2019) has applied it to queer farmers' resistance to heterosexism and processes of accessing farmland. *Collective agency* refers to social actors' ability to make and enact decisions that affect their political future. Extending studies of agency that often examine its psychological (vs. social) origins and impacts for individuals (vs. communities), collective agency captures the ways that communities organize based on a shared social identity. Relatedly, *community resilience* refers to a community's ability to adapt to extreme adversity. Drawing from the field of resilience science (Folke 2006; Masten 2007; Walker and Salt 2012), community resilience highlights how communities respond and adapt to social and ecological disasters, emphasizing indigenous knowledges, emotional experiences, and racial dynamics and interactions pertinent to community adaptation. CACR expands preexisting understandings of everyday strategies of resistance (e.g., Scott and Tria Kerkvliet 1986), by focusing on efforts that are not only disruptive (e.g., protests, marches, and boycotts), but also constructive in turning energy inward to create

---

[1]In this chapter, we focus on Black and Latinx farmers and 20th and 21st century agricultural policies. We recognize the shortcomings of this limited scope, but still choose to use the broader term "farmers of color" to illustrate that similar themes of racism and resistance in food systems also apply to other non-white racial and ethnic groups. See, for instance, the excellent research done on the oppression of, and resistance by, Native American (e.g., Cleveland 1998; Norgaard et al. 2011) and Asian farmers (e.g., Bauer and Stewart 2013; Cheng and Bonacich 1984; Daniel 1982; Minkoff-Zern et al. 2011).

[2]We use "Latinx" to include all genders not accounted for in "Latino/a" or "Latin@" (Ramirez and Blay 2016).

[3]In contrast, 7% of Asian people (both LGBTQ+ and non-LGBTQ+) report not having enough money for food (Gates 2014: 5).

[4]As Eric Holt-Giménez explains, "The term is misleading and for many people living in these communities, insulting. These neighborhoods are not empty deserts, wastelands devoid of people or hope—or wealth…. They are areas of social, political and economic discrimination. In other words areas that have been subjected to a form of 'food apartheid.'" Furthermore, "the term 'food desert' is

also being used to justify land grabbing in the name of food security" (Holt-Giménez 2011; Wang et al. 2011).

[5]We use the term "farmer" to refer to anyone who works in agriculture, regardless of who owns the land, who works for whom, or who consumes what is produced. We use more specific terms when necessary.

alternative structures, institutions, and practices that demonstrate agency and resilience in peoples' efforts to feed themselves.

Demonstrating CACR, communities enact three primary, interrelated strategies to build self-reliance and self-determination. First, *commons as praxis* emerges when communities think and organize around shared social identities and statuses of race and class, using shared resources, ideologies, and behaviors in opposition to "dominant practices of ownership, consumerism, and individualism." Second, *prefigurative politics* develop when communities recognize their exclusion from formal political structures, and create spaces where they may freely develop independent, democratic decision-making processes to strategize liberation. Third, *economic autonomy* describes the ways that communities move away from preexisting conditions of economic exploitation and resource extraction toward the creation of alternative, independent systems for exchanging resources, which are necessary for articulating independence, building capacity and self-governance, and being regenerative (White 2018).

To demonstrate the ways that food production and distribution are used as sites of resistance for underserved communities, our approach emphasizes four areas considered central by scholars of race and food systems. First, we share the perspective that race pervades every step in the food system: farm to plate to waste, and every stage in between (Billings and Cabbil 2011). Second, we take a historical approach to the study of food justice activism to contextualize the ways that power and racial violence are reproduced and how they may be disrupted today (Ramírez 2015). Third, we focus on policy as a primary area where racism is institutionalized in the U.S. food system (Ammons 2014). Fourth, we shift the narrative by not only discussing racism, but also "historic and current working models" of resistance, which simultaneously take into account "the impact of White colonization, slavery, and deportation" (Ammons 2014: 6), and illuminate the ways these communities demonstrate agency and resilience. We follow in the footsteps of

White (2018) and Bowens (2015) by focusing on resistance and resilience alongside racism to give a more complete narrative of the rich and varied experiences of agriculturalists of color throughout U.S. history.

Using the theoretical framework of CACR, we examine prominent examples of racism in, and resistance to, (1) policies targeting U.S.-born[6] Black farmers, (2) policies targeting immigrant Latinx farmers, and (3) the Alternative Food Movement. Conversations about race and food are often viewed through the lens of oppression, especially in discussions that center on slavery, sharecropping, and tenant farming. However, these examples show that food production is also a site for resistance and collective agency, where farmers of color coopt an oppressive condition and use it as a strategy for taking an active position toward liberation. In doing so, they build community resilience to systemic racism's disastrous impact on food production and consumption in the U.S. by not only disrupting oppression, but constructing alternatives that contribute to building healthy and empowered communities. We argue that race and agriculture, seen through the framework of CACR, provides a way to shift the discussion from one focused

---

[6]We adopt Harrison and Lloyd's (2013: 287) explanation and use of the terms "U.S.-born," "immigrant," and "unauthorized": "First, we refer to nonimmigrant workers as 'U.S.-born'.... Second, we prefer to use the term 'migrant' to describe foreign-born people living in the United States, because the term does not presume that the individual intends to reside in the United States permanently. However, because the workers we describe typically live and work at one place on a full-time, year-round basis, we use the term 'immigrant' in this article to avoid the ways that 'migrant farm worker' conjures up an image of a roving person who moves with the harvests...Third, we use the term 'unauthorized' rather than 'undocumented' to describe immigrants without legal status, as they commonly work and live with forged or stolen identification documents in order to appear 'legal' and thus conduct basic activities such as acquiring a job, paying taxes, opening a bank account, and renting housing...We avoid the common term 'illegal,' as it does not point to the specific legal infraction committed but instead portrays the immigrant as generally criminal in nature."

solely on oppression to one that has the potential to inform contemporary movements' efforts toward self-sufficiency, self-determination, and liberation.

19.2 U.S.-Born Black Farmers

19.2.1 New Deal Policies and the Farm Bill

U.S. government agencies and policies have systematically disadvantaged farmers of color throughout U.S. history (Daniel 2013). Since its establishment in the 1860s, The United States Department of Agriculture (USDA) has racially discriminated in areas such as credit assistance, program delivery, and employment, leading to increased rates of land loss among farmers of color (Carpenter 2012; Gilbert et al. 2002).[7] Such oppression is not a thing of the past; the USDA continues to be challenged in court for discriminating against Hispanic, Native American, Black, and women farmers (Carpenter 2012; Feder and Cowan 2013). New Deal policy decisions and the Farm Bill have had significant impacts on the historical and current racial geographies of U.S. agriculture.

New Deal politicians excluded African Americans from social and agricultural support systems. In the 1930s, 60% of Black workers were employed in agricultural or domestic work. In the South, 75% of Black workers and 85% of Black women worked in these two sectors (Ayazi and Elsheikh 2015: 25). Politicians chose to exclude domestic and agricultural workers from the Social Security Act of 1935, despite NAACP warnings to Congress that this would impact 3.5 of 5.5 million Black workers (Linder 1987: 1365). Domestic work was not included until 1950, and agricultural work not until 1954, leaving an entire generation of workers with no

or limited retirement income, truncating their ability to accrue wealth for future generations (Giancatarino and Noor 2014). Furthermore, politicians refused to set minimum wages for jobs worked mostly by African Americans, excluded Black workers from agricultural union programs, and denied Black landowners federal farm support (Ayazi and Elsheikh 2015). These federal policy decisions contributed to a massive decline in the number of Black-owned farms: from 900,000 in 1930 to only 6,996 in 1978 (Ayazi and Elsheikh 2015: 25). This was not simply part of the broader trend toward farm consolidation; the total number of acres of U.S. Black-owned farmland declined from 14 million in 1920 to 2 million by the turn of the century (Gilbert et al. 2002). Proponents of New Deal reforms conceded to southern congressmen who sought "to obtain modifications of New Deal legislation that preserved the social and racial plantation system in the South—a system resting on the subjugation of [African Americans] and other minorities. As a result, New Deal legislation, including the [Fair Labor Standards Act], became infected with unconstitutional racial motivation" (Linder 1987: 1336).

The Farm Bill, first implemented in 1933 and renewed about every five years, is the legislation with the most significant impact on U.S. agriculture and food systems. Between 2014 and 2024, the Farm Bill designates $956.46 billion for nutrition programs like Supplemental Nutrition Assistance Program (SNAP) ($756.43 billion), crop insurance ($89.83 billion), conservation ($57.6 billion), commodity programs ($44.46 billion), and other areas such as trade, research and Extension, and rural development ($3.7 billion or less) (Ayazi and Elsheikh 2015: 15). The Farm Bill's economic structuring has had a disproportionate impact on farmers of color. Because farmers of color have been historically excluded from owning farmland, especially quality farmland, they tend to have small farms, made economically viable through labor-intensive specialty crops or livestock production. It is no accident that white farmers grow 98.6% of all grain and oilseed crops (considered cash crops), commodities that require large

---

[7]For a thorough examination of the history of racism against Black farmers in U.S. history, from slavery to exclusion on land today, see Hinson and Robinson (2008).

expanses of land, farmed with expensive machinery. In 2012, 63.6% of Asian farmers grew crops such as fruits and vegetables, while only 8.5% of white farmers did. That same year, 46.8% of Black farmers raised cattle, compared to 9.1% of white farmers. However, because the Farm Bill's subsidies are weighted toward large farms and commodity crops like grains, in 2012, 40% of white farmers and only 30% of Black farmers received subsidies. Small farms received an average of $5,003, while large farms received $47,732. Consequently, average payments to white farmers were $10,022 and only $5,509 to African Americans. White farmers receive 97.8% of government payments (Ayazi and Elsheikh 2015: 58–59). Furthermore, 34% of rural African Americans compared to 14% of rural white people live in poverty, yet the Farm Bill's Rural Development program is miniscule compared to its overall budget. The Trump administration's proposed cuts to the Farm Bill, especially to SNAP, would likely exacerbate these inequalities (Evich et al. 2017).

The Farm Bill is both a product and a tool of neoliberal economic policies, which fuel racial disparities in three primary ways, according to Ayazi and Elsheikh (2015: 11). First, since the 1930s, but especially since the 1970s, the Farm Bill has been restructured to increasingly support corporate agribusiness, ultimately disadvantaging communities of color. Even the recent shift from minimum prices or direct payments for farmers to subsidizing crop insurance primarily benefits private insurance companies. Furthermore, access to the democratic process for changing the bill has been limited, leaving corporate agribusiness with the most power to affect policy. Second, while the Farm Bill funds SNAP, a lifeline for many people of color, in doing so "they ultimately maintain structural inequality" by guaranteeing profits for large food retailers like Walmart, which channel wealth outside of communities and only offer low wage work. Third, the Farm Bill is contradictory to combating structural racism and poverty because by favoring large-scale, industrial agriculture, it supports a food system where producers are forced to reduce expenses in all realms, resulting in unjust, racialized labor practices and the production of toxic environmental hazards and climate change that disproportionately affect communities of color (Downey 2015; Mohai et al. 2009).

These examples suggest the discrimination that Black farmers have experienced because of federal policies and show how they have exacerbated land dispossession and economic disenfranchisement among the Black farmers who have contributed their labor to food production. The repercussions of these policies, and of other federal, state and local actions, have had a devastating impact on African American land loss. It was this economic exploitation, and not the hardship of agricultural work, that fueled Black migration from southern and western states in search of better employment and educational opportunities.

19.2.2 Black Resistance

While much of the scholarship that investigates the relationship between African Americans and agriculture concentrates on slavery, sharecropping, tenant farming, and their historical legacies, an important, yet overlooked counter-narrative is the rich history of African Americans who have used food and food production as a strategy of resistance from plantation slavery to the present day. Today's urban agricultural resurgence in cities across the U.S. continues these efforts to incorporate access to land, food production, and distribution into social justice movements.

One of the earliest examples of this resistance is found in the captured Africans who suffered the Middle Passage and who carried contraband seeds in their hair while in the cargo bellies of ships. Once on dry land they planted these seeds to be able to consume foods that reminded them of their homelands, culture, religion, and language. Oral histories of enslaved Africans passed down through generations to their descendants tell stories of seeds such as okra, yams, millet, plantains, purslane, and many others that served as the foundation of their diet and that journeyed from the continent of Africa to the Americas (Carney 2004).

The institution of slavery was also a site of resistance in the ways that those who labored on the plantation negotiated for access to space to grow food for themselves and their communities. Those who were enslaved created provision grounds or "slave gardens" on small plots of land, usually directly outside of the slave quarters, where they grew healthy fruits and vegetables that added nutrition to the paltry diet of food scraps enslavers allowed them (Barickman 1994). The enslaved had limited time for these provision grounds after they completed their hard day's labor working with the cash crops of plantation agriculture, however on Sunday those who produced edibles might sell them in markets. In these shared spaces, they exerted agency, independent production, and marketing (Tomich 2016).

After slavery and under Jim Crow, Black farmers began, as early as the 1880s, to build agricultural collectives and cooperatives of farmers to demand better wages and working conditions for sharecroppers, day laborers, and tenant farmers, and to seek equal treatment for Black landowners. The Colored Farmers Alliance began in 1894; at its peak 1.2 million farmers were members across 175 chapters and every southern state (Ali 2010; Dann 1974; Miller 1972). The agrarian approach to freedom included access to land and knowledge of food production as part of their political platforms for freedom and liberation throughout the twentieth century.

Civil rights and Black power organizations such as the Universal Negro Improvement Association, the Nation of Islam, and the Black Panther Party all had a food and/or land component in their social justice platforms and they committed resources to facilitate a well-fed, well-employed membership (Abron 1998; Hill et al. 2011; Kirkby 2011; Patel 2011; Potorti 2014). In addition to the inclusion of food as strategy, Black farmers, many of whom were sharecroppers and tenant farmers, became politically involved in the civil rights movement, and organized cooperatives as an act of resistance against those who previously exploited their labor.

The Federation of Southern Cooperatives deserves special recognition for its 50-year history of responding to the needs of Black rural community development, with special attention to the use of cooperatives as a strategy of rebuilding an underserved and economically disadvantaged community. The Federation was founded in 1967 to provide training for cooperative development throughout southern Black states, assist former tenant farmers, sharecroppers, and domestic workers throughout the southern U.S., and to build cooperatives as an economic and resistance strategy. The founding members of the Federation were rooted in southern communities. They were committed to identifying solutions by providing technical and organizing resources that would ultimately allow the community to provide for itself. They had an intimate knowledge of community needs. To meet these community-identified needs, the Federation successfully submitted grants to private donors and the Office of Economic Opportunity to bring in experts to offer training in the mechanics of effective cooperatives as well as to support community members who wanted to put this training into action. The Federation taught record keeping, business planning, and other technical skills. Cooperative leaders who received training at Federation headquarters took these skills back to their home communities to improve their cooperatives. Eventually merging with the Emergency Land Fund in 1985, an organization established to save Black-owned land, the Federation is now known as the Federation of Southern Cooperatives/Land Assistance Fund. Both organizations have identified self-determination and self-reliance as essential to Black land ownership and as a strategy to building community wellness (Nembhard 2014).

Demonstrating the strategies of CACR, the Federation and its member organizations used cooperatives to create economic autonomy by encouraging value-added products, or the transformation of raw materials into goods and services. Organizationally, they emphasized prefigurative politics in enacting democratic principles of one person, one vote. Additionally, strategies of commons as praxis were essential to the day-to-day operations of the Federation and its member co-ops. Members pooled their resources such as money, labor, and land to share the economic benefits of their efforts. These strategies together allowed Black farmers to continue working the land, stay in the south, and work toward self-sufficiency in building healthy communities.

Recent scholarship has begun to embrace these historical legacies and reclaim them as a way forward (Williams and Holt-Giménez 2017). The legacies of these organizations offer the backdrop for current conversations regarding the resurgence of agriculture in the context of food justice/sovereignty movements in urban spaces like Detroit, Chicago, Los Angeles, Milwaukee, New Orleans, and New York City.

19.3 Immigrant Latinx Farmers

19.3.1 The Bracero and H-2 Guestworker Programs

Today's U.S. food system relies on the exploitation of immigrant farm workers, six of every ten of whom are unauthorized (Bauer and Ramirez 2010: 4). Mexican workers moved feely across the border until they were first regarded as "illegal" in 1924 (Bauer and Stewart 2013), 76 years after the U.S. forcibly seized over half of Mexico's territory (Valerio-Jiménez 2016). During the labor shortages of World War I and World War II, Mexican workers were encouraged to migrate, yet during the Great Depression they were perceived to be a threat to U.S. citizens' job prospects, and a half million were deported (Bauer and Stewart 2013).

The U.S. and Mexico established the Bracero program during World War II, which created conditions for Mexicans to work in the U.S. It filled 4.5 million jobs between 1942 and 1964 (Bauer and Stewart 2013: 3). Even before reaching their workplace in the U.S., Mexican farmers were subject to racialized human rights abuses, such as humiliating physical exams where they were sprayed with the toxic pesticide

DDT (Mitchell 2010; Mize and Swords 2010). Agricultural employers ignored legal protections, such as minimum wage and adequate housing, and routinely exploited immigrants (Bauer and Stewart 2013). Employers created "violent landscapes" to maintain a system of capitalist production focused exclusively on profit (Mitchell 2010). Even the Bracero program's manager in the U.S. Department of Labor called it "a system of 'legalized slavery'" (Bauer and Stewart 2013: 4).

Current U.S. policy on immigrant workers, the H-2A guestworker program, is a renewal of the Bracero program. Many have interpreted the H-2A program as a system of modern-day indentured servitude because workers are bound to a single employer without opportunities for legal recourse or a path to citizenship (Bauer and Stewart 2013). The U.S. issues about 55,000 H-2A agricultural visas annually, 80% to Mexicans (Bauer and Stewart 2013: 5). Labor recruiters target people living in poverty and charge high interest for travel costs; workers have starting debts that range from $500 to $10,000 and have little opportunity to free themselves from that debt (Bauer and Stewart 2013: 9; Harrison and Lloyd 2013). Because firing someone means deportation, employers leverage that threat as a means of power and control. Employers routinely confiscate legal documents, such as passports and social security cards, so workers entering local communities fear being perceived as unauthorized and possibly deported (Bauer and Stewart 2013). Workers are further dependent on employers because of rural geographies, lack of transportation, and the threat of visibility. For many without authorization, immigration is not simply the often-portrayed choice of individuals, but "forced movement for survival," due to a web of structural conditions (including policies like the North American Free Trade Agreement), which rely on the racialization and normalization of human rights abuses (Holmes 2013: 186; Mize and Swords 2010).

Structural power asymmetries lead to similar patterns of exploitation in the H-2A and Bracero programs, including contract violations, wage theft, squalid housing conditions, no recourse for workplace injuries, and workplace hazards such as toxic pesticide exposures and heat stress (Bauer and Ramirez 2010; Bauer and Stewart 2013; Bon Appétit Management Company Foundation and United Farm Workers 2011; Estabrook 2012). Women have been sexually abused and raped, and often stay silent for fear of deportation if they fight back (Bauer and Ramirez 2010). Families are torn apart, as H-2 visas do not permit families to travel with workers (Bauer and Stewart 2013). Such abuses are institutionalized; agricultural workers can be fired for joining a union under the National Labor Relations Act, they cannot obtain unemployment insurance from the Social Security Act, and most U.S. farms are exempt from the workplace safety and health standards of the Occupational Safety and Health Administration (Bon Appétit Management Company Foundation and United Farm Workers 2011). While enduring these abuses, "[b]etween 2005 and 2009, about a third of farm workers earned less than $7.25/hour and only a quarter of all farm workers reported working more than nine months in the previous year" (Bon Appétit Management Company Foundation and United Farm Workers 2011: iii).

Agricultural policies contribute to the reproduction of overt, as well as more subtle forms, of white racism in rural areas. Immigrant workers endure racist epithets and discrimination over their "foreign" and "temporary" statuses (Hjalmarson et al. 2015). Fear of deportation renders farm workers invisible, to the advantage of farm owners who would rather not attract attention to unauthorized workers on their farm (Harrison and Lloyd 2013). This invisibility also benefits other industries in places like Vermont, which relies on its image of whiteness for tourism and its state brand (Vanderbeck 2006). Vermont's population is officially only 1.5% Latinx (Baker and Chappelle 2012: 278). However, its primary agricultural industry is highly dependent on Latinx workers: about two-thirds of Vermont dairy farms employ Mexican farmers, roughly 90% of whom are unauthorized (Radel et al. 2010: 190). White farm owners who abuse, or are complicit in the abuse of, farm workers do not only do so

exclusively out of economic necessity; Harrison and Lloyd (2013: 282) studied the stories farm owners tell about their own whiteness, and found that they uphold such labor relations "to maintain profits within a changing industry context, meet their own middle-class aspirations, comply with their peers' middle-class lifestyle expectations, manage their own concerns about immigration policing, assert their own class identity, justify the privileges that they and their white, U.S.-born employees enjoy on the farm, and maintain the advantages they have gained."

19.3.2 Latinx Resistance

In the mid-60s, organized Filipino grape workers joined forces with a new Latinx agricultural union and established the United Farm Workers (UFW) (Minkoff-Zern 2014b). The UFW helped expose the Bracero program's human rights abuses, leading to its abolishment (Carrasquillo 2011). Iconic leaders Cesar Chavez and Dolores Huerta led strikes and marches, protesting worker conditions and toxic pesticide exposure. The UFW earned a 40% increase in grape workers' wages and the right for farm workers to unionize (Bauer and Ramirez 2010: 13). Together with the Student Nonviolent Coordinating Committee (SNCC) and Students for a Democratic Society (SDS), UFW organized the most extensive food boycott in U.S. history, helping table grape workers unionize by the 1970s (Minkoff-Zern 2014b). After the 1970s, however, farm worker unions lost power. The UFW declined for a combination of internal and external reasons, such as employers' use of contractors instead of direct hiring (Minkoff-Zern 2014b). Nevertheless, the UFW had lasting impacts within and beyond agriculture; it spread tactics for organizing within hostile political climates, stimulated organizing across and outside of the U.S., and became an important component of the Chicanx and broader civil rights movements (Levy and Chavez 1975; Mize and Swords 2010; Rodriguez 2011).

Contemporary farm worker resistance groups learned valuable lessons from the UFW. The

Coalition of Immokalee Workers (CIW), for instance, has sustained a powerful campaign since the early 1990s. Latinx farmers in Immokalee, Florida, began CIW's tactic of leading boycotts and pressuring large food purchasers, such as Taco Bell, McDonalds, Whole Foods, and others, to agree to pay higher prices designated to farm worker wages and to enforce a Code of Conduct, which is regulated by farm workers themselves (Minkoff-Zern 2014b). Their first major campaign famously earned farm workers an extra penny for every pound of tomatoes they pick (Estabrook 2012). They advocate not only for better pay; their agenda includes raising attention to human trafficking, gender oppression, toxic exposure, and other areas of exploitation, described above. CIW's organizing structure is non-hierarchical. CIW builds on farm workers' peasant and indigenous struggles in their home countries in Central America and the Caribbean, creating one of the strongest farm worker-led, rural agricultural movements in the U.S. today (Estabrook 2012; Minkoff-Zern 2014b). In many ways, these organizations demonstrate their efforts toward economic autonomy and independence. In speaking out against the white, capitalist, economic power structure, they not only speak out about their economic oppression, but they also seek ways to work toward self-reliance and autonomous political community.

The UFW and CIW's strategies of community unionism have deep roots in the earlier *mutualista* movement—mutual aid societies in Mexican communities in the U.S.—that provided community-based economic, cultural, and education programs. Today's Hometown associations draw on the history of *mutualista* community organizing to support communities in Mexico that have social ties to immigrants in the U.S. (Mize and Swords 2010). Prefigurative politics occur when social justice organizations of politically disenfranchised members, like these, emphasize political participation in deciding the ways that these organizations work internally. Unauthorized workers also employ formal community-based strategies, such as worker centers for accessing basic needs and legal services, and less-formal tactics, such as co-residence strategies for sharing economic and social resources (Chavez 1990; Mize and Swords 2010). For prefigurative politics to occur, communities must establish these safe spaces that contribute to the politicization and education of the aggrieved community but also allow for efforts that demonstrate and expand agency and resilience.

19.4 The Alternative Food Movement

19.4.1 Racism in the Alternative Food Movement

The AFM includes a variety of initiatives that emerged in response to the ecological and health-related harms of capitalist industrial agriculture. However, as many scholars have argued, whiteness pervades and organizes AFM spaces and practices (e.g., Alkon and Agyeman 2011; Alkon 2012; Pilgeram 2012; Rice 2015; Slocum 2007). When white AFM organization leaders notice its overwhelming whiteness, it is usually perceived as a problem of insufficient diversity, rather than a systematic reproduction of power and privilege (Slocum 2006), let alone a call for participants to examine their own responsibility in its reproduction. Communities of color are often encouraged to embrace the organic agriculture of the AFM "as if it were never a pre-existing reality" for farmers of color (Slocum 2006: 334). Ignorance of historical and current racism, resistance, and cultural practices in agriculture permeates AFM projects, such as food policy councils (Henson and Munsey 2014), and often results in the exclusion of immigrant farmers and farmers of color (Flora et al. 2012). Even organizations focused on justice may fall into similar patterns of racial exclusion, despite the best intentions of white members. Their rhetoric of "bringing good food to others" and "getting your hands dirty" may actually primarily serve their own interests and "missionary zeal," and it cries ignorance of the history of U.S. agricultural race relations (Guthman 2008c: 436).

Racialized patterns and interactions are reproduced in institutions where people learn about agriculture and how to farm. For instance, land grant institutions are often overwhelmingly white and may fail to provide systematic education of the racialized aspects of food systems (Peña 2015). Organic agricultural apprenticeships may exclude people of color both because of the pervasive whiteness in these spaces, and also their reliance on low or unpaid labor that may not be an option for individuals with few resources (Biewener 2016; MacAuley and Niewolny 2016). Because of racialized gaps in income and wealth accrual over generations, farmers of color and immigrants are at a disadvantage when it comes to the three most common ways of obtaining a farm—marriage, inheritance, or purchase—and must also confront real and perceived racism in rural areas (Leslie 2019; Morales 2011). Farmers of color face additional racialized barriers when navigating the relationships necessary for accessing farmland, such as with landlords, real estate agents, and the USDA Farm Service Agency (Calo and De Master 2016).

Such racialized interactions are particularly evident where farmers sell their goods—spaces critical for farmers' economic success. Guthman (2008b) identifies two common discourses in farmers markets and CSA schemes[8]—color blindness and universalism—that reflect ignorance and dismissal of current and historical racism in food systems. The pervasive whiteness of farmers markets not only contributes to a lack of culturally appropriate foods, but to a racialized coding of these spaces as white and unwelcoming, uninteresting, or unsafe for people of color (Alkon and McCullen 2011; Pilgeram 2012; Slocum 2008). Farmers markets are more likely to be located in communities with a higher white population and socioeconomic status (Schupp 2017). Even when they are located in communities of color, some farmers markets have disproportionately high levels of white shoppers

compared to the racial makeup of the community (Rice 2015), which is perhaps explained by unaffordability and the racial coding of farmers markets as white. Thus, as farmers markets are increasingly used by local policy makers as a tool for community development and food access, greater attention must be paid to diverse and authentic stakeholder input, cultural relevance, profitability for farmers, and affordability and availability (such as hours of operation) for consumers (Fang et al. 2013).

19.4.2 Resistance in the Food Justice Movement

The AFM has paid more attention to environmental harms than human inequities, despite their inextricability (Pellow 2007). No longer in existence, but an important precursor to the FJM was the Community Food Security Coalition, founded in 1994 (Holt-Giménez and Wang 2011). Community food security advocates call for adequate, equitable access to nutritious, culturally appropriate foods. Building on this activism, the U.S. Food Justice Movement (FJM) emerged to confront racial disparities in food insecurity. The FJM encompasses a vast array of organizations, priorities, and tactics (Alkon and Agyeman 2011; Sbicca 2012; Slocum et al. 2016). Although there is ongoing debate about the movement's goals and the process of defining them (Loo 2014), the FJM has tended to focus beyond food access to draw attention to structural inequalities. The FJM calls for systemic change rather than reform, echoing the earlier food work of the Black Panther Party, although explicit critiques of racism and capitalism were less common in the early 2000s (Holt-Giménez and Wang 2011; Morales 2011).

Largely under the umbrella of the FJM, there are encouraging examples of communities of color building Collective Agency and Community Resilience through food and agriculture. Prominent examples of urban agriculture in Detroit, Michigan (White 2010, 2011b), and Holyoke, Massachusetts (Slocum 2006), demonstrate how communities of color are using

---

[8]Community Supported Agriculture (CSA) is a model where consumers typically pay in advance of the growing season for a share of the weekly harvest.

agriculture to organize around shared experiences of race and class, instantiating the concept of commons as praxis. Black women organizers of the Detroit Black Community Food Security Network utilize urban agriculture to build self-reliance, which they see as aligned with a history of Black resistance using food (White 2011a). Cities in California are developing creative policies to increase access to land for urban agriculture (Havens and Roman-Alcalá 2016). Other FJM organizations work with immigrant farm workers. One, for instance, organizes a community garden for food insecure immigrant farm workers to grow organic, culturally important produce (Minkoff-Zern 2014a). Justicia Migrante, an organization of immigrant farmers who primarily work in Vermont's dairy industry, has taken a similar approach to the Coalition of Immokalee Workers by pressuring powerful actors in the supply chain, like Ben and Jerry's, for better wages and working conditions. It has recently been fighting the detention of several of its immigrant leaders by Immigration and Customs Enforcement, which has been emboldened by the Trump administration (Justicia Migrante 2017). Importantly, these communities are creating safe spaces for prefigurative politics, necessary for democratic governance, self-determination, and strategizing liberation. These are just a few of many examples of initiatives led by Latinx, Black, Hmong, Native American, and other groups (Blue Bird Jernigan et al. 2012; Morales 2011).

Farmers markets are increasingly incorporating Electronic Bank Transfer systems so customers may purchase food using nutrition assistance programs like SNAP (Jones and Bhatia 2011). Whereas SNAP has been criticized for subsidizing corporate interests, such as Walmart (Ayazi and Elsheikh 2015), recycling SNAP monies back into the local economy is an important step toward economic autonomy. One study found that the introduction of a farmers market into a food insecure community had the effect of lowering neighborhood grocery prices by 12% (Larsen and Gilliland 2009). Programs like Double Up Food Bucks and Philly Food Bucks, which offer consumers extra money to buy food when they spend SNAP dollars at farmers markets, support local farmers and increase fruit and vegetable consumption (Hagan and Rubin 2013; Young et al. 2013). Importantly, more support is needed for farmers of color to participate in, and earn a fair wage at, farmers markets. Markets with high participation rates of farmers of color help to address the exclusionary whiteness of famers markets, increase offerings of culturally appropriate foods, and build farmers markets as sites for racial solidarity and resistance (Alkon 2012; Myers 2015).

For farmers of color to sell their goods, and to increase the food security of communities, it is necessary to have marketing avenues that extend beyond farmers markets. Other strategies include food hubs, co-ops (Zitcer 2015), mobile markets (Satin-Hernandez and Robinson 2015), corner store partnerships (Short et al. 2007), and sidewalk vending (Morales and Kettles 2009). Such models can help increase communities' economic autonomy (Hagan and Rubin 2013). There are benefits and drawbacks to each, so it takes a diversity of marketing options to build this aspect of community resilience. Marketing in alternative food systems is just one example of the importance of diversity to the resilience of socioecological systems (Folke 2006).

19.5 Toward Food Justice *and* Food Sovereignty

A key critique of the FJM is that it is limited by neoliberal practices and ideologies, which emphasize social change strategies that work through markets rather than government. Understandably, food justice organizations have been reluctant to partner with government because government has been responsible for many of the racist policies they seek to combat. Their alternatives, however, often use market-based strategies for social change, such as farmers markets, which are limited in their potential to make structural anti-racist change (Alkon and Mares 2012; Alkon 2014; Guthman 2008a; Leslie 2017). The FJM faces the dual challenges of neoliberal capitalism and racism, which are inextricably intertwined systems of oppression (Holt-Giménez 2015). Sbicca and Myers (2017) argue that because the process of neoliberalization is uneven, it leaves room for "food justice racial projects" to make radical change. We, however, put greater weight on neoliberal capitalism's constraints on AFMs and follow Holt-Giménez and Shattuck (2011) in calling for more strategic alliances between progressive and radical food organizations to embrace a systemic critique of neoliberal capitalism's impacts on just food systems.

Such a critique is already well integrated in the food sovereignty framework, first articulated by the international peasant movement La Vía Campesina. Food sovereignty intends to replace corporate control with community self-determination of food systems (Grey and Patel 2015; Holt-Giménez and Wang 2011). Food sovereignty resists neoliberalism and capitalist industrial agriculture, in which markets determine food access (Carney 2012). Whereas the U.S.-based food security movement has its roots in neoliberal notions of economic development (Jarosz 2014), the food sovereignty movement understands food security as a precondition for food sovereignty. Importantly, food sovereignty connects local community self-determination to global struggles of oppression (Wald and Hill 2016). Whereas FJM organizations often focus on urban consumers, food sovereignty has its roots among rural small-scale producers. One Native American food sovereignty perspective reminds us that food is about more than access and consumption; food system change must account for cultural contexts and historical relations of power (Vernon 2015). The food sovereignty framework makes a valuable addition to the FJM because of its critique of neoliberal capitalism, strategies for connecting local to global social movements, focus on producers, integration of rural and urban food movements, prioritization of indigenous knowledges, and history of grassroots organizing. Many scholars and practitioners have thus called on the FJM to adopt a food sovereignty framework (Alkon and Mares 2012; Block et al. 2012; Clendenning et al. 2015; Wald and Hill 2016).

19.6 Conclusion: Building Collective Agency and Community Resilience

Our opponents in the agricultural industry are very powerful and farm workers are still weak in money and influence. But we have another kind of power that comes from the justice of our cause. So long as we are willing to sacrifice for that cause, so long as we persist in non-violence and work to spread the message of our struggle, then millions of people around the world will respond from their hearts, will support our efforts…and in the end we will overcome. (Chavez 1972)

Cesar Chavez made this statement after his 24-day fast for justice in 1972. It reminds us that agriculture has long been a key site of racism and resistance in U.S. history, as it continues to be today. As the AFM redesigns food systems for human and environmental health, the food justice and food sovereignty movements demand that they also be structured for racial justice.

Research that integrates race and food scholarship offers important advice to current food movements: we need to move beyond the idea of inclusivity to address power asymmetries and interconnected structures of oppression (Kepkiewicz et al. 2015; Ramírez 2015). Doing so involves changing the rhetoric of diversity to the action of disrupting structural racism (Moore and Swisher 2015; Reynolds 2015). This demands that white activists adopt a self-reflective, critical stance toward the impacts of their own whiteness (Roman-Alcalá 2015) and reasons for participating in the movement (Meek and Tarlau 2015). As practitioners engage in the process of decolonization, racism must be tackled simultaneously with interlocking systems of oppression, such as patriarchy (Bradley and Herrera 2016).

We build on this race and food scholarship by focusing on acts of resistance within the context of social movements resisting structural oppression. Contrary to the common academic model of examining communities from a deficit-based approach (e.g., referencing communities as "food deserts"), our approach is based on the idea that all communities have assets upon which to build and that those who are food insecure have strategies for community building that move them toward freedom. By embedding scholarship in communities that are actively engaged in agricultural resistance for self-determination, it is clear that race and food are inseparable. It is important to highlight the inseparability of race and food in scholarship so that race scholars do not miss the importance of food, and that food scholars, when talking about racism, do not miss how food is also used as a strategy of resistance.

Extending our asset-based approach to policy, CACR provides a useful lens for aligning policy proposals with the resistance strategies of agriculturalists of color. Policy experts on racial justice in food systems have articulated concrete, near and long term recommendations for national, state, and local levels (Ammons 2014; Ayazi and Elsheikh 2015; Bauer and Ramirez 2010; Bauer and Stewart 2013; Center for Social Inclusion 2013; Elsheikh 2016; Giancatarino and Noor 2014). To outline just a few examples that align with CACR: on the national level, there should be increased funding for land access initiatives, such as the Farm Bill's Section 2501: Funding for Socially Disadvantaged Farmers and Ranchers or the Transitions Incentive Program (Center for Social Inclusion 2013), and they should prioritize farmers of color and proposals designed to increase food access and economic autonomy in communities of color. SNAP benefits should be decoupled from the Farm Bill, and redesigned to benefit community and independent, rather than corporate, retailers. Labor rights must be overhauled, including increasing protections related to wages, workers compensation, and organizing, regardless of legal status. Immigration policies must be reworked so that immigrant farmers are not reliant on an employer to enter the country, have a path toward citizenship for themselves and their family, and are protected from recruitment fees that result in "debt peonage" (Bauer and Stewart 2013: 43). States should coordinate comprehensive plans to support the various actors in local and regional food systems, as is being done in Vermont (Vermont Sustainable Jobs Fund 2013). Plans should include actions such as promoting institutional food purchasing from local farms,

matching SNAP funds when used in places like farmers markets, and making vacant public lands available for cultivation by local FJM organizations. There should be increased support for FJM organizations that have a history of success and are led by people of color. Representatives from these organizations should be sought out for leadership at all levels, in positions with power to affect policy.

This chapter contributes to the conversation of food as a site and strategy of resistance by offering a historical view of communities of color who engage food production and distribution for self-sufficiency, self-determination, and community wellness in their efforts toward food security and sovereignty. Although this chapter has concentrated on Black and Latinx communities, there are many examples of other communities of color who have historically engaged agricultural resistance strategies to participate in the food system for liberation. Communities of color have organized against the economic exploitation of the capitalist industrial food system, which stands between consumers and healthy, affordable, and culturally appropriate food, and relies on the exploitation of food and farm workers. In creating urban agricultural projects and demanding land access, just wages and working conditions, members of these underserved communities are creating opportunities for justice that are rooted in food production, distribution, and consumption. The outcomes increase their access to healthy food in ways that counter the typical resource extraction model and create resource regeneration that benefits the community through their involvement and creation of alternative food systems. The theoretical frame of CACR and the subsequent strategies of commons as praxis, prefigurative politics, and economic autonomy, help us see how these communities challenge the idea that agriculture is oppressive, advancing an understanding of agriculture as essential to healthy communities and racial justice.

Acknowledgements Special thanks to Jane Collins and Luis Sánchez Artú for their valuable feedback.

References

Abron, J. M. (1998). 'Serving the people': The survival programs of the Black Panther Party. In C. E. Jones (Ed.) *The Black Panther Party [Reconsidered]* (pp. 177–192). Baltimore, MD: Black Classic Press.

Ali, O. (2010). *In the lion's mouth: Black populism in the New South, 1886–1900*. Jackson, MI: University of Mississippi Press.

Alkon, A. H. (2012). *Black, white, and green: Farmers markets, race, and the green economy*. Athens, GA: University of Georgia Press.

Alkon, A. H. (2014). Food justice and the challenge to neoliberalism. *Gastronomica: The Journal of Critical Food Studies, 14*(2), 27–40.

Alkon, A. H., & Agyeman, J. (Eds.). (2011). *Cultivating food justice: Race, class, and sustainability*. Cambridge, MA: MIT Press.

Alkon, A. H., & Mares, T. M. (2012). Food sovereignty in U.S. food movements: Radical visions and neoliberal constraints. *Agriculture and Human Values, 29*(3), 347–359.

Alkon, A. H., & McCullen, C. G. (2011). Whiteness and farmers markets: Performances, perpetuations…contestations? *Antipode, 43*(4), 937–959.

Ammons, S. (2014). Shining a light in dark places: Raising up the work of southern women of color in the food system. *Center for Social Inclusion*. Retrieved July 14, 2017. http://www.centerforsocialinclusion.org/wp-content/uploads/2014/07/Shining-a-Light-in-Dark-Places-A-Policy-Brief.pdf.

Anguelovski, I. (2015). Alternative food provision conflicts in cities: Contesting food privilege, injustice, and whiteness in Jamaica Plain, Boston. *Geoforum, 58*, 184–194.

Ayazi, H., & Elsheikh, E. (2015). The U.S. farm bill: Corporate power and structural racialization in the United States food system. *Haas Institute for a Fair and Inclusive Society*. Retrieved July 14, 2017. http://haasinstitute.berkeley.edu/farm-bill-report-corporate-power-and-structural-racialization-us-food-system.

Baker, D., & Chappelle, D. (2012). Health status and needs of Latino dairy farmworkers in Vermont. *Journal of Agromedicine, 17*(3), 277–287.

Barickman, B. J. (1994). 'A bit of land, which they call Roça': Slave provision grounds in the Bahian Recôncavo, 1780–1860. *Hispanic American Historical Review, 74*(4), 649–687.

Barker, C., Francois, A., Goodman, R., & Hussain, E. (2012). Unshared bounty: How structural racism contributes to the creation and persistence of food deserts. *Racial Justice Project*. Retrieved July 14, 2017. http://www.racialjusticeproject.com/wp-content/uploads/sites/30/2012/06/NYLS-Food-Deserts-Report.pdf.

Bauer, M., & Ramirez, M. (2010). Injustice on our plates: Immigrant women in the U.S. food industry. *Southern Poverty Law Center*. Retrieved July 14, 2017. https://www.splcenter.org/20101108/injustice-our-plates.

Bauer, M., & Stewart, M. (2013). Close to slavery: Guestworker programs in the United States. *Southern Poverty Law Center*. Retrieved July 14, 2017. https://www.splcenter.org/20130218/close-slavery-guestworker-programs-united-states.

Biewener, C. (2016). Paid work, unpaid work, and economic viability in alternative food initiatives: Reflections from three Boston urban agriculture endeavors. *Journal of Agriculture, Food Systems, and Community Development, 6*(2), 35–53.

Billings, D., & Cabbil, L. (2011). Food justice: What's race got to do with it? *Race/Ethnicity: Multidisciplinary Global Contexts, 5*(1), 103–112.

Block, D. R., Chávez, N., Allen, E., & Ramirez, D. (2012). Food sovereignty, urban food access, and food activism: Contemplating the connections through examples from Chicago. *Agriculture and Human Values, 29*(2), 203–215.

Blue Bird Jernigan, V., Salvatore, A. L., Styne, D. M., & Winkleby, M. (2012). Addressing food insecurity in a Native American reservation using community-based participatory research. *Health Education Research, 27* (4), 645–655.

Bon Appétit Management Company Foundation and United Farm Workers. (2011). *Inventory of farmworker issues and protections in the United States*. Retrieved July 14, 2017. https://www.oxfamamerica.org/static/oa3/files/inventory-of-farmworker-issues-and-protections-in-the-usa.pdf.

Bowens, N. (2015). *The color of food: Stories of race, resilience and farming*. Gabriola Island, BC, Canada: New Society Publishers.

Bradley, K., & Herrera, H. (2016). Decolonizing food justice: Naming, resisting, and researching colonizing forces in the movement. *Antipode, 48*(1), 97–114.

Calo, A., & De Master, K. T. (2016). After the incubator: Factors impeding land access along the path from farmworker to proprietor. *Journal of Agriculture, Food Systems, and Community Development, 6*(2), 111–127.

Carney, J. A. (2004). 'With grains in her hair': Rice in colonial Brazil. *Slavery & Abolition, 25*(1), 1–27.

Carney, M. (2012). 'Food security' and 'food sovereignty': What frameworks are best suited for social equity in food systems? *Journal of Agriculture, Food Systems, and Community Development, 2*(2), 71–88.

Carpenter, S. (2012). The USDA discrimination cases: Pigford, in re Black farmers, Keepseagle, Garcia, and Love. *Drake Journal of Agricultural Law, 17*, 1.

Carrasquillo, N. (2011). Race and ethnicity from the point of view of farm workers in the food system. *Race/Ethnicity: Multidisciplinary Global Contexts, 5* (1), 121–131.

Center for Social Inclusion. (2013). *Immediate policy opportunities for an equitable and sustainable food system*. Retrieved July 14, 2017. http://www.

centerforsocialinclusion.org/publication/immediate-policy-opportunities-for-an-equitable-and-sustainable-food-system/.

Chavez, C. (1972). *Statement by Cesar Chavez at the end of his 24-day fast for justice*. http://chavez.cde.ca.gov/ModelCurriculum/Teachers/Lessons/Resources/Documents/EXR1_Cesar_E_Chavez_Statements_on_Fasts.pdf.

Chavez, L. R. (1990). Coresidence and resistance: Strategies for survival among undocumented Mexicans and Central Americans in the United States. *Urban Anthropology and Studies of Cultural Systems and World Economic Development, 19*(1/2), 31–61.

Cheng, L., & Bonacich, E. (Eds.). (1984). *Labor immigration under capitalism: Asian workers in the United States before World War II*. Berkeley, CA: University of California Press.

Clendenning, J., Dressler, W. H., & Richards, C. (2015). Food justice or food sovereignty? Understanding the rise of urban food movements in the USA. *Agriculture and Human Values, 33*(1), 165–177.

Cleveland, D. A. (1998). Indian agriculture, United States agriculture, and sustainable agriculture: Science and advocacy. *American Indian Culture and Research Journal, 22*(3), 13–29.

Daniel, C. E. (1982). *Bitter harvest: A history of California farmworkers, 1870–1941*. Berkeley, CA: University of California Press.

Daniel, P. (2013). *Dispossession: Discrimination against African American farmers in the age of civil rights*. Chapel Hill, NC: University of North Carolina Press.

Dann, M. (1974). Black populism: A study of the Colored Farmers' Alliance through 1891. *The Journal of Ethnic Studies, 2*(3), 58–71.

Downey, L. (2015). *Inequality, democracy, and the environment*. New York, NY: NYU Press.

Elsheikh, E. (2016). Race and corporate power in the U.S. food system: Examining the farm bill. *Food First, 2*, 1–7.

Estabrook, B. (2012). *Tomatoland: How modern industrial agriculture destroyed our most alluring fruit*. Kansas City, MO: Andrews McMeel Publishing.

Evich, H. B., Boudreau, C., & Hopkinson, J. (2017). Trump's budget takes aim at SNAP, crop insurance. *Politico*. Retrieved July 14, 2017. http://www.politico.com/story/2017/05/23/trumps-budget-takes-aim-at-snap-crop-insurance-238724.

Fang, M., Buttenheim, A. M., Havassy, J., & Gollust, S. E. (2013). 'It's not an "if you build it they will come" type of scenario': Stakeholder perspectives on farmers' markets as a policy solution to food access in low-income neighborhoods. *Journal of Hunger & Environmental Nutrition, 8*(1), 39–60.

Feder, J., & Cowan, T. (2013). Garcia v. Vilsack: A policy and legal analysis of a USDA discrimination case. *Congressional Research Service*. Retrieved July 14, 2017. http://www.nationalaglawcenter.org/wp-content/uploads/assets/crs/R40988.pdf.

Flora, J. L., Emery, M., Thompson, D., Prado-Meza, C. M., & Flora, C. B. (2012). New immigrants in local food systems: Two Iowa cases. *International Journal of Sociology of Agriculture & Food, 19*(1), 119–134.

Folke, C. (2006). Resilience: The emergence of a perspective for social-ecological systems analyses. *Global Environmental Change, 16*(3), 253–267.

Gates, G. J. (2014). Food insecurity and SNAP (food stamps) participation in LGBT communities. *Williams Institute: UCLA School of Law*. Retrieved July 14, 2017. http://williamsinstitute.law.ucla.edu/wp-content/uploads/Food-Insecurity-and-SNAP-Participation-in-the-LGBT-Community.pdf.

Giancatarino, A., & Noor, S. (2014). Building the case for racial equity in the food system. *Center for Social Inclusion*. Retrieved July 14, 2017. http://centerforsocialinclusion.org/wp-content/uploads/2014/07/Building-the-Case-for-Racial-Equity-in-the-Food-System.pdf.

Gilbert, J., Sharp, G., & Sindy Felin, M. (2002). The loss and persistence of Black-owned farms and farmland: A review of the research literature and its implications. *Southern Rural Sociology, 18*(2), 1–30.

Grey, S., & Patel, R. (2015). Food sovereignty as decolonization: Some contributions from Indigenous movements to food system and development politics. *Agriculture and Human Values, 32*(3), 431–444.

Guthman, J. (2008a). Neoliberalism and the making of food politics in California. *Geoforum, 39*(3), 1171–1183.

Guthman, J. (2008b). "If they only knew": Color blindness and universalism in California alternative food institutions. *The Professional Geographer, 60*(3), 387–397.

Guthman, J. (2008c). Bringing good food to others: Investigating the subjects of alternative food practice. *Cultural Geographies, 15*(4), 431–447.

Hagan, E., & Rubin, V. (2013). Economic and community development outcomes of healthy food retail. *Policy Link*. Retrieved July 14, 2017. http://www.rwjf.org/content/dam/farm/reports/reports/2013/rwjf406490.

Harrison, J. L., & Lloyd, S. E. (2013). New jobs, new workers, and new inequalities: Explaining employers' roles in occupational segregation by nativity and race. *Social Problems, 60*(3), 281–301.

Havens, E., & Roman-Alcalá, A. (2016). Land for food justice? AB 551 and structural change. *Food First / Institute for Food and Development Policy 8*. Retrieved July 14, 2017 (https://foodfirst.org/wp-content/uploads/2016/06/UrbanAgS2016_Final.pdf).

Henson, Z., & Munsey, G. (2014). Race, culture, and practice: Segregation and local food in Birmingham, Alabama. *Urban Geography, 35*(7), 998–1019.

Hill, R. A., Garvey, M., & Universal Negro Improvement Association. (2011). *The Marcus Garvey and Universal Negro Improvement Association papers, Vol. XI: The Caribbean Diaspora, 1910–1920*. Duke University Press.

Hinson, W. R., & Robinson, E. (2008). 'We didn't get nothing:' The plight of Black farmers. *Journal of African American Studies, 12*(3), 283–302.

Hjalmarson, E., Bunn, R., Cohen, A., Terbasket, E., & Gahman, L. (2015). Race, food, and borders: Situating migrant struggle in the Okanagan Valley, British Columbia. *Journal of Agriculture, Food Systems, and Community Development, 5*(4), 77–82.

Holmes, S. M. (2013). *Fresh fruit, broken bodies: Migrant farmworkers in the United States.* Berkeley, CA: University of California Press.

Holt-Giménez, E. (2011). Note about Food First Backgrounder 'Grabbing the Food Deserts'. Retrieved July 14, 2017. https://foodfirst.org/publication/grabbing-the-food-deserts/.

Holt-Giménez, E. (2015). Racism and capitalism: Dual challenges for the food movement. *Journal of Agriculture, Food Systems, and Community Development, 5*(2), 23–25.

Holt-Giménez, E., & Shattuck, A. (2011). Food crises, food regimes and food movements: Rumblings of reform or tides of transformation? *The Journal of Peasant Studies, 38*(1), 109–144.

Holt-Giménez, E., & Wang, Y. (2011). Reform or transformation? The pivotal role of food justice in the US Food Movement. *Race/Ethnicity: Multidisciplinary Global Contexts, 5*(1), 83–102.

Jarosz, L. (2014). Comparing food security and food sovereignty discourses. *Dialogues in Human Geography, 4*(2), 168–181.

Jones, P., & Bhatia, R. (2011). Supporting equitable food systems through food assistance at farmers' markets. *American Journal of Public Health, 101*(5), 781–783.

Justicia Migrante. (2017). Updated press release on recent ICE dententions." *Migrant Justice/Justicia Migrante.* Retrieved July 14, 2017. https://migrantjustice.net/news/updated-press-release-on-recent-ice-detentions.

Kepkiewicz, L., Chrobok, M., Whetung, M., Cahuas, M., Gill, J., Walker, S., & Wakefield, S. (2015). Beyond inclusion: Toward an anti-colonial food justice praxis. *Journal of Agriculture, Food Systems, and Community Development, 5*(4), 99–104.

Kirkby, R. J. (2011). 'The revolution will not be televised': Community activism and the Black Panther Party, 1966–1971. *Canadian Review of American Studies, 41*(1), 25–62.

Larsen, K., & Gilliland, J. (2009). A farmers' market in a food desert: Evaluating impacts on the price and availability of healthy food. *Health & Place, 15*(4), 1158–1162.

Leslie, I. S. (2017). Improving farmers markets and challenging neoliberalism in Argentina. *Agriculture and Human Values, 34*(3), 729–742.

Leslie, I. S. (2019). Queer farmland: Land access strategies for small-scale agriculture.

Levy, J. E., & Chavez, C. (1975). *Cesar Chavez: Autobiography of La Causa.* Minneapolis, MN: University of Minnesota Press.

Linder, M. (1987). Farm workers and the Fair Labor Standards Act: Racial discrimination in the New Deal. *Texas Law Review, 65,* 1335–1393.

Loo, C. (2014). Towards a more participative definition of food justice. *Journal of Agricultural and Environmental Ethics, 27*(5), 787–809.

MacAuley, L. E., & Niewolny, K. L. (2016). Situating on-farm apprenticeships within the alternative agrifood movement: Labor and social justice implications. *Journal of Agriculture, Food Systems, and Community Development, 6*(2), 195–223.

Masten, A. S. (2007). Resilience in developing systems: Progress and promise as the fourth wave rises. *Development and Psychopathology, 19*(3), 921–930.

Meek, D., & Tarlau, R. (2015). Critical food systems education and the question of race. *Journal of Agriculture, Food Systems, and Community Development, 5*(4), 131–135.

Miller, F. J. (1972). Black protest and white leadership: A note on the Colored Rarmers' Alliance. *Phylon (1960-), 33*(2), 169–174.

Minkoff-Zern, L.-A. (2014a). Knowing 'Good Food': Immigrant knowledge and the racial politics of farmworker food insecurity. *Antipode, 46*(5), 1190–1204.

Minkoff-Zern, L.-A. (2014b). Challenging the agrarian imaginary: Farmworker-led food movements and the potential for farm labor justice. *Human Geography, 7*(1), 85–101.

Minkoff-Zern, L. -A., Peluso, N., Sowerwine, J., & Getz, C. (2011). Race and regulation: Asian immigrants in California agriculture. In A. H. Alkon & J. Agyeman (Eds.), *Cultivating food justice: Race, class, and sustainability* (pp. 65–86). Cambridge, MA: MIT Press.

Mitchell, D. (2010). Battle/fields: Braceros, agribusiness, and the violent reproduction of the California agricultural landscape during World War II. *Journal of Historical Geography, 36*(2), 143–156.

Mize, R. L., & Swords, A. C. S. (2010). *Consuming Mexican labor: From the Bracero program to NAFTA.* Toronto, Ontario, Canada: University of Toronto Press.

Mohai, P., Pellow, D., & Roberts, J. T. (2009). Environmental justice. *Annual Review of Environment and Resources, 34*(1), 405–430.

Moore, K., & Swisher, M. E. (2015). The food movement: Growing white privilege, diversity, or empowerment? *Journal of Agriculture, Food Systems, and Community Development, 5*(4), 115–119.

Morales, A. (2011). Growing food *and* justice: Dismantling racism through sustainable food systems. In A. H. Alkon & J. Agyeman (Eds.), *Cultivating food justice: Race, class, and sustainability* (pp. 149–176). Cambridge, MA: The MIT Press.

Morales, A., & Kettles, G. (2009). Healthy food outside: Farmers' markets, taco trucks, and sidewalk fruit vendors. *The Journal of Contemporary Health Law and Policy, 26*(1), 20–48.

Myers, G. P. (2015). Decolonizing a food system: Freedom Farmers' Market as a place for resistance and analysis. *Journal of Agriculture, Food Systems, and Community Development, 5*(4), 149–152.

Nembhard, J. G. (2014). *Collective courage: A history of African American cooperative economic thought and practice.* University Park, PA: Penn State University Press.

Norgaard, K. M., Reed, R., & Van Horn, C. (2011). A continuing legacy: Institutional racism, hunger, and nutritional justice on the Klamath. In A. H. Alkon & J. Agyeman (Eds.), *Cultivating food justice: Race, class, and sustainability* (pp. 23–46). Cambridge, MA: MIT Press.

Patel, R. (2011). Survival pending revolution: What the Black Panthers can teach the US Food Movement. In *Food movements unite!: Strategies to transform our food systems* (pp. 115–137). Oakland, CA: Food First Books.

Pellow, D. N. (2007). *Resisting global toxics: Transnational movements for environmental justice.* Cambridge, MA: MIT Press.

Peña, O. A. (2015). Diversity education at land-grant universities from the perspective of a female student of color. *Journal of Agriculture, Food Systems, and Community Development, 5*(4), 121–124.

Pilgeram, R. (2012). Social sustainability and the white, nuclear family: Constructions of gender, race, and class at a Northwest farmers' market. *Race, Gender & Class, 19*(1/2), 37-60.

Potorti, M. (2014). Feeding revolution: The Black Panther Party and the politics of food. *Radical Teacher, 98,* 43–50.

Radel, C., Schmook, B., & McCandless, S. (2010). Environment, transnational labor migration, and gender: Case studies from Southern Yucatán, Mexico and Vermont, USA. *Population and Environment, 32*(2–3), 177–197.

Ramírez, M. M. (2015). The elusive inclusive: Black food geographies and racialized food spaces. *Antipode, 47*(3), 748–769.

Ramirez, T. L., & Blay, Z. (2016). Why people are using the term 'Latinx'. *The Huffington Post.* Retrieved July 14, 2017. http://www.huffingtonpost.com/entry/why-people-are-using-the-term-latinx_us_57753328e4b0cc0fa136a159).

Reynolds, K. (2015). Disparity despite diversity: Social injustice in New York City's urban agriculture system. *Antipode, 47*(1), 240–259.

Rice, J. S. (2015). Privilege and exclusion at the farmers market: Findings from a survey of shoppers. *Agriculture and Human Values, 32*(1), 21–29.

Rodriguez, M. S. (2011). *The Tejano Diaspora: Mexican Americanism and ethnic politics in Texas and Wisconsin.* Chapel Hill, NC: The University of North Carolina Press.

Roman-Alcalá, A. (2015). Concerning the unbearable whiteness of urban farming. *Journal of Agriculture, Food Systems, and Community Development, 5*(4), 179–181.

Satin-Hernandez, E., & Robinson, L. (2015). A community engagement case study of the Somerville mobile farmers' market. *Journal of Agriculture, Food Systems, and Community Development, 5*(4), 95–98.

Sbicca, J. (2012). Growing food justice by planting an anti-oppression foundation: Opportunities and obstacles for a budding social movement. *Agriculture and Human Values, 29*(4), 455–466.

Sbicca, J., & Myers, J. S. (2017). Food justice racial projects: Fighting racial neoliberalism from the Bay to the Big Apple. *Environmental Sociology, 3*(1), 30–41.

Schupp, J. L. (2017). Cultivating better food access? The role of farmers' markets in the U.S. Local Food Movement. *Rural Sociology, 82*(2), 318–348.

Scott, J. C., & Tria Kerkvliet, B. J. (Eds.). (1986). *Everyday forms of peasant resistance in South-east Asia.* London: Routledge.

Short, A., Guthman, J., & Raskin, S. (2007). Food deserts, oases, or mirages? Small markets and community food security in the San Francisco Bay Area. *Journal of Planning Education and Research, 26*(3), 352–364.

Slocum, R. (2006). Anti-racist practice and the work of community food organizations. *Antipode, 38*(2), 327–349.

Slocum, R. (2007). Whiteness, space and alternative food practice. *Geoforum, 38*(3), 520–533.

Slocum, R. (2008). Thinking race through corporeal feminist theory: Divisions and intimacies at the Minneapolis farmers' market. *Social and Cultural Geography, 9*(8), 849–869.

Slocum, R., Cadieux, K., & Blumberg, R. (2016). Solidarity, space, and race: Toward geographies of agrifood justice. *Justice Spatiale/Spatial Justice, 9.*

Tomich, D. W. (2016). *Slavery in the circuit of sugar: Martinique and the world-economy, 1830–1848.* Albany, NY: State University of New York Press.

Valerio-Jiménez, O. (2016). The U.S.–Mexico War. *Oxford Research Encyclopedia of American History.* Retrieved July 14, 2017. http://americanhistory.oxfordre.com/view/10.1093/acrefore/9780199329175.001.0001/acrefore-9780199329175-e-23.

Vanderbeck, R. M. (2006). Vermont and the imaginative geographies of American whiteness. *Annals of the Association of American Geographers, 96*(3), 641–659.

Vermont Sustainable Jobs Fund. (2013). *Farm to plate strategic plan.* Retrieved July 14, 2017. http://www.vtfarmtoplate.com/plan/.

Vernon, R. V. (2015). A Native perspective: Food is more than consumption. *Journal of Agriculture, Food Systems, and Community Development, 5*(4), 137–142.

Wald, N., & Hill, D. P. (2016). 'Rescaling' alternative food systems: From food security to food sovereignty. *Agriculture and Human Values, 33*(1), 203–213.

Walker, R. E., Keane, C. R., & Burke, J. G. (2010). Disparities and access to healthy food in the United States: A review of food deserts literature. *Health & Place, 16*(5), 876–884.

Walker, B., & Salt, D. (2012). *Resilience thinking: Sustaining ecosystems and people in a changing world*. Washington DC: Island Press.

Wang, Y., Holt-Giménez, E., & Shattuck, A. (2011). Grabbing the food deserts: Large-scale land acquisitions and the expansion of retail monopolies. *Food First Backgrounder, 17*(1).

White, M. M. (2010). Shouldering responsibility for the delivery of human rights: A case study of the D-town farmers of Detroit. *Race/Ethnicity: Multidisciplinary Global Contexts, 3*(2), 189–211.

White, M. M. (2011a). Sisters of the soil: Urban gardening as resistance in Detroit. *Race/Ethnicity: Multidisciplinary Global Contexts, 5*(1), 13–28.

White, M. M. (2011b). D-town farm: African American resistance to food insecurity and the transformation of Detroit. *Environmental Practice, 13*(4), 406–417.

White, M. M. (2018). *Freedom farmers: Agricultural resistance and the Black Freedom Movement*. Chapel Hill, NC: University of North Carolina Press.

Williams, J. M., & Holt-Giménez, E. (Eds.). (2017). *Land justice: Re-imagining land, food, and the commons in the United States*. Oakland, CA: Food First Books.

Young, C. R., Aquilante J.L., Solomon S., Colby L., Kawinzi M.A., Uy N., & Mallya G. (2013). Improving fruit and vegetable consumption among low-income customers at farmers markets: Philly Food Bucks, Philadelphia, Pennsylvania, 2011. *Preventing Chronic Disease, 10*.

Zitcer, A. (2015). Food co-ops and the paradox of exclusivity. *Antipode, 47*(3), 812–828.

Bureaucratic Capitalism, Mass Incarceration and Race and Ethnicity in America

20

Karen Manges Douglas, Gideon Sjoberg, Rogelio Sáenz and David G. Embrick

Contents

Abstract

Much scholarly attention has focused on the negative aspects of mass incarceration and rightly so. However, we know of no one that has paid attention to the role of large-scale organizations (or the millions of people they employ) that profit from or derive their livelihood off of mass incarceration and ancillary industries. We argue that the US system of mass incarceration is foundational to the reconfigured post-industrial economy. Millions of Americans, indeed entire communities, are dependent upon the millions of convicts and ex-convicts for their very sustenance. Every year, universities across the US graduate more than 60,000 students with majors in Homeland Security and Law Enforcement. These "controllogy" disciplines are perfecting the science of keeping people under control. Furthermore, race and racism undergird this system. Residents of highly policed "million dollar block" neighborhoods characterized by failing schools, low rates of home ownership, and limited access to credit, fuel the now multi-generational school-to-prison pipeline. Consequently, society has grown dependent upon black and brown incarcerated bodies to maintain a significant

K. M. Douglas (✉)
Department of Sociology, Sam Houston State University, Huntsville Texas, TX, USA
e-mail: KMD007@shsu.edu

G. Sjoberg
Department of Sociology, University of Texas at Austin, Austin, TX, USA
e-mail: gsjoberg@utexas.edu

R. Sáenz
Dean of the College of Public Policy, University of Texas at San Antonio, San Antonio, TX, USA
e-mail: rogelio.saenz@utsa.edu

D. G. Embrick
Department of Sociology and African Studies, University of Connecticut, Storrs, CT, USA
e-mail: david.embrick@uconn.edu

© Springer International Publishing AG, part of Springer Nature 2018
P. Batur and J. R. Feagin (eds.), *Handbook of the Sociology of Racial and Ethnic Relations*,
Handbooks of Sociology and Social Research, https://doi.org/10.1007/978-3-319-76757-4_20

part of the US economy. We conclude the chapter by advancing a counter-system to this system of mass incarceration that allows us to reverse course.

In a stump speech during the 2016 U.S. presidential campaign, candidate Hillary Clinton recited an oft-repeated statistic about the United States comprising 5% of the world's population but one quarter of the world's incarcerated population. The *Washington Post* verified the accuracy of the statement within a few percentage points (Lee 2015). While this statistic has become fairly commonplace, the full ramifications of this transformation in US society have remained unexamined. For example, while there is an extensive body of research on the negative consequences to those imprisoned, very little attention has been given to the beneficiaries of this expanded prison state or how the architecture of the prison industrial complex cuts through a broad swath of American institutions. This paper represents our effort to reveal the centrality of the expanded penal system to the system of stratification and the overall functioning of the U.S. economy. In a perverse way today's prison industrial complex is yesterday's Works Progress Administration (WPA).

Our purpose is to highlight the importance of the prison industrial complex in shaping the American economy and to underscore the need for an alternative political economy. In order to do this, we advance several thoughts. First, today's prison industrial complex is a product of the economic, social and political transformation associated with market-oriented policies over the past forty-plus years. Second, race and racism are defining features in present-day mass incarceration. Third, few social scientists recognize the importance of knowledge in the development and advancement of the modern-world political economy, a perspective which we seek to rectify. Lastly, we advance a multi-faceted counter system that will serve to buttress the population as we transition away from the prison economy and reverse course from the undemocratic path we have been traveling.

The sociological foundation from which we analyze the social organization and structure of the prison industrial complex is different from many social scientists. Sociologists rarely reckon with the fundamental role that knowledge plays, much less the types of support necessary for knowledge proliferation, in modern society. On this front, we are influenced by the work of economic historian, Mokyr (2002, 2005) and his explication on the role of knowledge to modern life. As Mokyr makes clear, the growth of scientific knowledge in Western Europe not only predates the industrial era but also is an essential element in its development. Furthermore, the keys to knowledge development and proliferation happened prior to and operated independent of the market economy. Europe… "discover[ed] the fundamental processes through which knowledge can create more knowledge and creat[ed] the institutional environment that facilitated these processes, the Industrial enlightenment unlocked the path to cumulative growth in the West" (Mokyr 2005, p. 324). The institutional arrangements that gave rise to the growth of scientific knowledge including open access, transparency, scrutiny, debate, criticism in place of closed knowledge systems like trade guilds and secret societies.

Further, we are cognizant of the dominant role that large-scale organizations, public and private, have in shaping institutional priorities. Some years back, Gideon Sjoberg spelled out the defining features of world bureaucratic capitalism.[1] This serves as the backdrop for this paper. As Sjoberg (1999) points out, large-scale organizations are the "engines that run modern bureaucratic capitalism" (43–44). Over the past forty years our institutional priorities have changed. As a result, the corporate sector is both closer to the state and further away as their multinational reach extends well beyond the state's territorial boundary. In particular, the ascent of multinational corporations coincides with a confluence of events involving the re-alignment with free-market principles that favor business and market-oriented solutions

---

[1]We only sketch Sjoberg's elaboration of bureaucratic capitalism. Refer to Abu-Lughod's *Sociology for the Twenty-first Century* (1999) for complete details.

including financial and industry deregulation. Significant advances in telecommunications and computation further propelled the growth of "corporate globalization" (Ruggie 2013: xv). Computerization and the development of the Internet allowed multinational corporations near instant access to capital and the ability to easily and cost-effectively transfer capital around the world (Massey 2007). Global trade was further institutionalized by the development of the World Trade Organization. Policies adopted by the World Bank and the International Monetary Fund solidified a global operating platform. The results are a greatly enhanced corporate bureaucratic power the world over.

The adoption of market-oriented solutions that promulgated financial and business deregulation prompted a contraction to the welfare state. A transference of responsibilities previously borne by government and business onto individuals in the name of market-efficiency (what Hacker (2008) dubbed "The Great Risk Shift") has contributed to the growing income and wealth inequality, diminishing life chances, and the rise in debt-saddled young people who have grown increasingly pessimistic about matching, much less exceeding, their parents standard of living. Correspondingly, these transformations have aided and abetted the growth of the prison industrial complex that now serves as a major economic driver of the US economy. While we devolved institutional supports for the social safety net we grew the institutional capacity for mass incarceration.

The paper is divided into two sections. We begin the first section with a brief elaboration on the role of knowledge in society before summarizing the major transformations of the economy and the growth of the prison industrial complex. We note the salient features in the rise of mass incarceration highlighting the role of race and racism. Given the substantial state and federal budget allocated for corrections, the prison industrial complex is now mainstream with most major institutions involved in the maintenance of the carceral system. While a complete accounting is beyond this paper, we provide key examples to illustrate the breadth of the prison industrial complex in American society. The second section offers recommendations to rectify the undemocratic turns this nation has taken over the past forty years including ways of depriving the system of mass incarceration its fuel. Here we build upon Feagin and colleagues' (2014) liberation sociology—an expansion and operationalization of Sjoberg and Cain's (1971) counter system. We make an extended case for both a guaranteed annual income and significant investments in education specifically targeting the poor. We also argue for the need to revisit the legal structure of corporations so as to advance the broader cause of human rights and democracy over the much narrower shareholders' interests as it stands now.

We should note that we introduce many ideas in delineating the major transformations to American society and its consequences. We follow a path traveled by others in our focus on the state and market nexus. However, we are somewhat unique in the incorporation into our analysis the centrality of knowledge for social and economic advancements. This element, while acknowledged by economic historians including Mokyr (2002), Cowen (2011) and Gordon (2016), remains under-theorized in sociology. By the end of the paper, we link these ideas in a fashion that we hope are both coherent and compelling. At a minimum, this paper is a call to action for sociologists to better understand the role of knowledge in an advanced economic order that is being undermined by the development of the prison industrial complex—the US's response to the changing world economy and for which we remain the undisputed world leader.

20.1 Moving Away from the New Deal

At the apex of the New Deal era all segments of society were growing with the fastest growth occurring at the bottom of the income distribution (Stiglitz 2015). One of the New Deal era's major achievement was creating a mixed economy that married government and market in ways that served "to overcome failures of the market and to translate economic growth into broad advances in human well-being—from better health and education to greater knowledge and opportunity" (Hacker and Pierson 2016: 7). This guiding philosophy promoted broad-based policies from which all sectors of society would benefit. Social turmoil of the 1960s gave way to economic turmoil in the 1970s and the philosophy began to unravel. The federal bureaucracy began to be seen as part of the problem rather than the solution. Keynesian economics came under fire; different ideas—market ideas, supported by neo-classical economists including Milton Friedman, George Stigler and other Chicago School economists–entered economic and political discourse (Hacker and Pierson 2016). The election of Ronald Reagan in 1980 put the adoption of market-oriented policies on a fast track. Running on a "Let's Make America Great Again" platform, Reagan declared that "...government is not the solution to our problem, government is our problem" (Reagan 1981). During his two administrations, Reagan worked to promote market-oriented policies and diminish the role of the federal government on social welfare programs.

Financial deregulation begun under the Carter administration escalated in the 1980s under Reagan. Thrifts were allowed to operate more like banks, and banks more like investment houses. In addition to rules being relaxed, regulatory oversight was also eased (called forbearance) allowing the industry broader discretion to engage in a wide array of practices.[2] In short order, the financialization of the economy in which finance, private equity and investment decisions dominate organizational decisions over direct business investments. As Mason (2015) explains, there is a

> ... strong empirical relationship of corporate cash flow and borrowing to productive corporate investment has disappeared in the last 30 years and has been replaced with corporate funds and shareholder payouts. Whereas firms once borrowed to invest and improve their long-term performance, they now borrow to enrich their investors in the short-run. This is the result of legal, managerial, and structural changes that resulted from the shareholder revolution of the 1980s. Under the older, managerial, model, more money coming into a firm—from sales or from borrowing—typically meant more money spent on fixed investment. In the new rentier-dominated model, more money coming in means more money flowing out to shareholders in the form of dividends and stock buybacks.

With regulations relaxed, the financial industry began to consolidate its power. Large organizations now dominate the financial industry. Three American banks (J. P. MorganChase, Bank of America and Wells Fargo) rank among the world's top 10 largest banks each having more than one trillion dollars of assets (Martin 2017). Today a handful of banks control most of the country's banking assets (Baradaran 2015). Relaxed financial regulations have transformed the creditor-debtor relationship (Ingham 2004). The Federal Reserves' preoccupation with inflation (rather than employment) has resulted in "growing indebtedness of the poor and social polarization" (Ingham 2004:158). Because credit is the avenue to wealth, those without are excluded and remain at the bottom of the stratification ladder (Baradaran 2015).

These economic transformations extend beyond the United States. As Gilpin explains, "Since the mid 1970s, financial deregulation and the creation of new financial instruments such as derivatives, and technological advances have contributed to a much more highly integrated international financial system" (Gilpin 2001: Kindle Location 250). Stiglitz notes growing

---

[2]See Timothy T. Taylor's "What Financial Risks are Lurking?" for discussions on the risks confronting financial institutions in the online blog, *Conversable Economist* (December 6, 2017)

income inequality in Europe and Japan. Nevertheless, the United States is by far "winning the race to be the most unequal country" among developed economies (White 2015: 4). Between 1980 and 2013, the median income for the top 1% increased by 142%. Median household income, on the other hand, only increased by 9% and this due to workers working more hours (White 2015). Put another way, for every dollar gained by the bottom 90%, the top 0.01% gained $18,000 (Girdner 2007).

The social contract between business and labor has also been redefined. A labor force that is "flexible" (easily hired and fired) is now the norm. Current labor laws, endorsed by the federal government, incentivize employers' use of contingent labor: "The use of independent contractors and part-time, temporary, seasonal and leased workers has expanded tremendously in recent years. The Commission views this change both as a *healthy* development and a cause for concern" (italics added, Department of Labor n. d.). The heavy use of contract soldiers during the Gulf War provides one example that also raises moral questions about outsourcing war to private mercenaries (Sjoberg 2005). That contingent workers are drawn from vulnerable segments of society; their use grows the gap between high and low wage workers ultimately increasing insecurity for all workers are the identified 'causes for concern' (Department of Labor n.d.).

Knowledge is an essential but taken for granted element to modern society. Scientific and technological knowledge were key to the development of the industrial revolution and advances in public welfare and remain critical to these developments today. Piketty (2014), discussing China's remarkable economic growth and inroads into reducing inequality, acknowledges the importance of knowledge acquisition in this process:

> Consider first the mechanisms pushing toward convergence, that is, toward reduction and compression of inequalities. The main forces for convergence are the diffusion of knowledge and investments in training and skills. The law of supply and demand, as well as the mobility of capital and labor … may always tend toward convergence as well, but the influence of this

economic law is less powerful than the diffusion of knowledge and skill and is frequently ambiguous or contradictory in its implications. Knowledge and skill diffusion is the key to overall productivity growth as well as the reduction of inequality both within and between countries …. The technological convergence process may be abetted by open borders for trade, but is fundamentally a process of the diffusion and sharing of knowledge—the public good par excellence—rather than a market mechanism (2014: 21).

Hacker and Pierson (2016) remind us that market mechanisms fall short in a number of areas including in the provision of education, infrastructure support and in basic scientific research. Key aspects of the public welfare including health and knowledge and its nurturance and transmission are not amenable to market solutions. Educating children, especially those marginalized by race and class, takes considerable investments of both money and time. Instead, as we detail next, monies that could have been spent on education were being diverted to grow and maintain the prison industrial complex.

20.2 The Prison Industrial Complex

Paradoxically, while Ronald Reagan ran on a platform to diminish the role of the federal government—and slashed social safety net programs extensively—his other policies greatly expanded the federal footprint including the prison industrial complex. Like Nixon, Reagan declared war on crime and drugs. He authorized sentencing modifications that lengthened prison sentences; extended the use of the death penalty to drug cases; and mandated minimum sentences for certain drug crimes. Under Reagan's watch, the incarcerated population reached the one million milestone (Kilgore 2015).

In the subsequent years, the incarceration population continued to grow with the highest rates occurring during in the 1990s. Under Clinton's watch the incarcerated population expanded at an average annual rate of 6.5% per year. Incarceration peaked in 2008 with 2,300,700 individuals locked away in state or federal prisons or jails. An additional 5 million people were under some form of community supervision (Glaze 2010).

Most prisoners are confined in one of the 1700 state prisons or 3300 local jails. Of the more than 600,000 jail inmates, 70% have not been convicted of a crime but are awaiting trial (Wagner and Rabuy 2017). The churn of inmates to ex-prisoners (and back) is enormous. One report found that "every year, 641,000 people walk out of prison gates" and "people go to jail over 11 million times each year" (Wagner and Rabuy 2017).

Still, these data do not reveal the full extent of the carceral reach as physical incarceration is but one measure. Millions more are convicted of felony offenses but serve no prison time. Additionally, there are millions more who are released from prison each year. When all are taken into account, some 19 million American adults—8% of the adult population—are either current or former felons (Shannon et al. 2017).

The focus on total number of people incarcerated obscures state-by-state variations. In 2010, estimates show that every state but one (West Virginia) registers at least 2% of its adult population as a current or former felon; and 18 states have more than 2% of their adult population with prison records; and 3 states—Alaska, California and Louisiana—tally more than 4% of their adult population as felons. Florida leads the nation with 10% of its total adult population having spent time under felony supervision (Shannon et al. 2017).

Yet, the pool from which the incarcerated originate is not random but geographically concentrated to a few neighborhoods in the major urban centers of the country. Kurgan and Cadora (2006) coin the term "Million dollar blocks" to illustrate this geographic concentration of incarceration. The term was derived from the $11 plus million dollars in incarceration costs associated with an 11-block area in Brooklyn. These maps reveal the highly imbalanced nature of mass incarceration with some neighborhoods disproportionately feeding the prison system. For example, in Houston, Texas, in 2005 10 of 88 neighborhoods were classified "super neighborhoods" with the incarceration costs totaling more than $100 million (Kurgan and Cadora 2006).

Another defining feature of mass incarceration is that it is highly racialized. Garland emphasizes that in the United States, the phenomena of mass incarceration is characterized by "the systematic imprisonment of whole groups of the population" (as quoted in Shannon et al. 2017: 1797)—in this case, whole groups of poor, uneducated, urban black men and increasingly, black women (Wacquant 2009). Historian Elizabeth Hinton (2016) notes that African Americans are more likely to be in prison or jail compared to other racial groups. The odds are 50–50 that young black urban males are in jail, in a cell in one of the thousands of state and federal prisons across the United States, or on probation or parole" (2016: 5).

A full one-third of adult African American males have a felony conviction compared to 13% of adult males overall. In almost every state in the nation, African Americans with prison records exceeded 5% of the adult population. Almost half of African American men have been arrested at least once by the time they reach 23 years of age; and for uneducated black men "incarceration has become a routine life event … more common than serving in the military or earning a college degree" (Shannon et al. 2017: 1797).

20.3 Mainstreaming the Prison Industrial Complex

Aware or not, the prison industrial complex touches every American. The networks that grew and now sustain the prison industrial complex are broad. While it is impossible to delineate every link to the prison industrial complex, we highlight key ones that help sustain the system. These include the organizations charged with designing, building, and renovating prisons; the corporations that supply the industry with food and clothing and sundries; the corporations that equip the guards with protective gear and weapons; and the institutions that supply the prison industrial complex its labor.

The last forty-plus years have been fruitful for the architecture firms, like HO+K, that design correctional facilities. "Justice buildings must be designed to advance the values and aspirations of society," declares HO+K's website (HO+K website n.d.). Building Designs + Construction identifies HOK as the top architecture firm for the government sector. The justice-related buildings that HOK has designed over the past 5 years are valued at over $3 billion. HOK has designed 2500 courtrooms and 100,000 detention and correction beds held in HOK-designed facilities. Some HOK designed projects include the Miami-Dade Children's Courthouse, San Francisco Public Safety Campus, and the Iowa State Penitentiary. HO+K employs more than 1700 people across three continents (HO+K website n.d.)

Between 2001 and 2012, correction-related construction averaged $2.8 billion per year (Kilgore 2015). Two of the largest builders are Turner Construction and Gilbane. Turner Construction, a subsidiary of German conglomerate Hochtief, employs more than 5000 people and lists annual revenue at $10 billion (Turner Construction website n.d.). Between 2005 and 2012, Turner's annual income from corrections construction was approximately $278 million annually (Kilgore 2015). Correction construction projects include the Cobb County Detention Center in Georgia, and the State of Indiana Forensic and Health Sciences Laboratories. Turner Construction also built the Arts and Architecture Addition and Renovations for Yale University, Temple University's Science, Education and Research Center, and the National Constitution Center in Philadelphia, to name just a few projects (Turner Construction website n.d.).

Gilbane Building Company, headquartered in Rhode Island, averaged $153 million annually in corrections construction (Kilgore 2015). U.S. Engineering News Record ranked Gilbane as the #3 correctional facilities builder in the United States. Gilbane employs 4000 people and tallies $4 billion in annual revenue. A few Gilbane construction projects include the Arizona State Forensic Hospital for mentally ill prisoners, the State of New Hampshire's Women's Correctional Facility, the Salinas Valley State Prison and Mental Health Facility in California. Education related Gilbane projects include the student recreation center at Bowling Green State University, the fitness complex at Arizona State University, Cal State Poly's engineering building (Gilbane website n.d.).

Prisons and jails incorporate a host of technology to monitor inmates. Multinational conglomerate 3 M makes more than PostIt Notes; they also sell a range of products including finger and palm print identification systems, house arrest tracking devices, breath alcohol testing and facial recognition devices. 3M employs over 90,000 people around the world (3M website n.d.).

The two million prisoners must also be fed, clothed and provided medical care. Bob Barker Industries (BBI) and Anchortex are two large suppliers to the prison industry. BBI proclaims it is "America's leading detention supplier" (Bob Barker website n.d.). The company supplies prisons with mattresses, bedding, clothing, and personal hygiene products. They also supply prison personnel with uniforms, handcuff holsters, riot gear, batons and shields, restraints, and metal detectors (Bob Barker Industries website n. d.). Anchortex supplies inmate uniforms, socks and underwear, footwear, discharge and release clothing, and transport clothing. Their client list extends to all branches of the military, the Department of Homeland Security, and the Department of Justice (Anchortex website n.d.).

Aramark Industries is a prominent food supplier on many college campuses. Their 270,000 employees serve more than 500 million meals annually to education, health care and sporting venues (Aramark website n.d.). Aramark also services 600 correctional institutions across the country serving more than a million meals per day to prisoners. Sodexo, a French multinational company, is another major campus food supplier that services correctional facilities. In addition to the U.S., Sodexo manages correctional facilities in Belgium, France, the Netherlands and the United Kingdom (Oceguera and Sager 2016).

Providing medical care to prisoners is revenue generator for organizations. Healthcare contracts to one of the largest prison healthcare contractors, Corizon Healthcare, total $1.5 billion annually (Kilgore 2015). The state of Texas contracts with Texas Tech University Health Sciences Center and the University of Texas Medical Branch (UTMB) for services at a cost of $431 million per fiscal year (Legislative Budget Board 2013). UTMB operates Hospital Galveston, a skilled medical facility for state prisoners. The hospital includes a staff of 496 people and offers surgical units, intensive care, acute care, and specialty clinics (TDCJ 2016). "The future looks promising for UTMB Correctional Managed Care employees," boasts the UTMB website (UTMB n.d.). Texas Tech University Health Sciences Center provides healthcare services for 31 correctional facilities in west Texas (Texas Tech University Health Sciences Center n.d.).

Across the United States, 3.4 million people are employed in protective-services occupations (Department of Labor 2017a). Jobs in this area include correctional officers and jailers, police and detectives, bailiffs, criminal investigators and private investigators, and security guards. Local governments employ 41% of protective-service workers and almost 95,000 protective-service workers work in primary and secondary schools (U.S. Department of Labor 2017b).

The International Security Conference and Exposition (ISCE) allows conference goers the opportunity to "meet with technical reps from over 250+ leading brands in the security industry…" (ISCE East website 2017). Leading brands include *NAPCO Securities Technology, Inc.* "one of the world's leading solutions provider and manufacturer of high-technology electronic security" (NAPCO website n.d.). *Continental Access* manufactures and installs the a system that reads identification badges upon building egress and exit for police, correctional facilities, and military installations throughout the United States (NAPCO website n.d.). *Breifcam Ltd.,* an Israeli company, develops media imaging software for the military, border control, security and transportation authorities, and retailers (Business Insights 2017). Other companies represented at the conference include *Drone Nerds, FacialStats.com, Garrett Metal Detectors, Genetec, Innovative Video Technology, Secure Watch 24, Talkaphone, VideogeniX,* (ISCE East website 2017).

Colleges and universities are a supplier of personnel to the corrections and protective services sectors. Across the country, new programs in criminal justice have been developed to meet the demand created by growing the prison industrial complex. Since 1970, bachelor degree conferrals in Homeland Security, Law Enforcement and Firefighting experienced the highest growth of all bachelor's degrees growing 30-fold from 2045 conferrals in 1970–71 to 62,743 in the 2014–15 (U.S. Department of Education 2016). Popular programs include Counterterrorism, Computer Forensics, Homeland Security, Criminology, Forensic Science, Forensic Nursing, and Cybersecurity (Criminal Justice Degree Schools n.d.).

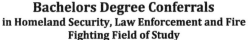

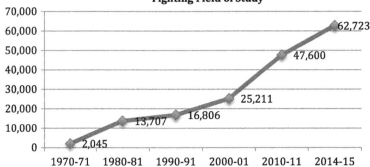

Source National Center for Education Statistics (2016). Table 322.10 Bachelor's degrees conferred by postsecondary institutions, by field of study: Selected years, 1970–71 through 2014–15

As the numbers of felons in society grew, so too did the numbers of judges and lawyers. Most of the twentieth century growth in lawyers and judges occurred after 1970. Employment more than tripled from 272,000 in 1970 to 927,000 in 2000 (Wyatt and Hecker 2006).

Street are propping up the prison industrial complex. The system is simply part of the mainstream of life in the United States.

Before turning to the next section, we highlight the implications of the material we have just covered. Because of financial deregulation,

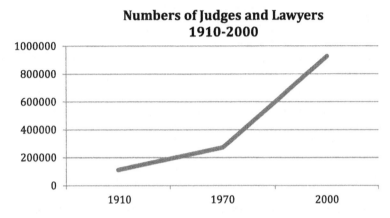

Numbers of Judges and Lawyers 1910-2000

Source Wyatt and Hecker (2006) "Occupational Changes during the 20th Century" *Monthly Labor Review*, March

Judges and lawyers are needed to serve in the plethora of specialty courts that have been created over the past twenty years. The first specialty court, a drug court, was established in 1989 in Miami-Dade County in Florida (Jensen and Mosher 2006). There are now 2734 drug courts and 1122 other problem-solving courts across all 50 states including DWI courts, theft courts, mental health courts, veterans courts, community courts, juvenile drug courts, and family courts (Rogers 2014).

Oceguera and Sager (2016) call for colleges and universities to divest from the prison system and from organizations that profit from the prison system. The reality is that colleges and universities train a significant number of people that work directly in the system. Further, major corporations have a stake in the prison industrial complex not only in building, maintaining prisons and jails but also in their use of prison labor in making products. Beyond that, the food we eat, the clothes we wear, the banks that hold our deposits, the jobs that provide our livelihood, the colleges we send our children, or the ones in which we teach, are all supporting the prison industrial complex. Both Main Street and Wall

banking institutions no longer have an incentive, nor are they compelled to service small account holders. Where once they encouraged small depositors to open accounts, they are now bombarded with a host of fees to access their money —charges to open an account, use a teller, use an ATM machine, for not maintaining certain balances, and even to close an account. On the opposite end, large account holders are exempted from these fees. Small account holders are subsidizing large account holders.

Lower-income, less educated, younger, Black and Latino households characterize the unbanked or loosely banked, who pay high fees to access their money.[3] Those without a bank account must forfeit a portion of their income to check-cashing establishments; and a growing number of establishments no longer accept cash for payments. Consequently, this group is forced to use expensive pre-paid credit cards. When cash runs short, financially strapped households

---

[3]Ex-prisoners won an enrichment claim against JP MorganChase for excessive fees charged to ex-prisoners associated with JP MorganChase issued debit cards that were distributed upon release (Mount 2016).

often turn to predatory lending companies or pawnshops to cover the shortfall. With poor or no credit scores, the loosely banked or unbanked are excluded from the traditional wealth generating activities including home ownership, locking them to a lower-class position.

Rental property and government housing are concentrated in poor minority neighborhoods linked to under-funded neighborhood schools. Schools deemed to be failing and designated as drop-out factories (less than 60% graduate) are overwhelming located in poor, minority neighborhoods (Balfanz and Legters 2004). For example, all of the Johns Hopkins identified drop-out factory schools in the Houston Independent School District (HISD) are economically disadvantaged and minority-serving schools—predominantly African American and/or Latino. Whites are largely absent from these schools accounting for an average of 2.4% of all students in Houston dropout factory schools.[4]

These schools are located in neighborhoods that are heavily policed. Police indoctrination begins early in a child's life and has a long-term effect. Instead of feeling protected, children feel targeted (Shedd 2015). Further, children become acclimated to prison-like settings through their schools. Many schools are equipped with metal detectors, security guards, police officers and surveillance cameras (Shedd 2015). Resources are being diverted away from educating students to supporting the security apparatus. In 2014, Chicago Public Schools spent almost $100 million on school security (Shedd 2015).

The extension of policing into neighborhood schools weds two systems—education and criminal justice—to detrimental effect. The surveillance apparatus socialize children into a criminal justice habitus, treats all children as suspects and criminalizes their behaviors. Attorney Kathryn Seligman (2004) describes a variety of real-life cases in which pre-teen and teenage behavior has been criminalized including a child

accidentally breaking their classmates arm after throwing a ball and being charged with battery causing serious bodily injury. One reason she gives for criminalized behavior is the "increase [ed] presence of police officers and security personnel on school campuses" (2004, p. 1).

In addition to providing prisons their occupants, poor, black neighborhoods serve as revenue generators for government budgets. The Department of Justice (2015) Report on Ferguson, Missouri found that the motivating factor for enhanced policing is to generate revenue for the city and that fines levied against African Americans by the police are integral to this revenue. This focus on making money has corrupted the entire system—police, courts, judges, attorney—who collude to keep the money-bilking cycle in place: "the municipal court does not act as a neutral arbiter of the law or a check on unlawful police conduct. Instead, the court primarily uses its judicial authority as the means to compel payment of fines" (3). The report is an alarming indictment of a municipal system motivated by money and budget rather than public safety or concern.

Ferguson is not alone in the practice of using poor, typically minority residents to bolster budgets. After Sandra Bland's arrest in Waller County, Texas, we learned local law enforcement officials are incentivized to make traffic stops because it subsidizes the county's budget (Nathan 2015). The town of Prairie View, home to historically black Prairie View A&M University, is a prime location for all levels of law enforcement and all are on the take. Nathan describes Prairie View as a cash cow with the cow being a cow of color. Perversely, even the historically black university's Juvenile Justice Center derives revenue from the traffic stops and arrests of its students (Nathan 2015).

The Department of Justice (2015) report on Ferguson revealed that pervasive racial bias, excessive use of violence and arrests and derogatory racial language are commonplace as African Americans are mocked, disparaged, ridiculed, and—as in the case of Michael Brown —killed. Other empirical accounts support this reality for poor African American males. The U.

---

[4]Data compiled using HISD-identified dropout factory schools and Texas Education Agency 2011–12 Academic Excellence Indicator System Campus Reports. See Appendix.

S. Department of Justice (2016) found similar violations by the Baltimore Police Department (BPD) in Baltimore, Maryland. DOJ investigators conclude that "BPD deployed a policing strategy that, by its design, led to differential enforcement in African American communities" (2016: 8). They document many instances of discrimination against African Americans including unconstitutional stops, searches and arrests, the use of excessive force, and the use of retaliation against citizens engaging in constitutionally protected activities. As in Missouri, the Baltimore police department ignored the use of racial slurs and epithets by Baltimore police officers which serves to "undermine the community's trust in the fairness of the police" (U.S. Department of Justice 2016: 8).

Recent ethnographic studies recount similar systemic racism against poor black and brown residents. Nicole Gonzalez Van Cleve (2016) documents the pervasive racism that permeates the entire Cook County courts from prosecutors, defense attorneys and judges. Ironically, these professionals are quick to acknowledge the system is racist while holding themselves apart from the same system. Alice Goffman's (2014) ethnography *On the Run* provides a rare glimpse of the violent policing tactics poor residents are subjected to in the hunt to capture elusive fugitives; Rios's (2017) study set in southern California paints a similar picture for young Latino males with policing tactics that waffle between *mano suave* (soft-handed) and *mano dura* (hard-handed and punitive). Collectively these ethnographies tell a story of a system run amok with little accountability to the targeted population. The broader story of racial injustice and overt racial discrimination is harder to deny especially in the context of the Department of Justice reports that find exactly the charges described in the ethnographies.

While the ethnographic and investigative data are not comprehensive in scope, they are highly suggestive of disparate and racialized police activity beyond that documented by the Department of Justice. This provides an explanation for why Blacks and Whites perceive the police so differently. Further, as the data on the

Houston ISD dropout factory schools reveals, White students do not attend minority-serving schools and are largely unacquainted with the tactics deployed in minority spaces. Negative opinions about the police start young and endure. These opinions are rooted in very different interactions that occur between police and citizen on the basis of race.

The war on poverty has morphed into a war on the poor.[5] The punitive war against the poor serves like Monopoly's "go to jail" card except this is no game. Misdemeanor crimes like truancy, sleeping in public, urinating in public, driving without insurance, trigger a round of fines and court costs, which the poor cannot pay prompting further arrest and jail time. As law professor Natapoff (2015) describes:

> Teachers are calling the police and sending students to probation offices. Welfare case managers monitor their clients for fraud and refer them to prosecutors. Emergency rooms are providing opportunities to catch and arrest people with open warrants. In other words, these institutions of the welfare state are engaged in a wide array of criminal functions that make them look less like service providers and more like law enforcement officers….
>
> …brushes with the criminal system tend to make people poor. They do so directly by imposing fines and fees, and indirectly by making it harder to get jobs, credit, and other resources. Moreover, because the social safety net itself is retracting, the criminal justice system has become a "peculiar social service" for the incarcerated and their families. In all these ways, the criminal system and the welfare state knit poverty and criminality together, functionally as well as ideologically, norm by norm, and encounter by encounter (445–446).

Sentencing reform, like three strikes legislation and the removal of judicial discretion has lengthened the time inmates spend in prison. Even misdemeanor crimes can activate a life sentence if the misdemeanor crime is the third offense (National Research Council 2014).

---

[5]States have employed private corporations (Maximus is one) to identify ways of diverting federal money designated for children with disabilities, nursing home patients and others in need to state budgets instead. For more about these practices see Hatcher's (2016) *The Poverty Industry: The Exploitation of America's Most Vulnerable Citizens.*

Budget cuts and creative financing schemes have incentivized harsher policing. We have in a sense reconstituted a debtors' prison with some of the churn through prison and jail doors due to a person's inability of to pay an assessed fee (Martin 2014). The difficulty with reforming the system is the vested interests attached to the financing schemes. The state of North Carolina recently passed legislation requiring judges to notify all public agencies that derive a portion of an assessed fee if they plan on waiving the fee knowing full well that these agencies will oppose such action (McKevers 2017).

There is also the issue of prison gerrymandering. While most prisoners are from urban areas, most of the prisons are now in rural areas (Huling 2002). Congressional districts are drawn utilizing population counts that include the incarcerated—enhancing the political power of these rural districts at the expense of the urban neighborhoods that contribute most of the prison population (Kilgore 2015). Like with banks where the least well-off are subsidizing the most well-off, the truly disadvantaged are perversely contributing millions of dollars to state budgets through fees and fines, and their very incarceration is subsidizing millions of jobs all-the-while they lose political power (and all the other forms of capital).

Eighty billion dollars is spent every year in maintaining the system of mass incarceration (Kearney et al. 2014)—almost three times as much as is spent by the state and federal government combined for children and support (US Department of Health and Human Services 2016). State expenditures on corrections has grown tremendously over the past forty years diverting funds from education, family support, healthcare, and poverty support among other areas. The nation's prosperity is in no insignificant part due to the knowledge that came before us. The elevation of market-based principles has resulted in neglect to knowledge-generating activities. There are too many examples for us to list of the ways in which market trumps knowledge development. One example involves the development of new antibiotics to address the matter of antibiotic resistance, which has stalled

in the United States because it is "no longer considered to be an economically wise investment for the pharmaceutical industry" (Ventola 2015: 279). Academic research on antibiotics has been "scaled back as a result of funding cuts" (Ventola 2015: 279). In the meantime, people are dying of bacterial infections contracted in hospitals (where they have gone to be cured) that could be successfully treated with new antibiotics, if only we had them. Public health suffers. Data marshaled by Hacker and Pierson show that we are already backsliding on a number of fronts including mortality, obesity, addictions, violence, and education, to name a few. For two years running (2015 and 2016), life expectancy in the United States has declined, a phenomena experienced by no other western democracy (Bernstein and Ingraham 2017).

As noted earlier, across the country record numbers of criminal justice-related majors go to work in the maintenance of the prison system. We are, Christie suggests, "refining the science on how to keep people under control" and "professionalizing the controllers" (2002: 6).

Scarce resources are going to feed the prison industrial complex rather than educate the nation's children. A 2016 Department of Education report found that government spending on corrections far outpaced state and local spending on all levels of education. Further, study authors note that: "All too often, children growing up in poor communities not only do poorly in school but also are disproportionately arrested and incarcerated during their teen-age and young adult years" (Stullich et al. 2016: 6).

We are failing to impart knowledge on the very group that needs it most. If demography is destiny, we are not charting a hopeful future as minority children, who are already the majority in several states including Texas and California (two of the largest prison states as well), have the worst educational outcomes. Demographer Steve Murdoch, former state of Texas demographer and US Census Bureau chief warns that "unless we reverse the trends that we're seeing now, we will be a poorer, less-educated state" (DeGrave 2017). While he was talking specifically about Texas, the same warning holds for the United

States more broadly. Unlike money, which can be inherited by the next generation, there is no guarantee that knowledge will, for knowledge is cumulative and like a garden must be carefully tended or risk being overrun by weeds.

20.4 Where Do We Go from Here?

In the United States, the prison industrial complex has grown in tandem with the rise of market ideology and is now an integral part of the economy. The irony of the dogma of market solutions and limited government is that with nary a blink of the eye, we shifted the meager resources from the social safety net and grew a behemoth prison industrial complex in its stead. Government has not shrunk; it has super-sized its surveillance and social control arms. For those at the bottom of the social hierarchy, we have replaced a social democracy with authoritarianism.

Our criminal justice system is no longer just about punishing law-breakers or removing the most dangerous elements from society; we have made being poor a crime. Furthermore, the rules are designed to regenerate the prison population across multiple generations in the targeted neighborhoods in support of the millions of jobs across a variety of industries that now derive a portion of their bottom line from the prison industrial complex. So large is this system of incarceration, the data collected and collated for use by public policy officials is no longer reliable because of the excluded population (Pettit 2012). These "invisible men," as Pettit calls them, and their exclusion from the data used to calculate employment statistics, educational achievement, poverty rates, etc. overstates black progress. But it is not just black progress that is affected by this. All Americans are paying a heavy price; our democracy is in a precarious state.

The new American stratification system is more rigid and mutually reinforcing than in the past. Deregulation of the financial industry has resulted in a population trapped at the bottom of the social order with marginal labor force opportunities. These groups live in highly policed neighborhoods with failing schools. Not only is this population feeding the prison industrial complex, they are subsidizing its costs through a bevy of fines and fees that fill local, state and federal coffers from their traffic stops, searches and seizures—many of which are unconstitutional. They are, as the title of Gottschalk's (2015) book makes clear, "caught". The racialized prison industrial complex serves as a stimulus to the economy as incarcerated bodies and the millions more under community supervision support millions of jobs—the better paying of which go to the university-trained graduates.

So where do we go from here?

Let us be unequivocal—the prison industrial complex must be dismantled. It is indefensible in a democratic society. The difficulty in undoing the system should not be underestimated as we have greatly expanded the vested interests in the system's maintenance. Fully cognizant of this difficulty, we advance a counter system that we believe will offset many of the negative impacts while simultaneously reconfiguring the economy back towards a knowledge society supported by a market economy[6].

Nils Christie's insights offer a good starting point for dismantling the system. Christie reminds us that crime is a social definition of certain unwanted acts. In different contexts the same acts do not yield the same criminal label. "Look at family matters," explains Christie, "teenagers often act in ways that if it were outside the family would be labeled as 'crime' but because it's just your son who takes some money from the kitchen table or hitting his brother, you don't call that 'theft' or 'violence' because you have reasons for his behavior…." (Swift 1996).

Unpacking Christie's statement yields several important considerations. As we teach in Sociology 101, when situations are defined as real, they become real in their consequences as well. Today we label acts 'criminal' that were not so in an earlier era. For example, we devolved the

---

[6]For a discussion on distinction between a market society and market economy, we recommend Michael Sandels' *What Money Can't Buy: The Moral Limits of Markets* (2012).

capacity to address the mentally ill, so their behavior has become criminal; drug addictions are treated as criminal rather than medical problems; improper teenage behavior previously addressed by teachers and school principals are now referred to police, and so on. This labeling is highly racialized. Acts, especially when done by young, black and Latino men are much more likely to be seen as criminal[7]. Secondly, we have responded with increasing punitiveness to criminal acts. For example, the Anti-Drug Abuse Act of 1986 imposed mandatory minimum sentences and reduced judicial discretion in sentencing decisions (Swann and Sylvester 2006). Procedural and policy changes account for some of the inconsistent divergence between crime and incarceration rates.

Thus, step one in dismantling the system is to decriminalize behavior. If the behavior is not a crime, police have no basis for an arrest.

Christie raises a second important point relevant to the social arrangements in the United States. Because we have—by design—segregated ourselves along racial and socioeconomic lines we do not know each other. Instead we rely upon media to describe and give meaning to everyday events. One consequence of racial unfamiliarity is that we are quick to label the strangers' behavior as criminal. In our isolation we do not have a network other than the police to deal with this undesirable behavior. Thus, we have both created the conditions that give rise to crime and inscribed the meaning of crime to the unwanted behavior (Swift 1996).

We have isolated the population that fuels the penal system—from good schools, safe neighborhoods, and wealth opportunities—which perpetuates and compounds their disadvantages. We have removed many aspects of citizenship from offenders (especially if they were drug offenders)—the right to vote; to sit on juries; for eligibility for federal financial aid for college; for

occupational certifications (barbers, hairdressers, etc.); for food stamps, government housing, and so on. We label this group criminal and inflict upon them incredible violence ostensibly to make us safer which ironically has the opposite effect.

Political decisions and attendant policies with an underlying of racism produce a new generation of prison inmates. Present incarceration is the largest contributor to the growth in foster care (Swann and Sylvester 2006). Incarcerated parents with children in foster care are more likely to have their parental rights terminated because their average sentence is 80 months and federal law mandates that states begin the termination process if a child has been in foster care for at least 15 months of a 22-month period. Foster children have "emotional, behavioral, developmental, and physical health problems … that almost certainly lead to personal and professional problems later in life" (Swann and Sylvester 2006: 309). African American children enter and stay in foster care at disproportionately higher rates than other children (USGAO 2007). The GAO further finds that bias among decision makers is a contributing factor in this disproportionality (USGAO 2007). Heavily policed, poor, African Americans have their children overrepresented in foster care which often leads to having their parental rights terminated. Children who spent time in foster care do not fare well as adults. Upwards of a third have a "high level of involvement in the criminal justice system" (McCarthy and Gladstone 2011). The carceral cycle continues.

Step two: Social exiles must be integrated into the broader social and political life.

How to we end the cycle and reintegrate exiled populations? "Give the populations an ordinary share of ordinary society—education, work and political and cultural participation," says Christie (2002: 9). The best alternatives to incarceration and the greatest opportunities for an "ordinary life" include (1) a guaranteed annual income; and (2) significant upgrades to the education of the poor; (3) revising the legal structure of corporations. We take up each of these in turn next.

---

[7]Law enforcement labeled white offenders "troublesome" and sent them to community rehabilitation centers; black and Latino youth were labeled "delinquent" and sent to juvenile detention centers. "The police … criminalized black children … and decriminalized white youth," asserts Hinton (2016, p. 222).

The idea of a guaranteed basic income is an old one. In the United States, serious consideration of the idea was given during the 1960s. President Nixon presented the idea to Congress where it passed in the House only to be scuttled by the Senate (BIEN website n.d.). Given the size and scope of the prison industrial complex, a guaranteed basic income would serve multiple purposes. First, it would provide a means of support to those who lose their job as the system downsizes. Secondly, as economists will attest, those at the lower end of the income spectrum who receive these monies will spend it, which would serve as a stimulus to the economy. This idea is not as far-fetched as it may appear at first blush. For example, Finland is trialing a basic income for their unemployed; the Netherlands is on course to pilot their own basic income program. Some cities already have guaranteed basic income programs in place including Livorno in Italy and Ontario, Canada (Henley 2017).

Another major advantage of a guaranteed basic income is that it would be a step forward in addressing issues of caring in modern society. The caring society is an area that has been a particular concern for women who undertake the disproportionate share of this type of work, much of it unpaid. Economist Folbre (2009) points out that the economic models beginning with Adam Smith have been founded by and around the interests of men seeking to advance their interests in the market. Women and caring have been excluded from these models. But one cannot think of a society without caring and especially an aging one like the United States. Thus, the universal basic income would provide monies for everyone over 18 including women engaged in the caring work.

During the 1970s and 1980s of his illustrious sociological career, Wilson (1980) called for jobs, jobs, jobs as the solution for poor black men. Given the contingent nature of jobs at the lower end of the pay scale, jobs alone are not sufficient. There is reason to believe that with automation and outsourcing, good jobs will not be returning any time soon—especially not for those with limited education. One thing seems clear—education is crucial to upgrading the knowledge and quality of life of the most disadvantaged members of U.S. society particularly black males and Latinos, and poor whites.

As ample empirical evidence attests, poor children for a variety of reasons—lack of medical attention, a less nutritious diet, more stress and disruption—have worse educational outcomes (Ravitch 2014). Given the disadvantages that already adhere to their class position, we owe these children the best education that can be had in order to maximize their odds for a better life. We envision federally funded, small, neighborhood schools. Federal funding, rather than local funding, is necessary because not only is this costly, but because local communities would likely set up districts to benefit the privileged as they have already done. Universal federal funding is necessary so that the poor can get as least as good as, if not better funded schools than do the rich. As Ravitch (2014) contends: "We know what works. What works are the very opportunities that advantaged families provide for their children …We want to extend the same advantages to children who do not have them …"(6).

Ravitch's solutions, which we support, include pre-kindergarten for all children and in addition to age-appropriate curricula; small classroom sizes; and making the learning environment more conducive to learning and fun for children. However, we believe that support should begin before pre-k to include quality daycare and enrichment programs beginning at birth through pre-kindergarten levels. There is empirical support for starting enrichment at birth. According to economist James Heckman, "we should invest in the foundation of school readiness from birth to age 5 by providing early childhood education for disadvantaged children. We should build on that foundation with high-quality elementary and secondary education to sustain the development of successful lives. That kind of equality will build a more productive society for all" (2011: 9).

At upper levels, Ravitch advocates a balanced curriculum to include music and art, foreign language, and physical education along with after-school programs that allow students to explore a variety of interests "whether in athletics, chess, robotics, history club, dramatics, science club, nature study, Scouting, or other activities" (2014, 7). Curricula once part of the classroom but shouldered out by the high-stakes, multiple choice "drill and kill," teaching-to-the-test curriculum that has accompanied *No Child Left Behind* has resulted in American students being left behind on the global scene.

All schools should be equipped with libraries and librarians and media specialists; school nurses, guidance counselors, psychologists, and social workers (Ravitch 2014). Some readers may be surprised to learn that many schools do not already have these features. For example, two-thirds of Houston Independent School District schools do not have a librarian; half do not have a counselor or social worker (Binkovitz 2016). All public schools in the Houston area, however, have police (Barnum 2016).

Which brings us to another point: schools need to return to being institutions of learning, not the police zones described by Shedd and Rios. Teachers, school administrators and parents should administer discipline *not* police and security forces. This no-police zone should extend to contiguous areas around school campuses as well. Police in and around schools criminalize the settings. In this environment, children become suspects. If there is any doubt about this, the recorded message the first-named author received from her daughter's suburban school notifying of a random search of children should dispel these idyllic notions. Parents were to be reassured that this random search only turned up a few forbidden contraband including a lighter, tobacco and prescription and over-the-counter medications. But this obfuscates the point that in these types of situations, *all* of the children morph into suspects and the situation is rife with the possibility of disparate racial, ethnic and class profiling. Children should not fear police harassment either in their journey to and from school, or while in school. These and other surveillance activities violate the trust of children-first policies and elevate a police culture over nurturing educational ones.

Building upon Ravitch's solutions, the school we envisage is public in character and the classroom building would be part of larger complex wherein there is an athletic facility and community meeting rooms. Further, small class sizes with no more than 6–10 students per class are essential. Small classes will also foster the discourse-reading connection that reinforces learning. Small classes also have the added benefit of allowing students and teachers to get to know each other on a much different level than would be allowed in a large class setting. "Where people do not know each other, they feel a need to have officials fix matters," explains Christie. Small, intimate classrooms obviate the need for officials beyond the teacher to address behavioral issues. Students become accountable to each other and to the teacher and vice versa.

Clearly teachers are an important element in this process. Teachers serve as important role models for students and especially so in the early years. However, a 2013 study found that disadvantaged students have less access to effective teachers (Isenberg et al. 2013). This must change. The type of broad-based, hands-on education requires patience on the part of teachers. Teachers must be devoted to teaching and compensated handsomely for this devotion.

We must remember that the students who are expected to read and write standard English often do not come from families where Standard English or use of a wide-ranging vocabulary are the order of the day. Given the racial and class segregation mentioned earlier, combined with the fact that teachers are overwhelmingly middle class and white, teachers themselves will need additional training to address the multiple challenges confronting disadvantaged students. Teachers must also be made aware of their own cultural and class biases. For example, with regards to language, Delpit reminds us that teachers "should recognize that the linguistic form a student brings to school is intimately connected with loved ones, community and personal identity. To suggest that this form is "wrong" or even worse, ignorant, is to suggest that something is wrong with the student and his or her family" (Delpit 1997). Instead, teachers should include a study of language diversity as part of the curriculum for all students. In this way, "children can learn that there are many ways of saying the same thing, and that certain contexts suggest particular kinds of linguistic performances" (Delpit 1997). Still children must learn to speak Standard English.

Early on, school curriculum must also emphasize discussion. Children learn to internalize abstract concepts first through discussion, followed by reading then writing. Discussion is critical for supporting and advancing the written material, and for developing the use of proper grammar, complex vocabularies and abstractions. Curriculum must also emphasize reading for it is only through reading (reinforced by extensive discussion) that children can place themselves in a larger context. A broad vocabulary is necessary to be a proficient reader. Beyond that, students must also be aware of factual knowledge. All writers assume the reader has a level of knowledge that allows them to comprehend the points being made (Willingham 2015). Knowledge about a broader world allows readers to imagine a world beyond their own. Further, reading is a necessary precursor to writing—another skill that is best advanced in small classrooms where children can receive immediate, ongoing and extensive feedback.

In addition to reading, writing and arithmetic, children need to understand that what they put in their bodies has a direct bearing on their health. Public health has to be part of the curriculum. Children need to learn about proper nutrition including reading food labels; the importance of and reasons for immunization; the importance of hygiene, etc. These types of practical knowledge aimed at improving knowledge at the bottom of the income and social hierarchy benefits everyone in society—everyone is the healthier for it. Furthermore, high school students must be exposed to sustained information about the world economy in such a way that they begin to realize that although they live in a local community, they are part of a larger world economy as well. It is imperative that students understand that what goes on in the broader world economy impact their lives as well.

Clearly knowledge is an important component of a prosperous society. Today, money is the symbol of success and much of the modern economy is geared towards making money. But scientific and medical knowledge is absolutely essential too as what we are able to do in the modern world is predicated on knowledge. Knowledge needs to be nurtured and disseminated—not hoarded for profit or undeveloped because it is not efficient or too costly. Young minorities are increasingly becoming victims of a system that is emphasizing the role of charter schools. Charter schools are grounded on the principle that one can make money on education all the while catering to the privileged sector of the social orders. Charter schools did not start out this way. The original idea for charter schools were not to be "profit-making opportunities for entrepreneurs" but innovation laboratories to reach and teach the "lowest performing students, the dropouts, and the disengaged" and to then share the most successful methodologies with fellow public school teachers (Ravitch 2014: 12–13). Abrams (2016) while acknowledging the "commercial mindset" has taken hold among policymakers points out a few business principles education should adopt. Improving teacher training, raising teacher pay, allowing teachers creative autonomy are all pages taken straight from the business playbook that should be adopted. Abrams points to Finland's successful adoption and perfection of these business principles to tremendous positive effect. We must understand that children are not commodities to enrich the lives of shareholders but *our future*. The emphasis should be on instilling knowledge about the social and natural world and not just knowledge about making money, which we acknowledge is important as well.

The responsibility for ensuring their future resides with adults with whom we should have faith are putting the interests of children before their own. We are alone in the way we finance education which advantages the already advantaged. All other industrial nations invest equally if not more in the children who need it most—the financially least well off. This egregious funding mechanism, which most sociologists fully acknowledge is unfair, must flip to where the poorest children receive the most resources to offset as much as possible the other disadvantages that adhere to poverty.

Skeptics may say we are unrealistic—unrealistic in the sense that US society will not financially support the schools that we have sketched out nor the idea of a guaranteed annual income. We think not. Certainly, higher taxes are in order to advance education as a public good. In the end, this will also advance the cause of democracy. The ideal has somehow disappeared in the proclivity to make money. The critics of a guaranteed annual income believe that it will undermine the role of work in modern society. We believe such criticisms are false. Research cited by Surowiecki (2016) indicates this not to be the case as well. Work will remain meaningful for large sections of the population despite the emergence of a guaranteed annual income.

Per Feagin et al. oppression consists of "systematic institutional processes which prevent some people from learning and using satisfying and expansive skills in socially recognized settings or institutionalized social processes which inhibit people's ability to communicate with others or to express their feelings and perspective on social life in contexts where others can listen" (2014: 14). By any vantage points, what we describe in this chapter is an oppressive environment for impoverished racial and ethnic minorities. Detailing the empirical reality for this group was necessary so that an alternative course of action could be sketched out. We believe that the guaranteed annual income and upgrades in education are necessary first steps to advancing the social welfare of racial and ethnic minorities. We envisage a better future and a more robust democracy as a result of dismantling the prison industrial complex.

We are fully aware that the costs of the types of programs we are proposing in our counter system will be expensive. But we are a rich country. Economists like Adair Turner (2016) have steadily been redefining and clarifying the meaning of debt in the modern industrial world. For sure, big corporations cannot escape taxation in order to achieve the counter system we have proposed. Organizations have to be held accountable in ways that they currently are not.

Zucman, a student of Piketty's, believes that national debt would be significantly lessened if the revenues lost from tax evasion and tax havens could be recovered (Leslie 2014).

It is fitting to return to the issue of bureaucratic capitalism and the role that large-scale organizations played in the scenarios we have spent this essay describing.[8] As Hacker and Pierson detail, the story over the past thirty years is one of organizational triumph. In particular, the organizations that have triumphed over the past thirty years are business. During the 1970s, "[e]mployers learned how to work together to achieve political goals. As members of coalitions, firms could mobilize more proactively and on a much broader front. Corporate leaders became advocates not just for the narrow interests of their firms but also for the shared interests of business as a whole" (Hacker and Pierson: 118).

Since the 1970s, businesses have become multinational in scope and their sphere of influence has magnified. And inequality has continued its relentless rise. Sjoberg (2009) asks a question that government officials as of yet have not been able to answer: Can human rights standards be employed so as to hold large bureaucratic structures morally accountable? Advancing a case for human rights is ever more complicated by the fractured nature of U.S. politics which renders a political solution to the problems raised in this essay much more difficult to resolve. On the positive front, there is growing international concern as the task of Ruggie as a Special Representative to the United Nations to "identi[fy] what international human rights standards currently regulate corporate conduct, as opposed to the conduct of states and individuals; and [to] clarify[y] the respective roles of states and business in safeguarding these rights" (2013: xi) reveals.

In this essay, our agenda has been to draw attention to the bottom of the social hierarchy,

---

[8]For more about the relationship between corporations and state government, see "State Contracting with Private Corporations is Big Business," by the Service Employee International Union Local 1000, February 2012.

which is tied heavily to the prison industrial complex, and offer a way to improve the life chances for this group. Our concern for the bottom of the stratification and human rights is not misplaced. The United Nations undertook its own investigation of extreme poverty in the United States (Alston 2017). The U.N. asked a difficult question: Is it possible, in one of the world's leading democracies, to enjoy fundamental human rights such as political participation and voting rights if you are unable to meet basic living standards? (Pilkington 2017a). The picture of poverty painted by the U.N. is a grim one (Pilkington 2017b). It raises serious questions about the path we have taken these past forty years that have grown these types of inequality.

We fully acknowledge that our analysis is incomplete. For one, it does not address the growth of the 1%. Hacker and Pierson (2010) outline how the corporate agenda and lobby rose to dominate U.S. politics, but this alone cannot explain the phenomenal rise of the 1%. This group is tied to an international ruling class the boundaries of which extend beyond any one nation-state. As globalization has advanced this group is less reliant upon what the United States contributes to their bottom line.

We remind the reader of the dramatic rise of the prison industrial complex over the past 40 years—a system that houses disproportionately poor minorities—particularly black men, with increasing numbers of Latino men and black and Latina women. As sociologists we are deeply troubled by the fact that the U.S. houses 5% of the world's population but about 25% of the world's prisoners. The rise of the prison industrial complex came into its own during the 1970s with the law-and-order campaign of Richard Nixon and flourished thereafter. Ironically, Reagan viewed the federal government as the problem, but governments at the local and state levels, and their police forces were expanding as they pushed forward the prison industrial complex.

What is striking about the prison industrial complex is how many Americans are dependent upon it for their livelihoods. Vested interests go beyond the prison guard unions that make the national news for opposing proposals to ease the carceral grip (Fang 2016). Reporters have taken note of the fact that corporations are making money on variety of facets of the prison system. But so too are the thousands of college-trained students who are assuming administrative and operational mantels for system maintenance.

We reiterate Sjoberg's (2009) contention for the need to hold large-scale bureaucratic organizations accountable to human rights standards. Corporate structures must be congruent with the principles of human rights and democracy. In this essay, we have provided a counter system analysis geared to advancing democracy and human rights. Advocating for democracy is not a radical idea—in fact it is uniquely American harkening back to our founding principles. What is happening in this country is highly undemocratic from the gerrymandered political districts to the gerrymandered prison districts. Corporate charters must be re-aligned to be accountable to the broader public and not just their own bottom line.

Ruggie's (2013) attempts at the United Nations to establish a universally acceptable standard to hold corporations accountable to human rights standards is a starting point. At a minimum, we echo Ruggie who argues that "states must protect; companies must respect; and those who are harmed must have redress" (2013: xx–xxi). Human rights should encompass both social and *economic* rights (Sjoberg et al. 2001). Towards this end, the legal structure of corporations will have to change including the privileging of shareholders above all other interests; the notion of corporations as 'natural persons' that "insulate them from moral accountability to human rights standards" (172).

As far as we can determine, there has been very little attention to these issues either by mass media or social scientists. From our point of view, it is clear that the current organizational structures are inadequate to the task of dealing with these issues. The relationship forged between the state and market ideologues over the past forty years contributes to this situation. Thus, we are forced to think of a counter system—and one that takes into account that so many people depend upon the prison industrial system for their livelihood.

There is an urgency in combatting this broad magnitude of human suffering—and it is suffering. Christie reminds us that "punishment means delivery of pain intended as pain." Mass incarceration is an "act with the intention to get other humans to suffer" (2002: 8). We are inflicting inordinate amounts of pain on poor men of color particularly African American men, and increasingly Latino men (and their families), to lasting effect. As a society we seem blind to or worse still, uncaring of this pain. As we have demonstrated, racism—institutional and cultural—factored heavily in growing mass incarceration and remains a key element in its maintenance. How do we reconcile this institutional intent with human rights? Sjoberg (2005) argues that given the world economy, the nation-state, citizen-rights based approaches are not adequate. Indeed, non-citizens comprise a major portion of the federal expansion of the prison industrial complex and multinational corporations have been integral in detention center construction and operations (Douglas and Sáenz 2013). Instead, institutions must be held to a moral standard. The moral foundations of organizational activities that directly affect human life and death (and suffering) require attention and must be brought under a universal human rights umbrella. Corporations specifically and organizations more broadly should not profit from coercion, violence and pain. We have grown the prison industrial complex to behemoth levels. No matter Harcourt's (2011) efforts to link our use of punishment to 18th century France, we stand alone amongst our peers in this enterprise. We take for

granted the size of the system, indeed assume its continued growth. Christie asks a question we extend to the reader: "How large a prison population can you have before you change the kind of country you live in?" (Swift 1996).

Appendix

2011–2012 TEA

Column1	% Hispanic	% African Amer	% White	% Ec disadvan
Austin HS	94.4	4.1	1.3	83.3
Chavez HS	81.7	12.7	1.6	82.7
Davis HS	88.5	10.3	1	93.4
Furr HS	80.4	16.6	2.5	92.3
Jones HS	27	72.3	0.2	76.4
Kashmere HS	17	81.3	0.2	80.2
Law Enfr-Cr Jus HS	72.2	23.4	3.1	83
Lee HS	74.3	13.3	4.3	78.7
Madison HS	52.9	45.1	0.6	81.2
Milby HS	95.6	3.1	0.7	81.3
Reagan HS	85.2	9.8	3.9	78.9
Scarborough HS	65.9	26.6	6.3	87.2
Sharpstown HS	66	29.1	2.4	94
Sterling HS	25.8	71.5	1.3	79.7
Waltrip HS	73.5	13.4	11.5	75.1
Washington BTS HS	32.1	64	1.5	85.2
Westbury HS	48	41.9	2.5	78.4
Worthing HS	10.5	88.4	0.8	76.7
Yates HS	8.3	90.5	0.2	75.9
			2.415789474	82.29473684

Texas Education Agency 2011–2012 Academic Excellence Indicator System Campus Reports available online at: https://rptsvr1.tea.texas.gov/perfreport/aeis/2012/campus.srch.html

References

Abrams, S. E. (2016). *Education and the commercial mindset*. Cambridge, MA: Harvard University Press.

Abu-Lughod, J. L. (1999). *Sociology for the twenty-first century*. Chicago: The University of Chicago Press.

Alston, P. (2017). Extreme poverty in America: Read the UN special monitor's report. *The Guardian*. 15 December. Accessed online.

Balfanz, R., & Legters, N. (2004). Locating the Dropout Crisis: Which high schools produce the nation's dropouts? Where are they located? Who attends them? Accessed online.

Baradaran, M. (2015). *How the other half banks: Exclusion, exploitation and the threat to democracy*. Cambridge: Harvard University Press.

Barnum, M. (2016). Data shows 3 of the 5 biggest school districts hire more security officers than counselors. *The 74*. 27 March. Accessed online.

Bernstein, L., & Ingraham, C. (2017). Fuled by drug crisis, U.S. life expectancy declines for a second straight year. *Washington Post*, 21 December.

Binkovitz, L. (2016). New recommendations says every school should have a nurse. Many Don't. *The Urban Edge*. 24 August. Accessed online.

Bloom, N. (2017). Corporations in the Age of Inequality. *Harvard Business Review*. 21–29 March. Accessed online.

BreifCam website (n.d.). "About us," *BreifCam*. Accessed online 17 December 2017: http://briefcam.com/about-us/.

Anchortex. (n.d.). About us. Anchortex website. Accessed online.

Aramark website. (n.d.). Company profile. *Aramark*. Accessed online.

BIEN (Basic Income Earth Network). (n.d.). Basic Income History. Accessed online.

Bob Barker Industries (n.d.) "Products" and "Officers-only," *Bob Barker Industries website*. Accessed online.

Business Insights. (2017). Global. "BreifCam Ltd.," *Gale Business Insights*. Accessed online.

Cowen, T. (2011). *The great stagnation: How America Ate all the low-hanging fruit of modern history, got sick, and will (eventually) feel better*. New York: Dutton.

Child Welfare Information Gateway. (2016). *Racial disproportionality and disparity in child welfare*. Washington, DC: U.S. Department of Health and Human Services, Children's Bureau. Accessed online.

Christie, N. (2002). Out of Control: Prisons as a Growth Industry. *Prison Reform Trust*. Accessed online.

Criminal Justice Degree Schools. (n.d.). Home page *Criminal Justice Degree Schools website*. Accessed online 15 December 2017: https://www.criminaljusticedegreeschools.com.

DeGrave, S. (2017). Texas demographer has given the same speech for 25 years. Is anyone listening? *Texas Observer*. 11 April. Accessed online.

Delpit, L. (1997). The real Ebonics debate: What should teachers do? *Rethinking Schools*. Accessed online.

Douglas, K. M., & Sáenz, R. (2013). The criminalization of immigrants and the immigration-industrial complex. *Daedalus, 142*(3), 199–227.

Fang, L. (2016). Police and prison guard groups fight Marijuana Legalization in California. *The Intecept.* 18 May. Accessed online.

Feagin, J. R., Vera, H., & Ducey, K. (2014). *Liberation sociology.* New York: Taylor and Francis, ProQuest Ebook Central.

Folbre, N. (2009). *Greed, lust & gender: A history of economic ideas.* New York: Oxford University Press.

Gilpin, R. (2001). *Global political economy: Understanding the international economic order* (Kindle Edition). Amazon.com.

Girdner, E. J. (2007). From sea to shining sea: The degradation of social welfare under neoliberalism in the United States. *Nature, Society, and Thought, 20*(3–4), 395–400.

Glaze, L. E. (2010). Correctional population in the United States, 2009. *U.S. Department of Justice Bureau of Justice Statistics*, December. Accessed online.

Goffman, A. (2014). *On the run: Fugitive life in an American City.* Chicago: The University of Chicago Press.

Gordon, R. J. (2016). *The rise and fall of American growth: The U.S. standard of living since the civil war.* Princeton: Princeton University Press.

Gottachalk, M. (2015). *Caught: The prison state and the lockdown of American Politics.* Princeton: Princeton University Press.

Gottschalk, M. (2006). *The prison and the gallows: The politics of mass incarceration in America.* New York: Cambridge University Press.

Hacker, J. S. (2008). *The great risk shift: The new economic insecurity and the decline of the American Dream.* New York: Oxford University Press.

Hacker, Jacob S., & Pierson, Paul. (2010). *Winner-take-all politics: How Washington made the Rich Richer—And turned its back on the middle class.* NY: Simon and Schuster Paperbacks.

Hacker, J. S., & Pierson, P. (2016). *American Amnesia: How the war on government led us to forget what made America Prosper.* NY: Simon & Schuster.

Harcourt, B. E. (2011). *The illusion of free markets: Punishment and the myth of natural order.* Cambridge, MA: Harvard University Press.

Hatchter, D. L. (2016). *The poverty industry: The exploitation of America's most vulnerable citizens.* New York: New York University Press.

Heckman, J. J. (2011). The economics of inequality: The value of early childhood education. *Education Digest, 77*(4), 4–11.

Henley, J. (2017). Finland trials basic income for unemployed. *The Guardian.* 3 January. Accessed online.

Hinton, Elizabeth. (2016). *From the war on poverty to the war on crime: The making of mass incarceration in America.* Cambridge, MA: Harvard University Press.

Huling, T. (2002). Building a prison economy in Rural America. In M. Mauer & M. Chesney-Lind (Eds.), *Invisible punishment: The collateral consequences of mass imprisonment.* New York: The New Press.

Ingham, G. (2004). *The nature of money.* Cambridge, UK: Polity Press.

International Security Conference and Exposition (ISCE). (2017). ISCE East website. Accessed online.

Isenberg, E., Max, J., Gleason, P., Potamites, L., Santillano, R., Hock, H., & Hansen, M. (2013). *Access to Effective Teaching for Disadvantaged Students* (NCEE 2014–4001). Washington, DC: National Center for Education Evaluation and Regional Assistance, Institute of Education Sciences, U.S. Department of Education.

Jensen, E. L., & Mosher, C. (2006). Adult drug courts: Emergence, growth, outcome evaluations, and the need for a continuum of care. *Idaho Law Review, 42,* 443–470.

Kearney, M. S., Harris, B. H., Jácome, E., & Parker, L. (2014). *Ten economic facts about crime and incarceration in the United States.* Accessed online: The Hamilton Project. May.

Kilgore, J. (2015). *Understanding mass incarceration: A people's guide to the key civil rights struggle of our time.* NY: The New Press.

Kurgan, L., & Cadora, E. (2006). Million Dollar Blocks. *Spatial information design lab.* Accessed online 15 February 2017. http://www.justicemapping.org.

Lee, M. Y. H. (2015). Does the United States really have 5 percent of the world's population and one quarter of the world's prisoners? *The Washington Post.* 30 April. Accessed online.

Legislative Budget Board. (2013). *Correctional managed health care for state incarcerated adult offenders in Texas.* Accessed online: Legislative Budget Board.

Leslie, J. (2014). The true cost of hidden money: A Piketty Protégé's theory on tax havens. New York Times. 15 June. Accessed online.

Martin, R. (2014). Supreme Court ruling not enough to prevent Debtors Prisons. *Morning Edition* from NPR, 21 May 2014, Accessed online.

Mason, J. W. (2015). Disgorge the cash: The disconnect between corporate borrowing and investment. Roosevelt Institute. 25 February. Accessed online.

Martin, W. (2017). These are the 23 biggest global banks —all with more than $1 trillion in assets. *Business Insider.* 21 April. Accessed online.

Massey, D. S. (2007). *Categorically unequal: The American stratification system.* New York: Russell Sage Foundation.

McCarthy, S., & Gladstone, M. (2011). What percentage of the state's polled prison inmates were once foster care children? *Policy Matters, California Senate Office of Research.* December. Accessed online.

McKevers, K. (2017). North Carolina Law makes it harder for judges to waive fees and fines. *All Things Considered* from NPR, 4 December 2017.

Mokyr, J. (2002). *The gifts of Athena: historical origins of the knowledge economy.* Princeton: Princeton University Press.

Mokyr, J. (2005). The intellectual origins of modern economic growth. *The Journal of Economic History, 65*(2), 285–351.

Mount, I. (2016). J.P. Morgan just settled a suit over sticking ex-cons with unfair debit card fees. Fortune. 3 August. Accessed online.

Natapoff, A. (2015). Gideon's servants and the criminalization of poverty. *Ohio State Journal of Criminal Law., 12*(2), 445–464.

Nathan, D. (2015). The real reason Sandra Bland got locked up. *The Nation.* 16 December. Accessed online.

National Research Council. (2014). *The growth of incarceration in the United States: Exploring causes and consequences.* Washington, DC: The National Academies Press.

Oceguera, E., & Sager, M. (2016). The Prison Industry on your campus. *Investigate.* 8 June. Accessed online.

Pettit, B. (2012). *Invisible men: Mass incarceration and the myth of black progress.* New York: Russell Sage Foundation.

Piketty, T. (2014). *Capital in the twenty-first century.* Cambridge, MA: Harvard University Press.

Pilkington, E. (2017a). Why the UN is investigating extreme poverty … in America, the world's richest nation. *The Guardian.* 1 December. Accessed online.

Pilkington, E. (2017b). A journey through the land of extreme poverty: Welcome to America. *The Guardian.* 15 December. Accessed online.

Ravitch, D. (2014). *Reign of error: The Hoax of the privatization movement and the danger to America's Public Schools.* New York: Vintage Books.

Reagan, R. (1981). "Inaugural Address," January 20, 1981. Online by Gerhard Peters and John T. Woolley, *The American Presidency Project.*

Rios, V. M. (2017). *Human targets: Schools, police, and the criminalization of Latino Youth.* Chicago, IL: The University of Chicago Press.

Rogers, D. (2014). Problem-solving courts: Changing lives. *Corrections forum.* September/October. Accessed online.

Ruggie, J. G. (2013). *Just business: Multinational corporations and human rights.* New York: W.W. Norton & Company.

Sandel, M. (2012). *What money can't buy: The moral limits of the market.* New York: Farrar, Straus and Giroux.

Seligman, K. (2004). Challenging the criminalization of immature preteen and teenage behavior. In *Federal District Appellate Project* (FDAP.org). Accessed online.

Shannon, Sarah K. S., Uggen, Christopher, Schnittker, Jason, Thompson, Melissa, Wakefield, Sara, & Massoglia, Michael. (2017). The growth, scope, and spatial distribution of people with Felony records in the United States, 1948–2010. *Demography, 54,* 1795–1818.

Shedd, Carla. (2015). *Unequal city: Race, schools and the perception of Injustice.* New York, NY: Russell Sage Foundation.

Sherman, M. (2009). A short history of financial deregulation in the United States. In: *Center for Economic and Policy Research* (CEPR). July. Accessed online.

Sjoberg, G. (1999). Some observations on bureaucratic capitalism: Knowledge about what and why? In J. L. Abu-Lughod (Ed.), *Sociology for the twenty-first century: Continuities and cutting edges.* Chicago: The University of Chicago Press.

Sjoberg, Gideon. (2005). The corporate control industry and human rights: The case of Iraq. *Journal of Human Rights, 4,* 95–101.

Sjoberg, G. (2009). Corporations and human rights. In R. Morgan & B. Turner (Eds.), *Interpreting human rights: Social science perspectives.* NJ: Routledge.

Sjoberg, G., & Cain, L. D. (1971). Negative values, counter system models, and the analysis of social systems. In H. Turk & R. L. Simpson (Eds.), *Institutions and social exchange: The sociologies of Talcott Parsons and George Homans* (pp. 312–329). Indianapolis, IN: Bobbs-Merrill.

Sjoberg, G., Gill, E. A., & Williams, N. (2001). A sociology of human rights. *Social Problems, 48* (1), 11–47.

Stiglitz, J. (2015). Inequality and Economic Growth. *The Political Quarterly, 86*(51), 134–155. Accessed online.

Stullich, S, Morgan, I, Schak, O. (2016). *State and local expenditures on corrections and education.* U.S. Department of Education Policy and Program Studies Services. Accessed online.

Surowiecki, J. (2016). The case for free money: Why don't we have a universal basic income? *The New Yorker.* 20 June. Accessed online.

Swann, C. A., & Sylvester, M. S. (2006). The foster care crisis: what caused caseloads to grow? *Demography, 43*(2), 309–322.

Swift, R. (1996). Crime and civilization. In: *New internationalist.* 5 August. Accessed online.

Texas Department of Criminal Justice (TDCJ) (2016). Texas Department of Criminal Justice website. Accessed online.

Texas Education Agency. (2012). *Academic excellence indicator system—Campus reports.* Accessed online: Texas Education Agency.

Turner, Adair. (2016). *Between debt and the devil: money, credit, and fixing global finance.* Princeton, NJ: Princeton University Press.

U.S. Department of Education, Institute of Education Sciences, National Center for Education Statistics. (2016). *Table 322.10 Bachelor's degrees conferred by postsecondary institutions, by field of study: Selected years, 1970–71 through 2014–15.* Accessed online.

U.S. Department of Health and Human Services, Administration for Children and Families, Office of Family Assistance. (2016). *State TANF spending in FY 2015: A Fact Sheet.* Accessed online.

U.S. Department of Justice Civil Rights Division (2015). *Investigation of the Ferguson Police Department.* March 4. Accessed online.

U.S. Department of Justice Civil Rights Division. (2016). *Investigation of the Baltimore City Police Department.* 10 August. Accessed online.

U.S. Department of Labor, Bureau of Labor Statistics. (2017a). *May 2016 national occupational employment and wage estimates—United States*. 31 March.

U.S. Department of Labor, Bureau of Labor Statistics. (2017b). *May 2016 national occupational employment and wage estimates—33-0000 protective service occupations (Major Group)*. 31 March. Accessed online.

U.S. Government Accountability Office. (July 2007). *African American Children in Foster Care (Publication No. GAO-07-816)*. Accessed online.

Van Cleve, N. G. (2016). *Crook county: Racism and injustice in America's Largest Criminal Court*. Stanford: Stanford University Press.

Ventola C. L. (2015). The antibiotic resistance crisis, part 1: Causes and threats. *Pharmacy and Therapeutics, 40* (4), 277–283 (April accessed online).

Wacquant, Loic. (2009). *Punishing the Poor: The Neoliberal Government of social insecurity*. Durham, NC: Duke University Press.

Wagner, P. & Rabuy, B. (2017). Mass incarceration: The whole pie 2017. In: *The Prison Policy Initiative*. March 14. Accessed online.

White, G. B. (2015). Stiglitz: Here's How to Fix Inequality," *The Atlantic*. November 2 Accessed online.

Willingham, D. T. (2015). *Raising kids who read: What parents and teacher can do*. San Francisco, CA: Jossey-Bass.

Wilson, W. J. (1980). *The declining significance of race: Blacks and changing American Institutions*. Chicago: The University of Chicago Press.

Wyatt, D., & Hecker, D. (2006). Occupational Changes during the 20th Century. In: *Monthly Labor Review, Bureau of Labor Statistics, U.S. Department of Labor*. March. Accessed online.

Gilbane Building Company. (n.d.). "Projects overview" "projects, criminal justice, correctional facilities" "projects college-university," *Gilbane Building Company*. Accessed online.

Hochtief website (n.d.). Accessed online.

HO + K website (n.d.). "Design: Justice," and "About" HO + K. Accessed online.

NAPCO website. (n.d.). Continental access enterprise integrated security management. *NAPCO*. Accessed online.

Sodexo USA. website (n.d.) "About us," *Sodexo USA*. Accessed online.

Texas Tech University Health Sciences Center—Correctional Managed Health Care (TTUHSC CMHC). (n. d.). *CCMC home—Services we offer*. Accessed online.

3M (n.d.). *"About us" 3M website*. Accessed online.

Turner Construction Company. (n.d.). "About us" and "our experience"—government. *Turner Construction Company Website*. Accessed online.

U.S. Department of Labor. (n.d.). *Commission on the Future of Worker-Management Relations—Section 5: Contingent Labor*. Accessed online.

University of Texas Medical Branch (UTMB) (n.d.). *Correctional managed care—employment*. Accessed online.

The Influence of Sexual Racism on Erotic Capital: A Systemic Racism Perspective

Jesus G. Smith, Maria Cristina Morales
and Chong-Suk Han

Contents

Despite the rapid growth in "queer studies," as a field of academic inquiry, there remains a gap in the literature examining the ways that race and racism influence sexual desire for, and among, gay men of color. This is particularly interesting given that the development of the Black Feminist paradigm (Lorde 1984; Hill Collins 2004) was helpful in developing new theories and analytics in order to help scholars better grasp how race and racism intersected in terms of sexuality. According to this perspective, the racial construction of "Black" has always been intimately linked to notions of sexuality. For instance, Black men and women were historically constructed as being sexually deviant as a contrast to "pure" White sexuality. More importantly, being constructed as sexually deviant has had, and continues to have, negative consequences for Black women and men that extend outside of the bedroom. Yet much of the work using this approach focused on the experiences of Black heterosexual women and men. Similarly, in sexuality studies, the sexual fields approach (Green 2008; Martin and George 2006) helped to expand theorizing around how micro interactions and structural forces arrange sexual desire and produce erotic capital, or "the quality and quantity of attributes that an individual possesses, which elicit an erotic response in another"

J. G. Smith (✉)
Ethnic Studies, Lawrence University, Appleton, WI, USA
e-mail: smithj@lawrence.edu

M. C. Morales
Department of Sociology and Anthropology, University of Texas at El Paso, El Paso, TX, USA
e-mail: mcmorales@utep.edu

C.-S. Han
Department of Sociology and Anthropology, Middlebury College, Middlebury, VT, USA
e-mail: chongsukh@middlebury.edu

© Springer International Publishing AG, part of Springer Nature 2018
P. Batur and J. R. Feagin (eds.), *Handbook of the Sociology of Racial and Ethnic Relations*,
Handbooks of Sociology and Social Research, https://doi.org/10.1007/978-3-319-76757-4_21

idual (Green 2008: 29). Per this perspective, otic life is organized around different sexual fields that produce different ideas of what is desirable in which those who more closely align with those ideas will accrue more erotic capital. For example, some sexual fields may value men who are trim and neatly shaven while other sexual fields may value men who are muscular and rugged appearing. Within different sexual fields, different characteristics are given more erotic "worth" and individual actors within a given sexual field attempt to maximize their erotic capital by highlighting those characteristics that are considered desirable within the sexual field in which they compete for sexual partners. However, these studies largely ignored the ways that sexual desires are racialized. So, while these theories and concepts have brought us far in our understanding of the ways that race and sexuality are intimately linked and how social structures influence sexual desires, there is still a lack of perspective when it comes to the ways that race and racism influences sexual desire for, and among, gay men of color.

At the same time, the notion of "sexual racism" has become widely distributed in popular narratives about the seemingly racialized sexual "preferences" of gay White men. Using the concepts developed within the black feminist paradigm and the sexual fields approach, we argue that sexual racism, or racial discrimination in a sexual context (Plummer 2008), greatly impacts the ways that individual actors are organized into sexually racist hierarchies that situate Whites as the most desirable and Blacks as the least desirable within the gay marketplace of desire. Because of this, we argue that while different sexual scenarios can produce different erotica that is based on those scenarios, racism remains systematically reproduced nonetheless, thus maintaining White supremacy through what becomes considered "universally desirable" among gay men.

In this chapter we explore how sexual racism impacts erotic capital among gay men who identify as Black and/or Black-mixed race. We argue that sexual racism influences erotic capital in four ways. First, sexual racism limits dating choices for Black and Black-mixed men. In other

words, systemic racism (Feagin 2006) in society maintains a rigid color line that is difficult to navigate if one is Black or mixed with Black, even in the realm of desire. This means that Black racial stereotypes about sexuality are imposed onto gay Black and mixed race men regardless of how they may actually racially identify, which are difficult to overcome. As a result, even changes in outer appearance, such as attempting to offset racist stereotypes about "Black thugs" by modifying their attire or their speech patterns, can do little to control the manner in which others perceive them. Without the power to determine how others position them in the racial hierarchy, the erotic capital of Blacks and Black-mixed gays are negatively affected by sexual racism. Second, although it has been suggested that mixed race individuals are positioned higher in the racial hierarchy than Blacks (Bonilla-Silva 2010), we suggest that Black-mixed individuals still experience sexual racism based on their Blackness. The salience of race in sexual interactions in turn constrains erotic capital. The third point is in regards to sexual fields. A sexual field (Green 2011: 247) is a pattern of relations where individual people come together in a single space and produce, through their "erotic sensibilities," an "overarching, transpersonal structure of desire." This structure of desire determines the status order within the sexual field of "specific characteristics that qualify as desirable" (Green 2011: 247). We argue that while different sexual fields produce different erotica specific to that field, sexual racism is nonetheless persistent across all sexual fields, resulting in Black men still accruing less erotic capital, even when they possess all of the qualities that should make them desirable within a given sexual field. This is particularly true of the online sexual market where people are allowed to be more open about their sexual desires due to the anonymity afforded to them (Smith 2017). Finally, we discuss how Black men navigate sexually racist assumptions about them in order to increase their erotic capital, although still operating within a context of hegemonic Whiteness. To arrive at this understanding, we explore the recent literature on race and sexuality as they pertain to desire.

21.1   Race and Racism in Sexual Desire

Within the mainstream gay community, race and racism greatly impacts the lives of gay men of color, particularly within the realm of dating and sexual behaviors, as well as how members of this group come to see themselves as both a racial and sexual minority (Ro et al. 2013). While Black gay men have intersecting views of their race and sexuality, they often do not adhere to a gay identity (Hunter 2010). Han (2007) theorized that a lack of acceptance within gay spaces has greatly contributed to gay men of color prioritizing their racial identity over their sexual identity, or refusing to identify as "gay" even when they are open about their sexual behaviors and same sex attractions (Han 2007, 2015a, b). For example, Han (2007) revealed that gay organizations worked towards acceptance from the mainstream rather than liberation from it through "various whitening practices" (p. 54) that include actively excluding men of color from "gay" public spaces (p. 54). These practices included requesting multiple IDs at the doors of gay clubs in order to keep men of color out, championing "universal gay issues" like marriage equality over other issues that may be of more critical importance to gay people of color, and creating barriers to leadership roles within "gay" organizations that dramatically impacted gay men of color (Han 2007, 2008a, b). The lack of being able to see themselves in the gay community as well as the active whitening of what it means to be "gay," has often resulted in internalized racism whereby gay men of color, including gay Black men, have come to see themselves as less desirable than gay White men (Loiacano 1989). In doing so, many gay men of color come to reject other men of color as unsuitable sexual partners (Han 2007) and/or adopt the language of White gay men to maintain racial hierarchies of desire (Han et al. 2014).

While racism in the gay community takes multiple forms, we are specifically interested in the concept of "sexual racism." Plummer (2008) discovered that sexual racism, or discrimination in sexual contexts, is manifested through the internet, pornographic media, gay clubs and bars, casual/anonymous sexual encounters, and romantic relationships. Plummer (2008) also noted that within these locations, sexual racism was reported to take the forms of sexual stereotypes, racial fetishism, as well as race-based sexual rejection. Similarly, Raymond and Mcfarland (2009) found that, Black men were the least preferred as sexual partners due to stereotypes such as being at higher risk for HIV than other ethno-racial groups, less likelihood of being among friendship networks, perception that they are harder to meet, and generally being less welcomed in venues that cater to gay men (Raymond and McFarland 2009).

As in heterosexual spaces, although in different forms, sexual racism against Black men may be intimately tied to the historic ways that Black sexuality has been constructed in the White imagination. As Nagel (2003) stated, "claims and concerns about the physical sexual endowments of Black men and the sexual appetites of Black women circulated back and forth across the Atlantic in the minds and publications of Europeans who settled the Americas" (11). Hill Collins (2004) also argued that African men's sexuality was seen as dangerous and in need of control (4)." Similarly, D'Emilio and Freedman (1997) suggested that "by labeling them [Black people] sexual savages, Whites reassured themselves that their own race was indeed the civilized one it aspired to be" (17) reinforcing the racial hierarchy between colonizers and the colonized (Hill Collins 2004). Black men continue to be socially constructed as aggressive, dominant and hyper-masculine tops with large penises and Asian men as smooth, feminine and passive bottoms (Grov, Parsons, and Bimbi 2010; Han 2008a, b; Wilson et al. 2009). Given the way that Black sexuality has been constructed, White men are seen as the default of desire, and as the preferred sexual partner, with other racial groups competing for their attention (Han 2008a, b). White gay men yield the largest influence in dictating the physical requirements of potential sex partners including race, being the group to reject men of color most often (Callander et al. 2012).

21.2 Understanding Sexual Racism

For this study, we have chosen to utilize Systemic Racism Theory (Feagin 2006) as a basis for understanding how Whites constructed sexual stereotypes about Blacks, which are meant to maintain White Supremacy, including within in the gay community. Unlike Racial Formation Theory (Omi and Winant 1994) that explores the various historic processes that have shaped racial hierarchies, Systemic Racism Theory examines "the White racist ideologies and attitudes created to maintain and rationalize White privilege and power," investigating how racism is reworked from the past and continues on into the present through "racial images, interpretations, emotions, and actions" (Feagin 2001: 6). Thus, the racist sexual stereotypes of the past created by Whites in the White imagination get replicated through, and then reinforced by, racist images and emotions in the present. Despite this strength in examining White racial attitudes and beliefs in maintaining White supremacy, systemic racism lacks a complex understanding of sexuality. In order to explore the ways that racism operates within the context of gay desire, we couple Systemic Racism Theory with the sexual fields framework developed by Green (2008).

Building on the work of Levi Martin and George (2006), the sexual fields framework highlights the ways that different characteristics are seen as being desirable in different erotic spaces which, in turn, influence sexual actor's self-presentations (Green 2008). Some components of the sexual field include a set of relations based on sexual partner competition and selection, how others are perceived within a particular field based on that fields ideals of sexual attractiveness, and the ways that individuals adjust their "front", or outward appearance, in order to increase their competitiveness in relation to sexual partner selection (Green 2011). Within different sexual fields, tiers of desirability are influenced by bodies, fashion, media, sexual practices and sexual identities that stratify the groups based on physical, affective and stylistic features (Green 2008). By adapting a particular "front" (Goffman 1956) through manipulation of personal appearance, behavior, or demeanor, particular classes of actors are able to elevate their status within the tiers of desirability (Green 2008).

Green's (2008) research revealed that "Black gay men engaged in a pattern of effective and behavioral negotiations," that is, presenting a "front," that includes taking up Black sexual stereotypes such as playing into White men's racial stereotypes about Black men's hyper-sexuality or presenting a "thug aesthetic" in order "to offset sexual marginality" (Green 2008: 27). By adjusting their "fronts" in accordance with what is seen as sexually attractive in different sexual fields, men can accrue erotic capital, "the quality and quantity of attributes that an individual possesses, which elicit an erotic response in another (Green 2008: 29)." Therefore, Blacks who are more masculine in appearance can be considered more desirable than feminine Black men within the gay community that values masculinity over femininity, particularly among Black men (Green 2008).

While there is much to be gained with the sexual fields framework, it lacks a strong understanding of how racism impacts sexuality and often works from a White logic (Zuberi and Bonilla-Silva 2008). For instance, Green (2011) gives the case of a gay Leather bar in Chicago as an example of a particular site where different sexual frames dictate what is sexually attractive (men wearing leather for example). Based on Green's argument, one would assume that individuals can move up the hierarchy of desire by incorporating the trappings of desirability into their "fronts." Similarly, a muscle bar can also be seen as a site where men can improve their erotic capital by developing larger muscles. However, regardless of the site and the sexual fields that populate those sites, systemic racism is replicated throughout. So a Leather bar with predominately White patrons might still find a Black patron invisible. In addition, frame adjustment is limited for people of color based on perceptions of their degree of blackness. Last, even if people of color adapt or engage in negotiations to offset marginality, White Supremacy can and often does remain situated as most desirable. For example, Han (2015a, b) found that gay Asian men who attempt to build muscles by going to the gym find little success at gay bars, despite possessing the "type" of body that is considered desirable within these venues.

Based on the limitations of both systemic racism in regards to sexuality and sexual fields framework in regards to race, a synthesis of the two can bring clarity to the way sexual racism influences erotic capital. That is, as an offspring of the sexual component of systemic racism, we can see how sexual racism organizes people into racial hierarchies with Whites on top and Blacks on bottom. From this hierarchy, erotic capital is dispersed among the different racial groups, with those seen as "White" gaining more capital and those seen as non-White gaining less.

21.3 Data and Methods

Data for this study was collected in El Paso, a predominately working class city consisting of 82% people of Mexican-origin, followed by 14% non-Latino-Whites, and 3% Blacks located along the U.S.–Mexico border (U.S. Census Bureau 2010). Participants were primarily recruited through the popular online gay men's dating site, adam4adam.com (A4A) that markets itself as an online space where gay men can find "friendship, romance or a hot hook up" (https://www.adam4adam.com/), posting and announcements placed on craigslist.com in the "men seeking men" section, the city's gay magazine titled Bloke, on Facebook, and through e-newsletters for Metropolitan Community Church (El Paso's sexually inclusive church). This purposeful sampling frame resulted in 16 participants, (4 Latinos, 4 non-Latino Whites, 4 Blacks, and 4

mixed race (Black and Latino and White and Latino, and Black and White) (N = 4) (Appendix A). For purposes of this study, we will focus on the experiences of Black and Black-Mixed men.

For our interview guide, we followed insights from Plummer's (2008) study on sexual racism. We also included questions relevant to the context of the study (i.e. the border), race and condom usage, and online profile identity. Interviews were recorded and transcribed verbatim and all respondents were assigned pseudonyms. Data were analyzed using NVivo 9, beginning with theory-derived concepts and expanding to include common themes across interviews. We sought to gain an understanding of how respondents identified in terms of race/ethnicity and sexuality. Other questionnaire items/themes included socio-economic status, education, perceptions of race in the gay community versus the straight community, and experiences of racism.

21.4 Sexual Racism and Its Impact on Erotic Capital

Sexual racism systematically organizes desire in a way that elevates Whites as more sexually desirable than Blacks and other men of color within the gay marketplace of desire. It also highlights the primacy and permanence of race in sexual relationships. As a result of this, sexual racism impacts how those who are perceived as White and light-skinned gain more erotic capital than those who are not. Below we describe the four ways in which sexual racism impacted erotic capital: (1) Race is central to identity; systemic racism imposes a strong racialized identity on Black gays, negatively impacting their erotic capital, (2) They see you as Black; how Black-mixed gays also experience sexual racism based on their Blackness and how it constrains their erotic capital, (3) It's the same across all fields; across sexual fields, sexual racism greatly decreases erotic capital for men of color, particularly Black men and especially online and, (4) Now I can't say I don't play on it; Blacks can play on the sexually racist stereotypes Whites have created of them in order to attempt to increase their erotic capital.

21.4.1 Race Is Central to Identity

Despite being both gay and Black, race was central to how many of the men in the study defined themselves. More importantly, the participants often believed that they had no choice but to consider themselves as Black before they considered themselves as gay. For example, when asked if he would prioritize his racial identity over his sexual identity, 47-year-old Joseph responded:

> Yes, because it's obvious, you know people always ask about racial identity as opposed to sexuality, and well, as an African American, you don't have a choice. You're Black when you're seen, so that's first. That's always first priority.

Therefore, race for Black gays is not what Gans (1979) referred to as *symbolic ethnicity* where individuals get to decide if they make ethncity a part of daily interactions. As the above quote demonstrates, Joseph makes clear that a racialized identity is unavoidable for Black people, and that they do not have a choice when it comes to how they are racially identified. Because of this, Black gay men must always address their racial identity over their sexual identity because their blackness is always visible while there sexuality can be hidden during social interaction with others. As a result, Black men prioritize their racial identity over their sexual identity. This is extremely important because it reflects how the history of racism in the United States continues to greatly limited Black men's ability to operate outside of racial categories (Feagin 2006). Another participant, a 57-year-old named Peter explained:

> One of the challenges that a lot of dark-skinned people have, I think in America, is they don't have a choice. You go for a job interview, they see your skin and automatically they make assumptions. They hear you speak, they make assumptions, they see how you're dressed and make assumptions. You can hide your sexuality but your race you can't hide.

The permanence of race meant that there was not much Black people could do to overcome being seen as Black before anything else.

When Peter describes going to a job interview, he ties it to the history of racism in the U.S. that perceives Black men as less professional (Feagin 2010). In this case, wearing a suit and tie does not change the idea of race already deeply planted inside the minds of individuals. When Peter mentions that "they hear you speak" and "they make assumptions," he is again tying this to a history that perceives Black men as inarticulate and uneducated; Black people who speak "proper" English are still Black. Race in these scenarios is viciously tied to the racist past of the U.S. and embedded with expectations and assumptions, constructed and used by Whites as a means of racial control and subordination. Thus, attempting to present a certain type of front, for example "appropriate job candidate" in Peter's case, by wearing a suit and tie does not negate his Blackness.

Ideas about race are implicated in the way sexual racism impacts erotic capital for men of color as being Black takes precedent over any other identities in the sexual market, and greatly impacts how other gays interact with Black people. When asked to explain how his race impacts his sexuality, 31-year-old Dorian stated:

> Well I think people consider me to be…they expect me to be more ghetto, rough, and thuggish, based on the way that I look…I hear it a lot when they get to know me they tell me I'm nothing about what I look like…. people automatically assume me to be this straight up "top."

In the quote above, we see how first appearance again leads to the socially prescribed behaviors expected of Black men. The expectation that Black people will be "ghetto, rough, and thuggish," reflects a history of systemic racism in the U.S., as beliefs about Black hyper-sexuality continues to dictate the sexual expectations of Black men. In this case, Dorian again has no choice in his own racial identity but must navigate the racist assumptions about him. Due to the racialization of Black bodies, Blacks gays, such as Dorian, are stereotypically assumed to be the assertive top partner during sex and aggressive and "rough" in the bedroom.

While sexual racism at times expects aggressive sexual behavior from Blacks, it can also result in exclusion. Take for example the case of 55-year-old Phillip. When asked how his race impacted his sexuality, he surmised:

> I guess when I was growing up, you would meet guys in the clubs and they'll talk to you, but they wouldn't walk out with you.

While Blacks bodies are racialized as over-sexualized when it comes to sex, White gays are still reluctant to be seen with them in public. Thus, the implication is that Black men are good for sex but not to build a relationship with. For Phillip, being Black eroded his erotic capital if it meant meeting up outside a sexual site like the club. What needs to be considered in this context is how White ideas about Black aggression have constructed these stereotypes and Black men have been and continue to be trapped by them. This reinforces the idea that race has built-in assumptions that impact how others are perceived and limits what people can do based on this, thus again effecting the way erotic capital is distributed in the sexual market.

21.4.2 They See You as Black

While it has been argued that mixed race men with "ambiguous phenotypes" can engage in deceptive front work to increase their erotic capital (Green 2011), we find that Black-mixed gays are nonetheless still perceived as Black, thus complicating the argument that they can engage in deceptive front work. To illuminate this scenario, take 23-year-old Black and Latino mix Leo who claimed:

> Here on the border, um, well when people, I guess, take a look at me, they see a Black person first even though I am mixed.

Given the sexual field of the U.S./Mexico border, Blackness resonates in unique ways that nonetheless still reflect the durability of a binary Black and White system in society. In the above

quote Leo makes it clear that despite being mixed race, he is perceived as a Black person. This sentiment was echoed by 40-year-old mixed Black and Latino Michael who stated:

> I think the stereotype is still there as far as you know, people they look at me first and they assume that I'm Black… the majority of Mexicans hit on me and…they assume that I don't speak Spanish and you know, they're talking to their friends and they're speaking in Spanish and I'm playing my coy little self and being very quiet and they say something stupid about me and I turn around and answer them in Spanish and they're all, you know, they're floored. They're kind of embarrassed of the fact that…they make assumptions, thinking that I didn't speak the language, they made the assumption and then I turn around and you know, basically clap them with you know, what did you say about me?

Michael's account helps us see how even being racially mixed does not lead to the men being perceived as "mixed" but rather still leads to them being perceived as Black. In actuality, when part Black, gay men are perceived as *only* Black. In the scenario that Michael describes, he is hit on by Mexican men who assume he is only Black, despite being mixed with Latino. In this case, the association with Blackness also makes him a cultural outsider who is assumed to not know Spanish. His status as a Black gay man becomes apparent when the gay Latino men speak Spanish in his presence assuming that he will not understand them.

Interestingly, mixed race Blacks that are mixed with White, as oppose to Latino, have some White privilege, as is the case with 20-year-old White and Black mixed James. James surmised:

> I think I've had far more positive than negative experiences because of my lighter skin intonation so I guess like because I guess I don't look more African American, that's kind of a good thing in that sense…. Like I've never had anyone say, "Oh you Black I don't like you," but I've heard people say that about Blacks… like me myself for example, I can personally say I don't find Black people attractive so I know there has to be other's that feel that way.

In this case, being mixed with White on the U.S./Mexico border increases James's erotic capital. Yet the most significant extraction from his comments come from the way he rationalizes how he feels about other seemingly full Black men and what he thinks others feel about them. While James does not have to deal with the blatant discrimination that many dark-skinned men face among gay men, his comments demonstrate how White standards of sexual desire reduces erotic capital for Black gays and Black-White mixed gays look down on their own Blackness and privilege the part of themselves. James has heard people denigrate Black people and even sympathizes with them, all the while finding it "good" that he does not have to experience this form of discrimination.

21.4.3 It's the Same Across All Fields

While the internet has a limitless set of sexual fields (Green 2011) where personal profiles aim to gain erotic capital, we maintain that the permanence of racism across various sexual fields limits erotic capital for people of color. The internet has created new ways for systemic racism to replicate itself not only digitally, but globally (Daniels 2012). In the context of this study, adam4adam.com presents a popular hookup app where men can select different cities and locations. That is, users can pick the city of El Paso, which is a minority majority city in the southwest of Texas, and be confronted with different aspects that yield different erotic capital based on the people of that city, in this case Mexican-Americans and Mexican immigrants. In practice, the internet's added layer of anonymity as real names are virtually never used in online profiles and "interaction" is never face-to-face in person. This encouraged sexual racism to prosper, allowing men to express blatantly what they prefer as well as what they reject. As 30-year-old Areli stated:

> I think people are more specific to what they're looking for and aren't afraid to ask for what they're looking for online so I think racism can present itself stronger online, where as you know, if you're in person, live, I think there's different forms of subtle racism that sometimes people don't really pay attention to.

Areli expressed how he sees racism online as "stronger" than the more "subtle racism" some experience offline. In particular, being online actually allows people to be more themselves because they know what "they're looking for and aren't afraid to ask for it." This might mean that even though being online can reflect many different sexual fields and different erotica pertaining to those fields, the internet is also a space where people can feel more comfortable expressing their racial prejudices regardless of location and audience. 40-year-old mixed Black and Latino Michael further supported this idea when he stated:

> I think online people have a definite idea of what they want. But if you're not what they want, they let you know. Or if you don't fit a certain mold, they let you know and they move on. Um, you know, so I think online, it's easier because you're not in front of that person so they can be more of their own selves.

This idea that a person can be more of "their own selves" is striking for many reasons. First, sexual racism is blatant online. Based on the perceptions that gay men can be "more of themselves" online and have a "definite idea of what they want," the internet is an ideal location to express varying sexual preferences and erotic desires. The prevalence of racial preferences online is illuminated by 44-year-old Matt:

> I think the best reference would be the online hookup applets that more clearly express what they're into and what they're not into. And you can see a number of profiles that say Whites only, White and Latino only, no Black, no fat, no older.

Matt stated that "a number of profiles" explicitly make statements that work to exclude certain men of color. In the case of the U.S./Mexico border, Black men are excluded, as White men are usually preferred, and in many cases "White and Latino only" is blatantly stated. Matt also expressed that Blackness is lumped together with other non-desirable traits such as fatness and old age. Where some men are able to disguise their age online or engage in activities that increased weight loss (Green 2011), Blackness is seen as unchangeable, not preferred and similar to other less desirable traits. Despite this, men can and often do choose to play on the ideas associated with race in order to increase their erotic capital.

21.4.4   Now I Can't Say that I Don't Play on It

While sexual racism in the gay community greatly reduces Black men's erotic capital, some men may utilize racist sexual stereotypes in order to increase both their erotic capital and their potential pool of sexual mates. Michael explained how this is possible:

> And so you know that stereotype, I think the first impression people see of me they say, oh who is this Black guy and hey come here, I have some chocolate and whatever. But you know it's just one of those things, that you know, I think it's something that, I think as a Black male, you kind of enjoy.

While Michael is a mixed Black and Latino male he expressed how people see him as Black and knowing he has "some chocolate," he mentions how the sexual stereotype, such as the one described below by Joseph, associated with Black men can be enjoyable. As Joseph stated:

> Hmmm, well it impacts it in ways that people perceive you based on stereotypes. Um of course, in an average society you're perceived as dominant, um you have a big dick, athletic, hum so it impacts it from that perception. For me personally, it, it, it's just normal. I mean it doesn't matter. Now I can't say I don't play on it sometimes (laughs) like when I use to live in Juarez [Mexico].

Joseph understood that the sexually racist stereotype of Black men with "big dicks," "athletic" bodies and "dominance" are common in an "average society," regardless of the sexual field. This is so common, that for Joseph it is "normal" and "doesn't matter" for him much. Knowing this, he plays on the stereotype, especially in a border town like Juarez (Mexico) where he, as a Black man, is a rarity. In both Joseph and Michael's cases, sexual racism has limited their erotic capital as Black and mixed with Black men, but if they play on the sexual stereotypes assigned to them through their race, they can

offset the marginalization brought on by racism as long as it affirms the racist ideas of non-Blacks. This is especially true online where Black men are more likely to be confronted with sexual racism. As Leo explained when asked about stereotypes online, he stated "Um by pictures, by numbers, by if you see on their profile a Black guy and it has their cock size it's like ten plus or it'll be like 8 plus or some outrageous number…" Similarly, Matt stated, "well definitely the one in terms of reference to African Americans, you know big dick profiles." For both Leo and Matt, Black men utilized their online profiles to highlight their above average penis sizes with "some outrageous number." By using their profiles Black men can counter some of the sexual racism they experience by emphasizing parts of them that may increase their erotic capital in one way while lowering it in another. Regardless, the potential of Whiteness to increase erotic capital seems overwhelming. As Dorian explained when adjusting the race on his adam4adam.com profile:

> The funny thing was I put that I was Black on there and I didn't get as many hits. As soon as I put mixed, hits came from everywhere… And the number 1 question was, "What are you mixed with?" Same body, same picture, the only thing I changed was Black to mixed…."

Dorian presented a clear example of how whiteness increases erotic capital online for gay men. When Dorian showed his race as he actually identifies, as Black, his chances of finding a sexual partner were not as high as when he changed it to mixed. Even then, the interest was sparked by questions about his racial mix. Here, sexual racism decreases erotic capital when people identify as Black but increases it for mixed-race, demonstrating the power of race and anti-Blackness in sexual desire.

21.5   Conclusion

In this study we started to explore how sexual racism impacts erotic capital for Black and Black-Mixed gay men. Sexual racism in sexual relations results in the desire and privileging of Whiteness and the subjugation and stereotyping of Blackness. In the gay community, racial identity even takes primacy over the sexual identity, which limits their "fronts" and even decreases erotic capital. Even Black-Mixed individuals experienced sexual racism associated with their Blackness. In the case of the internet website adam4adam.com it allowed men to visit different cities with entirely different sexual fields. Yet the internet was still seen as a field where people are allowed to be more open with their racist beliefs those supporting sexual racism.

In such racialized contexts, gay Black and Black-Mixed men find ways to increase their erotic capital, mostly by playing up to sexual racists stereotypes of Black bodies. In particular, Black and Black-Mixed gay men use stereotypes of being aggressive and over-sexualized to increase their erotic capital. Yet, there are some indications that such strategies only matter for sex and not for building relationships. In the end, Black and Black-Mixed gays are measured against Whiteness and ideas of what is desirable and White-created stereotypes of Blacks, limiting how much they can actually transcend the dominance of White supremacy.

Theories of racism and sexuality have aided researchers in revealing the unique ways race is reproduced in sexual scenarios. One such theory is that of sexual fields, which suggests that different sexual fields produce different ideas of what is desirable and those who more closely align with those ideas will accrue more erotic capital. This can be seen in the case of Adam4adam.com, a website where all sorts of men from all parts of the U.S. can convene to discuss sex and relationships. Yet, despite the access that the website brings men from different backgrounds to others, systemic racism remains in place. This results in White men cleansing Blacks and other people of color from their searches, resulting in them just talking to other Whites exclusively (Robinson 2015). This reality reveals how certain perspectives lack a strong

racial lens to accurately capture the experiences of people of color.

To improve on this limitation, we have intersected the sexual fields framework with systemic racism theory. Systemic racism theory considers "White racist ideologies and attitudes created to maintain and rationalize White privilege and power," by means of "racial images, interpretations, emotions, and actions" (Feagin 2001: 6) in order to arrive at a greater understanding of how racism replicates itself from the past to the present through social structures. This helps explain how despite everyone having their own erotic capital, what is determined as the most desirable traits that will yield that greatest erotic capital is usually dictated by White standards of beauty and normalcy. With both these perspectives in mind, there can be a greater understanding of how sexual racism, or racial discrimination in sexual contexts, takes place and why. More importantly it is clear how it organizes racial groups into hierarchies of desire with Whites as most desirable and non-Whites as least and erotic capital distributed along this hierarchy accordingly.

References

"Adam4adam.com,". Accessed January 30, 2012. https://www.adam4adam.com/.

Bonilla-Silva, E. (2010). *Racism without racists: Color-blind racism and the persistence of racial inequality in the United States*. Lanham: Rowman & Littlefield Publishers.

Callander, D., Holt, M., & Newman, C. E. (2012). Just a preference: Racialised language in the sex-seeking profiles of gay and bisexual men. *Culture, Health & Sexuality, 14*(9), 1049–1063.

D'Emilio, J., & Freedman, E. B. (1997). *Intimate matters: A history of sexuality in America*. Chicago: University of Chicago Press.

Feagin, J. (2001). *Racist America: Roots, current realities, and future reparations*. London: Routledge.

Feagin, J. (2006). *Systemic racism: A theory of oppression*. New York: Routledge.

Feagin, J. (2010). *The white racial frame: Centuries of racial framing and counter framing*. London: Routledge.

Gans, H. J. (1979). Symbolic ethnicity: The future of ethnic groups and cultures in America. *Ethnic and Racial Studies, 2*(1).

Goffman, E. (1956). *The presentation of self in everyday life*. New York: Anchor Books.

Green, A. I. (2008). Erotic habitus: Toward a sociology of desire. *Theory and Society, 37*(6), 597–626.

Green, A. I. (2011). Playing the (sexual) field: The interactional basis of systems of sexual stratification. *Social Psychology Quarterly, 74*(3), 244–266.

Grov, C., Parsons, J. T., & Bimbi, D. S. (2010). The association between penis size and sexual health among men who have sex with men. *Archives of Sexual Behavior, 39*(3), 788–797.

Han, C.-S. (2007). They don't want to cruise your type: Gay men of color and the racial politics of exclusion. *Social Identities, 13*(1), 51–67.

Han, C. S. (2008a). A qualitative exploration of the relationship between racism and unsafe sex among Asian Pacific islander gay men. *Archives of Sexual Behavior, 37*(5), 827–837.

Han, C.-S. (2008b). No fats, femmes, or Asians: The utility of critical race theory in examining the role of gay stock stories in the marginalization of gay Asian men. *Contemporary Justice Review, 11*(1), 11–22.

Han, C.-S. (2015). No brokeback for black men: Pathologizing black male (homo)sexuality through downlow discourse. *Social Identities, 21*(3), 228–243.

Han, C. W. (2015). *Geisha of a different kind: Race and sexuality in gayasian America*. New York: NYU Press.

Han, C. S., Han, C. S., Ayala, G., Paul, J., Boylan, R., Gregorich, S. E., et al. (2014). Stress and coping with racism and their role in sexual risk for HIV among African American, Asian/Pacific islander, and latino men who have sex with men. *Archives of Sexual Behavior, 44*(2), 411–420.

Hill Collins, P. (2004). *Black sexual politics: African Americans, gender, and the new racism*. New York: Routledge.

Hunter, M. A. (2010). All the gays are white and all the blacks are straight: Black gay men, identity, and community. *Sexuality Research and Social Policy, 7*(2), 81–92.

Loiacano, D. K. (1989). Gay identity issues among black American's: Racism, homophobia, and the need for validation. *Journal of Counseling and Development., 68*(1), 21–25.

Lorde, A. (1984). *Sister outsider: Essays and speeches*. Trumansburg, NY: Crossing Press.

Martin, J. L., & George, M. (2006). Theories of sexual stratification: Toward an analysis. *Sociological Theory, 2*(2), 107–132.

Nagel, J. (2003). *Race, ethnicity, and sexuality: Intimate intersections, forbidden frontiers*. New York, NY: Oxford University Press.

Omi, M., & Winant, H. (1994). *Racial formation in the United States: From the 1960s to the 1990s*. New York: Routledge.

Plummer, M. D. (2008). Sexual racism in gay communities: Negotiating the ethnosexual marketplace. *Dissertation Abstracts International: Section B: The Sciences and Engineering, 68*(8–B), 5636.

Raymond, H. F., & McFarland, W. (2009). Racial mixing and HIV risk among men who have sex with men. *AIDS and Behavior, 13*(4), 630–637.

Ro, A., Ayala, G., Paul, J., & Choi, K. H. (2013). Dimensions of racism and their impact on partner selection among men of colour who have sex with men: Understanding pathways to sexual risk. *Culture, Health & Sexuality, 15*(7), 836–850. Retrieved http://search.proquest.com/docview/1449309742?accountid=14523%5Cnhttp://ucelinks.cdlib.org:8888/sfx_local?url_ver=Z39.88-2004&rft_val_fmt=info:ofi/fmt:kev:mtx:journal&genre=article&sid=ProQ:ProQ:psycinfo&atitle=Dimensions+of+racism+and+their+impact+on+partn.

Robinson, B. A. (2015). 'Personal preference' as the new racism: Gay desire and racial cleansing in cyberspace. *Sociology of Race and Ethnicity, 1*(2), 317–330.

Smith, J. G. (2017). Two faced racism in online gay sex: Preferences in the frontstage or racism in the backstage? In P. G. Nixon and I. K. Dusterhoft (Eds.), *Sex in the digital age* (pp. 134–146). Howick Place, London: Ashgate/Routlegde Publishing Co.

U.S. Census Bureau. (2010). Race alone or in combination. *2010 Census Summary File*, El Paso, TX. Retrieved March 23, 2012. http://factfinder2.census.gov/faces/tableservices/jsf/pages/productview.xhtml?pid=DEC_10_SF1_QTP5&prodType=table.

Wilson, P. A., Valera, P., Ventuneac, A., Balan, I., Rowe, M., & Carballo-Dieguez, A. (2009). Race-based sexual stereotyping and sexual partnering among men who use the internet to identify other men for bareback sex. *Journal of Sex Research, 46*(5), 399–413.

Zuberi, T., & Bonilla-Silva, E. (Eds.). (2008). *White logic, White methods: Racism and methodology*. Lanham, MD: Rowman & Littlefield Publishers Inc.

Lost and Damaged: Environmental Racism, Climate Justice, and Conflict in the Pacific

22

Danielle Falzon and Pinar Batur

Contents

Abstract

Pacific Island Nations are at great risk from climate change impacts such as storms and sea level rise. In the next century, they face the possibility of losing their homes and land, and having to relocate elsewhere; though questions of to where, how, and when remain open. To better understand these uncertain futures, we look to the past for answers on how these precarious circumstances have come about, examining the contribution of racist colonialism to environmental destruction and climate vulnerability. Telling the story of two islands —Nauru and Banaba—we imagine how it may be possible to begin approaching climate justice through international policy. Thus far, climate negotiations at the international scale have failed to meet the needs of the world's poorest and most vulnerable. However, we see a possibility for just futures with the incorporation of a mechanism on loss and damage that must hold countries accountable for their destructive pasts.

The world is actively failing Pacific Islanders. As of this writing, the planet has passed the threshold of 400 parts per million of carbon dioxide in the atmosphere, a key indicator that we have moved into an era of massive changes in the global climate (Khan 2016). And as the concentration of CO_2 and other greenhouses continue to rise due to human industry and energy production, the islands of the Pacific disappear into the ocean.

D. Falzon (✉)
Department of Sociology, Brown University, Providence, RI, USA
e-mail: danielle_falzon@brown.edu

P. Batur
Department of Sociology and the Program in Environmental Studies, Vassar College, Poughkeepsie, NY, USA
e-mail: pibatur@vassar.edu

© Springer International Publishing AG, part of Springer Nature 2018
P. Batur and J. R. Feagin (eds.), *Handbook of the Sociology of Racial and Ethnic Relations*,
Handbooks of Sociology and Social Research, https://doi.org/10.1007/978-3-319-76757-4_22

The Pacific is home to 22 island nations, each with its own culture, language, and people. Though the Pacific Island Nations cannot be reduced to a singular set of characteristics and histories, they are similarly positioned in their vulnerability to global climate change. Pacific Island Nations are largely low-lying and a great risk from climate change impacts such as storms and sea level rise. In the next century, they face the possibility of losing their homes and land, and having to relocate elsewhere; though questions of to where, how, and when remain open. To better understand these uncertain futures, we look to the past for answers on how these precarious circumstances have come about, examining the contribution of racist colonialism to environmental destruction and climate vulnerability. Telling the story of two islands—Nauru and Banaba—we imagine how it may be possible to begin approaching climate justice through international policy.

Ulrich Beck explored alternative perspectives on climate change, pointing out that the first question framing this issue is often: "What can we do against climate change?" He posits, though, that this is difficult to answer without considering an alternative question: "What does climate change do to us, and how does it alter the order of society and politics?" (Beck 2016: 36). While the first framing question could lead many of us to apathy, feelings of incapacity, worsened by the acceptance of "premeditated catastrophe," we want to instead emphasize the importance of striving for and working toward justice through global policy. In considering how climate change alters social and political order, we argue that society and politics can be mobilized to build a more egalitarian world. This is only possible, however, if there is a concerted global commitment.

This chapter begins with a discussion of the meanings and interconnections of concepts such as colonialism, systemic racism, and environmental justice. These concepts are crucial for understanding this historic and racialized nature of climate injustice in the Pacific Islands. We then move on to detail key pieces of the colonial histories of the islands, highlighting Nauru and

Banaba (now part of Kiribati) as places of extreme environmental destruction for the benefit of the colonizers, and to the detriment of the people living there. These histories illustrate the connections between colonialism and climate injustice. Next, we turn to the context of international climate policy under the United Nations Framework Convention on Climate Change (UNFCCC), and raises the possibility of using the new component of "loss and damage" to move toward just solutions. Finally, we conclude by discussing the uncertain futures of Pacific Island Nations and the urgency of developing just global policies to actively correct for the century of collective failure in protecting their people.

22.1 Racism, Colonialism, and Climate Justice

Pacific Island Nations, along with regions across what is now termed the "Global South," have faced injustices for centuries. Their current vulnerability and lack of capacity to adapt to climate change on their own is premised on years of rapid resource depletion, oppression, and exploitation under colonialism, and post-colonial political marginalization on the global stage. Their current prospective of loss of land, cultures, homes, and potentially sovereignty are therefore part of a complex web of interconnected injustices, which diminishes the agency of these nations and their citizens to shape their futures. While the histories of the Pacific Island Nations do not begin with their colonization by the Western world, such colonization is the beginning of the oppression, marginalization, and exploitation that creates the nations' realities today. In this section, we outline the key concepts and theories employed in this chapter to better understand the potential for justice in the Pacific Islands.

First, colonialism refers to the economic exploitation, political oppression, and cultural and social marginalization of the Global South by the Global North. Direct and indirect colonial rule and post-colonial oppression remain a dominant force in the 21st century. The history of formerly colonized nations cannot be clearly divided into a colonial past and an independent present, since culture, values, landscapes, and political and economic structures are all inevitably marked by the influence of the colonizer. This highlights the role of formal and informal domination in the relationship between colonizers and colonized, legitimized and maintained by discourses and knowledge systems that were produced to justify them. This justification is rooted in systemic racism, which operates under the global white racial frame.

Systemic racism is the coalescence of economic, political, cultural and social forces that foster the articulation of racial inequality through institutional structure. Globally, it allows for the succession of overt individual and collective racist attitudes and practices into more covert operations, integrating racism in all past, present, and future contexts. Under global systemic racism, color means powerlessness, and to struggle against it means working to alter such discourse so that the meaning and impact of race can be changed (Marable 1996: 5).

The "white racial frame" is an associated tool of systemic racism that rationalizes white dominance, made global through racist colonial oppression. It incorporates the colonizer's construction of reality into the colony, and legitimizes the continued supremacy of white values and systems that oppress colonized societies. Racism becomes part of the system of knowing, and is perpetuated even after the end of formal colonial rule through a conceptual dominance, through the "colonization of the mind." The power in colonizing the mind is malleable adaptability to the skewed balance of power in the contemporary post-colonial era. Goldberg (1993) analyzed this ideological component of racism to understand how it has become pervasive and universal. He pointed out that once the racist discourse was set, it molded to fit new contexts and time periods to rationalize and validate the hierarchical division of people along racial lines (Goldberg 1993).

Together, racial oppression and capitalist exploitation through colonialism imposes violence on people, on all species, on the environment, and on the planet as a whole (Batur 2007). Three core elements of systemic racism also work to normalize and reinforce global environmental racism: the explicit discrimination against and exploitation of people of color; institutional economic and political practices that both create racial hierarchy and destroy the environment; and the "white racial frame," discussed above, that rationalizes ongoing white oppression in every facet of life and justifies the domination of the environment globally (Feagin et al. 1999; Batur and Weber 2017). Thus, when climate change impacts the world's poorest and most vulnerable populations first, while predominantly rich, white, industrialized nations, that are most responsible for climate change, it is evidence for the persistence of systemic racism into the 21st century. There are clear ties between historical colonialism and the present vulnerability of nations to ecological crises, which enables the conceptualization of the global climate change within the context of white racial frame. For this reason, Timmons Roberts and Parks (2007) argue, "the issue of global climate change is fundamentally an issue of injustice and inequality," (97).

Environmental racism is not exclusively a product of the disproportionate impacts of climate change, however, it is more broadly the product of all systemic racial power resulting in the environmental degradation, pollution, and exploitation of the natural resources of racially oppressed communities. Bullard (1994) defines environmental racism as, "any policy, practice, or directive that differentially affects or disadvantages…individuals, groups, or communities because of their race or color" (32). Pulido (1996) states that environmental racism gives insights into the "intersection of racism, social justice, and political economy" (142). She has furthermore demonstrated that the driving factor for inequitable exposure to pollutants and environmental destruction is racial differentiation, rather than class hierarchy (Pulido 1996). The environmentally destructive practices of colonizing nations for their profit and progress are then the inception and establishment of environmental racism.

The struggle against global environmental racism necessitates the struggle against what David Pellow argues is a "unified practice:" the domination of people via the domination of their environment (Pellow 2007: 20). Colonization is an important example of such a "unified practice." This must entail the introduction of five principles of environmental justice: "guaranteeing the right to environmental protection, preventing harm before it occurs, shifting the burden of proof to polluters, obviating proof of intent to discriminate, and redressing existing inequalities," (Westra and Wenz 1995: 9). By using these principles of environmental justice to combat the legacies of colonialism and the persistence of global racism through the white racial frame, there is the possibility to, as Adamson et al. (2002) put it, "secure political, economic and cultural liberation that has been denied for over 500 years of colonization and oppression," (5).

Katherine Teaiwa asks, "What remains in the aftershocks of empire? How do imperial formations persist in their material debris, in ruined landscapes and through the social ruination of people's lives?" (Teaiwa 2014). In the case of Pacific Island Nations, the answer to these questions is that they are left bare and vulnerable to the next wave of challenges brought on by the industrialized world from climate change. They continuously confront racist colonial legacies, and environmental and climate injustice synchronistically. Thus, understanding racism as more than just prejudice and discrimination is crucial to recognizing how it is structurally built into modern society and policymaking, and how it includes the domination of both peoples and their environments. In the next section we will outline two illustrative cases of these dynamics in the Pacific.

22.2 Environmental Racism in the Pacific

The Pacific islands entered the colonial imagination in the late 17 and 18th century, fostering images of the "noble savage," with descriptions of the people living there as being in their most natural, animal-like, and uncivilized state,

yet also uncommonly pleasant and naïve, on idyllic white beaches untouched by civilization (Batur and Weber 2017). As the Pacific peoples' resistance to the colonial intrusion grew, however, so did a narrative of the "dangerous immoral savage," portraying islanders as sexually predatory and spiritually undeveloped, living in primitive societies. These discourses, both positive and negative, were formulated to serve the same purpose: justifying the need of continuing European intervention to civilize, bring religion, and continue colonial control.

The journals of European explorers reflect this progression, such as that of Milo Calkin, who explored the islands in the 1830s. He wrote of the "immense depravity and ignorance" of man in a completely uncivilized environment: fierce, savage, animal-like, and sexual. According to these accounts, island nations were without history, and could have a future only if they remained under the rule of Western colonial powers. The islanders were both blamed for, and judged according to, the colonial conditions that they endured. Their struggles against colonial exploitation were folded into the "dangerous immoral savage" framework—reflective of the "colonial mind" structured by the white racial frame—and enabled the unified practice of oppressing, exploiting, and devastating the lives of the people and their environment (Batur and Weber 2017).

This section outlines two stories of colonialism and environmental degradation. The exploitation of peoples and their environments that occurred in both cases must be understood as actions spurred by, not only the racist actions of the past, but also by the continued injustices faced on the populations as effects of these actions and the persistence of the global white racial frame. These are furthermore stories of how islanders have been left vulnerable to the impacts of climate change.

22.2.1 Nauru

In Nauru, the previously lush and beautiful forest now exists only around the small island's perimeter, with the entire center of the island contaminated after intensive phosphate mining. Journalist Jack Hitt described the island as "one of the scariest things [he's] ever seen." Schlanger (2015) described, "Almost all of Nauru is missing, picked clean, right down to the coral skeleton supporting the island…all blindingly white."

In the early years of the 20th Century, the small island was visited by Western travelers and was discovered to have a wealth of highly sought-after phosphate. From 1908, when Nauru was made part of the German protectorate for access to this resource, through World War II when it was occupied by Japan, there was continuous phosphate mining. After World War II, both Great Britain and the Australia/New Zealand Commonwealth administered control over the island and its mineral reserves. Through these colonial occupations, Nauru became dependent on the mining of phosphate as its primary tradable good. The island maintained the industry even after it gained independence in 1968, until reserves were exhausted in the early 21st century.

Phosphate was once the miracle mineral that enabled global industrial agriculture to achieve high rates of growth, but the phosphate mines on Nauru now stand as a sign of toxic pollution and environmental devastation. Phosphate in high concentrations burns the earth, leaving charred land in its wake. In addition, the island is now laden with additional heavy metal byproducts of mining, such as lead, uranium, and cadmium, which continue to poison the land and water, destroying the surrounding ecosystem (http://www.unep.fr/shared/publications/pdf/2890-PhosphateMining.pdf).

Though the environmental and social costs of phosphate mining were high, Nauru had no economic option but to mine and sell its supply to the point of exhaustion, even after colonization. When the phosphate ran out, Nauru became desperate for foreign investment, and set itself up as a tax haven for the economic elite to store their money. The island now houses an Australian detention center, upon which its economy is now entirely dependent. Nauru was the chosen site of the Australian "Pacific Solution," policy to locate asylum seekers on island detention centers from 2001 to 2007.[1] Though the first regime of detention centers was ended, a second regime has begun, though its details have been closely guarded (Doherty 2016).

Thus, Nauru continues to be "informally" dominated by colonial forces to this day, despite the nation's formal independence. The people of Nauru now live in impoverished conditions, as the island becomes increasingly unrecognizable due to exploitative and destructive international interventions, while they are experiencing impacts of climate change. Nauru has also been experiencing drought due to inconsistent rainfall, straining the island's only source of freshwater (Schlanger 2015). Residents are increasingly concerned about their futures; about what climate change will do to the island, and whether they will be able to stay there for much longer.

22.2.2 Banaba

The story of Banaba is one of exploitation through the extraction economy. Captain Neill Green, reporting in *Life* in 1929 under the heading of "Modern Treasure Island," described Banaba as "…a small insignificant speck, set in the midst of a vast expanse of water, Banapa [sic], or Ocean Island, as it is generally called, is one of Britain's most valued possessions of its size in Pacific." At that time, the British took 70,000 tons of phosphate from the island each year. In her 1948 prize-winning book *It's a Bigger Life*, Lucille Iremonger, writing about her life as the wife of a colonial officer stated that "Every time anyone opened his mouth on Ocean Island the word 'phosphate' came out…. For hundreds of thousands of years the slow process

---

[1]After international protests, Australia established new "relocation" centers on the Christmas Islands, a policy carried out in order to circumvent the arrival of "boat people" on the mainland until 2013. Presently, a new policy has been designed to deter refugees, called "Operation Sovereign Borders." Carried out as a military operation, the policy mandates mandatory detention for all refugees, about 10,000 per year, with numbers only increasing, especially since 2010 (https://www.theguardian.com/environment/2013/apr/16/australia-climate-change-refugee-status).

of making an island like this had gone on…Then one day a man struck his foot against a 'coral' door-stop in a Sydney office, and phosphate was discovered. The life of a Pacific island was changed before the inhabitants knew anything about it," (quoted in Teaiwa 2014: 39). Iremonger also described that the mining left, "Row upon row of gnarled pinnacles of porous rock as tall as trees gave the place a look as some mediaeval inferno," (quoted in Teaiwa 2014).

Though it was never officially a colony of Great Britain, Banaba was incorporated as part of the British Gilbert and Ellice Islands Protectorate in 1901. The island was so heavily mined for phosphate that by 1940, it was clear that it was becoming less and less capable of sustaining both locals and the mining industry, much like what occurred in Nauru. Then, during World War II, Japanese forces took control of the island and moved the Banabans to internment camps on neighboring islands such as Tarawa in Kiribati, creating greater distress and devastation for the population (Edwards 2013).

After the war, Australian forces took control of Banaba and the British reinitiated the intensive mining of phosphate, to revive their post-war agriculture. To facilitate the growing mining industry, they forcefully moved the Banabans to the island of Rabi in north-eastern Fiji, once again displacing them from their homes. This move also resulted in their further distancing from their traditional connection to the land and their traditional knowledge of fishing, putting their cultural identity at risk (Campbell 2010) gold.

Though the island of Rabi seemed similar enough to Banaba in the eyes of the British, Banabans had to develop entirely new ways of sustaining themselves and coping with their losses. This forced move, in addition to negatively impacting the island of Rabi, was accompanied by the destruction of the peoples' sustainable lifestyle because of their unfamiliarity with this new environment (Teaiwa 2014). Furthermore, by the time mining stopped on Banaba in 1979, 90% of the surface soil had been removed, destroying the landscape, including sacred water caves (Edwards 2013). Now only a

few Banabans return to the island (now part of Kiribati) periodically as keepers to maintain the peoples' connection to it.

These cases of Nauru and Banaba exemplify the dynamics of colonialist exploitation driven by racism and mechanisms of unified practice that have been described thus far. The result has been social, cultural, and environmental injustice that has left the island poorly positioned to adequately respond to the impending impacts of climate change on their own. Because they did not contribute to climate change, and were not the beneficiaries of the industrialization that caused it, climate injustice is another component of their domination. As the Pacific Islands depend on action at the global scale to generate just solutions for their survival, we now turn to international climate negotiations to gauge the potential for justice through policy.

22.3 Challenges to Justice in International Climate Policy

Negotiations in climate policy are fraught with the same power imbalances that characterized colonial and post-colonial hierarchies. The interests of economically dominant countries are given priority, as they have the resources needed to confront climate change, and therefore they control the direction of policy-making. Meanwhile, the needs of those most impacted by climate change in primarily non-White, historically exploited, Global South nations are sidelined. Pacific Islanders, along with other small island states and developing nations, have fought to have their concerns addressed through global climate policy for decades, yet their demands, when they are incorporated, are done so only marginally and incrementally (Ciplet et al. 2015). This political marginalization, part and parcel of post-colonial politics, puts the islanders at greater risk form insufficient action, and exacerbates their already precarious position on the global stage.

International climate negotiations began in 1992 at the Rio Earth Summit, at which time the United Nations Framework Convention on

Climate Change (hereafter UNFCCC or "the Convention") was established. The Convention has now been ratified by 197 nations or "Parties" and as of the end of the year 2017, has had 23 annual Conference of the Parties (COP) meetings, in addition to numerous intercessional, working group, and other related meetings occurring between the COPs. Though the UNFCCC recognizes the "common but differentiated responsibilities" of Parties in contributing to climate solutions, there is a model of consensus built into the negotiations that equally allows any Party to object to proposals. While this seemingly constructs an egalitarian model of policy-making, history and scholarship has shown that this is not always the case in practice.

Since the beginning of the climate negotiations, there have been divisions between developed and developing countries.[2] In one of the UNFCCC's primary products, the Kyoto Protocol, developed countries were required to limit their emissions of greenhouse gases, while developing countries were not given the same restrictions. This was the result of a concerted effort by developing countries, demanding action from the Global North, and highlighting that they are most likely to feel the effects of climate change even though they were not the cause. Despite the differentiation in the Protocol, it was ultimately unsuccessful, largely because the United States, one of the world's largest polluters, never ratified it. This demonstrates that, despite formal equality between the Parties in the process of negotiations, there are power differentials in their ability to determine results.

The Kyoto Protocol is far from the only instance of division between developed and developing countries in the climate negotiations. The 2007 COP meeting in Bali underscored this division, as there were heated positions taken on how to set universal emissions reductions goals without going against the principle of common but differentiated responsibilities. Conflict arose again in Copenhagen in 2009, as developing nations pushed for a global goal of limiting average temperature increases to 1.5 °C; acknowledged as the maximum change that will still permit the survival of frontline communities in island nations. Rather than building an agreement around this goal, however, the Convention accepted the hastily put together "Copenhagen Accord," written by then United States President Obama and leaders from Brazil, South Africa, India, and China. Representatives from developing nations felt this marginalized both their inputs and their needs.

Most recently, the UNFCCC produced the Paris Agreement at COP 21 in 2015. This was a remarkable feat for the Convention and the text of the Agreement includes several priorities of developing countries, such as a 2 °C temperature rise limit with the added goal of limiting warming to 1.5 °C, as well as an article on "loss and damage," which is discussed in greater depth below. The Paris Agreement has now been ratified by 170 Parties and has officially entered into force, but the work that nations do to ensure its success remains to be seen. Until decisive action is taken on the promises made in the Paris Agreement, with regards to finance, support, and global goals for mitigation and adaptation, the policy will be useless for protecting vulnerable peoples.

One might now ask, if policy-making under the UNFCCC has done so little for the Pacific Islands and other vulnerable nations, why do they still participate? The answer is that removing themselves from the UNFCCC remains infeasible, given that they are reliant on the action of nations at the global scale to make the necessary changes to mitigate climate change and provide support for the islands' adaptation. Furthermore, as Ciplet et al. (2015) demonstrate, island nations' lack of power on the global stage also prevents their governments from obstructing negotiations until an adequate policy to combat climate change has been developed. Their consent in the process is thus manufactured by economically and politically powerful nations that control climate negotiations and policy-making and repeatedly subordinate the survival of Pacific Island Nations to their own

---

[2]These terms are problematic in themselves, but are common parlance within the UNFCCC to distinguish between these two groups and so will be utilized here.

economic interests. Vulnerable nations are then forced to accept even the smallest of concessions, because doing otherwise would prevent progress altogether and put them at greater risk.

Climate injustice is defined as the "heightened and disproportionate vulnerability to climate-related harm by disadvantaged social groups, who in general are far less responsible for the problem and are excluded from decision making about its resolution," (Ciplet et al. 2015: 5). From the UNFCCC negotiations, we learn that climate injustice also exists within the white racial frame, as nations with histories of colonialism and imperialism put people and environments of former colonies at the greatest risk for their own economic gain. It is not a coincidence that nations and peoples that are most at risk of climate change and most unable to correct this problem are also those in the global periphery with histories of colonization, exploitation, and environmental destruction. These nations have been marginalized and their capacity limited through racist and Global North-centric policies and practices that have dominated the world system for centuries. Collectively, Pacific islanders are responsible for less than 0.03% of global greenhouse gas emissions, and even the advanced target of 1.5 °C temperature increase has the potential to devastate their region because industrialized nations are unwilling to take decisive action. It is not that Pacific islanders are passive recipients of these changes—in fact they are fighting hard for their nations—but they have been systematically marginalized for too long to fix this issue on their own.

22.4 "Loss and Damage": The Policy Tool for Climate Justice?

"Loss and damage," did not suddenly appear in international climate policymaking in 2013. It is a mechanism for which island nations have been advocating since the very beginnings of the UNFCCC in the early 1990s (Millar et al. 2015: 444). Unlike its accompanying two pillars of climate actions—mitigation and adaptation—loss

and damage does not involve the prevention of climate change impacts, but rather acknowledges the impacts that do occur, and plans an appropriate response. The effects of climate change that fall into the realm of loss and damage include, but are not limited to, loss of land from rising seas, loss of critical industries such as agriculture and fishing, destruction of homes from increased intensity and frequency of storms, and loss of nations altogether from a combination of these factors. Pacific islands facing numerous forms of loss and damage thus have much at stake in ensuring that the related text under the UNFCCC is clearly defined, supported, and implemented.

Loss and damage was first officially incorporated under the UNFCCC through the Warsaw International Mechanism on Loss and Damage (WIM), established at COP 19 in 2013. The WIM establishes an executive committee tasked with defining key issues under loss and damage, such as displacement and slow-onset events, and determining how to address those issues under the UNFCCC, on which they have been slowly making progress. It also includes differentiation between economic loss and damage and non-economic loss and damage (NELD), which is important both for accounting the economic losses properly, but also for identifying those losses, such as health and cultural sites, which cannot be fully monetized. These components also served as the basis for Article 8 of the Paris Agreement on Loss and Damage, which ensures that these issues will continue being addressed as the Convention moves forward under this new agreement. It is a problem that these texts remain ambiguous and lack clear definitions and action plans for implementation, but they hold promise.

It is no wonder why loss and damage has been slow to be incorporated into international climate policy, primarily because it comes dangerously close to a topic that developed countries have actively prevented from entering the UNFCCC for years: liability. Under the Convention, there has never been a component of liability and therefore legal and financial responsibility for climate change, which would force industrialized nations to pay for their decades of pollution. Most recently, former United States Secretary of State John Kerry demanded that any liability language be struck from decision texts in the Paris Agreement because it would be a deal breaker for his country (Clémençon 2016).[3] Rather than being held responsible for addressing climate change, the developed world has preferred to fund mitigation and adaptation efforts through voluntary contributions. Since loss and damage cannot be converted into projects or programs that developed countries can willingly elect to fund, however, it is more difficult to approach in this way, and thus re-opens the question of liability. This is critical, because the incorporation of a liability component under this issue could be a key avenue for climate justice.

Though developed nations have attempted to skirt this issue by emphasizing insurance as a solution to defend against losses, this is not sufficient to cover NELD components, such as loss to sovereignty, culture, health, language, well-being, community, and tradition. Part of the difficulty in bringing NELD issues to the forefront in negotiations is the devaluation of the Global South. Just as the exploitation of Pacific Islanders is taken less seriously than threats to white bodies of Europeans and their descendants, the loss of Pacific cultures and traditions due to climate change is not taken up as an urgent issue requiring immediate action (Batur and Weber 2017). Finding just solutions to address such impending losses require more than insuring homes and finding a new place to put people once their nations become uninhabitable, but working together with islanders to find culturally appropriate solutions that do not further marginalize them. To do this in a truly just way, policies must incorporate a component of liability that requires nations to take responsibility for their historical actions.

In future UNFCCC negotiations, policymakers will have to address and important question:

what are the obligations of the world to nations facing inevitable loss and damage? Specifically, they will need to take seriously the demands of Pacific islanders that have been fighting for decisive action to be taken on climate change for years. There is room for progress in the existing texts, particularly under the issue of loss and damage. Now the Convention must do what has been resisted for decades: make those responsible for climate change pay for their damage, and implement decisive text that compensates vulnerable nations for their losses.

22.5 Climate Negotiations and the Future of Island States

Where are these island nations on a map? We need to locate them soon because they are on the brink of being lost. During the Humanitarian Summit in Istanbul in 2016, Baron Waqa, the president of Nauru, issued a global challenge. He argued for a special U.N. envoy on climate change and security to provide a collective answer to crisis that the island nations are facing due to global climate change. The rising seawaters are only one piece of this problem; they are also being challenged with depleting fishing stocks, ocean acidification, seawater temperature fluctuations, and destruction in sea ecology. Baron Waqa's position echoes Pacific Island nations proposal at the 2015 U.N. Climate Change Summit at Paris.

Tuvalu Prime Minister Enele Sopoaga is advocating for the need of all countries to develop and put in effect urgent and thoughtful action plans, not merely communicate them. At COP 21 in Paris, he stated, "Just imagine, you are in my shoes. What would you do? I believe no leader…, no leader around or in this room carries such level of worry or responsibility. No leader in this room can say a total of its territory and all citizens might disappear." The Fijian Prime Minister Frank Bainimarama has also pointed out that Fiji, where some at-risk islanders have migrated, is looking for relocation possibilities for some of its own communities. As Baron Waqa, President of Nauru, asked at the

---

[3]The concern in this case being that the Agreement would not pass through the U.S. Congress for ratification with such language, making its success on the international stage extremely doubtful.

opening of the 2015 climate negotiations in Paris: "The climate bill has finally come due. Who will pay? Right now, it is being paid by the smallest and most vulnerable."

The smallest and most vulnerable are marginalized in climate policy, and their powerlessness is rooted in racist constructions of the other, centuries of oppression and domination, capitalist logics that rationalize the exploitation of people and nature, and unjust power imbalances, which have created climate and environmental injustice as part of the global political economy. For Pacific Islanders, the result of both colonialism and climate change are the same: loss and damage to their homes and livelihoods, and a reduction in agency to construct their own futures.

The denial of responsibility and liability for climate change, and the absence of necessary mitigation and adaptation is particularly egregious given this context. It is not, however, surprising. An acknowledgement by modern Global North nations of their creation of these circumstances and consequent, legally binding action to alleviate the damages that they have caused in the realm of climate change, would open the door to leave them liable for damages caused by centuries of exploitation in all other realms. It also puts their economic gains at risk as they could be forced to cut off their practices of environmental and social exploitation and pull environmentally destructive industries out of developing countries. However, in working actively to avoid legally binding requirements for even monetary compensation to fund adaptation projects in vulnerable nations, Global North nations only further injustice. Therefore, a liability component for loss and damage under the UNFCCC is a step and not a solution, but without a minimum formal acknowledgement of these problems, no just policy is possible.

Leaders and activists of Pacific Island Nations have not been silent on this issue. Former President Anote Tong, of Kiribati, has been particularly vocal, referring to his home as a "sinking island" and stating to developed nations, "This is not caused by us. This is caused by you," (Goldberg 2013). The injustice that residents of

Nauru, Banaba (now Kiribati), and dozens of other Pacific Island Nations, are experiencing is multi-faceted and not reducible to a singular event or historical context. The uncertain fate of these nations begins with colonialism, is layered with environmental destruction, and a lack of power on the political stage. Only after considering all of these components can we understand how they are threatened by climate change and rising seas.

22.6 Toward Climate Justice

So, what would a truly just climate policy look like? The 1948 Universal Declaration of Human Rights states that everyone has "the right to life, liberty and security of person," and "the right to a nationality," that "no one shall be arbitrarily deprived of his nationality," and finally that "everyone is entitled to a social and international order in which [these] rights and freedoms…can be fully realized." This is all in addition to the right not to be discriminated against based on race or national origin, and yet we continue to see people being deprived of these rights in Global South, predominantly non-White nations. A just climate policy would renew these rights. It would guarantee a political basis in which Pacific Islanders can determine their own futures that are economically and socially secure and that minimize both their economic and non-economic loss and damage. Already Islanders are being turned away from the developed world as they attempt to leave their vulnerable islands under the status of "climate refugees." Justice in climate policy would mean acknowledgement of this status, with liability for climate change included explicitly, and funding provided in abundance for relocation and other expenses that are incurred as Pacific islanders work to build their own futures.

This year, 2017, is the hottest on the record, we are now edging to a symbolic milestone set at Paris COP: the need to limit the increase in average global temperatures to 1.5 °C. This limit is not symbolic for Pacific Island Nations, however. They can see rising waters, coral bleaching, land salinization, and drought. They suffer from the Global North's greedy consumption of fossil fuels and resources. The violence of this injustice accentuates the past and present terms of oppression. Though the islands are formally independent nations now, they reflect the scar of exploitation under colonial rule, evident in deforestation, extinctions, depleted resources, and pollution, in addition to lacking adequate education systems, accessible health care facilities, clean water, sewage treatment systems, roadways, and electricity facilities. Living as post-colonial economies, many centered on tourism, their markets and production continues to be directed to serve wealthy foreigners. For example, islanders often consume unhealthy, imported and processed food rather than the local fish off of which they have lived for centuries, in order to sell the fish to restaurants and other tourist facilities (Parry 2010).

The lesson in this is that international climate policymakers must step back and listen to what Pacific Islanders and their leaders have been saying for decades. Climate change should be the final straw in the centuries-long marginalization and exploitation of these islands and their people, and must finally push the Global North to correct the damage it has caused. The world must make the decision to work toward a just future; otherwise Pacific Islanders will be left to drown.

References

Adamson, J., Evans, M. M., & Stein, R. (Eds.). (2002). *The environmental justice reader: Politics, poetics, & pedagogy.* Tucson, AZ: University of Arizona Press.

Batur, P. (2007). Heart of violence: Global racism, war and genocide. In H. Vera & J. Feagin (Eds.), *Handbook of the sociology of racial and ethnic relations* (pp. 441–454). New York: Palgrave.

Batur, P., & Weber, K. (2017). Water connects it all: Systemic racism and global struggle for water. In R. Thompson-Miller & K. Ducey (Eds.), *Systemic racism: Making liberty, justice and democracy real.* New York: Palgrave.

Beck, U. (2016). *The metamorphosis of the world.* Cambridge MA: Polity.

Bullard, R. D. (Ed.). (1994). *Unequal protection: Environmental justice and communities of color.* San Francisco: Sierra Club Books.

Campbell, J. (2010). Climate-induced community relocation in the Pacific: The meaning and importance of land. In J. McAdam (Ed.), *Climate change and displacement: Multidisciplinary perspectives* (pp. 57–79). Oxford: Hart.

Ciplet, D., Timmons Roberts, J., & Khan, M. (2015). *Power in a warming world: The new global politics of climate change and the remaking of environmental inequality.* Cambridge, Massachusetts London, England: The MIT Press.

Clémençon, R. (2016). The two sides of the Paris climate agreement: Dismal failure or historic breakthrough? *The Journal of Environment & Development, 25*(1), 3–24.

Doherty, B. (2016). A short history of Nauru, Australia's dumping ground for refugees. *The Guardian.* <https://www.theguardian.com/world/2016/aug/10/a-short-history-of-nauru-australias-dumping-ground-for-refugees>.

Edwards, J. (2013). Phosphate and forced relocation: An assessment of the resettlement of the Banabans to Northern Fiji in 1945. *The Journal of Imperial and Commonwealth History, 41*(5), 783–803.

Feagin, J. R., Vera, H., & Batur, P. (1999). *White racism* (2nd ed.). New York: Routledge.

Goldberg, D. T. (1993). *Racist culture: Philosophy and the politics of meaning.* Oxford: Blackwell Publishers.

Goldberg, J. (2013). Drowning Kiribati. *Bloomberg Businessweek.* 21 November 2013. Web. <http://www.businessweek.com/articles/2013-11-21/kiribati-climate-change-destroys-pacific-island-nation#p2>.

Khan, B. (2016). The world passes 400 PPM threshold. Permanently. *Climate Central.* http://www.climatecentral.org/news/world-passes-400-ppm-threshold-permanently-20738. Retrieved December 12, 2017.

Marable, M. (1996). *Speaking truth to power: Essays on race, resistance, and radicalism.* Boulder, CO: Westview Press.

Millar, I., Gascoigne, C., & Caldwell, E. (2015). Making good the loss: An analysis of the loss and damage mechanism under the UNFCCC process. In M. Gerrard, & G. E. Wannier (Eds.), *Threatened island nations: Legal implications of rising seas and a changing climate.*

Parry, J. (2010). Pacific Islanders pay heavy price for abandoning traditional diet. *Bulletin of the World Health Organization, 88*(7). http://www.who.int/bulletin/volumes/88/7/10-010710/en/. Retrieved December 12, 2017.

Pellow, D. N. (2007). *Resisting global toxics: Transnational movements for environmental justice.* Cambridge, MA: MIT Press.

Pulido, L. (1996). A critical review of the methodology of environmental racism research*. *Antipode, 28*(2), 142–159.

Schlanger, Z. (2015). Can the Paris climate deal save this Tiny Pacific Island? *Mother Jones* 12 December.

Teaiwa, K. M. (2014). *Consuming Ocean Island: Stories of people and phosphate from Banaba*. Bloomington: Indiana University Press.

Timmons Roberts, J., & Parks, B. C. (2007). *A climate of injustice: Global inequality, North-South politics, and climate policy*. Cambridge, MA: MIT Press.

Westra, L., & Wenz, P. S. (Eds.). (1995). *Faces of environmental racism: Confronting issues of global justice*. Lanham, MD: Rowman & Littlefield.

Antiracism

23

Eileen O'Brien

Contents

Antiracism can be understood in its broadest sense as any theory and/or practice (whether political or personal) that seeks to challenge, reduce, or eliminate manifestations of racism in society. The question of what particular ideas and practices qualify as antiracist is difficult to answer without first acknowledging two important factors. First, scholars in the field of race and ethnic relations operate from several different definitions of racism (Yelman 2004). Thus, to identify something or someone as antiracist necessitates some common understandings of what it means to be challenging racism. Indeed, Bonnett (2000) argues that antiracism "cannot be adequately understood as the inverse of racism" (p. 2) because one entity might practice antiracism in a manner that may even perpetuate racism by another definition.

A second factor contributing to murky understandings of antiracism in the social sciences is that there is not a well-developed typology of antiracist theory and practice anywhere in the academic world. On the other hand, feminism enjoyed some good fortune in that many white, middle-class feminist scholars had access to the academy during a good part of the 20th century when feminist thought and politics proliferated. As a result there are now a plethora of textbooks outlining several fairly well-accepted and standardized types of feminism, including liberal feminism, radical feminism, Marxist feminism, lesbian feminism, and multicultural feminism (e.g., Lorber 2005; Tong 1998). Antiracism, by contrast, first was introduced into the field of sociology by scholars like W. E. B. DuBois and Oliver Cromwell Cox, who are only recently gaining recognition in their respective fields. Du Bois, although granted a Harvard Ph.D., did have to publicly accept his degree on stage by "passing" as a white man.

E. O'Brien (✉)
Saint Leo University, Virginia campus, St. Leo, FL, USA
e-mail: eileen.obrien@saintleo.edu

© Springer International Publishing AG, part of Springer Nature 2018
P. Batur and J. R. Feagin (eds.), *Handbook of the Sociology of Racial and Ethnic Relations*,
Handbooks of Sociology and Social Research, https://doi.org/10.1007/978-3-319-76757-4_23

413

Although all African Americans suffered degrading and humiliating racism regardless of their class status in Du Bois' day, Du Bois himself was of a fairly elite, academic class of African Americans, and one cannot help but wonder how much other antiracist practice and scholarship existed even then that has not been canonized and typologized as feminism has been. Those who publicly and vocally challenge racism have not had as much access to elite academic status as feminist scholars have in the latter decades of the 20th century. While most racial-ethnic relations textbooks now acknowledge some standardized types of racism (e.g., individual, institutional, structural, cultural), the same cannot be said for types of antiracism. As we shall see, several scholars have begun to outline types of antiracism, but no one scholar's schema has been widely accepted and used in any other context other than his or her own work.

For the purposes of this essay, we will focus mainly on two types of antiracism—individual and institutional—while acknowledging that these types are not mutually exclusive, and that within these two types themselves there are varying approaches to antiracist thought and praxis. To include these various types of antiracism, we will operate from a broad definition of racism; that is, a system of advantages for the dominant racial group (whites) in society (Tatum 2003). This definition of racism encompasses individual prejudices and acts of discrimination that bolster the position of the majority group, as well as material and cultural advantages that flow into the dominant group due to systemic societal arrangements (Feagin 2000). As we shall see, at times antiracist thought and/or practice may focus on one component of this definition of racism, to the detriment of other components. To begin with, we shall explore how scholars have attempted to craft definitions of antiracism by grappling with this multifaceted reality of racism itself.

23.1 Types of Antiracism

Alastair Bonnett, in his work on antiracism from a global perspective, points out that there are seven different reasons "why racism is claimed to be a bad thing." (2000: 4). Upon examining these reasons, it becomes more evident that antiracism might take incredibly different forms depending upon the definition of racism that underlies it. The seven reasons he outlines are: "Racism is socially disruptive; Racism is foreign; Racism sustains the ruling class; Racism hinders the progress of our community; Racism is an intellectual error; Racism distorts and erases people's identities; Racism is anti-egalitarian and socially unjust" (Bonnett 2000: 4–7). The third reason, "racism sustains the ruling class," is often a reason behind why neo-Marxist and/or socialist activists get involved in antiracist protest. People of color who organized around incidents of racism affecting their community will sometimes find white allies coming from this orientation, and the two may come into conflict if some people of color are highly invested (or dependent upon) their position in the capitalist structure. Much akin to the conflict between liberal and radical feminists, some antiracists simply want a more egalitarian or even colorblind capitalist social structure, while others would like to dismantle capitalism altogether, viewing it as the ultimate economic foundation of racism. The tension between these two goals is perhaps best illustrated in the various branches of black nationalist movements, to which we will return in a subsequent section.

George (2004) identifies a particular type of antiracism, *critical antiracism*, whose adherents would subscribe to five basic beliefs: (1) race is a social construct that functions to preserve the power of the majority group; (2) whites occupy a privileged position in this power dynamic; (3) there are multiple manifestations of racism, among these are overt hate crimes, cultural racism (in language, history, art, etc.) and institutional racism; (4) whites' place is not to change people of color, but to change others like themselves; (5) antiracism is not diversity or multicultural work, since one of its primary goals is to alter power relationships rather than to merely be more sensitive to the other. Of these five tenets, the second and the fifth ones in particular indicate a particular role for whites in contrast to that for people of color. Several scholars have noted that whites sometimes face challenges in accepting the idea of white privilege and how it applies to them (e.g., Kivel 2002; McIntosh 1998; Tatum 1994). For example, some whites respond with guilt, anger, and denial that disengage them from moving onto an antiracist identity (Tatum 1992, 1994). As a result, George's critical antiracism may be considered less palatable to whites than other forms.

Indeed, O'Brien's (2001) study of two different white antiracist organizations finds that the organization that adheres closest to George's critical antiracism was led by people of color and its membership was more racially mixed than the other predominantly white organization. Most members of the latter organization acknowledged white privilege in the abstract, and in their understanding of the legal institution, for instance, but did not have much of a sense of how that privilege applied to them personally. O'Brien identified this type of antiracism as *selective race cognizance*, and contrasted it with *reflexive race cognizance* in which participants clearly articulated their resistance to how racism operated institutionally as well as how it manifested itself in their own lives, particularly as whites experiencing white privilege. In some other work, O'Brien (2003) demonstrates how reflexively race cognizant antiracists spend a great deal of energy analyzing their personal relationships and how they can reduce the racism they may unintentionally perpetuate in those relationships, both intraracial and interracial. In contrast, O'Brien's selectively race cognizant antiracists deal mainly with challenging police brutality and neo-Nazi organizing in their communities, locating racism as an organizational evil outside themselves.

While O'Brien demonstrates types of antiracism by contrasting different organizations, Scott (2000) examines how a single organization may attempt to practice different types of antiracism simultaneously, with varying degrees of success. In her study of two feminist anti-violence organizations that had antiracism as an explicit part of their mission, Scott found that these groups had strategies to confront racism both structurally and interpersonally in their work settings. Structurally, the organizations took measures in their hiring process to ensure that people of color would be prominently located in key positions in order to effectively reach their diverse clientele ("affirmative action"). Additionally, the groups held "antiracism discussion groups" to share feelings coworkers had about interpersonal racism they had confronted in each other over each period prior to a meeting. One group even had a "calling out" policy where members were expected to interrupt individual racism in that moment. While members had certain criticisms about how both levels of antiracist work operated at their organizations, on the whole Scott's evaluation was that their structural "affirmative action" work was more successful than their interpersonal discussion work. Following points made by O'Brien's work, when the women in Scott's organizations had to look critically at themselves in the context of the discussion groups, it became painful and each "side" effectively shut down. This reaction would counter any shared perceptions of working together toward a common goal that the structural antiracist efforts would be more likely to foster.

While institutional or structural antiracist work might be less emotionally challenging for its participants and thus engender fewer internal difficulties, Feagin and his colleagues would argue that antiracist solutions at both levels are necessary to fully address the problem of he terms systemic racism (Johnson et al. 2000; Feagin 2000). In his book, Racist America, Feagin concludes by suggesting some antiracist strategies at the individual level, which he describes as "individual whites .... Becoming activists by working on their own racist attitudes, stereotypes and proclivities" (2000: 253). He profiles one group, the Institutes for the Healing of Racism, which forms small discussion groups for the purpose of addressing racism on the emotional level that the above research has deemed rarer and more challenging than other levels of antiracism. Some such groups have white participants emerging and referring to themselves as "recovering racists," borrowing from the Alcoholics Anonymous idea that one can transition into a process of unlearning racism, but that people cannot be suddenly "cured" of the racism of one short period that they have socialized into for their entire lifetimes. Some of O'Brien's (2001) respondents who were reflexively race cognizant took a similar view. For example, one member of the organization the People's Institute for Survival and Beyond declared that, as a white person, she would always be a racist, but that she could also be an antiracist and work against that. Coming to this realization was the "healing" aspect for her, to heal the typical guilt that tends to be associated with whites learning about racism in a deep way.

Johnson et al. (2000) also conclude that antiracism can be perpetuated on an individual level when individuals experience *transformative love* across the color line. When individuals traverse the rigid racial boundaries that separate them in the larger society and begin to think of themselves as a single unit (as in a long-term relationship between lovers, or a parent-child relationship), then racism becomes personal even for the white member of the relationship who might not have held a personal stake in eliminating racism prior to their cross-racial relationship. Feagin and O'Brien (2003) propose a term called autopathy—stronger than sympathy or empathy, the white member of the relationship would actually experience racism as an actual target, rather than as an empathetic observer. In this work, Feagin gives the example of an elite white man who is married to a black woman (and father of her child). This man enters a predominantly white social gathering with his family, and using the pronoun "we," observes that they are the only non-white people there. Even though he is white, he feels the sense of isolation at a segregated event as if he were a person of color, through the connection to his interracial family.

These findings should be interpreted with caution, however, and it safest to say that cross-racial relationships are a necessary, but not sufficient, condition for producing antiracism at the individual level. Work by Childs (2005), Korgen (2002), O'Brien and Korgen (2007) all point to colorblind racism as an obstacle for cross-racial relationships necessarily leading to antiracist outcomes, but this research will be reviewed in more detail in the next section.

However, Feagin does not end by suggesting these individual-level antiracist strategies. He envisions the several smaller antiracist organizations that exist across the United States networking together into one larger national organization. He cites Jesse Jackson's Rainbow Coalition effort of the 1980s and the New Party as possible models of such a strategy. Johnson et al. (2000) further identify three major U.S. institutions that could be targeted for some antiracist revamping: the political sphere, the educational system, and religious institutions. Following Feagin's earlier suggestion with Hernan Vera in White Racism (1995), Johnson et al. (2000) propose holding a new Constitutional Convention that is more representative in terms of gender, race, and other statuses than the original group was when it convened in the late 18th century to write the document that the United States still upholds today. For educational antiracism, these scholars suggest both an overhaul of the curriculum to remove cultural racism and a restructuring of funding so that schools are not perpetuating apartheid-like conditions for students who emerge from them (see also Kozol 2005). Finally, because society's religious institutions often form the basis for its moral compass, and those morals become encoded in law, it is suggested that the high degree of racial segregation in churches be addressed. All of these kinds of antiracist reform strategies parallel the structural antiracism practiced by organizations like those in Scott's (2000) research where shifts in racial-ethnic demographics are encouraged to break up the monopoly held by the majority group.

To summarize, although no standardized typology of forms of antiracism currently exist in the literature as a whole, it is evident that most scholars agree there are different levels or types of antiracism. While each scholar of antiracism tends to use his or her won terminology to describe them (e.g., Feagin's individual and institutional, Scott's structural and interpersonal, O'Brien's selective and reflexive race cognizance), a majority of the work exploring the different types of antiracism focuses on two distinct forms. It may be helpful to conceptualize them using Max Weber's tradition of ideal types (Weber as cited in Edles and Applerouth 2004). The first ideal type of antiracism functions largely at the level of interpersonal and micro-level interactions. It may even involve individual-level introspection that does not involve anyone but a single actor. This type of antiracism might involve a white person taking stock of all of the ways she unintentionally takes advantage of white privilege, and planning ways she can interrupt that privilege in her everyday life. However, this introspection would soon involve other people. In most situations, a white person would not be self-motivated to undertake this kind of action completely unprompted. She might be assigned it as part of a course assignment, or as part of a workshop held by the Institute for the Healing of Racism, the People's Institute for Survival and Beyond, or some other such organization. It is also important to note that such groups that encourage personal antiracist work usually do so in the context of a workshop that mandates interracial participation. The People's Institution for Survival and Beyond holds an Undoing Racism workshop, for example, that necessitates multiracial attendance. It includes break-out groups for same-race interactions, and large full group exchange and sharing of cultural differences (O'Brien 2001). Further, as soon as an individual white person takes stock of the white privilege in her life and devises strategies to challenge it, those strategies would almost always entail interactions with others.

This first ideal type of antiracism does not usually focus on implementing policy or institutional-level changes, but it could certainly have latent effects on such changes. For instance, part of the white person's plan to interrupt white privilege in her life could be to consciously choose to move to a more racially integrated neighborhood, and begin sending her child to a more racially diverse school. Although this person's action alone does not significantly alter structural arrangements in that locality, it sets an example that others may follow and creates a context that might eventually lead to parents coming together to protest their lack of adequate educational facilities, for example. People in positions of power might also be impacted by individual antiracist workshops or discussion groups to change their organization's hiring practices, as one grocery store CEO did in O'Brien's (2001) work. Thus, the ideal type of individual-level antiracism is not exclusively limited to challenging individual friends' and family members' prejudices. It can also have an impact on larger social structures in various ways.

The second ideal type, already alluded to above, is a structural or institutional form of antiracism. This antiracism tends to focus on public policy and/or the structural arrangements of organizations. While Scott's (2000) work cited above demonstrates how private nonprofit organizations can choose to commit themselves to "affirmative action" hiring, antiracists could also work at the level of local, state, or federal government to protest the ending of affirmative action strategies in higher education. Some antiracists have done this kind of work either at the level of grassroots organizing (e.g., educating voters on ballot initiatives, staging public protests) or as policy makers (e.g., candidates taking a public stand against such measures or lawyers seeking to challenge the policies in the courts). Nonpartisan efforts to make sure people of color are registered to vote, sponsored by nationally recognized groups such as the National Association for Advancement of Colored People (NAACP), would also fall under this type of antiracism. An antiracist group called Anti-Racist Action (ARA) started a program called "Copwatch" where members used video cameras to monitor the on-the-street behavior of police officers to guard against police brutality. One lead organizer for this group was also a police misconduct litigator who filed lawsuits against the city on behalf of victims of police brutality and donated his share of the settlements back to the ARA organization (O'Brien 2001).

As with the first type of antiracism, it is also difficult to draw a clear line separating the larger institutional type of antiracism from individual antiracism. Feagin and O'Brien (2003) profile one elite white man in their study, cited earlier as an example of autopathy at the individual level, who also is a police misconduct litigator. While we may be able to make a clear distinction between the autopathy he shares with his family at a social event and his legal activities, another example from his life is less clear cut. When his biracial son becomes the target of racial harassment at the hands of peers from school (and his family's home is the target of a vandalism hate crime), this man intervenes not only seeking justice for his son and their family, but also requesting various types of antiracist educational curricula at the school. Quite simply, he is not just interested in individual-level restitution, but in institutional-level change that will perhaps reduce the likelihood of others engaging in acts of discrimination in the future. O'Brien's (2001) study also provides an example of a participant in an Undoing Racism workshop who begins the individual-level process of unlearning racism, starts confronting racist comments in interpersonal interactions, but eventually institutes a multicultural arts program in the racially segregated (predominantly black) elementary school where she teaches. This antiracist credits her individual, interpersonal work of building allies at her school with creating the institutional context that was eventually supportive enough of her to allow the program to become part of the school's agenda. She also continually returned to her antiracist discussion group as a source of support when her efforts to start this program were difficult or painful. Thus, like Weber's ideal types, neither type of antiracism is mutually exclusive, and the two can overlap and mutually reinforce each other. However, **individual/ interpersonal antiracism** and **institutional/ structural antiracism** are useful concepts to convey the patterns established thus far in the field.

23.2 A Brief History of Antiracism in the United States

The term "antiracism" itself is fairly recent in human history. However, if we use the definition laid out at the start of this essay, surely there has been thought and practice that could be characterized as antiracist since racism itself began. Although ethnic conflict existed long before the idea of "race" emerged, we will limit ourselves here to racism as opposed to ethnic conflict, prejudices, and disagreements. Racism, fueled by the socially and politically constructed concept of distinct "races," has been linked by most scholars to the development of capitalism, colonization, and the slave trade—particularly chattel slavery in the Western world. Although scholars disagree on the exact date, most focus sometime between the 17 and 18th centuries as the origin of racism (e.g., Allen 1994; Aptheker 1992). As such, Aptheker (1992) begins his book *Antiracism in the United States: The First Two Hundred Years*, around the turn of the 18th century and ends with the emancipation of African American slaves in 1865. Thus, his work centers upon the abolitionist or antislavery movement. As Aptheker's work shows, much pre-antiracist work was largely done through multiracial coalitions. Slave rebellions led by such notable figures as John Brown, Nat Turner, and Denmark Vesey necessitate the participation of both blacks and whites —either in actually taking up arms against slaveholders to attempt escape or in simply securing hideouts for escaped African Americans. The basis of Thomas's (1996) entire work, *Understanding Interracial Unity*, is to advance this thesis that most antiracist work has been accomplished by bridging racial dividing lines. Using a timeline that extends a bit beyond Aptheker's into the U.S. civil rights movement itself, Thomas demonstrates how groups like the NAACP, for example, were co-founded by both blacks and whites. Using legal test cases to take before the Supreme Court to challenge institutional segregation, and nonviolent direct action to raise public awareness of the issues, these antiracists effectively challenged social conventions uniformly accepted that few politicians dared even address them. To even question them put one at risk for white terrorism, resulting in slander, torture, and even death. Aptheker's work includes names too many to count, of both blacks and whites, who were martyred to antiracism. In this era, antiracism was a risky venture, to be sure.

Antiracism, however, was not always decidedly interracial. At times, African Americans in particular advocated for necessarily black-only antiracist organizations. In their struggle against the devastating effects of racism on African-American communities, several prominent black scholars and activist called for various strategies of empowerment through separation. It should be noted that voluntary separation of a subordinated group in society is altogether different from legally enforced segregation and/or that of group by those in power. Various prominent black pre-antiracists have engaged with such strategies from time to time. Although in African-American history lessons, Booker T. Washington and W. E. B. Du Bois are often cast as opposites—the former as an accommodationist and the later as an assimilationist—legal scholar Brooks (1996) points out that both men agreed on certain strategies for fighting racism that did not demand equal treatment from the white establishment, but instead encouraged African Americans to hone their own skills and talents to work in service of each other. Many students of this history may be familiar with Washington's "up-by-your-bootstraps" self-help strategy, which was the impetus for the Tuskegee Institute and its training of African Americans in skilled trades (constraining them largely to the working class). However, Du Bois also advocated for a separatist strategy of sorts that would speak more to the "talented truth" elite African Americans of the day by encouraging them to do as much of their business as possible with other African American merchants (Brooks 1996). In these ways, black antiracists believed they could eschew the negative stereotypes attached to them by the larger society and "prove" themselves as well-functioning, talented, gifted members of the society, deserving of all the rights and privileges denied to them at the time.

A major tension running throughout the history of multiracial antiracist efforts has been this dichotomous "integration or separation" question upon which Brooks focuses his 1996 book of the same name. Brooks (1996) points out that some African Americans spend many years as dedicated antiracists committed to a strategy of integration, but become exasperated with the white establishment's lack of cooperation in such endeavors, and eventually prefers an antiracist strategy that incorporates some separatist elements. Brooks himself proposes one such strategy, calling it "limited separation." Du Bois, for example, in his long life, went from working with whites to establish the National Association for the Advancement of Colored People (NAACP) to emigrating to Ghana where he died (Edles and Applerauth 2004). This move seemed to mirror the path advocated by Marcus Garvey's Universal Negro Improvement Association (UNIA), whose work culminated in the establishment of the American-created African nation of Liberia in 1822. Such total separationist strategies, though, sometimes attracted curious allies. The Ku Klux Klan, obviously not an antiracist organization, but indeed an organization of racist terror, found itself supporting Garvey's emigration movement because they relished the logical outcome of fewer black citizens in the United States. Indeed, more contemporary separationist groups like the Nation of Islam have been criticized for their allegiance to more conservative ideologies such as the inferiority of women (Brooks 1996). Nonetheless, for some blacks, the ability to function independently of the negative stereotypes of the dominant group, and in an environment that ideally would nurture their unique contributions to society, was something attractive to many for whom integration seemed nothing but an empty promise.

In his book, We Are Not What We Seem, Bush (1999) argues that the key factor distinguishing between the different black-led antiracist movements is not so much whether they were integrationist or separationist, but whether they were able to mobilize the masses of working-class African Americans or had more conservative aims of inclusion into the system for those with middle-class aspirations and credentials. For example, Bush contrasts Du Bois' NAACP with Garvey's UNIA to show that even at the height of the NAACP's public support in the 1960s, it still could not surpass the UNIA's effective recruitment of working-class blacks, boasting a membership somewhere between one and six million in the 1920s (Bush 1999: 96). Similarly, in the 1920s, another militant black group was able to mobilize thousands of members on the basis of both race pride and fighting worldwide related oppression—the African Blood Brotherhood (ABB). One difference between the UNIA and the ABB was that the latter encouraged alliances with majority white groups who were fighting class-based oppression. Thus, even black militant groups whose names suggest a separationist platform actually did work within multiracial coalitions. The main difference between the above groups and organizations like the NAACP, as Bush sees it, was not that the former pursued separation and the latter opted for integration, but that the latter pursued civil rights within the existing American capitalist framework, while the former demanded that the United States own up to its neglect of *human rights* on a global scale.

During the U.S. civil rights movement of the 1950s and 1960s, as the legal victories that the NAACP won on behalf of people of color did not translate into immediate changes in the everyday lives of blacks in the Jim Crow south, the Student Nonviolent Coordinating Committee (SNCC) and the Congress of Racial Equality (CORE) effectively mobilized students and working-class blacks to use direct action to demand the rights they deserved. In the meantime, in several northern cities, the plight of the urban black poor was being tapped by more conservative nationalist groups like the Nation of Islam. Northern blacks understood that even with "civil rights," they still were unable to secure full economic access to society. Groups like the Nation of Islam took a stance similar to Booker T. Washington and Marcus Garvey, that blacks must "do for self" in the context of a society clearly hostile to their equal participation. Although the Nation of Islam, like SNCC and CORE, was successful at reaching the black working class in large numbers, they did not have a strategy that challenged structural racism directly. They challenged the system's ideology, but not its practices. In Bush's analysis, black-led antiracist groups were at their most effective when they used a race-pride ideology to counteract hegemonic cultural racism and attract the black working class, but then challenged the system in ways from which all oppressed peoples could benefit. Thus, groups like the UNIA and the Nation of Islam limit themselves not necessarily because they do not include whites in their membership, but because their agenda does not make demands on the system to attend to the human rights of its peoples.

Malcolm X's journey from conservative nationalism to a more radical human-rights-focused antiracism over the course of his lifetime exemplifies the kind of ideological shift which Bush advocates. Malcolm X began his antiracist career as a member of the separationist Nation of Islam, but later broke with that organization and started his own, the Organization of Afro-American Unity (OAAU), which was less based in fundamentalist religion and more based on economic and social justice with a racially inclusive membership (Malcolm X and Haley 1965). Soon groups like the Black Panther Party (BPP) began forming to emphasize black pride and economic justice. Although the BPP and the Nation of Islam both agreed that blacks needed to take it upon themselves to ensure their economic and cultural survival in a U.S. system hostile to their full inclusion, the Nation of Islam demanded a conservative transformation of its members, who would then serve each other's needs. By contrast, all the BPP asked of its members was agreement with its 10-point plan, and then many of its programs, such as free breakfast and school clothes for children, liberation schools, and buses to visit prisons were open to and served all, regardless of racial background or organizational membership. While the Nation of Islam's conservative strategy mirrored the dominant capitalist ideology of self-denial ("work hard and you too can succeed"), the BPP's actions clearly projected an ideology that every-one's basic needs should be met regardless of merit but rather due to their innate worth as human beings. Like the ABB before it, the BPP was also open to building coalitions with other like-minded organizations that empowered other oppressed groups, such as the Puerto Rican Young Lords, the Chinese American Red Guards, and the white working-class Young Patriots (Bush 1999: 199).

Other racial-ethnic groups from the late 1960s to the 1980s followed the BPP's model of racial empowerment, such as La Raza and the American Indian Movement (AIM) (Feagin 2000). While race-specific antiracist groups like these formed as an attempt to cast off negative imagery perpetuated by the white majority and encourage economic and political empowerment, many such groups were never entirely nonwhite. In O'Brien's (2001) work on white antiracists, one activist recalls that she was allowed to stay in SNCC even when they "kicked out" the white members, and she also reports working with the Black Panthers to help them serve breakfast to low-income children in their communities. Further, even when certain antiracist organizations limited majority-group membership, many con-tinued to build coalitions with other kindred groups, as we have seen above. Thus, a brief examination of history reveals that people of color have always been at the forefront of anti-racist struggles, but more often than not they have worked alongside white allies. Moreover, the key difference among the various antiracist efforts is not as much about the racial identities of who they have included, but in the goals, tactics, and strategies they have utilized to attain racial equality.

23.3 What Conditions Tend to Foster Antiracism?

While history demonstrates that both whites and people of color have involved themselves in antiracist efforts, there is a basic assumption underlying much of the contemporary research on antiracism that people of color are essentially prone to be antiracism without qualification or precondition. In fact, Johnson, Rush, and Feagin assert: "To some degree, most Americans of color are forced routinely to engage in anti-racist work, at least in regard to their own group." (2000: 105). Whites, by contrast, have more ground to traverse to become aware of racism and commit to acting against it. As Du Bois noted with his concept of double consciousness, the system of racism results in a keen awareness on the part of people of color about not only their own condition, but of whites' own perceptions of them. Indeed, their position in the social structure compels them to be experiential experts on racism. They have gotten to know whites inti-mately and have had to understand them for survival in a world where they are the dominant group. People of color have had to play by whites' rules, in a sense, so they know them well. By contrast, whites are relatively ignorant about people of color and their cultures and can func-tion largely without penalty not having to know about them. As a result, one of the most promi-nent questions in the more contemporary litera-ture examining antiracism is, "What drives whites to become antiracist?" Although the remainder of this essay will summarize the basic findings of that literature, it will also examine why research on antiracism is so heavily centered upon the question of whites' alignment with antiracism and less concerned with people of color as "antiracists."

Several scholars have identified "colorblind-ness" as the major obstacle to antiracism today, particularly among whites (Bonilla-Silva 2003; Carr 1997; Frankenberg 1993). Their work demonstrate how colorblindness (or, as Frankenberg calls it, color and power evasive-ness) prevents people from acknowledging the structural realities of racism, leading them to instead interpret the "racial" differences they sometimes claim not to see (but do see) as caused by biological, psychological, or cultural factors intrinsic to individuals. This kind of thinking results in a blame-the-victim ideology, which does not believe structural antiracism is neces-sary. Some scholars have likened this colorblind ideology to "nonracism," which is characterized by a denial of racial realities and set in contrast to antiracism. For example, Joseph Barndt writes that "Nonracists deny that the prison exists," while antiracists "work for the prison's eventual destruction" (1991: 65). These scholars assert that being colorblind and claiming not to notice racial differences usually results in an absence of antiracist activities.

It should come as no surprise, then, that the research shows that whites are much more likely to subscribe to this strategy of denial than are blacks. Carr (1997) surveyed college students to find that 77% of whites agreed with the statement "I am colorblind when it comes to race" (while only 40% of blacks agreed). Bonilla-Silva (2003), who also relied on two samples, found that only 15% of his white student sample and 12% of his Detroit Area study were considered racially progressive. This would mean that, like Carr's study, over three quarters of the whites Bonilla-Silva studied espoused the dominant colorblind ideology. These findings may shed some additional light upon why the literature on antiracism is so preoccupied with identifying the motivating factors behind whites' becoming antiracist. Whites are likely to hold a colorblind ideology that is generally deemed incompatible with antiracism. O'Brien (2000) does pose some qualified challenges to this uniform incompatibility thesis with her selective race cognizant category of white antiracists who tend to acknowledge racial differences at the abstract, structural level, but are not articulate about their own white privilege nor the racial identities of others. However, on the whole, the fact that a majority of whites subscribe to some aspect of the dominant colorblind ideology means there are major barriers to moving whites in particular to an antiracist identity. As such, scholars of antiracism have been particularly interested in examining the processes by which individual whites break with the dominant colorblind ideology and become antiracist.

Even before colorblindness was the dominant ideology of racism in the United States, though, whites were still considered a curious group to be involved in antiracist activities. John Brown, a white man involved in a slave rebellion, was

executed for his role in the uprising and later portrayed in folklore as a "nut case." Malcolm X argued that such a negative portrayals of him were strategic to prevent white people from perceiving antiracism as a viable focus of their time (O'Brien 2001). Although John Brown is a more well-known (relatively speaking) white abolitionist martyr, there are plenty of other lesser-known antiracists of all racial backgrounds who suffered consequences, including death, for their antiracist acts and publicly declared convictions. In his study of that particular era, Aptheker (1992) concluded that whites were more likely to be involved in such antiracist/ abolitionist practices if they were women, lower class, and/or had significant experiences with blacks. However, by the time the civil rights movement of the 1960s attracted significant white participation, class and gender in particular did not seem to have the same effect. Northern white college students who came to the U.S. south to participate in such activities as Freedom Summer (a voter registration drive in 1964) had more elite class backgrounds, and gender was sometimes a mitigating factor for such "high-risk" activism. That is, some white women who wanted to participate had to struggle against parental paternalism in order to do so, or were not able to go at all (McAdam 1988, 1992; Sherkat and Blocker 1994). Most of the research on white antiracists of the 1960s concludes that experiences with African Americans were not as influential for them as the predominantly white activist and religious networks of which they were a part of (McAdam 1988; Pinkney 1968).

There does not seem to be much attention paid in the literature to the question of hwat inspires white antiracists again until the 1990s Indeed, even much of the above studies on 1960s' antiracism were completed in the 1990s. By this time, scholars probed the question of what moves whites away from a colorblind ideology, rather than the question of "high-risk" activism, which was one of the major barriers to participation in the 1960s. Feagin and Vera (1995) focused on the concept of empathy, and the various routes through which whites could traverse the color line and develop empathy with people of color, realizing that racism is still a serious issue in their lives. They assert that white women who face sexism might be more likely to emphasize with African Americans and become antiracist than white men. Their graduate students, Hogan and Netzer (1993, as cited in Feagin and Vera 1995), did some unpublished work that identified three different types of "approximating experiences" through which white women developed empathy for people of color and became antiracist: (1) overlapping approximations, where they had faced some other type of oppression (e.g., anti-Semitism or homophobia) and made connections from that to racism; (2) borrowed approximations, where they had gained their understandings of racism through stories told to them by people of color in their lives; and (3) global approximations, where they drew upon democratic ideas of social justice and fairness to develop a sense of outrage about contemporary racism. Some subsequent work by O'Brien (2001) and Eichstedt (2001) pointed out that some white antiracists who were survivors of sexual abuse and/or incest—although not considered dimensions of "oppression" in the traditional sociological sense—had also made empathic connections with people of color through these "abuses of power" in their own lives.

Much of this research pointing to the role of empathy in white antiracism, though, was based on samples of white women only, so did not include white male antiracists. Even in O'Brien's (2001) mixed-gender sample of white antiracists, it was only the women who discussed the "overlapping approximations" where whites empathisized with people of color due to some other non-racial form of oppression they had faced themselves. This not to say white men are not also antiracist, but that they more often commit to antiracism due to reasons besides empathy. Consistent with McAdam's (1988) research on the 1960s' civil rights workers, some contemporary white antiracists also become involved through activist networks—their activist friends invited them to a meeting or a workshop (O'Brien 2001). Some become involved because their religious organization is committed to issues of social justice—one person's church even had an "antiracism committee' (O'Brien and Korgen 2007). Still others reported an influential college class, book read, song heard, or lecture attended (O'Brien 2001). For most, there was usually not just one factor, but a series of factors in a "process of sensitization" that eventually led to an antiracist awareness (O'Brien and Korgen 2007).

It is important to note that many of these routes to becoming antiracist do not necessitate whites having actual relationships with people of color. This is significant since the contact hypothesis, a major tenet of race relations research, points to a connection between cross-racial contact and reduced racial prejudice (Allport 1958; Forbes 1997). Being unprejudiced, however, is not the same as being antiracist, as the above discussion of nonracism versus antiracism illustrates. Indeed, only about a third of one sample of white antiracists reported becoming antiracist due to an interracial relationship. In this same article, another sample of whites with a close black friend is analyzed, and less than a third (27.5%) of whites who had a close black friend (verified by the researchers through also meeting and interviewing the friend) were antiracist. Many close interracial friends tended not to even discuss race. The authors conclude that the dominant ideology of colorblindness is a major factor explaining why interracial contact is not more influential in motivating antiracism. Where interracial relationships are the impetus for becoming antiracist, they are almost always romantic and not merely platonic. Interestingly, a great deal of the sample in the above study had some type of interracial relationships, but they had either occurred after the person become antiracist, or the respondent felt that s/he was not antiracist yet during the relationship (O'Brien and Korgen 2007). This questionable correlation between interracial relationships and antiracism is further substantiated by Childs' research. Childs (2005) studied partners in romantic inter-racial relationships and found that they tended to fall into one of two categories: antiracists or colorblind racists. The latter group used colorblind language to discuss why they chose their partner (e.g., "I do not notice his/her race") but used racialized language to discuss people of color as a whole (e.g., "blacks bring their problems on themselves").

Taking all of this research together, from early abolitionism to the present, it is evident that antiracism among whites is motivated by a number of factors, including interracial relationships, interactions with other activists and their organizations, religious organizations, and other experiences with non-racial forms of oppression, particularly for women. Though social class appears to be less of a factor than it once was, class (especially when measured by educational level) may not influence whether or not someone becomes antiracist as much as it influences the *type* of antiracism to which s/he subscribes (O'Brien 2001). And gender continues to be influential, not in terms of necessarily making one more or less likely to be antiracist, but rather in the ways in which one perceives and interprets his or her involvement in antiracism (McAdam 1992; Sherkat and Blocker 1994).

One's racial identity bears a complex relationship to antiracism. Possession of a racially progressive ideology, the usual precursor to antiracist activities, is much more common among people of color—blacks in particular—than it is for whites (Bonilla-Silva 2003). If we limit antiracism to individual/interpersonal antiracism, then some scholars would argue that most people of color engage in antiracism on a near daily basis (Johnson et al. 2000). If, however, we analyze structural antiracism's relationship to race, it would depend upon the ideological bent of the particular antiracist organization in question. Those groups that stress a critical antiracism (George 2004) that holds whites explicitly accountable for various dimensions of racism generally have lower levels of white involvement than the antiracist groups that target "hate in any form" and are more "color-blind" in their ideology. In fact, these latter groups tend to be predominantly white (O'Brien 2001). Most analysts agree that much more white involvement is needed, both individually/interpersonally and structurally/institutionally, if

there is to be any major systemic and enduring antiracist transformation of the social structure.

References

Allen, T. W. (1994). *The invention of the White race volume I; racial oppression and social control.* New York: Verso.

Allport, G. W. (1958). *The nature of prejudice.* New York: Doubleday/Anchor.

Aptheker, H. (1992). *Anti-racism in the United States: The first two hundred years.* Westport, CT: Greenwood Press.

Barndt, J. (1991). *Dismatling racism: The continuing challenge to White America.* Minneapolis, MN: Augsberg Fortress.

Bonilla-Silva, E. (2003). *Racism without Racists: Color-blind racism and the persistence of Racial Inequality in America.* Lanham, MD: Rowman and Littlefield.

Bonnett, A. (2000). *Anti-racism.* London: Routledge.

Brooks, R. L. (1996). *Integration or separation? A strategy for racial equality.* Cambridge, MA: Harvard University Press.

Bush, R. (1999). *We are not what we seem: Black nationalism and class struggle in the American century.* New Yoek: New York University Press.

Carr, L. (1997). *"Color-blind` racism.* Los Angeles: Sage Publications.

Childs, E. C. (2005). *Navigating interracial borders: Black-White couples and their social worlds.* Rutgers, NJ: Rutgers University Press.

Edles, L. D., & Applerouth, S. (2004). *Sociological theory in the classical era.* Thousan Oaks, CA: Pine Forge Press.

Eichstedt, J. (2001). Problematic White identities and a search for racial justice. *Sociological Forum, 16,* 445–470.

Feagin, J. R. (2000). *Racist America: Roots, current realities and future reparations.* New York: Routledge.

Feagin, J. R., & Vera, H. (1995). *White racism: The basics.* New York: Routledge.

Forbes, H. D. (1997). *Ethnic conflict: Commerce, culture, and the contact hypothesis.* New Haven, CT: Yale University Press.

Frankenberg, R. (1993). *White women, race matters: The social construction of whiteness.* Minneapolis: University of Minnesota Press.

George, M. P. (2004). *Towards a critical antiracism: Redefining and rethinking the term 'Antiracism.'* Paper presented at the annual meetings of the American Sociological Association, August, San Francisco, California.

Hogan, T., & Netzer, J. (1993). Knowing the other: White women, gender, and racism. Unpublished manuscript, University of Florida, Department of Sociology.

Johnson, J., Rush, S., & Feagin, J. R. (2000). Doing anti-racism: Toward an EgalitarianAmerican Society. *Contemporary Sociology, 29*, 95–110.

Kivel, P. (2002). *Uprooting racism: How White people can work for racial justice*. St. Paul, MN: New Society Publishers.

Korgen, K. (2002). *Crossing the racial divide: Close friendships between Black and White Americans*. Westport, CT: Praeger.

Kozol, J. (2005). *The shame of the nation: The restoration of Apartheid Schooling in America*. New York: Crown.

Lorber, J. (2005). *Gender inequality: Feminist theories and politics* (3rd ed.). Los Angeles: Roxbury Publishing Company.

Malcolm X, & Haley, A. (1965). *The autobiography of Malcolm X*. New York: Ballantine Books.

McAdam, D. (1992). Gender as a mediator of the activist experience: The case of freedom summer. *American Journal of Sociology, 97*, 1211–1240.

McAdam, D. (1988). *Freedom summer*. New York: Oxford University Press.

McIntosh, P. (1998). White privilege and male privilege. In M. L. Anderson & P. H. Collins (Eds.), *Race, class and gender: An anthology* (3rd ed.). New York: Wadsworth.

O'Brien, E. (2000). Are we supposed to be colorblind or not? Competing frames used by Whites against racism. *Race and Society, 3*, 41–59.

O'Brien, E. (2001). *Whites confront racism: Antiracists and their paths to action*. Boulder, CO: Rowman and Littlefield.

O'Brien, E. (2003). The political is personal: The influence of white supremacy on white antiracists' personal relationships. In W. Doane & E. Bonilla-Silva (Eds.), *White out: The continuing significance of racism*. (pp. 253–270) New York: Routledge.

O'Brien, E., & Korgen, K. (2007). It's the message not the messenger: The declining significance of Black-White contact in a colorblind society. *Sociological Inquiry, 77*(3).

Pinkney, A. (1968). *The committed: White activists in the civil rights movement*. New York: New College and University Press.

Scott, E. K. (2000). Everyone against racism: Agency and the production of meaning in the anti-racism practices of two feminist organizations. *Theory and Society, 29*, 785–818.

Sherkat, D. E., & Blocker, T. J. (1994). The political development of sixties activists: Identifying the influence of class, gender and socialization on protest participation. *Social Forces, 72*, 821–842.

Tatum, B. D. (2003). *Why are all the Black kids sitting together in the cafeteria? And other conversations about race*. New York: Basic Books.

Tatum, B. D. (1994). Teaching White students about racism: The search for White allies and the restoration of hope. *Teachers College Record, 95*, 462–476.

Tatum, B. D. (1992). Talking about race, learning about racism: The application of racial identity development in the classroom. *Harvard Educational Review, 62*, 1–24.

Thomas, R. W. (1996). *Understanding interracial unity*. Thousand Oaks, CA: Sage Publications.

Tong, R. (1998). *Feminist thought: A more comprehensive introduction*. Boulder, CO: Westview Press.

Yelman, N. (2004). Prejudice and discrimination. In J. F. Healey & E. O'Brien (Eds.), *Race, ethnicity and gender: Selected readings* (pp. 8–20). Thousand Oaks, CA: Sage.

Part VI
Conclusion

Future Challenges: The Sociology of Racial and Ethnic Relations

24

Joe R. Feagin and Hernán Vera

Contents

Writing in the late 1960s, the great sociologist W. E. B. Du Bois perceptively wrote this overview of the United States:

> [T]oday the contradictions of American civilization are tremendous. Freedom of political discussion is difficult; elections are not free and fair.... The greatest power in the land is not thought or ethics, but wealth.... Present profit is valued higher than future need.... I know the United States. It is my country and the land of my fathers. It is still a land of magnificent possibilities. It is still the home of noble souls and generous people. But it is selling its birthright. It is betraying its mighty destiny (Du Bois 1968: 418–419).

This diagnosis of U.S. civilization is still accurate. The contemporary contradictions of this country's political, economic, and other institutions remain extensive, immense, and potentially destructive of U.S. democracy. Aggressive white male apologists and implementers openly celebrate white nationalism, hyper-masculinity, and an unregulated "free market" economy. Still, the country is also a land of progressive possibilities, with many and growing citizens' groups opposing these oppressive racial, class, and gender trends.

Most of the articles in this volume illuminate aspects of what sociologist Joe Feagin has termed the *elite-white-male dominance system*. Historically, a European and European American elite, mostly male, has crafted and sustained this dominance system in North America, a system with great shaping effects on most of the planet's other countries. This elite is a very small percentage of the U.S. and global populations, yet still dominates in very powerful and highly undemocratic ways—economically, politically, and socially. Strikingly, it is largely unknown to most of those it so extensively dominates. The concept of the elite-white-male dominance system encourages us to think about *who* and *what*

J. R. Feagin (✉)
Department of Sociology, Texas A&M University, College Station, TX, USA
e-mail: feagin@tamu.edu

H. Vera
Emeritus Professor of Sociology, University of Florida, Gainesville, FL, USA

© Springer International Publishing AG, part of Springer Nature 2018
P. Batur and J. R. Feagin (eds.), *Handbook of the Sociology of Racial and Ethnic Relations*,
Handbooks of Sociology and Social Research, https://doi.org/10.1007/978-3-319-76757-4_24

this distinctive elite is, and how it has dominated much of the world historically and in the present. This dominance system encompasses several major subsystems of societal oppression, not only the systemic racism central to all chapters in this volume, but also the systemic sexism (heterosexism) and systemic classism (capitalism) sometimes examined in them as well (Feagin and Ducey 2017: 1–50).

In North America, at the very top of all three of these major subsystems of oppression sit elite white men who are dominant in both numbers and power. In this volume we focus principally on the racial oppression they enforce, social subjugation that reaches into every major nook and cranny of U.S. society, and thus is systemic (Feagin 2006). As we suggested in the introduction, systemic racism involves the institutionalized patterns of subordinate and dominant societal positions, respectively, for people of color and for whites in a white-controlled, hierarchically arranged society. Our chapters demonstrate the systemic reality of white-imposed racism in the past and present, as it is seen in the exploitative and discriminatory practices of whites targeting people of color–and thus in the significant resources and privileges unjustly gained (and legitimated) by whites in that process.

24.1 The Countersystem Approach: Black Pioneers in Sociology for Change

The goals of sociology and much other social science have long revealed a major tension between seeking to remedy racial and other social injustice and seeking mainstream acceptance as legitimate academic disciplines, especially legitimacy from the powerful white male elite. While a majority of sociologists and other social scientists have generally accepted the academic status quo and the larger elite-white-male dominance system, from the late 19th century onward some have aggressively developed a *countersystem* framework oriented to a much more critical view of social science and society. These social scientists have undertaken

much significant research aimed at understanding, and then reducing or eliminating, key elements of systemic racism. This countersystem approach involves stepping outside mainstream social science reluctance to directly theorize and research white-racist institutions and to develop theory-based and data-based critiques of these persisting institutions central to systemic white racism (see Sjoberg and Cain 1971). As a result, such countersystem analyses have frequently led to studied considerations of alternative, more just societies.

Thus, in the late nineteenth and early twentieth centuries, a number of black male and female sociologists did much innovative countersystem research on U.S. racial matters, leading them to take informed positions on the country's ending the oppression of black Americans and other Americans of color. Among these often forgotten black sociologists were W. E. B. Du Bois, Ida B. Wells-Barnett, and Anna Julia Cooper. All developed important sociological ideas and research projects, especially attacking the racist ideas generated by whites' scientific racism of their era. In our considered view it is well past time for sociologists and other social scientists to reclaim their important ideas, insights, and methods. Note too that they are among the earliest founders of sociology as a scholarly discipline.

Consider, for example, the brilliant W. E. B. Du Bois. In 1896 he was hired by the University of Pennsylvania to do a study of black Philadelphians using the "best available methods of sociological research" (Du Bois [1899] 1973: 2). His resulting book, *The Philadelphia Negro* ([1899] 1973), was the first book-length sociological study of an urban (black) community. Soon, with this book in hand, Du Bois sought to create an academic program that would focus on social scientific research on black Americans. Since no white-run institutions were interested in hiring him or setting up such a program, he accepted a professorship at Atlanta University, a historically black institution. There in the first decade or two of the 20th century, working with numerous scholars at other historically black institutions, he built up the *first* truly scientific program of research in the history of U.S. sociology. Yet, their pioneering efforts are still rarely recognized in mainstream social science disciplines.

Using innovative conceptual frameworks and empirical research methods (e.g., field observations, surveys, interviews, U.S. census materials), this Du Bois-Atlanta school of sociology made early and important contributions to the sociological study of black community, family, and racial problems, as well as to important historical studies. They insistently challenged the white racist categories and theories inside and outside the academia of their era (Morris 2015: 57–69). In addition, in this early period there were important black women sociologists, including Ida B. Wells-Barnett and Anna Julia Cooper, whose work has recently also been rediscovered (Cooper 1892; Wells-Barnett 1895). Because of institutional racial and gender exclusion they did most of their sociological research and analysis outside of academia.

More recently, and accenting this black countersystem tradition, sociologist Ladner ([1973] 1998) has underscored how contemporary scholars of color have regularly forced issues of racial oppression to be seriously assessed by academic sociology. She and other sociologists of color have also pressured the discipline to consider multiple oppression statuses and intersectionality, especially linkages of racial and gender oppression (Baca Zinn and Dill 1994).

24.2 Countersystem Analysis and Social Justice

Unmistakably, these scholars of color have not only developed an alternative fund of social science knowledge, but also moved the recognition and use of this knowledge from the societal margins into ever more central research efforts of sociology and other social sciences. Over several decades, this accumulating knowledge from the margins has become extraordinarily important in understanding how systemic white racism actually operates, and thus in contributing to organized societal-change efforts by community and national activist groups seeking to reduce systemic racism's many institutionalized patterns. Additionally, these pioneering sociologists of color, women and men, have offered critical role models in their commitments to gaining social-scientific knowledge by utilizing both a solid countersystem conceptual framework and frequently innovative research methods. By the 1960s and 1970s, their critical scientific work was finally being recognized by more contemporary social scientists of color in various fields–and increasingly by a slowly growing number of white social scientists who adopted their perceptive countersystem approach (Feagin 2001).

In our view many more contemporary sociologists and other social scientists need to engage in, cultivate, and enlarge this long-standing countersystem approach, not only in regard to investigating systemic racism and its racial inequalities, but also with regard to advocating for alternative social systems that are far more just and egalitarian. Systemic racism needs much more research showing the *how* and *why* of its maldistribution of goods and services, as well as of the oppressive intergroup relations responsible for that massive and unjust maldistribution. These hierarchical racial relations encompass inegalitarian power relationships and unjustly unequal access to essential socioeconomic resources. Such coerced inequality determines whether individuals, families, and community groups are included or excluded from society's important decision-making processes. It centrally shapes the development of individual and group racial identities, as well as the sense of personal dignity. It is clear from earlier and contemporary countersystem research that ending systemic racism must entail a thorough restructuring of U.S. society's unjust, alienating, and inegalitarian racial relationships (Feagin et al. 2015).

A *countersystem* approach involves serious reconsideration of methods, that is, of how we actually do sociology and other social sciences. Numerous sociologists, including many in this book, have done considerable and pathbreaking analyses of the character and impact of racial and class subordination. They have pioneered in new methods with a countersystem dimension. For example, some social science researchers on several continents have utilized participatory-action-research strategies that incorporate countersystem ideas and methods. Many have worked collaboratively with ordinary people at the grassroots level; these efforts often target how to dismantle the oppression of, and develop societal alternatives to, the established status quo (see, for Latin America, Fals-Borda 1960). These countersystem researchers eschew sterile analyses aimed at academic readers and instead regularly work to construct resource and power bases for those faced with local or national patterns of racial and class discrimination and impoverishment, and associated political disenfranchisement. In our view, if sociology and the other social sciences are to make a difference in a world of countries under constant threat and reality of severe racial and class inequalities, the legitimacy and extent of countersystem research strategies must be greatly enhanced. Extensive research involving collaboration between social scientists and community organizations seeking solutions to local problems of discrimination and inequality must be pushed to the forefront, and thus should be positioned in the respected core of serious social science research—where it was at the birth of U.S. sociology in the late 19th and early 20th centuries (Sjoberg and Cain 1971; Feagin 2001).

Also very important is the significant social justice morality of this countersystem approach. It is often forgotten that the everyday practice of all social science involves *moral* activity. US society is greatly structured by racial and other societal oppressions, and much sociological theory and research methodology reflects this oppressive reality to some degree. Indeed, all social science perspectives incorporate an underlying view of what society should be like. Unsurprisingly, countersystem approaches often accent a broad human rights framework in which each person and group is entitled to fair treatment and to social justice–and to a society in which all are entitled to social institutions backing up these rights. Some countersystem social scientists (e.g., Sjoberg 1996) have suggested that the Universal

Declaration of Human Rights (UDHR) developed by the new and more diverse United Nations in the late 1940s could be an important starting place for developing a lasting human rights framework to guide social scientists in their everyday research.

Consider the UDHR that was finally approved in 1948. This great international document was constructed by several UN drafting and vetting committees and adopted by a multinational and multiracial United Nations General Assembly. Among its pathbreaking rights is Article 1, which firmly states human equality: "All human beings are born free and equal in dignity and rights. They are endowed with reason and conscience and should act towards one another in a spirit of brotherhood." Many other articles lay out the specific rights that fall within this overview. For example, Article 29 emphasizes democratic societal structures and individual community responsibilities: "Everyone has duties to the community in which alone the free and full development of his personality is possible… everyone shall be subject only to such limitations as are determined by law solely for the purpose of securing due recognition and respect for the rights and freedoms of others and of meeting the just requirements of morality, public order and the general welfare in a democratic society." Numerous other human rights that fall within this framework are laid out in rich and thoroughly vetted detail (United Nations 2016).

Some have argued that the UDHR is only a western (white) human rights document. This is incorrect, as a long drafting period insured that representatives of many countries and subnational groups—many of them people of color—actually reviewed, revised, and then supported it. Western rights concepts did greatly influence the Declaration, but major ethical and communal rights concepts stemming from all continents–Asia, the Middle East, Africa, Europe, North America, and Latin America–were imbedded in language stating human rights principles then and now considered universal. For instance, a Chinese delegate, the scholar P. C. Chang, made sure that Asian understandings of human rights and duties were considered well and concretely imbedded. Working with representatives of non-western areas, he insisted that the UDHR accented broadly relevant concepts of brotherhood, moral growth, pluralistic tolerance, the "will of he people" as governments' basis, and community duties as balancing individual rights (Chu 2016; Twiss 2010: 110–112).

Even more importantly, this non-western group was anti-colonialist and thus forced an emphasis on the right of all peoples to *self-determination* to be part of the document. This viewpoint of subordinated peoples of color directly challenged the extensive western colonialism still dominant in this postwar era. As a result, the Declaration opens with a relatively radical opening asserting that stated UDHR principles represent a "common standard of achievement for all peoples and all nations, to the end that every individual and every organ of society... shall strive by teaching and education to promote respect for these rights and freedoms... [and] to secure their universal and effective recognition and observance, both among the peoples of Member States themselves and *among the peoples of territories under their jurisdiction*." The latter phrase referenced the people in then (e.g., European) colonized territories as having full human rights and freedoms. These strikingly prescient assertions more or less insured that this UDHR would be used by many countries in preparing international agreements; it has also been cited in numerous legal decisions by various country's courts, as well as by the international courts (Henkin et al. 2009: 216). Subsequently, the general statements for human rights and against racial and other discrimination in the UDHR have been further developed, specified, and framed by subsequent implementing covenants on economic, social, and political rights–which have been agreed to, albeit sometimes with reservations, by most United Nations members. They include the International Covenant on Civil and Political Rights (ICCPR), which was added to the UDHR and thereby created an International Bill of Human Rights (Feagin and Ducey 2017: 251–254).

24.3 Peoples Movements for Racial Justice

Today, issues of racial and other social injustices are being forced to the forefront by tens of thousands of people's movements, most of which have been developed by people of color, in many countries around the globe. These currently include numerous indigenous rights movements and other anti-racist organizations. These movements usually accent concepts of racial justice, and emphasize human rights such as those in the UDHR that are viewed as requiring resource equity, fairness, and respect for cultural and racial diversity. This necessarily includes demands for, and efforts at, eradicating well-institutionalized societal structures of racial oppression. Many peoples' movements have also made clear that effective racial justice requires substantial resource redistributions away from those who have unjustly secured them and then socially moved to those justly deserving them.

As the UDHR and associated conventions insist, this also necessitates the creation of truly democratic structures guaranteeing real participation of ordinary people in a country's everyday political-economic decision-making. Western political theory commonly accents that ordinary people have a right to self-rule, but much theory also notes that in practice this right is delegated to a people's elected representatives—thereby suggesting that better-educated people serve as government leaders who act in the general public interest and under impartial laws. However, countersystem and other research shows that there is *no* such impartial political and legal system in supposedly democratic countries such as the United States. In fact, the actual U.S. reality is one of a hierarchically arranged society in which a mostly white and male elite has created and sustained over centuries an economic, political, and legal structure that disproportionately reflects and achieves their distinctive and inegalitarian societal goals and interests. As we suggested earlier, this elite-white-male dominance system, and its component systemic racism, must be fully recognized for its thoroughly oppressive character, and then if social justice is desired, must be fully dismantled. Clearly, only a decisive redistribution of unjustly gained socioeconomic resources and decision-making power to those from whom these resources and power were unjustly stolen can ensure real socio-racial justice and authentic popular democracy (Feagin 2001).

References

Baca Zinn, M., & Dill, B. T. (Eds.). (1994). *Women of color in U.S. society*. Philadelphia, PA: Temple University Press.

Chu, L. H. (2016). *Interview*. East Asian Institute Newsletter. http://weai.columbia.edu/professor-lydia-h-liu-on-human-rights-pioneer-and-columbia-alum-p-c-chang/. Accessed August 18, 2016.

Cooper, A. J. (1892). *A voice from the south by a black woman from the south*. Xenia, OH: Aldine.

Du Bois, W. E. B. (1968). The autobiography of W. E. B. Du Bois: A soliloquy on viewing my life from the last decade of Its first century. New York, NY: International Publishers.

Du Bois, W. E. B. ([1899] 1973). *The Philadelphia Negro: A social study*. Reprint. Millwood, NY: Kraus-Thomson.

Fals-Borda, O. (1960). *Acción comunal en una vereda colombiana: Su aplicación, sus resultados y su interpretacíon*. Bogota, Colombia: Universidad Nacional de Colombia, Departamento de Sociologia.

Feagin, J. R. (2001). Social justice and sociology: Agendas for the twenty-first century. *American Sociological Review, 66*, 1–20.

Feagin, J. R. (2006). *Systemic racism: A theory of oppression*. New York: Routledge.

Feagin, J. R., & Ducey, K. (2017). *Elite white men ruling: Who, what, when, where, and how*. New York: Routledge.

Feagin, J. R., Vera, H., & Ducey, K. (2015). *Liberation sociology* (3rd ed.). Boulder, CO: Paradigm Publishers.

Henkin, L., Cleveland, S. H., Helfer, L. R., Newman, G. L., & Orentlicher, D. F. (2009). *Human rights*. New York: Foundation Press.

Ladner, J. A. ([1973] 1998). Introduction to the black classic press edition. In J. A. Ladner (Eds.), *The death of white sociology: Essays on race and culture*. Reprint. Baltimore, MD: Black Classic Press.

Morris, A. D. (2015). *The scholar denied: W. E. B. Du Bois and the birth of modern sociology*. Oakland, CA: University of California Press.

Sjoberg, G. (1996). The human rights challenge to communitarianism: Formal organizations and race and ethnicity. In D. Sciulli (Ed.), *Macro socio-economics: From theory to activism* (pp. 273–293). M. E. Sharpe: Armonk, NY.

Sjoberg, G., & Cain, L. D. (1971). Negative values, countersystem models, and the analysis of social systems. In H. Turk & R. L. Simpson (Eds.), *Institutions and social exchange: The sociologies of Talcott Parsons and George C. Homans* (pp. 212–229). Bobbs-Merrill: Indianapolis, IN.

Twiss, S. B. (2010). Confucian contributions to the universal declaration of human rights: A historical and philosophical perspective. In A. Sharma (Ed.), *The world's religions: A contemporary reader*. Minneapolis, MN: Fortress Press.

United Nations. (2016). *Universal declaration of human rights*. United for Human Rights. http://www.humanrights.com/what-are-human-rights/universal-declaration-of-human-rights/preamble.html. Accessed August 18, 2016.

Wells-Barnett, I. B. (1895). *A red record*. Chicago, IL: Donohue and Henneberry.

Printed by Printforce, the Netherlands